VARIETY

International Film Guide
2006

the definitive annual review of world cinema
| edited by Daniel Rosenthal
| founding editor Peter Cowie

43rd edition

BUTTON
live communications

London   Los Angeles   Cannes

Silman-James Press
Los Angeles

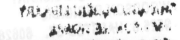

IN OUR BUSINESS
IT'S ALL IN THE CREDITS.

PUERTO RICO'S
ADD UP TO **40%**

Commonwealth of Puerto Rico

For more information, visit ▶ www.**PuertoRicoFilm**.com

PUERTO RICO
FILM
COMMISSION

Editor & Associate Publisher
Daniel Rosenthal
Publisher
Robert Bingham
Founding Editor
Peter Cowie
Assistant Editor
Danny Graydon
Consulting Editor
Derek Elley
Editorial Assistant
Sara Tyler
Sales Managers
Raquel Escobar
(Spain, Latin America),
Patricia Hutchins
(North America),
Sara Tyler
(Film Festivals)
Design
Button Group plc
Photo Consultants
The Kobal Collection
tel +44 (0) 20 7624 3300
www.picture-desk.com

Editorial and Business Offices
Button Group plc
246 Westminster Bridge Road
London SE1 7PD
tel +44 (0) 20 7401 0400
fax +44 (0) 20 7401 0401
e london@buttonplc.com

ISBN 0-9548766-2-8 (UK)
ISBN 1-879505-90-8 (US)

British Library Cataloguing in
Publication Data
International Film Guide 2006
1. Rosenthal, Daniel 1971-

Published in the UK by
Button Group plc

Published in the US by
Silman-James Press, Los Angeles

Copyright © 2006 by
Button Group plc

Printed and bound in Milan by
Rotolito Lombarda
www.rotolitolombarda.it

Distributed in the UK by
Combined Book Services, Tonbridge
www.combook.co.uk

59th Locarno International Film Festival.
August 2-12 2006.

Winners 2005

GOLDEN LEOPARD: "NINE LIVES"
by Rodrigo Garcia (USA)

SILVER LEOPARD: "FRATRICIDE"
by Yilmaz Arslan (Germany/France/Luxembourg)

SILVER LEOPARD: "3 GRAD KAELTER"
by Florian Hoffmeister (Germany)

SILVER LEOPARD: "WE ARE ALL FINE"
by Bizhan Mirbaqeri (Iran)

SPECIAL JURY PRIZE:
"UN COUPLE PARFAIT"
by Nobuhiro Suwa (Japan/France)

GOLDEN LEOPARD VIDEO C.P. COMPANY:
"MASAHISTA"
by Brillante Mendoza (Philippines)

GOLDEN LEOPARD VIDEO C.P. COMPANY:
"LES ÉTATS NORDIQUES"
by Denis Côté (Canada)

Via Ciseri 23, CH -6600 Locarno,
Tel:+ 41 91 756 21 21,
Fax: + 41 91 756 21 49
email:info@pardo.ch
www.pardo.ch

Sponsors et partenaires principaux du festival
UBS   AET   MANOR swisscom

International Liaison

Afghanistan: Sandra Schäfer
Algeria, Morocco, Tunisia,
rest of West Africa: Roy Armes
Argentina: Alfredo Friedlander
Armenia: Susanna Harutiunian
Australia: Peter Thompson
Austria: Gunnar Landsgesell
Azerbaijan, Belarus,
Georgia: Goga Lomidze
Bangladesh: Ahmed
Muztaba Zamal
Belgium: Erik Martens
Bosnia & Herzegovina:
Rada Sesic
Brazil: Nelson Hoineff
Bulgaria: Pavlina Jeleva
Canada: Tom McSorley
Central America:
Maria Lourdes Cortés
Central Asia: Gulnara Abikeyeva
Chile: Andrea Osorio Klenner
China: Sen-lun Yu
Colombia: Jaime E. Manrique,
Pedro Adrián Zuluaga
Croatia: Tomislav Kurelec
Cuba: Luciano Castillo,
Alberto Ramos
Cyprus: Theo Panayides
Czech Republic: Eva Zaoralová
Denmark: Jacob Neiiendam

Ecuador: Gabriela Alemán
Egypt: Fawzi Soliman
Estonia: Jaan Ruus
Finland: Antti Selkokari
France: Michel Ciment
Germany: Rüdiger Suchsland
Greece:
Yannis Bacoyannopoulos
Hong Kong: Tim Youngs
Hungary, United States:
Eddie Cockrell
Iceland:
Ásgrímur Sverrisson
India: Uma da Cunha
Indonesia: Lisabona Rahman
Iran: Jamal Omid
Ireland: Michael Dwyer
Israel: Dan Fainaru
Italy: Lorenzo Codelli
Japan: Tomomi Katsuta
Kenya, Tanzania, Uganda:
Ogova Ondego
Latvia: Andris Rozenbergs
Malta: Daniel Rosenthal
Mexico: Carlos Bonfil
Namibia, South Africa,
Zimbabwe: Martin P. Botha
Nepal: Uzzwal Bhandary
Netherlands: Pieter van Lierop
New Zealand: Peter Calder

Nigeria: Steve Ayorinde
Norway: Trond Olav Svendsen
Pakistan: Aijaz Gul
Peru: Isaac León Frías
Philippines: Tessa Jazmines
Poland: Barbara Hollender
Portugal: Martin Dale
Puerto Rico:
José Artemio Torres
Romania: Cristina Corciovescu
Russia: Kirill Razlogov
Rwanda: Daddy
Youssouf Ruhorahoza
Serbia & Montenegro:
Goran Gocic
Singapore: Yvonne Ng
Slovakia: Miro Ulman
Slovenia: Ziva Emersic
South Korea: Nikki J.Y. Lee
Spain: Jonathan Holland
Sri Lanka: Amarnath Jayatilaka
Sweden: Gunnar Rehlin
Switzerland: Michael Sennhauser
Taiwan: Ian Gabriel Rowen
Thailand: Anchalee Chaiworaporn
Turkey: Atilla Dorsay
Ukraine: Volodymyr Voytenko
United Kingdom: Philip Kemp
Uruguay: Jorge Jellinek
Venezuela: Martha Escalona Zerpa

Front Cover
Lee Young-ae as the heroine of **Sympathy for Lady Vengeance.** *The final part of Park Chan wook's revenge trilogy, it was one of 2005's most popular releases in South Korea, attracting 3.6 million admissions.*
Picture: Tartan Films.

UTAH. SHOOT HERE. LOVE LIFE.

FILM.UTAH.GOV

Notes from the Editor

This year's *IFG* records numerous milestones – and passes one of its own. The silver jubilee of the modern film movement that has produced Neil Jordan, Liam Neeson and Damien O'Donnell, to name but three, is explored by Michael Dwyer in "25 Years of Irish Cinema". It's Ireland, too, whose distributors and exhibitors are gearing up for the introduction of the world's first all-digital cinema circuit (part of our "Digital Cinema in Focus" feature).

Last year, Sarunas Bartas became the first Lithuanian director ever to be selected for Cannes, with *Seven Invisible Men*, and Roya Sadat's *Three Dots*, a tragedy of feudalism and forced marriage, became the first feature film ever made by an Afghan woman.

Afghanistan is featured in a "World Survey" that for the first time has reached the 100-country mark. As ever, we cover film-making in many forms, from bloated, loss-making Hollywood blockbusters with $150m price tags, to hugely profitable, hour-long 'Riverwood' comedies, shot for as little as $500 each in Kenya, and the 'Nollywood' video films produced at the rate of roughly three a day in Nigeria.

Maria Lourdes Cortés, our new Central America correspondent, reports on small but vibrant local film industries whose directors continue to work in spite of the absence of any state support, and welcomes "an exceptional burst of creativity" in Guatemala, after a decade in which not a single theatrical feature was completed there.

In Hollywood, meanwhile, the budgets keep getting bigger and the films longer (*two* hours for a trifle such as *Wedding Crashers*?), even as theatrical audiences dwindle alarmingly and the window between cinema and home video release narrows. This gap has become so short on both sides of the Atlantic that when *Meet the Fockers* made its UK DVD debut in mid-May

Daniel Rosenthal

2005, posters for its theatrical release had yet to be peeled off the sides of some London buses.

The Sixth Sense director M. Night Shyamalan, speaking at America's ShowEast exhibitor conference last October, called this trend "the worst idea I have ever heard… It's greed. It's heartless and soulless and disrespectful." He implored the studios to "wait for the thing to finish its life. If you inspire audiences, theatres will be packed. That's when the collective soul is talking. Great movies connect everybody. That's when humanity grows."

Yet M. Night's nightmare – the death of traditional cinemagoing – seems unthinkable when one reads Ogova Ondego's *IFG* report from Uganda. There, audiences pay about $0.07 to sit in flimsy video shacks and watch DVDs of action movies that are 'dubbed' live into the local luganda language by video jockeys. This simultaneous translation may not be accurate, Ogova writes, "but the viewers hang on the VJs' every word." In this high-tech age, their role is a remarkable throwback to the silent era, when Akira Kurosawa's love of film was fuelled by his elder brother, Heigo, a *benshi* (film narrator) who specialised in commentating on foreign films.

A digital dream

In the 1990s, the cinema-building boom in the UK came with an oft-repeated promise: one screen at the local multiplex, we were told, would provide a regular, perhaps permanent, home for arthouse fare. What we have ended up with at larger sites, of course, is *Fantastic Four*, *War of the Worlds* and *Wedding Crashers* starting every half-hour in three screens each. Some in the industry believe that digital cinema could finally see that broken promise fulfilled, and one personal experience from last year made me hope they're proved right.

On a midweek evening in the middle of blockbuster season, I turned up at my local Odeon in north London, and found myself in arthouse heaven. I was planning to see *Bombón El perro*, from Argentina's Carlos Sorin (one of our five Directors of the Year in this edition), but I could just as easily have bought tickets for Israeli thriller *Walk on Water* or Paolo Sorrentino's *The Consequences of Love*, from Italy, all three starting within 10 minutes of each other. Granted, I was at a cinema with an exceptionally world cinema-hungry local clientele, yet I couldn't help wishing that this singular experience might just have been a taste of screens to come.

In theory, digital cinema can deliver the low-cost flexibility that could allow one corner of a multiplex to act as a new-generation arthouse rep, with almost on-demand programming. Anyone who wishes to see a broader audience base for foreign-language cinema must hope that the theory can become practice.
– *Daniel Rosenthal*
(dmr2000@gxn.co.uk)

WORLDWIDE BOX-OFFICE 2005	$m
1. Revenge of the Sith	849
2. War of the Worlds	589
3. The Goblet of Fire*	561
4. Madagascar	526
5. Charlie and the Chocolate Factory	471
6. Mr. & Mrs. Smith*	429
7. Batman Begins	372
8. Hitch	368
9. Fantastic Four	329
10. Wedding Crashers	283
11. Robots	261
12. Howl's Moving Castle**	232
13. Constantine	230
14. Kingdom of Heaven	211
15. The Pacifier	199
16. The Longest Yard	190
17. Wallace & Gromit...*	175
18. Flightplan*	174
19. The 40-Year-Old-Virgin*	166
20. The Interpreter	163

*Still in release. **Excludes 2004 gross.

Source: Variety.
Figures are provisional, for Jan 3 – Dec. 4, 2005.

Directors of the Year

Patrice Chéreau by Adrien Gombeaud

CNC/Kobal

I n the past 30 years, Patrice Chéreau has directed 10 films that have taken him to every major festival, both in competition and as a jury member. Yet in France he is not fully accepted as a real film-maker. He is still seen as a stage director who steps briefly into cinema before returning to theatre or opera. This misunderstanding is a consequence of Chéreau's original vision. He sees cinema not only as a continuation of his stage work, but as a synthesis of all the forms that feed his life as an artist: literature, music, painting, sculpture, dance.

The youngest son of a family of painters, PATRICE CHÉREAU was born on November 2, 1944 in Lézigné, Maine et Loire, and spent most of his childhood in Paris. He is part of the generation that grew in the shadow of the *nouvelle vague*. His biggest influence is probably Orson Welles, whose films he discovered at the Paris Cinémathèque. Like Welles, Chéreau started on stage. He directed his first plays at the prestigious Louis Le Grand high school, before studying classical literature and German at university. His first professional productions were

highly political and had a big impact on French theatre. He worked both in France and in Italy at the Piccolo Teatro di Milano. In the mid-1970s, he was a renowned stage director whose inspiration came from cinema.

From Bertrand Tavernier to Alain Corneau or Claude Miller, French film-makers from the post-war era grew up digging jazz, Hollywood films and other pieces of American pop culture that GIs carried in their bags. Many of them later brought American noir classics to the screen. Chéreau also safely chose to make his film debut within this genre, backed by experienced co-writer Jean-Claude Carrière. *Flesh of the Orchid (La chair d'orchidée)* is an adaptation of James Hadley Chase, starring Charlotte Rampling, Bruno Cremer and, in supporting roles, two French legends, Simone Signoret and Edwige Feuillére. It tells the story of a young woman from a rich family, who escapes from a mental asylum where she was sent by the aunt who wanted to steal her inheritance. It was a good way for the young director to get accustomed to his new medium. However, the film, visually too ambitious and over-sophisticated,

Charlotte Rampling in **Flesh of the Orchid**

was not well received when it opened in 1975.

On the set, Chéreau had met Hervé Guibert, a 20-year-old journalist who also wrote for children. They started working on a project that would become The Wounded Man in 1983. Guibert's personality and his premature death, years later, would play a key role in Chéreau's life and creative inspiration.

Shot in 1978, Judith Therpauve was brought to Chéreau by Simone Signoret. Shot in realistic style, in total contrast to Flesh of the Orchid, it tells the true story of a woman who tries to sustain the moral values of her small, independent local newspaper in the face of takeover pressure from a major newspaper group. Some 30 years later, it looks like a prophetic movie, bringing out topics such as the threat to press freedom. In terms of visual style, it is obvious that Chéreau was still looking for a personal way to use the camera. It would be five years before he returned to cinema, to direct what he now calls his real first film: The Wounded Man.

Simone Signoret and Marcel Imhof in **Judith Therpauve**

Breaking taboos

The Wounded Man (L'Homme blessé) is Chéreau's first film in many ways, but mostly because it was neither an adaptation, nor made at the instigation of a star. It is the result of a long and personal collaboration between Guibert and Chéreau. They shared the César for Best Script in 1984, for this story of a young innocent (newcomer Jean-Hugues Anglade) who

prostitutes himself in a Paris train station for the love of a handsome lout (Italian idol Vittorio Mezzogiorno, dubbed in French by Gérard Depardieu). It was one of the events of the 1984 Cannes Competition: one of the first films to deal with homosexuality and to film gay sex scenes in a direct manner.

Vittorio Mezzogiorno, left, and Jean-Hugues Anglade
in **The Wounded Man**

A year after its release, all the stakes, motivations and fears of the characters suddenly belonged to the past: AIDS had appeared and The Wounded Man became the last filmic testimony of the pre-AIDS era. Most of all, along with Jean-Jacques Beneix's Diva and other films, it started a modern, melancholic aesthetic, a sophisticated urban poetry, perhaps the defining spirit of French cinema in the 1980s. Jean-Hugues Anglade would become one of the icons of this cinema in Beneix's Betty Blue and Luc Besson's Subway. One of Chéreau's major contributions to French cinema has always been his talent for discovering actors.

Chéreau was still a very active play producer and director. In 1982, he had become the director of the Théâtre des Amandiers in Nanterre, outside Paris. There, he directed classics by Genet, Marivaux and Shakespeare and original creations by a young playwright and friend, Bernard-Marie Koltès. His theatre was also a drama school and his next films gave him the opportunity to put his students on screen. Shot in 1987, Hôtel de France is an adaptation of Chekhov's Platonov, which Chéreau produced at Nanterre the same year. Set in a contemporary environment, it tells the story of old friends reunited after 20 years.

The film was co-produced by Théâtre des Amandiers and featured students who would later become important French actors: Valeria Bruni-Tedeschi, Agnès Jaoui, Vincent Pérez. During the 1970s and 1980s, Chéreau also acted himself, playing revolutionary figure Camille Desmoulin in Andrej Wajda's *Danton* (1982) and Napoleon for Youssef Chahine in *Farewell Bonaparte* (1985).

Around 1992, scriptwriter Danièle Thompson gave him a copy of Alexandre Dumas' *La Reine Margot*. The project grew into one of the biggest productions in the history of French cinema, chosen as the opening at Cannes in 1994. Everyone expected a beautiful costume drama produced by Claude Berri, served by the glamorous presence of Isabelle Adjani and an all-star European cast (Daniel Auteuil, Jean-Claude Brialy, Virna Lisi, Miguel Bosé). Though the film received the Prix du Jury and Best Actress for Virna Lisi, it was a box-office disappointment.

Chéreau did not regard Dumas' novel as Saturday night family entertainment: the characters wear dirty shirts and long greasy hair; Lisi looks like Nosferatu; Goran Bregovic's music gives the film a hip-hop pulse. The dialogue, has a strange contemporary and poetic echo ("I am smelling my own death," says Jean-Hugues Anglade as the dying king). The film shocked the audience with its brutal violence. Piles of dead bodies floated in the mud, as Chéreau was probably influenced by the revolutions in Eastern Europe and the horrific images of a mass grave in Timisoara.

With detailed autopsy scenes and the blood bath of the St. Bartholomew massacre, this is a crude and realistic reconstitution of history. More than any of his other films, *La Reine Margot* reveals Chéreau's dramatic architecture, a structure that looks like a solar system: a strong character as a sun (like Adjani as Margot), around which dance numerous satellites. In 1998, *Those Who Love Me Can Take the Train (Ceux qui m'aiment prendront le train)* brought this configuration to its highest point.

A symphony of actors

Like *Hôtel de France, Those Who Love Me...* follows the familiar plot of a reunion of old friends. As in *The Big Chill* (a cult movie in France), the starting point is a funeral. This time, the central figure is a dead artist who has decided to be buried in Limoges, far away from Paris, because "those who love him can take the train".

Chéreau's camera, usually as still as a painter's canvas, flies like a squash ball between the painter's friends, lovers and family, who all remember him in different ways. As an opera director, Chéreau has worked with conductors

Isabelle Adjani and Vincent Pérez in **La Reine Margot**

Kobal

such as Daniel Barenboim and Pierre Boulez and here he plays his 10 actors like musical instruments. The energy of Valeria Bruni-Tedeschi, the cold mineral power of Pascal Greggory, the delicate fragility of Charles Berling, the ambiguous seduction of Jean-Louis Trintignant (as the painter and his brother) – all these faces and voices meet in a harmonic symphony of actors. This masterful orchestration earned Chéreau the 2000 César for Best Director.

Delphine Schlitz, left, and Sylvain Jacques in
Those Who Love Me Can Take the Train

Those Who Love Me... opens in the train station that Chéreau had filmed in *The Wounded Man*. By now, Hervé Guibert had died of AIDS, after writing a major book and having shot a film on his own disease. Chéreau came back to the topic of homosexuality and included in *Those Who Love Me...* a young, HIV-positive man. In a way, *The Wounded Man* was the story of a violent birth, describing how a man finds out who he is. *Those Who Love Me...* revolves around death – of the main characters, of love between couples – but also involves re-birth.

One of the best characters is Viviane, the transvestite played by Vincent Pérez, who takes the decision to re-invent himself as a woman. With this film, Chéreau was looking back at his own work, the changes his generation had gone through, but he was also moving on to a different chapter, and ends the film with a spectacular, symbolic aerial shot: in a large cemetery, the camera flies over hundreds of tombs, before reaching the railway tracks. Each track is a

possibility, a new destination. Chéreau was on his way to another kind of cinema.

Three duets

In the new century, Chéreau has tried to find greater simplicity, in films that rely not on an ensemble but on just two leading characters. On stage, Chéreau had already experienced this kind of duet in one of his best productions: *In the Loneliness of Cotton Fields*, a play by Bernard-Marie Koltès exploring the hate and dependence between a drug addict and his dealer. Chéreau appeared in it twice, in 1987 and in 1995, with Pascal Greggory, and it may be the origin of his three films exploring relations between pairs: lovers, brothers, husband and wife. All of them could bare the same title: *Intimacy*.

Shot in London and in English, *Intimacy* is an adaptation of a Hanif Kureishi novel. Every Wednesday, a divorced man (Mark Rylance) meets a married actress (Kerry Fox) in his apartment; they make love without exchanging a word and she leaves. The ritual is destroyed when he tries to find out who she is. Shot in cold grey and green tones, with explicit but unerotic sex scenes, the film describes urban loneliness and the slow destruction of a couple. Most of all, it is served by a very sharp, clear storyline, a flow that takes the character and the viewer in one coherent direction, all the way to an inevitable ending.

Mark Rylance and Kerry Fox in **Intimacy**

This marked Chéreau's first collaboration with scriptwriter Anne-Louise Tridivic, who would also write his next films. Whereas his previous work

Canal +/Telema/Kobal

Jack English/Azor Films//France 2/Greenpoint/Kobal

flourished in several directions, the stories seemingly open to multiple possibilities, the three duets co-written with Tridivic share a simple and readable arc. After *Intimacy* received a Golden Bear and the prize for Best Actress for Kerry Fox in Berlin 2001, Chéreau announced a return to the epic: a biopic on Napoleon starring Al Pacino. But after two fruitless years this ambitious project was abandoned.

In a very short time, almost to fill the emptiness left by this unborn film, Chéreau adapted a novel by Patrick Besson, directed, and for the first time produced, what probably remains his best film to date: *His Brother (Son frère)*. A man suffering from a blood disease (Bruno Todeschini) comes back to his younger brother (Eric Caravaca), whom he has not seen for 10 years. Through his slow death, he restarts a broken relationship.

CNC/Kobal

Eric Caravaca, left, and Bruno Todeschini in **His Brother**

This film, which won a Silver Bear at Berlin, can be seen as a sequel to *Intimacy*. Under the pale neon light of the hospital, we witness the same meticulous work of destruction, the same slow burn, but death has replaced desire in the bodies. Once again, the film bears no surprise or twist ending: the brother cannot be saved. Acceptance is the only possibility. Therefore, it is perhaps Chéreau's calmest piece; at peace with the horrific truth: that life sometimes does end after just 30 years.

Though *His Brother* is not about AIDS, Chéreau rooted it in his personal experience by quoting the last shot from Hervé Guibert's film on his own death: a man walks in the sea and is brutally swallowed by the depths. As a requiem, Marianne Faithfull sings "safe to sleep alone". The same fatal brutality characterises Chéreau's latest film, *Gabrielle*, an adaptation of a little-known short story by Joseph Conrad, "The Return".

In the early 1900s, a wealthy man (Pascal Greggory) comes home to his wife (Isabelle Huppert). He sees both house and spouse as symbols of his success. His life falls apart when he finds a letter: his wife has left with another man. One hour later, she comes back. Shot in Italy, *Gabrielle* is possibly Chéreau's most audacious project. In the vein of Ingmar Bergman, it tries to marry the simplicity of *Intimacy* and *His Brother* to the visual flamboyance of *La Reine Margot*. The result is almost experimental. The unusual voiceover describes the past, not the present, the film shifts from black-and-white to colour, and uses slow motion. Though Chéreau's most baroque movie, *Gabrielle* still revolves around his obsession with decomposition; the faces of Huppert and Greggory seem to be melting like wax.

If Chéreau's films are about wounded men, they are not really morbid. In *Intimacy*, Chéreau takes us to an acting class and gives a key to his conception of cinema: the students play basketball with an imaginary ball. *The Wounded Man* and *La Reine Margot* show the back streets of Paris, the toilets of train stations, places where loners look for fast love in the night. They slowly walk around, senses opened to a glimpse, a brief invitation or brutal opposition. These scenes are not only about sex; they are similar to the fancy dinner parties in Gabrielle's living room, where decent women walk around with their opened fans, where eyes meet or hit like daggers. Chéreau sees cinema as a way to catch this silent energy, the fluid power that circulates between bodies, the invisible streams of life – like a phantom basketball.

ADRIEN GOMBEAUD (AGombeaud@aol.com) is a member of the editorial board of *Positif*, a film critic and a travel journalist for the daily paper *Les Echos*.

Patrice Chéreau
Filmography

[Feature film directing credits only]

1974
LA CHAIR D'ORCHIDEE
(Flesh of the Orchid)
Script: PC and Jean-Claude Carrière, based on the novel by James Hadley Chase. Direction: PC. Photography: Pierre Lhomme. Sound: Harald Maury. Editing: Pierre Gilette. Players: Charlotte Rampling (Claire), Bruno Cremer (Louis Delage), Edwige Feuillère (Miss Wegener), Simone Signoret (Lady Vamos), François Simon (Bekerian), Hans-Christian Blech (Bekerian's brother), Alida Valli (mad woman in the train station). Produced by Vincent Malle. 110 mins.

1978
JUDITH THERPAUVE
Script: PC and Georges Conchon. Direction: PC. Photography: Pierre Lhomme. Costume: Thérèse Ripaud. Editing: Françoise Bonnot, Jacques Audiard. Players: Simone Signoret (Judith Therpauve), Philippe Léotard (Jean-Pierre Maurier), François Simon (Claude Hirsh-Balland), Robert Manuel (Droz), Bernard-Pierre Donnadieu (Laindreaux). Produced by Alfred de Graaf. 125 mins.

1983
L'HOMME BLESSE
(The Wounded Man)
Script: PC and Hervé Guibert. Direction: PC. Photography: Rénato Berta. Production design: Richard Peduzi. Editing: Denise de Casabiancca. Players: Jean-Hugues Anglade (Henri), Vittorio Mezzogiorno (Jean), Roland Bertin (Bosmans), Liza Kreuzer (Elizabeth), Gerard Desarthe (crying man), Claude Berri (client), Gérard Depardieu (dubbed voice of Jean). Produced by Marie-Laure Reyre. 109 mins.

1987
HOTEL DE FRANCE
Script: PC and Jean-François Goyet, based on Anton Chekhov's play Platonov*. Direction: PC.*

Photography: Pascal Marti. Editing: Albert Jurgenson. Players: Laurent Grevill (Michel), Valeria Bruni-Tedeschi (Sonia), Vincent Perez (Serge), Laura Benson (Anna), Thibault de Montalembert (Nicolas), Marc Citti (Philippe Galtier), Marianne Denicourt (Catherine), Isabelle Renault (Marie), Bruno Todeschini (Bouguereau), Agnès Jaoui (Miss Bouguereau). Produced by Claude Berri. 98 mins.

1994
LA REINE MARGOT
Script: Danièle Thompson and PC, based on the novel by Alexandre Dumas. Direction: PC. Photography: Philippe Rousselot. Sound: Dominique Hennequin, Guillaume Sciama. Editing: François Gédigier, Hélène Viard. Costume: Moidele Bickle, Bernadette Villard. Players: Isabelle Adjani (Margot), Daniel Auteuil (Henri de Navarre), Jean-Hugues Anglade (King Charles IX), Vincent Pérez (La Môle), Dominique Blanc (Henriette de Nevers), Virna Lisi (Catherine de Médicis), Pascal Greggory (Duc d'Anjou), Miguel Bosé (Duc de Guise), Asia Argento (Charlotte de Sauve), Jean-Claude Brialy (Coligny), Emmanuel Salinger (Du Bartas), Barbet Schroeder (The adviser), Bruno Todeschini (Armagnac), with Grégoire Colin, Valeria Bruni-Tedeschi, Hélène de Fougerolles. Produced by Claude Berri. 162 mins.

1998
CEUX QUI M'AIMENT PRENDRONT LE TRAIN
(Those Who Love Me Can Take the Train)
Script: PC, Danièle Thompson, Pierre Tridivic. Direction: PC. Photography: Eric Gautier. Sound: Jean-Pierre Laforce. Editing: François Gédigier. Players: Pascal Greggory (François), Valeria Bruni-Tedeschi (Claire), Charles Berling (Jean-Marie), Jean-Louis Trintignant (Lucien, Jean-Baptiste Emmerich), Bruno Todeschini (Louis), Sylvain Jacques (Bruno), Vincent Pérez

(Viviane), Roschdy Zem (Thierry), Dominique Blanc (Catherine), Olivier Gourmet (Bernard), Guillaume Canet (hitchhiker). Produced by Charles Gassot. 120 mins.

2001
INTIMACY
Script: PC and Anne-Louise Tridivic. Direction: PC. Photography: Eric Gautier. Sound: Guillaume Sciama, Jean-Pierre Laforce. Artistic director: Jacqueline Abrahams. Editing: François Gédigier. Costume: Caroline de Vivaise. Music: Eric Neveux. Players: Mark Rylance (Jay), Kerry Fox (Claire), Timothy Spall (Andy), Alastair Galbraith (Victor), Philippe Calvario (Ian), Marianne Faithfull (Betty). Produced by Charles Gassot. 119 mins.

2003
SON FRERE (His Brother)
Script: PC and Anne-Louise Tridivic, based on the novel by Philippe Besson. Direction: PC. Photography: Eric Gautier. Costume: Caroline de Vivaise. Sound: Guillaume Sciama. Players: Bruno Todeschini (Thomas), Eric Caravaca (Luc), Nathalie Boutefeu (Claire), Catherine Ferran (Doctor), Maurice Garrel (The old man on the bench), Robinson Stevenin (Manuel), Sylvain Jacques (Vincent). Produced by Pierre Chevalier. 95 mins.

2005
GABRIELLE
Script: PC and Anne-Louise Tridivic, based on a short story by Joseph Conrad, "The Return". Direction: PC. Photography: Eric Gautier. Editing: François Gédigier. Sound: Guillaume Sciama, Benoît Hillebrant, Olivier Dô Hùun. Production design: Olivier Radot. Music: Fabio Vacchi. Players: Isabelle Huppert (Gabrielle), Pascal Greggory (Jean Hervey), Claudia Coli (Yvonne), Thierry Hancisse (the chief editor), Chantal Neuwirth (Madeleine), Thierry Fortineau (one of the guests). Produced by: Serge Catoire. 90 mins.

David Cronenberg By Eddie Cockrell

Kobal

Among the most imaginative and thematically consistent film-makers at work anywhere over the last 30 years, David Cronenberg has forged a career that began with startling and groundbreaking low-budget horror movies in the 1970s. It has blossomed into a linked series of dark genre exercises that, in addition to providing thrills and gore, pose thought-provoking questions about the pervasive and often insidious influence of technology and organised medicine on humanity (*The Fly*, *Dead Ringers*), the darker side of psychological behaviour (*Naked Lunch*) and the dangerous intersection of sexual aberration and extreme violence (*Videodrome*, and just about every other film he's made).

Cronenberg's work has been aptly described as "body horror". Most genre fans of a certain age are intimately familiar with his bloody early work, including the sex-virus scare *Shivers* (1975); the Montreal epidemic thriller *Rabid* (1976); the killer children shocker *The Brood* (1979); and the head-exploding mutant horror saga *Scanners* (1981). Along with George Romero (*Dawn of the Dead*, 1978), Brian De Palma (*Sisters*, 1973), Wes Craven (*The Hills Have Eyes*, 1977), Larry Cohen (*God Told Me To*, 1976) and other then-

cult directors, Cronenberg defined the 1970s horror movie, albeit in a more pungently visual, thematically cohesive and purely personal way than his peers. Or, as another member of that exclusive club, John Carpenter, director of *Halloween* (1978), once said: "Cronenberg is better than the rest of us combined."

But with each new film in the most recent third of his career – from the chrome-cold perversity of *Crash* (1996), to the almost playful biotech shenanigans of *eXistenZ* (1999), and the focused brilliance of Ralph Fiennes as the profoundly disturbed *Spider* (2002) – the depth and richness of Cronenberg's vision have been coming to the fore. As Mark Irwin, who shot his early efforts, once said: "Probably the sum total of his works will be more impressive than any single film."

Exhibit A in the case for and against that theory is his 15th feature, the thoughtful, focused and deeply resonant *A History of Violence* (2005). Thirty years after *Shivers* sent shockwaves through the then marginalised horror genre, this magisterial new work continues Cronenberg's explorations of identity and fate, via a low-key, B-movie-ish plot about a smalltown American everyman who may or may not have a dark past that is rapidly catching up with him. It is at once the quietest of Cronenberg's works and among the most accomplished films of 2005.

There is a wealth of written material on Cronenberg, much of which includes the participation of the apparently affable and certainly eloquent film-maker; of particular interest is Faber's *Cronenberg on Cronenberg*, (1991; updated in 1997). Yet, as he confesses early in the commentary track for the 1996 Criterion Collection laser disc of *Dead Ringers* (1988), Cronenberg finds it "very difficult to come to terms with looking at my old films, much less analysing them and discussing them."

DAVID CRONENBERG was born on March 15, 1943, in Toronto, Ontario, to a journalist father and pianist mother. His middle-class childhood was spent surrounded by books and music. "I loved insects and science and animals as a kid," Cronenberg remembers on the *Dead Ringers* commentary. "But I don't think I was as strange as these kids [the Mantle twins, played by Jeremy Irons]. However, I think that I managed to avoid the other side of it, which was a kind of a shrivelling up, a deficiency of the emotional and the effective faculties."

An aspiring writer with a fondness for Vladimir Nabokov and William S. Burroughs, Cronenberg chose instead to study science at the University of Toronto, with an ambition towards biochemistry, but dropped out after less than a year. Re-enrolled for English Honours, he was soon distracted by film-making and founded a society called the Toronto Film Co-op with a group of like-minded students that included the Czech-born Canadian citizen Ivan Reitman, who would co-produce *Shivers* and enjoy a hugely successful directing–producing career in Hollywood (*Ghostbusters*, *Twins*).

Weird science

After making two short films, a psychiatrist–patient conversation, *Transfer* (1966), and a surrealist conspiracy thriller, *From the Drain* (1967), Cronenberg wrote and directed two 65-minute futuristic thrillers. In *Stereo* (1969), seven young adults are subjected to strange experiments by the Canadian Academy for Erotic Inquiry. In *Crimes of the Future* (1970), the assistant to a missing, insane dermatologist investigates Rouge's Malady, the cosmetics-borne disease discovered by his boss. Cronenberg considers these featurettes his first "finished, complete and autonomous" films. They also planted the seed for his enduring fascination with visionary scientists and their bizarre, inevitably doomed experiments.

Shivers and *Rabid* expand these themes: in the former, a parasite originally bred to bolster failing organ functions mutates into a sexually transmitted aphrodisiac that turns a luxury high-rise into a chaotic orgy of death. The latter extends this idea, as botched plastic surgery turns an innocent girl (porn queen Marilyn Chambers) into a vampiric runaway whose disease infects very nearly all of Montreal. Despite the extreme reactions generated by these startlingly original films – audiences of the day either loved or hated them – money, as always, did the talking: *Shivers* cost $385,000 and returned $5m; *Rabid* cost a little over half a million and returned more than $7m.

Cinema Ent. Enterprises/Kobal

Joe Silver under attack in **Rabid**

His third feature, *Fast Company*, is a melodrama set in and around the world of drag racing, and represents a startlingly commercial manifestation of Cronenberg's fondness for machinery, and automobiles in particular. Featuring the final performance of B-movie queen Claudia Jennings, the spottily distributed *Fast Company* has only recently surfaced on DVD, in a special edition that features both *Stereo* and *Crimes of the Future* on a second disc.

Then came *Scanners*, and the famous exploding head. A telepathic outsider, Vale (Stephen Lack) is one of a handful of so-called "scanners" being rounded up by a mysterious scientist (Patrick McGoohan) to serve the shadowy military combine Consec through their potent form of telekinesis. Yet a rival group of mutants, led by demented scanner Revok (Michael Ironside), is determined to thwart them, forcing a showdown between him and Vale. The weekend it opened, *Scanners* was the number one film in North America.

Michael Ironside in **Scanners**

Film Plan Intl./Kobal

Though it was "the most classic horror film I've done", as he told Rodley, and had his then largest budget ($1.5m) and most recognisable stars (Oliver Reed and Samantha Eggar), *The Brood* (1979) was not a commercial success. Inspired in part by his divorce which was happening at the time, Cronenberg imagined "Psychoplasmics" and the manifestation of one woman's rage into murderous children.

The commercial *Zone*

The chunk of his career post-*Brood* and pre-*M. Butterfly* (1993) is Cronenberg's most commercial to date. In *Videodrome*, James Woods plays an unscrupulous cable TV hustler whose discovery of the titular snuff show and sadomasochistic affair with the beautiful Nicki Brand (Blondie singer Deborah Harry) lead him down the path to madness. *The Dead Zone* (1983) was his first film to be set

James Woods and Debbie Harry in **Videodrome**

Universal/Kobal

in the United States, although Cronenberg shot it on Canadian locations, approximating the feel of smalltown America. Adapted – distilled is a better word – from Stephen King's novel, it stars Christopher Walken as Johnny Smith, a schoolteacher who awakens from a five-year coma to a new career peering into people's futures. Cronenberg remains mildly bitter over the commercial fate of *The Dead Zone*, which didn't meet expectations. He explained in a 2000 AFI documentary on his career: "You have to be lucky... because there are so many things that can happen on the way that have nothing to do with the movie. Corporate politics, internal struggles in a studio, in a distribution company. All of these things were happening at Paramount... and they really, really did interfere with the release of the movie. I think by all rights it should have been my biggest hit. And it was not."

Between *The Dead Zone* and *The Fly*, Cronenberg spent by his own estimation a year doing rewrites on *Total Recall*, a famously unproduced script from the Phillip K. Dick short story "We Can Remember it for You Wholesale" which had at one time also enthralled a clutch of other film-makers. During this period Cronenberg was also offered, and turned down, *Flashdance*, *Witness*, *Top Gun* and *Beverly Hills Cop*.

Out of money and feeling "very despondent", he was approached by Mel Brooks to helm a remake of a 1950s horror film. Quickly sensing what he called the "body-conscious" elements of the story of a scientist (Jeff Goldblum) who accidentally mixes his own DNA with that of the title insect and mutates horribly in front of his journalist girlfriend (Geena Davis), Cronenberg rewrote it to balance the horror with the relationship. The result was a resounding mainstream success. "It might be the biggest hit I'll ever have," he said in the AFI documentary, adding to Rodley: "I don't think *The Fly* is mainstream. No horror film is truly mainstream. When people say, 'Great, another Cronenberg movie! Let's take everybody and have popcorn!' – then I'll know I'm mainstream." This has yet to occur.

Jeff Goldblum in **The Fly**

Twin freaks

His next film, *Dead Ringers*, was inspired by a newspaper headline – "Twin Docs Found Dead in Posh Pad" – and the subsequent novelisation of this grim tale, and starred Jeremy Irons as gynaecologists Beverly and Elliot Mantle. Its disturbing imagery, non-graphic but suggestive, ended up giving Cronenberg another commercial success.

For his next film, *Naked Lunch*, Cronenberg drew on his love of William S. Burroughs to combine the titular novel with events from the author's life and the writing of the novel into something original and eye-catching. Peter Weller gives a supremely deadpan performance as exterminator and former junkie Bill Lee (a Burroughs pen name), who becomes involved with bizarre talking bugs in the Interzone, after accidentally shooting his wife. Funding challenges forced Cronenberg to cancel a planned shoot in Tangiers and recreate the milieu in a Canadian studio; the resulting sequences drew critical praise for their distinctive stylisation.

Though *M. Butterfly* is among his least-seen works, it's easy to imagine Cronenberg being attracted to David Henry Hwang's play, based on the true story of a 1930s French diplomat (Irons again) whose love for a Peking opera star was so idealised that for 20 years he never learned that the woman was actually a man – and a spy. "The central question of the case," wrote Roger Ebert,

with tangible reluctance, "'Why didn't he realise this was a man?'… was never answered in the courtroom, and now it is not answered in the movie, either. And without that answer, there is no story."

Peter Weller in **Naked Lunch**

A test of metal

"I could never make this into a movie," Cronenberg remembers thinking of J.G. Ballard's cult novel, *Crash*. "And so that was another instance where somehow that damn book had just gotten its hooks like a little parasite into my intestines, and took up residence there, and demanded to be dealt with." Horrified at the very idea, his then agent begged him to do *The Juror* instead.

Though maligned by critics, and the subject of much controversy, the story of a TV director (James Spader) sucked into a netherworld of fetishists whose goal is automotive destruction – and what one character calls "the reshaping of the human body by modern technology" – retains a certain ghastly power not unlike the urge that commands drivers to slow down to look at car wrecks. It is also perhaps the most organic collaboration yet from the skilled technicians Cronenberg uses for all his films, particularly the cold and lonely electric guitar wails of composer Howard Shore. *Crash* won the Special Jury Prize at Cannes.

eXistenZ signalled Cronenberg's first entirely original script since *Videodrome*, and covered vaguely similar material, updated to reflect new technologies. Inspired by the *fatwa* against

Salman Rushdie, it stars Jennifer Jason Leigh as fugitive game designer Allegra Geller, who enlists young marketing trainee Ted Pikul (Jude Law) to help her when the organic gaming device she's developed becomes damaged. "This is unquestionably Cronenberg Lite," wrote David Stratton in *Variety*, "but there is plenty of fun to be had from the absurdities and convoluted plotting."

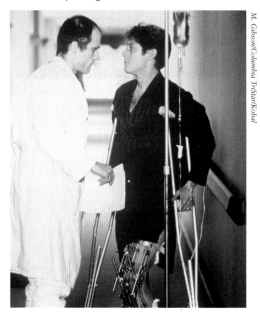

Elias Koteas, left, and James Spader in **Crash**

Said Cronenberg of his next film, adapted from the 1990 novel by Patrick McGrath: "*Spider* is an austere psychodrama with a profound human mystery at its heart. It has the feel of Samuel Beckett confronting Sigmund Freud." Ralph Fiennes gives one of his better performances as the unfortunate Spider, whose release from a British mental institution prompts harrowing hallucinations in which his troubled past blends with his current situation. Sadly, this superlative drama failed to find a wide audience.

A more detailed account of Cronenberg's latest film, *A History of Violence*, may be found in my report on the United States in this edition. Suffice it here to say that this perfectly controlled work, adapted from a graphic novel whose existence Cronenberg was unaware of until well into production, exhibits in its very title a multi-levelled

pun, not only on the theme of the film itself, but also in the way in which the director has pared away the genre excesses of his previous work to arrive at concentrated human truths. We all have a capacity for violence, says the film, and it might just be for the best if we admit it.

Cronenberg shooting **Spider** *with Ralph Fiennes*

Cronenberg still lives in the city of his birth, and prefers to work in Canada; to this date he has not officially exposed a foot of film in the United States (though sequences from *Spider* were shot in London). At press time it was reported that he was teaming with HBO on a TV series adaptation of *Dead Ringers*; *Cape Fear* scribe Wesley Strick will write, Cronenberg will direct. He acted in the recently cancelled ABC spy drama *Alias* (after proving his worth as an actor in, among numerous projects, Clive Barker's 1990 self-referential horror thriller, *Nightbreed*) and is attached to direct and produce the big-screen adaptation of Martin Amis' 1991 novel, *London Fields*, about a promiscuous psychic troubled by disturbing premonitions. It seems a snug fit. The Palm Springs International Film Festival has made Cronenberg the recipient of its "Vision Award" for January 2006; should *A History of Violence* figure prominently in the Oscar race, look for more such tributes in 2006 and beyond.

Cronenberg's films show us an artist whose life's work has been to connect lowbrow horror to deeper elements of shared humanity. "I do feel that in a way I'm a card-carrying Existentialist," he mused to the AFI. "I feel we have to create our own meaning: there is no outside meaning that comes from God or outer space or anywhere else. And yet… we need to feel that our lives have meaning and significance in some way. And we have to create that meaning. I think that's why we have that creative impulse. And so each person has to find his own means of responding to that impulse. And for me, for various reasons, some of them very mysterious to me, film-making is that means."

EDDIE COCKRELL (eddiec4370@aol.com) is a *Variety* film critic and freelance programming consultant who, when not reviewing from festivals in Europe and Canada, splits his time between Maryland and Sydney.

Bender/Spink/Kobal

Viggo Mortensen and Maria Bello in **A History of Violence**

David Cronenberg
Filmography

[Feature film directing credits only]

1975
SHIVERS (aka THEY CAME FROM WITHIN, THE PARASITE MURDERS)
Script and Direction: DC. Photography: Robert Saad. Editing: Patrick Dodd. Players: Paul Hampton (Roger St. Luc), Joe Silver (Rollo Linsky), Lynn Lowry (Forsythe), Allan Migicovsky (Nicholas Tudor), Susan Petrie (Janine Tudor). Produced by Ivan Reitman, John Dunning, Andre Link for DAL Productions Ltd., with the participation of the CFDC. 87 mins.

1977
RABID
Script and Direction: DC. Photography: Rene Verzier. Editing: Jean Lafleur. Production design: Claude Marchand. Players: Marilyn Chambers (Rose), Frank Moore (Hart Read), Joe Silver (Murray Cypher), Howard Ryshpan (Dr. Dan Keloid), Patricia Gage (Dr. Roxanne Keloid), Susan Roman (Mindy Kent), J. Roger Periard

(Lloyd Walsh), Lynne Deragon (Nurse Louise). Produced by John Dunning for Cinema Entertainment Enterprises (for DAL Productions Ltd.), with the participation of the CFDC. 91 mins.

1979
FAST COMPANY
Script: Phil Savath, Courtney Smith, DC, from an original story by Alan Treen. Direction: DC. Photography: Mark Irwin. Editing: Ronald Sanders. Production design: Carol Spier. Players: William Smith (Lonnie Johnson), Claudia Jennings (Sammy), John Saxon (Phil Adamson), Nicholas Campbell (Billy Brooker), Cedrick Smith (Gary Black), Judy Foster (Candy). Produced by Michael Lebowitz, Peter O'Brian, Courtney Smith for Michael Lebowitz Inc. (for Quadrant Films Ltd.), with the participation of the CFDC. 91 mins.

1979
THE BROOD
Script and Direction: DC. Photography: Mark Irwin. Editing: Alan Collins. Production design: Carol Spier. Players: Oliver Reed (Dr. Hal Raglan),

Samantha Eggar (Nola Carveth), Art Hindle (Frank Carveth), Cindy Hinds (Candice Carveth), Henry Beckman (Barton Kelly), Nuala FitzGerald (Juliana Kelly), Susan Hogan (Ruth Mayer), Michael Magee (Inspector Mrazek). Produced by Claude Heroux for Les Productions Mutuelles and Elgin International Productions, with the participation of the CFDC. 91 mins.

1981
SCANNERS
Script and Direction: DC. Photography: Mark Irwin. Editing: Ron Sanders. Production design: Carol Spier. Players: Jennifer O'Neill (Kim Obrist), Stephen Lack (Cameron Vale), Patrick McGoohan (Dr. Paul Ruth), Lawrence Z. Dane (Brandon Keller), Michael Ironside (Darryl Revok), Robert Silverman (Benjamin Pierce), Adam Ludwig (Arno Crostic). Produced by Claude Heroux for Filmplan International Inc., with the participation of the CFDC. 103 mins.

1983
VIDEODROME
Script and Direction: DC.

Photography: Mark Irwin. Editing: Ron Sanders. Production design: Carol Spier. Players: James Woods (Max Renn), *Sonja Smits* (Bianca O'Blivion), *Deborah Harry* (Nicki Brand), *Peter Dvorsky* (Harlan), *Les Carlson* (Barry Convex), *Jeck Creley* (Brian O'Blivion), *Lynne Gorman* (Masha). *Produced by Claude Heroux for Filmplan International II Inc., with the participation of the CFDC. 87 mins.*

1983
THE DEAD ZONE
Script: Jeffrey Boam, from the novel by Stephen King. Direction: DC. Photography: Mark Irwin. Editing: Ron Sanders. Production design: Carol Spier. Players: Christopher Walken (Johnny Smith), *Brooke Adams* (Sarah Bracknell), *Martin Sheen* (Greg Stillson), *Sean Sullivan* (Herb Smith), *Jackie Burroughs* (Vera Smith), *Herbert Lom* (Dr. Sam Weizak), *Tom Skerritt* (Bannerman). *Produced by Debra Hill for Dead Zone Productions, in association with Lorimar Productions Inc. 100 mins.*

1986
THE FLY
Script: Charles Edward Pogue, DC, from a story by George Langelaan. Photography: Mark Irwin. Editing: Ronald Sanders. Production design: Carol Spier. Players: Jeff Goldblum (Seth Brundle), *Geena Davis* (Veronica Quaife), *John Getz* (Stathis Borans), *Joy Boushel* (Tawny). *Produced by Stuart Cornfeld for Brooksfilms. 92 mins.*

1988
DEAD RINGERS
Script: DC, Norman Snider, from the novel "Twins" by Bari Wood and Jack Geasland. Photography: Peter Suschitzky. Editing: Ronald Sanders. Production design: Carol Spier. Players: Jeremy Irons (Beverly Mantle/Elliot Mantle), *Genevieve Bujold* (Claire Niveau), *Heidi von Palleske* (Cary), *Barbara Gordon* (Danuta), *Shirley Douglas* (Laura), *Stephen Lack*

(Anders Wolleck), *Nick Nichols* (Leo), *Lynn Cormack* (Arlene), *Damir Andrei* (Birchall), *Miriam Newhouse* (Mrs. Bookman). *Produced by DC, Marc Boyman for Mantle Clinic II Ltd., in association with Morgan Creek Productions, with the participation of Telefilm Canada. 115 mins.*

1991
NAKED LUNCH
Script and Direction: DC, from the novel by William S. Burroughs. Photography: Peter Suschitzky. Editing: Ronald Sanders. Production design: Carol Spier. Players: Peter Weller (Bill Lee), *Judy Davis* (Joan Lee, Joan Frost), *Roy Scheider* (Dr. Benway), *Ian Holm* (Tom Frost), *Julian Sands* (Yves Cloquet). *Produced by Jeremy Thomas for Recorded Picture Company, with the participation of Telefilm Canada and the Ontario Film Development Corporation. 115 mins.*

1993
M. BUTTERFLY
Script: David Henry Hwang, from his play. Direction: DC. Photography: Peter Suschitzky. Editing: Ronald Sanders. Production design: Carol Spier. Players: Jeremy Irons (Rene Gallimard), *John Lone* (Song Liling), *Barbara Sukowa* (Jeanne Gallimard), *Ian Richardson* (Ambassador Toulon), *Annabel Leventon* (Frau Baden). *Produced by Gabriella Martinelli for Geffen Pictures, Miranda Productions Inc. 101 mins.*

1996
CRASH
Script and Direction: DC, from the novel by J.G. Ballard. Photography: Peter Suschitzky. Editing: Ronald Sanders. Production design: Carol Spiers. Players: James Spader (James Ballard), *Holly Hunter* (Helen Remington), *Elias Koteas* (Vaughan), *Deborah Kara Unger* (Catherine Ballard), *Rosanna Arquette* (Gabrielle), *Peter MacNeill* (Colin Seagrave). *Produced by DC for Alliance*

Communications. 110 mins.
1999
eXistenZ
Script and Direction: DC. Photography: Peter Suschitzky. Editing: Ronald Sanders. Production design: Carol Spier. Players: Jennifer Jason Leigh (Allegra Geller), *Jude Law* (Ted Pikul), *Willem Dafoe* (Gas), *Ian Holm* (Kiri Vinokur), *Don McKellar* (Yevgeny Nourish), *Callum Keith Rennie* (Hugo Carlaw), *Sarah Polley* (Merle), *Christopher Eccleston* (Levi). *Produced by Robert Lantos, Andras Hamori, DC for Robert Lantos. 97 mins.*

2002
SPIDER
Script: Patrick McGrath, from his novel. Direction: DC. Photography: Peter Suschitzky. Editing: Ronald Sanders. Production design: Andrew Sanders. Players: Ralph Fiennes (Spider), *Miranda Richardson* (Yvonne/Mrs. Cleg/Mrs. Wilkinson), *Gabriel Byrne* (Bill Cleg), *Lynn Redgrave* (Mrs. Wilkinson), *John Neville* (Terrence), *Bradley Hall* (Boy Spider), *Gary Reineke* (Freddy). *Produced by DC, Samuel Hadida, Catherine Bailey for Capitol Films, Artists Independent Network, Grosvenor Park. 98 mins.*

2005
A HISTORY OF VIOLENCE
Script: Josh Olson, from the graphic novel by John Wagner and Vince Locke. Direction: DC. Photography: Peter Suschitzky. Editing: Ronald Sanders. Production design: Carol Spier. Players: Viggo Mortensen (Tom Stall), *Maria Bello* (Edie Stall), *William Hurt* (Richie Cusack), *Ashton Holmes* (Jack Stall), *Stephen McHattie* (Leland Jones), *Peter MacNeill* (Sheriff Sam Carney), *Ed Harris* (Carl Fogarty), *Heidi Hayes* (Sarah Stall), *Greg Bryk* (William "Billy" Orser). *Produced by Chris Bender, JC Spink for Benderspink. 96 mins.*

Michael Haneke By Eddie Cockrell

Studio Kanal +/CNC/Kobal

It's an oft-quoted line, first delivered with layers of meaning by one of the most demanding of contemporary film-makers – and perhaps the most misunderstood. Introducing a 1998 screening of one of his dark, emotionally terrifying films in London, Michael Haneke told the audience: "I wish you a disturbing evening".

Consider the evidence. Seemingly consumed by ennui, a well-to-do Austrian family commit suicide together after destroying their well-appointed flat (*The Seventh Continent*, 1989). A young high-schooler, fascinated by home-movie footage of a bolt gun destroying a pig, uses the same weapon to kill a classmate he meets in front of the video shop; his parents cover up the crime (*Benny's Video*, 1992). An Austrian youth's apparently unprovoked killing spree in a bank lobby is the centre of a dramatic ripple effect that reveals seemingly random sequences from the lives of his victims (*71 Fragments of a Chronology of Chance*, 1994). Two teenagers mock, torture and kill a family vacationing at their lakeside home (*Funny Games*, 1997).

In Paris, a chance encounter affects a handful of lives as it slowly but inevitably peels back the veneer of civility masking racial and social tensions (*Code Unknown*, 2000). Among the arts elite of Vienna, a repressed, spinsterish piano instructor takes a vain young lover who brutally turns the tables on her (*The Piano Teacher*, 2001). In the chaotic wake of an unspecified global catastrophe, one fragmented family attempts to make sense of their post-apocalyptic world, while holed up with other survivors in an abandoned train depot in the European wilderness (*Time of the Wolf*, 2002). Back in Paris, a literary talk show host and his increasingly exasperated wife attempt to connect the sinister videotapes that seem to threaten them and their teenage son with a childhood event involving the husband's Algerian playmate (*Hidden*, 2005).

What do these chilling synopses tell someone who has seen only one, or a few, of the eight theatrical features Haneke has directed to date? Described superficially, as above, the films sound like nothing so much as latter-day Hitchcock, probably hyped for the jittery, post-Michael Bay thrills crowd. After all, didn't Hitchcock become famous for gleefully toying with his audience? And isn't the goal of Hollywood genre film-making, locked into a doomed spiral of technological advances, to provide precisely that cheap adrenaline rush to an increasingly dulled and jaded public?

Pilloried by some as unbearably mannered and almost fascistically cold, held up by others as unsparing pleas to halt the unravelling of a fundamentally flawed social order, the films of Michael Haneke are... well, a good bit of both. From *The Seventh Continent* to *Hidden*, Haneke has concerned himself with the insidious influence of pre-packaged media – particularly television – on the individual, and with collective, gossamer-thin social veneers and the cold-blooded random violence that inevitably follows when the former tears the latter.

The average filmgoer resists his movies for the same reasons most sensible folk shudder to look into an open grave: these are hard truths, coldly inevitable. "There but for the grace of God go I," viewers think. In fact, one Haneke newbie, posting online after an autumn 2005 festival screening of *Hidden* in upstate New York, fussed: "I never want to think that hard again to figure out what a film means, or whether a dead rooster is just a dead rooster." Earlier, she had overheard another patron proclaim that *Hidden* "ruined my Saturday night".

Juliette Binoche andn Daniel Auteuil in **Hidden**

Somewhere, the director may be chuckling. Yet these are the films of an artist completely aware of his provocations and their impact. Yet, rather than provoking for the sake of the shock, his remarkable consistency of vision suggests that Haneke is a supreme moralist at heart.

These are harrowing journeys, and many mainstream audiences are unwilling to make them. Yet, as committed as Haneke is to telling hard truths, and as keen as he is to discuss his vision, he will only go so far to soften the blow to the unwary viewer, and brushes off most questions about specific deeper meanings. "You can lead a horse to water, but you can't make him drink," is one variation on his stock answer. "I can't force the audience into anything. It can take or leave my offer. I am not a social worker." This might be misinterpreted as a sadistic form of evasion, when a more reasonable explanation is that, having put himself through the trauma of

making these confrontational works, there's little energy left to advocate their messages beyond the work itself.

Manipulating the viewer

MICHAEL HANEKE was born on March 23, 1942, in Munich, Germany. His father, Fritz Haneke, was a director and actor from Düsseldorf; his mother was Austrian actress Beatrix von Degenschild. His childhood and youth were spent in Wiener Neustadt, Austria, the regional centre of south-east Lower Austria, nestled in the "Magic Mountains" approximately 40 minutes' drive south of Vienna. After pursuing his interests in acting and piano-playing, Haneke studied psychology and philosophy at university in Vienna. During this time he also worked as a film and literary critic. From 1967 to 1971, he was an editor and television feature *Dramaturg* at the Südwestfunk TV and radio stations in Baden-Baden, Germany.

It was there that he directed his first stage production, *Whole Days in the Trees with Marguerite Duras*, in the early 1970s. This led to plays by Strindberg, Goethe, Kleist and others in more than a half-dozen German and Austrian cities. Haneke began making films for television in 1974 and the two decades between his beginnings in television and his move to theatrical features afforded him plenty of time to observe the effect of TV on the populace. "I don't believe that television provides us with that much information about what is going on in the world," he told an interviewer years later. "We see images that are manipulated – because there is no such thing as an objective image – but that give us the illusion of knowledge. And that is very dangerous, because we end up being manipulated by that illusion."

By the time of his debut feature, *The Seventh Continent* (*Der siebente Kontinent*), the foundations of his world-view are already evident. As with many subsequent Haneke protagonists, the married couple on view are named a variation of Georg/Georges and Anna/Anne, a partial nod to *Who's Afraid of Virginia Woolf?* that

Artifical Eye Films

establishes faintly ironic monikers for his archetypal upper-middle-class characters and their strange melodrama. The antiseptic modernity of their lives, revealed in fragments that substantially avoid faces, subtly emphasises the coldness of their comfort. The final components in his cinema of apprehension are city streets themselves, filmed with a flatness that literally prevents the viewer from anticipating what will enter the frame and from where.

As the family wordlessly prepares for an end they've described as emigration to Australia (hence the mythical title), a blaring television is never far away, underscoring the medium's ability to soothe even those in inarticulate turmoil. It's a bleak commentary, to be sure, but the clarity of vision and emotional remorselessness announced a substantial new voice.

Video, nasty

"Don't you think there'd be better ways to rebel?" exasperated father Georg (Ulrich Muehe) asks his son Benny (Arno Frisch), in *Benny's Video* (1992), after the lad has just shaved his head. Unfortunately, Georg has yet to learn of Benny's real act of defiance, an extension of the action movies he watches on TV in his cocoon-like bedroom (dismissing them to a schoolmate as "all ketchup and plastic"). The genuine revolt is the grisly murder of a girl, seen only through the fixed gaze of Benny's unblinking video camera. "I don't know," he tells Georg later, when asked why he killed her. "I wanted to see what it's like." An unrelenting and remorseless meditation on the deadening distance of media,

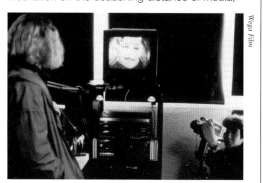

Arno Frisch as Benny in **Benny's Video**, *with Ingrid Stassner*

Benny's Video remains a soul-chilling exercise that prefigured the well-to-do lethargy of *American Beauty* (1999).

Perhaps Haneke's least seen film, *71 Fragments of a Chronology of Chance* (*71 Fragmente einer Chronologie des Zufalls*, 1994) marks the dawning of a new strain of global awareness, his first steps towards a goodbye – or at least a farewell – to the insular criticism of his home country, and a warm-up for *Code Unknown* (2000). *71 Fragments* is worthy of rediscovery. Together, these first three films have been referred to as the "Glaciation Trilogy" for obvious reasons. Though unavailable on Region 1 DVD, Cinema Parallel offers an NTSC VHS tape of *The Seventh Continent*, and there's a French Region 2 boxed set of the German-language trilogy (minus English subtitles).

Haneke's third feature, **71 Fragments of a Chronology of Chance**

Asked to contribute to the compilation film *Lumière and Company* (1996), in which prominent directors from all over the world shot a minute-long sequence using the Lumières' original hand-cranked camera, Haneke responded by filming chunks of the news – including a space shuttle, the Queen, a bombing, sports, weather – broadcast on March 19, 1995, one hundred years to the day since the first exhibition of the brothers' films. "Is cinema mortal?" he is asked on-camera. "Of course," comes the inevitable reply, "like everything."

A few years later, Haneke directed a distinctly personal feature version of Franz Kafka's unfinished novel, *The Castle*, for television.

Featuring the same three lead actors who would feature in perhaps his most shocking work, *Funny Games*, it was an exercise rife with contradictions. "My attitude is that TV can never really be any form of art," he told an interviewer, "because it serves audience expectations. I would not have dared to turn *The Castle* into a movie for the big screen; on TV, it's okay because it has different objectives."

A holiday from hell

In the midst of the domestic carnage in *Funny Games*, as a family is about to be exterminated in their lakeshore holiday villa by a pair of teenagers dressed in – of all things – tennis whites, one of the attackers (Arno Frisch again) glances casually at the camera and asks: "What do you think? Do you think they've a chance of winning? You are on their side, aren't you?" It is this jarring complicity, along with a bold melding of the film itself with the video convenience of rewind, that make this rapidly growing cult favourite so shocking. Later, when the exhausted mother manages to grab a shotgun and to even the score, the family's fate is sealed when the film itself is rewound so the weapon can be snatched from her. At once a horrific film and a subversion of the very idea of a horror film, *Funny Games* is a singularly terrifying experience. It was around this time that Haneke began to feel constricted by the scarcity of film finance in Austria, not to mention whatever pressure he may have felt as a result of the harsh criticisms of contemporary society levelled by his work (even years later, as his reputation grew, *Hidden* would be delayed as crucial funding sources fell through). French backers came to the rescue,

apparently stimulated by the interest of Juliette Binoche, who is said to have called the director one day with a request that they work together. The resulting relocation clearly recharged Haneke, as his French films explore deeper emotional and societal issues.

Paris by nightmare

The first of his French films, *Code Unknown: Incomplete Tales of Several Journeys* (*Code inconnu: Récit incomplet de divers voyages*, to give it its full title), finds an inspired metaphor in its very title: characters cannot enter their supposedly safe apartments because electronic key codes have been mysteriously changed. Beginning with a chance meeting on a Paris street between actress Anne (Binoche) and her husband's younger brother, Jean (Alexandre Hamidi), events soon spiral out of control when the angry boy throws a piece of paper at a Romanian street beggar, Maria (Luminita Gheorghiu). As the ripple effect takes hold, the film is intercut with scenes of Anne working, including an acting exercise with chunks of a horror film for which Anne is rehearsing that upend the veracity of the racially charged drama being played out for real. Given the explosive tensions in and around Paris in late 2005, *Code Unknown* now crackles with a new urgency.

Juliette Binoche in **Code Unknown**

Haneke's first theatrical feature adapted from an existing novel (by feminist playwright and kindred spirit Elfriede Jelinek, winner of the 2004 Nobel Prize for Literature) and his most prominent US release to date, *The Piano Teacher* (*La pianiste*), is nearly atypical in the Haneke œuvre, and not

Arno Frisch, left, and Stefan Clapczynski in **Funny Games**

only for these two distinctions. It is more of a struggle among individuals than an indictment of a group or milieu, and draws its power more from character flaws than blind chance or cruel fate. *The Piano Teacher* won the Grand Jury Prize at Cannes, as well as festival awards for Isabelle Huppert, in the title role, and Benoît Magimel, as her lover.

Canal +/CNC/Kobal

Isabelle Huppert, left, Annie Girardot and Benoît Magimel in **The Piano Teacher**

As a follow-up, Haneke decided to twist the speculative fiction genre in much the same way as *Funny Games* had subverted horror films; where the fate of the latter's doomed family is inexorably sealed, *Time of the Wolf* (*Le temps du loup*) presents a mother (Isabelle Huppert) and her children, Eva (Anais Demoustier) and Ben (Lucas Biscombe), as survivors of an off-screen apocalypse whose lot in the rubble of society seems to be wandering and waiting. As they stumble about, literally in the dark, there's little to prepare the viewer for the unexpectedly moving grace note of the climax, in which Ben seems to reverse the fate of his namesake in *Benny's Video* by sacrificing himself for the good of the group.

Apollo Media/Chesler/Perlmutter Prods./Kobal

Isabelle Huppert in **Time of the Wolf**

The all-seeing television, now suspended in a mammoth wall full of books, resurfaces in *Hidden* (2005), which may well be Haneke's most accessible film to date. When mysterious videotapes, showing static shots of the front of the upscale Paris townhouse of TV literary show host Georges (Daniel Auteil) and publisher Anna (Binoche again), begin showing up on their doorstep, the pair are mystified. When the tapes are appended by crude drawings of a child or a rooster with crayoned blood, a memory from Georges' past is dislodged. This involves former playmate Majid (Maurice Benichou), an Algerian now struggling to make ends meet, whose mystification at Georges' increasing agitation results in a shocking act.

That few secrets are revealed throughout the course of this chilling, masterful inquiry into fear and culpability should come as no surprise to long-time Haneke observers. An exquisite political metaphor is there for those who want it; others can, as Haneke asserts, "take or leave my offer". *Hidden* was a hot tip for the Palme d'Or at Cannes in 2005, but instead earned him the arguably more appropriate Best Director award.

As with many directors in complete control of their visions, Haneke has shown a preference for familiar faces in front of and behind the camera. More than a half-dozen actors have appeared in several films (reinforcing the George-and-Martha interchangeability of the pawns in Haneke's games), and he calls upon the same key colleagues to photograph, edit and handle production design. The same man, Wega Film's Veit Heduschka, has produced or co-produced all his theatrical features, and *The Castle*.

The protracted international rollout and ongoing critical acclaim for *Hidden*, which in December 2005 added four European Film Awards, including Best Film and Best Director, to its Cannes triumph, feel like another plateau for Haneke. For the future, rumours have circulated that he has considered remaking at least one of his films in English. At Cannes, he announced that his next film would be the opera *Don Juan*, to be made in Paris. Whatever material he chooses, the resulting film will probably "ruin" many more Saturday nights.

Michael Haneke
Filmography

[Feature film directing credits only]

1989
DER SIEBENTE KONTINENT
(The Seventh Continent)
*Script and Direction: MH.
Photography: Toni Peschke.
Editing: Marie Homolkova.
Production design: Rudi Czettel.
Players: Birgit Doll (Anna), Dieter
Berner (Georg), Leni Tanzer
(Eva), Udo Samel (Uncle Alex),
Silvia Fenz (woman at the
optician). Produced by Veit
Heduschka for Wega Film. 90 mins.*

1992
BENNY'S VIDEO
*Script and Direction: MH.
Photography: Christian Berger.
Editing: Marie Homolkova.
Production design: Christoph
Kanter. Players: Arno Frisch
(Benny), Angela Winkler (Anna),
Ulrich Muehe (Georg), Ingrid
Stassner (young girl). Produced
by Veit Heduschka, Bernard Lang
for Wega Film. 105 mins.*

1994
71 FRAGMENTE EINER
CHRONOLOGIE DES ZUFALLS
(71 Fragments of a Chronology
of Chance)
*Script and Direction: MH.
Photography: Christian Berger.
Editing: Marie Homolkova.
Production design: Christoph
Kanter. Players: Gabriel Cosmin
Urdes (Marian Radu), Lukas
Miko (Max), Otto Gruenmandl
(Tomek), Anne Bennent (Inge
Brunner), Udo Samel (Paul
Brunner), Branko Samarovski
(Hans), Claudia Martini (Maria),
Georg Friedrich (Bernie).
Produced by Veit Heduschka for
Wega Film. 96 mins.*

1997
FUNNY GAMES
*Script and Direction: MH.
Photography: Juergen Juerges.
Editing: Andreas Prochaska.
Production design: Christoph
Kanter. Players: Susanne Lothar
(Anna), Ulrich Muehe (Georg),
Arno Frisch (Paul), Frank Giering*

(Peter), *Stefan Clapczynski*
(Georgie), *Doris Kunstmann*
(Gerda), *Christoph Bantzer*
(Fred), *Wolfgang Gluck* (Robert),
Susanne Meneghel (Gerda's sister),
Monika Zallinger (Eva). *Produced
by Veit Heduschka for Wega Film.
108 mins.*

2000
CODE INCONNU:
RECIT INCOMPLET DE
DIVERS VOYAGES
(Code Unknown: Incomplete
Tales of Several Journeys)
*Script and Direction: MH.
Photography: Juergen Juerges.
Editing: Andreas Prochaska,
Karin Hartusch, Nadine Muse.
Production design: Manuel de
Chauvigny. Players: Juliette
Binoche (Anne), Thierry Neuvic
(Georges), Sepp Beirbichler (the
farmer), Alexandre Hamidi (Jean),
Helene Diarra (Aminate), Ona Lu
Yenke (Amadou), Djibril Kouyate
(Youssouf), Luminita Gheorghiu
(Maria), Crenguta Hariton Stoica
(Irina), Bob Nicolescu (Dragos),
Bruno Todeschini (Pierre), Paulus
Manker (the station agent), Didier
Flamand (the director [voice
only], Walide Akfir (the young
Arab), Maurice Benichou (the old
Arab), Carlo Brandt (Henri),
Philippe DeMarle (Paul), Arsinée
Khanjian (Francine). Produced by
Marin Karmitz, Alain Sarde for
MK2 Productions, Les Films
Alain Sarde. 112 mins.*

2001
LA PIANISTE
(The Piano Teacher)
*Script and Direction: MH, from
the novel by Elfriede Jelinek.
Photography: Christian Berger.
Editing: Monika Willi, Nadine
Muse. Production design:
Christoph Kanter. Players: Isabelle
Huppert (Erika Kohut), Annie
Girardot (the mother), Benoît
Magimel (Walter Klemmer),
Susanne Lothar (Mrs. Schoeber),
Anna Sigalevitch (Anna Schoeber),
Udo Samel (Dr. Blonski), Cornelia
Koendgen (Mrs. Blonski), Thomas
Weinhappel (Baryton), Philipp
Heiss (Napravnik). Produced by
Veit Heduschka, Marin Karmitz,*

*Alain Sarde, for Wega Film, MK2,
Les Films Alain Sarde, Arte
France Cinema. 125 mins.*

2002
LE TEMPS DU LOUP
(Time of the Wolf)
*Script and Direction: MH.
Photography: Juergen Juerges.
Editing: Monika Willi, Nadine
Muse. Production design:
Christoph Kanter. Players: Isabelle
Huppert (Anne), Anais
Demoustier (Eva), Lucas
Biscombe (Ben), Hakim Taleb
(young runaway), Béatrice Dalle
(Lise Brandt), Patrice Chéreau
(Thomas Brandt), Brigitte Rouan
(Bea), Olivier Gourmet
(Koslowski), Daniel Duval
(Georges), Branko Sanarovski
(policeman), Thierry van Werveke
(Jean), Maurice Benichou (Mr.
Azoulay), Maryline Even (Mrs.
Axoulay), Florence Loiret-Caille
(Nathalie Azoulay). Produced
by Margaret Menegoz, Veit
Heduschka for Les Films du
Losange, Wega Film, Bavaria Film.
113 mins.*

2005
CACHE (Hidden)
*Script and Direction: MH.
Photography: Christian Berger.
Editing: Michael Hudecek,
Nadine Muse. Production design:
Emmanuel de Chauvigny
(France), Christoph Kanter
(Austria). Players: Daniel Auteuil
(Georges), Juliette Binoche
(Anne), Maurice Benichou
(Majid), Annie Girardot (Georges'
mother), Bernard Le Coq
(Georges' editor-in-chief), Walid
Afkir (Majid's son), Lester
Makedonsky (Pierrot), Daniel
Duval (Pierre), Nathalie Richard
(Mathilde), Denis Podalydes
(Yvon), Aissa Maiga (Chantal),
Caroline Baehr (nurse), Christian
Benedetti (Georges' Father
[young]), Annette Faure (Georges'
Mother [young]), Hugo Flamingni
(Georges [as a child]). Produced
by Margaret Menegoz, Veit
Heduschka for Les Films du
Losange, Wega Film, Bavaria
Film, Bim Distribuzione. 121 mins.*

Deepa Mehta By Cameron Bailey

When Deepa Mehta opened the 2005 Toronto International Film Festival with the world premiere of *Water*, it was more than an industry honour. It was a film-maker coming home. With Atom Egoyan's *Where the Truth Lies* and David Cronenberg's *A History of Violence* in the running for the same Toronto slot, *Water*'s prime position elevated Mehta to the top rank of her adopted country's directors. To both friends and journalists, she pointed out that her film, written and directed by an Indian immigrant and filmed entirely in Hindi, was considered Canadian enough to open Toronto. It was a statement of both pride and a little amazement.

Mehta had a right to be amazed. Not only have her Indian stories been embraced by Canada, but the scope of her films marks a break with the astringent tone of directors like Cronenberg and Egoyan. Over the seven features she has directed since her debut in 1991, Mehta's work has become central to Canadian cinema, even as her films offer more heat and colour than the film world expects from the great white north.

In fact, Mehta is an exact hybrid of Canadian and Indian cinema. Her trilogy of *Fire* (1996), *Earth* (1998) and *Water* (2005) is liberal and western enough to be attacked or even banned by conservative elements in India, yet rich with Indian tradition and history. She embraced Mumbai's all-singing, all-dancing style in *Bollywood/Hollywood* (2002), but with typical Canuck irony. Even her WASP romance, *The Republic of Love* (2003), set in a wintry Toronto, featured *tabla* music by UK artist Talvin Singh.

Love across the divides

If any one theme can be discerned in Mehta's films, it is her interest in pushing against the grain. Her "elemental trilogy" is marked by an almost activist desire to question authority. *Fire* tells the story of two Hindu wives who become lovers, defying their husbands and their faith. *Earth* chronicles the destruction of a multicultural community in 1947 Lahore, as Partition whips up factional sentiment and pits Hindus against Muslims, with Parsees caught in between. And *Water* follows two Hindu widows in 1938 who resist the lives of privation and suffering to which they have been condemned. In each case the villain is not an individual, so much as the power that individuals invest in tradition and group loyalty. Each of these films is also a love story, but in each case love demands that Mehta's protagonists cross sometimes lethal cultural boundaries.

Often those boundaries are the trenches between men and women. Mehta's films speak not just against the injustice of male dominance over women, but also against the separation of male and female spheres. In *Fire*, Sita (Nandita Das) begins her rebellion by trying on her husband's oversized trousers and smoking a cigarette. In *Camilla* (1994), octogenarian Jessica

Tandy takes the active, typically male role in her own romantic life, pursuing a long-lost love (played by real-life husband Hume Cronyn).

With *Water*, Mehta has reached a new peak. The film's original production in 2000 had been beset by violent protests. Hindu fundamentalists burned down the set, seized negatives and launched a public campaign against Mehta. Eventually the government of the Indian state of Uttar Pradesh halted production. It took five years to remount the film, which was shot in Sri Lanka in 2004 under the fake title *Full Moon*. Having recently made *Bollywood/Hollywood* and *The Republic of Love*, Mehta hid *Water* under the cover of innocuous romance.

Those five years also saw Mehta honing her craft. "In cinematic terms,' she told Indian online publication Rediff.com, "I began to realise I could use the camera and the actors to convey emotions, and rely less on dialogue." The result is a film powered by Mehta's longstanding commitment to individual liberty in the face of groupthink, crafted with new grace and maturity. Covering the film at the 2005 Pusan Film Festival, *The Economist* wrote: "*Water* combines a humanist message, political courage and visual poetry in a way not seen since the death of Satyajit Ray. It is the finest Indian film for a generation." That's praise any Indian film-maker would kill for – but complicated acclaim for a woman who also considers herself fully Canadian.

DEEPA MEHTA was born in 1949 in Amritsar, India, to a father who distributed Hindi movies. Her younger brother, Dilip, is a well-known photo-journalist. She studied philosophy at the University of New Delhi, where she was first drawn to making her own films. "I met someone who had a small documentary house in Delhi," she told indieWIRE. "I was wondering if I should do my dissertation or not and it seemed a good stop-gap thing to do was to help make documentaries or learn something about them."

In India, she met the Canadian film-maker Paul Saltzman, who had photographed the Beatles at the Maharishi Mahesh Yogi's ashram during his first trip to the country in 1968. Mehta married Saltzman in Delhi in 1973, and moved to Canada with him. She began her career in Toronto shooting documentaries and writing scripts for children's films. She founded Sunrise Films with Saltzman, and worked as an editor, producer and director. In 1987, she produced and co-directed the omnibus film *Martha*, *Ruth & Edie* with Norma Bailey and Danièle J. Suissa. Its three stories explored the emotional lives of three women who meet at a feminist seminar. Both its themes and its mix of light comedy and social drama foreshadowed later work, especially *Camilla* and *The Republic of Love*.

A beautiful friendship begins

In 1991, Mehta made her feature debut with *Sam & Me*, the story of an Indian immigrant to Toronto who takes work as carer to a cantankerous, older Jewish man. Although the script mined Mehta's own culture-clash story, it was written by Ranjit Chowdhry, who also co-starred, with Peter Boretski. The film marked the beginning of Mehta's collaboration with Chowdhry, who excelled at playing comic servile characters, capturing the complex mix of wit, innocence and passive-aggression of a particular Indian type. After his starring turn in Mehta's debut, he took supporting roles in *Camilla*, *Fire* and *Bollywood/Hollywood*. *Sam & Me* premiered at Cannes, where it was awarded a Special Mention for the Camera d'Or.

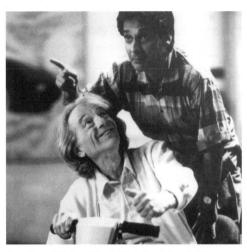

Peter Boretski, left, and Ranjit Chowdhry in **Sam & Me**

Sam & Me was released at a time of cultural foment in Toronto. The city was seeing a wave of immigrant artists set new agendas for local culture, with film-makers often leading the way. Egoyan's unsettling early dramas, *Next of Kin* and *Family Viewing*, had already shown Armenian identity to be a source of stark alienation, while Srinivas Krishna's *Masala*, also released in 1991, tossed Indo-Canadian angst into a post-modern blender. Mehta's work was far less adventurous formally, but her arguments were every bit as pointed. From her first film onwards, she pushed for a complex notion of identity that could include multiple traditions and individualism all at the same time.

It was three years before her next feature. In the interim, she directed an episode of *The Young Indiana Jones Chronicles* (1992) television spin-off for George Lucas, shooting in Benares, India, where years later she would attempt to film *Water*. When fundamentalists were burning her in effigy in India, Lucas was among the prominent film-makers to come to her defense.

Jessica Tandy, left, and Bridget Fonda in **Camilla**

For her sophomore feature, Mehta was hired to direct Oscar-winner Jessica Tandy in her penultimate role. *Camilla* matched Tandy's high-spirited performance with Bridget Fonda's more buttoned down role, as an aspiring musician undermined by the scepticism of her husband (Elias Koteas). The result is a road movie driven by a kind of feminist euphoria, as the women come alive once they leave men behind. Indeed, men are often peripheral to the main story in Mehta's films, as she pursues the contours of female relationships. At the same time, she is a sucker for romantic love. *Camilla* climaxes in a touching reunion between Tandy's character and her old love (Hume Cronyn), no doubt deepened by the half-century the two actors had spent together.

The power of three

Reportedly not completely happy with the finished cut of *Camilla*, Mehta decided to commit to more personal projects. In 1996, she launched *Fire* at the Toronto International Film Festival. In an unprecedented move, she announced the film as the first in a trilogy. Few Canadian indie film-makers can count on completing three films. But Mehta had clear ideas in mind. "The trilogy is about elements on one level that nurture and destroy us," she later told indieWIRE. "They are very tangible elements. *Fire* is about the politics of sexuality, *Earth* is about the politics of nationalism and *Water* is about the politics of religion."

Fire, as it turned out, was also very much about the politics of religion in India. When the drama about a lesbian affair between two New Delhi wives debuted in India it was greeted by violent protests, stoked by Shiv Sena, a Hindu fundamentalist party. Men smashed up the lobbies of cinemas where it played. Women tore down posters. Politicians denounced it as un-Indian. The federal Minister of State for Information and Broadcasting stepped in, but took the side of the protesters. "The country's law and order situation cannot be jeopardised for a mere film," he told *The Statesman*.

Shabana Azmi and Ranji Chowdhry in **Fire**

Shaftesbury/Skreba/Kobal

Trial by Fire/Kobal

Surprisingly, *Fire* was cleared by India's censorship board, not once but twice, after the protests forced the board to reconsider its original verdict. Although the storm had centred on lesbianism, the film clearly struck deeper chords with audiences. Nandita Das plays Sita, a new wife whose husband neglects her and continues an affair. Shabana Azmi, not coincidentally a progressive member of India's parliament, plays Radha, a wife whose husband has long withheld sexual affection in the pursuit of spiritual transcendence. Both women are frustrated and confined within their marriages. As Das noted: "When women come to see this film they're not seeing it as a lesbian film. They're probably relating to the loneliness that women go through."

In one of the film's defining scenes, Mehta dramatises both that loneliness and the intimacy of domestic repression. Sita is a virgin when she marries. After a joyless consummation, her husband rolls over and falls asleep. Sita gets up and starts scrubbing the bloodstained sheet clean, as her husband lies slumped unconscious beside her. This is classic Mehta: a picture of injustice, emotionally wrenching and beautifully lit.

A nation split in two

If *Fire* told an intimate story with national repercussions, *Earth* flipped the script. Mehta took on nothing less than the defining wound of both India and Pakistan: the 1947 partition of one country into two, following the departure of the British colonisers. The film is set in a Lahore neighbourhood where a Parsee family – descendants of Persian migrants – employs a Hindu nanny who is being wooed by a Muslim man. All is harmonious until the country is divided into mostly Hindu India and mostly Muslim Pakistan. One of the largest migrations in human history begins, and slaughter erupts on all sides.

Partition remains the testing ground for the subcontinent's great artists. While *Earth* could never attempt the scope of Salman Rushdie's *Midnight's Children*, for instance, it is surprisingly successful in clarifying the complex forces at work in 1947, by showing how they affect one

neighbourhood. It is also Mehta's strongest articulation to date of her ideal of pluralism. The multi-faith, multi-cultural community that is torn apart in this film is reflected in smaller details elsewhere, like the cross-dressing eunuch pimp who works among the widows in *Water*, or the fact that the philandering husband in *Fire* has a Chinese-Indian girlfriend. Canada likes to think it has a monopoly on multiculturalism; Mehta makes it global.

David Hamilton/Jhamu Sughand/Kobal

Nandita Das and Aamir Khan in **Earth**

After *Earth*, Mehta was on schedule to complete the trilogy with *Water* in 2000, but the violent protests shut her down. Speaking to Rediff.com, she recalled that she never gave up hope of making Water. "But I did two [other] films – *Bollywood/Hollywood* and *Republic of Love* – because I needed to move far from the controversies, bitterness and sense of betrayal." Both films are light compared to *Fire* and *Earth*, perhaps reflecting the relative safety of her adopted Toronto.

Different Tree Same Wood/Kobal

Lisa Ray in **Bollywood/Hollywood**

Bollywood/Hollywood sends up the conventions of Hindi musicals and American romantic comedies in a story of an Indo-Canadian man who hires a "Hispanic" woman to pretend to be his fiancée, then finds out she is actually Indian. *The Republic of Love* brought her into Nora Ephron territory, with a story, adapted from a novel by Carol Shields, of a woman with impossible romantic ideals (Emilia Fox) who falls for a man too quick to marry (Bruce Greenwood). In one of the film's funniest scenes, Kristen Thompson plays a demanding lover to Greenwood's character: "Could you start by rubbing my instep? Talk to me, baby. Feel free to use your tongue. Come up here and lie beside me. Let's just hold each other and talk." Mehta is not above making fun of the kind of female self-actualisation her films generally champion.

These two films stand apart from *Fire* and *Earth* aesthetically, too. For the past 10 years, Giles Nuttgens has shot Mehta's films in India, while Douglas Koch has shot her films in Canada. While that is surely a reflection of production realities in each country, it results in different palettes as well. Nuttgens' images are more colourful, and also carry a misty, romantic quality. Koch's Toronto look is cleaner and sharper.

The shift in consensus

Both *Bollywood/Hollywood* and *The Republic of Love* received mixed reviews. In fact, Mehta has never been a critics' darling. Reviewing *Bollywood/Hollywood* in *Variety*, Derek Elley described it as "lacking any kind of nuance, and oozing a self-satisfied smirk at its own dandy cleverness", while Andrew Pulver in *The Guardian* claimed the film's "germ of a good idea" was "sunk by toe-curling dialogue and transparently awkward emoting".

With *Water*, critics noticed a pronounced evolution in Mehta's work. "Gone is the tendency toward heart-on-the-sleeve emotions that marred both her previous trilogy entries and interim pics *Bollywood/Hollywood* and *The Republic of Love*," wrote Eddie Cockrell in *Variety*. He hailed *Water* as "profoundly moving" and "deeply satisfying". And then there is the rapturous *Economist*: "Like *La terra trema* and *The Battleship Potemkin*, *Water* uses great artistry to challenge orthodox views. It is in the grand humanist tradition of Ray, Ms. Mehta's mentor, and Vittorio De Sica."

David Hamilton Productions

Lisa Ray and John Abraham in **Water**

Mehta is unique among Canadian directors, and unprecedented among Indians. Her films play festivals and attract academic scrutiny, but she is one of the few independents to cross the C$1m mark at the box-office, which she did with both *Bollywood/Hollywood* and *Water*. She champions the Canadian ideals of fairness and pluralism, and the Indian principle of secular freedom in the face of religious or cultural dogma. And yet the comforts and responsibilities of family are central to all of her films, as are the pleasures of romantic love. Her work continues to be activist – a recent TV documentary, *Let's Talk About It*, allows children to question their own parents about domestic abuse within the family – but her images are never less than gorgeous. Reviewing *Earth* in the *New York Times*, Stephen Holden remarked on the film's "amber glow", which gave it "a ruddy twilit sensuality along with a sense of nocturnal foreboding".

Having completed her trilogy at last, Mehta will next take on the story of the *Komagata Maru*, a ship full of British Indian migrants that the Canadian government blocked from landing at Vancouver in 1914. "This is going to be a big project," Mehta says, "bigger than everything I have done so far." *Exclusion* will be shot both in India and in Canada – uniting Mehta's two worlds for the first time.

CAMERON BAILEY (dubwise63@yahoo.com) is a film critic and programmer, based in Toronto. He reviews for *NOW* magazine and CBC Radio One and programmes for the Toronto International Film Festival, where his responsibilities include the Indian selection.

Deepa Mehta Filmography

1991
SAM & ME
Script: Ranjit Chowdhry.
Direction: DM. Photography:
Guy Dufaux. Editing: Boyd
Bonitzke. Production Design:
Linda Del Rosario, Richard Paris.
Players: Ranjit Chowdhry
(Nikhil), Peter Boretski (Sam
Cohen), Om Puri (Chetan
Parikh), Heath Lamberts (Morris
Cohen), Kulbhushan Kharbanda
(Boldev), Javed Jaffrey [as Javid
Jafri] (Xavier), Jolly Bader (Ali),
Leonard Chow (Keith Wong),
Marcia Diamond (Hannah Cohen),
Gina Wilkinson (Mariana), Howard
Jerome (Mr. Klugman), Lance Koyata
(Takahito), Andy Marshall
(Vincent) Kay Tremblay (Mrs.
Rohrlich), Gene Mack (Lucas).
Produced by DM, Robert Wertheimer
for Sunrise Films. 96 mins.

1994
CAMILLA
Script: Paul Quarrington, Ali
Jennings (story). Direction: DM.
Photography: Guy Dufaux.
Editing: Barry Farrell. Production
Design: Sandra Kybartas. Players:
Jessica Tandy (Camilla Cara),
Bridget Fonda (Freda Lopez),
Elias Koteas (Vincent Lopez),
Maury Chaykin (Harold Cara),
Graham Greene (Hunt Weller)
Hume Cronyn (Ewald), Ranjit
Chowdhry (Kapur), George Harris
(Jerry), Sandi Ross (Border Guard),
Gerry Quigley (Border Official),
Atom Egoyan (Director), Devyani
Saltzman (Girl). Produced by
Christina Jennings, Simon Relph
for Shaftesbury Films. 95 mins.

1996
FIRE
Script: DM. Direction: DM.
Photography: Giles Nuttgens.
Editing: Barry Farrell. Production
Design: Aradhana Seth. Players:
Shabana Azmi (Radha), Nandita
Das (Sita), Javed Jaffrey [as Jaaved
Jaaferi] (Jatin), Kulbhushan
Kharbanda (Ashok), Ranjit
Chowdhry (Mundu), Alice Poon
(Julie), Karishma Jhalani (Young
Radha), Ramanjeet Kaur (Young

Radha's mother), Dilip Mehta
(Young Radha's father), Vinay
Pathak (Guide at Taj Mahal),
Kushal Rekhi (Biji), Ram Gopal
Bajaj (Swamiji), Ravinder Happy
(oily man in video shop), Devyani
Mehta Saltzman (girl in video
shop), Sunil Chabra [as Sunil
Chhabra] (milkman on bicycle),
Avijit Dutt (Julie's father), Shasea
Bahadur (Julie's brother).
Produced by DM, Bobby Bedi for
Trial By Fire Films. 104 mins.

1998
EARTH
Script: DM, based on Bapsi
Sidhwa's autobiography, Cracking
India. Direction: DM. Photography:
Giles Nuttgens. Editing: Barry
Farrell. Production Design: Aradhana
Seth. Players: Aamir Khan (Ice
Candy Man), Nandita Das (Ayah
Shanta) Rahul Khanna (Hasan),
Maia Sethna (Lenny), Kitu
Gidwani (Bunty Sethna), Kulbushan
Kharbanda (Imam Din), Arif Zakaria
(Rustom Sethna), Gulshan Grover
(Mr. Singh), Eric Peterson (Mr.
Rogers). Produced by Delip
Mehta, Anne Masson, DM for
Cracking the Earth Films. 110 mins.

2002
BOLLYWOOD/HOLLYWOOD
Script and Direction: DM.
Photography: Douglas Koch.
Editing: Barry Farrell. Production
Design: Tamara Deverell. Players:
Rahul Khanna (Rahul Seth), Lisa
Ray (Sue (Sunita) Singh), Rishma
Malik (Twinky Seth), Jazz Mann
(Bobby), Moushumi Chatterjee

(Mrs. Seth), Dina Pathak (Mrs.
Seth (grandmother), Kulbhushan
Kharbanda (Mr. Singh), Ranjit
Chowdhry (Rocky), Leesa
Gaspari (Lucy), Arjun Lombardi-
Singh (Govind), Jessica Paré
(Kimberly). Produced by David
Hamilton for Different Tree Same
Wood. 105 mins.

2003
THE REPUBLIC OF LOVE
Script: DM, Esta Spalding, from
the novel by Carol Shields.
Direction: DM. Photography:
Douglas Koch. Editing: Barry
Farrell. Production Design: Sandra
Kybartas. Players: Bruce Greenwood
(Tom), Emilia Fox (Fay), Edward
Fox (Richard), Martha Henry
(Audrey), Jan Rubes (Strom),
Gary Farmer (Ted), Lloyd Owen
(Peter), Jackie Burroughs (Betty),
Claire Bloom (Onion). Produced
by Anna Stratton, Julie Baines for
Triptych Media/Dan Films. 96 mins.

2005
WATER
Script and Direction: DM.
Photography: Giles Nuttgens.
Editing: Colin Monie. Production
Design: Dilip Mehta. Players:
Seema Biswas (Shakuntala), Lisa
Ray (Kalyani), John Abraham
(Narayan), Sarala (Chuyia),
Manorama (Madhumati), Vidula
Javalgekar (Patiraji, aka "Auntie"),
Raghuvir Yadav (Gulabi), Kulbushan
Kharbanda (Sadananda), Vinay
Pathak (Rabindra). Produced by
David Hamilton for David
Hamilton Productions. 117 mins.

Different Tree Same Wood/Kobal

Bollywood/Hollywood sends up Hindi musicals

Carlos Sorin By Alfredo Friedlander

ike many other Argentine directors, before Carlos Sorin worked on feature films he was heavily involved in other areas of production. He was particularly successful in producing commercials in Argentina, Colombia and Ecuador during the 1970s, and only in the 1980s did he become a movie director. His emergence as one of the most relevant world film-makers is rather recent, and with a new project already under way he has a strong chance of achieving a third hit in a row, following the national and international success of *Minimal Stories* and *Bombón El perro*. This would constitute an almost unprecedented feat in Argentina, where production is erratic for the majority of its most famous directors.

What makes Sorin such a special personality is his peculiar approach to film-making. His reliance on non-professional performers, whom he calls "non-actors", has to do with his preference for working with real people. He admits that he makes an initial draft of the script and only when he finds the "non-actors" does he rewrite everything, according to their personalities.

Another recurring element in Sorin's films is his preference for Patagonia as a location. "Ever since I was a child," he explains, "I have had some kind of weakness for Patagonia. Maybe for me it has the same meaning as for many Europeans. It is a mysterious area in a world where mystery has become rare. In Patagonia you can drive for several hours without seeing a single human being. You really feel that you are at the end of the world. I find that attractive in many ways, especially to place these small, intricate little stories of ordinary people in these epic backgrounds."

CARLOS SORIN was born in Buenos Aires on October 10, 1944. Aged eight, he was given a movie projector – a toy that used movies made from paper. What he really wanted was a projector with celluloid film, and at 12 he obtained a proper kit that included his first 16mm camera. He studied at the School of Cinema in La Plata, a city near Buenos Aires, and started working as assistant director to the late Alberto Fischerman.

His consolidation came in the advertising industry, where over a 20-year period he produced so many commercials that their combined length, as he himself points out, is equivalent to 15 feature films. He gained invaluable experience in those days, especially in the technical aspects of film-making, but had to change direction when he turned to features, as he explains: "Advertising is a formalism, a baroque style, which may work or dazzle for 30 seconds, but which might be absolutely unbearable during 90 minutes. Its objective is to seduce in order to sell. It is completely different from a feature where one has to produce emotions for the audience." It took him 18 months to finish his first feature, shooting only at weekends, because he was unable to find anybody interested in buying it.

It all started in Patagonia

Several directors before Sorin had wanted to film the true story of a Frenchman, Orllie-Antoine de Tounens (born in 1825 in Périgueux), who proclaimed the Kingdom of Araucania and Patagonia and declared himself King Orllie I. Two of the projects, both known as *The New France* (*La nueva Francia*), were aborted in the early 1970s. The second attempt, which was to have been directed by Juan Fresán and Jorge Goldenberg, was never finished because of lack of funds. Then Sorin and Goldenberg, a popular screenwriter, decided to co-write what became *A King and His Movie* (*La película del rey*, 1986).

Sorin took 18 months to shoot **A King and His Movie**

It tells the story of a young director, David Bass (played by the talented actor Hugo Chávez), who, together with his production manager, Arturo (Ulises Dumont), has difficulties in getting financial support. Consequently, they are unable to secure "stars" for their film and have to content themselves with a hippie as King Orllie I, a real prostitute as a brothel owner and a construction worker as an Araucano Indian chief. Once they have assembled their cast and crew, they travel to southern Patagonia, only to discover that their main financial backer has abandoned them. When most of their collaborators desert the shoot, they are obliged to live in an orphanage and, finally, to share a tent. There is an unforgettable moment close to the end in which the stubborn director, determined to finish the

movie, dons the wig of King Orllie and shoots a delirious scene using mannequins as extras.

The irony of the film-making travails depicted in *A King and His Movie* is that Sorin himself faced severe difficulties during the protracted shoot. At one point, for example, the crew were waiting for some horses to move a chariot, but the animals proved reluctant and the crew had trouble finding a truck to replace them. No doubt, reality sometimes surpasses fiction.

Sorin's first movie was released in Argentina at the end of August 1986 and immediately competed at Venice, where it won the Silver Lion for a First Film. It was also the winner of Spain's Goya award for Best Spanish-Language Foreign Film. Critics all over the world praised its qualities, and perhaps one of the most appropriate views was expressed by the late Argentinean critic, Jorge Abel Martín, when he wrote: "This beautiful initial film should be declared suitable only for those who are passionate, crazy and delirious, and therefore absolutely forbidden for indolent people."

Dentist on a motorbike

Next, Sorin directed a TV production co-written with Alan Pauls. *La era del ñandú* (literally, *The Age of the Ñandú*) was pure fiction about a miracle drug, obtained from a gland of the *ñandú* (a large bird commonly found in the Pampas), that could supposedly prevent people from getting old, thereby posing a dangerous challenge to multinational pharmaceutical laboratories. This impressive pseudo-documentary was very warmly received by TV viewers.

In 1989, the same year that Daniel Day-Lewis won a well-deserved Oscar for Best Actor for *My Left Foot*, he came to Argentina to shoot *Eversmile, New Jersey* (*Eterna sonrisa de New Jersey*), Sorin's second feature. An offbeat comedy, it followed Dr. Fergus O'Connell (Day-Lewis), a dentist travelling through Patagonia on his motorcycle and fighting tooth decay as if he were a missionary. A rather atypical road movie, it has episodes in which O'Connell has to face reluctant patients and old-fashioned colleagues. Then he meets Estela. Although about to get married, she decides to join O'Connell and become his assistant and friend.

Films del Camino/Kobal

Daniel Day-Lewis in **Eversmile, New Jersey**

Estela was played by Serbian actress Mirjana Jokovic, who had starred one year earlier in *Journey to the South*, a co-production with Yugoslavia, directed by Argentina's Juan Bautista Stagnaro. Interestingly, the Eversmile crew included a young Fabián Bielinsky as First Assistant Director, who would go on to become famous with his two features, *Nine Queens* and *El Aura*. *Eversmile, New Jersey*, which took its name from a fictitious "Eversmile Foundation of New Jersey", was never released in Argentina and remains a little-seen comedy. For the final cut, the producers required significant alterations and cuts to, among other elements, the soundtrack. It is clearly not Sorin's best movie.

On the road again

It is hard to understand why 13 years elapsed between *Eversmile* and *Minimal Stories* (*Historias mínimas*). But the long wait was worthwhile, since Sorin's third feature had some important

changes in its conception. For the first time, he decided to cast mostly "non-actors", which, strangely enough, was what David Bass had done in *A King and His Movie*.

When asked about the conditions in which *Minimal Stories* was shot, the director once said: "I feel comfortable in Patagonia. First of all, it is as if I was in my own movie study. When I am there, immediately I have the feeling that I am on the verge of shooting a film or that I am in a movie project. It is difficult to shoot a picture in Patagonia: the food is not good, accommodation is at a one-star hotel, the wind is unbearable, and there is dust everywhere. But at the same time I have the sensation that this challenge stimulates the whole crew and most notably the actors. The other advantage is that when you are 2,500 kilometres from Buenos Aires you feel as if you are retreating in a monastery. The movie becomes the centre of attraction of the whole group, even for people only slightly involved, like the electrician."

Javier Lombardo and Rosa Valsecchi in **Minimal Stories**

Minimal Stories follows three characters travelling along the solitary roads of southern Patagonia. Don Justo (Antonio Benedictis), 80, has escaped from his son's stifling care. He is looking for his missing dog, which someone reports seeing in San Julián, but mostly he is aiming to find peace of mind before his death. Roberto (Javier Lombardo, one of the few professional actors in the cast) is 40 and a travelling salesman. He is carrying a specially ordered birthday cake for the son of a young widow whose love he hopes to win. That very same day, Maria, 25 and very poor, travels by bus with her baby girl to a distant TV contest, where she may win a food processor. Each character travels separately, but their paths cross along the deserted Patagonic roads.

In a director's note, Sorin recalls an experience that strongly influenced his decision to cast "non-actors", which is worth quoting at length: "Some years ago, I was hired to shoot a commercial for a telephone company in the Patagonia steppe, where the telephone was about to be connected for the first time. We had cast actors in Buenos Aires, who were there to play the anxious villagers. Upon my arrival in the little village, one day before shooting, I had the feeling that the great excitement among the 150 inhabitants was not due to the shooting but to the arrival of the telephone.

"I realised it was pointless to shoot the fictionalisation of something that was really happening right in front of me. So I left the actors in a nearby hotel and the next day I filmed the villagers. They brought their kids, wives and telephone numbers written down on the palms of their hands (many of them talked with relatives for the very first time). They roasted lamb and turned the shooting into a great party. The film negative, not only sensible to light, registered that feeling, and the impact of the commercial was amazing. It transmitted something real, authentic and absolutely strange to the artificial world of advertising and television.

"Since then I have had the idea of making a fictional film with "non-actors", as another way of facing reality and its representation. *Minimal Stories* is born from this idea." The film stayed on screens for many months in Argentina, thanks to powerful word of mouth, and received, among other prizes, the Special Jury Award at the San Sebastián Film Festival.

A dog's life

Sorin admits to being responsible for the failure of Eversmile and knows that 13 years was far too long a gap between that film and *Minimal Stories*. Only two years later, in 2004, he released his fourth movie, *Bombón El perro* (*El Perro*), which, as he says, is his way of recovering lost time.

Juan Villegas, a mechanic who has lost his job at a gas station, now earns his living by selling hand-made knives and doing odd jobs. When he repairs the car of an elderly woman, she offers to pay him with a huge white dog, an amazing example of Dogo Argentino. At first Juan refuses, since a dog of this size, he says, probably eats more than he does. But the widow finally convinces him that Bombón has pedigree, making him valuable and also good company for a lonely man like Juan. With the help of Walter, a dog trainer, Juan discovers that his life may change if he enters Bombón in dog shows. Then they consider another possibility, which is for the dog to become a breeding "stud".

When asked why he chose to use dogs prominently in his last two films, Sorin replies that "dogs are important in our lives. People who live in the countryside, they all have dogs, so everybody has their own story with a dog. It is not the relationship between the man and the dog that is important; the dog represents some kind of fuel in the development of the man's character... In *Bombón*, there is someone who is unemployed and in his 50's. In Argentina, with the current economic problems, you don't normally get a second chance in life at that age. But Bombón becomes his second chance."

Referring to Gregorio, the dog used in the film, Sorin says: "He was a very obedient dog. From the first time I wrote the script I was looking for a dog that was not particularly effusive and affectionate, that would be reserved. Of course the dog is exactly like us, some moments you actually see that it is thinking. Look, he's got his internal conflicts." Here, Sorin relies more than ever on non-actors (Gregorio included!) and once again shoots in his beloved Patagonia. The movie was praised by local critics and shown in many festivals. In San Sebastián it won the FIPRESCI Prize and was well received in Europe, particularly in England, where it was a major word-of-mouth success, and France.

Also in 2004, Sorin participated in *18-J*, a compilation of 10 shorts conceived as a tribute to the 85 victims of the bomb that exploded on July 18, 1994 at the Argentine–Israeli Mutual Association. Sorin's short, the last of ten, showed, one after the other, photos of the victims, accompanied by very touching and sad music. In February 2006, he was scheduled to begin shooting his fifth feature – and the first not set in Patagonia. Its working title is *El camino de San Diego* and again "non-actors" will be the main participants. Sorin continues to make up for lost time, and critics and audiences look forward to being transported once again by the scenes of great emotion produced by this exceptional director.

ALFREDO FRIEDLANDER

(fredyfriedlander@fibertel.com.ar) is a member of the Asociación de Cronistas Cinematográficos de Argentina. He writes regularly for www.leedor.com, presents movies at the 51-year-old Cine Club Núcleo, and is, above all, a film buff.

Juan Villegas and Gregorio in **Bombón El perro**

Guacamole Films/OK Films/Kobal

Carlos Sorin
Filmography

[Feature film directing credits only]

1986
LA PELÍCULA DEL REY
(A King and His Movie)
*Script: Jorge Goldenberg and CS.
Direction: CS. Photography:
Esteban Courtalón. Editing:
Alberto Yaccelini. Production
design: Margarita Jusid. Music:
Carlos Franzetti. Players: Ulises
Dumont (Arturo), Julio Chávez
(David), Miguel Dedovich (Oso),
Villanueva Cosse (Desfontaine),
David Llewelyn (Lachaise), Ana
María Giunta (Madama), Roxana
Berco (Lucía), Marilia Paranhos
(Lula), Rubén Szuchmacher
(German translator), César García
(Bonnano), Eduardo Hernández
(Rosales), Rubén Patagonia
(Quillapan), Ricardo Hamlin
(Maxi). Produced by Perla
Lichtenstein, Gustavo Sierra and
Ezequiel Abalos for Carlos Sorin
Cine SA. 107 mins*

1989
ETERNA SONRISA DE NEW
JERSEY (Eversmile, New Jersey)
*Script: Jorge Goldenberg, Roberto
Scheuer and CS. Direction: CS.
Photography: Esteban Courtalón.
Editing: Luis César D'Angiolillo
and Bryan Oates. Production
design : María Luisa Bertotto.
Music: Steve Levine. Players:
Daniel Day-Lewis (Dr. Fergus
O'Connell), Mirjana Jokovic
(Estela), Gabriel Acher (Celeste),
Julio de Grazia (Dr. Ulises),
Ignacio Quirós (the boss), Miguel
Ligero (Brother Felix), Ana María
Giunta (lady in a small town),
Boy Olmi (radio announcer),
Eduardo D'Angelo (manager),
Alberto Benegas (sheriff), Roberto
Catarineu (López), Miguel
Dedovich (Brother Conrad).
Produced by Oscar Kramer for
Los Films del Camino
Productions. 91 mins.*

2002
HISTORIAS MÍNIMAS
(Minimal Stories)
*Script: Pablo Solarz. Direction:
CS. Photography: Hugo Colace.
Editing: Mohamed Rajid.
Production design: Margarita
Jusid. Music: Nicolás Sorin.
Players: Javier Lombardo
(Roberto), Antonio Benedictis
(Don Justo), Javiera Bravo
(María), Francis Sandoval
(María's daughter), Carlos
Montero (Losa), Aníbal
Maldonado (Don Fermín), Julia
Solomonoff (Julia), María Rosa
Cianferoni (Ana), Mariela Díaz
(friend of María), María del
Carmen Jiménez (baker woman
1), Rosa Valsecchi (baker woman
2), Mario Splanguño (baker),
Enrique Otranto (Carlos).
Produced by Martín Bardi for
Guacamole Films, Wanda Vision
(Spain). 94 mins.*

2004
EL PERRO (Bombón El perro)
*Script: Santiago Callori, Salvador
Roselli and CS, from an original
idea by CS. Direction: CS.
Photography: Hugo Colace.
Editing: Mohamed Rajid.
Production design: Margarita
Jusid. Music: Nicolás Sorin.
Players: Juan Villegas (Juan
Villegas), Walter Donado
(Walter), Gregorio (Bombón the
dog), Mico Estevez (Gracielita),
Pascual Condito (Pascual),
Claudina Fazzini (Claudina), Kita
Ca (Claudina's mother), Carlos
Rossi (manager), Mariela Díaz
(Villegas' daughter), Rosa
Valsecchi (Susana), Sabino
Morales (Sabino), Rolo Andrada
(Barreiro). Produced by Oscar
Kramer for Guacamole Films,
OK Films, Wanda Vision (Spain),
Chemo-Romikin, with the support
of INCAA. 96 mins.*

25 Years of Irish Cinema

From *Excalibur*
to *Adam and Paul*
by Michael Dwyer

To understand cinema's place in Irish culture and society today, you need to look back more than a century, to the first public exhibition of films in Ireland, at a Dublin music hall in 1896. The country's first cinema opened in Dublin city centre in 1909 – the Volta – and its first manager was James Joyce, who soon tired of the job and went off to Trieste to write.

A year later, The Kalem Company made the first fiction film ever shot in Ireland, *The Lad From Old Ireland*, which also was the first fiction film shot by Americans outside the US. When it became a commercial success, Kalem sent over a larger crew the following summer and made 17 films in 18 weeks. This could have been the start of a film industry in Ireland, but when the First World War broke out, Kalem stopped coming to Ireland.

In 1923, one of the first acts of the new Free State government was to introduce film censorship. Ireland's first film censor, James Montgomery, was a baker who famously stated that he knew little or nothing about movies, but that he knew the Ten Commandments, and took them as his code. In his first full year in the job, Montgomery banned 124 films and cut 166. Film censorship in Ireland remained draconian for the next 50 years, and numerous important films were cut or banned outright, without explanation.

Though Ireland produced a number of Oscar winners and Dublin-born Cedric Gibbons made a huge impact in Hollywood (appointed head of the art department at MGM in 1924, he designed

the Oscar statuette and won 11 of them across four decades), the country's principal role in film continued to be as a location. The great majority of films made in Ireland from the 1920s to the 1980s were directed by outsiders. They included Hitchcock's 1929 film of Sean O'Casey's *Juno and the Paycock; The Informer* (1935), *The Quiet Man* (1952) and several other movies directed by John Ford, the son of Irish immigrants to the US; Carol Reed's *Odd Man Out* (1947); *Moby Dick*, directed by John Huston in 1956; and David Lean's handsome epic, *Ryan's Daughter* (1970), which did wonders for Ireland as a tourist attraction.

However, Ireland did not have a dedicated film studio facility until 1958, when Ardmore Studios opened in Bray, Co. Wicklow, a 40-minute drive from the centre of Dublin. Unfortunately, Ardmore was to have a chequered history, and for decades was more often in receivership than in business. In the late 1970s, a number of Irish film-makers, notably Bob Quinn and Kieran Hickey, persevered against all the odds and produced indigenous feature films. These films were made on tiny budgets, but some were very impressive.

MGM/Kobal

Ryan's Daughter *showcased Ireland's stunning landscapes*

Enter Boorman

One of the visiting film-makers who used Ireland as a location was John Boorman. While shooting *Zardoz* in 1970, he decided to settle in Wicklow, where he has planted hundreds of trees. He also helped sow the seeds for an indigenous Irish film industry. Boorman's Arthurian epic, *Excalibur* (1981), was one of the largest productions shot in Ireland and a springboard for talent, marking the film debuts of Liam Neeson and Gabriel Byrne, who would be at the forefront as Irish actors began working in major Hollywood productions. And Boorman asked short-story writer and novelist Neil Jordan to direct a documentary, *Myth into Movie*, about the making of the film. "I didn't know one end of a camera from another," Jordan confessed at the time, but he learned quickly.

In 1981, following exhaustive campaigning, the government finally established the Irish Film Board. Boorman was among its first members and also executive producer of the first Board-funded feature, Jordan's *Angel*. *Angel* had its world premiere at the 1982 Celtic Film and Television Festival, held that year in Wexford in the south-east of Ireland. The festival provided a timely forum for debate but controversy flared when some Irish directors queried Boorman's dual role as Board member and executive producer of *Angel*. They called for a boycott of the screening, and the great majority of Irish film-makers at the festival stayed away.

"I could scarcely believe it," Boorman said at the time. "I thought it was some kind of joke." He pointed out that no other film was ready to go into production at the time *Angel* was shot, and that "the relatively small investment" by the Board in Angel would otherwise have been returned to the exchequer. He dismissed those who boycotted the film with the words, "I have to constantly remind myself that they are a group of malcontents and mad dogs."

Most of the finance for the film came from the then fledgling Channel 4, which intended to put it directly to television. However, at the 1982

Orion/Warner Bros./Kobal

Excalibur, *a pivotal film in Irish cinema history*

Cannes Film Festival, *Angel* was discovered by critics in the crowded festival market. One of its admirers was Stephen Woolley, a Londoner who had just set up a distribution company, Palace Pictures, and was on his first visit to Cannes in search of films to buy. "Neil brought such cinematic poetry to the story," Woolley said. "As soon as I got back from Cannes, I went straight to Channel 4 and asked to distribute *Angel*. They basically threw me out, saying they were putting it on TV in three months."

With the assistance of Boorman, Woolley eventually persuaded Channel 4 to let him show *Angel* for three weeks at the London repertory cinema, the Scala. "This meant all the critics reviewed *Angel*," Woolley said, "and it was regarded as a cinema film not just a TV movie, which was important in terms of Neil's career." Woolley produced Jordan's second feature, *The Company of Wolves*, and they have worked closely together ever since.

The next important director to emerge was Pat O'Connor, who had worked extensively in Irish television, making his breakthrough in 1982 with hour-long literary adaptations, principally *The Ballroom of Romance*, which won the BAFTA for Best Single drama, and *Night in Tunisia*, from a Neil Jordan short story. O'Connor made his feature film debut in 1984 with the emotional Northern Ireland drama, *Cal*, which remains the only film made in Ireland by an Irish director to be selected for the official competition at Cannes, where it won the Best Actress award for Helen Mirren. Two years later, the London-set *Mona Lisa* became the only Jordan film to date to compete at Cannes, where Bob Hoskins won Best Actor.

Kobal

Helen Mirren and John Lynch in **Cal**

The end of the affair

With the support of the Film Board, an indigenous industry was slowly beginning to develop, but Ireland was going through harsh economic times, losing many of its most talented and best-educated young people to emigration. In 1987, in what was widely regarded as a petty cost-cutting exercise, the government decided to "suspend" the Board. This was typical of the industry's long history of one step forward, two steps backward. Jordan and O'Connor had become established and were taking up offers to work abroad, while a cloud of gloom enveloped the burgeoning industry that produced them.

Movies continued to be made in Ireland, but once again, the higher-profile productions were the work of visiting film-makers: Huston's superb swansong, *The Dead* (largely shot in Los Angeles because of the director's declining health); Ken Loach's controversial political drama, *Hidden Agenda*; Peter Chelsom's whimsical *Hear My Song*; Ron Howard's historically sketchy emigration yarn, *Far and Away*, in which Tom Cruise's accent travelled the 32 counties of Ireland; and Alan Parker's boisterously funny *The Commitments*, which presented a radically different view of Dublin that shocked Irish–Americans and broke all box-office records in Ireland at the time.

Hope sprang again in 1989, as Jim Sheridan moved from theatre into film with his deeply affecting first feature, *My Left Foot*. Made on a low budget, it received five Oscar nominations,

winning Best Actor for Daniel Day-Lewis and Best Supporting Actress for Brenda Fricker. Ireland was on the international film map again, but to the government's shame, the Board remained suspended. It would take a change of government and another Oscar victory to restore the Board.

Granada/Miramax/Kobal

Daniel Day-Lewis and Fiona Shaw in **My Left Foot**

A new beginning

By 1991 Neil Jordan had directed six feature films in 10 years, but was deeply disillusioned. His sixth feature, *The Miracle*, a small, intimate and personal picture, had been very well reviewed but failed to find an audience, even in Ireland, and raising the budget for his next film, a drama about an IRA man's affair with a London woman, originally titled *When a Man Loves a Woman*, was proving exceedingly difficult. He and Stephen Woolley could not raise a penny of the finance in Ireland. "I just thought how making films is all so much work," he said at the time. "If I'm not going to be allowed to do anything interesting, and if people don't want to see the type of films I want to make, I don't want to make them any more." When the film eventually was completed on a small budget, Jordan was prepared to resume his life as a short-story writer and novelist, which had been dramatically interrupted by *Angel*. He settled down to write a novel.

Re-titled *The Crying Game*, the film took off as soon as it appeared on the festival circuit at Venice and Toronto in 1992. Miramax, which had enjoyed its first Oscar success with *My Left Foot*, had acquired the US rights and built a highly successful campaign around the movie's big secret, that the lover of the Stephen Rea character is really a man. It became one of the most profitable independent productions ever released in the US and received six Oscar nominations, including Best Picture and Director.

Jaye Davidson, left, and Stephen Rea in **The Crying Game**

Jordan won the Oscar for Best Original Screenplay, and the following morning, Michael D. Higgins, the first Irish arts minister to serve at cabinet level, welcomed the news from Los Angeles by re-establishing the Irish Film Board. Higgins also introduced an imaginative tax incentive scheme, now known as Section 481 (of the Finance Act), which made Ireland a highly attractive location for film-making and gave Irish crews a wealth of experience.

A charismatic and passionate combination of poet and politician, Higgins actively courted Mel Gibson to shoot his epic, *Braveheart*, in Ireland, even though it was set in neighbouring Scotland. The tax incentive helped, and when that was not quite enough, Higgins clinched the deal by offering Irish soldiers to participate in the movie's action sequences, which would have been too physically demanding for the average extra.

The new wave

The economic surge that was tagged "the Celtic Tiger" was kicking in, and as Ireland was rapidly transformed from the gloom of the 1980s to the boom of the 1990s, Irish culture thrived at home and abroad. U2 had become the biggest rock band in the world, the Riverdance phenomenon

Ten of the Best

Michael Dwyer's selection of 10 favourite Irish or Irish-made fims, 1981–2006:
The Ballroom of Romance (Pat O'Connor, 1982)
The Dead (John Huston, 1987)
My Left Foot (Jim Sheridan, 1989)
The Commitments (Alan Parker, 1991)
Ailsa (Paddy Breathnach, 1994)
Michael Collins (Neil Jordan, 1996)
The Butcher Boy (Neil Jordan, 1997)
The General (John Boorman, 1998)
Intermission (John Crowley, 2003)
Adam & Paul (Lenny Abrahamson, 2004)

burst out of an interval act in the Eurovision Song Contest, and the Irish film industry ended the twentieth century with an unmatched decade of activity that continued into the early 2000s.

Ardmore Studios, under managing director Kevin Moriarty, entered the busiest phase in its once troubled history. Steven Spielberg shot the first half hour's action of *Saving Private Ryan* on a beach in Wexford, not far from the cinema where *Angel* had been boycotted in 1982. Cinema's new James Bond was an Irishman, Pierce Brosnan, who doubled as a canny producer in his company, Irish Dreamtime. Jerry Bruckheimer set up a trio of big-budget pictures in Ireland (*The Count of Monte Cristo*, *Reign of Fire* and *King Arthur*), along with the more modest *Veronica Guerin*, starring Cate Blanchett as the murdered Irish crime journalist, which surpassed all three of Bruckheimer's action movies at the Irish box-office. Alan Parker returned to film Frank McCourt's best-selling memoir, *Angela's Ashes*.

Jim Sheridan continued to be a regular guest at the Oscars. A fine character actor, Brendan Gleeson, was given his first meaty leading role when John Boorman cast him as murdered Dublin criminal Martin Cahill (the subject of three films at the time) in *The General*, for which Boorman was named Best Director at Cannes. And a new wave of Irish directors emerged, including Sheridan's daughter, Kirsten, with *Disco Pigs,* and his brother, Peter, with *Borstal Boy*. Jim Sheridan set up Hell's Kitchen with producer Arthur Lappin, and produced, among others, *Borstal Boy*, Anjelica Huston's *Agnes Browne*, and *Some Mother's Son*, the first feature from Terry George, who later made *Hotel Rwanda*.

Jordan acted as producer or executive producer for other directors on Deborah Warner's *The Last September*, Conor McPherson's *The Actors* and John Crowley's *Intermission*, a huge Irish box-office hit that teamed the country's hottest new actors, Colin Farrell and Cillian Murphy, the successors to Gabriel Byrne and Liam Neeson.

Paddy Breathnach made a distinctive feature film debut with *Ailsa* and enjoyed two big hits with the road movies *I Went Down* and *Man About Dog*. Thaddeus O'Sullivan moved from shorts to features with *December Bride*, *Nothing Personal*, and *Ordinary Decent Criminal*, which featured Kevin Spacey as another character based on criminal Martin Cahill, and, in his first cinema role, Colin Farrell. Leonard Abrahamson turned from commercials to features and directed the gritty serious comedy, *Adam & Paul*, starring and scripted by Mark O'Halloran. Damien O'Donnell followed his multiple-award-winning short, *Thirty-Five-A-Side* with two notable British features, *East Is East* and *Heartlands*, before making his first Irish feature, *Inside I'm Dancing*, a touching and very funny film of two young disabled Dubliners.

The paying public

For centuries Ireland had a long tradition of storytelling through books, poetry and plays, and it seemed natural, then, after one of the country's greatest writers, James Joyce, threw open the doors of Dublin's first cinema in 1909, that the Irish would respond enthusiastically to this new medium for narrative. Ireland registered remarkably high cinema attendance figures throughout the twentieth century, with the exception of the late 1970s, when the business slumped internationally.

In recent years, Ireland has registered the highest cinema admissions per capita of all European Union countries, and Dublin the highest per capita of any European city. For a while, Irish audiences were somewhat suspicious of that new phenomenon that was the Irish movie, but, as more and more Irish productions were released, became more receptive.

In 2003, when cinema attendances in most European countries dropped, admission figures were up by more than 4%. The audience was getting the same American blockbusters as elsewhere, but what made the crucial difference was the substantial success of Irish-made movies, led by *Veronica Guerin*, which flopped everywhere else but was the biggest hit of the year in Ireland.

US productions continue to dominate the Irish market, as they do all over Europe, and of the 115 cinema screens in Dublin at present, only five are dedicated arthouse screens, although the 17-screen Cineworld (formerly UGC) complex has significantly broadened the range of fare on offer at a mainstream cinema (and now there is the prospect of further diversity thanks to the

Digital Cinema Ireland project examined on page 59). Two of the arthouse screens are based in the Irish Film Institute building, offering new releases, repertory programming and national film weeks, and that building also houses an education division, a library and the Irish Film Archive, which plays an invaluable role in preserving Ireland's film heritage.

For 30 years there was only one film festival in Ireland, the pioneering Cork Film Festival, which recently celebrated its 50th anniversary and continues to thrive, paying particular attention to the often neglected form that is the short film. The Dublin International Film Festival, of which I am artistic director, is features-driven with a policy of screening a diverse range of world cinema and bringing film-makers, writers and actors to discuss their work with the audience; recent retrospectives have been devoted to Claire Denis, Julio Medem and Gianni Amelio. In the west of Ireland, the Galway Film Fleadh is the busiest Irish film industry event of the year, doubling as exhibition outlet and spirited talking shop.

Going forward

The past two years have been another rocky period for the Irish film industry. The Section 481 tax incentive was under threat from the Department of Finance for most of 2003, but was rescued by the efforts of arts minister John O'Donoghue. Similar models are in place in many other countries now, and it has not been unusual for movies set in Ireland to be lured by the financial advantages offered by the Isle of Man, for example. The strength of the Euro against the US dollar has also been a disadvantage, along with the much cheaper labour rates available in eastern Europe. However, apart from that recent sustained hiccup with Section 481, the progress of the Irish film industry continues in the right direction, with all steps forward and no steps backward.

Milestones in Irish Cinema

1981 – John Boorman's *Excalibur* opens, featuring the film acting debuts of Gabriel Byrne and Liam Neeson; Neil Jordan's documentary on the making of the film is shown on television.
1981 – The Irish Film Board is established.
1982 – Jordan's first feature, *Angel*, opens. It is the first feature funded by the Board.
1984 – Pat O'Connor makes his feature film debut with *Cal*, for which Helen Mirren wins Best Actress at Cannes.
1987 – John Huston's final film, *The Dead*, from the James Joyce story, opens. The government "suspends" the Irish Film Board.
1989 – Jim Sheridan makes his film debut with *My Left Foot*, which gets five Oscar nominations and wins two of the four acting awards.
1991 – Alan Parker's film of Roddy Doyle's novel, *The Commitments*, breaks all records at Irish cinemas.
1993 – Neil Jordan wins the Best Original Screenplay Oscar for *The Crying Game*.

The day after the Oscars, the government re-establishes the Irish Film Board. Later in the year, it introduces a tax incentive scheme for film production.
1998 – John Boorman is named Best Director at Cannes for his Dublin crime drama, *The General*.
2000 – Colin Farrell makes his film debut down the credits of *Ordinary Decent Criminal* and within four years has become a Hollywood star and the highest-paid Irish actor of all time.
2001 – Producer Alan Moloney and Gate Theatre director Michael Colgan team up, working with Irish and international directors to bring all 19 of Samuel Beckett stage plays to the screen.
2003 – The Section 481 tax incentive is retained and extended, despite strong objections from the Department of Finance.
2003 – Irish-made productions boost Irish cinema admissions, while attendances decline in Europe.

Key Players

Michael Dwyer profiles 18 leading figures in Irish film.

CONSOLATA BOYLE, costume designer.

Boyle trained at Ireland's national theatre, the Abbey. Meticulous in her attention to detail when working on period pictures, she has been equally impressive when designing contemporary films. Her many notable credits include features by Thaddeus O'Sullivan (*December Bride*, *Nothing Personal*), Mike Newell (*Into the West*), John Sayles (*The Secret of Roan Inish*), David Mamet (*The Winslow Boy*), David Mackenzie (*Asylum*) and Alan Parker (*Angela's Ashes*). Her most recent credit is on *The Queen*, her fourth film for Stephen Frears, following *The Snapper*, *The Van* and *Mary Reilly*. She received an Emmy award in 2004 for Andrei Konchalovsky's *The Lion in Winter*.

PADDY BREATHNACH, director and producer.

Having made a few award-winning shorts and popular documentaries, Breathnach made an auspicious feature film debut in 1994 with the moody, haunting *Ailsa*, which earned him the Best New Director prize at the San Sebastián Film Festival. He went on to show his flair for more mainstream material with the boisterous road movie *I Went Down*, a major success at the Irish box-office. After a misstep with the UK-based *Blow Dry*, he returned home and to form with another hit road movie, *Man About Dog*. Breathnach co-founded Treasure Entertainment with producer Robert Walpole in 1992 and their other productions have included *Saltwater* and *The Mighty Celt*.

DAVID COLLINS, producer.

The first Film Officer appointed by the Arts Council of Ireland, Collins went on to establish Samson Films in 1984 and produced Cathal Black's *Pigs*, Thaddeus O'Sullivan's *The Woman Who Married Clark Gable*, Peter Ormrod's *Eat the Peach* and Sue Clayton's *The Disappearance of Finbar*. His many subsequent credits as producer or executive producer have included *A Further Gesture*, *I Went Down*, *The Most Fertile*

Man in Ireland, *Country*, *Blind Flight*, *The Honeymooners*, *Asylum*, *Short Order*, and the hit Irish TV series, *Pure Mule*.

I Went Down: *directed by PADDY BREATHNACH, produced by DAVID COLLINS and edited by EMER REYNOLDS*

BBC/Irish Films/Kobal

MARK GERAGHTY, production designer.

Ireland's most imaginative and resourceful production designer, Geraghty has worked extensively on home ground and in international productions. One of his earliest credits was on the award-winning 1994 RTE/BBC four-part drama, *Family*, written by Roddy Doyle and directed by Michael Winterbottom, with whom Geraghty later collaborated on *Welcome to Sarajevo*. He has worked with Stephen Frears (*The Snapper*, *The Van*), Pat O'Connor (*Dancing at Lughnasa*), Kevin Reynolds (*The Count of Monte Cristo*, *Tristan & Isolde*), Liev Schreiber (*Everything Is Illuminated*) and Jim Sheridan (*In America*, *Get Rich or Die Tryin'*).

ALAN GILSENAN, director, writer.

Arguably the least easily categorised of Irish film-makers, Gilsenan moves with enthusiasm and versatility between film, television and theatre, showing an openness to experimentation in his short films, features and documentaries. Fresh out of Trinity College in the mid-1980s, he tackled a Samuel Beckett adaptation, *Eh Joe*, as his first short film, and recently returned to the short format with visually and emotionally powerful results in *Zulu 9*.

His many documentaries have dealt with, among

other themes, Irish emigrants (the controversial *Road to God Knows Where*), American literature (*God Bless America*), Dublin lap-dancing clubs (*Private Dancer*) and the patients and staff of a psychiatric hospital (*The Asylum*). To date, he has directed just two fiction features, both uncompromising in style and ambition: *All Souls' Day* (1997) and the Sahara-set *Timbuktu* (2004). He is a member of the Irish Film Board and chairman of the Irish Film Institute.

ED GUINEY, producer.

Starting out as a producer while still in his 20s, Guiney produced the debut features of Paddy Breathnach (*Ailsa*), Gerard Stembridge (*Guiltrip*), Stephen Bradley (*Sweety Barrett*) and Kirsten Sheridan (*Disco Pigs*). He now runs Element Films, one of Ireland's busiest production companies, with former Irish Film Board executive Andrew Lowe. Over the past four years, he has been producer or executive producer on several award-winning films, including *The Magdalene Sisters*, *Omagh* (for which Guiney received the BAFTA award for best single TV drama), *Adam & Paul*, *The League of Gentlemen's Apocalypse*, *Boy Eats Girl*, *Isolation* and Charles Sturridge's new version of *Lassie*.

NEIL JORDAN, writer, director and producer.

Jordan was a critically acclaimed fiction writer before making his first feature, *Angel*, in 1982, and has directed a further 13 features, firmly establishing himself as Ireland's pre-eminent film-maker. Many of his finest films have come from original screenplays that illustrate his vivid imagination: *Mona Lisa*, *The Miracle*, *The Crying Game* and *Michael Collins*, a massive hit at the Irish box-office.

He has had mixed fortunes with previously filmed material: *We're No Angels*, *The Good Thief* and a very impressive Graham Greene adaptation, *The End of the Affair*. He has also been comfortable in adapting the work of other authors, such as Angela Carter (*The Company of Wolves*), Anne Rice (*Interview with the Vampire*) and, most fruitfully, Patrick McCabe (*The Butcher Boy* and *Breakfast on Pluto*). He has also been a

producer or executive producer on Deborah Warner's *The Last September*, Conor McPherson's *The Actors* and John Crowley's *Intermission*.

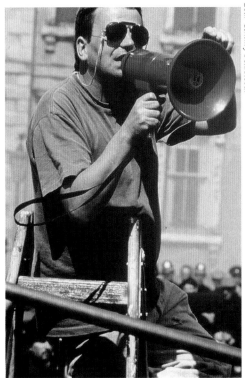

20th Century Fox/Kobal

NEIL JORDAN shooting **Michael Collins**

ARTHUR LAPPIN, producer.

A contemporary of David Collins (see above) at the Arts Council, where he was Drama and Dance Officer, Lappin has been a stage and film producer for the past 18 years. He is managing director of Hell's Kitchen Productions, which he established with director Jim Sheridan in 1992. Having been the line producer on Sheridan's first two features, *My Left Foot* and *The Field*, Lappin has produced all Sheridan's subsequent features: *In the Name of the Father*, *The Boxer*, *In America* and *Get Rich or Die Tryin'*. He also produced Terry George's directing debut, *Some Mother's Son*, Anjelica Huston's *Agnes Browne* and Peter Sheridan's *Borstal Boy*, along with the award-winning TV dramas, *Bloody Sunday*, which won the Golden Bear at the 2002 Berlin Film Festival, and *Omagh*.

BRENDAN McCAUL, distributor.

Vice-President and General Manager of Buena Vista International (Ireland), McCaul is the last of the great showmen in Irish cinema. Behind that image of gregarious entertainer and promoter, however, is a man whose business acumen has earned him universal respect in the business in which he has worked for 50 years. He started at a Dublin distribution company where he sent out stills and posters to exhibitors during the cinema boom of the late 1950s. In 1976, the Walt Disney Company hired him to head their Irish office. He became manager of the Irish office of 20th Century Fox in 1987, and three years later demonstrated his skill for releasing Irish movies with *The Commitments*, breaking all Irish box-office records.

The Commitments: *one of BRENDAN McCAUL's biggest Irish releases*

Even though the BBC insisted on showing the next Doyle adaptation, *The Snapper*, without a cinema release, McCaul picked up the Irish cinema rights and enjoyed remarkable success with a film so recently available on television throughout Ireland. Moving to Buena Vista, he has picked up Irish rights to more than a dozen indigenous productions, many of which proved lucrative investments, including *I Went Down*, *This Is My Father*, *A Love Divided* and *Intermission* (one of several recent hits he pre-bought at script stage).

NIAMH McCAUL, distributor.

Following her father, Brendan, into the film business, Niamh McCaul was head of theatrical distribution with the Irish film and video distribution company Clarence Pictures, from its formation in 1994 until 2002, when she set up her own distribution company, Eclipse Pictures, of which she is managing director.

Eclipse has acquired Irish rights to many local productions, among them Liz Gill's *Goldfish Memory*, Fintan Connolly's *Trouble with Sex*, Karl Golden's *The Honeymooners*, John Simpson's *Freeze Frame* and Perry Ogden's *Pavee Lackeen*, which won the Satyajit Ray Award for best first feature at the 2005 London Film Festival and the Irish Film and Television Award (IFTA) for Best Irish Film of 2005. Eclipse also represents UK independent distributors in Ireland, including Icon, Tartan, Metrodome and Verve, and has enjoyed particular success in the Irish market with *The Magdalene Sisters* and *The Passion of the Christ*.

ALAN MOLONEY, producer.

Having set up Parallel Film Productions with producer Tim Palmer in 1993, Moloney has been at the forefront of Irish production in recent years, with *Intermission*, Neil Jordan's *Breakfast on Pluto* and, in collaboration with Michael Colgan of the Gate Theatre, Dublin, as producer of the highly ambitious *Beckett on Film*, 19 films directed by the likes of Jordan, Atom Egoyan, Anthony Minghella and Karel Reisz. Moloney's many earlier credits have included *Into the West*, *A Love Divided* and *The Last of the High Kings* and hit TV series such as *Ballykissangel*, *Amongst Women*, *Showbands* and *The Clinic*.

JAMES MORRIS, facility house director.

Having trained as a film editor in London, Morris returned to Dublin in 1976 and founded Windmill Lane Pictures and Recording Studios, where U2 recorded many of their early albums. Windmill Lane is Ireland's premier facility house, providing editing, computer graphic effects, audio, telecine, DVD authoring and camera crews for commercials and television programming. In 1990, he founded The Mill, a film and TV post-production company in London. As chairman of the Irish Film Board and of the independent Irish television station, TV3, Morris is a hugely influential figure within the Irish industry.

JAMES MORRIS, Chairman of the Irish Film Board

PAT O'CONNOR, director.

Having studied film in Toronto, O'Connor returned home to Ireland in 1969, working with the national TV service, RTE, as a director on current affairs programmes, documentaries and a long-running soap opera. His breakthrough came in 1982 with the superb RTE/BBC TV drama, *The Ballroom of Romance*, based on a William Trevor story, which won the BAFTA for Best Single Drama. He followed it with two more outstanding TV dramas, *One of Ourselves* (another Trevor story) and *Night in Tunisia* (from a Neil Jordan story).

Merie W. Wallace/Warner Bros./Kobal

PAT O'CONNOR has directed in Ireland and America

O'Connor made his feature film debut in 1984 with *Cal*. His next film, *A Month in the Country*, starring a young Kenneth Branagh and Colin Firth, is arguably his best to date. His

subsequent features have included *Stars and Bars*, *The January Man* (on which he met his actress wife, Mary Elizabeth Mastrantonio), *Fools of Fortune* (another Trevor adaptation), *Circle of Friends*, *Inventing the Abbots* and *Dancing at Lughnasa*.

JOHN O'DONOGHUE, Arts Minister.

There was some dismay in Irish arts and culture circles when O'Donoghue was appointed as Minister for Arts, Sport and Tourism in 2002, principally because there appeared to be nothing in his background that suited him to the arts area of his new portfolio. A solicitor, he has been an elected representative since 1987 and was first appointed to the cabinet in 1997, when he was given a senior post as Minister for Justice. O'Donoghue has confounded his critics with his immersion in his current post, significantly increasing government spending on the arts in general and proving remarkably supportive of the Irish film industry, most importantly in persuading the government to retain the Section 481 tax incentive when it was threatened in 2003.

SIMON PERRY, Chief Executive, Irish Film Board.

Perry brings a remarkably broad range of experience to his new post as Irish Film Board chief executive, which he took up in January 2006. He worked for three years in late 1970s at the London bureau of *Variety*, for another three years from 1982 as head of the UK National Film Development Fund, and from 1991 to 2000 as chief executive of British Screen, which provided production support for 144 British and European films during his tenure.

SIMON PERRY now runs the Irish Film Board

He also has produced or co-produced 10 feature films, including three directed by Michael Radford – *Another Time, Another Place, Nineteen Eighty-Four* and *White Mischief*. Since 2000 he has been co-founder and president of Ateliers du Cinéma Européen (ACE), the Paris-based training initiative for European film producers; film financing consultant for a Swedish regional film centre; a course supervisor and lecturer at the International Film School in Cologne; and film production consultant for the republic of Macedonia's Ministry of Culture.

EMER REYNOLDS, film editor.

Reynolds started out as assistant editor to editor-turned-director Martin Duffy. She has worked twice with Paddy Breathnach (on *Ailsa* and *I Went Down*) and with Conor McPherson (*Saltwater* and *The Actors*). Her other notable credits include Cathal Black's *Korea*, Alan Gilsenan's *Timbuktu* and Dudi Appleton's *The Most Fertile Man in Ireland*. She won the 2004 Irish Film and Television Award for best film editing for *Timbuktu*, and took the award again in 2005 for her work on the Channel 4 TV series *Shameless*.

JIM SHERIDAN, writer, producer, director.

Sheridan worked extensively as a theatre director in Dublin and New York before making a remarkable film debut with *My Left Foot*, which won Oscars for Daniel Day-Lewis and Brenda Fricker. His second film, *The Field*, earned an

Oscar nomination for Richard Harris as best actor, and his third, *In the Name of the Father*, received seven Oscar nominations, including three for Sheridan as writer, producer and director. After *The Boxer*, he was back in the Academy arena with *In America*, sharing a Best Original Screenplay nomination with his daughters Kirsten (a director in her own right with *Disco Pigs*) and Naomi. His latest film is a departure from Irish themes, *Get Rich or Die Tryin'*, starring rapper 50 Cent. His screenplay, *Into the West*, was filmed by Mike Newell in 1992. Sheridan is also actively involved as a producer with Arthur Lappin (see above) in Hell's Kitchen Productions.

Granada/Michael Gibson/Kobal

JIM SHERIDAN's films have garnered many Oscar wins and nominations

LEO WARD, exhibitor, distributor.

Now 86, Ward continues to work five days a week running his Irish exhibition empire, and

checks opening weekend figures from his cinemas every Sunday morning. For decades, he has been the dominant player on the Irish exhibition circuit, controlling more than half the screens in the country and holding his own against the influx of UK-owned multiplexes in the 1990s. A former professional footballer with Manchester City, Ward returned to Ireland in the 1950s and set up a film distribution company, Abbey Films, with his half-brother, Kevin Anderson, now 90 and only recently retired. They acquired their first cinema in the Dublin suburbs in 1955 and firmly established their business during the lean years of the 1970s and 1980s, believing in the business while other exhibitors lost confidence, and buying up cinemas around the country as they closed during the slump.

When the Rank Organisation pulled out of the Irish market in the 1980s, the Ward-Anderson group bought their cinemas and one of those acquisitions, the Savoy in Dublin city centre, remains the company's flagship. The recently refurbished six-screen complex contains Ireland's largest cinema auditorium, which is a natural magnet for film premieres. Ward and Anderson's sons, both named Paul, are actively involved in the family business, but Leo Ward continues to rule the roost.

MICHAEL DWYER has been film correspondent of *The Irish Times* since 1988. He is co-founder and artistic director of the Dublin International Film Festival, which had its fourth edition in February 2006.

Irish Films at International Festivals, 2000-05: Selected Award-Winners

2000
Saltwater (Conor McPherson)
CICAE Prize (European Film), Berlin International Film Festival

2001
Accelerator (Vinny Murphy)
Best Actor (Stuart Sinclair Blyth), Festival of British and Irish Film, Cherbourg
The Most Fertile Man in Ireland (Dudi Appleton)
Best Director, US Comedy Arts Festival, Aspen
Best Film (International Competition), Noordelik Film Festival, The Netherlands

2002
The Magdalene Sisters (Peter Mullan)
Golden Lion, Venice Film Festival
Discovery Award, Toronto Internatioanl Film Festival
Audience Award, Ljubljana Film Festival
Audience Award for Best Narrative Feature, IFP Los Angeles Film Festival (2003)
Bloody Sunday (Paul Greengrass)
Golden Bear, Berlin International Film Festival
Hitchcock d'Or, Dinard Film Festival
Audience Award, Sydney Film Festival
World Cinema Audience Award, Sundance Film Festival
H3 (Les Blair)
Special Mention (Les Blair) and Best Screenplay, Avanca Film Festival
Silver "Rosa Camuna", Bergamo Film Meeting

2003
Song for a Raggy Boy (Aisling Walsh)
Audience Award and Best Actor (John Travers), Festival of British and Irish Film, Cherbourg
Best Film, Salerno Film Festival (2004)

2004
Dublin 1 (Jason Tammemägi)
Silver Hugo, Chicago International Film Festival
Omagh (Pete Travis)
Discovery Award, Toronto International Film Festival
Inside I'm Dancing (Damien O'Donnell)
Audience Award, Edinburgh International Film Festival
Goldfish Memory (Liz Gill)
Best Director, Peñíscola Comedy Film Festival
Audience Award, Turin Gay & Lesbian Film Festival
Audience Award, Copenhagen Gay & Lesbian Film Festival (2003)

2005
Adam & Paul (Lenny Abrahamson)
Best Director, Romanian Film Festival
Grand Prix for Best Film and FIPRESCI Jury Award, Sofia International Film Festival
The Ten Steps (Brendan Muldowney)
Grand Prize, New York International Children's Film Festival
Best Short, New York Film Feadh
Best Short, "Fantastic" Category, Sitges International Film Festival (2004)

Digital Cinema in Focus

D-Day for D-Cinema
by Ellen Wolff

A world beyond celluloid is no longer orbiting somewhere out in George Lucas' Star Wars universe. More than 100 commercial digital screens opened in 2005 in the US alone, according to the online database DCinemaToday.com. This unprecedented increase nearly doubled the number of America's existing D-cinema screens, and announcements of future openings arrive regularly. While most investments in digital exhibition thus far seem to be in mainstream metropolitan theatres, it's just a matter of time before digital projection arrives at US arthouses.

In fact, that's the goal of Landmark Theatres, whose 57 venues make it America's largest arthouse chain. Co-founders Todd Wagner and Mark Cuban, who made their fortunes with Broadcast.com, have ordered Sony's SXRD 4K digital projectors for their theatres and expect to be screening movies digitally from early 2006. That will allow Steven Soderbergh to present his new, all-digital indie film, *Bubble*, without having to transfer it to 35mm film for its theatrical debut. *Bubble* is the first of six digital films that Soderbergh is making for Wagner and Cuban's Magnolia Pictures, and Wagner admits this synergy is unique. "The only reason we've made progress is because we don't need anybody's permission," he explains. "We have theatres and the ability to make movies, so we just do it."

With installation costs around $100,000 per theatre, digital refitting is not readily affordable for typical arthouse exhibitors. And they think distributors will reap digital's initial windfalls, by sending movie files to theatres via fibre optics or

Debbie Doebereiner in **Bubble:** *a digital release for 2006*

satellite instead of making and shipping film prints. That process ultimately will be especially cost-effective for independent distributors, but at the moment, asks Wagner, "what's the incentive for an exhibitor to change over?"

Taking the Initiative

Some key developments have altered the situation in recent months. Last July, the major Hollywood studios agreed upon the Digital Cinema Initiative (DCI) specifications, to ensure that movie files could play in digital theatres worldwide. Without that, D-cinema's situation resembles the early days of celluloid, when Pathé films would not play on Edison machines and vice versa, observes Gwendal Auffret of France's Eclair Digital. "Now that the DCI spec is set, we'll start to get out of the chicken-and-egg situation where there were no digital releases because there were no screens," she says. "With a common standard, it becomes economically viable to create digital masters."

Another key development has been the emergence of companies willing to pay for the installations, including Technicolor (owned by

Magnolia Pictures

France's Thomson) and a partnership between two US companies, projector manufacturer Christie and Access Technologies. These companies expect to recoup their installation costs by charging distributors "virtual print fees." An electronic distribution fee will also be charged by the companies that send a distributor's master file to theatres. In addition to Technicolor, two satellite communications companies poised to offer this service are US-based Microspace and T-Systems, a subsidiary of Deutsche Telecomm.

This delivery chain leaves some independent distributors sceptical about how much they will benefit. At InDigEnt, the New York City-based distributor that has backed the recent digital production, Greg Harrison's *November*, starring Courteney Cox, producer Jake Abraham says: "I have a feeling that the fees will be high for indies, because we don't do large volumes. Warner Bros. will get good transmission fees on a 2,000 'print' run and we're going to pay hundreds of dollars each. That being said, those costs will be offset by our not having to take a digital production to film for exhibition."

Will digital prove costly for US indie pictures like **November**?

Perhaps ironically – given the high cost of digital installations – the places where *November* and *Bubble* have screened digitally have been film festivals, at Sundance and Toronto respectively. The commercial run of *November* was on film, and *Bubble* may have to be offered in a 35mm version to play outside the Landmark chain. So at present, festivals remain the best place to see digital indie films.

Charles Swartz, who heads the Digital Cinema Lab at the University of Southern California, notes: "There was a big emphasis at Venice [in 2005], which made a major commitment to set up digital projection, and even created a 'sidebar' for digitally made films." At the Skip City International D-Cinema Festival in Japan, $110,000 in prize money was shared by two digital indies that have US distribution by IFC Films: Miranda July's *Me and You and Everyone We Know*, and the Danish film *Brothers*. "Without digital," observes Swartz, "those films probably would not have been made because of cost."

InDigEnt's Abraham admits: "We go to festivals as digital and that's where we try to get distributors on board. Then we usually start working on going to film because there's still really no other way to get a US release." But some alternatives are emerging. Wagner laments the fact that "so many movies go to film festivals and if no distributor picks them up they just sit on a shelf. So we've announced 'Truly Indie', an arrangement where film-makers pay a certain amount of money [to exhibit their films] but they keep the box-office [returns]. If you believe in your movie, it's ideal." Another interesting model comes from New York-based Emerging Pictures. They are arranging exchanges with foreign distributors, taking advantage of the fact that digitally encoding multiple language tracks is cheaper than creating subtitled or dubbed film prints. As Abraham explains: "Let's say you're working with the Mexican producers of *Y tu mamá también* and it's encoded by the producers in Mexico. When it comes to the US for certain screens, you can show it for free – in exchange for sending a US-made indie film down there."

At Eclair, which conforms many of France's digital masters, Auffret believes that digital distribution will help the circulation of foreign films to other continents, and not only because of the ease of creating multiple language tracks. "When a medium becomes digital, it creates 'stock', which in digital won't be ruined over time. Therefore, in the future, exhibitors will have access to a large database of movies to programme for targeted audiences."

The movies that have been helped the most thus far – at least by digital production methods – are documentaries. At Think Film (based in New York and Toronto), Mark Urman remarks: "Digital has been an extraordinary boon. 'Fly-on-the-wall' documentaries can be made with extremely light but proficient cameras. The price at which documentaries can be made has been revolutionised by digital. We distributed the hugely acclaimed movie *The Aristocrats*, which made millions. It was made with a camera that probably cost under $500 and the tape cost under $50." Think Film recently distributed the documentaries *Murderball* and the Oscar short-listed *Boys of Baraka*, which were exhibited digitally only in New York City.

Think Film

Digital may revolutionise distribution of documentaries like **Murderball**

One of the biggest financial benefits of digital exhibition for indies will be that money saved in print costs can be diverted to marketing. Urman notes: "One of the great expenses is creating trailers on 35mm. If I can do a trailer digitally, that's a windfall." But even great marketing cannot counteract today's limited release windows. Urman adds: "We're staggeringly successful in creating awareness through reviews, and staggeringly unsuccessful in being able to reach our customers. For us, a big release is 250 screens, which is less than a drop in the bucket. If digital movies could be beamed everywhere simultaneously, geography wouldn't be our enemy."

A side-effect of limited indie releases is that distributors have to re-launch their marketing campaigns for subsequent DVD releases. But that may change when movies are released day-and-date in theatres, on cable TV and on DVD, as Wagner plans to do with *Bubble*. But even he acknowledges, "Who knows how this plays out? We don't know for sure how digital will impact indies. It's just the first inning of a *long* baseball game."

ELLEN WOLFF is a Southern California-based writer who covers digital production, computer animation and visual effects.

In today's digital cinemas, the early technology leaders are evident, **writes Ellen Wolff**. Texas Instruments' DLP chip technology provides the brains behind the most widely used 2K projectors, which are made by US-based Christie, Japan's NEC and Belgium's Barco. Meanwhile, Japan's Sony and JVC are promoting 4K projectors, promising greater resolution and colour depth. Both the 2K and 4K projectors meet the industry's recently announced Digital Cinema Initiative (DCI) specifications.

When it comes to manufacturing the servers that feed digital master files to those projectors, several US-based companies are among the contenders: Dolby, QuVis and Kodak (which has aligned with Barco to equip theatres digitally) and early adopter Avica, which has announced an ambitious plan to spend $50 million to convert nearly 650 screens in Ireland to digital (see feature opposite).

According to Charles Swartz of USC's Digital Cinema Lab: "In general, the US has been leading the technical development. But at our lab, we've always had international delegations doing demos for the production and distribution sides of Hollywood. And that will only grow. I think we'll see more joint efforts between Europe and Asia. This will truly be a global industry."

While most vendors are developing equipment that's compliant with industry specs, Swartz notes: "There will be parts of this that will always be manufacturer-specific. Manufacturers will decide what they think is the best way to go."
Eclair Digital CEO Gwendal Auffret agrees. "Technology providers should compete to create something as good and as cheap as possible. It's in everyone's interest that we don't have one company totally dominating this technology."

Where Ireland leads, will Hollywood follow?
by Carol Nahra

While the movie industry has been talking about the digital cinema revolution for years, actually confirming how it could take place in practical terms has been slow going. It was not until 2002, when the Hollywood studios endorsed digital light projectors as having quality better than analogue that the majors began seriously looking at the prospect of digital cinema. But while they have now agreed on system requirements and specifications for digital projection – through a consortium called Digital Cinema Initiatives – they have yet to produce a business plan that demonstrates the enormous shift in practice that needs to take place.

Enter Avica Corp. of Santa Monica, California, who are determined to lead the way in digital cinema. Convinced that the best way to persuade Hollywood of what the future could look like was to set up a pilot operation, they looked for a reasonable sized territory. They settled on Ireland, for its high per capita cinemagoing, strong interest in Hollywood product, keen industry professionals and, above all, its manageable size.

The Avica project, called Digital Cinema Ltd., is an ambitious one: to equip each of Ireland's 648 screens with digital projection by the end of 2006; making the project almost three times larger than the Digital Screen Network being set up concurrently by the UK Film Council and Arts Alliance Digital Cinema. Fifty Irish screens per month are set to be converted in 2006, a major challenge for Japan-based NEC, which is providing the projectors, having previously manufactured them at a rate of two or three per month.

The hardware installation costs, roughly $100,000 per screen, are borne not by the exhibitors or distributors but by venture capitalists, whose investment will be recouped through a fee tacked onto the digital distribution costs. Even with this premium added, distribution costs will be significantly cheaper than current rates with celluloid prints. So distributors currently paying around $3,000 euros for a film print might pay 25% less for a "digital print".

Today Ireland, tomorrow the world

"It can work for the whole world," enthuses Kevin Cummins, Avica's Director of Operations in Ireland. "If it's demonstrated in a side territory like Ireland it means it can then be replicated to other sites; it's just a larger amount of money. And once you have a model up and going, banks are very keen to invest in something when they can see the viability of the model." Indeed Ireland's tiny size makes the amount of money needed to be raised a manageable concept: roughly $50m, as opposed to the $3.2 billion needed to convert the 30,000-plus screen network in the US.

In Ireland, the digital projectors are being set up alongside the celluloid portholes. While USB hard drives can be used at each of the sites to project the film digitally, the real economies of scale and ease of technology come into play with the envisaged satellite distribution system. A centralised "content management system" in Tipperary is set to distribute films via satellite, in the long run allowing for films to be beamed down to any configuration of cinemas in the country. Avica has developed a watermark encryption system, which can track pirated copies down to the screen where the crime occurred.

Cummins sees the centralised content system as having the potential to be a huge warehouse of film. "For a minimal fee, a theatre can download that movie to their site then play it for example for a film house club that you could have in there on a Monday night. It will make content more widely acceptable." The technology also has the potential to transform exhibition space, opening up theatres during the daytime for video conferencing or satellite transmissions of live concerts and sporting events.

Independent producers wanting to take advantage of Ireland's digital landscape need to build in the cost of a digital master into their post-production budgets, currently around $20,000. Avica is working with post-production houses in Ireland, France and the UK to enable them to have digital mastering systems available.

In addition to the transformation of distribution practice, digital cinema also greatly eases the way in which censors can make cuts to films. When the system is fully operational, the Irish censor board will be able to block individual frames electronically. Likewise, advertisers will find it much easier to provide ad packages for film programmes via digital rather than celluloid, tailoring content to the local market.

A watching brief

Irish industry professionals are keen on the theory of the country as the world's first fully digital cinema nation, but cautious in practice, waiting to see both how the technology kinks work themselves out, and how distributors embrace the new model. "The Avica project is clever and ambitious, to take a small territory that has a high cinemagoing population and plays all the mainstream stuff," says Brian O'Gorman, head of the Cinema Exhibition Association of Ireland, and an owner of two multiplexes. "It's the chance for distribution companies to see their project working in digital. But it's ultimately up to Avica to convince the distribution companies to supply their products in a digital format."

For distributors, the advantages of a fully realised digital cinema delivery system are clear: eliminating the freight, management and disposal of prints, greatly increasing flexibility of delivery and reducing costs. Brendan McCaul, VP and General Manager of Buena Vista International, Ireland, says he is one of the "very keen optimists" about the future role of digital cinema in Ireland. "I know it's going to come," he says. "I'm just nervous that when it's breaking in that we don't rush it and make too many mistakes along the way." According to McCaul one of the biggest concerns for the studios is the security of the planned satellite delivery system, with

Hollywood majors unlikely in the short term to want to use satellite delivery until they are convinced that piracy-prevention measures are watertight.

The digital dividend

The Irish Film Board has been a supporter of the project since its early days, without becoming involved in any formal way. "At the moment we're still slightly playing a wait and see game," says Teresa McGrane, Head of Business Affairs. But McGrane sees an enormous potential benefit for the distribution of Irish films. "We would see this as a really good way to look at opening up Irish films to an Irish audience."

McGrane cites as an example 2004's big Irish hit, *Man About Dog*. The film, directed by Paddy Breathnach, played much better in the regions than inside Dublin – an expensive lesson to learn when distributing 35mm prints. "If we'd been able to take *Man About Dog* and put it through the digital distribution network in 15 cinemas around the country for the opening week, you could get a much better and much cheaper feel of how the film is going to play" says McGrane. "With a digital distribution network, instead of the print and advertising costs going on prints and shipping, you can use it to direct more into advertising and to raise awareness before the film opens, so there is an idea that a big Irish film is actually opening."

Potboiler Prods./Treasure Ent./Kobal

Man About Dog *might have been a bigger local hit with digital distribution*

Jerome Maison/Bonne Pioche/Buena Vista/APC/Kobal

March of the Penguins: *waddling onto digital screens in Ireland in 2006.*

Julieanne Crothers-Gibson, Director of Policy Development at the Northern Ireland Film and Television Commission, is equally enthusiastic about the flexibility of the new system. "It will revolutionise the whole cinemagoing experience, not just for the customer but for the whole cinema operation," she says. "At the moment you're having to book a print for a number of days, but if you decide that a certain film is doing much better than you originally envisaged you can just send it to another screen at a touch of a button."

Both McGrane and Crothers-Gibson remain concerned about compatibility, and how competition among digital providers will play out. But Avica's Cummins insists that many of the compatibility issues will go away as the hardware manufacturers all begin to comply with MXF, the newly agreed upon standard format set by the DCI.

So, most importantly for cinema fans, will it be the major Hollywood blockbusters or independent films that benefit more from digital cinema? "I suppose that's the million dollar question," says McGrane. "Everyone says, 'Look

there really are new opportunities to be gained here from digital distribution.' But the question remains, what those opportunities actually are. Is it going to change the appetite for films?"

According to McCaul, independent films stand to benefit from going digital. "The notion abroad is that with the advent of digital it will be cheaper to produce movie on digital for exhibition purposes and therefore it will make independent movies, or international cinema or arthouse movies – call them what you like – much more accessible," he says. As for the major studios, McCaul says only time will tell: "It all has to be seen to be working and that it can deliver some of the things that we have aspirations for, namely security and economies of scale."

For theatre-owner O'Gorman, though, the future is bright. "In a way it's going to be good for both parties, for both independents and Hollywood studios. There's a bigger chance than ever for people to see everything."

CAROL NAHRA (carolnahra@homechoice.co.uk) is a freelance journalist based in London.

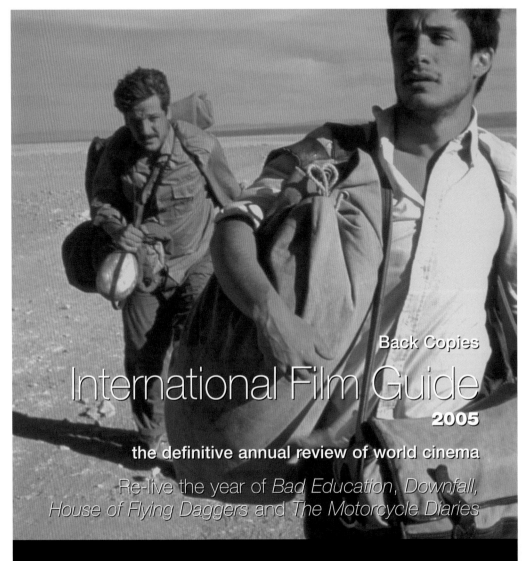

DVD Round-Up
by Daniel Rosenthal

Andrzej Wajda's **Three War Films** (Criterion, R1) from the 1950s ought to be part of the syllabus for all young Poles studying their country's history; not to mention viewers of any other nationality who wish to appreciate the idealism and bravery of the Poles' resistance during the Second World War.

The trilogy's action starts in 1943 with the young resistance fighters of *A Generation* (1955), Wajda's feature film debut, then follows the last hours of doomed remnants of the Home Army in 1944 in *Kanal* (1957), making their way through Warsaw's reeking sewers, and, as the war ends, takes a leap into more heightened, satirical territory with *Ashes and Diamonds* (1958), the film that saw Zbigniew Cybulski give Polish youth their answer to James Dean.

It's astonishing to watch Wajda's innate artistry deployed with increasing confidence across films made over such a short period of time. His handling of actors, his visual flair, in collaboration with cinematographers Jerzy Lipman and Jerzy Wojcik (both magnificently served by the Criterion restorations and transfers), and his ability to blend realism with blatant symbols or wild satire all help to make this box-set my DVD highlight of 2005.

The documentaries accompanying each film are packed with revelatory detail, whether it is Wajda's assistant director explaining why they used live ammunition for a night-time firefight in *Kanal*; or the director himself on how they outwitted the Polish censors with visual rather than verbal criticism of the Russians' failure to aid the Home Army in Warsaw in 1944, and why he chose to alter the source novel for *Ashes and Diamonds*, by making Cybulski's character,

Zespol Kimowy Kadr/Kobal

Tadeusz Janczar, left, and Teresa Izewska in **Kanal**

Maciek, the hero, instead of the Communist commissar he has been sent to assassinate.

Another of the year's best European box-sets, **Werner Herzog** (Anchor Bay, R1 & 2), collects *Even Dwarfs Started Small* (1970), *Fata Morgana* (1970), *The Enigma of Kaspar Hauser* (1974), *Heart of Glass* (1976) and *Stroszek* (1976), with absorbing commentary by Herzog and Norman Hill on each film.

Jean-Luc Godard called Robert Bresson's **Au hasard Balthazar** (1966; Criterion, R1) "the world in an hour-and-a-half" and the eponymous beast of burden's ability to provoke extremes of tenderness and cruelty in the humans around him – the virginal Marie (Anne Wiazemsky), the chorister rebel, Gérard (François Lafarge), the vagrant Arnold (Jean-Claude Guilbert) – leaves us with images as indelible as they are inscrutable (there's much more going on here than straightforward Christian allegory).

Pinning down the film's multiple meanings has proved impossible for critics as distinguished as Donald Richie, who in a video interview on this disc talks of Bresson moving "in mysterious ways", not least in his use of 'models' rather than professional actors. Bresson's methods are less mysterious in **Pickpocket** (1959; Criterion, R1), the brief tale of a nihilistic young hero's redemption through love. In the sequences showing Michel (Martin LaSalle) and his accomplices relieving Parisian race-goers and train passengers of wallets, cash and wristwatches, the film-making takes the breath away, the harmony between editing and camerawork as perfect as that between the thieves.

Deadly journeys

One of Jules Dassin's assignments for Twentieth-Century Fox, **Thieves' Highway** (1949), would make a sensational double-bill with Henri-Georges Clouzot's **The Wages of Fear** (1953; both Criterion R1). Dassin manages to invest a race to transport a truckload of Californian apples to market with almost as much tension and danger as Clouzot gives Yves Montand's mountainous journey to the blazing South American oil well with a cargo of nitro-glycerine.

Dassin's hero is Nick (Richard Conte), the ex-soldier out for revenge against Lee J. Cobb, the corrupt market trader responsible for crippling Nick's father. A new interview with Dassin reveals that the clunky ending, as a cop tells Nick not to take the law into his own hands, was tacked on at the behest of studio boss Darryl Zanuck. As ever, the inclusion of a vintage trailer is a delight ("Never more virile!" proclaims the voiceover at a shot of Conte with his shirt off). Extras on the two-disc *Wages of Fear* set include a 1988 interview with Montand, *The Enlightened Tyrant*, a profile of Clouzot from 2004, and *Censored*, a close look at how the film was cut for its 1955 US release.

A year after *Thieves' Highway*, Dassin packed the shadowy streets of post-war London with an almost Dickensian cast of lowlifes for another urgently told and economical noir, **Night and the City** (Criterion, R1), adapted from a novel by Gerald Kersh. Richard Widmark is at his most wild-eyed and desperate as the amoral Harry Fabian, getting fatally involved with a famous,

Richard Widmark on the run in **Night and the City**

ageing Greco-Roman wrestler (Stanislaus Zbyszko) and a ruthless rival promoter (Herbert Lom).

Kurosawa and Cox

Kagemusha (1980; Criterion, R1), Akira Kurosawa's tale of the condemned criminal who doubles for a samurai warlord (a dual performance from Tatsuya Nakadai), was his penultimate masterpiece, and shares the epic scale, splendour and tortured production history of his last, *Ran* (1985). This sumptuous two-disc presentation features interviews with George Lucas and Francis Ford Coppola, explaining how their involvement as executive producers enabled the man they so revered to raise the money he needed after being rejected by all the major Japanese studios.

Tatsuya Nakadai in **Kagemusha**

The British Film Institute, meanwhile, continues its bare-bones Kurosawa reissues for Region 2 with the melodramatic but socially acute **Drunken Angel** (1948), which marked the beginning of the director's partnership with Toshiro Mifune, and **The Bad Sleep Well** (1960), his riveting and tragic blend of corporate thriller and *Hamlet*.

Alex Cox has never quite matched the weird charm of *Repo Man* or the compassion of *Sid and Nancy*, but his other films, made with funding from Japan, Mexico, Spain and the Netherlands, as well as Britain, display ambition, humour and a deep knowledge of film history. For Region 2 the British Film Institute has paired the Spaghetti Western homage, **Straight to Hell** (1987), and the futuristic Jorge Luis Borges adaptation, **Death and the Compass** (1996), featuring Peter Boyle and Christopher Eccleston, on one disc, while another disc offers the grim **Highway Patrolman** (1991), shot in Cox's beloved Mexican landscapes, and the Buñuel-esque **Three Businessmen** (1998). Always an engaging talker, Cox provides commentary for all four titles.

Hollywood Classics

In Ernst Lubitsch's **Heaven Can Wait** (1943; Criterion, R1), a sensational restoration of Edward Cronjager's Technicolor photography gives a dazzling sheen to Rene Hubert's costumes and the lavish sets for the anteroom to hell and the interiors of the Van Cleve family's Fifth Avenue mansion. As the playboy looking back from the underworld on his life, and the wife who can only suffer his indiscretions for so long, Don Ameche and Gene Tierney are all charm, elegance and deadpan comic timing.

Cary Grant, Katharine Hepburn and James Stewart (who won the year's Best Actor Oscar) were seldom better – or given better material – than in George Cukor's **The Philadelphia Story** (1940; Warner Home Video, R1 & 2), and the repartee still sparkles. The film has been exquisitely remastered for a two-disc edition, with commentary from historian Jeannine Basinger and documentaries on Hepburn and Cukor.

Gene Tierney as Don Ameche's long-suffering wife in **Heaven Can Wait**

British Cinema

The death of Ismail Merchant cast a shadow over the latest DVD releases from the Merchant Ivory Collection, which included a two-disc edition of arguably the pair's most accomplished and moving work, **Howards End** (1992; Criterion R1). Ruth Prawer Jhabvala's screenplay and the exceptional acting of Emma Thompson, Anthony Hopkins, Helena Bonham Carter and Samuel West help define each complex social and emotional layer of the E.M. Forster novel. Extras include an in-depth look at Luciana Arrighi's Oscar-winning production design and an archive documentary on the first 20 years of the Merchant Ivory partnership.

Anthony Hopkins in **Howards End**

The vigorous ensemble acting of Alexander Mackendrick's **Whisky Galore!** (1949; Optimum, R2) has matured well over time, and this two-disc release features audio commentary from John Ellis, an archive documentary, with contributions from Mackendrick and his crew, and a new conversation with the director's widow, Hilary.

James Anderson, left, and James Robertson Justice in **Whisky Galore!**

Anthony Asquith's **The Browning Version** (1951; Criterion, R1), adapted by Terence Rattigan from his play, contains buttoned-down English acting of the highest class, not only from Michael Redgrave as Crocker-Harris, the boarding school classics master reflecting on a wasted life and a loveless marriage, but also from Jean Kent as his unfaithful spouse, and Wilfred Hyde White as the blithely insensitive headmaster. In a new video interview, Mike Figgis analyses the Asquith film and explains why he chose to remake it in 1994, with Albert Finney donning the Crocker-Harris gown.

Michael Redgrave and Brian Smith as master and pupil in **The Browning Version**

Rattigan and Asquith's England of immaculate lawns, marquees and Latin prep seems like another planet when set against the dark, forbidding London of Mike Leigh's **Naked** (1993; Criterion, R1). David Thewlis' Johnny rants and rails, his aggressive alienation all the more disturbing because he's far too intelligent to be considered a mere thug. Director and lead actor, who both took away prizes from Cannes, look back on the film on a commentary track.

David Bowie and Rip Torn in **The Man Who Fell to Earth**

Nicolas Roeg

It has, sadly, been a very long time since Nicolas Roeg displayed the masterful control of atmosphere and performances that make **The Man Who Fell to Earth** (1976) and **Bad Timing** (1980; both Criterion, R1) so unsettling. As the lonely alien in the former, David Bowie's first screen role remains his best, and the Criterion edition restores almost 20 minutes deleted from the American theatrical release, further enhancing the hallucinatory spell cast by Roeg and Bowie (who both provide audio commentary), as well as production designer Brian Eatwell and cinematographer Anthony

Richmond. Also included is a reprint of the source novel by Walter Tevis, who, thanks to Roeg, and Robert Rossen's film of his earlier novel, *The Hustler*, has a more secure place in cinematic history than literary circles.

Roeg's preoccupation with sex reached its darkest point in *Bad Timing*, and the last act of the film's doomed, obsessive affair between a psychoanalyst (Art Garfunkel) and an aimless married woman (Theresa Russell) in Vienna remains almost as shocking as the finale of Roeg's *Don't Look Now*.

Contemporary Cinema

Set against alternately beautiful and bleak winter scenery in and around Jindabyne, New South Wales, Cate Shortland's feature debut, **Somersault** (Metrodome, R2) was the best Australian film of 2004, a coming-of-age tale dominated by a raw, star-making performance from Abbie Cornish as Heidi, a 16-year-old runaway learning to define herself by more than just whom she sleeps with. Extras include Shortland's fine short, *Flowergirl*, and an interview with director of photography Robert Humphreys on the film's distinctive colour scheme.

Beckett on Film (Tyrone Productions, all regions) is a four-disc record of the UK/Ireland collaboration of 2001, which saw 19 directors commit all of Samuel Beckett's work for the theatre to film – a mammoth task made all the more difficult by the need to adhere to Beckett's notoriously strict stage directions.

The outstanding elements are John Hurt's reservoir of regret in *Krapp's Last Tape*, directed by Atom Egoyan, and the hopelessly dependent master-and-servant act between Michael Gambon and David Thewlis in Conor McPherson's *Endgame*. The bonus material includes interviews with Hurt and 10 of the directors, and *Check the Gate*, an hour-long 'Making of' documentary. This is a collection that deserves a place in every school and university library.

Tai Seng Entertainment were welcome newcomers to the Region 2 market in 2005, offering a strong selection of recent Asian mainstream and arthouse titles, including Kim Ki-duk's disturbing portrait of the artist as revenger, **Real Fiction** (2000), and a two-disc edition of his compatriot Kim Ji-woon's farcical, pitch-black comedy, **The Quiet Family** (1998).

Eschewing prison movie clichés in favour of mordant wit and a bold dose of spirituality, Annette K. Olesen's Dogme drama, **In Your Hands** (2004; Metrodome, R2), has the superb ensemble acting that has been a hallmark of Danish cinema in the last decade, whether or not the 'Vow of Chastity' is observed. A Q&A with Olesen and several cast interviews are among the extra features.

The box-set **4 Films by Lukas Moodysson** (Metrodome, R2) brings together the first four features from one of Europe's most gifted and certainly least predictable young directors. The shift in tone from light to dark is astonishing: the teen-photo-story optimism of *Show Me Love* (1998) and the wild, affirmative humour of *Together* (2000) are succeeded by *Lilya 4-ever* (2002), with its damning vision of male exploitation, and the unwatchable (and in box-office terms almost totally unwatched) degradation of the wannabe porn stars in *A Hole in My Heart* (2004).

Memfis/SVT/Keyfilms/Zentropa/Kobal

Together *features in the Lukas Moddysson box-set*

Documentaries

Released to coincide with the 25th anniversary of the Beatle's murder, the two-disc edition of Andrew Solt's **Imagine: John Lennon** (1988; Warner, R1 & 2) adds new home-movie footage and interviews to what was already a fascinating combination of self-portrait and 'greatest hits' musical celebration.

A surprise ratings success when broadcast on BBC television in 2005, **The Lost World of Mitchell & Kenyon** (British Film Institute, R2) is a remarkable piece of social and film history. More than 100 years ago, Sagar Mitchell and James Kenyon travelled up and down the UK, recording the British at work, rest and play. Their footage of schoolgirls, policemen, holidaymakers, football fans and many others, had lain undiscovered in a shop basement in Blackburn, Lancashire, for 70 years, until accidentally unearthed by a businessman. The BFI's restoration compiles almost three hours' worth of footage and new interviews with descendants who are suddenly confronted with their long-dead ancestors' walk-on parts in some of Britain's earliest documentaries.

Burden of Dreams (1982; Criterion, R1), Les Blank's account of Werner Herzog and Klaus Kinski's jungle misadventures on *Fitzcarraldo*, gains even greater value in an edition that has audio commentary by Blank, editor and sound recordist Maureen Gosling and Herzog, plus a new interview with Herzog and an 80-page booklet of excerpts from Blank and Gosling's production journals, which draw attention to the tedium of the Amazon shoot ("I hadn't played cards so much since my eight days in a Louisiana jail on a pot offence", writes Blank).

Until Michael Moore took on American gun culture, the $8m gross of **Hoop Dreams** (1994; Criterion, R1) was a US box-office record, and it's easy to see why audiences responded in such numbers. The contrasting and unpredictable fortunes of Arthur Agee and William Gates, the two Illinois basketball stars pursuing college scholarships and NBA glory, gave Steve James' three-hour film more drama than the formulaic setbacks and last-reel victories of a dozen Hollywood sports pictures. It is a powerful account of inner-city life for poor African-American families. The reissue sees Gates, now a pastor, and Agee, who runs his own Role Model Foundation, commenting on their younger selves.

Fine Line/Kartemquin/Kobal

Hoop Dreams *once held a US box-office record*

Released to coincide with a new book on his work (see Books Round-Up) the six-disc boxed-set **Nick Broomfield: Documenting Icons** (Metrodome, R2) compiles some of the British directors' best investigations: *Soldier Girls* (1981), *Chicken Ranch* (1983), *The Leader, His Driver and the Driver's Wife* (1990), *Tracking Down Maggie* (1994), *Heidi Fleiss: Hollywood Madam* (1995), which has never previously been available on video in the UK, and the notorious *Fetishes* (1996), with additional material deemed too outré for the theatrical release. Broomfield's son, Barney, directs *Nick Broomfield – A History*, a feature-length documentary that sees his father looking back over his 35-year career, and the set even includes the Volkswagen TV commercials in which he sent up his on-screen persona.

Books Round-Up
by Daniel Rosenthal

While its $1.8 billion gross may make *Titanic* "king of the world" in the all-time movie chart, the only true and timeless test of a film's popularity is the number of tickets it sold. This was the criterion used by Phil Wickham and Matt Ker, the researchers whose labours for **The Ultimate Film** (British Film Institute, London) have produced such arresting revelations. Who would have thought that Anna Neagle and Michael Wilding's romantic comedy double-act in the frothy *Spring in Park Lane* (1948) would waltz into fourth place on the list of the most popular films ever at UK cinemas, its estimated 20.5 million admissions placing it three places above James Cameron's epic? Or that *The Guns of Navarone* outsold *Harry Potter and the Prisoner of Azkaban*?

The entry on each of the top 100 titles includes stills, memorable dialogue, a synopsis and an excerpt from the film's original *Monthly Film Bulletin* or *Sight & Sound review*. All in all, this is one of the most fascinating and valuable reference works of recent times, a wonderful barometer of changes in public taste, cinemagoing habits and film-making styles.

Few comic actors have made me laugh more than Gene Wilder, who has produced a sweet-natured, episodic and engaging autobiography, **kiss me like a stranger** (Harper Collins Entertainment, London and New York). Wilder's performing life began as Jerry Silberman, an eight-year-old Milwaukee kid who put on Jewish and German accents and sang Danny Kaye songs to make his mother laugh and, so her doctor told him, help ward off her next heart attack. We learn how Jerry became Gene, and ended up in *The Producers*, in partnership with Mel Brooks and Zero Mostel ("the two most

Imperadio/British Lion/Kobal

Spring in Park Lane: *a surprisingly high entry in* **The Ultimate Film** *chart*

unusual people I ever met"). He writes movingly of the loss of his second wife, Gilda Radner, to cancer, and his own brush with the disease.

Arnold Schwarzenegger's *Crusade*, Ridley Scott's *The Hot Zone*, 'Alien-on-a-train' thriller *ISOBAR* and the fourth *Indiana Jones* film are among a dozen abortive or long-gestating projects examined by David Hughes in **Tales from Development Hell** (Titan Books, London and New York). Hughes tells his stories with great verve, and makes no apology for siding with the long-suffering Hollywood scriptwriters whose work is constantly at the mercy of executives, stars and their 'people', confessing in his Introduction that "several of my own screenplays are currently rotting in development hell".

Interviews

Alistair Owen's *Story and Character* (2003) was a memorable collection of interviews with British screenwriters and in **Hampton on Hampton** (Faber, London and New York) he applies the same craft to his extended conversations with one of the UK's most prolific writers for stage and screen, Christopher Hampton. Highlights include Hampton's recollections of his

Jill Furmanovsky/Polygram/Canal +/Kobal

Carrington: explored in **Hampton on Hampton**

misadventures on the abortive adaptation of Donna Tartt's *The Secret History*, his triumphant directing debut, *Carrington*, and his work on the novels of Joseph Conrad: the unfilmed *Nostromo* for David Lean, and his own, hit-and-miss film of *The Secret Agent*. The other addition to the Faber series is Chris Rodley's **Lynch on Lynch**, which adds *The Straight Story* (Lynch's most humane film since *The Elephant Man*) and the infuriating *Mulholland Drive* to the original edition's account of his career up until 1997.

Jason Wood's **Nick Broomfield: Documenting Icons** (Faber, New York and London) finds Britain's best-known documentary director in typically frank and expansive mood, whether recalling his on-screen pursuit of Margaret Thatcher, Eugene Terre'Blanche and Courtney Love, or explaining why his only fiction feature to date, the incoherent *Diamond Skulls* (1989), was such a failure that, Broomfield says, "I still don't think I've entirely recovered from the pain of it." For **Screenwriters' Masterclass – Screenwriters Talk About Their Greatest Movies** (Faber, London and New York), Kevin Conroy Scott draws advice and anecdotes from 21 international scribes whose original scripts (Guillermo Arriaga's *Amores perros*, David O. Russell's *Three Kings*) and adaptations (Alexander Payne and Jim Taylor's *Election*) have contributed to some of the best features of the past decade.

Tim Adler's experience as editor of *Screen Finance* informs his illuminating profiles of and interviews with the likes of Michael Douglas, Dino De Laurentiis and Jeremy Thomas in **The Producers** (Methuen, London). Christopher Frayling has distilled more than 30 hours of conversation with his subject for **Ken Adam – The Art of Production Design**, a revealing retrospective on the man whose exceptional artistry, from the *Dr. Strangelove* war room to the Oscar-winning royal splendour of *The Madness of King George*, has been based on his belief, that "the point of production design is to create an idea of a place rather than a real place."

National Cinema Studies

Donald Richie has extensively revised and updated his **A Hundred Years of Japanese Film** (Kodansha International, Tokyo, New York and London) since its first appearance in 1990. It now includes directors he groups together in a chapter on "The New Independents", including Takeshi Kitano, Takashi Miike and Yoichi Sai, and a concise guide to Japanese films on DVD and video. Though sparsely illustrated, it is yet another reminder that, as Paul Schrader writes in the Foreword: "Whatever we in the West know about Japanese film, and how we know it, we most likely owe to Donald Richie."

In **Cool & Crazy** (Norwegian Film Institute, Oslo), *IFG* founding editor Peter Cowie looks back on the remarkable range of feature films produced by Norwegian directors from 1990–2005, a period in which international acclaim for the likes of Hans Petter Moland, Erik Skjoldbjærg and Knut Erik Jensen has, Cowie writes, "demonstrated the appeal of Norwegian cinema beyond its borders, and its right to be assessed alongside work from neighbouring Denmark and Sweden". Accompanied by a fine selection of large colour stills, his concise, evocative assessments of dozens of features always root them in the wider context of Norwegian society.

The late Edward Said called the work of Iran's post-Revolutionary film-makers "one of the most extraordinary artistic and social adventures of our time", and in **Close Up – Iranian Cinema Past, Present and Future** (Verso, New York and London), Hamid Dabashi paints compelling portraits of several leading adventurers: Abbas Kiarostami, Bahram Beiza'i, Bahman Farmanara and Mohsen Makhmalbaf.

In **The Heart of the World: Films from Central Asia** (Complex Print House, Almaty; ISBN 9965-471-79-7), Gulnara Abikeyeva provides an invaluable English-language survey of the first decade of post-Soviet film-making in Kazakhstan, Kyrgyzstan, Tajikistan, Turkmenistan and Uzbekistan, through reviews of more than 30 features, and interviews with 15 Central Asian directors.

The New Brazilian Cinema (I.B. Tauris, New York and London), edited by Lúcia Nagib, collects 16 essays exploring the complex social, political, economic and cultural factors that have influenced and been so memorably dramatised in the films of Walter Salles, Andrucha Waddington and Bruno Barreto, amongst others. Contributors include José Álvaro Moisés, who as a former National Secretary for Audiovisual Affairs, brings a true insider's perspective to the Brazilian industry.

Art and Photography

Two major cinematic events of 2005 – the release of *Revenge of the Sith* and the 50th anniversary of James Dean's death – inevitably unleashed a stream of tie-in publications. By far the weightiest and most impressive of the *Star Wars* books is Marcus Hearn's **The Cinema of George Lucas** (Abrams), which takes us from *THX-1138* to *Episode III*, using a wealth of material from the Lucasfilm archives (shooting schedules, concept drawings, a *Star Wars* preview questionnaire) to highlight Lucas' work as director and producer. Amongst more than 500 photographs, the most remarkable is a fish-eye image of Lucas, Coppola and the other founders of American Zoetrope, all looking impossibly young, pictured against the San Francisco skyline in April 1970. John Knoll's **Creating the Worlds of Star Wars – 365 Days** (Abrams) is for die-hard fans only, packing too many photographs into a cramped, awkward format.

The Magnum photographer Dennis Stock met James Dean at the start of 1955 and for the remainder of the star's short life took hundreds of pictures of him in New York, Indiana and Hollywood. Eighty of these have been immaculately reproduced in Stock's **James Dean – Fifty Years Ago** (Abrams). While the walking-and-smoking street scenes have been reproduced (and imitated) ad nauseam, other shots prompt gasps (Dean posing in a half-open coffin) or broad smiles (the star emulating Eartha Kitt at a New York dance class).

For more than 80 years, Los Angeles-based *Architectural Digest* has been assessing stars', directors' and moguls' taste in bricks, mortar and furnishings. **Hollywood at Home** (Abrams), edited by the magazine's editor-in-chief, Paige Rense, feels like the world's most stylish real estate catalogue, giving discrete peaks inside the (mostly) elegant homes of Cukor, De Mille, Garland, Monroe and others. Note John Travolta's Gulfstream jet, parked beside his lawn as casually as a Volvo.

Five years after his fine biography of the Spaghetti Western king, Christopher Frayling follows up with **Sergio Leone – Once Upon a Time in Italy** (Thames & Hudson, London and New York), which complements wonderful illustrations (stills, location shots, international posters, album sleeves, design sketches) with Frayling's archive interviews with key Leone collaborators, including Clint Eastwood, cinematographer Tonino Delli Colli and production designer Carlo Simi.

Two European screen icons are celebrated in Mark A. Vieira's **Greta Garbo – A Cinematic Legacy** and **Isabelle Huppert – Woman of Many Faces** (both Abrams), edited by Ronald Ariel Chammah and Serge Toubiana, which features photographs by the likes of Cartier-Bresson, Avedon and Brigitte Lacombe. Finally, **The Independent Movie Poster Book** (Abrams), selected from the collection of New York's Posteritati Gallery, features some dazzling European imagery inspired by American directors such as Lynch, Jarmusch and Hartley.

Other Recent Publications

American Splendor – Our Movie Year – Harvey Pekar (Titan Books)
The Cleveland everyman's latest curmudgeonly collection traces the transformation of his cartoon strip into one of the quirkiest, most compassionate American film comedies of the decade.

Batman Begins – Christopher Nolan and David S. Goyer (Faber, New York and London)
The only summer blockbuster of 2005 to offer entertaining dialogue as well as explosions. Nolan and Goyer's screenplay is augmented by interviews with both, and almost 200 pages of black-and-white storyboards.

British Film Guides: Brighton Rock – Steve Chibnall; **My Beautiful Laundrette** – Christine Geraghty (I.B. Tauris, London and New York)
In *Brighton Rock*, Chibnall reminds us that one of the greatest of all Graham Greene adaptations was savaged by the *Daily Mirror* as "false, cheap, nasty sensationalism", while Geraghty assesses the political and cultural impact of Stephen Frears' *My Beautiful Laundrette* and its influence on British-Asian film-makers.

Michael Caine – Christopher Bray (Faber, London)
Solid biography of the man whose work from *Zulu* (1964) to *Get Carter* (1971) dwarfs the dozens of mostly forgettable roles that followed.

The Cambridge Companion to David Mamet – Edited by Christopher Bigsby (Cambridge University Press)
Philip French provides a typically witty and perceptive assessment of Mamet's films up until *Heist* in this strong collection of essays.

Ciné-Files: French Film Guides (I.B. Tauris, London and New York)
This welcome new series of compact monographs blends scene-by-scene analysis with contextual study. Chris Darke tackles Godard's *Alphaville*, Susan Hayward chooses Clouzot's *Les Diaboliques*, Julianne Pidduck picks her way through the corpses of Patrice Chéreau's blood-drenched *La Reine Margot*, and the series' editor, Ginette Vincendeau, takes a timely look at Mathieu Kassovitz's *La Haine*, given shocking new relevance by the Paris riots in November 2005.

A History of Violence – John Wagner and Vince Locke (Vertigo, New York)
A chance to compare David Cronenberg's justly acclaimed film with its source: Locke's grainy monochrome artwork and Wagner's clipped dialogue (first published by DC Comics in 1997).

Hollywood Italians – Peter Bondanella (Continuum, London and New York)
Bondanella puts his deep knowledge of Italian cinema and history to engaging use in a book whose subtitle, "Dagos, Palookas, Romeos, Wise Guys, and Sopranos", covers everyone from Valentino and Sinatra to De Niro, Stallone and James Gandolfini.

Once Upon a Time in the Italian West – Howard Hughes (I.B. Tauris, London and New York)
Hughes' lively and astute "Filmgoers' Guide to Spaghetti Westerns" focuses in depth on 20 titles made between 1964 and 1973, mixing the Leone classics with lesser-known titles such as Sergio Sollima's *Face to Face*.

Postcolonial Images: Studies in North African Film – Roy Armes (Indiana University Press)
First comprehensive account in English of film-making in the Maghreb (Algeria, Tunisia, Morocco). It offers a detailed historical survey, in-depth studies of 10 key films, a dictionary of film-makers and chronology of films.

Carol Reed – Peter William Evans (Manchester University Press, Manchester and New York)
Part of MUP's admirable "British Film Makers" series, this is an in-depth study of Reed's entire career, with an especially good chapter on his three great collaborations with Graham Greene.

Mae West – It Ain't No Sin – Simon Louvish (Faber, London and New York) Louvish's access to West's unpublished papers enlivens this enjoyable new account of the life, movies and writing of "a vaudeville baby" who "carved her own identity out of a patchwork of influences".

Westerns – Philip French (Carcanet Press, Manchester). Welcome reissue, in revised and expanded form, for French's superb study of the genre that has had a (mostly) rough ride since the book first appeared in the 1970s.

World Survey

6 continents | 100 countries | 1,000s of films...

Afghanistan Sandra Schäfer

The Year's Best Films

Sandra Schäfer's selection:
Three Dots (Roya Sadat)
Nilofar in the Rain
(Hamayoun Karimpour)
Impossible State
(Docu. Atiq Rahimi)

Gul Afrooz in **Three Dots**

Recent and Forthcoming Films

QANOON (The Law)
*[Action drama, 2005] Script:
Saba Sahar. Dir: Ghafar Zalan,
Sahar. Phot: Mirwais Arash.
Players: Sahar. Prod: Saba
Film, GTZ, German Ministry
for Economic Cooperation
and Development.*
A policewoman fights corruption.

Saba Sahar, right, in **Qanoon**

SAYEH (Shadows)
*[Documentary, 2004] Script and
Dir: Mary Ayubi, Polly Hyman.
Phot: Shakiba Adil, Ayubi,
Parwin Ayubi, Mehria Azizi,*

Approximately 50 feature films have been produced in Afghanistan since 1965. After proscriptive production controls under Soviet occupation, the country then lived through the absolute prohibition of images under the Taliban. Happily, employees of the national film production agency and archive, Afghan Film, somehow managed to save its collection from destruction. It is even more astonishing that Siddiq Barmak's **Osama** could be shot on the streets of Kabul in 2002–03. Made with amateur actors, it tells the story of Taliban repression against women, from the perspective of a young girl, disguised as a boy so that she can can earn a living for her mother and grandmother. Her ruse echoes the traditional tale of Rostum, according to which walking under a rainbow could turn a girl into a boy. *Osama* won the 2004 Golden Globe for Best Foreign Film.

In spite of the misogynist climate, in 2004, Roya Sadat became the first Afghan woman feature director, with **Three Dots** (*Se noughta*). Realistically staged, it is set on the Iran/Afghanistan border, and its heroine is a young widow, Gul Afrooz, struggling to survive with her three children. By refusing to marry her late husband's brother, she violates traditional laws and is treated as a renegade. Desperate to keep her children, she starts smuggling drugs for a local boss, Khan. Symbolic clues hint at Gul's tragic fate, as Sadat sharply analyses family structures, feudalism and forced marriage.

Short, sharp lessons

The film landscape is dominated by Afghan Film, the Culture and Art Center in Kabul, the Film-makers' Union and Aina, an NGO, along with private production companies. Didactic short films, shot on digital, with independent finance or grants from humanitarian organisations, are commonplace. In Razi Mohebi's short, **Kite** (*Kaghaz paran*), children are afraid to play with kites because a Talib lives nearby, but they befriend his son and manage to persuade him to make an exception. In Mirwais Rekab's short, **Kabul Cinema**, a boy collects discarded reels from a demolished cinema and turns a wooden cart into a mobile screening unit, which he takes around Kabul, despite bombings and constant fear of discovery. In **Stoning** (*Sangsar*), engineer Latif Ahmadi tells the striking story of a married woman, who after being raped commits suicide to avoid the punishment of stoning. Her 13-year-old sister is forced to marry the rapist.

After finishing a journalism course paid for by Aina, five Afghan camerawomen produced the reportage **Afghanistan Unveiled** (2003), which gained a 2005 Emmy award nomination. Travelling for the first time without their families, the quintet toured Afghanistan asking women about their living conditions. They followed up with a series of video portraits of engaged women, **If I Stand Up** (*Man agar barkhezam*).

Hamayoun Karimpour and Atiq Rahimi are Afghan film-makers living in France. Karimpour produced, wrote, directed and edited a low-budget feature, **Nilofar in the Rain** (*Nilofar der baran*). Shapour, an Afghani living in France, narrates this psychologically dense story, full of unexpected turns, in which family relations damaged by war and exile put an end to his love affair with Nilofar.

Mamnoun Maqsoudi, Nassim Khoshgwar and Afrouz Nikzad in **Nilofar in the Rain**

Rahimi shot a documentary, **Impossible State** (*Etat impossible*), followed by his first fiction feature, **Earth and Ashes** (*Khak wa khakestar*), based on his own novel. In this parable, set during the Soviet occupation, a grandfather waits for a ride with his grandson, left deaf by a bomb explosion. Haunted by nightmares, the man chews tobacco to ease his hunger, and hopes that he can find his son, a miner, to bring news of their survival. Finally, **The Giant Buddhas**, by Christian Frei, contains astonishing video footage from an Al-Jazeera journalist who, while disguised as a Talib, secretly documented the destruction of these giant statues in Bamiyan.

SANDRA SCHÄFER (mazefilm@gmx.net) is a film-maker and curator. She co-curated a film festival, "Kabul/Tehran 1979ff", in Berlin in 2003 and is co-editor of a book of the same title (b_books Verlag). With Elfe Brandenburger she is working on a documentary about women's resistance under the Taliban.

Polly Hyman, Gul Makai Rangebar, Habib Samin, Daoud Wahab. Prod: Daoud Wahab & Florent Milesi (AINA).
Journalist Mary Ayubi interviews a female construction worker and the only policewoman in Kandahar, and asks students about bribery and sexual harassment.

KABOUTHAR (Pigeon)
[Video essay, 2004] Script and Dir: Soheila Muhd Ibrahim. Phot: Kaouther Ben H'nia. Prod: La Femis, The Ministry of Foreign Affairs.
A poetic essay made during the director's stay in Paris.

FIRE DANCER
[Drama, 2004] Script and Dir: Jawed Wassel. Phot: Bud Gardner. Players: Baktash Zaher-Khadem, Mariam Weiss, Yunis Azizi. Prod: Khaled Wassel, John G. Roche & Kate Wood.
A love story between Laila and Haris, Afghanis living in New York.

HIJRAT (Migration)
[Social drama, 2004] Script, Dir and Phot: Wahid Nazari.
A bin liner thrown out of a bus at a station in Germany contains Ali, a refugee from Afghanistan, who travels to the Netherlands and applies for asylum.

ENTEHAYE ZAMIN (End of the Land)
[Documentary, 2003] Script, Dir and Phot: Malek Shafi'i. Prod: CACA, Kabul.
In 2001, a group of Afghans wants to cycle from Iran to Geneva to demonstrate for peace, but entry permits divert them to Athens, where they interview Afghan refugees and see the 9/11 attacks on TV.

Algeria Roy Armes

Recent Films

EL MANARA
[Drama, 2004] Script: Salim Aïssa. Dir: Belkacem Hadjadj. Phot: Ahmed Messead. Players: Samia Meziane, Tarek Hadj Abdelhafidh, Khaled Benaïssa. Prod: Machahou Production.

LE THÉ D'ANIA (Ania's Tea)
[Drama, 2004] Script and Dir: Saïd Ould Khelifa. Phot: Marc Koninck. Players: Sonia Koudil, Abdelkader Bouaiche, Omar Oujdit, Mustapha Ayad. Prod: Agat Films/ENTV/CIM Audiovisuel/Djazair 2003.

LES SUSPECTS (The Suspects)
[Drama, 2004] Script: Kamal Dekane and Mahmoud Ben Mahmoud. Dir: Kamal Dehane. Phot: Michel Baudour. Players: Nadia Kaci, Kamel Rouini, Sid Ali Kouiret. Prod: Saga Film.

BAB EL WEB
[Comedy, 2004] Script and Dir: Merzak Allouache. Phot: Antoine Roch. Players: Samy Nacéri, Faudel, Julie Gayet, Hacène Benzerari, Boualem Benani. Prod: Maïa Films/Baya Films/ France 3 Cinéma/Les Productions JMH/Pyramide Productions/ ENTV/Gimages Développement.

Merzak Allouache's **Bab el Web**

Only four features were completed by Algerian directors in 2004. Belkacem Hadjadj is best known for his courageous first feature, *Once Upon a Time* (*Machaho*), a key feature in mid-1990s Algerian cinema, and a political event in its own right, being one of only three films to have used the previously forbidden Berber language, Tamazight. Since then, Belkacem has remained in Algeria, despite all the pressures, making a number of socially committed documentaries on contemporary issues. His new film, **El Manara**, looks back to the Algerian riots of October 1988, chronicling the experiences of three young people.

The three other 2004 features were all made by directors based outside Algeria. Saïd Ould Khelifa returned after a 12-year gap, with **Ania's Tea** (*Le thé d'Ania*). The protagonist is Mehdi, an author living in Algiers in the 1990s, blocked in his writing and cowed by the events around him. Mehdi is dominated by thoughts of the 150,000 Algerian dead whose names it is his job to chronicle and is helped only by his neighbour, Ania, who brings him tea daily. This is a slow film of looks and silences, not actions or words.

Kamal Dehane had from 1989 onwards established an international reputation with widely seen social and cultural documentaries. He made his fiction feature debut with **The Suspects** (*Les suspects*), another understated love story dominated by the violent Algerian past, which threatens to overwhelm a young psychiatrist, Samia, and the man she comes to love.

Paris-based Merzak Allouache has established himself as the most prolific of Maghrebian directors without sustaining the high quality of his early work, and has become, in effect, a French film-maker. His tenth feature, **Bab el Web**, is a slight, French-language comedy about a young man who invites all the French girls he chats up on the internet to come to Algiers – and is horrified when one takes him at his word. While all these films to some extent look back, the key event of 2004 is likely to have been the founding of a new National Film Centre (the CNCA) in Algiers.

ROY ARMES (royarmes@btinternet.com) is Emeritus Professor of Film at Middlesex University and a long-time student of African film-making. His most recent book is *Postcolonial Images: Studies in North African Film* (Indiana University Press, 2005).

Argentina Alfredo Friedlander

The Year's Best Films

Alfredo Friedlander's selection:
Whisky Romeo Zulu
(Enrique Piñeyro)
Trelew
(Docu. Mariana Arruti)
Bombón el perro
(Carlos Sorín)
Little Sky
(María Victoria Menis)
Enlightened by Fire
(Tristán Bauer)

Rodrigo Silva, left, and Leonardo
Ramírez in Little Sky

Recent and Forthcoming Films

LOS MUERTOS (The Dead)
[Drama, 2004] Script and Dir:
Lisandro Alonso. Phot: Cobi
Migliora. Players: Argentino
Vargas. Prod: Micaela Buye.
Vargas, 54, is released after
several years in prison. His only
wish is to see his daughter, who
lives in a distant place
surrounded by water and forests.

TRELEW
[Documentary, 2004] Script
and Dir: Mariana Arruti. Phot:
Javier Miquelez. Prod:
Fundación Alumbrar.
Examination of how, in 1972,
members of revolutionary
armed organisations planned a
massive escape from confinement

Almost 70 Argentine features (including co-productions) were released in 2004 – the highest number in the country's history – and compared to 2003 there was a general improvement in quality, with many pictures receiving awards at major festivals. At press time it looked as though around 60 local films would have reached cinemas by the end of 2005, though of generally inferior quality when set against 2004, making it difficult to choose five as the year's best domestic features. Only one local movie, **Dad is Crazy** (*Papa se volvió loco*), a very dull comedy, will be among the year's top 10 hits, with almost two million admissions. Overall, comedies, including the enjoyable **Elsa & Fred**, were largely responsible for giving local movies a market share of around 10–12%.

In March 2005, the 20th International Film Festival of Mar del Plata showed notable improvements. The inaugural Mercosur Film Market offered 300, mainly Argentine movies, for sale. Among the fairly limited number of international guests attending were Volker Schlöndorff, István Szabó and Norman Jewison, who gave masterclasses, which have become a feature of the festival. The jury, headed by Spanish critic Roman Gubern and including Hugh Hudson and Robert Lantos, awarded the Golden Astor to Ismaël Ferrouji's *The Great Journey*. A local production, Anahí Berneri's **A Year Without Love** (*Un año sin amor*), won the FIPRESCI award.

In April 2005, the seventh Buenos Aires International Film Festival (BAFICI), under new management, showed more than 350 films, including shorts, with almost 50 features from Argentina. The jury unanimously chose Spaniard Mercedes Alvarez's *The Sky Turns* (*El cielo gira*) as best movie. The festival dedicated retrospectives to Chantal Akerman and Monte Hellman, who both attended. For the first time the BAFICI had two competitions, one dedicated exclusively to Argentine films, most awaiting release.

Argentina had one film, Albertina Carri's **Géminis**, which had already screened out of competition as Closing Film at BAFICI, in the Directors Fortnight at Cannes 2005, alongside a co-production with France, Juan Solanas' **Northwest** (*Nordeste*), in Un Certain Regard. In sharp contrast with 2004, when many well-established directors released new movies, 2005 saw only a handful of famous names at work, among them Eduardo Mignogna, with **The Wind**

in the maximum security prison of Rawson, close to Trelew in Patagonia.

EL CIELITO (Little Sky)
[Social drama, 2004] Script and Dir: María Victoria Menis, Alejandro Fernández Murray. Phot: Marcelo Iaccarino. Players: Leonardo Ramírez, Darío Levy, Mónica Lairana, Rodrigo Silva. Prod: Héctor Menis, Sophie Dulac, Michel Zana.
Félix, 20, a small-time thief, begins to work in a modest farm, owned by a couple who live with their baby boy, Chango. Based on a true story, the film reflects on parental roles.

UN AÑO SIN AMOR
(A Year Without Love)
[Drama, 2004] Script: Pablo Pérez, Anahí Berneri. Dir: Beneri. Phot: Lucio Bonelli. Players: Juan Minujín, Mimi Ardú, Carlos Echevarría, Javier van de Couter, Bárbara Lombardo, Osnar Nuñez, Ricardo Merkin. Prod: BD Cine/Wap.
Pablo is a young writer with Aids. The "year without love" is 1996, when retroviral therapies with drug cocktails replace the AZT therapy. Pablo fears this prescription is not the right one.

NO SOS VOS, SOY YO
(It's Not You, It's Me)
[Comedy, 2004] Script: Cecilia Dopazo, Juan Taratuto. Dir: Taratuto. Phot: Marcelo Iaccarino. Players: Diego Peretti, Soledad Villamil, Cecilia Dopazo, Hernán Jimenez, Marcos Mundstock, Luis Brandoni. Prod: Rizoma Films/Filmanova Invest.
Javier, 30, a surgeon, and María decide to move to the US. She leaves first and calls to tell him that she has met another man. He buys a dog and meets Julia at the vet's. When María comes back he is no longer the same person.

ORO NAZI EN ARGENTINA
(Nazi Gold in Argentina)
[Documentary, 2004] Script: Jorge Camarasa, Rolo Pereyra. Dir: Pereyra. Phot: Pacho

(*El viento*), and Fabián Bielinsky with **The Aura** (*El aura*). More and more releases are from young directors presenting their first or second movie, such as *A Year Without Love*, Enrique Piñeyro's **Whisky Romeo Zulu**, Jorge Gaggero's **Bed Inside** (*Cama adentro*) and Julia Solomonoff's **Sisters** (*Hermanas*).

Antonella Costa and Federico Luppi in **The Wind**

Distribution remains difficult. Once again many Argentine films (often documentaries) were screened at one or two cinemas for only a few weeks. In addition, the number of films from new Argentine directors awaiting release is still increasing, and some will never reach theatres. During 2004 there was a 30% increase in total admissions, with a 75% market share for the US productions and only 13% for Argentina. The average number of prints per release for American movies was 40 and only 10 for Argentina. Only one local feature was released on more than 100 copies (*Patoruzito*) while the top 10 US titles surpassed this barrier. At press time, 2005 was on track to reflect the worldwide trend, with a reduction in admissions of around 15% (*Madagascar* was on course to be the number one release).

Diego Peretti in It's Not You, It's Me

Florencia Blanco

Guerty, Mariano De Lucca.
Prod: Ledafilms/HBO Ole
Partners/INCAA.
Shot in Argentina, Switzerland,
Spain, Germany and Italy, the film
uncovers controversial evidences
about the arrival of Nazi war
criminals in Argentina, implicating
Swiss banks and the Vatican.

WHISKY ROMEO ZULU

[Drama, 2004] Script and Dir:
Enrique Piñeyro. Phot: Ramiro
Civita. Players: Piñeyro,
Mercedes Morán, Alejandro
Awada, Adolfo Yanelli, Carlos
Portaluppi. Prod: Aqua Films.
Piñeyro, a former pilot of LAPA
Airlines, narrates the hidden story
behind the Boeing 737 accident
that caused 67 deaths in 1999.

HERMANAS (Sisters)

[Drama, 2004] Script and Dir:
Julia Solomonoff. Phot: Ramiro
Aisenson. Players: Valeria
Bertucelli, Ingrid Rubio, Adrián
Navarroa, Nicolás Pauls, Horacio
Peña, Mónica Galán, Eusebio
Poncela. Prod: Cruzdelsur zona
audiovisual/Tornasol Films
(Spain)/Patagonik Film Group/
Videofilmes (Brazil).
Two sisters meet again in Texas
in 1984, where Elena (Bertucelli)
has set up home with her
husband. Natalia (Rubio) comes
from a long exile in Spain and
together they relive terrible
moments during the military
dictatorship in Argentina.

CAMA ADENTRO (Bed Inside)

[Comedy-drama, 2004] Script and
Dir: Jorge Gaggero. Phot: Javier
Juliá. Players: Norma Aleandro,
Norma Argentina, Marcos
Mundstock, Raúl Panguinao,
Susana Lanteri, Claudia Lapacó,
Elsa Berenger, Mónica Gonzaga.
Prod: LibidoCine/Aqua Films/
Filamonova.
Beba (Aleandro) tries to conceal
the fact that she can no longer
keep up with her sophisticated
lifestyle. Conflict arises when
Dora, her maid, decides to
leave her.

ELSA & FRED

[Comedy, 2005] Script: Marcela

Norma Argentona in **Bed Inside**

Guerty, Lily Ann Martin, Marcos
Carnevale. Dir: Carnevale. Phot:
Juan Carlos Gómez. Players:
Manuel Alexandre, China
Zorilla, Carlos Álvarez-Novoa,
Roberto Carnaghi, José Ángel
Egido, Fanny Gautier, Federico
Luppi, Gonzalo Urtizberea.
Prod: Shazam/Tesela P.C.
Two 80-year-olds, Elsa (Zorilla)
and Fred (Alexandre), fall in love
and her everlasting dream, to
step into the Trevi Fountain like
Anita Ekberg in La dolce vita
comes true.

EL VIENTO (The Wind)

[Drama, 2005] Script: Graciela
Maglie, Eduardo Mignogna. Dir:
Mignogna. Phot: Marcelo
Camorino. Players: Federico
Luppi, Antonella Costa, Pablo
Cedrón, Mariana Briski, Esteban
Meloni, Ricardo Díaz Mourelle.
Prod: Retratos/Tesela P.C./
FilmSuez.
Frank (Luppi) travels for the first
time from Patagonia to Buenos
Aires to meet Alina (Costa), his
grandchild. He has just buried
his daughter, Alina's mother,
and reveals two secrets about
her father.

FAMILIA RODANTE (Rolling Home)

[Road movie, 2004] Script and

Dir: Pablo Trapero. Phot:
Guillermo Nieto. Players:
Graciana Chironi, Liliana
Capurro, Ruth Dobel, Federico
Esquerro, Bernardo Forteza,
Laura Glave, Leila Gómez,
Nicolás López, Marianela
Pedano, Carlos Resta, Raúl
Viñoles. Prod: Matanza Cine/
POL-KA Producciones Buena
Onda Films.
On her 84th birthday,
Grandmother announces that she
has been asked to be matron of
honor at a niece's wedding in her
home town in Misiones. In a
motor home the family of 12
makes an unforgettable trip.

GEMINIS

[Drama, 2004] Script: Santiago
Giralt, Albertina Carri. Dir: Carri.
Phot: Guillermo Nieto. Players:
Critina Banegas, Daniel Fanego,
María Abadi, Lucas Escariz,
Julieta Zylberberg, Beatriz
Spelzini, Damián Ramonda, Silvia
Bayle, Gogó Andreu, Viviana
Tellas, Lucrecia Capello. Prod:
Matanza Cine/Slot Machine/
INCAA/Fonds Sud Cinéma/
The Global Film Initiative.
A love story between a brother
and his sister in an upper-class
family where the mother, Lucía
(Banegas), believes she has
everything under control.

COMO PASAN LAS HORAS (The Hours Go By)

[Drama, 2005] Script: Daniel
Veronese, Inés de Oliveira Cézar.
Dir: de Oliveira Cézar.
Phot: Gerardo Silvatici. Players:
Roxana Berco, Guillermo Arengo,
Agustín Alcoba, Susana Campos,

Florencia Blanco

On the road: Pablo Trapero's **Rolling Home**

Pedro Recalde, Javier Fainzaig,
María del Rosario Quaranta.
Prod: Barakacine Producciones.
A woman has a last encounter
with her mother while her
husband is with their son at
the seaside.

ILUMINADOS POR EL FUEGO
(Enlightened by Fire)
[Drama, 2005] Script: Edgardo
Esteban, Gustavo Romero Borri,
Tristán Bauer, Miguel Bonasso.
Dir: Bauer. Phot: Javier Juliá.
Players: Gastón Pauls,
Virginia Innocenti, Pablo Ribba,
César Albarracín, Arturo Bonín,
Víctor Hugo Carrizo, Marcelo
Chaparro, Juan Leyrado. Prod:
Universidad Nacional General
San Martín/ INCAA/
Canal Plus (Spain).
A 40-year-old man sent to fight
in the Falklands War in 1982
returns to the islands to come to
heal old wounds.

Gastón Pauls in **Enlightened by Fire**

EL AURA (The Aura)
[Thriller, 2005] Script and Dir:
Fabián Bielinsky. Phot: Checo
Varese. Players: Ricardo Darín,
Dolores Fonzi, Alejandro Awada,
Pablo Cedrón, Jorge D'Elia,
Manuel Rodal, Rafael Castejón,
Walter Reyno, Nahuel Pérez
Biscayant. Prod: Patagonik Film
Group/Tornasol Films (Spain)/
Davis Films Productions.
An introverted and honest
taxidermist becomes obsessed
with committing the perfect
robbery and a trip south gives
him an opportunity to make his
dream come true.

Quote of the Year

"This is the festival's 20th
birthday. We should have
been celebrating 51 years,
but were interrupted during
military governments. We
should have now the maturity
of a man of 50, but are still
like a kid of 20."
MIGUEL PEREIRA,
President of the Mar del Plata
International Film Festival.

The 53rd Silver Condor Awards

Presented by the Asociación de Cronistas
Cinematográficos de Argentina, Buenos Aires,
June 27, 2005.

Film: *Roma* (Adolfo Aristarain).
First Film: *Buena Vida Delivery*
(Leonardo Di Cesare).
Director: Adolfo Aristarain (*Roma*).
Original Screenplay: Leonardo Di Cesare,
Hans Garrino (*Buena Vida Delivery*).
Adapted Screenplay: José Rivera
(*Diarios de motocicleta/The Motorcycle Diaries*).
Screenplay (Documentary): *Trelew*
(Mariana Arruti).
Actor: Rodrigo De La Serna
(*The Motorcycle Diaries*).
Actress: Susu Pecoraro (*Roma*).
Supporting Actor: Daniel Fanego
(*Luna de Avellaneda/Avellaneda Moon*).

Supporting Actress: Adriana Aizemberg
(*El abrazo partido/A Lost Embrace*).
Male Newcomer: Adrián Navarro (*Ay Juancito*).
Female Newcomer: Moro Anghileri
(*Buena Vida Delivery*).
Cinematography: José Luis Alcaine
(*La puta y la ballena/ The Whore and the Whale*).
Music: Gustavo Santaolalla
(*The Motorcycle Diaries*).
Sound: Abbate & Díaz (*Avellaneda Moon*).
Editing: Camilo Antonini (*Avellaneda Moon*).
Art Direction: Mercedes Alfonsín
(*Avellaneda Moon*).
Costume Design: Horace Lannes (*Ay Juancito*).
Documentary: *Trelew* (Mariana Arruti).
Foreign Film: *Spring, Summer, Autumn, Winter...*
and Spring (Kim Ki-duk).
Foreign Film (Spanish Language):
María llena eres de Gracia/Mary Full of Grace
(Joshua Marston).

Armenia Susanna Harutyunyan

Recent and Forthcoming Films

POETI VERADARDZE (Return of the Poet)

[Docudrama, 2005] Script: Harutyun Khachatryan, Mikayel Stamboltsyan, Valery Gasparyan. Dir: Harutyun Khachatryan. Phot: Vrezh Petrosyan. Players: Mikayel Dovlatyan, Artashes Hovsepyan. Prod: Hayfilm Studio.
Modern Armenia through the eyes of poet and philosopher Jivani (1846–1909). We follow the construction of a monument to Jivani and its transportation from Yerevan to Javakh, his birthplace.

MARIAM (Mariam)

[Drama, 2005] Script and Dir: Edgar Baghdasaryan. Phot: Vahagn Ter-Hakobyan. Players: Janet Harutyunryan. Prod: Hayfilm Studio.
Young Mariam (the Armenian name for Virgin Mary) dwells on her virginity and behaves so strangely that even her psychotherapist cannot understand her. He chooses an unconventional path for her that ends with what appears to be a virgin birth.

Janet Harutyunyan as **Mariam**

LIALOUSIN (Full Moon)

[Historical drama, 2005] Script: Vigen Chaldranyan, Anahit Aghasaryan. Dir: Chaldranyan. Phot: Vahagn Ter-Hakobyan. Players: Ruzanna Vit, Karen Janibekyan, Marine Sargsyan,

The longstanding rumours of the privatisation of the biggest state film studio, Hayfilm (also known as Armenfilm), finally came true with its sale to American–Armenian businessman and art collector Kafesjian in August 2005 (he is also building a Modern Art Center in the capital, Yerevan, to house his remarkable collection). Under the privatisation agreement, the new owner has promised grand investments in new technology, and guaranteed the completion of all the Armenian films in pre-production, production or post-production.

However, the state will continue to support Armenian cinema, though at moderate levels. In 2006, total subsidy will be around $1.05m l (482m drams), with around 58% going to feature production, 26% to animation and 8% to documentaries (Hayk Documentary Film Studio remains under government ownership). Privatisation has clearly taken Armenian cinema into a new era, but it remains to be seen what the consequences will be.

Among projects completed by the end of 2005 was a large-scale historical drama, **Full Moon** (*Lialousin*) by Vigen Chaldranian, which takes us back to the start of the fourth century, when Armenia adopted Christianity. Hovhannes Galstyan's debut feature, **Bonded Parallels** (*Khchechvatz zugaherner*), a love story set in two different time periods, will be shot in Armenia and Norway with an international cast drawn from Armenia, France, Norway and Syria.

Mikayel Dovaltyan's **Landslide** (*Soghank*) is a fantasy thriller, a rare type of film in Armenian cinema. A co-production between Armenia, France and Russia, it has a hero sucked underground by a landslide who finds that life below is not so different from that on the surface. Don Askarian's **Ararat – Three Stories** (*Ararat – erek patmutyun*) is a co-production between Armenia, the Netherlands and Germany. In three contrasting stories, the director hopes to explore the mystical significance of Mount Ararat for Armenians, not only because of its beauty but because of its tragic history.

The second Yerevan International Film Festival "Golden Apricot" took place in July 2005 and built on the success of the first event. Deborah Young wrote in *Variety*: "Though still small in scale, [the festival] has already positioned itself as a regional contender in the Caucasus and a link with Russia and the Mideast." It opened with

Karen Jangirov. Prod: Gevorg Gevorgyan/Hayfilm Studio/ Symphony Pictures (US). Russian reports of a wooden structure on Mount Ararat send an international expedition up its slopes. They stumble upon a cave inhabited by an ancient priestess. We flash back to her story in 301AD.

ARARAT – EREK PATMUTYUN
(Ararat – Three Stories)
[Portmanteau drama, 2005] Script and Dir: Don Askarian. Phot: Karen Stepanyan. Prod: Askarian, Don Film/Film21/3Sat. Mount Ararat is the backdrop for three stories: a drama, a thriller and a romance.

KHCHECHVATZ ZUGAHERNER
(Bonded Parallels)
[Drama, 2006] Script and Dir: Hovhannes Galstyan. Phot: Vahagn Ter-Hakobyan, Players: Laurence Ritter, Sos Janibekyan, Siri Helene Muller, Vrej Kassouni. Prod: Galstyan, Hayfilm.
Laura, 41, lives a quiet, isolated life as a maths teacher in Yerevan. Then she receives documents about her father, who died in exile in Norway. As the papers reveal her parents' love story, she begins to experience a parallel, forbidden love with a 16-year-old student.

SOGHANK (Landslide)
[Fantasy thriller, 2006] Script: Vahram Martirosyan, Mikayel Dovlatyan, Alexander Mindadze. Dir: Dovlatyan. Phot: Vahagn Ter-Hakobyan, Players: Serge Avedikian, Simon Abgarian, Sergey Yursky. Prod: Hayfilm.
A man and the girl he has just picked up are sucked underground by a sudden landslide.

Quote of the Year

"It was like heaven to be in a city the size of Yerevan, full of such activity."

ABBAS KIAROSTAMI, receiving his Lifetime Achievement Award at the Yerevan International Film Festival.

the premiere of Edgar Baghdasaryan's psychological drama about a virginal teacher at a school for deaf children, Mariam. Opening the festival with a new national film is becoming a very important tradition for a festival that aims to promote local production and put Armenia on the world cinema map. The International Feature Competition jury, headed by Atom Egoyan, awarded the Grand Prix to "a great artist working at the height of his powers, Alexander Sokurov, and his astonishing film The Sun, a profound meditation on power and personality". Sokurov noted that this was his first Grand Prix at an international film festival. More information about the programme, guests and awards can be found at www.gaiff.am.

More and more Western producers and directors are using Armenia for their movies because it offers skilled, affordable professionals and extremely varied shooting locations. French director Robert Guediguian is to film La voyage en Arménie in the country, with his wife Ariane Ascaride as a woman who returns to Armenia to explore her national and cultural roots and her own identity.

SUSANNA HARUTYUNYAN (aafccj@arminco.com) graduated in film criticism from Moscow's State Cinema Institute in 1987. She has been film expert of the daily Respublika Armenia since 1991 and is president of Armenia's Association of Film Critics and Cinema Journalists.

A memorial to Jivani is built in **Return of the Poet**

Australia Peter Thompson

The Year's Best Films

Peter Thompson's selection:
Look Both Ways
(Sarah Watt)
Little Fish (Rowan Woods)
The Proposition
(John Hillcoat)
Peaches (Craig Monahan)

Recent and Forthcoming Films

PEACHES
[Romantic social drama, 2004]
Script: Sue Smith. Dir: Craig
Monahan. Phot: Ernie Clark.
Players: Jacqueline McKenzie,
Hugo Weaving, Emma Lung,
Matthew Le Nevez, Sam Healy,
Tyson Contor. Prod: Craig
Monahan, Don Reynolds,
Peach Films Pty Ltd.
A love story that deals with
accepting loss and change, and
learning to move on.

A MAN'S GOTTA DO
[Comedy, 2004] Script and Dir:
Chris Kennedy. Players: John
Howard, Rebecca Frith, Alyssa
McClelland, Gyton Grantley.
Prod: Chris Kennedy, John
Winter, Oilrag Productions.
What a guy's gotta do to marry
his daughter off.

BONDI TSUNAMI
[Adventure, 2004] Script, Dir
and Phot: Rachael Lucas.
Players: Taki Abe, Keita Abe,
Nobu-Hisa Ikeda, Miki Sasaki.
Prod: Anthony Lucas-Smith,
Naomi Lucas-Smith,
Burlesque Productions.
Four Japanese surfers travel up
the spectacular east coast of
Australia on a psychedelic road trip.

Readers of last year's *IFG* may recall that the dire problems of Australian cinema were reported here in some detail. There were some solid films that year – notably *Somersault* and *Tom White*. Audiences showed their indifference to the opinions of film reviewers by endorsing Dean Murphy's disarming comedy, *Strange Bedfellows*. But it was too little too late, and Australian film was left looking shaky and open to attack. There's a sense of relief that 2004, perceived as an *annus horribilis*, has given way to brighter days and bluer skies, because 2005 saw a welcome turnaround and some modest commercial success.

Audiences were drawn to the homegrown, folksy charm of *Oyster Farmer*, the darkly comical but deeply compassionate *Look Both Ways*, the passionate intensity of *Little Fish* and the epic scale of *The Proposition*. There were fresh faces such as Scott Ryan and Emma Lung. And *Wolf Creek* looks like becoming an international ambassador for the 'charms' of the Outback on a par with *Crocodile Dundee*.

These titles obscure, for a moment, the crisis gripping the arts in Australia, and film in particular. There are more and more people with knowledge and experience going back decades, to the rebirth of Australian cinema in the 1970s. And there is the annual crop of talented and ambitious youngsters pouring out of our schools and universities. But a film culture cannot be built on low-budget miracles. The shrinkage of the investment base for Australian film is starving it to death.

This betrayal is largely a political failure. But it's not party-political. Both our major parties (Liberal, i.e. conservative, and Labor, somewhere in the middle) have retreated from the generous optimism of 30 years ago, when there was enlightened bipartisan support for film. And they've done so because they see it as politically expedient. John Howard's Liberals strengthened their grip on power in the 2004 elections with yet another scare campaign (this time about rising interest rates). So there is no prospect of change to cultural policy.

A fresh *Look*

But it's hard to be totally pessimistic. *Look Both Ways* is a remarkably original and moving story. Writer-director Sarah Watt's

THE OYSTER FARMER

[Romantic comedy, 2004] Script and Dir: Anna Reeves. Phot: Alun Bollinger. Players: Alex O'Lachlan, Diana Glenn, Kerry Armstrong, David Field, Jim Norton, Jack Thompson. Prod: Anthony Buckley, Piers Tempest, Anthony Buckley Films Pty Ltd./ Oyster Farmer Ltd.

LOOK BOTH WAYS

[Romantic comedy-drama, 2005] Script and Dir: Sarah Watt. Phot: Ray Argall . Players: Justine Clarke, William McInnes, Anthony Hayes, Lisa Flanagan, Andrew S. Gilbert, Daniela Faranacci, Sacha Horler, Maggie Dence, Edwin Hodgeman, Andreas Sobik. Prod: Bridget Ikin, Hibiscus Films Pty Ltd.

LITTLE FISH

[Drama, 2005] Script: Jacqueline Perske. Dir: Rowan Woods. Phot: Danny Ruhlmann. Players: Cate Blanchett, Hugo Weaving, Sam Neill, Noni Hazlehurst, Dustin Nguyen, Martin Henderson. Prod: Vincent Sheehan, Liz Watts, Richard Keddie, Porchlight Films Pty Ltd.

THE PROPOSITION

[Drama, 2005] Script: Nick Cave. Dir: John Hillcoat. Phot: Benoit Delhomme. Players: Guy Pearce, Ray Winstone, Danny Huston, Emily Watson, John Hurt, David Wenham. Prod: Chris Brown, Jackie O'Sullivan, Chiara Menage, Cat Villiers, The Proposition Pty Ltd.

WOLF CREEK

[Horror-thriller, 2005] Script and Dir: Greg McLean. Phot: Brandon Trost. Players: John Jarratt, Cassandra Magrath, Kestie Morassi, Guy Petersen, Nathan Phillips, Jenny Starwell. Prod: McLean, David Lightfoot, True Crime Channel Pty Ltd.

THE EXTRA

[Romantic comedy, 2005] Script: Jimeoin. Dir: Kevin Carlin. Phot: Mark Wareham. Players: Jimeoin, Rhys Muldoon, Katherine Slattery, Colin Lane,

international success with her short animated films signalled an unusual talent, but her first live-action feature transcends them. Meryl (Justine Clarke) and Nick (William McInnes) are two lonely souls, crushed by the mortal perils of human existence. They meet at the site of a fatal railway accident, a real event that throws their imaginary terrors into sharp relief, and they reach out to each other with touching and often comic results.

Justine Clarke and William McInnes in **Look Both Ways**

Watt weaves in several parallel stories that unfold with extraordinary economy and imagination, especially that of the train driver, told without dialogue. The use of music is particularly fresh and Watt uses her signature animation techniques to explore the inner lives of her characters. But the originality of *Look Both Ways* lies deeper, in the themes it tackles and the deceptively simple wisdom it displays. It won the major categories at the Australian Film Institute awards in November 2005 and was also endorsed by the Film Critics Circle of Australia. Perhaps more importantly, word-of-mouth suggests that people fall in love with it.

Such success notwithstanding, it's now socially acceptable in Australia to pour scorn on local films. It's cool to declare that you avoid them like the plague. We take comfort that our wonderful actors, from Russell Crowe to Naomi Watts and Heath Ledger, from Nicole Kidman to Guy Pearce and Toni Collette, can appear in foreign films with flawless American and English accents, giving not a hint of their humble origins. It reminds me of the Australia I grew up in – the Australia of the 1950s. Back then, Australian accents, when they did creep onto the airwaves or screens, were an embarrassing joke. Many well-informed and intelligent people now feel the same way. They want Australian films to disappear. And they want all financial support and regulatory protection erased.

A *Fish* out of her depth

Countering this, our international stars invariably confess loyalty to the ideal of a national film culture and many have redeemed that commitment in practical ways. The glorious Cate Blanchett, for example, took the central role in one of the year's most significant films, **Little Fish**. With her usual uncanny sensibility, she inhabits the world of Tracy Heart, a reformed heroine addict living in Cabramatta, a leafy but modest suburb west of Sydney, which is home to the recently arrived Vietnamese community. She's struggling to create an independent life for herself but the past keeps wrenching her back. Her old boyfriend and drug dealer, Jonny (Dustin Nguyen), shows up, declaring his love for her. And her stepfather, Lionel (an electrifying performance from Hugo Weaving), makes her pay for his emotional support by begging her to connive at his uncontrollable drug habit.

Myriad Pictures

Cate Blanchett in Little Fish

But *Little Fish* is about much more than addiction. It's about people of limited cultural resources trying to match aspirations with social and economic reality. It's about the hunger for intimacy and the dimensions of personal courage. Confronted by our shared humanity, it suggests, we're all little fish. Writer Jacqueline Perske and director Rowan Woods (*The Boys*, 1998) invest their film with a dynamic, almost documentary authenticity.

To their great credit, Australian film-makers haven't given up. They're fuelled mostly by passion, by enthusiasm, rather than the promise of seats on the gravy train. At its best, their work is tight and lean and rooted in the native soil. Writer-director Anna Reeves dreamed of a film that would entertain her boisterous older brothers and she was inspired by the marine community that has survived for several generations on the tranquil stretches of the Hawkesbury River, just a few miles north of Sydney. The so-called Sydney rock oyster, a rare, slow-growing mollusc, has long thrived there, along with diverse human fugitives from the modern world.

Shaun Micallef, Kristy Hinze, Taylor Kane, Raj Ryan, Helen Dallimore. *Prod: Charlesworth Josem Partners, Stephen Luby, Mark Ruse, Ruby Entertainment/ Republica Films/Extra Extra.*
An average guy sees movie stars making big money and getting the girls and thinks he has what it takes to do the same.

DECK DOGZ
[Adolescent adventure, 2005] Scriptand Dir: Steve Pasvolsky. Phot: Denson Baker. Players: Sean Kennedy, Richard Wilson, Ho Thi Lu, Tony Hawk. Prod: Bill Bennett, Jennifer Cluff, Deck Dogz Films.
Fast-paced story tracks three boys as they go to meet their hero, a legendary skateboard champion. The journey catapults them from adolescence to manhood.

THE BOOK OF REVELATION
[Erotic mystery, 2005] Script: Andrew Bovell, Ana Kokkinos. Dir: Kokkinos. Phot: Tristan Milani. Players: Tom Long, Greta Scacchi, Colin Friels, Anna Torr, Deborah Mailman. Prod: Al Clark, Wildheart Zizani Pty Ltd.
Sex and power, gender issues, a man's search for his lost self. From the director of *Head On* (1998).

CANDY
[Drama, 2005] Script: Luke Davies, Neil Armfield from the novel by Davies. Dir: Armfield. Phot: Garry Phillips. Players: Heath Ledger, Geoffrey Rush, Abbie Cornish. Prod: Margaret Fink, Emile Sherman, Candy Prods. Ltd.
Locked in the vicious circle of drug addiction, two young lovers battle their conflicting loyalties. Based on a savagely funny novel.

IRRESISTIBLE
[Psychological thriller, 2005] Script and Dir: Ann Turner. Phot: Martin McGrath. Players: Susan Sarandon, Sam Neill, Emily Blunt. Prod: Tatiana Kennedy, David Parker, Cascade Partners Pty Ltd.
Wife and mother Sophie is

convinced she's being stalked. Suspicious of her husband, she becomes the stalker and makes a discovery more shocking than her worst fear.

JINDABYNE
[Mystery, 2005] Script: Beatrix Christian. Dir: Ray Lawrence. Players: Laura Linney, Gabriel Byrne, Deborra-Lee Furness, Max Cullen, John Howard, Chris Haywood. Prod: Catherine Jarman/April Films. A modern day, adult ghost story.

LIKE MINDS
[Mystery, 2005] Script and Dir: Gregory J. Read. Players: Toni Colletee, Richard Roxburgh, Eddie Redmayne, Tom Sturridge. Prod: Jonathan Steinman, Piers Tempest, Bluewater Pictures. A forensic psychologist investigates a killing apparently carried out by a strangely charismatic 16-year-old schoolboy.

OPAL DREAMS
[Family drama, 2005] Script: Peter Cattaneo, Ben Rice, Phil Trail. Dir: Cattaneo. Phot: Robert Humphreys. Players: Christian Byers, Sapphire Boyce, Vince Colosimo, Jacqueline McKenzie. Prod: Lizzie Gower, Nick Morris, Emile Sherman, Sherman Pictures. Nine-year-old Kellyanne lives in an opal mining town with her invisible, imaginary friends, Pobby and Dingan. But one day they disappear.

THE MAGICIAN
[Crime comedy, 2005] Script and Dir: Scott Ryan. Phot: Massimiliano Andreghetto. Players: Andreghetto, Ryan, Ben Walker, Kane Mason, Nathaniel Lindsay. Prod: Ryan, Nash Edgerton, Will Films. An Italian film student sets out to make a film about Ray Shoesmith, a cold-blooded Aussie hitman.

FEED
[Thriller, 2005] Script: Kieran Galvin. Dir: Brett Leonard. Phot: Steve Arnold. Players: Patrick Thompson, Alex

Alex O'Lachlan in **Oyster Farmer**

Reeves' **Oyster Farmer** features rising star Alex O'Lachlan as a young man on the run from the law, who falls into the arms of Pearl (Diana Glenn), a daughter of the river with an extreme shoe fetish. Kerry Armstrong and David Field are husband-and-wife fisherfolk, estranged but still mad for each other. And Jack Thompson provides one of many colourful cameos, as a half-crazy Vietnam war veteran. *Oyster Farmer* found an appreciative audience, although, ominously, the oysters of the Hawkesbury were recently wiped out by a virulent disease, throwing the community into disarray.

Nick Cave and the bad deeds

In sharp contrast to Anna Reeve's intimate focus, singer-songwriter Nick Cave scripted a myth of tragic dimensions in **The Proposition**, An Australian-UK co-production, directed by John Hillcoat, it's a brutally uncompromising vision of colonial times and frontier life in the 1880s. Marooned in the Outback (stunningly photographed by Benoit Delhomme), Captain Stanley (Ray Winstone) sets bushranger Charlie Burns (Guy Pearce) on the murderous trail of Charlie's own psychotic brother, Arthur (Danny Huston). The consequences are violent in the extreme, with every character, including Stanley's innocent-seeming wife, Martha (Emily Watson), revealed as morally culpable.

Hillcoat made an impressive feature directing debut in 1988 with the ultra-violent *Ghosts… of the Civil* Dead and he's lost none of his fire in the intervening years. With its hugely ambitious production values and prestige international cast, *The Proposition* is on a scale seldom attempted in the currently constricted climate of Australian film-making, and its greatest virtue is the courage of its convictions. While the morbid darkness of Cave's conception is too much for some, the film has won passionate adherents, harking back to grander days, when Fred Schepisi could contemplate something of the scope of *The Chant of Jimmie Blacksmith* and Peter Weir helmed his romantic epic, *Gallipoli.*

Horror, Aussie-style

Just as Australian actors continue to shine on world screens, some younger Australian film-makers are scoring in the international market. Aussie director James Wan and actor-screenwriter Leigh Whannel made a box-office killing with the American horror film *Saw* in 2004, and Greg McLean's **Wolf Creek** has captured a similar audience with a genre melodrama about imperilled British backpackers. With a spine-tingling performance by John Jarratt and echoes of the grim murders of several tourists in the 1980s by serial killer Ivan Milat, the film revives primitive fears of the wilderness and its ghastly dangers, reinforced by the disappearance of another British tourist, Peter Falconio, in the Northern Territory in 2001. Whatever chords *Wolf Creek* strikes in contemporary audiences, McLean has proved himself, like Wan and Whannel, adept at the manufacture of horror.

Optimum Releasing

Kestie Morassi in **Wolf Creek**

The commercial success of the latter films will not go unnoticed by other ambitious young film-makers. For those still attached to perhaps more socially responsible notions of a national cinema, the future may appear clouded. But others are encouraged by the promise of a more diverse production slate, exploiting Australia's natural advantages, not the least of which is the positive image of the country in the eyes of many Americans. Erroneous or not, there's still a bit of "last frontier" glamour about Australia, even if *Crocodile Dundee* laid claim to that myth 20 years ago.

PETER THOMPSON is a writer, film-maker and critic who appears regularly on Australian television.

O'Lachlan, Gabby Millgate, Jack Thompson, David Field. *Prod: Melissa Beauford, Springer Films.*
An Internet detective discovers the world of gamblers who bet on the time of death of grossly obese women whose minders are force-feeding them.

M
[Drama, 2006] Dir: Geoffrey Wright. Phot: Will Gibson. Players: Sam Worthington, Victoria Hill, Lachy Hulme. Prod: Martin Fabinyi, Film Victoria/Mushroom Pictures.
Contemporary telling of the Macbeth legend, set in Melbourne's gangland.
From the director of *Romper Stomper* (1992).

GUESTS
[Drama, 2006] Script: Dave Warner. Dir: David Denneen. Phot: Simon Duggan. Players: Teresa Palmer, Stephen Moyer, Travis Fimmel. Prod: Anna Fawcett, Mark Lazarus, Todd Fellman, FGE Holdings/ Story Bridge Films.
A dangerous young couple on the run take refuge in a private country estate whose agoraphobic owner becomes their hostage.

Austria Gunnar Landsgesell

The Year's Best Films

Gunnar Landsgesell's
selection:
Hidden (Michael Haneke)
Sleepers
(Benjamin Heisenberg)
*F.A.Q. – Frequently Asked
Questions* (Stefan Hafner,
Alexander Binder)
You Bet Your Life
(Antonin Svoboda)
Workingman's Death
(Michael Glawogger)

Georg Friedrich in You Bet Your Life

Recent and
Forthcoming Films

SCHLÄFER (Sleepers)
*[Thriller, 2005] Script and Dir:
Benjamin Heisenberg. Phot:
Reinhold Vorschneider. Players:
Bastian Trost, Mehdi Nebbou,
Loretta Pflaum. Prod: coop99
Filmproduktion/ZDF (Germany).*

F.A.Q. – FREQUENTLY ASKED
QUESTIONS
*[Documentary, 2004] Script and
Dir: Stefan Hafner, Alexander
Binder. Featuring: the Hafners,
Rudi Vouk, Jörg Haider. Prod:
meter film.*
Highly entertaining, smart
documentary about the Slovenian
minority in Carinthia.

I n **Hidden** (*Caché*), one sees the intriguing progression of Michael Haneke's cinematic vision. Without abandoning his habitual theses on violence, family and the media, Haneke's story of a Paris literary TV show host (Daniel Auteuil), who is secretly filmed by an unknown person, presents a complex psychological thriller about guilt and oblivion that has been repeatedly cited as his best feature (see this edition's Director of the Year profile). Among young Austrian auteurs, alienation on an individual and social level has been crucial to recent films. Maybe this is because of the nation's unsettled recent history, or just part of the Austrian psyche. However, in May 2005, Cannes' invitation to the inaugural "Tous les cinémas du monde" programme gave a chance to trace the roots of this young cinematography: ten emblematic films from 1982 to 2002 were shown on an "Austrian Day".

In 2004, Austrian film recorded an astonishing 391 festival invitations. A growing number of films are promoted by world sales and international co-productions are increasing. Special challenges were faced by **Dallas Pashamende**, which dramatises the life of a Roma community living on a garbage dump in Romania. The set was stormed by police, then the Romanian Prime Minister denounced the film for "ridiculing our country". *Dallas* was finished in Hungary and shown at the Berlinale Panorama 2005.

To realise a fiction feature or feature documentary in Austria, financial support of one of the three major institutions is almost always essential: Austrian Film Institute (ÖFI), Film-Funds Vienna (FFW) and ÖRF (the Austrian Broadcasting Corp., which is increasingly short of funds). Rejection by them often means a serious delay or a desperate search for new partners. Antonin Svoboda's fierce drama about a notorious gambler, **You Bet Your Life** (*Spiele leben*), was turned down three times by ÖRF and Svoboda eventually found a Swiss TV partner, Triluna Film. This directorial debut from the experienced coop99 producer (*Hotel, The Edukators*) screened at Toronto and San Sebastian. Another coop99 co-production was **Sleepers** (*Schläfer*; Un Certain Regard, Cannes 2005), Munich-based director Benjamin Heisenberg's remarkably unpretentious tale of two young scholars and calamitous jealousy in a climate of growing paranoia.

When Austrian films open theatrically at home a strong presence at international festivals is generally followed by small audiences at home. According to the ÖFI, Austrian market share is 2.1%; various reasons are being investigated. The potential comedy hit **High Octane** (*Die Viertelliterklasse*), directed by and starring popular cabaret artist Roland Düringer in five wacky roles, did not meet commercial expectations; nor did Salzburg-set satirical murder-mystery **Silentium**. Starring Josef Hader as grouchy inspector Brenner, it nonetheless attracted respectable attendance of just under 200,000. **Crash Test Dummies** is the kind of film that might bridge the gap between arthouse and mainstream audiences. There are moments pitched somewhere between melodrama and comedy in this story of a young Romanian couple coming to Vienna to make some fast money.

Kathrin Resetarits in **Crash Test Dummies**

Michael Glawogger's **Workingman's Death** may be the most staggering, visually breathtaking documentary of recent years. It visits the most extreme working environments one could imagine, from self-organised coalminers who squeeze into perilous narrow rifts to sulphur gatherers in Indonesia. The route from producer to consumer features in another documentary debating globalisation, Erwin Wagenhofer's **We Feed the World**, which focuses on the perverseness of industrial food production in the Western world and presents yet another different case of alienation.

GUNNAR LANDSGESELL (gunnar.landsgesell@chello.at) is a freelance writer. He works for the Austrian monthly *RAY Kinomagazin* and the German *Blickpunkt:Film* and is co-editor of a book on Spike Lee, to be published by Bertz-Verlag in spring 2006.

SPIELE LEBEN
(**You Bet Your Life**)
[Drama, 2005] Script and Dir: Antonin Svoboda. Phot: Martin Gschlacht. Players: Birgit Minichmayr, Georg Friedrich, Gerti Drassl. Prod: coop99 Filmproduktion/Triluna Film/ Bavaria Film (Germany).

SILENTIUM
[Murder mystery, 2004] Script: Wolfgang Murnberger and Josef Hader, based on the novel by Wolf Haas. Dir: Murnberger. Phot: Peter von Haller. Players: Hader, Simon Schwarz, Maria Köstlinger. Prod: Danny Krausz, Kurt Stocker/Dor Film.

WORKINGMAN'S DEATH
[Documentary, 2005] Script and Dir: Michael Glawogger. Phot: Wolfgang Thaler. Prod: Erich Lackner/Lotus Film.

WE FEED THE WORLD
[Documentary, 2005] Script, Dir and Phot: Erwin Wagenhofer. Featuring: Jean Ziegler, Karl Otrok, Peter Brabeck. Prod: Helmut Grasser/Allegro Film.

CRASH TEST DUMMIES
[Comedy-drama, 2005] Script: Jörg Kalt, Antonin Svoboda. Dir: Kalt. Phot: Eva Testor. Players: Maria Popistasu, Simon Schwarz, Kathrin Resetarits. Prod: Amour Fou Film.

DALLAS PASHAMENDE
[Drama, 2005] Script and Dir: Robert Adrian Pejo. Phot: Vasile Vivi Dragan. Players: Szolt Bogdan, Dorka Gryllus, Mikos Szekely. Prod: Helmut Grasser/ Allegro Film.

Azerbaijan Goga Lomidze

Recent Films

ARKHADA GALMYSH
GIALIAJIAK (*literally,*
Future That Was Left Behind)
[Drama, 2005] Script: Yusif
Sheikhov. Dir: Rufat Asadov.
Phot: Amin Novruzov. Players:
Fuad Poladov, Agamekhdi
Abidov, Azerin, Anakhanym
Tagieva, Abbas Gakhramanov,
Ramiz Sarkalov, Omur Nagiev.
Prod: Azerbaijanfilm.

ZALOZHNIK (Hostage)
[Drama, 2005] Script: Eldar
Kuliev and Natig Rasulzade.
Dir: Kuliev. Phot: Rafig Kuliev.
Players: Afag Bashirgyzy, Giuliar
Nabieva, Vidadi Aliev, Gurban
Ismailov, Giulshad Bakhshieva.
ProdL Azerbaijanfilm.

On August 2, 2005, the country celebrated a national day of film: it was exactly 107 years since the first Azeri film was shot. To celebrate, several local film-makers received state awards. The government continues to support film, although some independent studios and producers are emerging. In Baku, Hollywood and some Russian productions dominate the box-office, mostly shown in the same high-tech cinema that hosts domestic premieres. October 2005 witnessed the international film festival "East West", which tried to connect Western and oriental film cultures, with guests from all the former Soviet states and other parts of Europe and Asia.

The leading state-backed studio, Azerbaijanfilm, released in 2005 two feature films, with two more in post-production at press time. **Hostage** (*Zalozhnik*), by prominent director Eldar Kuliev, is a tragic story about the war in Nagorny Karabakh. A married villager has to survive alone after enemies capture her husband. Then her neighbours bring her a captured enemy as compensation. Kuliev highlights with emotion and power the meaninglessness of war. There are no winners, only victims – simple people on both sides. Kuliev has been in the industry since 1959, graduated from Moscow's VGIK film school in 1966 and is the winner of many national and international awards.

The First International Festival of Muslim Film in Kazhan, Russia, presented a number of films from Azerbaijan. The event was part of the millennium celebrations for the founding of the city. The Grand Prix of the festival went to *Wizard* (*Ovsunchu*) by Oktai Mir-Kasym (*IFG 2004*) and Ayan Mir-Kasim took Best Actress for her lead role in the movie. Also shown at the festival was **Arkhada galmysh gialiajiak** (literally, *Future That Was Left Behind*) by Rufat Asadov, in which a child from a refugee camp finds himself back in the middle of the tragic war in Nagorny Karabakh. Asadov, a graduate of the Technical University in Saint Petersburg, has a background in shorts and documentary films.

GOGA LOMIDZE (gnl_98@hotmail.com) works in the Netherlands as a freelance translator.

Bangladesh Ahmed Muztaba Zamal

Recent and Forthcoming Films

SHANKHONAD
[Thriller, 2004] Script and Dir:
Abu Sayeed. Phot: Mahfuzur
Rahman Khan. Players: Zahid
Hasan, K.S.Firoz, Nazma Anwar.
Prod: Aangik Communications/
Maasranga Productions Ltd.

Zahid Hasan in **Shankhonad**

RANI KUTHIR BAKI ITIHASH
(Memories of Rani Kuthi)
[Thriller, 2006] Script: Dewan
Shamsur Rakib. Dir: Samia
Zaman. Phot: Maksudul Bari.
Players: Alamgir, Ferdous, Popy.

KHELAGHOR (Doll's House)
[Romance, 2006] Script:
Morshedul Islam, based on
a novel by Mahmudul Huq.
Dir: Islam. Players: Reaz, Saba,
Parvez Murad. Prod:
Manan Chalachitra.

AHA! (Sometime or Never)
[Drama, 2006] Script and Dir:
Enamul Karim Nirjhar. Phot:
Saiful Islam Badal. Players: Tariq
Anam Khan, Humayun Faridi,
Sathi Yasmeen, Khaled Khan.
Prod: 9 Steps.

SAPNA DANAY
(Wings of Dream)
[Drama, 2005] Script and Dir:
G.R.Biplob. Phot: Mahfuzur
Rahman Khan. Players:
Mahmuduzzaman Babu, Rokeya
Prachi, Fazlur Babu. Prod:
Impress Telefilms.

Cinema in Bangladesh is passing through a transitional phase and, like the country's economy, facing a tough time. The situation deteriorated notably in 2003, when bomb blasts rocked cinema halls in Mymensingh, killing more than 20 people. In many parts of the country cinemas have closed down because of the loss of business and the buildings turned into shopping malls. Many viewers, especially among the middle class, have been driven away not only by security fears but also by the 'obscene' sequences and 'excessive vulgarity' of the local films.

The industry has failed to attract new investment, and, in the age of globalisation, has continued to rely on market protection. Infrastructure has not been developed because of the monopoly operated by the state-owned Film Development Corporation (FDC), which controls most of the production facilities, and this remains a huge obstacle to positive development.

However, private television channels and certain exhibitor–distributors have played more positive roles, by promoting independent cinema. In particular, satellite station Channel I has become the most important patron of superior local film-making, producing as many as nine films a year through its subsidiary, Impress Telefilms, and then broadcasting the results. The other two TV stations, ATN and NTV, have hosted the broadcast premieres of many independent productions, alongside screenings of local studio-produced fare. Two cinemas in the capital, Balaka Star Cineplex and Modhumita, regularly exhibit independent productions, as well as studio titles, but the vast majority of independent films struggle to find local distribution.

Street children, boat people

Among recent films, two are worthy of special mention: Abu Sayeed's **Shankhonad** is the story of a man who returns to his ancestral village after many years and starts searching for childhood memories. Morshedul Islam's **Duratta** (literally, *The Distance*) follows a child, Putul (Fahad), aged about seven, who, despite the affection of his parents, runs away from home and finds friends among some street children. His parents search anxiously for him. At last he returns home with two of his friends, but they soon decide to return to their original haunts, which creates real sorrow all round.

MADE IN BANGLADESH
[Fantasy thriller, 2005] Script and Dir: Mostafa Sarwar Faruqi. Phot: Saiful Islam Badal. Players: Zahid Hasan, Tania Ahmed, Sachchu. Prod: Impress Telefilms.

ANTAR JATRA (Inner Journey)
[Drama, 2005] Script and Dir: Tareq Masud, Catherine Masud. Players: Harold, Buno, Anushey, Sara Zaker. Prod: Audiovision.

NIRONTAR
[Drama, 2006] Script and Dir: Abu Sayeed. Phot: Mahfuzur Rahman Khan. Players: Shabnoor, Litu Anam, Dolly Zahur. Prod: Impress Telefilms.

MEHERNIGAR
[Romance, 2005] Script: Kazi Nazrul Islam. Dir: Mowshumi and Gulzar. Players: Mowshumi, Ferdous, Nadir Khan. Prod: Impress Telefilms.

RAKKHOSHI
[Drama, 2006] Script: Kazi Nazrul Islam. Dir: Matin Rahman. Players: Rozina, Ferdous, Purnima. Prod: Impress Telefilms.

Refugees flee civil war in **The Land of Peace**

Two other notable productions, both produced outside the studio system on low budgets, explored the war of liberation in 1971. Toukir Ahmed's **The Victory** (*Joyjatra*) and Humayun Ahmed's **The Land of Peace** (*Shaymol Chaya*) both trace the suffering and misery faced by people during the war, through identical plots: a boat journey by groups fleeing slaughter. More independent films were scheduled for release in December 2005, most targeted at discerning middle-class audiences.

AHMED MUZTABA ZAMAL (amzamal@bdcom.com) is Secretary General of FIPRESCI Bangladesh and Festival Director of the Dhaka International Film Festival.

Fox/Kobal

ROBERT WISE shooting Star! *with Julie Andrews in 1968. The Oscar-winning director of* The Sound of Music, The Day the Earth Stood Still *and, with Jerome Robbins,* West Side Story, *died in September 2005, aged 91.*

Belarus Goga Lomidze

Recent and Forthcoming Films

ESHSHO O VOINE
(Still About War)
[Drama, 2004] Script: Izolda Kavelashvili. Dir: Piotr Krivostanenko. Phot: Tatyana Loginova. Players: Svetlana Kodzhemiakina, Anatoly Krot, Vera Poliakova. Prod: Belarusfilm.

DUNECHKA
[Drama, 2004] Script: Svetlana Shafranskaya. Dir: Aleksandr Efremov. Players: Maria Vozba, Zinaida Sharko, Mikhail Efremov, Vladimir Zherebtsov, Igor Bochkin, Valeria Arlanova, Zvelina Sakuro. Prod: Belarusfilm.

MALENKI BEGLETSY
(Little Fugitives)
[Family film, 2004] Script: Boris Berzner and Liana Koroliova. Dir: Renata Grutskova. Players: Liudmila Arinina, Dasha Brankevich, Maxim Darulis, Ilia Siniavski, Jora Gaiduchik, Evelina Sakuro, Oleg Akulich, Aleksandr Kashperov. Prod: Belarusfilm.

VAM ZADANIE
(You Have a Mission)
[War drama, 2004] Script: Nikolaj Cherginets and Aliona Kaliunova. Dir: Yuri Berezhitski. Players: Vitaly Khodin, Valentin Klemetiev, Albinas Keleris. Prod: Belarusfilm.

In September 2005 the fifth annual festival of Belarusian films was held in Brest, with support from the Belarus Ministry of Culture, the major national film studio, Belarusfilm, and Belarusian TV. The programme included *Anastasya Sluckaya* and *Ball Dress* (both reviewed in *IFG 2005*), and some new movies. The fifteenth-century drama *Anastasya Sluckaya* was a big hit in domestic cinemas, making it into the top 10 alongside Russian and American titles. Each November, Belarus also hosts an international festival in Listopad, which in 2004 chose French, Russian, Romanian, Italian and Belarusian films.

The most recent Kinoshok festival of films from the Baltic states and CIS presented several Belarusian productions. **Little Fugitives** (*Malenkie begletsy*) by Renata Grutskova is about a child's protest against parental behaviour. After conflict with her mother, a young girl leaves home and with her peers goes on an adventure. Belarusfilm in 2004 produced four new movies that at press time were still in post-production. *Still About War* (*Eshsho o voine*) by Piotr Krivostanenko is about young lovers Masha and Volodya, separated by the Second World War. *Dunechka*, by Aleksandr Efremov, is a co-production with Russia and features a number of popular Russian actors. The script is about a young actress who gets a role in the theatre, falls in love with an older boy and learns that life in the artistic world can be more complicated than outside the theatre. *You Have a Mission* (*Vam zadanie*) by Yuri Berzhitski is a Second World War drama, a family saga about the fight against fascists. The deaths of millions in Belarus in the war, with many towns and villages totally destroyed, makes this a subject to which film-makers often return.

Kola, a documentary by Victor Asliuk, won a number of international awards. It's a black-and-white film about country life. It seems that nothing happens up there, in a village inhabited only by old people. But Asliuk skilfully films this 'action', and there are no dull moments. Another documentary, **My God** (*Boze moy*), by Galina Adamovich, won the Documentary Grand Prize at Karlovy Vary in 2005. It's a humane film about an old woman who lives in a village on the border with Lithuania.

Belgium Erik Martens

The Year's Best Films

Erik Martens' selection:

The Child (Luc and Jean-Pierre Dardenne)

Ordinary Man
(Vincent Lannoo)

Ultranova (Bouli Lanners)

Private Madness
(Joachim Lafosse)

Gilles' Wife
(Frédéric Fontaine)

Bouli Lanners' **Ultranova**

Recent and Forthcoming Films

L'ENFANT (The Child)
[Drama, 2005] Script and Dir: Luc and Jean-Pierre Dardenne. Phot: Alain Marcoen. Players: Jérémie Renier, Déborah François, Jérémie Segard, Fabrizio Rongione. Prod: Jean-Pierre and Luc Dardenne, Denis Freyd/Les films du fleuve, Archipel 35.

QUAND LA MER MONTE (When the Tide Comes in...)
[Drama, 2005] Script and Dir: Yolande Moreau, Gilles Porte. Phot: Gilles Porte. Players: Yolande Moreau, Wim Willaert, Nand Buyl, Olivier Gourmet. Prod: Catherine Burniaux, Philippe Bonami/ Stromboli Pictures.

What a great year for Belgian cinema! In May 2005 Luc and Jean-Pierre Dardenne won the Palme d'Or for *The Child* (*L'enfant*), emulating their golden triumph with *Rosetta* in 1999. The importance of these awards goes beyond personal recognition; they have consequences for the whole Belgian production scene. Since cinema's earliest days, there have always been interesting Belgian pictures and interesting directors, but never a local name of truly international stature, who could establish this small country – divided as it is into two language communities, each with more or less its own film community – on the map of world cinema. Since 1996, the Dardenne brothers have been doing exactly that.

Their four films – *La promesse, Rosetta, The Son* and *The Child* – have all received instant worldwide acclaim. *Rosetta* and *The Son* were both extremely direct films, the camera almost totally restricted to the point of view of the main character, with plots that eliminated the smallest sense of conventional drama. Both tried to recreate the daily struggles of people living in the underclass. In **The Child** these elements are still evident, but the formal concept seems to have become less rigid, which makes the audience experience somewhat more comfortable. There are a few modest elements of suspense, even a Dardenne-style car chase, making *The Child* seem closer to *La promesse* than *Rosetta* or *The Son*.

Déborah François and Jérémie Renier in **The Child**

The main character is again played by Jérémie Renier: in *The Promise* he was the son, now he has become the (very young) father, Bruno, a street criminal of about 20, who lives from day to day and, with the help of two teenaged gang members, steals what he needs to survive. Occasionally that also includes a small luxury. The idea that life sometimes entails responsibility, for example for his new-born child, Jimmy, is beyond him. Indeed, in order to get money, he sells Jimmy to a shady adoption gang. This is a step too far for Sonia (Déborah François), Jimmy's young mother. When she breaks down, slowly and gradually a sense of deeper human consciousness seeps into Bruno. As usual in a Dardenne film, the acting is first-class, and with minimal means achieves maximum effect.

There was also French recognition this year for actress Yolande Moreau as writer-director of **When the Tide Comes in...** (*Quand la mer monte*), a French–Belgian co-production, which won two Césars and the Louis Delluc Prize for 2004. The film is a romantic road movie about Irene, who travels through the north of France with her one-woman show, and has a romance with Dries, the porter for a carnival giant.

Dutroux's movie legacy

Despite the critical succes of several Belgian features and a slight rise in cinema attendance, Belgian audiences had a pretty gloomy year watching local fare. It seemed as though all Belgian film-makers had conspired to produce only the darkest social drama, so dark that it often came close to sheer horror. One cannot help noting that 2004 was also the year of the long-awaited trial of Marc Dutroux, the man who kidnapped, raped and murdered a number of young girls in the mid-1990s. One of the most disturbing things about him was his utter ordinariness, and the fact that nothing in his appearance would have led anyone to suspect the horrors in his mind and home. In several new Belgian films it seemed as though Dutroux was in the directors' minds. Several dealt with child abuse. Several friendly-looking characters turned out to be monsters.

The title of Vincent Lannoo's brilliant second film, **Ordinary Man** (*Un homme ordinaire*), speaks for itself. George is a rather dull-looking furniture salesman, living in the rural Ardennes, with a wife and a daughter. No one suspects that he's a murderer who keeps a woman imprisoned in his car trunk. Also set in the Ardennes and with a similarly horrific plot, was Fabrice du Welz's debut, Calvaire, which follows Laurent Lucas as a travelling performer, who ends up in a deserted hotel whose owner turns out to be a psychopath, while the nearby village is inhabited by zombies. Lucas is extensively tortured and trash fans worldwide should love this film.

UN HOMME ORDINAIRE
(Ordinary Man)
[Thriller, 2005] Script and Dir: Vincent Lannoo. Phot: Gilles Bissot. Players: Carlo Ferrante, Christine Grulois, Stefan Liberski, Georges Siatidis, Elladé Ferrante, Vera Van Doren, Olivier Gourmet. Prod: Anthony Rey/Hélicotronc/ Pomme Production (France).

Joachim Lafosse's **Private Madness**

FOLIE PRIVEE (Private Madness)
[Drama, 2004] Script: Kris Cuppens, Joachim Lafosse. Dir: Lafosse. Phot: Frederico d'Ambrosio. Players: Kris Cuppens, Catherine Salée, Vincent Cahay, Mathias Wertz. Prod: Eric Van Zuylen/RYVA/ Joseph Rouschop/Tarantula.

CALVAIRE
[Horror, 2005] Script: Fabrice du Welz, Romain Protat. Dir: du Welz. Phot: Benoît Debie. Players: Laurent Lucas, Jackie Berroyer, Philippe Nahon, Jean-Luc Couchard. Prod: Michael Gentile/Eddy Géradon-Luyckx/Vincent Tavier.

ULTRANOVA
[Drama, 2005] Script and Dir: Bouli Lanners. Phot: Jean-Paul De Zaeytijd. Players: Vincent Lecuyer, Hélène De Reymaeker, Michaël Abiteboul, Marie du Bled, Vincent Belorgey, Viviane Robert. Prod: Antonino Lombardo/Prime Time/ Versus Production.

LA FEMME DE GILLES
(Gilles' Wife*)*
[Drama, 2004] Script: Philippe Blasband based on the works of Madeleine Bourdhouxe. Dir: Frédéric Fonteyne. Phot: Virginie Saint Martin. Players: Stefano

Accorsi, Emmanuelle Devos.
Prod: Patrick Quinet/Artémis,
LiaisonCinématographique
(France)/Samsa Film
(Luxembourg).

DE INDRINGER (The Intruder)
[Thriller, 2004] Script: Ward
Hulselmans. Dir: Frank Van
Mechelen. Phot: Lou Bergmans.
Players: Koen De Bouw, Filip
Peeters, Els Dottermans, Axel
Daeseleire, Maaike Neuville,
Vic De Wachter. Prod: Eric
Wirix/Skyline Entertainment.

CONFITUUR (Sweet Jam)
[Comedy, 2004] Script: Lieven
Debrauwer, Jacques Boon. Dir:
Debrauwer. Phot: Philippe
Guilbert. Players: Marilou
Mermans, Rik Van Uffelen, Chris
Lomme, Ingrid De Vos, Jasperina
de Jong, Viviane De Muynck.
Prod: Dominique Janne/K-Line.

DE KUS (The Kiss)
[Drama, 2004] Script and Dir:
Hilde Van Mieghem. Phot: Jan
Vancaille. Players: Marie Vinck,
Van Mieghem, Ides Meire, Fedja
Van Huet, Veerle Baetens, Jan
Decleir, Josse De Pauw,
Els Dottermans. Prod: Michel
Houdmont/Signature Films.

ELLEKTRA
[Drama, 2004] Script: Rudolf
Mestdagh, Daniel Lamberts. Dir:
Rudolf Mestdagh. Phot: Danny
Elsen. Players: Julien
Schoenaerts, Matthias
Schoenaerts, Axelle Red, Gert
Portael, Serge-Henri Valcke,
Manou Kersting, Herwig
Illegems, Catherine Kools. Prod:
Rudolf Mestdagh/Cosmokino.

BUNKER PARADISE
[Drama, forthcoming] Script and
Dir: Stefan Liberski. Phot: Jean-
Paul De Zaetijd. Players: Jean-
Paul Rouve, François Vincentelli,
Audray Marnay, Bouli Lanners,
Sacha Bourdo, Yolande Moreau,
Jean-Pierre Cassel. Prod: Patrick
Quinet/Artémis Productions.
John Deveau is a member of a
band of wealthy youngsters who
fight boredom by experimenting
with alcohol, drugs and sex at

Private Madness (*Folie privée*), by newcomer Joachim Lafosse, has less horror, more psychology and realism, but the result is equally frightful. Jan (Kris Cuppens, who co-wrote the screenplay) reluctantly allows his ex-wife, Pascale, custody of their seven-year-old son, then suddenly changes his mind. The resulting conflict leads to a dramatic climax: Jan kills his son. Another very interesting first film is **Ultranova**, directed by actor Bouli Lanners, which won the CICAE prize at Berlin in 2005. Lanners needs few words to create atmosphere and establish the right tone. We are introduced to a handful of characters, all lonely people struggling to give meaning to their lives. The main character, Dmitri, and his two colleagues sell dream houses to people in the most desolate corners of southern Belgium. But even in bleak films, heroes and anti-heroes alike fall in love, and so does Dmitri.

Visually Frédéric Fontaine's **Gilles' Wife** (*La femme de Gilles*), is the exact opposite of the cold and desaturated *Ultranova*. Yet even here, the warm, chocolate box storytelling is anything but uplifting: Fontaine details the breakdown of Elise and Gilles' marriage, ending in Elise's suicide. The story is told in a subtle but distant way, as in Fontaine's *A Pornographic Affair* (1999). Images, shot by Virginie Saint Martin, and music are handled in a very sensitive manner.

Koen De Bouw as a doctor searching for his daughter in **The Intruder**

Different language, same agony

In comparison to the French-speaking production output in the south of Belgium, the Dutch-speaking part of Belgium had relatively little to offer. Frank Van Mechelen's **The Intruder** was the most notable film in terms of ticket sales. Its concept (horror suspense thriller) was to a great extent modelled on *The Alzheimer Case*, Flanders' 2003 box-office smash (which was released in the US in summer 2005). Again, a great deal of the action takes place in the Ardennes, a region we have come to associate with mystery and horror, as a 40-year-old doctor, Tom Vansant (Koen De Bouw) searches for his missing daughter. His inquiries lead him to the Ardennes, where he is confronted by a hostile community that seems to have much to hide.

Sweet Jam (*Confituur*), the long-awaited follow-up to *Pauline and Paulette* by Lieven Debrauwer, is another Flemish title that performed reasonably well at the box-office. Like *Pauline and Paulette*, this is another tale of old people and old loves, as Tuur leaves his wife at their wedding anniversary party. Debrauwers' characteristic 'light opera' style does not always meet approval from the critics, but the universe he creates is unique.

Lieven Debrauwer's **Sweet Jam**

Two other Dutch-speaking films tried in their own way to create this kind of world apart. Perhaps they tried too hard, because both **The Kiss** (*De kus*) by actress Hilde Van Mieghem and **Ellektra** by Rudolf Mestdagh were complete misfires. *The Kiss* is yet another exploration of cruelty to children, in which the director plays the abusive mother and her real-life child, Marie Vinck, plays the daughter. *Ellektra* also fails to get the tone right. Seven mysterious characters who have all experienced dreadful events contact a girl called Ellektra. Although Mestdagh convinced popular singer Axelle Red to take one of the lead roles, he, like the rest of the year's Flemish directors, could not match the sense of ease or self-confidence shown by most of the year's French-speaking productions.

ERIK MARTENS is a film critic and editor-in-chief of DVD releases for the Royal Belgian Film Archive.

wild parties. When Mimmo, a taxi driver and aspiring actor, is caught in Devau's underground bunker, he turns out to be the perfect prey.

BUITENSPEL (Gilles)
[Comedy, forthcoming] Script: Ed Vanderweyden. Dir: Jan Verheyen. Phot: Danny Elsen. Players: Ilya Van Malderghem, Filip Peeters, Joke Devynck. Prod: Dirk Impens/Menuet. Every weekend across Belgium, thousands of proud, nervous football fathers cheer their sons. One of them is Bert, who is only too happy that his 12-year-old son Gilles is a talented and passionate player. When Bert dies Gilles' life falls apart.

EEN ANDER ZIJN GELUK (Someone Else's Happiness)
[Drama, forthcoming] Script and Dir: Fien Troch. Phot: Frank van den Eeden. Players: Ina Geerts, Johan Leysen, Natali Broods, Peter Van den Begin, Johanna ter Steege, Josse De Pauw. Prod: Antonino Lombardo/Prime Time. Christine's life changes after she discovers the body of a child killed in a hit-and-run accident. The whole village is in a state of uproar and the longer the search for the driver goes on, the more secrets are revealed.

Quote of the Year

"Recreating the experience of people's suffering within the spectator is a way for art to reconstruct human experience."
LUC DARDENNE, *in his book* Au dos de nos images 1991-2005.

Bolivia José Sánchez-H.

The Year's Best Films

José Sánchez-H.'s selection:
The Robbery (Paolo Agazzi)
The Children of the Last Garden (Jorge Sanjinés)
Jesus' Heart (Marcos Loayza)

Diego Bertie in **The Andes Don't Believe in God**

Recent and Forthcoming Films

LOS ANDES NO CREEN EN DIOS (The Andes Don't Believe in God)
[Drama, 2006] Script and Dir: Antonio Eguino. Phot: Ernesto Fernandez. Players: Adolfo Diego Berti, Claudina Carla Ortiz, Joaquin Milton Cortez, Colta Gloria Lazo, Genaro Jorge Ortiz. Prod: Cinema Ventura.

NO LE DIGAS... (Don't Breathe a Word ...)
[Drama, 2006] Script and Dir: Mela Márquez. Phot: Guillermo Medrano. Players: Jorge Ortiz, David Mondacca, Teresa Del Pero. Prod: Amacord Producciones/Paolo Agazzi.

AMERICAN VISA
[Drama, 2005] Script and Dir: Juan Carlos Valdivia. Phot: Nestor Fernández. Players: Demián Bichir, Kate del Castillo, Carla Ortiz, Jorge Ortiz, Claudia Lobo. Prod: Paolo Agazzi/Fondo Ibermedia/Bola Ocho Producciones.

Much like the country itself, Bolivian cinema persevered in 2004–05, despite seemingly insurmountable odds. Only a fraction of a movie's budget comes from CONACINE, the Bolivian film council, and although cinemas are continually closing, as more and more of the audience, especially families, choose cheaper home-viewing on DVD, film-makers remain determined. They create their films in co-production with other countries and have turned to low-cost digital video. There also seems to be a resurgence of Super-16mm, particularly with the advent of new film stocks, which give excellent results when blown up to 35mm.

Bolivian audiences made Paolo Agazzi's local thriller **The Robbery** (*El atraco*) number six at the box-office in 2004, beating *Harry Potter and the Prisoner of Azkaban*. A co-production with Spain and Peru, it won Best Picture at the Festival of New Latin American Cinema in Trieste in 2004. Set in 1980s La Paz, but based on events that occurred in Bolivia in the 1960s, it masterfully explores a heist and its aftermath with a strong script, performances and cinematography.

Acclaimed director Jorge Sanjinés' first digital production, **The Children of the Last Garden** (*Los hijos del último jardín*), a drama set in La Paz, saw him resume his role as interpreter of indigenous culture. Five characters function as a collective protagonist in a story that begins in the future and shifts to the past, its structure reflecting the Andean view of time as cyclical. Marcos Loayza premiered his third film, **Jesus' Heart** (*El corazón de Jesús*), an engaging black comedy set in La Paz, which unveils the emotions of a marginalised character, Jesus (Cacho Mendieta), who has learned to survive in the jungle that is state bureaucracy and must now learn to live with those who have lost everything.

Agazzi to the fore

Paolo Agazzi produced *American Visa* by Juan Carlos Valdivia and *Don't Breathe a Word... (No le digas...)* by Mela Márquez, as well as directing an entertaining comedy, **Sena/Quina: The Immortality of the Crab** (*Sena/quina: La inmortalidad del cangrejo*), whose title borrows a phrase, *sena/quina*, from a popular local dice game, *cacho*. It is a contemporary story about two ingenious low-life swindlers who withstand the unemployment crisis but find their

Cacho Mendieta in **Jesus' Heart**

lives taking a 180-degree turn when they try to swindle a person they think is just another victim. Set in the Altiplano lowlands and valley regions, the film was shot chronologically on digital for a 35mm blow-up.

American Visa, a thriller set in La Paz and based on a novel by Juan de Recacochea, tells the story of a professor searching for a visa to go to the US. Unable to obtain one legitimately, he plans to rob a gold smuggler to pay for an illegal visa and becomes a killer. Forthcoming in 2006, **Don't Breathe a Word …** is a drama of memories, dreams and reality, based on the life of one of Bolivia's leading writers of the twentieth century, Jaime Sáenz (1921–1986).

Fernando Vargas' debut **Say Good Morning to Dad** (*Di buen dia a papá*) takes its title from the code phrase used to give the order to kill Ernesto "Ché" Guevara in Bolivia. Set in the town of Vallegrande from 1967 to 1997, this drama tells four personal stories of love, conflict and reconciliation, examining what happened in Vallegrande, where "Ché" was captured before his execution. Veteran director Antonio Eguino's long-awaited **The Andes Don't Believe in God** (*Los Andes no creen en Dios*), marked his return to feature film-making after 20 years. Based on three literary works by Adolfo Costa du Reis, the story takes place in the 1920s and tells of passions and ambitions in the search for minerals in a mining town, and includes scenic locations of the Altiplano in Uyuni.

JOSÉ SÁNCHEZ-H. (sanchezh@csulb.edu) is a film-maker and author of *The Art and Politics of Bolivian Cinema*. He teaches in the Film and Electronics Art Department of California State University, Long Beach.

SENA/QUINA:
LA INMORTALIDAD DEL
CANGREJO (Sena/quina:
The Immortality of the Crab)
[Comedy, 2005] Script and Dir: Paolo Agazzi. Phot: Guillermo Medrano. Players: Cristian Mercado, Rosendo Paz, José Veliz, Soledad Ardaya, Davis Mayo. Prod: Ute Gumz/ Pegaso Producciones.

DÍ BUEN DIA A PAPÁ
(Say Good Morning to Dad)
[Drama, 2005] Script and Dir: Fernando Vargas V. Phot: Juan Pablo Urioste. Players: Isabel Santos, Paola Rios, José Veliz, Bismark Virhuez, Jorge Ortiz. Prod: Verónica Córdovas/Imagen Propia srl (Bolivia)/Matanza Cine (Argentina)/ICAIC (Cuba).

EL ATRACO (The Robbery)
[Drama, 2004] Script and Dir: Paolo Agazzi. Phot: Ernesto Fernández. Players: Diego Bertie, Salvador del Solar, Lucia Jimenez, Jorge Ortiz, Jorge Jamarlli. Prod: Paolo Agazzi, Pegaso Producciones/Javier Castro/Filmart P.C.

Victor Salinas in **The Children of the Last Garden**

LOS HIJOS DEL ÚLTIMO
JARDÍN (The Children of the
Last Garden)
[Drama, 2004] Script and Dir: Jorge Sanjinés. Phot: César Pérez. Players: Victor Salinas, Alejandro Zárate, Carlos Mendoza, Henry Unzueta, Luis Bolivar. Prod: Beatriz Palacios/GrupoUkamau.
Five young friends take justice into their own hands, giving back to the country the money stolen by a corrupt politician.

Bosnia and Herzegovina Rada Sesic

Recent and Forthcoming Films

DOBRO USTIMANI MRTVACI
(Well-tempered Corpses)
*[Black comedy, 2005] Script:
Fedja Isovic, Benjamin Filipovic.
Dir: Filipovic. Phot: Ven Jemersic.
Players: Lazar Ristovski, Boro
Stjepanovic, Tanja Sojic, Miralem
Zupcevic. Prod: Dunja Klemenc/
Studio Maj (Slovenia).*

GO WEST
*[War drama, 2005] Script:
Ahmed Imamovic, Enver Puska.
Dir: Imamovic. Phot: Mustafa
Mustafic. Players: Tarik Filipovic,
Mario Drmac, Mirjana
Karanovic, Rade Serbedzija,
Nermin Tulic. Prod: Samir
Smajic/Imamovic/COMPREX.*

*Mario Drmac, left, and Tarik
Filipovic in* **Go West**

SASVIM LICNO
(Totally Personal)
*[Docu-drama, 2005] Script, Phot
and Dir: Nedzad Begovic.
Players: Amina, Sabrina, Naida
and Nedzad Begovic. Prod: Ismet
Nuno Arnautalic/SAGA.*

GRBAVICA
*[Drama, 2006] Script and Dir:
Jasmila Zbanic. Phot: Christine
A. Maier. Players: Mirjana
Karanovic, Jasna Zalica, Leon
Lucev, Ermin Bravo. Prod:
Damir Ibrahimovic/Deblokada.*

Although the country's annual output still consists of only three fiction features, the situation for production, distribution and exhibition improved in 2005. Most importantly, Bosnia and Herzegovina became eligible for funding from Eurimages and regional ministers of culture from Bosnia and Herzegovina, Croatia, Serbia and Montenegro, Slovenia, Macedonia, Hungary, Bulgaria, Romania, Turkey, Albania and Austria signed a crucial political agreement. Each state contributes equally to a fund for production and the rebuilding of movie theatre infrastructure. Scripts from member states compete for support, so that if one government cannot invest a large sum in any one year, continuous production should still be guaranteed to a certain extent by the fund, and producers should have less trouble raising a budget than the makers of **Well-tempered Corpses** (*Dobro ustimani mrtvaci*), a project that stalled for three years in search of state funding.

Benjamin Filipovic's satirical black comedy, set in present-day Sarajevo, finally opened the Regional Competition at the 11th Sarajevo Festival in August 2005, where audiences responded more warmly than the jury. Two weird morgue guards (Boro Stjepanovic and Zan Maroltpass) pass their time betting on how many bodies they will receive. Within this frame, the lives of peculiar characters destined for the slab are told separately, uniting at their deaths. We follow, among others, a train machinist (Lazar Ristovski), an unscrupulous, ambitious young woman (representative of the upcoming generation of leaders), a disillusioned Bosnian veteran and a crazy inventor dreaming of visiting his daughter in New York in a home-made flying machine.

Another film that took several years to be realised is the feature debut of Ahmed Imamovic, **Go West**. This intriguing blend of spaghetti Western and mystical local voodoo, about a gay couple during the war, stirred great controversy while still in production, not only because homosexuality was a new subject for Bosnian cinema but also because Imamovic depicted an intimate relationship between a Muslim and a Serb. They try to flee besieged Sarajevo and to escape the Serbs the young Muslim dresses up as a woman. They shelter in a village packed with Serbian fascists (Chetnicks) and gamble with their lives at every moment. The beauty and sophistication of actor Mario Drmac made him the discovery of the year, and young Imamovic, following his acclaimed short, *10 Minutes* (2003), skilfully blends surrealism and bold naturalism.

Lazar Ristovski, right, in **Well-tempered Corpses**

"Dear Diary…"

Received at home with roars of laughter, **Totally Personal** (*Sasvim licno*) is a very low-budget docu-drama by Nedzad Begovic. As if reading from his confidential personal journal, Begovic takes us through the 46 years of his life, mocking the time of Tito's enthusiastic pioneers and youth activists, then switching to the painful decay of former Yugoslavia and the horrible siege of Sarajevo and ending with sharp comments on the post-war era. The director, a conceptual artist and cartoonist, combines many different techniques, including animation, Super-8 and poetry.

Last season was also quite fruitful for short films. *Paycheck* (*Prva plata*), the graduation work of Alen Drljevic, is a blackly comic contemplation of the post-war crisis, in which a brave young Bosnian, desperate to earn money, races a motorbike through a minefield. Directed in minimalist style by gifted Elmir Jukic, *Frame for the Picture of My Homeland* (*Ram za sliku moje domovine*), starts in the pre-war era, with Muslims and Serbs living happily together. The war provokes evil in a Serb who kills his former friends.

Among some 30 new documentaries, two of the best are **Borderline Lovers** (*Ljubav preko granice*), by Miroslav Mandic, about three young couples of mixed ethnicity facing post-war obstacles. Haris Pasovic's **A Propos de Sarajevo** is a visual ode to the city and its spirit, set to jazz. Eleven years after the war destroyed 60% of the cinemas, a new enterprise, Art Company, has promised to build new multiplexes and renovate old theatres. The Sarajevo Film Festival has become indispensable, by facilitating a co-production market and nourishing the local audience for domestic productions.

RADA SESIC (sesic@worldonline.nl) is a film-maker and critic from Sarajevo. Based in the Netherlands, she teaches at the University of Amsterdam and collaborates on the programme of the Rotterdam Festival and IDFA, Amsterdam.

KROVNI TALAS
(*literally*, **Roof Wave**)
[*War satire, 2006*] *Script and Dir: Jasmin Durakovic. Phot: Mirsad Herovic. Players: Aleksandar Seksan, Lucija Serbezija, Senad Basic. Prod: Davor Pusic/FIST.*
On New Year's Eve during the siege of Sarajevo, an African–American woman gets trapped and meets a wounded, amnesiac soldier.

SNIJEG (**Snow**)
[*Post-war drama, 2006*] *Script: Aida Begic, based on a story by Faruk Sabanovic. Dir: Begic. Prod: Elma Tataragic/ Mamafilm/Karsten Stoeter/ Rohfilm (Germany).*

NEBO IZNAD KRAJOLIKA
(*literally*, **Skies Above the Landscape**)
[*Comedy, 2005*] *Dir: Nenad Djuric. Players: Haris Burina, Rastko Jankovic, Audrey Hamm. Prod: Almir Sahinovic/HEFT.*

KARAULA (**Border Post**)
[*Political comedy-drama, 2006*] *Script: Rajko Grlic, based on a novel by Ante Tomic. Dir: Grlic. Prod: Ademir Kenovic/ Refresh Production.*

ZIVI I MRTVI
(*literally*, **Alive and Dead**)
[*War drama/horror, 2006*] *Script: Josip Mlakic, Miro Barnjak. Dir: Kristijan Milic. Phot: Mirko Pivcevic. Players: Filip Sovagovic, Enes Vejzovic, Izudin Bajrovic, Ljubo Jurkovic. Prod: Miro Barnjak/Porta Mostar.*

Quote of The Year

"We should go to the video stores and check which of the Bosnian films is doing better."
BENJAMIN FILIPOVIC,
director of Well-tempered Corpses, *commenting on the sale of pirate copies of new Bosnian films as they premiered at the Sarajevo Film Festival.*

Brazil Nelson Hoineff

The Year's Best Films

Nelson Hoineff's selection:
Cazuza – Time Does Not Stop (Sandra Werneck and Walter Carvalho)
Movies, Aspirin and Vultures (Marcelo Gomes)
Vinicius (Miguel Faria, Jr.)
The Storytellers (Eliane Caffe)
Lower City (Sergio Machado)

Recent and Forthcoming Films

CIDADE BAIXA (Lower City)
[Drama, 2005] Script: Sergio Machado, Karim Ainouz. Dir: Machado. Phot: Toca Seabra. Players: Alice Braga, Wagner Moura, Lazaro Ramos, Jose Dumont. Prod: Mauricio Andrade Ramos.
Deco and Naldinho live by using a motor boat to transport goods and by committing petty thefts on board. The two give a ride to Karina, a stripper who wants to get some money. The attraction between them grows and they consider living in a threesome. But jealousy arises.

CINEMA, ASPIRINAS E URUBUS (Cinema, Aspirins and Vultures)
[Drama, 2005] Script: Marcelo Gomes, Karim Ainouz, Paulo Caldas. Dir: Gomes. Phot: Mauro Pinheiro, Jr. Players: Peter Ketnath, João Miguel, Fabiana Pirro, José Leite, Zezita Matos. Prod: Sara Silveira, Maria Ionescu, João Vieira, Jr.
In the Brazilian hinterland in 1942, two men meet: Johann, a German who has fled from the war, and Ranulpho, a Brazilian who is running from the

Despite the political crisis faced by President Lula's government since the second quarter of 2005, the country's economy has been remarkably stable, the local currency achieving its strongest rate in many years. This has encouraged public and private companies to invest in audiovisual production, and, as a result, Brazil keeps producing around 40 feature films per year. Not all of them find commercial distribution, however. In fact, almost 100 features produced in recent years have yet to reach cinemas and many never will. With Rio's government-owned distributor Riofilme almost inactive, local production relies heavily on the major distributors, such as Fox, for release. These companies take advantage of Article Three of the Audiovisual Law, which allows distributors of foreign films to invest part of their income tax dues in the production and distribution of local films.

As for the market, 2004–05 cannot be compared to the boom of 2003, when seven Brazilian features sold more than one million tickets each. The market share for Brazilian films reached 22% in that year, falling to 14% in 2004 and around 10% inr 2005. However, the phenomenon of the musical biopic **Two Sons of Francisco** (*2 Filhos de Francisco*) took the whole industry by surprise in 2005. It was seen by almost six million spectators in less than three months, outgrossing champions like *Carandiru* and *Lisbela and the Prisoner*. It also did better than *Cazuza – Time Does Not Stop* (see *IFG 2005*), the remarkable rock biopic that was perhaps the best Brazilian film of 2004 and, with slightly more than three million admissions, the year's biggest hit. *Cazuza* is one of the best examples of how a film made with a major (Sony) under the Audiovisual Law can be attractive to audiences and the critics. By contrast, **Sex, Love and Treason** (Fox), which sold 2.2 million tickets, preferred to incorporate TV values to lure to cinemas some of the 70 million Brazilians who every evening watch the local *telenovela* soaps.

Many other good Brazilian films launched during this period were negatively received by the audience, especially **The Storytellers** (*Narradores de Javé*), directed by Eliane Caffe, an inspired and very funny tale about the preservation of local culture, set in the northeast, which was seen by only 65,000 spectators. Claudio Torres' long-awaited **The Redeemer** (*Redentor*), made with Warner, was a high-tech, remarkable vision of a society dominated by corruption, which sold 220,000 tickets, far fewer than expected.

Francisco and his family in the hugely popular **Two Sons of Francisco**

Kings of country

Breno Silveira's *Two Sons of Francisco*, based on the true story of the Zeze di Camargo e Luciano country music duo, who have sold more than 20 million CDs in Brazil, opened with expectations of reaching 1.5 million viewers, but quickly went far beyond that figure, and was Brazil's Oscar entry. Silveira chose to tell the story through the determination of Francisco, a peasant, to help two of his sons (he had nine children in all) to become singing artists. The film cleverly mixes the strong father's emotions with some dramatic incidents from the duo's life (like the death of another brother, who was part of the original singing duo, during a tour). The duo's songs are now being interpreted by celebrities like Caertano Veloso.

If Silveira's film was not exactly intellectually moving, then the second half of 2005 saw the opening of several outstanding Brazilian films. Directed by Miguel Faria, **Vinicius** is a feature documentary about composer Vinicius de Moraes, author (with Tomn Jobim) of "The Girl from Ipanema" and one of the founders of bossa nova. Filled with a rare sensitivity, it portrays, better than many other earlier films about the same era, the spirit of the late 1960s and early 1970s, which allowed the flourishing of this most prolific cultural movement in Brazil.

A first feature, directed by Sergio Machado, **Lower City** (*Cidade Baixa*) is set on the outskirts of the city of Salvador, in Bahia, and depicts a tale of criminality and love between two men and a woman. The trio is outstandingly portrayed by Alice Braga, Lazaro Ramos and Wagner Moura, and Machado achieves a perfect blend of action and sensuality, friendship and jealousy, in a story filled with complexities that still appealed to wide audiences.

drought that afflicts the region. Driving from village to village, they earn their living by screening a commercial film for a medicine, to people who have never seen a movie before. Above all, they look for new horizons in their lives.

CARREIRAS
[Drama, 2005]. Script and Dir: Domingos Oliveira. Phot: Dib Lutfi. Players: Priscilla Rozembaum, Paulo Carvalho, Oliveira. Prod: Renata Paschoal. Laura, a beautiful, well-informed television presenter, is 40. She faces a "long night of madness", snorting grams of cocaine and trying to "break the system". Her resentment follows the loss of her status at the TV station, where she has been replaced by a younger woman.

VINICIUS
[Documentary, 2005] Script: Miguel Faria, Jr., Diana Vasconcellos. Dir: Faria, Jr. Phot: Lauro Escorel. Featuring: Camila Morgado, Ricardo Blat, Chico Buarque, Ferreira Gullar, Carlos Lyra, Caetano Veloso, Maria Bethânia, Toquinho, Adriana Calcanhoto, Olívia Byngton, Mariana de Moraes. Prod: Faria, Jr., Susana Moraes.
The life, works, family, friends and loves of Vinicius de Moraes, author of countless poems and lyrics for many songs, none more famous than "The Girl from Ipanema".

2 FILHOS DE FRANCISCO
(Two Sons of Francisco)
[Drama, 2005] Script: Patrícia Andrade, Carolina Kotscho. Dir: Breno Silveira. Phot: André Horta, Paulo Souza. Players: Angelo Antonio, Dira Paes, Marcio Kieling, Thiago Mendonça, Paloma Duarte, Jackson Antunes, Natália Lage. Prod: Luciano Camargo, Leonardo Monteiro de Barros, Luiz Noronha, Pedro B. Hollanda, Pedro Guimarães, Emanoel Camargo, Breno Silveira, Rommel Marques.

The story of a very popular Brazilian country music duo, Zezé di Camargo & Luciano, focusing on the efforts of their father, a radio lover, to introduce his children to the music scene.

ARIDO MOVIE

[Drama, 2005] Script: Lírio Ferreira, Hilton Lacerda, Eduardo Nunes, Sergio Oliveira. Dir: Ferreira. Phot: Murilo Salles. Players: Guilherme Weber, Giulia Gam, Matheus Nachtergale, Renata Sorrah, José Dumont, Selton Mello, Mariana Lima. Prod: Salles, Lírio Ferreira.
The Brazilian hinterland is the real and symbolic setting for this film, which highlights the contrasts of a contemporary society in which modern technology plants cell phone antennae at every available location but fails to overcome the challenge of making water widely available.

SOY CUBA, O MAMUTE SIBERIANO (I Am Cuba, the Siberian Mammoth)

[Documentary, 2004] Script and Dir: Vicente Ferraz. Phot: Ferraz, Tareq Daoud. Prod: Isabel Martinez.
In the early 1960s, acclaimed Soviet director Mikhail Kalatozov filmed *Soy Cuba*. It was intended as a powerful propaganda weapon for the Cuban revolution, but the film was ignored in Havana and Moscow. Then it was rediscovered in the 1990s by Martin Scorsese and Francis Ford Coppola. This documentary reveals key moments in the story of the film and its recovery, through memories of people involved in Cuban history.

Wagner Moura, left, Alice Braga, and Lazaro Ramos in **Lower City**

Another debut film, **Movies, Aspirin and Vultures** (*Cinema, aspirinas e urubus*), calls attention to its director, Marcelo Gomes. It follows a German citizen on a road through near-desert areas in Brazil's north-east, when the country gets involved in the Second World War. A road movie set in inhospitable terrain, it stars João Miguel and Peter Ketnath as two men for whom there is no present, no past and certainly no future. The film incorporates some aesthetic values of the *cinema novo* and transforms them magically into one of the best Brazilian films of 2005.

The undeniable values of films like these prove the importance of sustaining different production models in Brazil: some film-makers working with the majors, others independently. The success of this system depends heavily on the expansion of the exhibition circuit and the distribution system. Nearly 140 screens were opened in Brazil in 2004, but some state companies, like the BNDES (a state-owned bank for development), are opening special credit arrangements for the creation of up to 1,000 new screens, especially in heavily populated areas. This may help give wider releases to smaller and more specialised local films, which currently find it difficult to compete in a market that deals largely in blockbusters.

NELSON HOINEFF (nhoineff@uol.com.br) is a member of the Association of Film Critics of Rio de Janeiro and the Superior Council of Cinema of Brazil. He is President of the Institute of Television Studies and writes regularly on cinema for several publications, including www.criticos.com.br.

Bulgaria Pavlina Jeleva

The Year's Best Films

Pavlina Jeleva's selection:
Lady Zee (Georgy Duilgerov)
Stolen Eyes
(Radoslav Spassov)
Georgy and the Butterflies
(Docu. Andrei Paunov)
The Ritual
(Short. Nadejda Koseva)
Get the Rabbit Back
(Short. Dimitar Mitovsky,
Kamen Kalev)

Anelia Garbova and Pavel Paskalev in
Lady Zee

Recent and Forthcoming Films

RAZSLEDVANE (Investigation)
[Drama, 2005] Script and Dir:
Iglika Triffonova. Phot: Rali
Ralchev. Players: Svetlana
Yancheva, Krassimir Dokov.
Prod: Klas Film/Flying Moon
(Germany)/Phanta Vision
(Netherlands).
A murderer and a detective face
each other in a merciless battle.

MAIMUNI PREZ ZIMATA
(Monkeys in Winter)
[Drama, 2005] Script: Milena
Andonova and Maria Stankova.
Dir: Andonova. Phot: Rali
Ralchev. Players: Bonka Ilieva-
Bonny, Diana Dobreva, Angelina
Slavova, Sava Lolov. Prod:
Proventus/Tatfilm (Germany).

The sustained efforts of different generations on behalf of the national industry helped to make 2005 a very hopeful year for Bulgarian film-makers. There was an increase in the number of projects supported by the National Film Center and Bulgarian National Television and some films returned home from international festivals garlanded with prestigious awards, bringing confidence to the industry. In the front rank stands Moscow VGIK graduate and now veteran Georgy Duilgerov (Silver Bear-winner at Berlin for *Advantage* in 1977) with his latest feature, **Lady Zee**. This love story between young Zlatina and Lechko, both brought up in institutions for abandoned children, shows the desperate feelings of those underestimated by society.

The film touched a large audience because of its deep link with the sad reality in more than 300 Bulgarian homes for orphans and Duilgerov makes a powerful argument on behalf of moral values such as justice, freedom and honesty. He also brought outstanding performances from non-professionals, especially Anelia Garbova as Zlatina and Pavel Paskalev as Lechko. *Lady Zee* was named Best Film at Sarajevo and was chosen as the audience favourite at the New Montreal FilmFest. This international success was well received in Bulgaria, where the film also won the Golden Aphrodite at the 13th Varna Film Festival "Love is Folly" and Anelia Garbova won Best Actress.

At Moscow in 2005, the expressive Bulgarian actress Vessela Kazakova won the Silver Georgy for her brilliant performance in Radoslav Spassov's Bulgarian–Turkish co-production **Stolen Eyes**. Having given several proofs of her exceptional talent as a mute girl in Svetoslav Ovcharov's *A Leaf in the Wind*, an orphan artist in Sylvia Pesheva's *Crazy Day* and a prostitute in Zornitza Sofia's *Mila from Mars*, in *Stolen Eyes* she plays Turkish schoolteacher Ayten, who, like many others, is forced to change her native name during the communist "regeneration process". Spassov, who has been for years Duilgerov's director of photography (he shot *Lady Zee*) builds a bittersweet love story between Ayten, who has lost her child, and a Bulgarian soldier, Ivan (Valery Iordanov), responsible for the official seals on the new identity documents. The film combines rough realism with naïve episodes and owes a lot to the performance of young Iordanov, who preaches a smooth, good-hearted, orthodox Muslim message of reconciliation.

Three young women defined by their social status: gypsy girl Dona in the communist 1960s, law student Lucrecia in the 1970s and childless Tana in post-communist Bulgaria.

OBARNATA ELHA
(Christmas Tree Upside-down)
[Portmanteau drama, 2005]
Script and Dir: Ivan Cherkelov
and Vassil Zhivkov. Phot: Rali
Ralchev. Players: Alexandra
Vassileva, Georgi Cherkelov,
Krassimir Dokov, Slava Dojcheva.
Prod: Klas Film/Filmkombinat &
Co. KG (Germany).
Six separate stories about celebration, linked by interacts that follow a Christmas tree as it is cut down and driven from mountains to city.

PAZACHAT NA MARTVITE
(Warden of the Dead)
[Black comedy, 2005] Script and
Dir: Iliyan Simeonov. Phot:
Dimitar Gochev. Players: Vladimir
Georgiev, Izhak Finci, Samuel
Finci. Prod: Camera/Adcom.
The Kid has spent all his 13 years in a city cemetery. Encountering death daily, he has come to sense more than ordinary people, and is determined to make his only friends, the Old Man and the Artist, happy.

PRIZNAT I PROSSIAKAT
(The Prince and the Pauper)
[Drama, 2005] Script: Maia
Daskalova. Dir: Mariana
Evstatiava. Phot: Luidmil
Hristov. Players: Dossi Dossev,
Ivan Rankov, Plamen Dimitrov,
Ivailo Gerasskov, Aneta Sotirova.
Prod: Gala Film.

Quote of the Year

"I am not afraid of Hollywood – not only because I was born on the 4th of July."
VESSELA KAZAKOVA, *on receiving her Best Actress award at Moscow.*

Vessela Kazakova and Valery Iordanov in **Stolen Eyes**

Another happy festival winner was **Georgy and the Butterflies** by 31-year-old Andrei Paunov from Sofia. His sensitive and ironic feature documentary won the Silver Wolf at the IDFA in Amsterdam and the Human Rights Award in Sarajevo. In contrast with the usually brief theatrical lives of most national titles, Paunov's film about the exceptional psychiatrist and director of a home for psychologically challenged men, Dr Georgy Lulchev, stayed in cinemas for months. The audience was strongly attracted by the enthusiasm of Lulchev, who treats his patients with love and compassion, humour and fun.

Among successful young Bulgarian film directors should also be mentioned Nadejda Koseva, whose *The Ritual* was part of **Lost and Found**, the collective Eastern Europe young generation surprise at the 2005 Berlinale, and Dimitar Mitovsky and Kamen Kalev, whose six-minute *Get the Rabbit Back* charmed the audience at Critics Week in Cannes. Finally, Svetla Tsotsorkova surprised with her Jameson Short Film Award-winner, *Life with Sofia* (also shown in Cannes).

PAVLINA JELEVA (geopoly@techno-link.com) has been a film critic and journalist since 1978, contributing to many Bulgarian newspapers and magazines. A former national representative on the boards of Eurimages and FIPRESCI, she now runs her own film company.

Canada Tom McSorley

The Year's Best Films

Tom McSorley's selection:
Water (Deepa Mehta)
The Hamster Cage
(Larry Kent)
The Novena (Bernard Emond)
Familia (Louise Archambault)
Memory for Max, Claire,
Ida and Company
(Docu: Allan King)

Recent and Forthcoming Films

THE HAMSTER CAGE
[Drama, 2005] Script: Daniel Williams, Larry Kent. Dir: Kent. Phot: Gilles Blais. Players: Patricia Dahlquist, Jillian Fargey, Scott Hylands, Carly Pope, Alan Scarfe, Tom Scholte. Prod: Robert French, Hamstercage Productions Inc.

C.R.A.Z.Y.
[Comedy, 2005] Script: Jean-Marc Vallée, François Boulay. Dir: Vallée. Phot: Pierre Mignot. Players: Michel Cote, Pierre-Luc Brillant, Marc-André Grondin, Danielle Proulx, Emile Vallée, Maxime Tremblay. Prod: Jacques Blain, Richard Speer, Cirrus Communications/Crazy Films.

FAMILIA
[Drama, 2005] Script and Dir: Louise Archambault. Phot: André Turpin. Players: Sylvie Moreau, Mylène St-Sauveur, Macha Grenon, Juliette Gosselin, Vincent Graton, Micheline Lanctot. Prod: Luc Dery, microscope.

A SIMPLE CURVE
[Drama, 2005] Script and Dir: Aubrey Nealon. Phot: David Geddes. Players: Kris Lemche, Michael Hogan, Matt Craven, Pascale Hutton, Sarah Lind.

To understand yet another of the Canadian cinema's seemingly perennial years of transition, one must leave the multiplex, head to a library and read two books. One is a slim volume entitled *Technology and the Canadian Mind*, by Arthur Kroker, describing Canada as an 'in-between' nation, perched between its founding European heritages and, of course, the United States of America, that future-obsessed economic and cultural juggernaut to its immediate south. The other is *Two Solitudes*, Canadian author Hugh MacLennan's seminal novel that explores the historical and cultural differences between English- and French-speaking Canada. And there you have 2005: a year of cinematic in-betweens and two solitudes.

The 'in-betweens' operate at a number of levels, from production to content, and mostly in English-speaking Canada. As in 2004, in English Canada the wrongheaded commercial re-orientation of the state funding agency, Telefilm Canada, under former head Richard Stursberg failed to produce the desired results. New Telefilm boss S. Wayne Clarkson should improve things, although at the moment Telefilm itself seems stalled in a transitional, in-between state. As the old policy fades away, films produced under its flawed assumptions of commercial appeal (the highest-profile of which is, arguably, Atom Egoyan's disappointing international co-production, the noirish murder mystery, *Where the Truth Lies*) have found little success.

Not surprisingly, a counter-revolution has begun. 2005 witnessed the slow resurgence of the traditional strength of Canadian cinema: low-budget, aesthetically daring, artist-driven films. Aubrey Nealon's well-observed coming-of-age debut feature about a young man being raised by back-to-the-land draft dodgers, **A Simple Curve**, Sean Garrity's gritty psychological thriller, **Lucid**, about a man whose life is turned upside-down after a night of infidelity, Michael Mabbott's raucous mockumentary about a fictitious Albertan country singer, **The Life and Hard Times of Guy Terrifico**, and newcomer Julia Kwan's first feature about a nine-year-old Chinese–Canadian girl with an overheated imagination, **Eve & the Fire Horse**, all demonstrate that the future of Canadian cinema remains firmly in the hands of its talented and budget-conscious writer–directors. While it is indisputable that film-making English-speaking Canada is in an in-between state, it also appears to be headed, however tentatively, in the right direction.

Prod: Aubrey Nealon, Idaho
Peak Productions Ltd.

3 NEEDLES
[Drama, 2005] Script and Dir:
Thom Fitzgerald. Phot: Thomas
M. Harting. Players: Lucy Liu,
Sandra Oh, Olympia Dukakis,
Chloe Sevigny, Stockard
Channing, Shawn Ashmore,
Tanabadee Chokpikultong.
Prod: Michael Gleissner, Bryan
Hofbauer, Thom Fitzgerald,
Emotion Pictures.

WHOLE NEW THING
[Drama, 2005] Script: Amnon
Buchbinder, Daniel MacIvor.
Dir: Buchbinder. Phot:
Christopher Ball. Players: Daniel
MacIvor, Rebecca Jenkins,
Robert Joy, Callum Keith Rennie,
Aaron Webber. Prod: Camelia
Frieberg, Kelly Bray, Whole
Thing Productions Inc.

PAPER MOON AFFAIR
[Drama, 2005] Script: David
Tamagi, Michael Parker, Jilena
Cori. Dir: Tamagi. Phot: Robert
New. Players: Misa Shimizu,
Brendan Fletcher, Sebastian
Spence, Philip Granger, John
Lone. Prod: Michael Parker,
Paper Moon Film Ltd.

**THE LIFE AND HARD TIMES
OF GUY TERRIFICO**
[Comedy–mockumentary, 2005]
Script and Dir: Michael Mabbott.
Phot: Adam Swica. Players:
Matt Murphy, Kris Kristofferson,
Phil Kaufman, Natalie Radford,
Donnie Fritts, Rob Bowman,
Lyriq Bent, Jane Sowerby,
Levon Helm, Merle Haggard.
Prod: Nicholas D. Tabarrok,
Darius Films Inc.

EVE & THE FIRE HORSE
[Drama, 2005] Script and Dir:
Julia Kwan. Phot: Nicolas
Bolduc. Players: Vivian Wu,
Chan Chit Man Lester, Phoebe
Jojo Kut, Hollie Lo, Ping Sung
Wong. Prod: Tom Brown, Erik
Paulsson, Shan Tam, Yves Ma,
Golden Horse Productions.

THESE GIRLS
[Drama, 2005] Script: John

Aubrey Nealon's **A Simple Curve**

That's one Canadian cinematic solitude. In the other, by way of contrast, the Quebec film industry again produced impressive box-office hits as well as more introspective, auteurist fare. Even without the presence of another international hit like Denys Arcand's Oscar-winning *The Barbarian Invasions*, Quebec audiences flocked to see Jean-Marc Vallée's family comedy set in east-end Montreal in the 1970s, **C.R.A.Z.Y.**, and Ricardo Trogi's **Dodging the Clock** (*Horloge biologique*), a droll take on whether or not men have biological clocks too. On the less commercial front, there is Bernard Emond's impressive, assured, arthouse-destined, third feature, **The Novena** (*La neuvaine*), already an award-winner at Locarno, capturing the Ecumenical Jury Prize. It is a moving drama about the nature of faith, which follows the journey of Dr. Jeanne Dion (played with authority by Elise Guilbault) who is seeking solace from her traumatic past.

In a more comedic vein but equally thoughtful is the debut feature from Louise Archambault, **Familia**. The darkly humorous story of Michele, a 30-something aerobics instructor with gambling debts and her 14-year-old daughter, Marguerite, this study of mother–daughter dynamics is deftly directed and written by Archambault. Even with the dominance of Hollywood releases, the 2005 cinematic output of Quebec, well supported by local audiences, reveals a well-balanced blend of locally produced commercial and arthouse fare. Outside the film festival circuit, however, the distribution of Quebec films in the rest of Canada remains woeful, almost non-existent. At the movies, sadly, Canada's two solitudes persist.

Return of the auteurs

One healthy sign in Canadian cinema in 2005, despite or perhaps because of Telefilm's previous misguided policy of funding commercial movies, is the return of many seasoned auteur directors to the scene, in both fiction and documentary modes. Most celebrated among them is Toronto-based Deepa Mehta. **Water**, the third instalment of her so-called 'elemental' dramatic trilogy of films (following her previous *Earth* and *Fire*) exploring the plight of women in her native India, opened the 2005 Toronto International Film Festival to much critical acclaim and a wide release in Canadian terms. Pioneer independent auteur Larry Kent also returned with **The Hamster Cage**, a searing family drama about sexual abuse, murder and revenge in one profoundly dysfunctional family.

On the documentary front, cinéma vérité legend Allan King delivered **Memory for Max, Claire, Ida and Company**, a moving observational feature documentary about elderly patients confronting memory loss, their fading pasts and time itself. Nova Scotia-based William D. MacGillivray returned to the scene with not one but two feature documentaries, **Silent Messengers**, about Inuit art and culture in Canada's north, and **Reading Alistair MacLeod**, an intimate biography of the internationally celebrated Canadian author. Even Winnipeg's cult fave auteur director Guy Maddin got in on the documentary act with his short experimental portrait of late Italian film legend Roberto Rossellini, **My Dad Is 100 Years Old**, written and narrated by the subject's daughter, Isabella Rossellini.

Canada's two most prominent auteur film-makers, Atom Egoyan and David Cronenberg, shared the official competition spotlight in Cannes in 2005, the first such double Canadian selection in over three decades along La Croisette. While Canadian film officials took pride in this fact, it bears remembering that Cronenberg's **A History of Violence** is a Hollywood film merely shot in Canada; Egoyan's **Where the Truth Lies**, which stars Kevin Bacon and Colin Firth, is less overtly Canadian and more 'international' and commercial, clearly aimed at the American arthouse market. Reflecting the transitional year for Canadian cinema in many respects, both auteurs delivered films which could be described as being from somewhere 'in between' Canada and the United States. One is successful; one is not. For his whole career, Cronenberg has been a master at navigating those spaces between arthouse movie and Hollywood, form and content, Canada and the United States. Egoyan, on the other hand, appears decidedly less comfortable in that 'in-between' territory, from the content of the film itself to his losing battles with the Motion Picture Association of America, which had rated it NC-17. Ultimately, Egoyan's distributor ThinkFilm opted for an NR (not rated) release in the United States.

TOM McSORLEY is Executive Director of the Canadian Film Institute in Ottawa. He teaches cinema studies at Carleton University, and is Associate Editor at *Take One* magazine and a freelance film and theatre critic for CBC Radio One.

Hazlett, based on the play by Vivienne Laxdal. Dir: Hazlett. Phot: Alex Vendler. Players: David Boreanaz, Caroline Dhavernas, Amanda Walsh, Holly Lewis. Prod: Anne-Marie Gelinas, Sam Grana, John Hamilton, Hazlett, Andrew Noble, Production Jeux d'Ombres.

LUCID
[Thriller, 2005] Script: Sean Garrity, Jonas Chernick. Dir: Garrity. Phot: Michael Marshall. Players: Jonas Chernick, Callum Keith Rennie, Michele Nolden, Lindy Booth, Brianna Williams, Ross McMillan. Prod: Garrity, Jamie Brown, Hypnogogic Images Inc.

HORLOGE BIOLOGIQUE (Dodging the Clock)
[Comedy, 2005] Script: Jean-Philippe Pearson, Patrice Robitaille, Ricardo Trogi. Dir: Trogi. Phot: Jean-François Lord. Players: Patrice Robitaille, Pierre-François Legendre, Jean-Philippe Pearson. Prod: Nicole Robert, Go Films.

LA NEUVAINE (The Novena)
[Drama, 2005] Script and Dir: Bernard Emond. Phot: Jean-Claude Labrecque. Players: Elise Guilbault, Patrick Drolet, Denise Gagnon, Isabelle Roy, Stéphane Demers. Prod: Nicole Hilareguy, Bernadette Payeur, Corporation ACPAV Inc.

THE FRENCH GUY
[Comedy, 2005] Script and Dir: Ann-Marie Fleming. Phot: C. Kim Niles. Players: Babz Chula, Tygh Runyan, Carly Pope, Serge Bennathan, Heidi Iro. Prod: Fleming, Adrian Salpeter, Sleepy Dog Films.

Quote of the Year

"I've been waiting for years to sell out. It's just that nobody offered me anything before now."

DAVID CRONENBERG, *joking during a media scrum at Cannes.*

Chile Andrea Osorio Klenner

The Year's Best Films

Andrea Osorio Klenner's
selection:
Machuca (Andrés Wood)
Cachimba (Silvio Caiozzi)
In Bed (Matías Bize)
Mi mejor enemigo
(Alex Bowen)
Play (Alicia Scherson)

Mariana Loyola and Pablo Schwartz in Cachimba

Recent and Forthcoming Films

MI MEJOR ENEMIGO
(*literally*, **My Best Enemy**)
*[Comedy-drama, 2005] Script:
Julio Rojas, Paula del Fierro. Dir:
Alex Bowen. Phot: José María
Hermo. Players: Nicolás
Saavedra, Erto Pantoja, Jorge
Román, Miguel Dedovich, Juan
Pablo Miranda, Pablo Valledor,
Felipe Braun. Prod: Alex Bowen,
Pablo Trapero, Adrián Solar,
Hugo Castro/Alce Producciones
S.A./Matanza Cine (Argentina)/
Wanda Vision (Spain).*
December 1978. Chile and
Argentina are close to armed
confrontation. In Patagonia, a
lost Chilean patrol digs in
opposite an Argentine patrol, but
tension leads to friendship
between enemies.

EN LA CAMA (**In Bed**)
[Drama, 2005] Script: Julio

The new domestic cultural set-up in Chile has begun to bear fruit. In 2004, the National Council of Culture and Performing Arts began to function, creating the Council for the Arts and Audiovisual Industry, and the Fund for the Promotion of Audiovisual Arts. In concrete, this has meant grants of about $2.25m (1.2 billion pesos) for the development of the audiovisual industry. About $1.85m was distributed in the first edition of the National Contest of Projects for the Fund for the Promotion of Audiovisual Arts. It is important to state that this funding has been created with an integral vision, designed to foster the production of audiovisual works of art, provide training (scholarships and internships) and broadcast and exhibit Chilean productions.

The coup d'état on September 11, 1973 has, undoubtedly, marked the history of Chilean cinema. Its deep and lasting effects on all levels of society help to explain why Andrés Wood's **Machuca** ranked fourth in the box-office chart for 2004, with 654,169 spectators, even though many earlier films had already tackled the coup. In this autobiographical tale, Wood, who was eight in 1973, views the lead-up to the overthrow of Salvador Allende's government through the eyes of two 11-year-olds in Santiago. Gonzalo Infante belongs to a family from a privileged social class and Pedro Machuca comes from an illegal shantytown nearby. Their two realities are separated by a great, invisible wall, but the boys are united thanks to the groundbreaking ideas of a priest, who integrates shantytown boys into the private school of which he is the principal. Wood gives audiences

Matías Quer, left, Manuela Martelli and Ariel Mateluna in **Machuca**

a clear insight into the complex political and social processes, without ever manipulating the viewer. The children's perspectives make this a thrilling movie, in which the work of the young actress Manuela Martelli, as Machuca's sister, once more stands out.

Another 2004 release was **Cachimba**, by acclaimed director Silvio Caiozzi. Based on Jose Donoso's novel, *Naturaleza Muerta con Cachimba (Still Life with Pipe)*, this comedy tells the story of Marcos and Hilda, who head for Cartagena for a romantic weekend. In a large house, they find a collection of paintings of unknown artistic value and have a series of misadventures when they try to rescue the paintings from the sudden interest of dark characters. *Cachimba* stands out for the delicacy and dexterity that have become Caiozzi's trademaks. The attention to detail only reaffirms the craft of a genuine master. However, the film's box-office performance (122,335 admissions) suggests that Caiozzi's cinema is for those with a more refined taste.

The streets of Santiago

The year 2005 was characterised by a renewed wave in film production. Even though some have dared to talk about the "New Chilean Cinema", it would perhaps be better not to get ahead of the facts, but merely to notice the work of a new generation of directors, and in particular Alicia Scherson. Her **Play** is the first Chilean movie filmed in High Definition and one of the very few directed by a woman. Furthermore, it was screened at the Tribeca Film Festival 2005, where it received the award for best first film and went on to become Chilean candidate for the 2006 Oscars. It is the story of Cristina and Tristán, who on the same day loses his wife and his briefcase. They walk through a warm and polluted Santiago de Chile. He is trying to recover what he never had, she is the silent witness of his collapse. In Scherson's film there is minimal dialogue and it is the narrative details that give shape to a compelling tale of encounters and misunderstandings.

ANDREA OSORIO KLENNER (produccionfestival@uach.cl) is a journalist and Executive Producer and Programme Co-ordinator of the Valdivia International Film Festival.

Viviana Herrera and Andrés Ulloa in **Play**

PLAY
[Drama, 2005] Script and Dir: Alicia Scherson. Phot: Ricardo de Angelis. Players: Juan Pablo Quezada, Aline Kuppenheim, Viviana Herrera, Andrés Ulloa. Prod: Sergio Gándara, Macarena López/Parox/La Ventura/Paraiso Production Difussion (France)/ Morocha Films (Argentina).

Rojas. Dir: Matías Bize. Phot: Gabriel Díaz, Cristian Castro. Players: Blanca Lewin. Prod: Adrián Solar, Cristoph Meyer-Wiel/Ceneca Producciones/CMW Films Company (Germany). Bruno and Daniela, two young strangers, have an intense sexual encounter that changes their lives forever.

EL BAÑO
(*literally,* **The Bathroom**)
[Drama, 2005] Script and Dir: Gregory Cohen. Phot: Piola Avalos. Players: Faryde Kaid, Alex Zisis, Pablo Macaya, Eduardo Marambio, Juan Barahona. Prod: Rodrigo Orellana, Antonino Ballestrazzi, Guillermo Álvarez, Igor Rosenmann.
Chilean history, from 1968 to 1988, viewed through a bathroom security camera.

MACHUCA
[Drama, 2004] Script: Roberto Brodsky, Mamoun Hassan, Andrés Wood. Dir: Wood. Phot: Miguel Joan Littin. Players: Matías Quer, Ariel Mateluna, Manuela Martelli, Aline Kuppenheim, Federico Luppi, Ernesto Malbrán. Prod: Gerardo Herrero, Mamoun Hassan, Andrés Wood.

LA SAGRADA FAMILIA
(**The Sacred Family**)
[Drama, 2005] Script and Dir: Sebastián Campos. Phot: Gabriel Díaz. Players: Sergio Hernández, Néstor Cantillana, Coca Guazzini, Patricia López, Macarena Teke. Prod: Úrsula Budnik, Antonino Ballestrazzi, Andrés Waissbluth, Cristián Jiménez/Horamágica/Retaguardia.

CACHIMBA
[Comedy, 2004] Script: Silvio Caiozzi, Nelson Fuentes. Dir: Caiozzi. Phot: Miguel Abal. Players: Pablo Schwarz, Mariana Loyola, Julio Jung, Patricio Contreras, Jesús Guzmán. Prod: Silvio Caiozzi, Guadalupe Bornard, José Luis Segura, Luis Sartor/Andrea Films S.A.

China Sen-lun Yu

The Year's Best Films

Sen-lun Yu's selection:

Shanghai Dream
(Wang Xiaoshuai)
Sunflower (Zhang Yang)
Waiting Alone (Dayyang Eng)
Dam Street (Li Yu)
You and Me (Ma Liwen)

Recent and Forthcoming Films

**QIANLI ZOU DAN JI
(Riding Alone for Thousands
of Miles)**
*[Drama, 2005] Script: Zhang
Yimou, Zou Jingzhi. Dir: Zhang.
Phot: Zhao Xiaoding. Players:
Ken Takakura, Kiichi Nakai,
Shinobu Terajima, Jiang Wen.
Prod: Zhang Weiping, Zhang
Yimou, Toho Company/Beijing
New Picture Co. Ltd.*
In the 1920s, a researcher
specializing in musicals and
operas is diagnosed with a fatal
disease. To fulfill the dying son's
wish, the father takes him to
China's Yunan province to learn
opera. On the way they meet a
Chinese girl and a group of bandits.

WU JI (The Promise)
*[Fantasy drama, 2005] Script and
Dir: Chen Kaige. Dir: Chen
Kaige. Phot: Peter Pau. Players:
Cecilia Cheung, Nicholas Tse,
Jang Dong-kun, Liu Ye, Hiroyuki
Sanada. Prod: Chen Hong/Han
Sanping/Kim Dong-ju/Ernst
Etchie Stroh/China Film
Group/Show East/Moonstone
Entertainment.*
Apoor and hungry girl accepts
charity from a goddess but pays
the price by being cursed. She
will become Queen, enjoying
fortune, beauty and power, but

The year 2005 saw progress and changes in Chinese cinema. More genres are emerging in an increasingly diverse and receptive market. As the production environment becomes more fertile, budgets escalate. And the film industry as a whole has benefited from the simultaneous rise in box-office revenue. While auteurs from the so-called sixth generation continue to make their voices heard at international festivals, their predecessors, the fifth generation, compete for the spotlight by making big-budget films, recruiting international crew members and stars. Taking another share of the pie are the Hong Kong film-makers, who enjoyed their second year of testing the mainland market under the Close Economic Partnership Agreement (CEPA); 2005 was very fruitful for co-productions: the top five most successful films were all Hong Kong/China co-productions.

Chinese cinema celebrated its centenary in 2005, and at least two films were made as part of the many commemorative events. **Electric Shadows** (*Dianying Wangshi*), by up-and-coming director Xiao Jiang, follows a similar structure to *Cinema Paradiso*, depicting a love story and a small town's craze for outdoor screenings, as well as a tragic accident in the cinema itself. **Focus: the Moment** (*Jujiao Zhe Yike*) is a collective project of eight shorts made by eight young directors as a tribute to the centenary. The project is produced by Tian Zhuangzhuang and recruits well-known names such as Jia Zhangke, Wang Xiaoshuai and Liu Hao, each making a three-minute film about a precious moment. The strongest of the eight films is Jian Zhangke's "Out in There", about a Hong Kong man's memory of Beijing snow.

A *Dream* of the 70s

Wang Xiaoshuai's **Shanghai Dream** (*Qinghong*) is a realistic story reflecting life in China in the late 1970s, a continuation of the 2004 trend for nostalgia-themed films. Its focus is on the intimate interaction between parents whose traumatic experiences of the Cultural Revolution lead them to put pressure on and build high hopes for their children, hoping they will not repeat the same mistakes. This leads to daily family conflict and, ultimately, tragedy. A 19-year-old girl has her first love hampered by the father. The family, having followed government policy by moving inland from the costal city of Shanghai to help developing factories, find

Fortissimo Films

Wang Xiaoshuai's **Shanghai Dreams**

themselves stuck in a mountain village. The father believes that their only hope is a return to Shanghai.

Director Wang maintains a tranquil beauty in landscape and a suffocating atmosphere, depicting the father's demands and the daughter's silent resistance. The film won him the Prix du Jury at Cannes. It also marks Wang's first "above the ground" movie, following a number of underground efforts, and it enjoyed an officially sanctioned nationwide release.

Another nostalgic, parent-child relationship is explored in Zhang Yang's **Sunflower** (*Xiangri Kuei*). Like his previous films, *Shower* (*Xizao*) and *Quitting* (*Zuotian*), it is yet another story dealing with a power struggle, love and care between father and son. This time the father is a former painter returning home from a labour camp with his hands permanently damaged. He begins a strict educational regime with his son, hoping that he will fulfill his own unfinished dreams as an artist. This autobiographical film vividly presents the changing landscape of Beijing, from courtyards to high-rises.

Waiting Alone (*Duzi Dengdai*) by debut feature director Dayyan Eng presents an entirely different perspective. Rather than looking back, the film focuses on the urban youngsters of contemporary Beijing, using caustic and humorous dialogue to explore their lifestyles, friendship and love. The American-Chinese Eng was nominated for three Golden Rooster awards, making him the first foreigner to be recognised in this way. The commercial success of this upwardly mobile independent film also reflects the demand of Chinese audiences for a wider choice of genres.

Good news for horror fans

Chinese moviegoers have also been enjoying a loosening of the rules concerning horror films. Traditionally, Chinese film policy ruled that stories of ghosts, violence and sex were not to be approved by the Film Bureau, in order to protect the young. But since 2004,

will never know true love. Twenty years later a martial slave fights battles to win the lonely queen's heart, without knowing there are more enemies in the battle: the duke, the general and a mysterious ghost.

WOMENLIANG (You and Me)
[Drama, 2005] Script and Dir: Ma Liwen. Phot: Wu Di, Wu Wei. Players: Jin Yaqin, Gong Zhe, Zhang Shufang. Prod: Han Sanping, China Film Group.
One snowy and windy day, a girl runs into a courtyard house, looking for a place to live. The owner of the house, an elderly widow, has lived there her whole life. The girl brings changes to the house as well as the old lady's ordered life. As time passes, caution and conflict turn into care and companionship. But the girl is only a passer-by. She is about to leave the courtyard.

YEYAN (The Banquet)
[Period drama 2006] Script: Sheng Heyu. Dir: Feng Xiaogang. Phot. Zhang Li. Players: Zhang Ziyi, Ge You, Zhou Xun, Daniel Wu. Prod: Wang Zhonglei, John Chong, Huayi Brothers Film Investment/Media Asia Films.
When her brother-in-law ascends the throne after the King's death, the Queen agrees to marry him in order to protect her stepson. Convinced that his uncle has murdered his father, the prince decides to return to the palace and take revenge. Everything culminates in a night banquet where all hell will break loose.

MOZI GONGLUE (Battle of Wisdom)
[Period drama, 2006] Script and Dir: Jacob Cheung. Phot: Yoshitaka Sakamoto. Players: Andy Lau, Ahn Sung-ki, Wang Zhiwen, Fan Bingbing. Prod: Cheung, Satoru Iseki, Huang Jianxin/Huayi Brothers /Sundream Motion Pictures /Comstock/Boram Entertainment.
During China's Warring States period (475-221 BC), the tiny

Kingdom of Liang fought against a 15,000-strong army by applying the strategies of the philosopher Mozi.

BAI FENGHUANG
(The White Phoenix)
[Period action-drama, 2006]
Script: David Hunsaker, Tsui Hark. Dir: Tsui. Prod: Peter Loehr, Francoise De Leu, Samuel Hadida /Ming Productions/Davis Film/D+ Productions/Metropolitan.
An Imperial Magistrate is sent to solve the mystery of the disappearance of the Crown Prince. As he faces danger from assassins, pirates, corrupt officials and ruthless businessmen in Tang Dynasty Guangzhou, Judge Dee only really discovers what he's up against when he reaches a chaotic southern port city.

JIQUAN BUNING
(One Foot Off the Ground)
[Comedy, 2006] Script and Dir: Chen Daming. Phot: Yang Shu. Players: Xu Fan, Xiao Xiangyu, Li Yixiang, Jin Hong, Ren Silu. Prod: Chris Lee, Wang Zhongjun, Huayi Brothers.
A traditional Henan opera troupe is facing bankruptcy. Performers are obliged to begin new careers. Some become dog-sellers while others run cockfights. But the new jobs are harsher than they expected and then the troupe office is burgled.

YUN SHUI YAO *(literally,* **The Cloud Water Ballad)**
[Drama, 2006] Script: Liu Heng. Dir: Yin Li. Phot: Mu Deyuan. Players: Vivian Hsu, Chen Kun, Li Bingbing. Prod: Han Sanping, China Film Group.
A Taiwan woman's extraordinary love story. Remembering her young love she crosses the strait and mountain to Lhasa, seeking the doctor who was sent to work on the plateau.

GEINI YIDIAN YANSE
(Show You Colour)
[Drama, 2006] Script and Dir: Cui Jian. Phot: Christopher Doyle. Prod: Philip Lee, Chen

The Beijing youth of Dayyan Eng's **Waiting Alone**

when the Film Bureau simplified the approval procedure for features, by vetting only plot synopses rather than full screenplays, many previously taboo topics have begun to appear on screen. While horror films featuring ghosts and spirits are still banned, more and more thrillers have appeared in mainstream cinemas.

The Game of Killing (*Tianhe Qing Biyan*) was the best-selling horror film of the year. Directed by Ah Gan, the film is adapted from a popular novel about a card game that turns out to be the scenario used by a real serial killer. Other popular horror films include **Suffocation** (*Zhixi*) and **Curse of Lola** (*Zuzhou*). The former, by Zhang Binjian, has been hailed as the first Chinese psycho-thriller in mainstream cinemas. It follows a photographer unraveling his nightmares and the death of his wife. *Curse of Lola* is about the mysterious murder of a dance troupe's lead performer.

With more horror films coming to the market, the next step in the industry will be the introduction of a ratings system. Film Bureau Director Tong Gang in early 2005 announced that the long-awaited Film Promotion Law would be enacted in 2006 and that it would bring with it the implementation of a rating system.

From epic to intimacy

Fifth-generation giants Chen Kaige and Zhang Yimou both presented big-budgeted films at the end of 2005. Chen's **Promise** (*Wu Ji*), a $30m costume extravaganza set in ancient China, is billed as the most expensive Chinese film ever. Zhang's *Riding Alone for Thousands of Miles* (*Qianli Zou Dan Ji*) is a China/Japan co-production, about a Japanese father and his ailing son traveling to China's Yunan province to learn opera. Both films were unreleased at press time.

Two women film-makers stood out in 2005. Li Yu's **Dam Street** (*Hong Yan*), set in 1980 in Sichuan, is the story of a traditional opera actress, Xiaoyun, and her ill-fated drifting through life at a time when traditional values were clashing with the new money-chasing trend. After being deserted by various men, she develops an ambiguous affection for a 10-year-old boy, without knowing that he is the illegitimate son she gave birth to at 16. The harsh reality and the honest and innocent affection between the woman and the little boy have helped the film win awards at the Venice and Vienna film festivals.

Ma Liwen took the Golden Rooster prize for Best Director for **You and Me** (*Womenliang*). The story, set in contemporary Beijing, sees an 80-year-old woman (Jin Yaqin) receive a 19 year-old girl as her housemate in her old and shabby courtyard. The simple setting is enriched by the intriguing daily interactions between the two characters, whose worlds could not be more different. In the changes of four seasons, a genuine affection develops, in director Ma's clean-cut but creative narrative. Jin won Best Actress at the Tokyo Film Festival and the Golden Rooster Awards.

The Hong Kong-China co-productions that topped the box-office charts for 2005 were Stephen Chow's action-comedy, **Kung Fu Hustle** (*Gong Fu*; see also Hong Kong section) and Feng Xiaogang's modern adventure, **A World Without Thieves** (*Tianxia Wuzei*). Jackie Chan and Stanley Tong's collaboration, **The Myth** (*Shenhua*), an action-adventure set in both ancient and modern China, was the biggest hit of the latter half of the year. Andrew Lau and Alan Mak's modern car-racing film, **Initial D** (*Tou Wenzi D*), and Tsui Hark's **Seven Swords** (*Qijian*), a martial arts drama set in China's Ming dynasty, were in fourth and fifth places on the charts. Peter Chan's modern musical-drama **Perhaps Love** (*Ruguo Ai*) also did good business.

In the second year of the implementation of CEPA, which lets Hong Kong film-makers work on the Chinese mainland through co-production deals, Hong Kong film-makers demonstrated a canny understanding of the mainland market – by opting for bigger budget and stars. It is expected that the mainland market will continue to dominate the production direction of the Hong Kong film industry.

The total gross for 2005 topped $250m (RMB 2billion) up 30% from 2004, mainly because of an increase in the number of releases and the success of the Hong Kong hits. Another factor was the introduction of half-price movie tickets on Tuesdays, a scheme implemented in June 2005 to encourage people to see movies in cinemas instead of buying pirated DVDs. The new policy is estimated to have contributed as much as 20% of the total gross in big cities' cinemas.

SEN-LUN YU (senluny@gmail.com) is a Beijing-based *journalist* who contributes to *The Hollywood Reporter* and Taipei-based newspaper *Pots*.

Weiming, Zonbo Media.
The film will be divided into three parts, with each part using red, yellow and blue to represent the aura of the time. Each story will be about the influence of the Cultural Revolution on an ordinary individual's life.

FANGXIANG ZHILU (Road)
[Drama, 2006] Script: Yuan Daju, Zhang Jiarui. Dir: Zhang. Phot: Lin Liangzhong. Players: Zhang Jingchu, Fan Wei, Nie Yuan. Prod: Ling Li, Guangcai Culture and Media Group /Beijing Qingnian Film Studio.
A woman's first love takes place during the Cultural Revolution, when pre-marital sex is not allowed. Her first boyfriend is sent to jail. She then goes to her second choice, a worker who was honoured by Mao Zedong. But a car accident puts him in a coma. In this repressed era, the only thing she can do is wait for another man.

Quote of the Year

"This year's top five best-selling movies are all Chinese. There is no such thing as the American blockbuster!"
ZHENG DONGTIAN, *director, at the Golden Rooster Awards Ceremony.*

Colombia Jaime E. Manrique and Pedro Adrián Zuluaga

The Year's Best Films

Jaime E. Manrique and Pedro Adrián Zuluaga's selection:
On the Path
(Short. Martín Mejía)
The Fence
(Short. Rubén Mendoza)
Additions and Subtractions
(Víctor Gaviria)
The Wandering Shadows
(Ciro Guerra)
The King (Antonio Dorado)

César Badillo, left, and Ignacio Prieto in The Wandering Shadows

Recent and Forthcoming Films

LA SOMBRA DEL CAMINANTE
(**The Wandering Shadows**)
[Drama, 2005] Script and Dir: Ciro Guerra. Phot: Emanuel Rojas. Players: César Badillo, Ignacio Prieto, Inés Prieto Saravia, Dubián Gallego. Prod: Tucán Producciones/ Cinematográficas Ltda./Ciudad Lunar.

COLOMBIANOS, UN ACTO DE FE
(**Colombians, an Act of Faith**)
[Drama, 2004] Script and Dir: Carlos Fernández de Soto. Phot: Humberto Carrizo. Players: Isabella Santodomingo, Nicolás Montero, Ana María Kamper.

Commercial Colombian cinema had decent results in the second half of 2004, Antonio Dorado scoring a hit with the tense, impressively directed and designed **The King** (*El Rey*), which explored the origins of the drugs trade in Cali, the country's third largest city, through the story of the legendary local dealer, Pedro Rey. Written by soap opera author Carlos Fernandez de Soto, **Colombians, an Act of Faith** (*Colombianos, un acto de fe*) drew on TV formulas and told the humorous story of a male foetus that, knowing he will be born in Colombia, refuses to leave the womb. Raúl García Jr.'s **The Corner** (*La esquina*) tried and failed to repeat the smashing success of *The King*. It told the story of two comedian friends whose relationship and shared values strain and ultimately shatter.

In March 2005, during the 45th International Film Festival of Cartagena, the Development Film Fund (Fondo para el Desarrollo Cinematográfico), created by the new film law (which came into force in January 2004) launched a promotional call (Convocatoria), offering access to approximately $2.6m – an unprecedented level of state support – for features, documentaries and short films. Cartagena screened seven Colombian features, four of which were national premieres. Bob Cecout's co-production **The Honest People ...** (*La gente honrada*) cartoonishly followed a French woman (Victoria Abril) who recklessly decides to adopt a Colombian child. Jaime Osorio's **Without Amparo** (*Sin Amparo*) was a small-scale, intimate failure, focusing on the pain and impotence of a grieving widower as he forms a new relationship with someone totally unlike his late wife.

Once upon a time in Medellín

Following *Rodrigo D* (1989) and *The Rose Seller* (*La vendedora de rosas*, 1998), **Additions and Subtractions** (*Sumas y restas*), reaffirmed the inner coherence of director Victor Gaviria's work. With a poignant, realistic style, Gaviria continued his surgical analysis of 1980s Medellín, with its easy-money lifestyle fostered by drug trafficking. Another fine example of low-budget auteur cinema at Cartagena was **The Wandering Shadows**, the debut of Ciro Guerra (b. 1981). Two characters are united by rural violence and are later reunited in the city, without recognising their shared pasts. The non-commercial elements – black-and-white cinematography, dramatic repetition and slow pacing – were not very appealing to the average moviegoer.

Sergio Cabrera's highly commercial and, by local standards, very expensive **The Art of Losing** (*Perder es cuestión de método*) followed the violent misadventures of a journalist (Daniel Giménez Cacho) caught up in a criminal investigation against a background of corruption and sex, including an affair with a young hooker (Martina García). Santiago Gamboa's novel was transferred to the big screen in cold, schematic fashion.

Daniel Giménez Cacho and Martina García in **The Art of Losing**

Despite limited audience response to feature films, Colombian short films performed well in 2004–05. *Od the Path* (*Od el camino*), the silent journey of a peasant's day, by Martín Mejía, took top honours at Oberhausen 2004. *The Fence* (*La cerca*) by Ruben Mendoza was selected for the Cinéfondation at Cannes 2005. It shows a father–son relationship against a backdrop of ancestral violence.

In August 2005, **Rosario Tijeras**, the Medellín-set story of a woman killer, directed by Mexican Emilio Maille and based on the bestselling book by Jorge Franco Ramos, became one of the biggest local box-office hits of recent years, despite bad reviews. Set during the terrorist violence brought about by drug wars, it was badly edited, unevenly acted and used family soap-opera tactics to confront a major national conflict. The year was set to end with new film openings that would again challenge the relationship between the Colombian industry and national audiences – the relationship on which depends the viability of a young, unstable cinema.

JAIME E. MANRIQUE (jaime@blackvelvetlab.com) is director of audiovisual production agency Laboratorios Black Velvet and general editor of digital bulletin Cine Colombiano Pantalla Colombia. **PEDRO ADRIÁN ZULUAGA** (pedroadrian@hotmail.com) is a journalist and film critic. He was editor of *Kinetoscopio* magazine for four years.

Prod: Jairo Serna Rosales/Carlos Fernández de Soto/R.C.N. Televisión/Ana Fernanda Martínez/Gustavo Carbonell.

LA ESQUINA (The Corner)
[Comedy-drama, 2004] Script: Dago García. Dir: Raúl García Jr. Phot: Juan Carlos Vasquez. Players: Enrique Carriazo, Fabio Pubiano, Jairo Camargo. Prod: Dago García/Caracol Televisión.

PERDER ES CUESTIÓN DE MÉTODO (The Art of Losing)
[Drama, 2005] Script: Jorge Goldenberg, based on the novel by Santiago Gamboa. Dir: Sergio Cabrera. Phot: Hans Burmann. Players: Daniel Giménez Cacho, Martina García, César Mora, Víctor Mallarino. Prod: Gerardo Herrero/Tomás Darío Zapata/ Marianella Cabrera/ Sergio Cabrera.

ROSARIO TIJERAS
[Drama, 2005] Script: Marcelo Figueras, based on the novel by Jorge Franco. Dir: Emilio Maillé. Phot: Pascal Martí. Players: Flora Martínez, Manolo Cardona, Unax Ugalde, Rodrigo Oviedo. Prod: Mathías Ehrenberg/Gustavo Ángel/Mano Producciones/United Angels Production/Maestranza Films/Dulce Compañía.

Manolo Cardona and Flora Martínez in **Rosario Tijeras**

SIN AMPARO (Without Amparo)
[Drama, 2005] Script: Iván Beltrán, Jaime Osorio, Jaime Escallón. Dir: Osorio. Phot: Raúl Pérez Ureta. Players: Germán Jaramillo, Luís Fernando Hoyos, Ruddy Rodríguez, Ana Soler. Prod: Tucán Producciones Cinematográficas Ltda./ TyM Films/A.T.P.I.P. SL.

Croatia Tomislav Kurelec

The Year's Best Films

Tomislav Kurelec's selection:
What's a Man Without Moustache? (Hrvoje Hribar)
What Iva Recorded on October 21st, 2003 (Tomislav Radic)
Sleep Sweet, My Darling (Neven Hitrec)
Two Players from the Bench (Dejan Sorak)
Somewhere Nowhere (Filip Sovagovic)

Recent and Forthcoming Films

SEX, PICE I KRVOPROLICE
(Sex, Booze and Short Fuse)
[Portmanteau drama, 2004]
Script and Dir: Boris T. Matic,
Zvonimir Juric, Antonio Nuic.
Phot: Vjeran Hrpka. Players:
Admir Glamocak, Matko
Fabekovic, Kreso Mikic, Leon
Lucev. Prod: Boris T. Matic/
Propeler Film.
Interesting debut of three young
directors with three different
stories, all connected with the
day of the greatest Croatian
football derby. A father and son,
supporters of the opposing teams,
go to the game together. Two
friends get into trouble with
police on their way to the
stadium. After the game four fans
of the local club deal with long-
unresolved secrets.

PUSCA BISTRA
(Somewhere Nowhere)
[Absurdist film, 2004] Script and
Dir: Filip Sovagovic. Phot:
Slobodan Trninic. Players: Enes
Vejzovic, Mladen Vulic, Ranko
Zidaric, Dragan Despot. Prod:

A record 180 film premieres in 2004 were watched by 2.9 million (just shy of the all-time record of 3 million, in 2001). The boom was caused by *The Return of the King* and *The Passion of the Christ*, which between them attracted almost 20% of total admissions, and the opening of the 13-screen Cinestar in Zagreb, with seats for 3,000. However, the first half of 2005 brought great disappointment. No films came even close to matching the two mega-hits of the previous year; Cinestar was no longer a novelty and, somewhat belatedly, video piracy presented a serious threat. Both commercial and public television aired more and more films, bringing not only the theatrical exhibition industry but also the DVD business to the brink of extinction.

At the same time, Croatian film production seemed to be facing a serious crisis. After two cinema seasons that had been probably the best in the country's history and seen eight or nine features produced annually – some winning significant international awards and reviving the public's fading interest – in 2004–05 only six new films emerged, from not altogether promising authors. Yet they surpassed all expectations, notably the films that marked and were mostly premiered at the 2005 Pula Film Festival.

What Iva Recorded on October 21st, 2003

Tomislav Radic's **What Iva Recorded on October 21st, 2003**, won the key awards: Best Film, Director and Best Leading Actress (Anja Sovagovic playing the role of the heroine's mother) and Actor (Ivo Gregurevic as the stepfather). Radic (b. 1940) works primarily in theatre and TV and, after several poorly received films, surprisingly offered one of the most original movies of recent years. Despite comparisons made by younger critics, who stressed the similarity between his film and the Danish *Dogma*, Radic's film follows more in the footsteps of his debut, *Living Truth* (1971), and what was then defined as cinéma-vérité. Iva, a young girl, is given a digital camera for her 14th birthday by her stepfather. She uses it to document preparations for her birthday celebrations, which do not include her peers but her father's business partner from abroad. The unusual, yet highly effective perspective that Radic chooses – that of the young protagonist – offers a complex presentation of relations within the family, the primitivism of the nouveaux riches and their vulnerability to the machinations of foreigners.

In the highly humorous comedy **What's a Man Without Moustache?**, Hrvoje Hribar presents amorous intrigues between three couples: the relationships between a young widow and a priest and a female ex-alcoholic and an ageing wealthy widower, recently returned from abroad, run in parallel to another storyline following the widower's daughter, who has grown up abroad, and the local poet, who is also an environmental activist. A further twist occurs with the ongoing manoeuvres of the Croatia army in the town. Grave issues underlie Hribar's highly entertaining film: the relationship to the Church, the army and authority in general, as well as the inherited patriarchal mentality hindering the development of smaller communities located in the magnificent, yet impoverished provincial landscape, which lend an intricate insight into one specific segment of modern Croatian society. Hribar created an unprecedented scandal at Pula by declaring only hours before the premiere that the film would not be screened because of technical post-production problems.

Two other films deservedly shared most of the other numerous awards at Pula: Dejan Sorak's film **Two Players from the Bench** also deals with contemporary issues: exposing the state's

Dejan Sorak's **Two Players from the Bench**

Ivan Maloca/Inter Film/HRT. Uneven but in some sequences very original and amusing directorial debut of a well-known actor. In a remote village certain characteristics of today's Croatian society are revealed in grotesque situations.

DVA IGRACA S KLUPE
(**Two Players from the Bench**)
[Drama, 2005] Script and Dir: Dejan Sorak. Phot: Vjekoslav Vrdoljak. Players: Goran Navojec, Borko Peric, Tarik Filipovic, Dora Lipovcan, Rene Gjoni. Prod: Ivan Maloca/Inter Film/HRT/Maj Film.

Sleep Sweet, My Darling

SNIVAJ, ZLATO MOJE
(**Sleep Sweet, My Darling**)
[Sentimental comedy, 2005] Script: Hrvoje Hitrec. Dir: Neven Hitrec. Phot: Stanko Herceg. Players: Ljubomir Kerekes, Ivan Glowatzky, Ines Bojanic, Alan Malnar, Frank Kos, Vlatko Dulic. Prod: Ivan Maloca/Inter Film/HRT.

STO JE IVA SNIMILA 21.LISTOPADA 2003. (What Iva Recorded on October 21st 2003)
[Drama, 2005] Script: Ognjen Svilicic, Tomislav Radic. Dir: Radic. Phot: Vedran Samanovic. Players: Anja Sovagovic, Ivo Gregurevic, Boris Svrtan, Masha Mati Prodan, Barbara Prpic. Prod: Korugva/HRT.

STO JE MUSKARAC BEZ BRKOVA? (What's a Man Without Moustache?)
[Romantic comedy, 2005] Script: Hrvoje Hribar, based on the novel by Ante Tomic (co-writers: Tomic, Ivica Ivanisevic, Renato Baretic). Dir: Hribar. Phot: Silvio Jesenkovic. Players: Leon Lucev,

Zrinka Cvitesic, Ivo Gregurevic, Bojan Navojec, Jelena Lopatic. Prod: Hrvoje Hribar/Mirko Galic/FIZ/ HRT/HFS.

LIBERTAS
[Historical drama, forthcoming]
Script: Mirko Kovac, Ivo Bresan, Feda Sehovic, Veljko Bulajic. Dir: Bulajic. Players: Sven Medvesek, Livio Badurina, Sandra Ceccarelli, Goran Grgic, Radko Polic. Prod: Libertas/Tuna Film/HRT/RAI TV, DDC Film (Italy).

KARAULA (The Blockhouse)
[Comedy-drama, forthcoming]
Script: Ante Tomic and Rajko Grlic, based on the novel by Ante Tomic. Dir: Grlic. Phot: Slobodan Trninic. Players: Toni Gojanovic, Sergej Trifunovic, Emir Hadzihafizbegovic, Bogdan Diklic, Verica Nedeska–Trajkova. Prod: Ademir Kenovic/Refresh Productions (Bosnia and Herzegovina)/Boris T. Matic/Propeler Film (Croatia)/ Vladimir Anastasov/Sektor Film (Macedonia)/Zoran Cvijanovic/ Milko Josifov/Yodi Movie Craftsman (Serbia and Montenegro)/Franz Novotny/ Novotny & Novotny Filmproduktion (Austria)/Thierry Lenouvel/Ciné-Sud Promotion (France)/Mike Downey/ Film & Music Entertainment (United Kingdom).

Quote of the Year

"There are so many books and movies about the downfall of Yugoslavia, but so little is said about the [previous] years. Who were these men who would transform themselves into murderers, refugees, victims? My movie [confronts] this period, these men."
RAJKO GRLIC, director, on his movie The Blockhouse.

hypocritical position regarding the International War Crimes Court in The Hague and the way in which those in power manipulate ordinary people. It is equally critical of the way international organisations treat a small country. The protagonists, the Croat Ante and the Serb Dusko, who fought on opposite sides during the war in the early 1990s, are seized by the Croatian secret service because they resemble two missing soldiers, who could prove the innocence of a general wanted for trial in The Hague.

Despite initial mutual animosity and a refusal to accept the assignment, threats and promises of a high reward soon change their minds. Sorak displays great skill in blending a comedy with a thriller: his only false step is the introduction of a love story between the Croat and a Ukrainian girl forced into prostitution by the local mafia. It adds several valid issues to the debate, but causes a loss of rhythm halfway through the film.

Neven Hitrec's **Sleep Sweet, My Darling**, which received the Audience Award at Pula, verged on greatness. It opens in the suburbs of Zagreb on the days before and after the end of the Second World War. The protagonists are a young boy and two girls whose day-to-day life includes a series of clearly profiled adults as seen through the eyes of the children. Hitrec succeeds in reawakening the atmosphere of this dramatic period through tragic and comic scenes, nostalgia and sincere emotions. He almost succeeds in doing the same in the second half, which shows the same protagonists in the same place 12 years later, this time as young adults witnessing the first signs of the decline of the rigid communist regime. However, the film's overall achievement is marred by an unconvincing ending.

That four of the six films produced in the last year were impressive represents an above-average achievement, but does not ease the prevailing anxiety about the future of the Croatian film industry, caused by ever-decreasing financial support, the absence of a law on cinema and the failure to grasp co-production opportunities with other European countries. The greatest hope resides in the vitality and ingenuity of Croatian film-makers under such trying circumstances.

TOMISLAV KURELEC (tomislav.kurelec@hrt.hr) has been a film critic since 1965, mostly on radio and television. He has directed five short films and many television items.

Cuba Luciano Castillo and Alberto Ramos

The Year's Best Films

Luciano Castillo and Alberto
Ramos' selection:
Viva Cuba (Juan C. Cremata)
deMolish
(Docu. Alejandro Ramírez)
Havana Blues
(Benito Zambrano)
Out of League
(Docu. Ián Padrón)
Fruits in the Coffee
(Humberto Padrón)

Recent and Forthcoming Films

VIVA CUBA

*[Comedy-Drama, 2004] Script:
Manolo Rodríguez, Juan C.
Cremata. Dir: Cremata. Phot:
Alejandro Pérez. Players: Malú
Tarrau, Jorgito Miló, Larisa
Vega. Prod: QUAD Productions
(France)/Casa Productora de la
Televisión Cubana/La Colmenita/
El Ingenio.*
Two kids try to save their
friendship, threatened by their
parents' opposing stands towards
the Cuban Revolution.

MATA, QUE DIOS PERDONA
(Kill, as God Forgives)

*[Thriller, 2005] Script and Dir:
Ismael Perdomo. Phot: Rafael
Solís. Players: Broselianda
Hernández, Cheryl Zaldívar,
Jorge Alí. Prod: Tercer Piso
Films/River Films (Mexico).*
Two women get involved in
a murder.

BARRIO CUBA
(Neighbourhood Cuba)

*[Drama, 2004] Script: Humberto
Solás, Elia Solás, Sergio
Benvenuto. Dir: Humberto Solás.
Phot: Rafael Solís. Players: Jorge*

The anthology shot by three debutants, *Three Times Two* (see *IFG 2005*), has paved the way for young directors involved in a handful of feature projects sheltered by the Film Institute (ICAIC) or seeking independent support. Six out of nine forthcoming films were shot on DV, offering minimal financial risk. New names include Pavel Giroud, Leonardo Pérez, Ismael Perdomo, Jorge Luis Sánchez (a prominent figure in the 1980s amateur avant garde) and Alejandro Brugués.

Simultaneously, works-in-progress from masters Humberto Solás and Fernando Pérez gave the industry symbolic continuity. Solás, presented with the National Prize of Cinema in March 2005, has completed **Barrio Cuba** (literally, *Neighbourhood Cuba*; formerly titled *Gente de pueblo*), a polyphonic take on contemporary life in Havana. Pérez has begun his long-awaited **Madrigal**, a second-chances tale of a young, spoiled couple. Animation is also gaining momentum after the introduction of digital design facilities at ICAIC. Add a growing interest in co-production from TV companies, the launch of a new TV studio and extended teaching at the San Antonio de los Baños Film School (EICTV) and everything points to 2006 as a crucial year for national cinema.

The year's event has been **Viva Cuba**, Juan Carlos Cremata's second feature, which became a hit at home (more than 500,000 admissions). It is a spirited, funny and affectionate road movie giving children a voice on Cubans' harrowing, longstanding dilemma: homeland versus exile. The odyssey of two runaway kids challenging their parents' disregard for individual aspiration in the name of political obstinacy highlights a disturbing generation gap. Cremata's screenplay was surprisingly taken up by television after ICAIC turned it down, a decision in line with the institute's move away from politically sensitive issues such as emigration towards a cinema of gender, race and cultural identity, hence the trend towards ICAIC-backed musicals and period pieces.

Life at the margins

Young directors working outside or on the margins of the state-run industry insist on more inquisitive visions. The gloomy, seedy realism of Enrique Colina's *Hurricanes* (2003) was picked up in three new features. Humberto Padrón's **Fruits in the Coffee** (*Frutas en el café*)

Isabel Santos in **Barrio Cuba**

*Perugorría, Isabel Santos, Rafael
Lahera, Adela Legrá. Prod:
ICAIC/FINE Productions (Spain).*

DIVINA DESMESURA
(**Divine Greatness**)
*[Musical-biopic, 2005] Script:
Abrahán Rodríguez, Jorge L.
Sánchez. Dir: Sánchez. Phot:
José M. Riera. Players: Renny
Arozarena, Enrique Molina,
Carlos E. Fonseca. Prod:
ICAIC/Coral Capital
Entertainment Ltd. (UK).*
The rise and fall of Cuban pop
star Benny Moré.

H2O
*[Comedy, 2005] Script: Anna
Assenza, Leonardo Pérez. Dir:
Pérez. Phot: Fabrizio
LaPalombara. Players: Jorge Alí,
Luis A. García.*
Luis invents a fantastic device
that could provide the South with
drinking water.

LA PARED (The Wall)
*[Drama, 2005] Script and Dir:
Alejandro Gil. Phot: Rigoberto
Senarega. Players: Héctor E.
Suárez, Aramís Delgado,
Amarilys Núñez. Prod: Gricel
González/ ICAIC.*

LA EDAD DE LA PESETA
(**The Age of the Coin**)
*[Drama, 2005] Script: Arturo
Infante. Dir: Pavel Giroud. Phot:
Luis Najmías. Players: Mercedes
Sampietro, Iván Carreiras,
Susana Tejera. Prod: ICAIC/
Mediapro (Spain)/Alter.
Producciones (Venezuela).*
A surprising complicity brings an
old lady and her grandson closer.

is an episodic, circular story of present-day Havana, depicting a
frenzied mix of underground, intellectual and ordinary lives. Ismael
Perdomo's Perdomo's debut, **Mata, que Dios perdona** (literally, *Kill,
as God Forgives*), is a thriller with an extreme, convoluted narrative,
set on January 8, 1959, the day the rebel army arrived triumphantly in
Havana, with an ironic focus on the trashiest, least redeemable side of
society. In **Havana Blues**, by EICTV-trained Spaniard Benito
Zambrano, fits of disenchanted humour and verbal violence punctuate
the agonising journey of two young musicians.

Derived from a United Nations project, Guatemalan Alejandro
Ramírez's documentary **deMolish** (*deMoler*) is a brief, intimate elegy
for the passing of a beloved Cuban icon. It deals with the impact on
workers and neighbours when a sugar mill is demolished. Ián
Padrón's controversial **Out of League** (*Fuera de liga*, 2002), a closely
observed portrait of Cuba's legendary baseball team, Industriales, as
told by stars, managers and fans, delivers a gripping statement on the
connections between sport, politics and mass communication. Its
interviews with exiled stars were presumably the main reason for the
film being banned, although it thrived via a proficient underground
video network. With the brief **Extravagant Beings** (*Seres
extravagantes*), EICTV graduate Manuel Zayas delivered a more
rigorous approach to the late Cuban writer Reinaldo Arenas than
Julian Schnabel in the self-indulgent, spurious biopic, *Before Night
Falls*, winning two international festival awards for this detached,
compelling reconstruction. Finally, the documentary essay **I'm Cuba,
the Siberian Mammoth** (*Soy Cuba, el mamut siberiano*), by Brazilian
Vicente Ferraz, made an inestimable contribution to Cuban cinema
history. Its infamous subject was a film *maudit:* Mikhail Kalatozov's
reviled then revered *I'm Cuba* (1964), a monumental and daring
experiment in cross-cultural dialogue.

LUCIANO CASTILLO (lcastillo@eictv.org) is a film critic and
scholar, director of the mediatheque at EICTV, Havana, and editor-
in-chief of *Cine Cubano* magazine.
ALBERTO RAMOS (arzhabana@cocc.co.cu) is a film critic and
editor of *ECOS* magazine.

Iván Carreiras and Mercedes Sampietro in **The Age of the Coin**

Czech Republic Eva Zaoralová

The Years Best Films

Eva Zaoralová's selection:
Something Like Happiness
(Bohdan Sláma)
Wrong Side Up (Petr Zelenka)
The City of the Sun
(Martin Sulík)
Papa (Jan Sverák)
Looking for Ester
(Vera Chytilová)

Recent and Forthcoming Films

KOUSEK NEBE
(A Little Piece of Heaven)
[Romantic drama, 2005] Script: Jirí Stránsky, based on his own novel. Dir: Petr Nikolaev. Phot: Martin Duba. Players: Jakub Doubrava, Tána Pauhofová, Petr Forman, Zuzana Stivínová. Prod: Premysl Prazsky/Luxor.

KREV ZMIZELÉHO
(Bonds of Blood)
[Period drama, 2005] Script: Vladimír Koerner, Milan Cieslar, Dir: Cieslar. Phot: Jirí Macháne. Players: Václav Jirácek, Radoslav Brzbohaty, Anna Cónová, Vilma Cibulková, Ester Geislerová. Prod: Milan Ciselar/Happy Celluloid/ Czech TV.

MILENCI A VRAZI
(Lovers and Murderers)
[Comedy-drama, 2004] Script: Viktor Polesny, Petr Polednák, based on the novel by Vladimír Páral. Dir: Viktor Polesny. Phot: Josef Spelda. Players: Jirí Langmajer, Jan Vlasák, Zlata Adamovská, Jakub Prachar, Kristina Koubková, Ondrej Vetchy. Prod: Filip Cervinka/ Arva/Czech TV.

In autumn 2005, the Czech film industry was still awaiting an amendment to the audiovisual law, which would increase state support for film production. The main obstacle to its approval by parliament remained the proposed tax on DVD and video sales, opposed by the producers' lobby. In 2004, average monthly cinema attendance fell by 9.5% year on year, while ticket prices rose slightly. Nevertheless, 17 feature films from 2004 competed for the annual Czech Lion awards in March 2005, which, in view of Czech population, is no paltry figure. As expected, many Lions were carried away by the bittersweet comedy by Jan Hrebejk, **Up and Down** (*Horem pádem*), a mosaic of satirical perspectives on contemporary society, which was one of the year's most popular Czech films and also the most highly regarded by local critics.

Life, or *Something Like…*

Although 2004 was so productive, Czech cinema had to wait until September 2005 before it saw any significant festival successes, when the Golden Shell at San Sebastian went to Bohdan Sláma's **Something Like Happiness** (*Stesti*) and the Silver Shell for Best Actress to its star, Ana Geisler (in 2002 Slama's *Wild Bees*/Divoké vcely was victorious at Rotterdam and several other festivals). Slama here portrays relationships between young people in a border town, living without any prospects for the future. He combines tragic elements with a dose of humour and his film is the most serious candidate for the Czech Lions for 2005 and an Oscar nomination.

Something Like Happiness was not the only film to emphasise its characters' psychology within a clearly defined social context. The relatively skilled adaptation of the 1970s bestselling novel by Vladimír Páral, **Lovers and Murderers** (*Milenci a vrazi*), develops in a similar spirit. Directed by Viktor Polesny, it interweaves the lives of several inhabitants of a provincial town, who fulfil their unrealised ambitions through sex. Petr Nikolaev, for his second film, **A Little Piece of Heaven** (*Kousek nebe*), also chose a literary model. The book's author, Jirí Stránsky, in his story about the love of two young people kindled under curious circumstances in a communist prison, wrote from his own experiences.

Milan Cieslar in the drama **Bonds of Blood** (*Krev zmizelého*) traces the development of his characters from the Second World War to the

NON PLUS ULTRAS
[Comedy, 2004] Script: Jiří Popel.
Dir: Jakub Sluka. Phot: Jakub
Dvorsky. Players: Vladimír
Dlouhy, David Novotny, Karel
Zima, Matej Hádek, Michal
Novotny, Oldrich Kaiser. Prod:
Lajka Film.

PÁTRÁNÍ PO ESTER
(Searching for Ester)
[Documentary, 2005] Script and
Dir: Vera Chytilová, Phot: David
Cálek. Prod: Bionaut Films/
Czech TV.
The life and the artistic activity
of Ester Krumbachová, one of
the leading persons of the Czech
nouvelle vague.

PRÍBEHY OBYCEJNÉHO
SÍLENSTVÍ (Wrong Side Up)
[Dark comedy, 2005] Script and
Dir: Petr Zelenka. Phot: Miro
Gábor. Players: Ivan Trojan,
Nina Divísková, Miroslav
Krobot, Zuzana Sulajová, Karel
Hermánek, Jiří Bartoska. Prod:
Negativ/Ceska produkcní/
SisaArt/Pegasos Film Verleih und
Produktion (Germany).

ROMÁN PRO ZENY
(From Subway With Love)
[Comedy, 2005] Script: Michal
Viewegh, based on his own novel.
Dir: Filip Renc. Phot: Petr Hojda.
Players: Zuzana Kanóczová,
Marek Vasut, Simona Stasová,
Miroslav Donutil. Prod: Ceska
produkcní 2000.

SAMETOVÍ VRAZI
(The New Breed)
[Crime thriller, 2005] Script and
Dir: Jiří Svoboda. Phot: Martin
Sácha. Players: Michal Dlouhy,
Jan Dolansky, Richard Krajco,
Alice Veselá, Lucie Benesová,
Dusan Urban. Prod: Czech
TV/Studio Ostrava.

Lucie Benesová and Michal Dlouhy
in **The New Breed**

1950s, set against the background of the historical transformation of
the Czech–German border regions. The crime thriller **The New Breed**
(*Sametoví vrazi*), set in recent times, is based on a real-life contract
killing, in which director Jiří Svoboda, a representative of the
generation now in their 50s, highlights more the motivation for crimes
than the depiction of the acts themselves. In the Czech–Slovak co-
production **The City of the Sun** (*Slunecní stát*), distinguished Slovak
film-maker Martin Sulík abandoned his characteristic, poetic magic
realism to recount a harsh tale of four unemployed men and their
families in multi-ethnic Ostrava, a Silesian mining town.

Riding the comedy wave

The films mentioned above attracted more attention from critics than
audiences, who flocked, as usual, to domestic comedy. The debut by
Karel Janák, **Snowboarders** (*Snowboard'áci*), became a true teen
cult with its laid-back story about two schoolboys enjoying the
mountains. Both actors – Vojta Kotek and Jiří Mádl – instantly became
the idols of Czech schoolgirls, and the film's success immediately
prompted Janák to embark upon another comedy with them, **Rafters**
(*Raft'áci*), where both heroes experience new adventures during a
summer spent skimming down the river.

Vojta Kotek, left, and Jiri Madl became overnight stars in **Snowboarders**

Women from the slightly older generation, in particular, enjoyed
experienced Filip Renc's comedy **From Subway With Love**
(*Román pro zeny*), about the amorous exploits of a mother and
daughter. It was based on the eponymous novel by easily the most
widely read contemporary Czech writer, Michal Viewegh. The black
comedy by Petr Zelenka, **Wrong Side Up** (*Príbehy obycejného*
sílenstvi), is unquestionably one of the most remarkable films of
2005, an adaptation of the author's highly successful stage play.
Like his debut, **Buttoners** (*Knoflíkári*, 1997), it speaks of the
somewhat indefinable and uncontrollable swings of the human
mind, manifested, above all, in intimate relationships.

The fragile border between "rational deviation" and so-called normality was also examined in the feature debut by young Marie Procházková, who had previously to achieved success in animation. Her **Shark in the Head** (*Zralok v hlave*) is an original portrait of an eccentric, middle-aged man (brilliantly portrayed by one of the most popular Czech actors, Old_ich Kaiser), who embarrasses those around him with his genial interest in everything going on outside the windows of his ground-floor flat. Procházková, granddaughter of a famous writer from the 1960s, Jan Procházka, used animation for the protagonist's visions and dreams. **Non plus ultras** is another noteworthy debut, in which Jakub Sluka uses humour to present young football fans who no longer indulge in hooliganism with their former verve.

There were mixed reviews and only a limited audience for the outlandish thriller, with elements of black comedy, **Vaterland – A Hunting Logbook** (*Vaterland – lovecky deník*), made by surrealism-oriented stage director David Jarab. Another debut, awaiting release at press time, is the social tale **The Indian and the Nurse** (*Indián a sest_i_ka*), in which young Dan Wlodarczyk describes relationships between the Romany community and the "whites".

A master's return

Before 2005 drew to a close, world-famous master of animation Jan Svankmajer was due to present **Lunacy** (*Síleni*), a philosophical horror set at the beginning of the nineteenth century, and freely inspired by two stories by Edgar Allen Poe. The next film by the makers of the controversial but critically acclaimed *Bored in Brno* (*Nuda v Brne*, 2003) will probably also generate considerable interest. Early reports on *Hrubes and Mares Are Best Friends – Come Rain, Come Shine* (*Hrubes a Mares jsou kamarádi do deste*) suggest that it would be even more provocative in its negation of film-making conventions.

Also worthy of note are several documentaries for which a system of DVD cinema distribution has finally been established. After the fictional documentary *Czech Dream* (*Cesky sen*, 2004), which made its mark at many foreign film festivals, director Erika Hníková presented **The Beauty Exchange** (*Zeny pro meny*), a series of interviews with women who surrender to ubiquitous advertising and allow themselves to be influenced by the ideals of the "perfect body", sacrificing everything they earn for the cult of beauty.

The charming documentary by Jan Sverák and Martin Dostál, **Papa** (*Tatínek*), spotlighting Zdenek Sverák, the screenwriter of all Jan Sverák's films, including the Oscar-winning *Kolya* (1996), and the lead player in most of them, is conceived as a kindly look behind the scenes of his creative and private lives. Renowned director Vera Chytilová endeavours in her documentary **Searching for Ester** (*Pátrání po Ester*) to capture her close friend and

SLUNECNÍ STÁT
(**The City of the Sun**)
[Comedy-drama, 2005] Script: Martin Sulík, Marek Lescák. Dir: Sulík. Phot: Martin Strba. Players: Oldrich Navrátil, Ivan Martinka, Lubomír Kostelny, Igor Bares, Anna Cónová, Petra Spalková, Anna Sisková. Prod: První verejnoprávní/ Czech TV/Studio Ostrava.

SNOWBORD'ÁCI
(**Snowboarders**)
[Comedy, 2004] Script and Dir: Karel Janák. Phot: Martin Sácha. Players: Vojta Kotek, Jirí Mádl, Ester Geislerová, Jiří Langmajer, Pavla Tomicová. Prod: Whisconti/ Czech TV/Cská produkce.

SÍLENÍ (**Lunacy**)
[Philosophical horror, 2005] Script and Dir: Jan Svankmajer. Phot: Juraj Galvánek. Players: Pavel Liska, Jan Tríska, Ana Geislerová, Pavel Novym Jaroslav Dusek. Prod: Athanor/ Czech TV.

ST'ESTÍ
(**Something Like Happiness**)
[Drama, 2005] Script and Dir: Bohdan Sláma. Phot: Divis Marek. Players: Tatiana Wilhelmová, Pavel Liska, Ana Geislerová, Marek Daniel, Zuzana Krónerová, Bolek Polívka, Simona Stasová, Martin Huba. Prod: Negativ/Czech TV/ Pallas Films.

Tatiana Wilhelmová in **Something Like Happiness**

TATÍNEK (**Papa**)
[Documentary, 2004] Script and Dir: Martin Dostál, Jan Sverák. Phot: Ivan Zachariás, Radka Splíchalová. Prod: Biograf Jan Sverák/Czech TV.

VATERLAND – LOVECKY
DENÍK (Vaterland –
A Hunting Logbook)
[Fantasy comedy-drama, 2004]
Script and Dir: David Jarab.
Phot: Marek Jícha. Players:
Karel Roden, Frantisek Rehák,
Petr Forman, Júlio Martin de
Fonseca, José Figueiredo, Vasil
Fridrich. Prod: Cineart TV
Prague/Czech TV/UPP/
Ateliéry Bonton Zlín.

ZENY PRO MENY
(The Beauty Exchange)
[Documentary, 2004] Script and
Dir: Erika Hníková. Phot: Marek
Janda. Prod: Endorfilm.

colleague Ester Krumbachová (1923–1996) in all her professional and human complexities.

EVA ZAORALOVÁ (zaoralova@kviff.com) is Artistic Director of the Karlovy Vary International Film Festival, editor of *Film a doba* magazine and author of books on Czech, French and Italian cinema.

Ivan Trojan, left, and Jiri Bartoska in **Wrong Side Up**

Kobal

RICHARD PRYOR gets to grips with Erland van Lidth de Jeude in **Stir Crazy** *(1980), the best of the comedies that paired this hugely influential comedian with Gene Wilder. Pryor, whose brilliance as a stand-up comic is preserved in several films, including* Richard Pryor Live on the Sunset Strip *(1982), died on December 10, 2005, aged 65.*

Denmark Jacob Neiiendam

The Year's Best Films

Jacob Neiiendam's selection:
Adam's Apples
(Anders Thomas Jensen)
Manslaughter (Per Fly)
Dark Horse (Dagur Kari)
Manderlay (Lars von Trier)
Allegro (Christoffer Boe)

Recent and Forthcoming Films

SOLKONGEN (The Sun King)
[Comedy, 2005] Script: Anders Thomas Jensen, Tomas Villum Jensen. Dir: Villum Jensen. Phot: Jacob Kusk. Players: Nikolaj Lie Kaas, Birthe Neumann, Thomas Bo Larsen, Niels Olsen, Peter Gantzler. Prod: Michael Obel, Carsten Holst, Thura Film.

NORDKRAFT (Angels in Fast Motion)
[Drama, 2005] Script: Ole Christian Madsen, Bo hr. Hansen, based on a novel by Jacob Ejersbo. Dir: Madsen. Phot: Jørgen Johansson. Players: Signe Egholm Olsen, Thomas L. Corneliussen, Claus Riis Østergaard, Thure Lindhardt. Prod: Meta Louise Foldager, Morten Kaufmann, Nimbus Film.

KINAMAND (Chinaman)
[Comedy-drama, 2005] Script: Kim Fupz Aakeson. Dir: Henrik Ruben Genz. Players: Bjarne Henriksen, Vivian Wu, Charlotte Fich, Paw Henriksen, Johan Rabeus. Prod: Thomas Gammeltoft, Fine & Mellow Productions.

ADAMS ÆBLER (Adam's Apples)
[Black comedy, 2005] Script and Dir: Anders Thomas Jensen.

While solid government funding and a good local market share continue to be the order of the day in the Danish film industry, the much-envied drive and success of recent years seem to be winding down. As has been the case since 1999, the revival year for Danish film, 2004 saw several local films in the box-office top 10. Nikolaj Arcel's political thriller, *King's Game*, was the strongest contender, behind only *Harry Potter* and *Lord of the Rings*. The other three top 10 entries were the family film *My Sister's Kids in Egypt*, Susanne Bier's drama *Brothers* and the anarchistic animation *Terkel in Trouble*. In total, the box-office gross increased slightly to €7.5m, but the local market share dropped 2% to 24%, not least because of a drop in the number of domestic releases in 2004, from 24 to 19.

Apart from *Brothers*, however, most new Danish films failed to perform well internationally. Denmark was represented at major festivals in 2005, by Jacob Thuesen's *Accused* in competition in Berlin; Lars von Trier's *Manderlay* and Dagur Kari's *Dark Horse* at Cannes and Un Certain Regard respectively; and Christoffer Boe's *Allegro* at Venice. However, substantial critical or commercial success failed to materialise. This would be less of a problem if local audiences had embraced the films, but in fact they did not.

The more the merrier?

With the total of new domestic releases back up to 29 in 2005, competition has been more intense than ever. The year got off to a great start when more than a million tickets for Danish films were sold in the first two months, a figure normally not reached until May. However, only three films did well: Carsten Myllerup's family film **Oskar & Josefine**, based on a popular TV series, Tomas Villum Jensen's broad comedy **The Sun King** (*Solkongen*), about a dim young guy who falls in love with a rich woman old enough to be his mother, and Ole Christian Madsen's **Angels in Fast Motion** (*Nordkraft*), based on a *Trainspotting*-like bestseller about urban youths.

A number of other films fell through the cracks, among them the aforementioned A-festival contenders. In **Accused** (*Angeklaget*), editor-turned-film-maker Jacob Thuesen displayed impressive technical craft in a psychological drama about a popular family man

Phot: Sebastian Blenkov. Players: Mads Mikkelsen, Ulrich Thomsen, Paprika Steen, Nicolas Bro, Ole Thestrup. Prod: Tivi Magnusson, Mie Andreasen, M&M Productions.

VOKSNE MENNESKER
(Dark Horse)
[Black comedy, 2005] Script: Rune Schjøtt, Dagur Kári. Dir: Kári. Phot: Manuel Alberto Claro. Players: Jakob Cedergren, Nicolas Bro, Tilly Scott Pedersen, Morten Suurballe. Prod: Birgitte Skov, Morten Kaufmann, Nimbus Film.

MANDERLAY
[Drama, 2005] Script and Dir: Lars von Trier. Phot: Anthony Dod Mantle. Players: Bryce Dallas Howard, Isaach De Bankole, Danny Glover, Willem Dafoe. Prod: Vibeke Windeløv, Zentropa Entertainments 13.

FLUERNE PÅ VÆGGEN
(Flies on the Wall)
[Political thriller, 2005] Script and Dir: Åke Sandgren. Players: Trine Dyrholm, Lars Brygmann, Kurt Ravn, Henrik Prip. Prod: Thomas Heinesen, Nordisk Film Production.

PUSHER III (I'm the Angel of Death – Pusher III)
[Crime drama, 2005] Script and Dir: Nicolas Winding Refn. Phot: Morten Søborg. Players: Zlatko Buric, Slavko Labovic. Prod: Henrik Danstrup, NWR Productions.

DRABET (Manslaughter)
[Drama, 2005] Script: Kim Leona, Per Fly, Dorte Høegh, Mogens Rukov. Dir: Fly. Phot: Harald Paalgard. Players: Jesper Christensen, Beate Bille, Charlotte Fich, Pernilla August. Prod: Ib Tardini, Zentropa Entertainments 12.

ALLEGRO
[Drama, 2005] Script: Christoffer Boe, Mikael Wulff. Dir: Boe. Phot: Manuel Claro. Players: Ulrich Thomsen, Henning Moritzen, Helena Christensen,

suddenly accused of sexually abusing his daughter. However, the script seemed too contrived and left many disappointed.

Icelandic-born Dagur Kari's first Danish-language feature, **Dark Horse** (Voksne mennesker), almost came a cropper, but it served up enough magical moments of sweet offbeat black comedy to counter its script problems. It follows a young graffiti artist, who's having a hard time adjusting to the fact that he's supposed to be a grown-up. Beautifully shot in black and white, with wonderful performances, the director's follow-up to festival favourite Noi Albinoi failed at the box-office, but has the making of, and deserves to become, a cult classic. It's possible the same might happen to Christoffer Boe's science-fiction drama **Allegro**, about a pianist (Ulrich Thomsen) in search of his memories. The film confirmed Boe as a bold, original and skilful visual storyteller, but ultimately failed to live up to the expectations set by his multiple award-winning debut, Reconstruction.

Helena Christensen and Ulrich Thomsen in **Allegro**

Acclaimed maverick Lars von Trier had the dubious distinction of having written two of the biggest box-office disappointments: his own highly anticipated follow-up to Dogville, **Manderlay**, and Dear Wendy, which was directed by Dogme-brother Thomas Vinterberg. Aside from the fact that they had cost three times as much as most Danish-language films, they confirmed the trend of recent years, which has seen local audiences ignoring 'Danish' films in English. Neither is without artistic merit, but both suffer from being too similar to Trier's more accomplished Dogville. In **Dear Wendy** two very different film-making styles – the calculating von Trier and the sensitive Vinterberg – failed to find a common language in the story of young pacifists with a fatal fascination with guns.

Despite Manderlay's brilliantly provocative script about slavery, equality, oppression and free will, the fact that Trier for the first time seemed to be repeating himself (at least visually) turned many off, and even the rave reviews could do nothing to convince local audiences to care for his take on the politics of 2005.

One film that deserved all its ample box-office and critical success was **Adam's Apples** (*Adams æbler*), Anders Thomas Jensen's third feature as writer–director. It seemed impossible that someone could pull off a black comedy about a neo-Nazi (Ulrich Thomsen) and a priest (Mads Mikkelsen), based on the "Book of Job", but Jensen's original, hilarious and thought-provoking film managed to gather together all of the humor and seriousness that he had previously shown in smaller quantities in his many scripts.

Mads Mikkelsen, left, and Ulrich Thomsen in **Adam's Apples**

Back to basics

The only good to come out of von Trier's lack of box-office draw in 2005 was his and Vinterberg's decision to return to lower-budget Danish-language projects, something neither has done since their 1998 Dogme hits *The Idiots* and *Festen*. Postponing the third instalment of his USA trilogy, *Washington*, von Trier is set to shoot the comedy *The Manager of it All*, which takes place in the world of trade and industry. At press time, Vinterberg was prepping *A Man Comes Home*, which he calls a tragic love story, but set in an uplifting party environment. Neither will be a strict Dogme film, but both will be shot in the same spirit.

Meanwhile, Lone Scherfig, the director of the most commercially successful Dogme film, *Italian for Beginners*, has been juggling several international projects, but is now also set to return to Danish film-making with *Erik Nietzsche – the Early Years*, a semi-autobiographical script by von Trier about his time at the National Film School.

However, the Dogme fathers' return to their roots does not mean that every new Danish film will be a low-budget digital feature. One happy consequence of the increase in feature production has been the willingness of film-makers to test genres not normally

Nicolas Bro. Prod: *Tine Grew Pfeiffer, AlphaVille Productions Copenhagen.*

Nikolaj Lie Kaas in **Murk**

MØRKE (Murk)
[Thriller, 2005] Script: Anders Thomas Jensen, Jannik Johansen. Dir: Johansen. Phot: Rasmus Videbæk. Players: Nikolaj Lie Kaas, Nicolas Bro, Laura Drasbæk, Lærke Winther Andersen. Prod: Thomas Gammeltoft, Hanne Palmquist, Fine & Mellow Productions.

NYNNE
[Comedy, 2005] Script: Mette Heeno, based on a novel by Henriette Lind, Lotte Thorsen, Anette Vestergaard. Dir: Jonas Elmer. Phot: Niels Reedtz Johansen. Players: Mille Dinesen, Lars Kaalund, Ole Lemmeke, Jimmy Jørgensen, Mette Horn. Prod: Christian E. Christiansen, Lars Feilberg, Angel Production.

DOMMEREN (The Judge)
[Drama, 2005] Script: Mikael Olsen. Dir: Gert Fredholm. Phot: Jørgen Johansson. Players: Peter Gantzler, Micky Skeel Hansen, Benjamin Boe Rasmussen, Nastja Maria Arcel, Heidi Holm Katzenelson. Prod: Mikael Olsen, Zentropa Entertainments 7.

DEN RETTE ÅND (True Spirit)
[Comedy drama, 2005] Script: Flemming Klem, Martin Strange-Hansen. Dir: Strange-Hansen. Phot: Adam Philp. Players: Ken Vedsegaard, Jesper Asholt, Sofie Gråbøl, Laura Bro. Prod: Mie Andreasen, M&M Productions.

1:1
*[Drama, 2005] Script: Kim Fupz
Aakeson. Dir: Annette K.
Olesen. Phot: Kim Høgh.
Players: Joy K. Petersen,
Mohammed-Ali Bakier, Anette
Støvelbæk, Helle Hertz, Subhi
Hassan. Prod: Ib Tardini,
Zentropa Productions.*

EFTER BRYLLUPPET
(After the Wedding)
*[Drama, 2005] Script: Anders
Thomas Jensen. Dir: Susanne
Bier. Phot: ?. Players: Mads
Mikkelsen, Rolf Lassgaard, Sidse
Babett Knudsen. Prod: Sisse
Graum, Zentropa Productions.*

VIKAREN
(*literally,* **The Substitute**)
*[Children's thriller, 2005] Script:
Ole Bornedal, Henrik Prip. Dir:
Bornedal. Phot: Dan Laustsen.
Players: Paprika Steen. Prod:
Michael Obel, Thura Film.*

DE FORTABTE SJÆLES Ø
(The Island of Lost Souls)
*[Children's adventure, 2005]
Script: Rasmus Heisterberg,
Nikolaj Arcel. Dir: Arcel. Phot:
Rasmus Videbæk. Players: Lukas
Munk Billing, Sara Gaarmann,
Lasse Borg. Prod: Sarita
Christensen, Zentropa.*

Quote of the Year

"It's a self-centred, vanity
project, so I chose to resign
from directing. By letting
Lone Scherfig direct, it will
hopefully be a little less
narcissistic."
LARS VON TRIER *on* Erik
Nietzsche – the Early Years.

associated with Danish cinema (although the trend may be short-lived if the films do not perform at the box-office), and several high-profile film-makers seem bent on burying the Dogme label. Ole Bornedal (*Nightwatch*) is finishing *Vikaren*, a science-fiction horror film for kids about a schoolteacher (Paprika Steen) who's really an alien. Nikolaj Arcel (*King's Game*) shot the family action adventure *The Island of Lost Souls* on a massive €5m budget. Nicolas Winding Refn, who made one of 2004's best films, *Pusher 2: With Blood on my Hands*, failed to reach the same heights with 2005's **Pusher 3: I'm the Angel of Death**, and has expressed interest in doing a $5m Viking movie, *Valhalla Rising*.

Nicolas Winding Refn's crime saga concluded in **Pusher 3**

Susanne Bier, whose Dogme drama *Open Hearts* and *Brothers* made her the most commercially successful Danish film-maker at home and abroad, made history when her new film, *After the Wedding*, became the first ever Danish feature to be pre-sold for US distribution. Anders Thomas Jensen wrote this drama, which sees Mads Mikkelsen return to Denmark to attend a wedding that will change his life forever. With or without Dogme as the driving force, Danish film should be able to stay in the international spotlight.

JACOB NEIIENDAM (neiiendam@film.dk) is a Danish film critic and journalist contributing to national and international media. Nordic correspondent for *Screen International* from 1999 to 2005, he is now head of programming at the Copenhagen International Film Festival.

Ecuador Gabriela Alemán

The Year's Best Films

Gabriela Alemán's selection:

Displaced (Short. Allan Jeffs)

Crossfire (Short. Gustavo
Abad and Galo Betancourt)

The Old Years
(Short. Juan Carlos Donoso)

The Duel (Alex Schlenker)

Country at War
(Short. Wilson Burbano)

Recent and Forthcoming Films

EL DUELO (The Duel)
*[Thriller, 2005] Script, Dir and
Phot: Alex Schlenker. Players:
Alejandro Monge, Pablo Velasco,
Ana María Vera, José Abdón
Calderón. Prod: Cooperativa de
Cine "San Elián"/Hasgafilms.*
The story involves a sniper and
the would-be grandson of
Ché Guevara.

ESAS NO SON PENAS
(*literally,* **Those Are Not Sorrows**)
*[Drama, 2005] Script and Dir:
Anahí Hoeneisen. Co-Dir and
Phot: Daniel Andrade. Players:
Amaia Merino, Francisca Romeo,
Paquita Troya, Carolina Valencia,
Anahí Hoeneisen. Prod:
Verónica Andrade.*
The lives of thirty-something
women who were classmates in
high school.

QUE TAN LEJOS (*literally,* **How
Far Are You Willing to Go?**)
*[Road movie, 2005] Script and
Dir: Tania Hermida. Phot:
Armando Salazar. Players: Cecilia
Vallejo, Tania Martínez, Pancho
Aguirre, Fausto Niño, Ricardo
González. Prod: Mary Palacios,
Paula Parrini.*
Two young women meet: a

To understand what happened in Ecuadorian cinema this year, one should trace four converging lines. First came news that Sebastián Cordero (director of the award-winning *Crónicas* in 2004) had become the first Ecuadorian director to accomplish the dream of going to Hollywood. Early in 2006, he was scheduled to shoot a historical thriller, *Manhunt: The 12-Day Chase for Lincoln's Killer*, starring Harrison Ford.

The next line would be the near-approval of a Film Law by Congress; the third would follow the consolidation of the Encuentros del Otro Cine documentary film festival (EDOC) and the Cero Latitud Latin American and Iberian film festival. The last line, the faintest of the four, concerns the public. After the surprising success (seven weeks in theatres) of **Viagra**, a misogynistic comedy full of sexual innuendo, a short-lived debate developed on what Ecuadorian cinema should be. Not much came out of it, except that it brought to attention the wide gap that separates audience reception from production. This needs to be bridged if there is to be any future for the developing industry. The success of Cordero and the possibility of a Film Law have enabled the previously divided film community to bond together and speak out publicly on such topics as the need for a national film board and an Ecuadorian promotion fund that would eventually lead to sustained film output.

EDOC, now in its fourth year, has promoted the exhibition and production of local documentaries. Cero Latitud, in its third edition, has formed a captive audience for a previously unknown cinema and helped to finance Andean production through "Work-in-Progress", a $10,000 post-production award. The festivals have also opened up new exhibition circuits, while the creation of three new awards ("Ojo en la Democracia" and "Padre Crespi", for documentary, and the "Violencia Cotidiana", with experimental, fiction and documentary categories), has led to a boom in the production of shorts.

Allan Jeffs' *Displaced* is an excellent three-minute animation-told-as-parable of war-torn Colombian refugees arriving in Ecuador's urban centres. Gustavo Abad and Galo Betancourt's *Crossfire*, an enormously powerful short with hardly any dialogue, follows a teenager who earns his living by spitting fire on street corners at night. Juan Carlos Donoso's playful *The Old Years* takes the point of view of an infant slowly coming to terms with the world around

Anahí Hoeneisen's **Esas no son penas**

Spanish tourist and an
Ecuadorian in search of hope.

TU SANGRE
(*literally,* **Your Blood**)
*[Documentary, 2005] Script, Dir
and Phot: Julián Larrea. Prod:
Tania Laurini.*
How long does a jungle election
count take when votes arrive by
canoe and bus?

DEMOCRACIA 25 AÑOS
(**25 Years of Democracy**)
*[Documentary, 2005] Script:
Manolo Sarmiento, Felipe
Terán, Andrés Barriga. Dir and
Phot: Andrés Barriga. Prod:
Polo Barriga/Odysea
Producciones Culturales.*

**ECUADOR VS. EL RESTO DEL
MUNDO** (*literally,* **Ecuador vs.
The Rest of the World**)
*[Documentary, 2005] Script:
Amaia Merino, Pablo
Mogrovejo. Dir: Mogrovejo.
Phot: Pepe Yépez, Simón Brauer,
Armando Salazar, Filippo
Burbano, Diego Araujo, Diego
Falconí, Pablo Mogrovejo. Prod:
Vista de Ojos Films/William
Chicha Producciones/Gato
Tuerto Producciones.*
Ecuador vs. Uruguay in
November 2001. Will Ecuador
reach its first World Cup Finals?
How do Ecuadorians overseas
experience this moment?

VIAGRA
*[Comedy, 2005] Script: Ramón
Serrano, Alfredo Cuesta, Ma.
Elena Vega. Dir: Cuesta. Players:
Napoleón Soria, Ana María
Valarezo, Gabriela Sánchez.
Prod: Ma. Elena Vega.*
After a 25-year marriage, a
couple renew their vows and take
a second honeymoon.

him. The allegorical *Country at War* recreates the world as a no-
man's-land of conflict and chaos.

Women on top

Two women have made their mark with new features. Anahí
Hoeneisen's **Esas no son penas** (literally, *Those Are Not Sorrows*)
was accepted in the "Cine en Construcción" category at San
Sebastián, and Tania Hermida's **Que tan lejos** (literally, *How Far Are
You Willing to Go?*) won the "Work-in-Progress" prize at Cero
Latitud. Both films sparked debate by exploring the mores of
contemporary middle-class women. Alex Schlenker's **The Duel**
(*El duelo*) is a welcome anomaly, an experimental feature partly shot
with a Super 8 camera, in black and white.

Two young women meet on the road in Tania Hermida's **Que tan lejos**

At EDOC there were many notable film-makers as guests, giving
lectures, workshops and masterclasses (including Patricio Guzmán,
Albert Maysles and Fernando Solanas). The breadth of EDOC's
programme has created a more conducive environment for
documentary production. The four feature documentaries produced
this year all have complex montage structures and are the result of
thorough investigative work and pre-production. **Ecuador vs. The
Rest of the World** (*Ecuador vs. el resto del mundo*) was all shot in
one day, November 7, 2001, in different cities and countries. **Tu
Sangre** (literally, *Your Blood*) follows a long election campaign trail in
the Amazon jungle. **25 Years of Democracy** (*Democracia 25 años*)
orchestrates interviews with several Ecuadorian presidents (some in
forced exile) and archival material rescued from TV vaults. Mateo
Herrera and François Laso, respectively the director and cameraman
on **The Committee** (*El comite*), were live witnesses (and hostages) of
a prison revolt. Documentaries came a long way in 2005.

GABRIELA ALEMÁN (gabrielaa@usfq.edu.ec) is a journalist with a
PhD from Tulane University, where she specialised in Latin American
film. She lectures at the universities of USFQ and Andina in Ecuador.

Egypt Fawzi Soliman

The Year's Best Films

Fawzi Soliman's selection:
Free of Cholesterol
(Mohammed Abu Seif)
In Love (Saad Hendawy)
Alexandria Private (Sandra)
My Soul Mate
(Khaled Youssef)
Ithaki
(Docu. Ibrahim Al-Batout)

Menna Shalaby and Hani Salama in
My Soul Mate

Recent and Forthcoming Films

HALET HOB (In Love)
[Drama, 2004] Script: Ahmed Abdel Fattah. Dir: Saad Hindawy. Phot: Nezar Shaker. Players: Hani Salama, Tamer Hosny, Hend Sabry, Mohammed Morshed. Prod: Fine Arts.

INTA OMRI (My Soul Mate)
[Tragic romance, 2004] Script: Mohammed Rifaat. Dir: Khaled Youssef. Phot: Samir Bahzan. Players: Nelly Karim, Hani Salama, Menna Shalabi. Prod: Media City.

ABU ALI
[Action, 2004] Script: Belal Fadl. Dir: Ahmed Galal. Phot: Ihab Mohammed. Players: Karim Abd Al-Aziz, Mona Zaki. Prod: Renaissance Egypt.
Two young men, flatmates wrongly accused of a crime, flee to an oasis.

The Egyptian Cinema Critics Association (EFCA), a member of FIPRESCI, condemned in its annual report for 2004 the predominance of farces in local film production and called on its members to oppose this trend, which distracts audiences from thinking about daily Egyptian reality. But what critics observed in 2004 was largely repeated in 2005, especially in the summer season. **Okal**, starring Mohammed Saad, was the biggest hit of 2004, and in 2005 his new film, **Booha**, exceeded all commercial expectations. As in his two previous films, *Al-Limby* and *Al-Limby 2*, Saad played slight variations on the same dim character, dependent on physical caricature, singing and dancing. He makes people laugh at his stupidity, crudeness, pratfalls and disastrous choices.

Another enormously popular comic whose only method of generating laughs is buffoonery is Mohammed Heneidy, whose recent hits were **The Great Fool of China** (*Fuul el Seen elazim*, 2004), shot mostly in China, and **Me or My Aunt** (2005), in which he disguises himself as a woman. **Sorry, We're Being Humiliated** (*Maalesh ehna binitbahdel*) gives a leading role to another comic star, Ahmed Adam. Its narrative, made up of comic sketches, is framed by the 9/11 attacks and the fall of Saddam Hussein, and begs to be viewed as political farce. **The Embassy in the Building** (*Al-sifara fil-imara*) is the second comedy with political overtones, directed by Amr Arafa and starring Adel Emam, king of comedy in Egypt for more than 25 years. With spirited humour, it explores some of the ironies and intellectual conflicts in Egyptian society, through the relationship between an Egyptian engineer, back in Egypt after 25 years away in the Gulf region, and staff at the Israeli Embassy.

The Egyptian Hitchcock?

Alexandria Private (*Mallaki Iskendriya*), directed by Sandra, is an action-packed crime thriller, shot at music video pace and with a good deal of suspense. Sandra said she set out "to make a film carrying shadows of Hitchcock. I love cinema because of him." After two political films, *The Storm* (*Al-asefa*) and *Marriage with Presidential Decision* (*Gawaz bekarar gomhoury*) Khaled Youssef (once an assistant to Youssef Chahine), delivered a romantic tragedy, **My Soul Mate** (*Enta omri*), the love story between a cancer patient and a similarly afflicted ballerina (Nelly Karim). She somehow resists death to fulfill her dream of dancing with the

MAALISH IHNA BINITBAHDEL
(Sorry, We're Being Humiliated)
[Comedy, 2005] Script: Youssef
Maaty. Dir: Sherif Mandour.
Phot: Mamdouh Abdel Aziz.
Players: Ahmed Adam. Prod:
Renaissance Egypt-Film House.

AL-SIFARA FIL-IMARA
(The Embassy in the Building)
[Political comedy, 2005] Script:
Youssef Maaty. Dir: Amr Arafa.
Phot: Wael Darwish. Players:
Adel Imam, Dalia Al-Beheiry,
Lotfy Labib. Prod: Essam Imam.

MALLAKI ISKENDRIYA
(Alexandria Private)
[Action, 2004] Script:
Mohammed Hefzy. Dir: Sandra.
Phot: Nezar Shaker. Players:
Ahmed Ezz, Nour, Khaled Saleh.
Prod: Oscar, Al-Nasr, Al-Masa.

FARHAN MULAZEM ADAM
[Drama, 2004] Script: Mohsen
Zayed. Dir: Omar Abd Al-Aziz.
Phot: Samir Farag. Players: Fathy
Abd Al-Wahab, Lebleba, Yasmin
Abd Al-Aziz. Prod: Al-Shorouk –
Motei Zayed.
Last work of the late scriptwriter
Mohsen Zayed, known for his
realistic films, the story explores
contradictions between rural
morality and urban corruption.

HAREEM KAREEM
[Social comedy, 2005] Script:
Zeinab Aziz. Dir: Aly Idris. Phot:
Ihab Mohammed Ali. Players:
Moustafa Qamar, Dalia Al-
Beheiry, Ola Ghanem, Basma,
Riham Abd Al-Ghafour. Prod:
Arab Screen/Unicorn.

Quote of the Year

"I refuse this classification
that fragments creation into
women's films and men's
films. Art is for all, the only
arbitrator is quality."
SANDRA, director of
Alexandria Private.

Ghadia Adel and Ahmed Ezz in **Alexandria Private**

Bolshoi. Karim won Best Actress at the Cairo International Film Festival 2004.

After several shorts, Saad Hendawy presented his first feature, **In Love** (Halet Hob), about an artist who emigrates to France after failing in Egypt. Hendawy gave famous singer Tamer Hosny his film debut and created a rich blend of themes: the problems of youth, culture clashes, Western views of a Middle East citizen and concepts of family and home country. **Hareem Kareem** is the first film collaboration between a real-life couple, scriptwriter Zeinab Aziz and director Aly Idris, and was dedicated to the class of 1987 from the High Film Institute. The film is an interesting variation on new-wave comedy, starring pop singer Moustafa Qamar, who gives refreshingly stylised performances as four female characters.

Central to the ongoing boom in the popularity of Egyptian fiction films is the construction of many new theatres, each with several screens, funded by the distributors of local and American films. American titles are still given a very limited release (sometimes only five prints), though distributors hope to change this.

Among recent documentaries, **About Feeling Cold** (An al-sheour bel berouda), directed by Hala Lotfy, deals with nine unmarried women of different ages, examining their attitudes towards love, society and morals, as well as education and upbringing. **Ithaki**, written, directed, photographed and produced by Ibrahim Al-Batout, is a fustion of documentary and fiction, capturing moments in the lives of 15 characters whose paths are woven together by a war cameraman, who wants to make his first film. Al-Batout highlights the thin line between reality and fiction.

FAWZI SOLIMAN (adifwzgm@hotmail.com) is a film journalist and critic who has contributed to magazines and newspapers in Egypt and the Arab world. He has served on the FIPRESCI jury of many film festivals.

Estonia Jaan Ruus

The Year's Best Films

Jaan Ruus' selection:
Revolution of Pigs
(Jaak Kilmi, René Reinumägi)
Frank & Wendy
(Animation. Kaspar Jancis,
Ülo Pikkov, Priit Tender)
Choose Order!
(Docu. Andres Maimik)
Stand Up to All the Winds
(Docu. Enn Säde)

US super-agents **Frank & Wendy**

Recent and Forthcoming Films

KÕRINI! (Fed Up!)
*[Comedy, 2005] Script: Valentin
Kuik, Peeter Simm. Dir: Simm.
Phot: Rein Kotov. Players: Heio
van Stetten, Thomas Schmauser,
Maarja Jakobson. Prod: Artur
Talvik, RUUT/Hans Honert,
Saxonia Media (Germany).*
Road movie about a long-distance
truck driver and a young
girl violinist.

Heio van Stetten in **Fed Up!**

stonian feature films of 2004 were premiered in the first half of the year (*IFG 2005* pp. 134-135). Then later in December, the full-length animation **Frank & Wendy** (*Frank ja Wendy*), directed by Kaspar Jancis, Ülo Pikkov and Priit Tender, opened the animation programme of the 8th Tallinn Black Nights Film Festival. This *South Park*-style political satire follows the adventures of two American super-agents determined to save the world in a dangerous place called Estonia. The film is largely based on absurdity humour with large doses of political incorrectness. Estonia's Grand Old Man of animation, Priit Pärn, has produced a delightfully ironic script for the voiceover.

The 2005 film season was opened by René Vilbre's **Mat the Cat** (*Röövlirahnu Martin*), the director's debut feature. This fantasy story follows a lonely boy in a seaside village whose imaginary friend, otherwise his pet cat, offers sage advice in a satisfying Scandinavian-style children's film. Accomplished director Peeter Urbla directed **Shop of Dreams** (*Stiilipidu*), a naïve-optimistic but somewhat simple melodrama about three novice and energetic businesswomen.

Businesswomen in their **Shop of Dreams**

The Õ-Fraktsioon group (Kaaren Kaer, Lauri Lippmaa, Tõnis Leht, Erik Moora, Andres Korberg), whose Monty Python-esque short productions have achieved near cult status among young Estonians, completed their first full-length feature, **Men at Arms** (*Malev*). The comedy parodied the Estonians' fight for freedom in the Middle Ages. The film met with mixed reviews, some considering it Estonia's first

FRANK JA WENDY
(Frank & Wendy)
*[Animation, 2005] Script:
Priit Pärn. Dir: Kaspar Jancis,
Ülo Pikkov, Priit Tender. Prod:
Kalev Tamm/Eesti Joonisfilm.*
Black comedy about two
American super-agents saving
the world.

KULDRANNAKE
(*literally*, **Golden Coast**)
*[Melodrama 2006] Script: Hans
Luik. Dir: Jüri Sillart. Phot: Mait
Mäekivi. Players: Mait Malmsten,
Taavi Eelma, Marika Korolev,
Hendrik Toompere jun. Prod:
Kristian Taska/Taska Film.*
Reunion of a pop band opens
old wounds.

Paul Oskar Soe as **Shipwreck Rudy**

RANNAKÜLA RUUDI
(Shipwreck Rudy)
*[Children's film, 2006] Script:
Aare Toikka, Aarne Mägi. Dir:
Katrin Laur. Phot: Rein Kotov.
Players: Paul Oskar Soe. Prod:
Piret Tibbo-Hudgins/Allfilm.*
A boy of seven organises a
contest to find a husband for his
single mother.

LEIUTAJAKÜLA LOTTE
(Lotte from Gadgetville)
*[Animation, 2006] Script: Heiki
Ernits, Andrus Kivirähk, Janno
Põldma, Alvis Lapins. Dir:
Põldma, Ernits. Prod: Riina
Sildos, Kalev Tamm, Eesti
Joonisfilm/Vilnis Kalnaellis,
Rija Films (Latvia).*
Life in a village where inventing
domestic gadgets is an
esteemed art.

full-length trash movie. A road-movie comedy **Fed Up!** (*Kõrini!*), filmed in Estonia and Germany and directed by another prominent film maker, Peeter Simm, will be premiered at the 9th Tallinn Black Nights Film Festival in December 2005.

The first film of 2006 is children's movie **Shipwreck Rudy** (*Ruudi*), directed by Katrin Laur. It follows a young boy, raised by his single mother, who is looking for a father in his life. In spring, a psychological melodrama, **Kuldrannake** (literally, *Golden Coast*) by Jüri Sillart, will open, which depicts a reunion of a one-time pop band in a glamorous villa. Several documentaries of particularly high quality were released in recent months: for example, a political satire, **Choose Order!** (*Vali kord*) by Andres Maimik, reminiscent of Ali G sketches, and another, **Stand Up to All the Winds** (*Mis teeb tuul müürile...*) by Enn Säde, a portrait of the accomplished film director Jüri Müür.

Television is the principal outlet for Estonian films. In 2004, Estonian films on TV drew a combined audience of some 9.4 million, while the overall attendance at domestic features in the cinemas was only 64,000. This triggered Estonian Film Foundation and Estonian public television (ETV) to sign a co-finance agreement to support the production of a number of domestic films. At the same time, some features originally produced for television also find their way to the big screen, such as **August 1991** by Ilmar Raag, a restoration of the footage of the 1991 putsch in Moscow, and **Meeting with the Unknown** (*Kohtumine tundmatuga*) by Jaak Kilmi, a comedy about Estonian star TV reporters.

Altogether, 131 feature films (including foreign films) were premiered in Estonia's cinemas with an overall attendance of 1.187 million, or 0.88 per capita. The multiplex cinema in Tallinn drew the largest number of viewers.The government's support of the film industry continues to increase annually. In 2005 the government allocated about $5.5 million, a 22% increase over the previous year. In 2006, the three Baltic countries of Estonia, Latvia and Lithuania will jointly establish the Baltic Film and Media School in Tallinn. The school's English-language curriculum will offer postgraduate studies in all aspects of film-making and other audiovisual media. The school will be open to international students.

JAAN RUUS is a film critic for the largest Estonian weekly, the Tallinn-based *Eesti Ekspress*. He is the president of the Estonian FIPRESCI.

Finland Antti Selkokari

The Year's Best Films

Antti Selkokari's selection:
***The Three Rooms of
Melancholia*** (Pirjo Honkasalo)
Beauty and the Bastard
(Dome Karukoski)
Frozen Land (Aku Louhimies)

Recent and Forthcoming Films

PAHA MAA (Frozen Land)
*[Episodic drama, 2004] Script:
Paavo Westerberg, Jari Rantala
and Aku Louhimies, inspired by
the Leo Tolstoy short story
False Coupon. Dir: Louhimies.
Phot: Rauno Ronkainen.
Players: Jasper Pääkkönen,
Mikko Leppilampi, Petteri
Summanen, Matleena
Kuusniemi, Pertti Sveholm,
Mikko Kouki. Prod: Markus
Selin, Solar Films.*

**ONNEN VARJOT
(Shades of Happiness)**
*[Drama, 2004] Script:
Anna-Leena Härkönen.
Dir: Claes Olsson. Phot:
Pertti Mutanen. Players:
Tiina Lymi, Nicke Lignell,
Milka Ahlroth, Härkönen,
Dick Idman. Prod: Leila
Lyytikäinen, Kinoproduction.*
Thirty-somethings mess up
their relationships.

**ELÄVILLE JA KUOLLEILLE
(For the Living and the Dead)**
*[Drama, 2005] Dir and script:
Kari Paljakka. Phot: Pekka
Uotila. Players: Hannu-Pekka
Björkman, Katja Kukkola,
Johannes Paljakka. Prod:
Ilkka Mertsola, Sputnik.*
A family mourns a dead son.

S ince 2000, Finland has produced about 12 films a year and 2005 saw this level surpassed: 11 fiction feature premieres, plus a strong dose of feature documentaries, making a total of 15. According to the Finnish Film Foundation's latest estimate, in November, the audience share for local films will have dropped slightly from 2004's 17% to around 13%. Three of the 11 fiction films were period pieces, which indicates producers' desire to reach a crossover audience.

Aku Louhimies's **Frozen Land** (*Paha maa*) uses the same Tolstoy short story that inspired Robert Bresson's *L'argent*. Louhimies and his writers, Paavo Westerberg and Jari Rantala, use the premise to study the unpleasant downside of market-oriented, high-tech contemporary Finland. The crisscrossing story uses a forged €500 banknote to connect characters who pass on all the misery they have experienced, much as the forged note circulates from hand to hand. This episodic film suffers badly from the director's reluctance to cut it shorter than 130 minutes, but is carried by wonderful performances from the main actors. Sulevi Peltola as a travelling vacuum-cleaner salesman reaches new tragic heights with his portrait of this lapsing alcoholic. Another peak is Matleena Kuusniemi's over-achieving policewoman, who has fallen into depression. As much as Louhimies wallows in the doom and gloom, he does it with consistency. On its own terms *Frozen Land* enchants with its cold logic.

Pertti Sveholm, left, in **Frozen Land**

KOTI-IKÄVÄ (Homesick)
[Drama, 2005] Script: Petri Kotwica, Selma Vilhunen. Dir: Kotwica. Phot: Harri Räty. Players: Julius Lavonen, Tarja Heinula, Janne Virtanen. Prod: Kai Nordberg, Making Movies.
A teenage boy hides his emotions and is put in a mental hospital.

GAME OVER
[Drama, 2003] Script: Juha Siltala, Pekka Lehto, Jaakko Heinimäki, William Aldridge. Dir and Prod: Lehto. Phot: Kasimir Lehto. Players: Reino Nordin, Julius Lavonen, Juuso Pekkinen, Jarkko Niemi, Lilli Aro, Karoliina Blackburn.
An immoral boy wants to outdo his rich father and ends up as a killer.

KAKSIPÄISEN KOTKAN VARJOSSA (Shadow of the Eagle)
[Historical drama, 2005] Script, Dir and Prod: Timo Koivusalo. Phot: Pertti Mutanen. Players: Vesa-Matti Loiri, Mikko Leppilampi, Helena Vierikko, Anneli Saaristo, Tapio Liinoja.

ÄIDEISTÄ PARHAIN (Mother of Mine)
[Drama, 2005] Script: Jimmy Karlsson, Kirsi Wikman. Dir: Klaus Härö. Phot: Jarkko T. Laine. Players: Topi Majaniemi, Marjaana Maijala, Maria Lundqvist, Michael Nyqvist, Esko Salminen. Prod: Ilkka Matila, MRP Röhr Productions.

VALO
[Comedy, 2005] Script: Markku Flink. Dir: Kaija Juurikkala. Phot: Harri Räty. Players: Vili Järvinen, Joni Kehusmaa, Sara-Maria Juntunen, Alina Sakko, Eveliina Uusitalo, Teijo Eloranta, Rea Mauranen. Prod: Outi Rousu, Periferia Productions.
Schoolchildren start running their own school, enraging the adults.

TYTTÖ SINÄ OLET TÄHTI (Beauty and the Bastard)
[Drama, 2005] Script: Pekko Pesonen. Dir: Dome Karukoski. Phot: Pini Hellstedt. Players: Pamela Tola, Samuli Vauramo,

A debuting director, film-school graduate Dome Karukoski, provided a welcome burst of youthful energy with the deft **Beauty and the Bastard** (*Tyttö sinä olet tähti*). Karukoski avoids the usual traps of Finnish film-making, by treating his edgy tale of a nice wannabe starlet who ends up in the arms of a hardcore hip-hop DJ on its own terms as a genre piece. Where he represented fresh talent, the absolutely final Uuno Turhapuro film signalled the end of an era in autumn 2004. The title character, a grown-up career slacker, was invented for television by the late entertainer Spede Pasanen in the early 1970s. Usually the films were directed by Ere Kokkonen and were hugely popular, especially with baby boomers, who mistook Uuno as an indispensable part of Finnish identity. His popularity faded along with plummeting admissions figures at Finnish cinemas. His nondescript exit, **Uuno Turhapuro – This Is My Life**, sees him enjoying his days in an old people's home and a reality TV show that lets him reminisce about his youth.

Vesa-Matti Loiri in all his glory as **Uuno Turhapuro**

Eagle **fails to soar**

Timo Koivusalo's **Shadow of the Eagle** (*Kaksipäisen kotkan varjossa*) plays along the lines of his previous film, the 2003 biopic Sibelius, with an emphasis on the surface: careful staging of period and heavy-handed symbolism. This is the story of a fictional Finnish poet who stands up to Russian oppression in nineteenth-century Finland. Koivusalo is a very ambitious director, who seeks a larger-than-life canvas on to which to project his entertainment, but he creates something more like a picture book than a cohesive, enthralling story.

Klaus Härö impressed with his 2002 debut feature, *Elina – As If I Wasn't There*, about the anguishes of a border-town schoolgirl seeking a cultural and personal identity in a troubled environment. His follow-up, **Mother of Mine** (*Äideistä parhain*) tells a comparable story, as a motherless schoolboy is sent to Sweden from Finland to escape the Second World War. Forced to speak Swedish, the boy suffers from the lack of his mother and his mother tongue. Härö was inspired in part by Erja Dammert's 2003 documentary about these so-called war children. He recreated the period carefully, shooting in Sweden and Finland. Quite emotional, *Mother of Mine* is the Finnish hopeful for the Oscars in 2006.

Another factually inspired war film was released in December 2005: **Promise** (*Lupaus*), by Ilkka Vanne, told the story of three girls who volunteered for Lotta Svärd, the women's unarmed defence organisation. Its members performed duties in hospitals and air raid precaution, thus releasing men to fight at the front. It was banned after the end of the war, since the Soviets considered it too fascist. The stories of Lotta women began surfacing after the collapse of the Soviet Union. In its heart, Vanne's film has an emotional plea for the recognition of women who selflessly worked for their country when most needed. Unfortunately it concentrates more on setting the historical record straight than on the narrative.

Kaija Juurikkala, a renowned director of chidren's films and TV series, made her third feature, **Valo**, to show that children's rights are to be respected at all times. *Valo* is set in a fairy-tale nineteenth-century Finnish village, where a local school teacher is laid off for paying too much attention to her pupils and their wishes. Her unhappy charges respond by setting up a school for and run by children. Juurikkala is honest in her approach, but *Valo*'s storyline is ruined by characters and situations far too black-and-white for grown-up taste. Pirjo Honkasalo's documentary **The Three Rooms of Melancholia** (*Melankolian kolme huonetta*) collected awards at many international festivals. She discovers how children are exploited by both sides in the Russians' war against the Chechens. Honkasalo directs, writes and shoots her films, creating a work of art that avoids clichés and respects the viewer's right to his own thoughts, a quality all too rare in many of today's documentaries.

ANTTI SELKOKARI (antti.selkokari@netti.fi) is a freelance film critic and journalist in Helsinki.

Joonas Saartamo, Eero Milonoff, Mikko Leppilampi, Mikko Kouki. Prod: Aleksi Bardy, Riina Hyytiä, Olli Haikka, Helsinki Filmi.

LUPAUS (Promise)
[Drama, 2005] Script: Inkeri Kilpinen, Elina Halttunen. Dir: Ilkka Vanne. Phot: Jani Kumpulainen. Players: Laura Birn, Karoliina Vanne, Hanna Lekander. Prod: Asko Apajalahti, Fantasiafilmi.

PAIMENET (Shepherds)
[Documentary, 2005] Script: Veikko Aaltonen, H.T. Partanen. Dir: Aaltonen. Phot: Marita Hällfors. Prod: Partanen, Alppiharjun Elokuva. Eight priests serve a neighbourhood undergoing radical changes, as yuppies move in to replace working-class residents.

MELANCHOLIAN KOLME HUONETTA (The Three Rooms of Melancholia)
[Documentary, 2005] Script, Dir and Phot: Pirjo Honkasalo. Prod: Kristiina Pervilä, Millennium Film. Visually stunning look at children affected by war in Russia and Chechnya.

Quote of the Year

"You can learn more from a bad movie than a good one."
PEKKA LEHTOSAARI,
scriptwriter, on analysing mistakes.

Tarja Matilainen and Karoliina Vanne in **Promise**

France Michel Ciment

The Year's Best Films

Michel Ciment's selection:
Hidden (Michael Haneke)
The Beat That My Heart Skipped (Jacques Audiard)
Gabrielle (Patrice Chéreau)
The Last Mitterrand (Robert Guédiguian)
Kings and Queen (Arnaud Desplechin)

Recent and Forthcoming Films

UN LONG DIMANCHE DE FIANCAILLES
(A Very Long Engagement)
[Historical Drama, 2005] Script:
Jean Pierre Jeunet, Guillaume
Laurent. Dir: Jean-Pierre Jeunet.
Phot: Bruno Delbonel. Players:
Audrey Tautou, Gaspard Ulliel,
Dominique Pinon, Ticky
Holgado, Chantal Neuwirth.
Prod: Francis Boespflug,
2003 Productions.

LA MOUSTACHE
(The Moustache)
[Drama, 2005] Script and Dir:
Emmanuel Carrère. Phot: Patrick
Blossier. Players: Vincent Lindon,
Emmanuelle Devos, Mathieu
Amalric, Hippolyte Girardot,
Cylia Malki. Prod: Anne-
Dominique Toussaint, Films
des Tournelles (Les).

INNOCENCE
[Drama, 2005] Script and
Dir: Lucile Hadzihalilovic.
Phot: Benoît Debie. Players:
Zoé Auclair, Alisson Lalieux,
Joséphine Van Wambeke,
Astrid Homme, Léa Bridarolli.
Prod: Patrick Sobelman,
Ex Nihilo.

The absence of laws creates chaos; too many laws lead to unwelcome rigidity. This was demonstrated by a lawsuit that shook the French film industry early in 2005. Jean-Pierre Jeunet's **A Very Long Engagement** (Un long dimanche de fiançailles) produced by '2003', an ancillary company linked to Warner Brothers France (which held 33% of its capital), had benefited from financial advantages granted to French productions by the Centre National de la Cinématographie (CNC). Two producers' associations, which included Pathé, Gaumont, UGC and MK2, took legal action against this decision, contending that '2003' was a Trojan horse financed by Hollywood and should not be considered as a European company.

The court ruled in their favour and Jeunet's film was denied any support – even though it was shot in France, in French, with French technicians and actors. The directors' and technicians' unions sided with Jeunet, on the grounds that the film had employed around 2,000 French people and that the benefits at the box-office would anyhow be reinvested in subsequent French films produced by '2003'. Paradoxically, Alexander, co-produced by a French company (Pathé), shot in English outside France with an Anglo-Saxon cast and crew and directed by Oliver Stone, was considered French!

Underlying the legal arguments was a battle between big French studios and an American potential rival capable of producing high-calibre films such as Jeunet's First World War epic. The outcome was a bitter lesson for Jeunet, who had been so determined to make A Very Long Engagement as a French film, and all the more regrettable because it is rare to find such originality in a big-budget French film (albeit one financed by America). A Very Long

Warner Bros./Kobal/Bruno Calvo

Jean-Pierre Jeunet's **A Very Long Engagement** divided the French film industry

Engagement confirmed Jeunet as a fearless artist working on a broad canvas, mixing pathos and humour with his habitually keen eye for oddball characters and lofty feelings.

The chauvinistic approach to production revealed by this case anticipated the results of the referendum in which 55% of French voters rejected the European Constitution. Among them were many film artists who might suffer from a less powerful and united Europe, more likely in future to cancel the French cultural exception, without which a fair number of commercially unsuccessful directors could hardly continue to work.

To add to industry gloom, box-office returns for the first six months of 2005 dropped by 10% on the previous year. This was the context in which Veronique Cayla, the former administrator of the Cannes Film Festival, took over as director of the CNC in June 2005. A decisive woman, and an expert on audiovisual matters, she will certainly need all her experience to face issues of paramount importance such as the impact of home video and the huge threat from piracy.

Strength in numbers

This downturn followed an exceptionally successful 2004. Cinema attendance had risen by 12.3% (the biggest increase in Europe), reaching the highest level since 1983, 194.8 million spectators, with a market share of 39% for French films (76.1 million tickets). This was the second-best domestic performance since 1985 and an increase of 25.6% from 2003. The market share for American films, at 47.4% (92.3 million tickets), showed an apparent decline of 4.8%, but only because of the byzantine accounting that considers *Harry Potter and The Prisoner of Azkaban* (6.89 million admissions) and *Troy* (2.71 million) as wholly British, and *The Return of the King* (2.17 million) as a wholly New Zealand feature.

All in all, however, France is still the European country where American films are least dominant. This does not mean that the French public shows a great curiosity for European films. Attendance for German (1.8 million), Spanish (1.37 million) and Italian (420,000) films has not improved and at Cannes 2005 the Competition featured only one European film (by Marco Tullio Giordana) spoken in a language other than French or English.

Though the statistics prove that the cinema audience is made up mostly of young, urban, well-off and educated spectators, they do not show – any more than their counterparts in neighbouring countries – a particular interest in non-Hollywood foreign films. Overall, 60% of France's population saw at least one film at the cinema during 2004 and the annual per capita attendance of six visits is one of the highest results in Europe.

LES REVENANTS
(They Came Back)
[Drama, 2004] Script and Dir: Robin Campillo. Phot: Jeanne Lapoirie. Players: Géraldine Pailhas, Jonathan Zaccaï, Frédéric Pierrot, Catherine Samie, Victor Garrivier. Prod: Caroline Benjo, Carole Scotta, Haut et Court.

L'ANNULAIRE
(The Ring Finger)
[Drama, 2004/5] Script and Dir: Diane Bertrand. Phot: Alain Duplantier. Players: Olga Kurylenko, Marc Barbé, Stipe Erceg, Edith Scob, Hanns Zischler. Prod: Bruno Berthémy.

L'AVION (The Plane)
[Drama, 2005] Script and Dir: Cedric Kahn. Phot: Michel Amathieu. Players: Isabelle Carré, Vincent Lindon, Roméo Botzaris, Nicolas Briançon, Alicia Djemaï. Prod: Olivier Delbosc, Marc Missonnier, Fidélité Productions.

L'INTRUS (The Intruder)
[Drama, 2004/5] Script and Dir: Claire Denis. Phot: Agnès Godard. Players: Michel Subor, Béatrice Dalle, Grégoire Colin, Katerina Golubeva, Bambou, Florence Loiret-Caille. Prod: Humbert Balsan, Oignon Pictures.

LA DEMOISELLE D'HONNEUR
(The Maid of Honour)
[Thriller, 2004/5] Script and Dir: Claude Chabrol. Phot: Eduardo Serra. Players: Benoît Magimel, Laura Smet, Aurore Clément, Anna Mihalcea, Bernard Le Coq. Prod: Patrick Godeau, Antonio Passalia, Alicéleo/Canal Diffusion.

A TOUT DE SUITE (Suddenly)
[Drama, 2004] Script and Dir: Benoît Jacquot. Phot: Caroline Champetier. Players: Isilde Le Besco, Ouassini Embarek, Nicolas Duvauchelle, Laurence Cordier, Fotini Kodoukaki. Prod: Georges Benayoun, Raoul Saada, Natan Productions.

LEMMING
[Drama, 2005] Script and Dir:

Dominik Moll. Phot: Jean-Marc
Fabre. Players: Laurent Lucas,
Charlotte Gainsbourg, Charlotte
Rampling, André Dussollier,
Jacques Bonnaffé. Prod: Michel
Saint-Jean, Diaphana Films.

LE COUPRET (The Axe)
[Drama, 2005] Script and Dir:
Costa Garvas. Phot: Patrick
Blossier. Players: José Garcia,
Karin Viard, Ulrich Tukur,
Olivier Gourmet, Geordie
Monfils. Prod: Michèle Ray
Gavras, KG Productions.

José Garcia in Costa-Garvas' **The Axe**

LES MAUVAIS JOUEURS
(Gamblers)
[Genre, 2005] Script and Dir:
Frédéric Balekdjian. Phot: Pierre
Milon. Players: Pascal Elbé,
Simon Abkarian, Isaac Sharry,
Linh Dan Pham, Teng Fei Xiang.
Prod: Fabienne Vonier,
Pyramide Productions.

MON PETIT DOIGT M'A DIT
(By the Pricking of My Thumbs)
[Mystery, 2005] Script: François
Caviglioli. Dir: Pascal Thomas.
Phot: Renan Pollès. Players:
Catherine Frot, André Dussollier,
Geneviève Bujold, Laurent
Terzieff, Valérie Kaprisky. Prod:
Alain Cadier, Ah, Victoria! Films.

LE PETIT LIEUTENANT
(The Little Lieutenant)
[Thriller, 2005] Script: Di Rand.
Phot: Xavier Beauvois. Players:
Nathalie Baye, Jalil Lespert,
Roschdy Zem, Antoine Chappey,
Beauvois. Prod: Why Not
Productions.

ENTRE SES MAINS
(In His Hands)
[Drama, 2004/5] Script: Julien
Boivent, based on the novel by
Dominique Barbaris. Dir: Anne

A total of 203 French films was produced in 2004 (nine fewer than
2003); 34 fewer features were co-produced with foreign partners; 130
were financed solely with French money (105 in 2003). Great Britain
and Belgium were privileged co-production partners, followed by Italy,
Germany and Spain. As usual, first films accounted for a high
proportion of the total (32%), and an increase in the number of
second features (35 in all) showed signs of a healthy, constantly
renewing industry. There were fewer films budgeted at less than €1m,
and more in the intermediate range (€5m-€10m). Public and cable
television channels remained vitally important, providing 32% of total
production finance and influencing the kind of films that are greenlit,
with an eye on ratings. This preoccupation with mainstream taste
does not encourage bold and controversial projects; nor does the
fragmented nature of the production system (133 companies financed
the 167 films initiated in France!) encourage big-budget productions.
French films, though faring less well overseas than in previous years,
still sold 46 million tickets, grossing €222m, a little more than half that
revenue coming from Europe, led by Germany, Belgium and Italy,
followed by the US (16.9%) and Japan (12%).

France is still the place where one can see the greatest range of
films: 560 features were distributed in 2004 (up 9.6%), with a
conspicuous increase in documentaries (68 titles) and animation
(23 releases). Hollywood films accounted for 48% of the prints in
circulation (French films for 40%) and *Harry Potter* and *Shrek 2*
opened in 900 theatres. The country's network of 5,302 screens
allows this massive exhibition, particularly as multiplexes attracted
48% of the attendance (up 18%). This of course makes life more
difficult for films with an unusual profile.

Fantasy in many forms

The 2004–05 season proved rich and varied, with all generations
contributing – from directors such as Chabrol, Deville and Lelouch,
who started in the 1950s, to newcomers instantly displaying
distinctive personalities. One striking feature has been a tendency to
break with the traditional psychological-cum-realistic style that has
characterised so many French films, often with very good results. A
taste for the uncanny, the oneiric, the fantastic has appeared in a
number of films, including debuts. Emmanuel Carrère, already noticed
for his documentary *Retour à Kotelnitch*, has adapted as his first
fiction his own novel **The Moustache** (*La moustache*) about a man
(Vincent Lindon) who shaves off his moustache, discovers that
nobody notices the difference, and descends into a spiral of paranoid
disorder. Another debutant, Lucile Hadzihalilovic, made probably the
year's most original feature, **Innocence**, about a group of girls trained
to become ballerinas in a domain surrounded by a forest. Some
mysteriously disappear, the atmosphere is heavy with ritualistic
gestures and the lush photography suggests a perverse eroticism

Ex Nihilo/Kobal

*Ballerinas are at the centre of **Innocence***

under the innocent surface. **They Came Back** (*Les revenants*), the first film of Robin Campillo, also belongs to the realm of the fantastic, with its subtle variation on the return of the living dead. The way in which Campillo shows a community learning to live again, neither rejoicing nor frightened, with those who were supposed to have disappeared forever becomes a social and metaphysical enquiry into the nature of a group's collective state of mind.

Diane Bertrand's second feature, **The Ring Finger** (*L'annulaire*), set in Hamburg with sets recalling Edward Hopper's compositions, spins the tale of a beautiful young woman hired by the male boss of a laboratory that transforms objects into specimens. A modern variation on *Cinderella*, it engenders a disquieting atmosphere both sensuous and eerie. In **The Plane** (*L'avion*), Cedric Kahn, one of the most gifted directors of his generation, presents another of his obsessional heroes, this time a boy whose pilot father gives him a toy plane just before he dies in a crash. The child imbues the model with life and the film enters a poetic territory where fantasy becomes a means of accepting loss.

Inspired by a philosophical text by Jean-Luc Nancy, the talented Claire Denis in **The Intruder** (*L'intrus*) traces the itinerary of a man (an impressive Michel Subor) who, before having a heart transplant in Korea, stops in Polynesia to look for his son. Denis' cerebral approach comes into conflict with the high sensuousness of Agnès Godard's photography and the film becomes unnecessarily convoluted and elliptical. Its disastrous reception at the Venice Film Festival and, later, at the French box-office, made it, not surprisingly, a cult object for a Parisian coterie.

Gangsters, and Moll

The crime film has attracted many directors in recent years and produced a great variety of films. One of its masters, Claude Chabrol, proved his skill yet again in **The Maid of Honour** (*La*

Fontaine. *Phot: Denis Lenoir. Players: Benoît Poelvoorde, Jonathan Zaccaï, Isabelle Carré, Valérie Donzelli, Agathe Louvieaux. Prod: Bruno Pesery, Philippe Carcassonne, Ciné B/ Soudaine Compagnie.*

UN FIL A LA PATTE
[Comedy, 2005] Script: Rosalinde Deville. Dir: Michel Deville. Phot: Pierre-William Glenn. Players: Emmanuelle Béart, Charles Berling, Dominique Blanc, Jacques Bonnaffé, Mathieu Demy. Prod: Rosaline Deville, Eléfilm.

LE COURAGE D'AIMER
[Drama, 2004/5] Script and Dir: Claude Lelouch. Phot: Jean-Marie Drejou. Players: Mathilde Seigner, Arielle Dombasle, Massimo Ranieri, Maïwenn Le Besco, Michel Leeb. Prod: Claude Lelouch, Les Film 13.

LES POUPEES RUSSES
(Russian Dolls)
[Drama, 2004/5] Script and Dir: Cédric Klapisch. Phot: Dominique Colin. Players: Romain Duris, Audrey Tautou, Cécile de France, Kelly Reilly, Kevin Bishop. Prod: Bruno Lévy, Ce Qui Me Meut.

TRAVAUX, ON SAIT QUAND CA COMMENCE ...
[Drama, 2005] Script: Eric Besnard. Dir: Brigitte Roüan. Phot: Christophe Pollock. Players: Carole Bouquet, Jean-Pierre Castaldi, Didier Flamand, Françoise Brion, Aldo Maccione. Prod: Humbert Balsan.

QUAND LA MER MONTE
[Drama, 2005] Script and Dir: Yolande Moreau, Gilles Porte. Phot: Porte. Players: Yolande Moreau, Wim Willaert, Olivier Gourmet, Jackie Berroyer, Philippe Duquesne. Prod: Humbert Balsan, Oignon Pictures.

LES MOTS BLEUS
(Words in Blue)
[Drama, 2005] Script and Dir: Alain Corneau. Phot: Yves Angelo. Players: Sylvie Testud, Sergi Lopéz, Camille

Gauthier, Mar Sodupe, Cédric Chevalme. Prod: Laurent Pétin, Michèle Halberstadt.

L'EQUIPIER
[Drama, 2004] Script: Emmanuel Courcol. Dir: Phillipe Lioret. Phot: Patrick Blossier. Players: Sandrine Bonnaire, Philippe Torreton, Grégori Derangère, Emilie Dequenne, Anne Consigny. Prod: Christophe Rossignon.

LA PETITE CHARTREUSE
[Drama, 2005] Script and Dir: Jean-Pierre Denis. Phot: Benoît Dervaux. Players: Olivier Gourmet, Marie-Josée Croze, Bertille Noël-Bruneau, Marysa Borini, Yves Jacques. Prod: Catherine Dussart.

DE BATTRE MON CŒUR S'EST ARRETE (The Beat That My Heart Skipped)
[Drama, 2005] Script and Dir: Jacques Audiard. Phot: Stéphane Fontaine. Players: Romain Duris, Aure Atika, Emmanuelle Devos, Niels Arestrup, Jonathan Zaccaï. Prod: Why Not Productions.

ROIS ET REINE (Kings and Queen)
[Drama, 2005] Script and Dir: Arnaud Desplechin. Phot: Eric Gautier. Players: Emmanuelle Devos, Mathieu Amalric, Catherine Deneuve, Maurice Garrel, Nathalie Boutefeu. Prod: Pascal Gaucheteux, Why Not Productions.

LE PROMENEUR DU CHAMP DE MARS (The Last Mitterrand)
[Drama, 2005] Script: Georges-Marc Benamou. Dir: Robert Guédiguian. Phot: Renato Berta. Players: Michel Bouquet, Jalil Lespert, Philippe Fretun, Anne Cantineau, Sarah Grappin. Prod: Marc Bayser (de), Frank Le Wita, Robert Guédiguian, Film Oblige/ Agat Films/Cie.

CACHE (Hidden)
[Drama, 2005] Script and Dir: Michael Haneke. Phot: Christian Berger. Players: Juliette Binoche, Daniel Auteuil, Maurice Benichou, Walid Afkir, Nathalie

demoiselle d'honneur), with his usual mixture of thriller and comedy of manners. Another of his scenes from provincial life, his new film is also the incisive portrait of a mythomaniac (Laura Smet, a new rising talent) who captures in her net a young bourgeois. **Suddenly** (A tout de suite) sees Benoît Jacquot put fresh spin on the story of the crook on the run with his girlfriend (Isilde le Besco, another stunning new actress), a proper adolescent seduced by a hoodlum.

Dominik Moll, after Harry, He's Here to Help, displayed in **Lemming** his usual mathematical precision in another view of antagonistic couples, one older and experienced (André Dussollier and Charlotte Rampling, the latter as an evil catalyst), set against an innocent, younger pair (Charlotte Gainsbourg and Laurent Lucas). Moll blurs the line between reality and fantasy, creating a psychoanalytical thriller. Costa Gavras in **The Axe** (Le couperet) pursues his political commentary on our society through the prism of a social thriller in which an unemployed executive kills his rivals for a job. This macabre fable (adapted from Donald Westlake) is greatly helped by the remarkable lead performance of José Garcia, who manages to inspire fear and laughter in the viewer.

For his first feature, **The Gamblers** (Les mauvais joueurs), Frédéric Balekdjian has also trusted the crime genre, in a tale of rival Armenian and Asian gangs in central Paris. Very much in the nitty-gritty style of Mean Streets, it reveals a new talent. At the other end of the spectrum, old-timer Pascal Thomas adapts an Agatha Christie novel in **By the Pricking of My Thumbs** (Mon petit doigt m'a dit), in which a couple of amateur sleuths (Catherine Frot and André Dussollier at their most delectable) meet an array of picturesque characters scattered in the Alps (a fair substitute for the novel's Scottish mountains). The virtue of working within a genre is also exemplified by Xavier Beauvois' fourth feature, **The Little Lieutenant** (Le petit lieutenant), a cop movie, reminiscent of Bertrand Tavernier's documentary-like L 627, about a police squad, led by Nathalie Baye, in search of drug smugglers. Beauvois' usual auteurist indulgence gives way to a straightforward, vivid account of the cops' daily life. Similarly, Anne Fontaine's **In His Hands** (Entre ses mains) is a convincing psychological thriller about a married woman (Isabelle Carré) attracted to an oddball personality (Benoît) who reveals himself as a psychopathic killer.

Laughs in short supply

Almost half the French films produced each year are comedies but few are worth noticing. Presented as his last film, Michel Deville's **Un fil à la patte** is an adaptation of Georges Feydeau's classic vaudeville with a star-studded cast including Emmanuelle Béart, Charles Berling, Dominique Blanc and Audrey Tautou, and the veteran director shows once more his sense of rhythm and virtuoso mise en scène. Another veteran, Claude Lelouch, too often prone to lofty subjects and pseudo-philosophical considerations, has opted in **Le courage d'aimer** for a more modest approach where his real talent for directing actors and weaving sentimental stories tinged with humour is shown at its best.

Cédric Klapisch has experienced a huge popular success with **Russian Dolls** (*Les poupées russes*), a sequel to *Europudding* (*L'auberge espagnole*), a truly European film in which the original film's characters pursue their amorous affairs in Paris, London, Moscow and St Petersburg. Brigitte Roüan in **Travaux, on sait quand ça commence…** gives an unusual comic role to Carole Bouquet, as a straight-laced posh lawyer with a compassion for the third world, who hires a team of Latin American refugees to transform her apartment. The result is a series of disasters, which gives this screwball comedy its original flavour, a mixture of social comments and absurdist gags.

The field of psychological studies has produced some worthy films on an intimate scale, like Yolande Moreau and Gilles Porte's first feature, **Quand la mer monte…**, an exploration of the bleak landscapes of Belgium and the north of France, with a funny and touching portrayal of its main character (Yolande Moreau), a kind of Belgian Gelsomina. **Words in Blue** (*Les Mots bleus*) is Alain Corneau's moving drama about a mother (Sylvie Testud) and her silent child who finds a path to recovery through the help of an educator (Sergi López). Philippe Lioret's **L'équipier** depicts, in the poetic realist style of a Duvivier or Grémillon, an adulterous love affair in the rugged landscape of the coast of Brittany in the context of the Algerian war. Perhaps the most accomplished of them all is Jean-Pierre Denis' **La pétite chartreuse** where an extraordinary Olivier Gourmet brings back to consciousness a little girl whom he ran over with his car and plunged into a coma. There is something magical about their relationship and the mountainous landscape that surrounds them gives the story a fable-like dimension.

Tales of keyboards, kings and a president

Finally come five excellent films whose diversity testifies to the richness of French cinema. Jacques Audiard's **The Beat That My Heart Skipped** (*De battre mon cœur s'est arrêté*), with its powerful and intense portrayal of a small-time crook (played in a virtuoso performance by Romain Duris), his love–hate relationship with his father and his dream of becoming a piano player, is closer to the energy of the best Asian and American cinema (it is a remake of James Toback's *Fingers*) than to the French tradition. Arnaud Desplechin's **Kings and Queen** (*Rois et reine*) mixes farce and drama to tell the story of a man (Mathieu Amalric) confined to a mental asylum and his former companion (Emmanuelle Devos), bruised by life and the animosity of her dying father.

Richard. Prod: Les Films du Losange Les Films du Losange.

GABRIELLE
[Drama, 2005] Script and Dir: Patrice Chéreau. Phot: Eric Gautier. Players: Isabelle Huppert, Pascal Greggory, Thierry Hancisse, Claudia Coli, Chantal Neuwirth. Prod: Azor Films.

French César Academy Awards 2005

Film: *The Dodge/L'esquive.*
Director: Abdellatif Kechiche
(*The Dodge*).
Actress: Yolande Moreau
(*Quand la mer monte…*).
Actor: Mathieu Amalric (*Kings and Queen/Rois et reine*).
Supporting Actress:
Marion Cotillard (*A Very Long Engagement/Un long dimanche de fiancailles*).
Supporting Actor:
Clovis Cornillac (*Mensonges et trahisons et plus si affinites*).
Female Newcomer:
Sara Forestier (*The Dodge*).
Male Newcomer:
Gaspard Ulliel
(*A Very Long Engagement*).
Foreign Film:
Lost in Translation.
Film from the EU:
Just a Kiss/Life Is a Miracle.
Screenplay:
Abdel Kechiche & Ghalis Lacroix (*The Dodge*).
First Film:
Quand la mer monte...
Short Film:
Cousins (Cousines).
Score: Bruno Coulais
(*The Chorus/Les choristes*).
Costumes:
Madeline Fontaine
(*A Very Long Engagement*).
Cinematography:
Bruno Delbonnel
(*A Very Long Engagement*).
Set Design: Aline Bonetto
(*A Very Long Engagement*).
Editing: Noëlle Boisson
(*Two Brothers/Deux frères*).
Best Sound: Daniel Sobrino, Nicolas Cantin, Nicolas Naegelen (*The Chorus*).

Canal+/UGC/Wellspring Media/Kobal

Romain Duris gives a virtuoso performance in **The Beat That My Heart Skipped**

In **The Last Mitterrand** (*Le promeneur du Champ de Mars*) Robert Guédiguian has abandoned for a while his usual world of the Marseilles suburbs to explore the last months of Mitterrand's life through a dialogue with a young, candid journalist. Michel Bouquet's exceptional performance as Mitterrand expresses all the complexities and ambiguities of the man and the politician. **Hidden** (*Caché*) is probably Michael Haneke's best film, in which the rigour of his style is not marred by gratuitous excesses. An ugly episode of his childhood comes back to haunt a TV journalist (Daniel Auteuil) via the threats of mysterious videotapes. The unrelenting suspense does not distract from the ethical questions raised by the film.

Last but not least, after *Intimacy* and *Son frère*, Patrick Chéreau concludes his trilogy of chamber dramas with **Gabrielle**, an adaptation of Joseph Conrad's novella *The Return*. Combining the soul-searching of a Bergman with the operatic aesthetics of a Visconti, Chéreau creates a harrowing atmosphere in which a husband (Pascal Greggory), who has always considered his wife (Isabelle Huppert) as a precious object, is confronted by a shocking act of rebellion: she leaves him, and then comes a return after which their life will never be the same.

MICHEL CIMENT is president of FIPRESCI, a member of the editorial board of *Positif*, a radio producer and author of more than a dozen books on cinema.

Film Oblige/Kobal

Michel Bouquet, left, as the former president, with Jalil Lespert as a journalist in **The Last Mitterrand**

Georgia Goga Lomidze

Recent and Forthcoming Films

TBILISI-TBILISI
[Drama, 2005] Script, Dir and Prod: Levan Zakareishvili. Phot: Archil Akhvlediani. Players: George Maskharashvili, Ek Nijaradze, Baadur Tsuladze, Berta Khapava, Rusiko Kobiashvili. Prod: Zaqareishvili.

TZAMETI (13)
[Drama, 2005] Script and Dir: Gela Babluani. Phot: Tariel Meliava. Players: Giorgi Babluani, Philippe Passon, Pascal Bonrand, Vania Villers. Prod: Mortze Mohammadi, Bruno Daniault, Les films de la strada/Solimane Production.

GASEIRNEBA KARABAGSHI
(A Trip to Karabakh)
[Drama, 2005] Script: Aka Morchiladze and Irakli Solomonashvili. Dir: Levan Tutberidze. Players: Levan Doborjginidze, Misha Meskhi, Nutsa Kukhianidze. Prod: Korinteli, Giorgi Kharabadze.

ZGVIS DONIDAN (Eye Level)
[Short, 2004] Script and Dir: Giorgi Ovashvili. Phot: Giorgi Gersamia. Players: Anna Talakvadze, Avto Makharashvili. Prod: Tomas Gakhokidze, G. Ovashvili, Imedi TV.

MEIDANI, SAMKAROS CHIPI
(Maidan, Nave of the World)
[Documentary, 2004] Script: Dato Janelidze, Pieter Jan Smit. Dir: Janelidze. Phot: Giorgi Gersamia. Prod: Pieter Jan Smit, PS Pictures/Studio 99/ImediTV.

Gogita Chkonia had been shooting his art movie **Pseudometamorphose** since 1991 and in 2004 it finally premiered. He chooses different styles, including animation, to tell five stories, including those of a painter, a country's struggle for independence and the builder of an ancient stone city. After the premiere, some critics talked of a "poetic revival" for Georgian cinema.

One of several Georgian films presented at the Kinoshok festival of work from the CIS and Baltic states, Levan Tutberidze's **A Trip to Karabakh** (*Gaseirneba Karabagshi*) took the event's Grand Prix. Two disappointed young people decide to make money drug-dealing on the Armenia–Azerbaijan border. It starts as an enjoyable adventure, moves through war and ends as they reach maturity. Tutberidze started his career as a leading actor in a historical drama, *Demetre II* (1982). Kinoshok's Best Director and Critics' awards went to Levan Zaqareishvili for **Tbilisi-Tbilisi**. In the Georgian capital, a film director is writing a script for his new film and during this artistic process he meets people from different social classes, learning that a great deal has changed in the city.

Dato Janelidze's documentary **Maidan, Nave of the World** (*Meidani, samkaros chipi*) was a lyrical, slightly melancholic film about a small district of Tbilisi, where geopolitical changes have altered the make-up of a neighbourhood that has traditionally been home to people from many ethnic and religious backgrounds. At the 2005 Berlinale, Giorgi Ovashvili was awarded a scholarship to study at the New York Film Academy for his short *Eye Level* (*Zgvis donidan*), a lyrical tale of first love. At Venice 2005, **13** (*Tzameti*) by Paris-trained Gela Babluani (son of prominent film-maker Temur Babluani) was named best first feature. Filmed in black and white, it is the story of a young emigrant accidentally caught up in a complicated crime.

Dato Janelidze's **Maidan, Nave of the World**

Germany Rüdiger Suchsland

The Year's Best Films

Rüdiger Suchsland selection:
Ghosts (Christian Petzhold)
The Forest for the Trees
(Maren Ade)
Katze im Sack
(Florian Schwarz)
Two or Three Things
I Know About Him
(Malte Ludin)
Netto (Robert Thalheim)

Recent and Forthcoming Films

DIE WEISSE MASSAI
(The White Massai)
[Drama, 2005] Script: Johannes W. Betz, from the novel by Corinne Hofmann. Dir: Hermine Huntgeburth. Phot: Martin Langer. Players: Nina Hoss, Jacky Ido, Katja Flint, Nino Prester, Janek Rieke. Prod: Guenter Rohrbach, Constantin Film.

WILLENBROCK
[Drama, 2005] Script: Laila Stieler. Dir: Andreas Dresen. Phot: Michael Hammon. Players: Axel Prahl, Inka Friedrich, Anne Ratte-Polle, Dagmar Manzel, Tilo Prueckner, Andrzej Szopa, Wladimir Tarasjanz. Prod: UFA Film & TV Produktion /WDR/MDR (Leipzig)/ SWR/ARTE (Strasbourg) /Trebitsch Produktion International/Studio Babelsberg.

NVA
[Comedy, 2005] Script: Thomas Brussig, Leander Haussmann. Dir: Haussmann. Phot: Frank Griebe. Players: Kim Frank, Oliver Broecker, Jasmin Schwiers, Detlev Buck, Maxim Mehmet,

In January 2005, **Go for Sugar!** (*Alles auf Zucker!*), the sparkling comedy by Dani Levy, was an instant hit. Everybody in the industry was surprised that a comedy about a dysfunctional Jewish family, reuniting at the grave of the dead mother, could be such a huge success. The film is full of black humour, taboo-breaking and politically incorrect jokes. Perhaps it was exactly this uncommon, free-spirited approach, combined with a general message of tolerance and reconciliation, that the audience liked. It was in marked contrast to all the sometimes well-meaning, sometimes politically naïve or even obscene films about the Third Reich that seemed to dominate German cinema in 2004–05.

After *Downfall* (*Der Untergang*) took almost €30m at German cinemas, some observers identified this sudden surge of interest as a "Nazi-Wave". Elder statesmen were part of the phenomenon, including Volker Schlöndorff with his honorable, fact-based **The Ninth Day** (*Der neunte Tag*), about a Luxembourg priest and concentration camp prisoner set free and given nine days to make a compromise with his homeland's Nazi oppressors.

Denis Gansel's **Napola**, about boys at a Nazi elite boarding school, combines personal drama with a general perspective on the daily suppression in Nazi Germany. Marc Rothemund presented his chamber piece, **Sophie Scholl: The Final Days** (*Sophie Scholl: Die letzten Tage*) at Berlin, where it won Best Director and Best Actress for Julia Jentsch, who gives a stunning performance as the doomed icon of the student resistance group, "White Rose".

Henry Hübchen and Hannelore Elsner in **Go for Sugar!**

X Verleih

Rothemund reminds audiences that not all young Germans became followers of the Nazis, as does Niko von Glasow's passionate and striking resistance tale, **Edelweiss Pirates** (*Edelweisspiraten*).

The documentary renaissance

Quite an important tendency in contemporary German cinema is the new popularity of documentaries. More than 20 German documentaries were shown on the big screen during 2005. Some dealt with the Nazi era, notably the brilliant and inventive **Two or Three Things I Know About Him** (*2 oder 3 Dinge, die ich von ihm weiß*), by Malte Ludin, and the less precise **Winter Children** (*Winterkinder*) by Jens Schanze. Both are bitter investigations into their directors' family histories. Marcel Schwierin's **Eternal Beauty** (*Ewige Schönheit*) is an impressive analysis of Nazi propaganda cinema, and Lutz Hachmeister tries in **The Goebbels Experiment** (*Das Goebbels-Experiment*) to deconstruct Goebbels' propaganda methods and language. Doris Metz's **Schattenväter** (literally, *Shadow Fathers*) is about the sons of Willy Brandt and Günther Guillaume, the spy who forced Brandt to resign in 1974.

Cinematographically, the most ambitious recent documentary is **Durchfahrtsland**, by Alexandra Sell, an essay about daily life in two provincial towns near Cologne that is cool and clear, full of laconic wit and sympathy for its protagonists, and told with an inventive visual language. Sell explores a landscape and stories that most German films ignore, and so does Philip Gröning, in his unique **Into Great Silence** (*Die große Stille*), which became a surprise success at German arthouse cinemas last November. For more than 150 minutes, the movie reveals the lives of tacit Carthusian monks (no more than a dozen words are spoken in the whole film); Gröning was one of the first non-members allowed to film the monks' world.

From Kenya to Berlin

In 2005 there was no huge local hit on the scale of 2004's *(T)Raumschiff Surprise – Period 1*, but Hermine Huntgeburth's **The White Massai** (*Die Weisse Massai*), about a European woman marrying a Massai warrior in Kenya, did surprisingly well – despite, or perhaps because of, its kitschy, sentimental tone. Another surprise at the box-office was **Barefoot** (*Barfuss*), a comedy-drama driven by the star power of Til Schweiger.

Christian Petzold shot the year's best arthouse film, **Ghosts** (*Gespenster*), a touching story of two very different girls who meet by chance one summer in Berlin and share some time together on the streets. The main character is the city itself, brilliantly photographed by Hans Fromm. The best of the rest came from

Robert Gwisdek, Philippe Graber, Daniel Zillmann. Prod: Boje Buck/7 Pictures.

SIEGFRIED
[Comedy, 2005] Script: Tom Gerhardt, Herman Weigel. Dir: Sven Unterwaldt. Phot: Peter von Haller. Players: Gerhardt, Dorkas Kiefer, Volker Buedts, Axel Neumann, Jan Sosniok, Daniela Wutte, Michael Brandner. Prod: Constantin Film/B.A. Produktion.

FREMDE HAUT (Unveiled)
[Drama, 2005] Script: Angelina Maccarone, Judith Kaufmann. Dir: Maccarone. Phot: Kaufmann. Players: Jasmin Tabatabai, Anneke Kim Sarnau, Hinnerk Schoenemann, Navid Akhavan, Jens Muenchow. Prod: MMM Film/Fischer Film (Vienna).

GESPENSTER (Ghosts)
[Drama, 2005] Script: Christian Petzold, Harun Farocki. Dir: Petzold. Phot: Hans Fromm. Players: Julia Hummer, Sabine Timoteo, Marianne Basler, Aurélien Recoing, Benno Fuermann. Prod: Schramm Film Koerner + Weber/Les films des Tournelles (Paris)/BR (Munich)/ARTE (Strasbourg)/ARTE France Cinema.

ALLES AUF ZUCKER!
(Go for Zucker!)
[Comedy, 2004] Script: Dani Levy, Holger Franke. Dir: Levy. Phot: Carl-F. Koschnick. Players: Henry Hübchen, Hannelore Elsner, Udo Samel, Golda Tencer, Steffen Groth. Prod: X Filme Creative Pool.

NAPOLA
[Historical drama, 2004] Script: Dennis Gansel, Maggie Peren. Dir: Gansel. Phot: Torsten Breuer. Players: Max Riemelt, Tom Schilling, Devid Striesow, Joachim Bissmeier. Prod: Olga Film/Constantin Film/Seven Pictures Film/Unterfoehring.

**SOPHI SCHOLL –
DIE LETZTEN TAGE**
(Sophie Scholl – The Final Days)
*Script: Fred Breinersdorfer. Dir:
Marc Rothemund. Phot: Martin
Langer. Players: Julia Jentsch,
Fabian Hinrichs, Gerald
Alexander Held, Florian Stetter,
Petra Kelling. Prod: Rothemund,
Breinersdorfer, Sven Burgemeister,
Christopher Müller.*

Julia Jentsch as **Sophie Scholl**

**CROSSING THE BRIDGE –
THE SOUND OF ISTANBUL**
*[Music documentary, 2005]
Script and Dir: Fatih Akin. Phot:
Hervé Dieu. Featuring: Ander
Hacke, Baba Zula, Orient
Expressions, Duman, Replikas,
Erkin Koray, Ceza, Mercan
Dede. Prod: Intervista Digital
Media/Corazón International/NDR.*

BARFUSS (Barefoot)
*[Romantic comedy, 2005] Script
and Dir: Til Schweiger. Phot:
Christof Wahl. Players:
Schweiger, Johanna Wokalek,
Nadja Tiller, Michael Mendl,
Steffen Wink, Eric Judor. Prod:
Schweiger, Barefoot Film/Buena
Vista International (Germany)
/Mr. Brown Entertainment.*

KEINE LIEDER UBER LIEBE
(No Songs of Love)
*[Drama, 2005] Script and Dir:
Lars Kraume. Phot: Alexa Ihrt.
Players: Florian Lukas, Jurgen
Vogel, Monika Hansen. Charlie
Rinn, Heike Makatsch. Prod: Film1.*

Quote of the Year

"I have beaten Hitler!"

HENRY HÜBCHEN, *star of*
Go for Sugar! *after winning the
German Film Award for Best
Actor, beating Bruno Ganz, who
played Hitler in* Downfall.

first- or second-time directors. Maren Ade's brilliantly directed **The Forest for the Trees** (*Der Wald vor lauter Bäumen*), is a character study of a young teacher unable to communicate adequately. It provides a good example of the concentrated and quiet, but nevertheless very ambitious film-making of the so-called "Berlin School", a lose group centred around the director Christoph Hochhäusler (who also founded a regular discussion group and *revolver*, a quarterly underground film magazine).

Hochhäusler's second movie was the impressive coming-of-age-drama **Low Profile** (*Falscher Bekenner*), about an 18-year-old slacker and his family. **Sleeper** (*Schläfer*), the debut of Hochhäusler's film school friend and scriptwriter, Benjamin Heisenberg, was a strong thriller, a story about suspicion and treason. Florian Schwarz made a noirish, wild and passionate debut, **Katze im Sack** (literary, *Cat in the Bag*), a stylish movie that brings together three lonely souls on one night in Leipzig. These young and ambitious film-makers undoubtedly represent the future of German cinema.

Art for Hartz sake

A third strand amongst the younger directors may be called "Hartz IV-Cinema" (named after one of the most important social reform laws). **Netto**, by Robert Thalheim, is the best example of the light, bittersweet tone and spontaneous, actor-driven ethos of these socially aware films, nearly all of which are set in east Berlin. *Netto* is the story of a 15-year-old who wants to move in with his father, who is unemployed and obsessed by the idea of becoming a bodyguard.

Other movies dealing lightly with economic crisis and social decline in contemporary Germany came from more experienced directors. Eoin Moore's fourth movie, **Im Schwitzkasten** (literally, *In a Headlock*), presents a group of people united by their sauna obsession. Some of its best comic moments are reminiscent of Billy Wilder. The prolific Andreas Dresen delivered two new films: the melancholic comedy **Sommer vorm Balkon** follows two young women in their search for love and happiness. The hero of **Willenbrock** is a dodgy car salesman in eastern Germany, whose life falls apart after he struggles with two burglars.

For 2006, we can look forward to new films from Hans-Christian Schmid (*Requiem*), Dominik Graf (*Der rote Kakadu*), Oskar Roehler (*Elementarteilchen*), Tom Tykwer (*Perfume*) and Wolfgang Becker.

RÜDIGER SUCHSLAND (suchsland@gmx.de) lives in Munich and Berlin and writes regularly for the daily *Frankfurter Rundschau*, *Berliner Zeitung* and *Kölner Stadtanzeiger* and the magazine *Filmdienst*.

Greece Yannis Bacoyannopoulos

The Year's Best Films

Yannis Bacoyannopoulos'
selection:
Delivery
(Nikos Panayotopoulos)
Rakushka (Fotini Siskopoulou)
Marseilles, A Greek Profile
(Marco Gastine)
Brides (Pantelis Voulgaris)
Real Life (Panos Koutras)

Nikos Panayotopoulos' **Delivery**

Recent and Forthcoming Films

**H CHORODIA TOU
CHARITONA (Chariton's Choir)**
*[Comedy, 2005] Script: Grigoris
Karantinakis, Giorgos Makris,
Dimitris Vakis. Dir: Grigoris
Karantinakis. Phot: Nikos
Kavoukidis. Players: George
Corraface, Maria Nafpliotou,
Akylas Karazissis, Dimitris
Piatas, Prod: Safe Company/
Odeon/Greek Film Centre/
CL Productions/Hellenic
Broadcasting Corp. ERT S.A./
NOVA/Cinefilm/Accelere/
Graal S.A.*
A comedy about life and the
people of a small country town in
the 60s. Love, passion, intrigue,
tenderness and lots of optimism
abound in a time of innocence
and beauty when people still
embraced life and its joys.

Although the total number of admissions rose only slightly during the year, many new multiplexes were created by the three major rival multinational companies. The reason? The huge investment in entertainment, especially for the young. On the outskirts of the cities huge malls are being built and equally gigantic fun parks, which must also offer the choice of film entertainment in order to provide maximum variety and ensure a maximum consumer spending by visitors. Traditional movie theatres are barely making ends meet or are on the verge of closing. Indeed, even more luxurious VIP theaters are being created that also provide dining facilities.

Greek cinema continues to find itself in a strange, crucial situation. In 2004–5, as in the previous year, a Greek film, **Brides** (*Nyfes*) climbed to the top of the box-office charts with 700,000 admissions and a second feature, **Honey and the Pig** (*Loukoumades ke meli*), a sex comedy by Olga Malea, reached 120,000. The rest went under. The change in government brought a severe cutback in state funding for production, which has already limited the number of new films (only low-budget films using DV technology increased) and has led to a crisis in the industry. The announcement of ambitious plans for the support of major international co-productions that will be shot in Greece remains vague and problematic.

Brides (*Nyfes*) is an imposing film by veteran top director Pantelis Voulgaris. Pre-production lasted four years because of the search for sufficient international capital, with the support of Martin Scorsese, who considered the project especially interesting. Although the huge initial budget had to be restricted, the film

Victoria Charalambidou and Damian Lewis in **Brides**

stands out for its rich, jam-packed production values and its effective adaptation to the American genre of the socio-sentimental drama. The film is based on true events – the mass transport of young women from poor European countries as mail-order brides for immigrants in the USA who are strangers to them. A young American photographer is aroused by their dramatic fate and falls in love with a seamstress. The film's weakness lies in its conformity with the model of mainstream cinema but Voulgaris once again develops his warm and tender look at human passions.

Nikos Panayotopoulos made his best film since the days of **Edge of Night** (*Afti I nichta meni*). With *Delivery* he takes a bold dive into the depths of Athens, in the slums where the homeless, the losers and the immigrants live. He wanders in the night, with shots that are raw and "dirty", and immerses his young hero in the black hole of our society, in absolute nothingness. Panayotopoulos is a dark pessimist but with a metaphysical sting. His hero is an angel who falls down here and flies away again.

With **Rakushka** Fotini Siskopoulou also takes up residence on the fringes of the city, amid the poor immigrants pressured into dead-end situations. Yet she too is more interested in the internal human landscape, relations of power, love and the inability to communicate. Siskopoulou adapted Dostoevski's short story "The Meek One" to the Greek reality and so dares to match herself with the Bresson of *Une femme douce*, succeeding by virtue of her feminine temperament and the social dimensions she maps out. The withdrawn man who marries the poor young immigrant from Tashkent in order to tame her with oppression, loses her in the war he wins and her soul escapes like a ray of sunshine.

In **Hostage** (*Omiros*), Constantine Giannaris is more directly social. He recreates the true hijacking of a bus by an angry Albanian worker who holds the passengers hostage. As always, Giannaris directs with a pulsing rhythm and power and focuses on the terrible injustice and the merciless pursuit that the Albanian faces at the hands of both the Greek and the Albanian authorities, but his perception wavers between subjective and objective narration.

With **Real Life** (*Alithini zoi*), Panos Koutras moves in a totally different climate and perspective of the cinema. The film drives this aspect to the limits, but does not restrict itself to a subversive irony in the John Waters style. On the contrary, with aesthetic sophistication and with vertical incisions in the dramatic substratum of the heroes, it attempts, even if it doesn't quite pull it off, a recuperation of the brash melodrama in the style of a modern Douglas Sirk. Indeed, Koutras is courageous enough not to lead his two young heroes to salvation, leaving them finally captives of their petty interests for survival or else of the irresistible forces of self-destruction.

Face Control

EFKOLI LIA (Face Control)
[Drama, 2005] Script and Dir: Vangelis Seitanidis. Phot: Seitanidis. Players: Ioannis Papazissis, Anna-Maria Papaharalambous, Michalis Iatropoulos, Emmanouella Alexiou, Eva Theotokatou, Prod: Vassilis Alatas (VA Films)/ Vangelis Seitanidis.
Savvas is a doorman at a fashionable Athens club and enduring a "midlife crisis" at 30! On Christmas Eve he's involved in a collision with Lia, the daughter of an infamous big businessman, in whom he sees his "other half". Subsequently interpreting coincidences as divine signs, he decides that her father is to blame for Lia's S&M proclivities and God arms him with a .45-calibre gun.

I KARDIA TOU KTINOUS (The Heart of the Beast)
[Drama, 2005] Script and Dir: Renos Haralambidis. Phot: Dimitris Theodoropoulos. Players: Renos Haralambidis, Giorgos Voultzatis, Manos Vakoudis, Alkia Panagiotidis, Gina Thliveri. Prod: Midnight Films/Lambros Trifyllis/FS Productions/Strada Productions/ Nova/Greek Film Centre.
Stephanos views everyone as inferior and when he is discharged from the army he thinks the world belongs to him. In reality, all he has are debts left by his dead mother and rejection by his formerly devoted girlfriend, who has replaced him with a new lover. Nikos, an old high-school classmate who distinguished himself as a criminal, proposes that they rob the bank where Aris works as a teller.

Angelos Frantzis' **A Dog's Dream**

Angelos Frantzis' **A Dog's Dream** (*To oniro tou skylou*) moves in the same post-modern direction but with elements of fantasy and magic realism. Embracing dreams and night vigils, film and reality, dual heroes and a weird city, he weaves an enchanted journey that constantly interrogates itself with a fair amount of sensitivity. The heroes sleep without sleeping and wake up because they dream. But the director fails to follow them and the film loses focus.

As in other countries, lately in Greece there has been a flourishing of the feature-length documentary, which has managed to attract audiences in commercial runs as well. The most interesting example of this type of documentary is Marco Gastine's **Marseilles, A Greek Profile** (*Massalia, makrini kori*) about the Greek community of the French city that was founded by the ancient Greeks. With succinct stories he makes us party to what those who arrived there to settle in a foreign land felt like, to the oblivion that sets in as they became assimilated by their new country and to the desire to return to the homeland that arises at some point. Yet he does not hesitate to point beyond the "bridges" of the Mediterranean and to the disappointment of some who returned and their unsettling position between two lives.

YANNIS BACOYANNOPOULOS has written about film since 1960 in many dailies, reviews and books. He was film critic of the Athens daily *Kathimerini* (1974–2003) and from 1975 to the present he is a critic for the Hellenic Broadcasting Corporation.

LOUCOUMADES KE MELI (Honey and the Pig)
[Comedy, 2005] Script: Olga Malea, Apostolos Alexopoulos. Dir: Malea. Phot: Elias Adamis. Players: Christos Loulis, Fay Xyla, Vladimiros Kyriakidis, Haris Mavroudis, Fotini Baxevani. Prod: Papandreou S.A./ Greek Film Centre/Mega Channel/ Prooptiki/ Attika/Olga Malea.
Despite great success with women, Manos steers clear of sex. To escape this, he goes to his village for a few days. There he finds his uncle secretly consuming honey buns with a 10 year-old boy. What is the uncle up to? With funeral home employee Fenia and Marikaki, a piglet who's crazy about honey buns, Manos tries to unmask his uncle's true intentions.

OMIROS (Hostage)
[Drama, 2005] Script and Dir: Constantine Giannaris. Phot: Panagiotis Theofanopoulos. Players: Stathis Papadopoulos, Theodora Tzimou, Giannis Stankoglou, Minas Hadjisavvas, Arto Apartian, Marilou Kapa-Valeonti. Prod: C. Giannaris Films/Highway Productions/ Samarsik Sanaltar/Greek Film Centre/Alpha TV/Graal S.A./ Strada Productions.
A 25-year-old Albanian immigrant boards an intercity bus on its daily route to Thessaloniki and hijacks it at gunpoint, taking seven passengers hostage. For the next 20 hours a wild and bleakly comic chase ensues through northern Greece at the head of a convoy of police cars, television crews, desperate relatives and bystanders, all the while heading towards the Albanian border.

Hostage

Espresso Studio

Looking for the new

GREEK FILM CENTRE
10, Panepistimiou Av., 106 71 Athens Greece
Tel. +30 210 3648007 Fax. +30 210 3614336
e-mail: info@gfc.gr www.gfc.gr

LIUBI

[Drama, 2005] Script and Dir: Layia Yiourgou. Phot: Dimitris Katsaitis. Players: Alexis Georgoulis, Eugenia Kaplan, Lena Kitsopoulou, Nikos Georgakis, Olga Damani. Prod: Highway Productions, VA FILMS, Greek Film Centre, NOVA TV/MAX Productions. Liubi enters a Greek family to become a companion for an elderly lady, happy that life has offered her this small but important opportunity. However, Dimitris yearns for a different opportunity: 'something' that will take him away from his role as the 'pillar' of his family. Liubi and Dimitris get together and live the illusion of freedom and love, which, sadly, cannot last for long…

I POLI TON THAVMATON
(Planet Athens)

[Drama, 2005] Script and Dir: Dimitris Athanitis. Phot: Spyros Papatriantafyllou. Players: Dimitris Alexandris, Katerina Didaskalou, Ekavi Douma, Babis Hadzidakis, Lida Matsangou. Prod: DNA Films/Cinegram/ DS Films/Greek Film Centre. August 2004. For ten days Athens becomes the centre of the universe as people arrive from all over the planet for the Olympic celebration. From Paris, Boston, Moscow and Tokyo, the paths of a disparate set of characters cross in unexpected ways. In this pulsing city anything can happen. Welcome to Planet Athens!

GLYKIA MNIMI
(Sweet Memory)

[Drama, 2005] Script and Dir: Kyriakos Katzourakis. Phot: Alekos Yiannaros. Players: Katia Gerou, Ekavi Douma, Maria Zorba, Nikos Arvanitis, Nikos Karathanos. Prod: CL Productions/Greek Film Centre. Irina returns to Greece from Russia after 20 years away, in order to find her stepbrother. Meeting her brother's friends, a chance encounter with an American saxophone player and

a young compatriot, a series of dramatic events that intervene, and her contact with a text by Genet, which she finds among her father's papers, all spark an internal journey of understanding and reconciliation.

TO GALAZIO FOREMA
(True Blue)

[Drama, 2005] Script: Panos Papadopoulos. Dir: Yannis Diamandopoulos. Phot: Andreas Sinanos. Players: Rania Economidou, Giorgos Nanouris, Maria Engelezaki, Electra Nikolouzou, Markella. Prod: Metavision S.A./Greek Film Centre S.A./EURIMAGES/ Hellenic Broadcasting Corp. ERT S.A./ ACT Ltd./Foundation Bulgarian Cinema Decade of the '50s. A widow is raising her three children and has a soft spot for her only son. The first signs of the son's self-destructive nature appear early on: clashes with the family, a break with social role models, and bisexual relationships. His passion for dancing leads him to Paris and his passions to a spiral towards tragedy.

I NOSTALGOS
(The Woman Who Missed Home)

[Drama, 2005] Script: Eleni Alexandrakis, based on the short story by Alexandros Papadiamandis. Dir: Alexandrakis. Phot: Vassilis Kapsouros. Players: Olia Lazaridou, Giorgos Tsoularis, Spyros Stavrinides and the people of the island of Nisyros. Prod: Eleni Alexandrakis/PPV S.A./ Lexicon Factory, S.A./New Star. A married woman, Anna, runs away from the island where she lives with her much older husband, to return to her native land. A young shepherd, Mathios, helps her escape in a small rowboat.

SIRINES STO AEGEO
(Sirens in the Aegean)

[Comedy, 2005] Script: Nikos Perakis. Dir: Perakis. Phot:

Giorgos Argyroiliopoulos. Players: Yannis Tsimitselis, Giorgos Seitaridis, Ioannis Papazissis, Socrates Patsikas, Stelios Xanthoudakis. Prod: CL Productions/Odeon/ Hellenic Broadcasting Corp. ERT S.A./Nova/Graal S.A./ Nikos Perakis. An optimistic comedy with dramatic moments.

ITHIKON AKMAIOTATON
(Morally Alive and Kicking)

[Comedy, 2005] Script: Stamatis Tsarouchas, Sophia Sotiriou. Dir: Tsarouchas. Phot: Dimitris Theodoropoulos. Players: Sakis Boulas, Renos Haralambidis, Dimitris Piatas, Tassos Pantzidis, Yannis Zouganelis. Prod: Midnight Films/FS Productions S.A./Lambros Trifyllis/Takis Veremis/Hellenic Broadcasting Corp. ERT S.A. The sudden death of a friend reunites a group of 50-year-olds who remain adolescents at heart.

KI AN FIGO THA XANARTHO
(Coming as a Friend)

[Drama, 2005] Script and Dir: Dora Masklavanou. Phot: Claudio Bolivar. Players: Yannis Stankoglou, Maria Kechagioglou, Meletis Georgiadis, Giorgos Tsoularis, Errikos Litsis, Yannis Economidis, Giorgos Xykomninos, Marios Ioannou. Prod: Panayotis Petropoulos/ Dora Masklavanou/ Dimitris Kalaitzis. A small-time crook who is released from prison meets a woman who lives "imprisoned" on a mountain and makes coal.

AGRIPNIA (The Wake)

[Drama, 2005] Script: Nikos Grammatikos, Nikos Panayotopoulos. Dir: Nikos Grammatikos. Phot: Simos Sarketzis. Players: Vangelis Mourikis, Michalis Tsourounakis, Angeliki Dimitrakopoulou, Iro Loupi. Prod: Graal S.A. Two brothers – Andreas, a dirty cop, and the younger Nikos, a priest – are a decade apart in age and a world apart in views. They have no common ground, until the moment when Andreas accidentally injures his wife with his service revolver.

I YINEKA INE SKLIROS ANTHROPOS
(Woman is a Tough Person)
[Comedy, 2005] Script: Alexis Kardaras, based on an idea by Antonis Kafetzopoulos. Dir: Kafetzopoulos. Phot: Elias Konstantakopoulos. Players: Kafetzopoulos, Jenny Roussea, Fay Kokkinopoulou, Yota Festa, Mania Papadimitriou. Prod: Bad Movies S.A./Odeon/ Alpha TV/ Nova.
A tender situation comedy about men's mistakes and women's desires, shot in modern Athens.

ME TIN PSICHI STO STOMA
(Heart in Mouth)
[Drama, 2005] Script and Dir: Yannis Economidis. Phot: Dimitris Katsaitis. Players: Errikos Litsis, Maria Kechayoglou, Vangelis Mourikis, Maria Nafpliotou, Yannis Voulgarakis. Prod: Argonauts S.A./Yannis Economidis Films Ltd./ Hellenic Broadcasting Corporation ERT S.A./Cassandra Films/Strada Productions S.A.
A penetrating and subversive look deep inside the microcosm of working-class Greek society. Takis is the film's main hero: middle-aged, a worker in a cottage industry; divorced, remarried and with a newborn infant; under pressure from everywhere. No one leaves him in peace. Wife, employer, relatives, friends. Violence and oppression. Verbal, mental, physical. All against one and God against everyone... The lighted fuse is just a few metres away from the gunpowder and in the end, reaches it.

KINETTA
[Drama, 2005] Script: Yorgos Lanthimos, Yorgos Kaknakis. Dir: Lanthimos. Phot: Thymios Bakatakis. Players: Evangelia Randou, Aris Servetalis, Kostas Xikominos. Prod: Haos Films/ Modiano S.A./Top Cut/ Stefi Productions.
Kinetta is a defunct Greek resort town inhabited during the off-season by migrant workers. A plainclothes cop with a passion for automobiles, tape recorders and Russian women investigates a series of recent murders in the area.

TO ONIRO TOU IKAROU
(Icarus' Dream)
[Drama, 2005] Script and Dir: Costas Natsis. Phot: Stamatis Yannoulis. Players: Angelos Sifonios, Nikos Aliagas, Anna Mouglalis, Renos Haralambidis, Lefteris Eleftheriadis, Dimitris Kamberidis. Prod: Cinegram S.A. – Haris Padouvas, Despina Mouzaki/Love Streams – Agnes B.
All 10-year-old Elias wants is to be a musician.

Quote of the Year

"I can't stand directors who think they're gods."
PANTELIS VOULGARIS, *director.*

Hong Kong Tim Youngs

The Year's Best Films

Tim Youngs' selection:

Crazy 'n the City
(James Yuen)

Beyond Our Ken
(Pang Ho-cheung)

Seven Swords (Tsui Hark)

AV (Pang Ho-cheung)

2 Young (Derek Yee)

Recent and Forthcoming Films

JOI SUET YAT CHI NGO NGOI NEI (All About Love)
[Drama, 2005] Script: Daniel Yu, Lee Kung-lok. Dir: Daniel Yu. Players: Andy Lau, Charlie Yeung, Charlene Choi. Prod: Focus Films.

TSING DIN DAI SING (A Chinese Tall Story)
[Fantasy, 2005] Script and Dir: Jeff Lau. Players: Nicholas Tse, Charlene Choi, Chen Bo-lin, Fan Bingbing. Prod: Emperor Classic Films.

BUN JEUI YAN GAAN (Cocktail)
[Drama, 2006] Dir: Herman Yau, Picas So. Players: Candy Lo, Race Wong, Endy Chow, Bobo Chan. Prod: Buddy Film Creative Workshop.

MAANG LUNG (Dragon Squad)
[Action, 2005] Script: Daniel Lee, Lau Ho-leung. Dir: Lee. Players: Shawn Yue, Eva Huang, Lawrence Chou. Prod: Visualizer Film Productions.

LUNG FU MUN (Dragon Tiger Gate)
[Martial arts, 2006] Script: Edmond Wong. Dir: Wilson Yip. Players: Donnie Yen, Nicholas

H ong Kong's film-industry fortunes looked mixed at the beginning of 2005, with output slipping despite a strong finale for 2004. **Kung Fu Hustle** filled cinemas over Christmas, returning hugely popular actor–director Stephen Chow to screens and drawing a record-breaking $7.9m (HK$61.3m) in ticket sales. But the film's success gave way to grim indicators later. The number of local releases continued the decline of recent years and overall box-office takings for the first half of 2005 dropped 18% year on year. Concerns about quality and ongoing video piracy were cited as contributors. Sixty-four Hong Kong movies reached cinemas in 2004, down from 77 the year before.

As 2005 progressed, film-makers exercised caution, while spending on movies fell and overseas blockbusters competed strongly. Chinese New Year, traditionally a highlight for popular cinema, saw slower ticket sales than usual for the local offerings, but summer was marked with a box-office smash for popular comic-book adaptation **Initial D**, which took $4.9m (HK$37.9m), alongside a handful of moderately successful pictures. Producers showed enthusiasm for the Chinese National Day and Golden Week holiday period that started ahead of October 1, fielding high-profile dramas and action films for concurrent Hong Kong and mainland release.

Hong Kong-China co-productions remain a steady part of the cinema landscape, aided by the Closer Economic Partnership Arrangement (CEPA) that came into force in 2003. Despite relaxations of some restrictions in early 2004, those forging cross-border partnerships must still juggle catering to the different tastes

Stephen Chow's **Kung Fu Hustle**

Tse, Shawn Yue, Dong Jie. Prod:
Mandarin Films/Beijing Polybona
Film Publishing (China)

HAK SEH WUI (Election)
[Action drama, 2005] Script:
Yau Nai-hoi, Yip Tin-shing.
Dir: Johnnie To. Players: Simon
Yam, Tony Leung Ka-fai, Louis
Koo, Nick Cheung. Prod.
Milkyway Image.

**YEE WOH WAI GWAI
(Election II)**
[Action drama, 2006] Script: Yau
Nai-hoi, Yip Tin-shing. Dir:
Johnnie To. Players: Louis Koo,
Simon Yam, Nick Cheung, Lam
Ka-tung. Prod: Milkyway Image.

SUM YUEN (Forest of Death)
[Thriller, 2006] Dir: Danny
Pang. Players: Shu Qi. Prod:
Universe Entertainment/Magic
Head Film Production Thailand).

SEUNG TSI (Futago)
[Horror, 2005] Script: Sam
Leong, Paul Chung. Dir: Fung
Yuen-man. Players: Hisako
Shirata, Tony Ho, Samuel Pang,
Emily Kwan. Prod: Same Way/
Art Port (Japan).

**GWAI MUT
(Home Sweet Home)**
[Horror drama, 2005] Script:
Szeto Kam-yuen, Tang Lik-kei.
Dir: Soi Cheang. Players: Karena
Lam, Hsu Chi, Alex Fong.
Prod: Filmko.

YI SA BUI LAI (Isabella)
[Drama, 2006] Script: Pang Ho-
cheung, Kearen Pang, Derek
Tsang, Jimmy Wan. Dir: Pang
Ho-cheung. Players: Chapman
To, Isabella Leong, JJ Jia, Derek
Tsang. Prod: Not Brothers.

**YEH MAAN BEI KAHP
(My Kung Fu Sweetheart –
working title)**
[Kung-fu comedy, 2006] Dir:
Wong Jing. Players: Leo Ku,
Cecilia Cheung, Yuen Wah, Yuen
Qiu. Prod: Wong Jing's
Workshop.

**TSING YI NGOR SUM JI
(Moonlight in Tokyo)**
[Comedy drama, 2005] Script

of Hong Kong and mainland audiences while ensuring their films
meet Chinese censorship standards. Further co-operation was
promoted at the revived Hong Kong–Asia Film Financing Forum in
March–April 2005, part of a larger Entertainment Expo that grouped
previously separate annual events including the Hong Kong
International Film & TV Market, the film awards and the Hong Kong
International Film Festival under a single banner.

Star attractions

Kung Fu Hustle and *Initial D* created the largest splashes in
2004–05, both eagerly anticipated and each gaining strong word-
of-mouth support. Action-spectacular *Kung Fu Hustle* built on the
meeting of martial arts and digital trickery. Director Stephen Chow
previously tapped this vein for *Shaolin Soccer* in 2001 to push
kung-fu cinema forward while paying tribute to local film heritage.
Chow cast himself within a colourful troupe as an underdog,
stumbling into a tenement block of skilled fighters and drawing the
ire of local gangsters. *Initial D,* based on a popular Japanese comic
book series, was brought to life by co-directors Andrew Lau and
Alan Mak. Set in Japan, the car-racing tale combined familiar print-
medium faces with idols from Hong Kong and Taiwan and used
slick technique to soup up showdowns on winding mountain roads.

Tsui Hark's **Seven Swords**

Also providing high-budget action in 2004 and 2005 were Tsui
Hark's **Seven Swords** and two new releases starring Jackie Chan.
In *Seven Swords*, Tsui returned to epic wuxia material, building a
set of heroes fighting to uphold tradition and save a village. Starring
Leon Lai and Charlie Yeung, with martial-arts aces Lau Kar-leung,
and Donnie Yen, Tsui's film staged rousing action in windswept,
dusty Xinjiang province locations and left scope for a sequel. In
2004 **New Police Story** had Chan fighting rich-kid urban terrorists
on Hong Kong turf but with some lively throwbacks to his action
classics thrown in. **The Myth**, a pricey Stanley Tong-directed
movie, scored the stronger opening of Chan's two, positioned
ahead of the 2005 National Day, as it sent its lead to India and

China in a time-travelling fantasy adventure.

Local arthouse crowds and overseas festivalgoers took in Wong Kai-wai's **2046** after years of waiting. In Wong's follow-up to *In The Mood For Love*, Tony Leung Chiu-wai reprised his role from the earlier film, this time as a writer engaged in liaisons with women (Zhang Ziyi, Carina Lau, Faye Wong) at a rundown hotel. Sumptuously shot, evoking a strong 1960s ambience and throwing in sci-fi diversion, *2046* walked off with six statuettes at the subsequent Hong Kong Film Awards – a haul equalled by *Kung Fu Hustle*. Stanley Kwan's **Everlasting Regret** captured further old-style charm, offering a tale of unfulfilled love between a society girl (Sammi Cheng) and photographer (Tony Leung Kar-fai) spanning decades from glamorous 1930s Shanghai origins.

Local flavours

A variety of smaller productions lit up screens with distinctly local flavour. Director Pang Ho-cheung shook off his earlier black-comedy label with **Beyond Our Ken**, an exceptional drama set around a teacher (Gillian Chung) finding risqué photos of herself posted online, supposedly placed there by a slimy ex-boyfriend. Built from a simple premise but leavened with scheming, twists and turns, *Beyond Our Ken* enlivened youth-oriented film-making with a distinct pop sensibility. Not leaving comedy for too long, Pang next served up **AV**, a clever affair about a team of college underachievers coaxing a Japanese adult-movie starlet to Hong Kong for a bogus film shoot but learning they're not so smart after all.

A mélange of themes and district details emerged in James Yuen's **Crazy 'n the City**, ostensibly a police-themed drama. Largely following two cops (Eason Chan and Joey Yung) on their beat, Yuen infused his feature with snippets of street life and peculiarities, alongside meatier romance and crime subplots to defy genre labels. Director Derek Yee meanwhile set about tackling teen drama and romantic comedy with **2 Young** and **Drink, Drank, Drunk**,

James Yuen's **Crazy 'n the City**

and Dir: *Alan Mak, Felix Chong. Players: Leon Lai, Chapman To, Yang Gwei-mei, Michelle Ye. Prod: Media Asia/Basic Pictures.*

YU GWO NGOI (Perhaps Love)
[Drama musical, 2005] Script: Aubrey Lam, Raymond To. Dir: Peter Chan. Players: Jacky Cheung, Takeshi Kaneshiro, Zhou Xun. Prod: Ruddy Morgan (US)/Applause Pictures.

GWAI WIK (Re-Cycle)
[Horror, 2006] Dir: Danny Pang, Oxide Pang. Players: Lee Sinje. Prod: Universe Entertainment/ Magic Head Film Production (Thailand).

JEUI NGOI LUI YAHN KAU MUT KWONG (Shopaholic – working title)
[Comedy, 2006] Script and Dir: Wai Ka-fai. Players: Cecilia Cheung, Lau Ching-wan, Jordan Chan. Prod: One Hundred Years of Film.

MAN JEUK (The Sparrow)
[Suspense drama, 2006] Dir: Johnnie To. Players: Simon Yam, Kelly Lin, Lam Ka Tung. Prod: Milkyway Image.

SA PO LONG (SPL)
[Action, 2005] Script: Szeto Kam-yuen, Ng Wai-lun. Dir: Wilson Yip. Players: Donnie Yen, Sammo Hung, Simon Yam, Wu Jing. Prod: 1618 Action.

Quote of the Year

"We only had one local film, *Kung Fu Hustle*, in the cinemas at Christmas and that's not healthy."
WOODY TSUNG WAN-CHI, Motion Picture Industry Association chief executive, on Hong Kong's reduced number of releases in 2004–05.

The 24th Hong Kong Film Awards

Best Film: *Kung Fu Hustle.*
Best Director: Derek Yee Tung-sing (*One Nite in Mongkok*).
Best Screenplay: Derek Yee Tung-sing (*One Nite in Mongkok*).
Best Actor:
Tony Leung Chiu-wai (*2046*).
Best Actress: Zhang Ziyi (*2046*).
Best Supporting Actor:
Yuen Wah (*Kung Fu Hustle*).
Best Supporting Actress:
Bai Ling (*Dumplings*).
Best New Actor:
Tian Yuan (*Butterfly*).
Best Cinematography:
Christopher Doyle, Lai Yiu-fai and Kwan Pun-leung (*2046*).
Best Editing:
Angie Lam (*Kung Fu Hustle*).
Best Art Direction:
William Chang Suk-ping and Alfred Yau Wai-ming (*2046*).
Best Costuming and Makeup:
William Chang Suk-ping (*2046*).
Best Action Choreography:
Yuen Wo-ping (*Kung Fu Hustle*).
Best Original Score:
Peer Raben (*2046*).
Best Original Song: "Gam, gam, gam" by The Pancakes (*Mcdull, Prince de la Bun*).
Best Sound Design:
Steven Ticknor, Steve Burgess, Rob Mackenzie and Paul Pirola (*Kung Fu Hustle*).
Best Visual Effects:
Frankie Chung Chi-hung, Don Ma Wong-on, Tam Kai-kwan and Franco Hung Yuk-leung (*Kung Fu Hustle*).
Best Asian Film:
Old Boy (South Korea).
New Director Award:
Wong Ching-po (*Jiang Hu*).
Lifetime Achievement Awards:
Jackie Chan, Yu Mo-wan.

earning box-office success. *2 Young* rolled themes of teen pregnancy, class boundaries and rebellion into a compelling whole, with newcomers Fiona Sit and Jaycee Chen both lending likeable performances to the leads. *Drink, Drank, Drunk* later cast popular comedienne Miriam Yeung as a beer salesgirl, immune to the effects of alcohol and catching the heart of a French chef (Daniel Wu) prone to booze binges.

A couple of high-budget productions reconfirmed actor Andy Lau

Derek Yee's teen drama **2 Young**

as one of the city's most bankable talents. Johnnie To's **Yesterday Once More** paired Lau with Sammi Cheng in a globetrotting tale of high-class thievery that packed an emotional punch after a playful opening. Teddy Chen's **Wait Til You're Older** clad Lau's features in heavy make-up for a *Big*-like transformation, going from schoolboy to senior citizen in a matter of days thanks to a magic potion. Chen's movie reached cinemas in the burst of National Day releases at the end of summer, leading the way for a diverse slate of upcoming movies with potential to lift the industry out of its doldrums. As October started, local movie fans were looking forward to the likes of Johnnie To's hotly anticipated triad-society tale, **Election**, Wilson Yip's dark actioner, **SPL**, Peter Chan's Shanghai-set musical, **Perhaps Love**, and a Christmas line-up set to include **A Chinese Tall Story**, the latest adventure fantasy from director Jeff Lau.

TIM YOUNGS is a Hong Kong-based writer who serves as Hong Kong consultant to the Far East Film Festival, Udine.

Hungary Eddie Cockrell

The Year's Best Films

Eddie Cockrell's selection:
Black Brush
(Dir: Roland Vranik)
Fateless (Dir: Lajos Koltai)
The Porcelain Doll
(Dir: Peter Gardos)
Who the Hell's Bonnie and Clyde (Dir: Krisztina Deak)

Lajos Koltai's **Fateless**

Recent and Forthcoming Films

CSUDAFILM (Miracle Film)
[Comedy, 2005] Script: Andras Kern, Elemer Ragalyi. Phot: Ragalyi. Phot: Ragalyi. Players: Katerina Didaskalou, Andras Kern, Peter Rudolf, Sandor Badar, Janos Derzsi. Prod: Gabor Kalomista, Blonde/ Megafilm/RTL Klub.
A bum in Budapest inherits a sprawling resort hotel on Crete.

EG VELED! (See You in Space!)
[Drama, 2005] Script: Francisco Gozon, Jozsef Pacskovsky, Pal Sandor. Dir: Pacskovsky. Phot: Gozon. Players: Eszter Balla, Dimitrij Pavlenko, Foso Nicoletta, Ferenc Kallai, Zsolt Laszlo, Marco Bonini, Natalia Sellverstova, Csaba Pindroch, Ildiko Toth. Prod: Andreas Kormos, Pal Sandor, Hunnia Film Studio.
In Budapest, Moscow and Rome,

f Steven Spielberg makes a movie in your country in 2005, it must mean you have appealing tax laws, solid infrastructure and skilled manpower. Thus it was for Hungary, as the Oscar-winning director of *Schindler's List* was just the most high-profile international film-maker to take advantage of the government's two-year-old Roosevelt-sounding "New Deal" legislation by filming sequences from his hotly anticipated Mossad thriller *Munich* in-country between location work in Malta and New York City. The shoot was originally planned for Germany, but relocated to take advantage of the highly touted scheme offering a generous 20% rebate on all production costs.

In truth, the continuing success and ever-higher profile of the tax law are, for the moment, the envy of such countries as the Czech Republic, Canada and Italy, which have seen their 1990s dominance of offshore Hollywood productions give way to such waiting-to-be-discovered destinations as Romania, the Baltic States and, of course, Hungary. A year after the passage of the law, in December 2004, Budapest-based investment bank Concorde Securities sweetened the deal by establishing a Film Trust that "definitely applies to foreign productions as well as Hungarian," as Concorde director Mike Boris told *Variety*. "I think this law and the Trust will once again make Hungary a beneficial area to make a movie." Just ask Steven Spielberg.

As if to echo the invigorating energy of these art-friendly financial and legislative machinations, the 36th Hungarian Film Week in February 2005 offered a number of exciting films from widely disparate genres that subsequently resonated with international

Gergely Banki, Csaba Hernadi, Karoly Hajduk and Andras Rethelyi get involved with the wrong crowd in **Black Brush**

a series of interconnected relationships play themselves out.

FEHER TENYER (White Palms)
[Sports drama, 2006] Script and Dir: Szabolcs Hajdu. Phot: Andras Nagy. Players: Miklos Zoltan Hajdu, Orion Radies, Silas Radies, Gheorghe Dinica, Kyle Shewfelt. Prod: Ivan Angelusz, Gabor Kovacs, Agnes Pataki, Peter Reich, Katapult Film/Filmpartners.

FEKETE KEFE (Black Brush)
[Comedy, 2005] Script: Roland Vranik, Gergely Poharnok. Dir: Vranik. Phot: Poharnok. Players: Gergely Banki, Csaba Hernadi, Karoly Hajduk, Andras Rethelyi. Prod: Istvan Major, Agnes Pataki, FilmTeam/Film Partners/ Inforg Studio.
Four slacker buddies become involved in underworld mischief.

**A FENY OSVENYEI
(Paths of Light)**
[Drama, 2005] Script: Attila Mispal, Emese Babette Solti, Sandor Tar. Dir: Mispal. Phot: Andras Nagy. Players: Annamaria Cseh, Gyorgy Cserhalmi, Balazs Czukor, Lajos Kovacs, Attila Soos, Eniko Szilagyi, Mari Torocsik. Prod: Peter Miskolczi, Attila Mispal, Andras Muhi, Gabor Varadi, Eurofilm Studio/Inforg Studio.
A scarred model and a blind goldsmith are drawn together.

JOHANNA
[Drama, 2005] Script: Kornel Mundruczo, Viktoria Petranyi. Dir: Mundruczo. Phot: Matyas Erdely, Andras Nagy. Players: Laszlo Boldog, Hermina Fatyol, Istvan Gantner, Denes Gulyas, Jozsef Hormai, Sandor Kecskes, Janos Klezil, Viktoria Mester, Orsi Toth, Zsolt Trill. Prod: Viktoria Petranyi, Bela Tarr, Proton Cinema/T.T. Filmmuhely.
A miraculously cured drug addict cures patients with her body.

KESZ CIRKUSZ (Bedlam)
[Action comedy, 2005] Script: Zsombor Dyga, Balazs Lovas. Dir: Dyga. Phot: Arpad Horvath.

audiences. Emerging as a dark horse from the strong field to win the main prize was director Roland Vranik's slacker saga **Black Brush** (*Fekete kefe*). A widescreen black-and-white stoner comedy about four twenty-something chimney sweeps and their adventures in a surreally hot Budapest nether region of listless criminals and missing drugs, the film relies on a leisurely but unerring interior logic that rewards the patient viewer with a Jarmusch-like sense of laissez-faire inevitability. The Film Week prize ensures that this very funny film will have the momentum to reach a target demographic Vranik dryly described as "elevated from reality."

Much more traditional, though no less risk-taking in its mood and construction, was **Fateless** (*Sorstalansag*), the triumphant directing debut of Lajos Koltai, whose distinguished career as a cinematographer has seen him working on numerous films with the great István Szabó. An astute adaptation of Imre Kertesz' novel about a teenaged boy in 1944 Budapest who survives a series of concentration camps with patience and inner peace, the co-production with the United Kingdom and Germany creates a remarkable mood of strength and tolerance unique for its sensitive subject matter.

Presented on the very last evening of the Hungarian Film Week before debuting in Berlin as a last-minute addition to that fest's competition section, at press time *Fateless* had been freshly nominated for two European film awards, recognising Gyula Pados' magnificent cinematography and Ennio Morricone's stirring score. The film also will represent Hungary in the balloting for Best Foreign Film at the 78th annual Academy Awards.

A more resolutely arthouse endeavour in the spirit of recent Hungarian success *Hukkle* and the country's track record of challenging, folk-drenched fables is Peter Gardos' **The Porcelain Doll** (*A porcelanbaba*). A gently humanistic and vaguely historic visualisation of three novellas by Ervin Lazar, this confident yet low-key work incorporates elements of resurrection, rural life and mystical realism into stories that are as thought-provoking as anything dreamed up by O. Henry or Rod Serling. Appropriately, this distinctly whimsical and sure-handed work—quite different in tone from Gardos' previous films, including 1986's *Whooping Cough* – picked up the Best Director award at the 36th Hungarian Film Week, along with the coveted foreign critics' prize named for venerated *Variety* correspondent Gene Moskowitz.

Also making positive impressions were vet director Krisztina Deak's astutely constructed teenaged outlaw homage **Who the Hell's Bonnie and Clyde** (*A miskolci boniesklajd*), Aron Gauder's unclassifiable animated sociopolitical urban rap musical comedy **The District** (*Nyocker*) and Zsombor Dyga's frenetic multi-character chase laffer **Bedlam** (*Kesz cirkusz*). A pair of sweet-tempered local comedies, vet funnyman Robert Koltai's circus-set **Colossal Sensation** and DP-turned-star/director Elemer Ragalyi's **Miracle Film** (*Csudafilm*) proved that the industry still makes room for conventional, older-skewing popular entertainments of modest ambitions.

Gabriella Hamori takes aim in Who the Hell's Bonnie and Clyde

Even the more thematically ambitious but less completely satisfying works, including Kornel Mundruczo's Joan of Arc-inspired grunge opera **Johanna** (which premiered in Cannes' Un Certain Regard), Attila Mispal's large-palette mismatched romantic drama **Paths of Light** (*A feny osenyei*) and Jozsef Pacskovsky's multi-character millennial meditation **See You in Space!** (*Eg veled!*) displayed marked signs of directorial talent needing only the discipline and focus that experience will provide. In all, during 2005 some dozen Hungarian features have screened at more than 120 international festivals, winning dozens of awards and special mentions. Add in the plethora of short films supported and encouraged by the industry, and those numbers more than double.

In other news, Hungarian-born Hollywood cinematographers Laszlo Kovacs (*Easy Rider*) and Vilmos Zsigmond (Spielberg's *Close Encounters of the Third Kind*), along with local legends Gyorgy Illes and Janos Toth, received the inaugural Legends awards from the Hungarian Society of Cinematographers; and Romanian director Cristi Puiu's *The Death of Mister Lazarescu* won the Best Film award at the inaugural Alba Regia festival in Szekesfehervar. The 15th edition of Germany's Cottbus festival spotlighted recent Hungarian film production by showing some 40 features and shorts organized into 15 separate programmes, while national treasure István Szabó—who received the life achievement award in Cottbus—lauded the "miracle of film and television" for recording "how an emotion is being experienced as it occurs" in his fervent Cinema Militans lecture, sponsored by *Variety*, at the Utrecht festival in the Netherlands.

Players: Imre Csuja, Ferenc Elek, Laszlo Gorog, Zoltan Nagy, Eszter Onodi, Peter Scherer, Zoltan Schmied, Jozsef Toth, Dorottya Udvaros, Gabor Welker. Prod: Gyorgy Durst, Akna Film/Duna Workshop/ Mediawave 2000.

A MISKOLCI BONIESKLAJD
(**Who the Hell's Bonnie and Clyde**)
[Drama, 2005] Script and Dir: Krisztina Deak, from the memoir by Tunde Novak. Phot: Tibor Mathe. Players: Ildiko Raczkevy, Gabor Karalyos, Gyorgy Gazso, Gabriella Hamori, Mate Haumann, Tamas Lengyel. Prod: Gabor Garami, Cinema-Film/TV2.
Two young lovers on the run.

Peter Gardos' The Porcelain Doll

A PORCELANBABA
(**The Porcelain Doll**)
[Historical fantasy drama, 2005] Script and Dir: Peter Gardos, from the novella by Ervin Lazar. Phot: Tibor Mathe. Players: Lajos Bertok, Sandor Csanyi, Judit Nemeth, people living on farms. Prod: Denes Szekeres, Tivoli/Duna Television.
A trio of rural fables.

SORSTALANSAG (**Fateless**)
[Holocaust drama, 2005] Script: Imre Kertesz, from his novel. Dir: Lajos Koltai. Phot: Gyula Pados. Players: Marcell Nagy, Aron Dimeny, Endre Harkanyi, Andras M. Kecskes, Jozsef Gyabronka, Bela Dora, Daniel Szabo, Zsolt Der, Daniel Craig. Prod: Andras Hamori, Peter Barbalics, Ildiko Kemeny, Jonathan Olsberg.

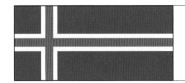

Iceland Ásgrímur Sverrisson

The Year's Best Films:

Ásgrímur Sverrisson's selection:

Africa United
(Docu. Hilmar Oddsson)
Screaming Masterpiece
(Docu. Ari Alexander)
I Nearly Lost My Head
(Short. Bjargey Ólafsdóttir)
Dark Horse (Dagur Kári)

Recent and Forthcoming Films

A LITTLE TRIP TO HEAVEN
[Thriller, 2005] Script and Dir: Baltasar Kormákur. Players: Forest Whitaker, Julia Stiles, Jeremy Renner, Peter Coyote. Prod: Palomar Pictures (US/ Blue Eyes Productions.

Forrest Whitaker in
A Little Trip to Heaven

AFRICA UNITED
[Documentary, 2005] Script and Dir: Ólafur Jóhannesson. Prod: Poppoli Films.

GARGANDI SNILLD
(Screaming Masterpiece)
[Documentary, 2005] Script and Dir: Ari Alexander. Prod: Palomar Pictures (US)/Zik Zak Filmworks (Iceland).

STRÁKARNIR OKKAR
(Eleven Men Out)
[Comedy, 2005] Script: Jón Atli Jónasson, Róbert I. Douglas. Dir:

The year's most energetic and entertaining Icelandic film, the documentary **Africa United** by Ólafur Jóhannesson, blurs the line between fact and fiction in a fresh and inventive way. It tells the story of a hapless soccer team made up entirely of immigrants, mostly of southern European and African descent, participating for the first time in the third and lowest league division after years of playing in the non-league ghetto. Their aim: to stay in the third division. To cut a long story short, they fail miserably, but with considerable style. The phrase "extensive incompetence" springs to mind.

Jóhannesson does not shy away from directing his documentary subjects in certain ways. He appears regularly throughout the film as a team manager of sorts, secures sponsorship and gives them a good kick in the rear when all seems lost. He also structures his film in the shape of the traditional sports movie: underdogs face impossible odds, etc. The portrayal of the immigrants is done with tender loving care and despite watching the team's spirit sinking lower by the minute we cannot but root for these all-too-human footballers.

Another fine documentary, **Screaming Masterpiece** (*Gargandi snilld*), by Ari Alexander, covers the Icelandic rock music phenomenon of recent years. Internationally known artists like Björk and Sigur Rós feature prominently, but it soon emerges that these big names did not come out of a vacuum. *Screaming Masterpiece* positions itself as the harvest of the seeds planted by the legendary rockumentary *Rock in Reykjavík* (*Rokk í Reykjavík*), made in 1982 by the then unknown Fridrik Thór Fridriksson. His film portrayed the thriving punk rock scene and showed us, for example, Björk's first musical steps.

Dagur's *Dark* ride

Icelandic film-makers continue to find work abroad and this year two directors presented their foreign-made films. Dagur Kári made **Dark Horse** (*Voksne mennesker*) in Denmark, and Marteinn Thorsson, along with Jeff Renfroe, shot his US-produced *One Point O* in Budapest. Both films received support from the Icelandic Film Centre. *Dark Horse*, Kári's second film, premiered in "Un Certain Regard" at Cannes in May. It's a low-key comedy about a young layabout (Jakob Cedergren) who has to shape up when life knocks him abruptly on the head. It features, among others, the excellent Nicolas Bro as the hero's friend; Bro is becoming one of the finest actors in Danish films. In November, the film received the Edda (the Icelandic Oscar) for film of the year.

Jakob Cedergren, left, and Tilly Scott Pedersen in **Dark Horse**

One Point O is Thorsson's and Renfroe's debut and premiered in the main competition of the Sundance Film Festival in 2004. It's a nightmarish urban sci-fi thriller, excellently photographed and designed by Chris Soos and Eggert Ketilsson respectively. The story is set in a decaying cityscape and deals with a young computer programmer who receives a computer virus in his body, which begins to take control of his life. The film features a well-known cast, including Jeremy Sisto (*Six Feet Under*), Deborah Unger, Lance Henriksen and Udo Kier.

Out and proud

The only fully "homegrown" feature this year was **Eleven Men Out** (*Strákarnir okkar*) by Róbert Douglas. It's a comedy about a Reykjavík football star (Björn Hlynur Haraldsson) who causes a sensation when he declares himself gay in a magazine interview, in order to get himself onto the front page. While poking fun at the narcissistic spirit of our times, the film deals with the effect this has

Douglas. *Players: Björn Hlynur Haraldsson, Jón Atli Jónasson, Helgi Björnsson, Lilja Nótt, Armundur Ernst. Prod: Icelandic Film Company/Solarfilm Inc. (Finland)/Borealis Production AS (Norway)/Film & Music Entertainment (UK).*

VOKSNE MENNESKER (Dark Horse)
[Drama, 2005] Script and Dir: Dagur Kári Pétursson. Players: Nicolas Bro, Jakob Cedergren, Anders Hove, Nicolaj Kopernikus. Prod: Nimbus Film Aps.

BÖRN (Children)
[Drama, 2006] Script: Ragnar Bragason and the actors. Dir: Bragason. Phot: Bergsteinn Björgúlfsson. Players: Gísli Örn Gardarsson, Nína Dögg Filippusdóttir, Ólafur Darri Ólafsson, Andri Snaer Magnússon. Prod: Kvikyndi, Vesturport.

Beowulf & Grendel

BEOWULF & GRENDEL
[Drama, 2006] Script: Andrew Rai Berzins. Dir: Sturla Gunnarsson. Phot: Jan Kiessel. Players: Gerard Butler, Sarah Polley, Ingvar E. Sigurdsson, Stellan Skarsgård, Benedikt Clausen. Prod: Arclight Films (US)/Spice Factory Ltd. (UK)/

The Film Works Ltd. (Canada) /Icelandic Film Corporation.

BLÓDBÖND (Ordinary Life)
[Drama, 2006] Script: Jón Atli Jónasson, Denijal Hasanovic, Árni Ólafur Ásgeirsson. Dir: Ásgeirsson. Phot: Tuomo Hutri. Players: Hilmar Jónsson, Margrét Vilhjálmsdóttir, Aron Brink, Elma Lísa Gunnarsdóttir, Ólafur Darri Ólafsson. Prod: Pegasus Productions/Zentropa Entertainment (Denmark)/Thalamus Films.

FORELDRAR (Parents)
[Drama, 2006] Script: Ragnar Bragason and the actors. Dir: Bragason. Phot: Bergsteinn Björgúlfsson. Players: Ingvar Sigurdsson, Nanna Kristín Magnúsdóttir, Víkingur Kristjánsson. Prod: Kvikyndi/Vesturport.

on the other team members, the player's family, alcoholic former beauty queen ex-wife and teenage son.

Left to right: Arnmundur Ernst, Björn Hlynur Haraldsson and Lilja Nott Thorarinsdottir in **Eleven Men Out**

Two big-budget films by Icelandic standards, both shot in 2004, are coming soon and eagerly awaited. Baltasar Kormákur's third film, **A Little Trip to Heaven**, features Americans Forest Whitaker, Julia Stiles, Jeremy Renner and Peter Coyote and uses the lowlands of south Iceland as a substitute for Minnesota. It's a noirish thriller about an insurance investigator (Whitaker) who's dispatched to a small town to try and piece together the mystery surrounding a dead body with a million-dollar life insurance policy.

The other large-scale feature is **Beowulf and Grendel**, directed by Icelandic-Canadian Sturla Gunnarsson and produced by Fridrik Thor Fridriksson, among others. It's a modern retelling of the ancient poem *Beowulf* and deals with the great Viking warrior of the same name who has to fight the ferocious troll Grendel, hellbent on revenge. Gerard Butler, Ingvar Sigurdsson, Stellan Skarsgaard and Sarah Polley head the cast.

On the political front, the industry applauded the recent government announcement that it intends substantially to increase film subsidies over the next few years. Along with the 12% refund of production costs spent in the country, it should give the energetic but chronically cash-strapped film-making community a much-needed shot in the arm.

ÁSGRÍMUR SVERRISSON (asgrimur@asgrimur.is) is a film-maker and editor of the film magazine and website *Land & synir* (www.logs.is).

India Uma da Cunha

The Year's Best Films

Uma da Cunha's selection:

Views from the Inner Chamber (Rituparno Ghosh)

Water (Deepa Mehta)

Reaching Silence (Jahar Kanungo)

Dreaming Lhasa (Ritu Sarin, Tenzing Sonam)

Memories in the Mist (Buddhadeb Dasgupta)

Trina Nileena Banerjee in **Reaching Silence**

Recent and Forthcoming Films

MIXED DOUBLES

[Social drama, 2005] Script and Dir: Rajat Kapoor. Phot: Rafey Mahmood. Players: Ranvir Shorey, Konkona Sen Sharma, Rajat Kapoor, Koel Puri. Producer: Sunil Doshi, Handmade Films.

In India's emerging middle-class, Sunil and Malati, ten years into their marriage, have the lifestyle they always wanted, but its excitement is dwindling.

Konkana Sensharma, left, and Koel Purie in **Mixed Doubles**

At the end of every year, Indian cinema throws up another enigma, and there was a new twist this time: should the business favour corporate or independent production? The year 2004 had ended on a high, with a starved industry lapping up unexpected successes such as Mukesh Bhatt's **Murder**; Priyadarshan's **Uproar** (*HulChul*), the motorcycling caper, **Fun** (*Dhoom*), which kick-started the screen careers of John Abraham and Esha Deol, to say nothing of Abhishek Bachchan; and Yash Chopra's **Veer-Zaara**. But spirits dampened when, in early 2005, as many as ten films bombed. Audiences bypassed hyped, would-be blockbusters such as Subhash Ghai's **Kisna**, Vikram Bhatt's **Announcement** (*Elaan*) and Leena Yadav's **Word** (*Shabd*).

Less ambitious but more creative ventures succeeded, like Sanjay Leela Bhansali's **Black**, which had top-notch Amitabh Bachchan and Rani Mukherjee, but was also a bleak subject, basically the Helen Keller story of a deaf and blind child in need of understanding and care. Another resounding hit was Madhur Bhandarkar's modest **Page 3**, on Mumbai's exhibitionist, destructive high society. By year-end 2005, industry coffers were filling nicely. Ten films grossed more than $77m between them. **Godfather** (*Sarkar*), **Married Woman** (*Parineeta*) and **Greetings** (*Salaam Namaste*) were among the films to bring a good return to their investors. The year proved that while star names posed a risk, the genre working wonders was comedy, and the more risqué the better.

Distributors tumbled over each other to oblige. Offerings spilled from the packed prime-time holiday season (*Diwali* in November)

Yashraj Films

Preity Zinta and Shabrukh Khan in **Veer-Zaara**

EK AJNABEE (A Man Apart)
[Thriller, 2005] Script: Manoj Tyagi, Apoorva Lakhia. Dir: Lakhia. Phot: Gururaj R. J. Players: Amitabh Bachchan, Perizaad Zorabian, Arjun Rampal. Prod: Bunty Walia, Jaspreet Singh Walia.
This tale of love and revenge traces an ageing man's (Bachchan) lonely journey to self-destruction, and how an eight-year-old girl helps bring him back to life.

MAINE GANDHI KO NAHIN MARA (I Did Not Kill Gandhi)
[Drama, 2005] Script: Sanjay Chouhan. Dir: Jahnu Barua. Phot: Raaj A. Chakravarti. Players: Anupam Kher, Urmila Matondkar, Parvin Dabas, Rajit Kapur, Boman Irani, Sudhir Joshi. Prod: Anupam Kher/ Curtain Call Co.
When a widower (Kher) develops signs of amnesia and distressing memories from his past, his daughter (Urmila Matondkar) does everything she can to help him regain his sanity.

ANTARMAHAL (Views from the Inner Chamber)
[Drama, 2005] Script and Dir: Rituparno Ghosh. Phot: Abhik Mukherjee. Players: Jackie Shroff, Abhishek Bachchan, Rupa Ganguly, Soha Ali Khan. Prod: A.B. Corp. Ltd./Puja Films.
An ageing, barren landowner takes a young second wife, hoping to father an heir. His seething first wife and a young handsome village artist force him to face the real world.

Soha Ali Khan, left, and Abhishek Bachchan in **Views from the Inner Chamber**

into fresh big-time releases, starting mid-December 2005. This march was led by Sujoy Ghosh's second film, **Home Delivery** (Vivek Oberoi's chance to regain the spotlight); **Neal 'n' Nikki**, the Yash Chopra film starring his son, Uday, and Tanisha Mukherjee; **Bluffmaster!** with Abhishek Bachchan, and Prakash Jha's **Kidnapped** (*Apaharan*), on the real-life kidnapping trade, with tough do-gooder Ajay Devgan heading the cast.

A world of giants

The 2005 successes could be attributed to big business houses backing new films and planning their marketing strategy well in advance. Among the giants here are UTV Motion Pictures, headed by Ronnie Screwalla. It has teamed up with Fox Searchlight to produce Mira Nair's **The Namesake**. Other major players are Sahara One, led by Sandeep Bhargava, whose animated **Hanuman** raked in a cool $1.5m in just six weeks, AB Corps, the brand name of mega star Bachchan, The Factory, run by the enterprising director Ram Gopal Varma, and Columbia TriStar. Newcomer Sunil Doshi's Handmade Films had two productions ready in December, Santosh Sivan's **Nine Emotions** (*Navarasa*) and Rajat Kapur's third film, **Mixed Doubles**.

Seeing the domestic market being dwarfed by big bucks coming from abroad, movie moguls have set up distribution outlets in India and abroad. The one-time monopoly held by 27-year-old Eros International, headquartered in London, is now challenged by the indomitable Yash Chopra. His golden touch is legendary and now reaches out to London where he has opened a distribution office, Yashraj Films.

In India, big-timers entering production and distribution are Manmohan Shetty's Adlab Films, which is backing the American co-production *Marigold*, directed by Willard Carroll and starring Salman Khan; Pritish Nandy Communications, picking newcomers and new scripts; and Subhash Ghai's Mukta Arts. Mukta launches three to five big- to low-budget films a year, and its modest offering, **Iqbal**, an uplifting tale of a deaf and dumb cricketer making the national team, ushered in a new star name, Shreyas Talpade. It was an immediate nationwide success. With corporate interest and money entering the lists, a welcome professionalism is entering the traditionally happy chaos of Indian film-making. Banks are arriving with open cheque books; in fact, payment by cheque, once the exception, is beginning to be the rule. Accountability is the silver lining.

Stars and strife

There had to be a downside. Big money means that stars get to call the tune. Astronomical fees and untold side benefits are also the rule. So budgets balloon. "Globalisation" is taking its toll of films' content and style. The watchwords are traditionalism and conformism. After all, the profits come from India's nostalgic and affluent expatriate millions. They account for Hindi films regularly hitting the Top Ten in the UK and doing strong business in the US. Scriptwriters in India strain to adapt their stories to Indian audiences abroad. On the whole, they strike a hollow and false note, though not always at the cash registers.

In such a climate, content is of little consequence. Indeed, content is leading Indian films to be increasingly shot abroad. The shoots have moved from familiar Swiss valleys, Paris riverbanks and UK mansions, to Bangkok, Singapore, New Zealand and, a first, South Korea. Foreign government delegations are wooing Indian producers with tax breaks and co-production offers. Shoots abroad, producers claim, are more disciplined, with the added bonus of stars being in their control. Besides, they say, Indian audiences now have a wanderlust. They crave new vistas and faces in the movies. So, suddenly, a family scene in an Indian city will switch to a lavish dance in Prague, with the heroine changing mini-skirts at every turn.

In late 2005, three Hindi films, *Never Say Goodbye* (*Kabhi Alvida Na Kehna*), *What if...* (*Yun Hota to Kya Hota*), Naseeruddin Shah's debut as director, and Shirish Kunder's *Beloved* (*Jaaneman*) were being shot concurrently in New York. Tanuja Chandra's *Hope and a Little Sugar* is set in New York and backed by an American producer. Two films due for imminent release at press time were shot in Bangkok: Apoorva Lakhia's *Ek Ajnabee* and Ashok Thakeria's *Dear Mohan* (*Pyare Mohan*). Hrithik Roshan was in Singapore in late 2005 shooting *Krrish*.

Bollywood, but not as we knew it

The little understood brand name "Bollywood" has turned the Hindi feature film into a parody of itself, with fun-loving group dancing and far-fetched plots. Film talk on Indian cinema today focuses entirely on stars, dance, song and music. They are called "Item Numbers". Lithe and lightly clad bodies are thrown in willy-nilly for diversion; dance directors prance all the way to the bank. Promotion becomes more and more lavish, and the smaller, independent film-maker finds it hard to cope with this costly glitz. There is an ever greater struggle to make thoughtful cinema in Hindi or the regional languages. The heartening news is that these films survive.

There is better planning as commerce links hands with art. More stars are accepting serious, non-glamorous roles. New producers like actor Anupam Kher are emerging. He followed up his

Tara as **Haseena**

HASEENA
[Drama, 2005] Script and Dir: Girish Kasaravalli. Phot: S. Ramachandra Aithal. Players: Tara, Chandrahasa Ullal, Bhodini Bhargavi, Soundarya. Prod: Chiguru Chitra.
Set in a deeply religious part of south India, the film follows the subjugation of Muslim women and their need to unite and establish their rights.

JOHN & JANE
[Documentary, 2005] Dir: Ashim Ahluwalia. Phot: Mohanan K. U., Mukul Kishore. Featuring: Glen Castinho, Sydney Fernandes, Oaref Irani, Vandana Malwe, Nikesh Soares. Prod. Future East Film.
Six 'call agents' answer American 1-800 numbers at a Mumbai call centre, working all night to cater to daytime callers in the US.

DREAMING LHASA
[Thriller, 2005] Script: Tenzing Sonam. Dir: Ritu Sarin and Tenzing Sonam. Phot: Ranjan Palit. Players: Jampa Kalsang, Tenzin Chokyi Gyatso, Tenzin Jigme. Prod. White Crane Films.
A New York-raised Tibetan woman, her love life in shambles, returns to Dharamsala to make a film about her community. She hooks up with a girl-chasing local and a mysterious ex-monk. They look for a missing CIA-trained resistance fighter.

ANANDABHADRAM
(All Is Well)
[Thriller, 2005] Script: Sunil Parameshwaran. Dir and Phot: Santosh Sivan. Players: Prithviraj, Kavya Madhavan, Manoj K Jayan, Riya Sen. Prod: Manian Pilla Raju, Ajaya Chandran Nair, Reghu Chandran Nair.
Digambaran, an expert at black

magic, covets the rare diamond, Nagamanikam, which is guarded by the snake gods and accessed by the virgin girl, Bhadra. Anandan falls in love with Bhadra, and black magic takes a sinister turn.

Santosh Sivan's **Anandabhadram**

NISSHABD (Reaching Silence)
[Drama, 2005] Script and Dir: Jahar Kanungo. Phot: Dilip Varma. Players: Trina Nilina Banerjee, Kaushik Chakravarty, Sudeshna Basu, Piyali Das Gupta, Debika Sinha, Robishankar, Ashok Lal. Prod: Joel Farges, Elise Jalladeau, ARTCAM (Paris)/Sudhir Mishra.
In the deafening metropolis of Delhi, 30-year-old Sarit develops a sudden, inexplicable sensitivity to sound, and seeks respite in his home village.

KRANTIKAAL
(Critical Encounter)
[Social drama, 2005] Script: Sekhar Das, based on the novel by Prafulla Roy. Dir: Das. Phot: P.B. Chaki. Players: Roopa Ganguly, Shilajit, Soumitra Chatterjee. Prod: Nobel Associate.
A 'secessionist' on the run seeks refuge in the home of a family of former maharajas, carrying with him weapons and radical ideology.

Shilajit in **Critical Encounter**

remarkable *Bariwali* with **I Did Not Kill Gandhi** (*Maine Gandhi ko Nahin Mara*), directed in Hindi by Jahnu Barua, the award-winning Assamese. Corporate entities Mukta Arts and A.B. Corps are backing independent-minded film-makers. Deepa Mehta (profiled at the front of this edition) made **Water** in Canada in Hindi, with John Abraham, Lisa Ray and Seema Biswas, and it was chosen as opening film at Toronto.

Urmila Matondkar, left, and Anupam Kher in **I Did Not Kill Ghandi**

Regional cinema tries to find a way through the minefield between artistic and commercial success. From Kerala, Malayalam films arrive in numbers at international festivals. In Bengal, Rituparno Ghosh, Aparna Sen, Buddhadeb Dasgupta and Gautam Ghose stick to their guns inventively, and newcomers arrive with regularity, such as Jahar Kanungo, with the award-winning debut feature, **Reaching Silence** (*Nisshabd*). Production of Marathi cinema, known for its stirring family stories, has doubled, with 90 films scheduled over 2005. Films that relate to reality are still being made in Hindi. Shyam Benegal's next will be based on the immortal tale of a little cigar-maker, Carmen, who will do without Bizet. It will star Urmila Matondkar.

India's offering for Oscar nomination, the ghostly romance, **Paheli**, is directed by the inventive Amol Palekar. It has megastar Shahrukh Khan and is produced by Khan's own company, Red Chillies. From Karnataka, Girish Kasarvalli has directed another original subject, **Haseena**, on Muslim women trying to break free in an orthodox society. For these diehard innovators, the show goes on, even if money and wide distribution evade them.

In the film statistics for 2004, the big news is that the American blockbuster continues to make minimal impact in India: US films have an market share of just 8%. Indian production rose form 877 features in 2003 to 934, made in 31 Indian languages, as against 23 in 2003 – confirming the need for local cinema in small states and distinct vernaculars.

In 2004, Hindi led with244 films, followed by Telugu (203), Tamil (130), Kannada (75), Malayalam (71), Marathi (56), Bengali (46), Bhojpuri (21), Oriya (19), Gujarati and English (13 each), Assamese (9), Punjabi (four), Rajasthani (four), Garhwali (three); two each in Sadri, Nepali and Konkani; one each in Kokbork, Punjabi-Urdu, Chattisgarhi, Bodo, Kumayani, Maithili, Nagpuri, Himachali, Aaodhi and Banjara. To cap it all, there was a silent film! Some 285 films were imported: 207 from the US, followed by Hong Kong (29), Italy (12), UK (seven) and other European and Asian countries with between one and five releases each.

UMA DA CUNHA (umadacunha2003@yahoo.com) is based in Mumbai, where she works as a casting director, researcher and freelance journalist and edits the quarterly *Film India Worldwide*. She is also a programmer for international film festivals, specialising in new Indian cinema, and organises film industry PR events.

Rani Mukherjee, left, and Amitabh Bachchan had a hit in 2005 with **Black**

NO ENTRY
[Comedy, 2005] Script and Dir: Anees Bazmee. Phot: Ashok Mehta. Players: Anil Kapoor, Salman Khan, Bipasha Basu, Fardeen Khan, Lara Dutta, Esha Deol. Prod: Sahara One Motion Pictures Creation.
Three fun-loving friends get into trouble when they encounter Bobby, a sexy club dancer.

SRINGARAM (Dance of Love)
[Social drama, 2005] Script: Indira Sounderraja. Dir: Sharada Ramanathan. Phot: Madhu Ambat. Players: Aditi Rao Hyderi, Hamsa Moily, Manju Bhargavi, Manoj K. Jayan, Chandrashekar. Prod: Pradhan Centre for Arts, Bangalore, Sunderesan & Sons, Mumbai.
Temple prostitute Madhura and her contemporary, Kama, search for art, emancipation and spiritual enhancement.

AAYE DIL
(Heart Goes Sha La La)
[Drama, 2005] Script and Dir: Saurabh Shukla. Phot: Fuwad Khan. Players: Rajat Kapoor, Ranvir Sheorey, Amrita, Anchal. Prod: Positive Pictures/ Married Print.
A balding middle-aged writer meets a Miss India finalist on the internet. She arrives for the pageant and wants to meet him. What can he do?

Quotes of the Year

"While mainstream cinema, for the most part, peddled candyfloss, offbeat regional cinema chased the truth."
SAIBAL CHATTERJEE, *writing in* Outlook *magazine.*

"Stars can cancel shootings at the drop of a camera, change their dialogues at the drop of a pen and shed their modesty at the drop of a dress."
KOMAL NAHATA, *industry analyst, in* The Times of India.

Indonesia Lisabona Rahman

The Year's Best Films

Lisabona Rahman's selection:
Banyu Biru
(Teddy Soeriaatmadja)
The Rainmaker
(Ravi Bharwani)
Gie (Riri Riza)
Janji Joni (Joko Anwar)
Ungu Violet (Rako Prijanto)

Ella Gayo and Ladya Cheryl in **Kara,**
the Daughter of a Tree

Recent and Forthcoming Films

PANGGUNG PINGGIR KALI
(*literally,* **A Stage by the River**)
[*Drama, 2005*] Script: Djuli Y.
Ismail. Dir: Ucik Supra. Phot:
Yustiman Maningka. Players:
Kristina, Agus Kuncoro, Lina
Budiati, Henky Solaiman. Prod:
Sri Hastanto, Harry Simon,
Panitia Tetap Film/Kompetitif
Budpar/PT Jatayu Cakrawala
Film & Video.

TENTANG DIA
(*literally,* **About Her**)
[*Drama, 2005*] Script: Titien
Wattimena. Dir: Rudi Soedjarwo.
Phot: Roy Lolang. Players: Sigi
Wimala, Adinia Wirasti, Fauzi
Baadila, Donna Agnesia. Prod:
Leo Sutanto, Elly Yanti Noor,
SinemArt Pictures.

The year 2005 was marked by a slight increase from the previous year's output, with more than 50 films released or going into production. The recent trend for political films ended with the hugely anticipated release of **Gie**, Riri Riza's biopic of Indonesian–Chinese student activist Soe Hok Gie. Its budget of around $720,000 (seven billion Indonesian rupiahs) made it one of the most expensive Indonesian films produced since 1998, and it was greeted warmly by audiences of all ages. Critical reaction was very mixed, creating a lively debate about the representation of the most mysterious period in Indonesia's modern history, namely the alleged slaughter of hundreds of thousands of Indonesians accused of being communists in the 1960s, and the establishment of the authoritarian regime.

The predominant themes in Indonesian cinema were, as usual, love, teenage romance and horror, with a handful of releases also tackling the pressing topic of drug-trafficking. Most titles offer a time-honoured and deadly combination of bad script, poor acting and abysmal cinematography, but some are worth noting. One is **Banyu Biru**, Teddy Soeriaatmadja's debut feature, a magical realist tale about a hyper-mart attendant on a comic journey while trying to fix his relationship with his father and find his roots. *Banyu Biru* offers some appealing irregularities in its storytelling pattern, avoiding a linear approach and playing with the notion of which events are real and which ones are dreams.

A tearjerker in Jakarta

Rako Prijanto's **Ungu Violet** has appealing cinematography of Jakarta cityscapes as the background to a love story between a rising-star model and a photographer who has to cope with his terminal illness. **Janji Joni** (literally, *Joni's Promise*) managed to sustain more than 60 consecutive days of screening at local cinemas in various cities. It tells the story of a film courier working at the local cineplex who struggles to fulfil his promise to deliver films in time so that he can meet the girl of his dreams. The film is a fair combination of comical happenings while also giving insights into film distribution in local cinema. The film attracted 600,000 viewers nationwide, which gave it a good chance of becoming the year's biggest hit, though it was sure to face competition for top slot from a teenage flick released in late October, **What Love**

Kotak Hitam Prods.

Dian Sastrowardoyo, left, and Rizky Hanggono in **Ungu Violet**

Means (*Apa artinya cinta?*), a clone of last year's box-office smash, *Eiffel I'm in Love*, (seen by 2.2 million viewers), with the same casts and shot in San Francisco.

Faced with difficulties in marketing their work at home, Indonesian film-makers have long used film festivals abroad as part of their strategies to boost popularity among local audiences. This year's achievement was quite uplifting. Director Ravi Bharwani's **The Rainmaker** (*Impian kemarau*) was selected as Best Film in the Asian New Talent Awards at the Shanghai Film Festival 2005 and young director Edwin's short film, *Kara, the Daughter of a Tree* (*Kara anak sebatang pohon*), made it to Directors Fortnight selection at Cannes. *The Rainmaker* is a very exotic depiction of a community dealing with drought and the nation's politics, while *Kara* tells the story of a little girl trying to seek revenge for her mother's death against the McDonald's mascot, Ronald McDonald.

Despite a murky economic forecast for 2006, movie production will try hard to keep up its pace. One of the most anticipated pictures is director Garin Nugroho's Javanese opera-film, *Obong* (an episode from the *Ramayana*), a production filmed after a commission from US opera director Peter Sellars, as part of the major commemorations in Vienna marking the 250th anniversary of Mozart's birth.

LISABONA RAHMAN (lisabona@centrin.net.id) is a Jakarta-based freelance writer on film, literature and visual arts. She took part in the Berlinale Talent Campus 2004.

ANNE VAN JOGJA
(*literally*, **Anne of Jogja**)
[*Historical drama, 2005*] Script: Maria Laurianti Stephanie, Nur Adhani, Pahala Sigiro, Pradikha Bestari, Yanwar. Dir: Bobby Sandy. Phot: Rus Y. Sapari. Players: Rachel Maryam, Arie Kristanto, Marie Vanena. Prod: Sri Hastanto, Harry Simon, Panitia Tetap Film Kompetitif Budpar/PT Jatayu Cakrawala Film & Video.

BANYU BIRU
[*Comedy-drama, 2005*] Script: Rayya Makarim, Prima Rusdi. Dir: Teddy Soeriaatmadja. Phot: Faozan Rizal. Players: Tora Sudiro, Didi Petet, Slamet Rahardjo. Prod: Shanty Harmayn/Salto Films.

JANJI JONI
(*literally*, **Joni's Promise**)
[*Comedy-drama, 2005*] Script and Dir: Joko Anwar. Phot: Ipung Rachmat Syaiful. Players: Nicholas Saputra, Mariana Renata, Rachel Maryam. Prod: Nia diNata, Kalyana Shira Film.

Kalyana Shira Film

Rachel Maryam and Nicholas Saputra in **Janji Joni**

UNGU VIOLET
[*Romantic drama, 2005*] Script: Jujur Prananto. Dir: Rako Prijanto. Phot: Yudi Datau. Players: Dian Sastrowardoyo, Rizky Hanggono, Rima Melati. Prod: Leo Sutanto, Elly Yanti Noor/SinemArt Pictures.

DETIK TERAKHIR
(*literally*, **The Last Second**)
[*Drama, 2005*] Script: Alberthienne Endah, Twen Tyaval. Dir: Nanang Istiabudi. Phot: Bambang Supariadi. Players: Cornelia Agatha, Sausan, Shanty, Mike Muliadro. Prod: Shanker RS/Indika Entertainment.

Iran Jamal Omid

Recent and Forthcoming Films

BAGHE FERDOWS, PANJE BADAZ ZOHR
(Baghe Ferdows, 5pm)
[Drama, 2005] Script, Dir and Prod: Siamak Shayeqi. Phot: Gholam Reza Azadi. Players: Reza Kianian, Ladan Mostofi, Azita Hajian, Hamed Behdad.
A tale of assignations at a park in northern Tehran at 5pm. Attar waits for his beloved Shirin, who does not show up. Then, 25 years later, Dr Attar waits for Darya (Shirin's young daughter), who is in love with him.

BEH AHESTEGI (In Slow Steps)
[Drama, 2005] Script: Parviz Shahbazi. Dir: Maziar Miri. Phot: Hassan Karimi. Players: Mohammad Reza Forutan, Niloufar Khoshkholq, Shahrokh Forutanian, Hassan Pourshirazi. Prod: Miri, Jahangir Kowsari.
What does a man do if one day he returns home to find that his life partner is missing?

TARDAST (Dextrous)
[Comedy, 2005] Script, Dir and Prod: Mohammad Ali Sajjadi. Phot: Hossein Maleki. Players: Gowhar Kheirandish, Shahram Haqiqatdoost, Amir Jafari, Sirus Ebrahimzadeh.
Asad progresses from stealing automobile parts to whole cars, despite objections from his mother's ghost.

ZEMESTAN AST
(Winter Is Here)
[Drama, 2005] Script: Rafie Petes, based on a story by Mahmoud Dolatabadi. Dir: Petes. Phot: Mohammad Davoudi. Players: Mitra Hajjar, Anushiravan Haddad, Alireza

When Mahmoud Ahmadinejad was elected president in June 2005, producers became apprehensive about the future of cinema. Ahmadinejad had previously made it known that he regarded film-making solely as a means of conveying social and religious values. There were also rumours that film-making would henceforward be monopolised by a limited group of ideologically oriented people. However, in late August, industry concerns were eased by announcements from the new Minister for Cultural Affairs, Hossein Saffar Harandi, and Mohammad Reza Jafari Jelveh, the new Deputy Minister for Film Affairs.

Harandi emphasised that "there should be a liberal atmosphere in the film-making field and film-makers with different points of view should have equal opportunities." Jafari Jelveh also dispelled rumours regarding the restriction of the private sector's activities. "We are aware," he said, "that co-operation between the public and the private sectors is much more necessary in cinema than in any other cultural field." These and subsequent remarks have created a hopeful attitude, but Jafari Jelveh still faces problems for which the previous group of officials could not find adequate solutions, in spite of their conscientious efforts.

The shortage of cinemas continues to be the most pressing problem. The Tehran municipality has recently built six movie complexes, with a total of 27 screens and 6,200 seats, and other government-aided theatre projects are under way in and outside the capital. Modern screening facilities will be crucial in attracting audiences, and a $3.4m (30 billion rial) government credit has been allocated towards this goal.

Meanwhile, plans continue for the construction of Hashtgerd Cinema City, billed as the greatest entertainment and film complex in the Middle East. Its eventual completion should diminish many problems in connection with domestic productions and co-productions. Another challenge facing the new Deputy Minister is the profiteering attitude of commercial producers and distributors, who have acquired monopolistic control of the best theatres and prime screening times, at the expense of the producers of arthouse and experimental films and films for young people, which deserve and need wider distribution. At press time, the industry was still awaiting confirmation of new policies on the preferred subject matter of films, support for production, the presentation of films at international festivals and the screening of foreign films.

Duel at the top

Ahmad Reza Darvish's **The Duel** was the top-selling film of 2004 and divided opinion. At the age of 40, Zainal is released from an Iraqi prison after a 20-year sentence. He had put up fierce resistance against Iraqi troops in Khorramshahr city at the start of the war. A number of comrades ask Zainal to retrieve from the Iraqis a cabinet containing secret documents. Darvish's war movie, produced at a cost of $4m (provided from the government's cultural budget), could compete with Hollywood blockbusters in terms of special effects, but has an uneven, two-part structure and is inadequate in terms of storyline and character development. It grossed some $6.9m, with the aid of unprecedented promotion, but this was still less than the 2003 takings for Kamal Tabrizi's *The Lizard*, which cost only about $250,000. *The Duel* has undoubtedly helped upgrade technical aspects of Iranian film-making; one only wishes it possessed the artistic values of Darvish's previous films, such as *Kimia* and *Land in the Sun*.

One of the artistically noteworthy films, which also made the year's top 10, is Majid Majidi's **The Weeping Willow**. Yusef, 45, a university professor (a fine performance from Parviz Parastui), regains the eyesight that he lost to illness aged eight. Following the initial excitement, this restoration creates difficulties. He falls in love with a young woman and the ensuing conflict between his desires and his attachment to his family brings back his blindness. His shouts of protest lead him to a mystical understanding of a profound truth, and Majidi manages to preserve artistic values while entertaining the spectators. Majidi has gradually shifted his focus and instinctively mystical outlook from children to young adults and finally to grown-ups.

The audience's warm reception for *The Weeping Willow* and **So Close So Far**, by Reza Mir-Karimi, demonstrates that spectators do appreciate films on profound topics. Mir-Karimi's film, selected as the Iranian entry for the Oscars, marks a career peak for this young director, who appeared on the scene with *The Boy and the Soldier*. It depicts ordinary daily lives and yet has transcendental significance. Dr Alem, a distinguished neurologist, is so engrossed with his work that he neglects his young son, Saman. When he finds out that his son is suffering from a brain tumour, he is overwhelmed with guilt and goes in search of Saman, who spends his time in the desert, observing the stars. Alem is caught in a sandstorm and his car is buried. When he has given up hope of rescue, he hears the voice of Saman, who has come to his father's rescue. This oft-repeated story has been turned into a lovable, pleasant movie by the director's intelligence and attention to detail.

Niksolat. Prod: Mohammad Mehdi Dadgu.
After the death of her husband, Khatun tries to support her family single-handed.

**SORKHIE SIBE KAAL
(Redness of the Raw Apple)**
[Family drama, 2005] Script: Mohammad Ali Talebi, Mohammad Reza Kateb, Dir and Prod: Telebi. Phot: Ali Loqmani. Players: Shirin Bina, Danial Monafi, Shokrane Shokrova.
Reza, 15, who lives with his mother and brother, is disturbed when a stranger arrives and plans to marry Reza's mother.

**SHAERE ZOBALEHA
(Poet of the Trash)**
[Family drama, 2005] Script: Mohsen Makhmalbaf. Dir: Mohammad Ahmadi. Phot: Mohammad Aladpush. Players: Leyla Hatami, Farzin Mohaddes, Mohammad Eskandari. Prod: Makhmalbaf Film House/ Karnameh Institute.
A young road sweeper composes a love letter for a girl, using the discarded manuscripts of a poet.

YEK SHAB (One Night)
[Drama, 2005] Script: Niki Karimi, Kambozia Partovi, based on a story by Mahmoud Aideen. Dir: Karimi. Phot: Hossein Jafarian. Players: Haniye Tavassoli, Saeed Ebrahimifar, Abdolreza Fakhar, Nader Turkman. Prod: Jahangir Kowsari, Hassan Rajabalinia (MK2, France).
A young girl spends a night wandering the streets and encounters three men.

SETAREHA (The Stars)
[Social drama, 2006] Script and Dir: Fereydun Jeyrani. Phot: Mohammad Aladpush. Players: Ezzatollah Entezami, Khosro Shakibai, Niki Karimi, Amin Hayai. Prod: Abdollah Esfandiari, Hamid Etebarian, Majid Molai.
Relationships among wannabe stars and disenchanted, famous actors.

Reza Mir-Karimi's **So Close So Far**

The *Fish*'s tale

Ali Rafiee's **The Fish Fall in Love** is a belated first feature from a 67-year-old former actor in French theatre and films, who has staged numerous plays in Iran. He tells the story of Aziz, a middle-aged man who harbours leftist tendencies and rebels against his own social class. After spending years in jail, he returns home and finds that his family house has been turned into a restaurant by several women. It is a simple, splendid film that makes one regret that Rafiee didn't start directing films earlier.

Wake Up, Arezu (*Kianush ayari*) is a sincere attempt to recreate the catastrophe of the earthquake that shook Bam in southern Iran in 2003, through the story of a young woman teacher and an escaped male prisoner, who relieve their personal anguish by helping quake survivors. Ayari arrived in the stricken area with his cast shortly after the catastrophe and uses the simple story as a framework for recording the aftermath of the disaster. It is a laudable endeavour, despite shortcomings resulting from the shooting circumstances, and has generally made a great impression on viewers.

I Saw Your Daddy Last Night, Aida, about 17-year-old Aida's discovery of a young woman in her father's life, is the third part of Rasul Sadr-Ameli's survey of young girls' encounters with love. It is not as engaging as the first two parts, *The Girl in the Sneakers* (1999) and *I Am Taraneh, 15* (2001). With *Café Transit*, Kambozia Partovi focuses on an outdated tradition. After the death of her husband, Reyhan is expected to marry her brother-in-law, but she rebels by running her husband's restaurant outside a border village. The familiar story, which could have lapsed into sentimentality, is saved by Partovi's intelligent treatment, and by fine performances, especially from Fereshteh Orafai as Reyhan.

ZIRE DERAKHTE HOLOU
(Under the Peach Tree)
[Comedy, 2006] Script: Hamid Jebeli, Iraj Tahmasb. Dir: Tahmasb. Phot: Aziz Sa'ati. Players: Hamid Jebeli, Fatemeh Motamed-Aria, Iraj Tahmasb, Shohreh Lorestani. Prod: Majid Modarressi, Hamid Modarressi (Sahra Film).
One member of a large family hates peaches and no one is permitted even to mention the fruit.

SHAM-E AROUSI
(Wedding Dinner)
[Comedy, 2006] Script: Peyman Moadi. Dir: Ebrahim Vahidzadeh. Phot: Dariush Ayari. Players: Amin Hayai, Niki Karimi, Maral Farjad, Pooya Amini, Sirus Ebrahimzadeh. Prod: Hamid Etebarian.
A magnificent wedding is arranged without anyone spending money.

YAD-DASHT BAR ZAMIN
(Signs on the Earth)
[Drama, 2005] Script, Dir and Phot: Ali Mohammad Qasemi. Players: Asiye Bakhshizad, Hossein Moslemi, Shirin Qasemi. Prod: Young Iranian Cinema Society/Center for Promotion of Documentary and Experimental Filmmaking/A.M. Qasemi.
A man whose wife cannot bear a child decides to kill all the children on Earth.

ZAGROS
[Social drama, 2006] Script: Shadmehr Rastin. Dir and Prod: Mohammad Ali Najafi. Phot: Hassan Karimi. Players: Reza Kianian, Merila Zarei, Keyhan Maleki.
Three civil engineers rush to finish work on a dam.

ZAMAN MI-ISTAD
(Time Stops)
[Social drama, 2006] Script and Dir: Alireza Amini. Phot: Reza Rakhshan. Player: Haniye Tavassoli. Prod: Taqi Alizadeh.
A pregnant young wife undertakes an arduous mountain journey.

JAZIRE AHANI (Iron Island)
[Social drama, 2005] Script, Dir

and Prod: *Mohammad Rasoulof.*
Phot: Reza Jalali. Players: Ali
Nasirian, Hossein Farzizade,
Neda Pakdaman.
Homeless people on the southern
coast reside on an old,
abandoned ship.

HOKM (The Warrant)
[Adventure drama, 2006] Script,
Dir and Prod: Masud Kimiaie.
Phot: Alireza Zarrindast. Players:
Ezzatollah Entezami, Khosro
Shakibai, Leyla Hatami, Bahram
Radan, Merila Zarei.
Three young people are involved
in crime.

BEH NAME PEDAR
(In the Name of Father)
[War drama, 2005] Script, Dir.
and Prod: Ebrahim Hatamikia.
Phot: Hassan Karimi. Players:
Parviz Parastoui, Mahtab Nasirpour,
Golshifteh Farahani, Kambiz
Dirbaz, Seyed Mehrdad Ziaie.
A father knows how much his
daughter depends on him, but
cannot shirk his duty to his
country in wartime.

YEK BOOSE KOUCHOULU
(A Little Kiss)
[Social drama, 2006] Script and
Dir: Bahman Farmanara. Phot:
Mahmoud Kalari. Players: Reza
Kianian, Jamshid Mashayekhi,
Hedye Tehrani, Fateme
Motamed-Aria, Fakhri Khorvash.
Prod: Ali Reza Shojanoori.
Two old writers, one just back in
Iran after 38 years because of his
son's recent suicide, travel to the
young man's grave.

PARVANDE HAVANA
(The Havana Case)
[Social drama, 2006] Script:
Farhad Tohidi. Dir: Alireza
Raisian. Phot: Mahmoud Kalari.
Players: Amin Tarokh, Niki
Karimi, Hamid Reza Pegah.
Prod: Seyed Zia Hashemi.
Dr Pezhman faces personal and
professional problems.

We Are All Fine is a promising debut film by Bizhan Mirbaqeri. The family of Jamshid, who has been living abroad, record their daily life in a film and send it for him. It is distinguished by the director's ingenious use of three camera angles: the view of Omid, the young son who acquires the camera; the family members' efforts at covering reality; and Mirbaqeri's view, which explores the truth and the false pretensions. The film won the Silver Leopard at Locarno 2005. **The Bitter Dream**, by Mohsen Amir-Yusefi, is another successful debut by a young film-maker. It depicts the life of Esfandiar, an old caretaker, who bargains about his imminent demise with the angel of death. With its impressive satirical approach, *The Bitter Dream* marks the emergence of a fine director. There are other notable films from the past 12 months, but they are beyond the scope of this report.

JAMAL OMID (fcf2@dpi.net.ir) has written more than 20 film scripts and 20 books on cinema, including the three-volume *History of the Iranian Cinema*. He is a member of the organising committees of the Tehran, Fajr and Isfahan international film festivals and produced the television series *The Detective and the Trial*.

Ali Rafiee, director of **The Fish Fall in Love**

Ireland Michael Dwyer

The Year's Best Films

Michael Dwyer's selection:
Breakfast on Pluto
(Neil Jordan)
Pavee Lackeen (Perry Ogden)
The Mighty Celt
(Pearse Elliott)
Isolation (Billy O'Brien)
Short Order (Anthony Byrne)

Recent and Forthcoming Films

BOY EATS GIRL
[Comedy-horror, 2005] Script: Derek Landy. Dir: Stephen Bradley. Phot: Balazs Bolygo. Players: Samantha Mumba, David Leon, Deirdre O'Kane, Bryan Murray. Prod: Element Films/Lunar Films.

BREAKFAST ON PLUTO
[Comedy-drama, 2005] Script: Neil Jordan, Patrick McCabe, based on the novel by McCabe. Dir: Jordan. Phot: Declan Quinn. Players: Cillian Murphy, Liam Neeson, Stephen Rea, Brendan Gleeson, Gavin Friday. Prod: Parallel Films.

DEAD LONG ENOUGH
[Romantic comedy, 2006] Script: James Hawes and Tommy Collins, based on the novel by Hawes. Dir: Collins. Phot: P.J. Dillon. Players: Michael Sheen, Jason Hughes, Angeline Ball. Prod: Grand Pictures.
Two Welsh brothers return to an Irish village after 16 years and meet a woman from their past.

ISOLATION
[Horror, 2005] Script and Dir: Billy O'Brien. Phot: Robbie Ryan. Players: John Lynch, Essie Davis, Sean Harris, Ruth Negga.

The Irish arts minister, John O'Donoghue, was upbeat when he opened the Irish Pavilion at Cannes in 2005. Acknowledging the problems in attracting inward production because of the strength of the Euro against the dollar, he described the retention of Ireland's Section 481 tax incentive scheme as "a critical decision" that "already has impacted on Irish film activity". Yet 2005 proved to be dismal for production in Ireland. It started promisingly enough in February, with **Studs** and **Dead Long Enough** going into production. Although two significant productions were shooting during the summer – Ken Loach's **The Wind That Shakes the Barley**, and Charles Sturridge's new version of **Lassie** (half of which was shot on the Isle of Man) – it was a remarkably lean year until production began to pick up in November.

The Irish Film Board was without a chief executive for seven months, following the resignation of Mark Woods in April 2005, after just 18 months in the job. After a thorough selection process (almost as long as the casting of the new James Bond), producer and former British Screen executive Simon Perry was appointed in November 2005. Only one Irish film figured on the Irish box-office top 10 for 2004: Paddy Breathnach's comedy, **Man About Dog**, about three Belfast men taking to the road when they fall foul of a corrupt bookie. It overcame lukewarm reviews. Overall cinema attendances remained steady, with multiplexes opening in three regional cities and a new Dublin site bringing the capital's screen count to 115.

Once again, the outstanding Irish film was directed by Neil Jordan. Like their fruitful collaboration on *The Butcher Boy*, **Breakfast on Pluto** was another potent mix of novelist Patrick McCabe's wonderfully weird and fertile imagination and Jordan's rich cinematic flair. At its heart is another remarkable performance from versatile Irish actor Cillian Murphy as one of life's pure innocents, a young transvestite, Kitten, who is the unplanned offspring of a priest (Liam Neeson) and his housekeeper (Eva Birthistle) in a border town in the 1960s. Like Candide, Kitten proves an eternal optimist as he undergoes various misadventures, comic and tragic. The film intoxicatingly fuses preoccupations familiar from Jordan's work – terrorism, cross-dressing, inter-racial relationships, lost parents, musicians and fairy tales – and amply justifies the audience's willing suspension of disbelief.

Prod: Element Films.

JOHNNY WAS
[Thriller, 2006] Script: Brendan
Foley. Dir: Mark Hammond.
Phot: Mark Moriarty. Players:
Vinnie Jones, Samantha Mumba,
Patrick Bergin, Roger Daltrey,
Lennox Lewis. Prod:
Borderline Productions.
A former IRA man on the run
and caught up in racial tension
in London.

LASSIE
[Canine adventure, 2005] Script
and Dir: Charles Sturridge. Phot:
Howard Atherton. Players: Peter
O'Toole, Samantha Morton, Peter
Dinklage. Prod: Element Films.

MICKYBO AND ME
[Drama, 2004] Script: Terry
Loane, based on the play by
Owen McCafferty. Dir: Loane.
Phot: Roman Osin. Players: Niall
Wright, John Jo McNeil, Julie
Walters, Ciaran Hinds, Adrian
Dunbar, Gina McKee, Susan
Lynch. Prod: New Moon Pictures.

THE MIGHTY CELT
[Drama, 2005] Script and Dir:
Pearse Elliott. Phot: Seamus
Deasy. Players: Robert Carlyle,
Gillian Anderson, Ken Stott,
Tyrone McKenna, Sean McGinley.
Prod: Treasure Entertainment.

PAVEE LACKEEN
(The Traveller Girl)
[Urban docu-drama, 2005]
Script: Perry Ogden, Mark
Venner. Dir: Ogden. Phot:
Ogden. Players: Winnie
Maughan, Rose Maughan, Paddy
Maughan. Prod: An Lár Films.

SHORT ORDER
[Musical, 2005] Script and Dir:
Anthony Byrne. Phot: Brendan
Maguire. Players: Emma de
Caunes, Cosma Shiva Hagen,
John Hurt, Jack Dee, Vanessa
Redgrave. Prod: Igloo Films.

STUDS
[Comedy, 2006] Script: Paul
Mercier, based on his stage play.
Dir: Mercier. Phot: Ronan Fox.
Players: Brendan Gleeson, David
Wilmot, Eanna MacLiam, Liam

Stephen Rea, left, and Cillian Murphy in **Breakfast on Pluto**

Darker sides of Dublin

Photographer Perry Ogden makes an impressive directing debut
with **Pavee Lackeen** (*The Traveller Girl*), which defies easy
classification in its blending of documentary and fictional drama.
The main 'roles' are taken by a large traveller family, the Maughans,
living in a trailer parked in a desolate area of Dublin, and Ogden
focuses on Winnie Maughan, 12. Ogden's observation is
consistently unpatronising as it challenges stereotypical images of
the traveller community, drawing us deep inside their world. It won
the Satyajit Ray Award for best first feature at the 2005 London
Film Festival.

The most successful indigenous production at Irish cinemas in
2005, Gillies MacKinnon's **Tara Road**, earned more than
€500,000, despite generally negative reviews. Based on Maeve
Binchy's best-selling novel, this melodrama follows the parallel lives
of two women (Andie McDowell and Olivia Williams) on opposite
sides of the Atlantic, as they swap houses while struggling to cope
with traumatic events. The result is sketchy and thoroughly
conventional and squanders the talent assembled on both sides of
the camera.

Zombies prowl the Dublin suburbs in **Boy Eats Girl**, an entertaining
transposition of US teen horror-comedy to a deftly employed Irish
context. Stephen Bradley's second feature, after *Sweety Barrett*,
this cheerfully unpretentious romp suffered at the box-office when it
opened on the same day as George Romero's **Land of the Dead**.
Fintan Connolly's mellow romantic drama, **Trouble with Sex**,
features the expressive Aidan Gillen as a lonely, unattached Dublin
bar manager tentatively getting involved with a fast-rising young
lawyer (radiant newcomer Renee Weldon). The consequences are
developed with honesty and credibility.

Growing pains

Man About Dog screenwriter Pearse Elliott turns director with the appealing coming-of-age drama **The Mighty Celt**, featuring Tyrone McKenna as a Belfast schoolboy who lives with his single mother (Gillian Anderson) and works enthusiastically for a greyhound trainer (Ken Stott). With the reappearance of a former IRA man (Robert Carlyle), the narrative extends subtly to explore contrasting attitudes in post-peace process Belfast. Brimming with energy and natural screen presence, newcomers Niall Wright and John Joe McNeill play schoolboy friends in another coming-of-age drama, Terry Loane's **Mickybo and Me**. Coming from opposite sides of the sectarian divide in 1970s Belfast, they escape from harsh realities into the fantasy world of movies, taking Butch Cassidy and the Sundance Kid as their role models.

Emma de Caunes in **Short Order**

Writer–director Anthony Byrne's highly assured first feature, **Short Order**, a distinctly offbeat musical, opens on a street scene so consciously presented as a film set that the lights are switched on at the outset. Emma de Caunes is wonderfully spirited as a short order chef in this wilfully eccentric movie, which is obsessed with connecting the pleasures of food and sex, fragmented and elusive in its structure, and exhibits dazzling visual style.

In **Isolation**, writer-director Billy O'Brien's unsettling first feature, the shadow of mad cow disease hangs over a dark tale set on a remote Irish farm. It wastes no time in setting up several ominous incidents, and as it reveals the consequences of tampering with nature, establishes and sustains a climate of fear. It closes with tongue firmly in cheek on a country song, *"I'm Going to Make You Love Me 'Til the Cows Come Home"*.

Carney, Eamon Owens. Prod: Brother Films.
A plain-speaking new coach takes on a losing football team.

TARA ROAD
[Melodrama, 2005] Script: Shane Connaughton, Cynthia Cidre, based on the novel by Maeve Binchy. Dir: Gillies MacKinnon. Phot: John de Borman. Players: Andie McDowell, Olivia Williams, Iain Glen, Stephen Rea, Brenda Fricker. Prod: Ferndale Films.

TROUBLE WITH SEX
[Romantic drama, 2005] Script and Dir: Fintan Connolly. Phot: Owen McPolin. Players: Aidan Gillen, Renee Weldon, Declan Conlon, Gerard Mannix Flynn. Prod: Fubar Films.

WILDERNESS
[Horror, 2006] Script: Dario Polini. Dir and Phot: Michael Bassett. Players: Sean Pertwee, Alex Reid. Prod: Ecosse Films. Young offenders are taken on a course on a supposedly deserted remote island.

THE WIND THAT SHAKES THE BARLEY
[Historical drama, 2006] Script: Paul Laverty. Dir: Ken Loach. Phot: Barry Ackroyd. Players: Cillian Murphy, Liam Cunningham, Padraic Delaney. Prod: Sixteen Films/ Element Films.
Young Irishmen's experiences during the War of Independence in the 1920s.

Quote of the Year

"Neil was possessed shooting the movie. He reminded me what an abstract painter would have been like, just applying colour all the time."
LIAM NEESON, *on making* Breakfast on Pluto *with* Neil Jordan.

Israel Dan Fainaru

The Year's Best Films

Dan Fainaru's selection:
Avenge but One of My Eyes
(Avi Mograbi)
What a Wonderful Place
(Eyal Halfon)
Free Zone (Amos Gitai)
Close to Home
(Dalia Hager, Vidi Bilu)

Avenge but One of My Eyes

Recent and Forthcoming Films

EIZE MAKOM NIFLA
(**What a Wonderful Place**)
*[Drama, 2005] Script and Dir:
Eyal Halfon. Phot: Nili Aslan.
Players: Uri Gavriel, Evelyn
Kaplun, Yossi Graber, Avi Oriah,
Yaiv Hait, Ramon Bagatsing.
Prod: Assaf Amir, Yoav Roeh.*

JANEM JANEM
*[Drama, 2005) Script and
Dir: Haim Buzaglo. Phot:
Yoram Millo. Players: Danny
Rytenberg, Avital Deker, Amos
Lavie, Dor Zeigenbaum,
Galina Auzerner, Raymond
Amsalem. Prod: Haim Buzaglo,
Amir Gedalia, Yoram Millo,
Nelly Kafsky.*
A high-school teacher pretends to
take some time off in Paris, but
instead joins a group of foreign
workers in Israel and finds out
how life in his own country looks
from a different perspective.

After producing in a relatively short time a string of notable successes, such as *Walk on Water*, *The Syrian Bride* and *Turn Left at the End of the World*, the Israeli film industry evidently felt it needed to sit back, take a deep breath and ponder the reasons for this sudden overflow, before the next step forward. The output of 2005 was not altogether disappointing, but was a period of transition, holding much promise for the immediate future.

The prolonged impact of 2004's fruits (all reviewed in last year's *IFG*) sweetened a rather bland selection of newer products. Avi Nesher's *Turn Left at the End of the World* became the domestic box-office sensation of the last decade, with more than 450,000 admissions. Eytan Fox's fine thriller *Walk on Water* is now Israel's top film export to the US, and has grossed in excess of $6m worldwide, and Eran Riklis' *The Syrian Bride* has done almost as well. *To Take a Wife*, *Or* and *Atash*, were hot items abroad, while Gidi Dar's surprise hit, **Ushpizin** (meaning "guests" in Aramaic), a picture about Orthodox Jews, had not only 160,000 admissions but also a successful unveiling at the Tribeca festival.

No wonder all these people had to savour their victories, then collect their wits before going back to work. This left the stage clear once again for the prolific Amos Gitai, whose **Free Zone** went to Cannes with Natalie Portman on the marquee, and came out of it

Natalie Portman, centre, in **Free Zone**

with an acting award for Hanna Laszlo, virtually unknown outside Israel before, and with international kudos for Hiam Abbass, a Palestinian actress who may well be on course for international stardom in 2006, following the release of Steven Spielberg's *Munich*, in which she appears and acts as an adviser. This was another road movie for Gitai, one more metaphor of the Middle East conflict and the need to let the people there work out a solution for themselves instead of constantly meddling in their affairs; it is by far superior to his earlier, pretentiously ambiguous **Promised Land**.

Demystifying the myths

The other Cannes entry and the foremost representative of the thriving documentary industry here was Avi Mograbi's **Avenge but One of My Eyes**, the first Israeli film ever given a special screening slot in the official programme of the world's leading film festival. Mograbi looks at some of the most highly respected Jewish national myths, such as Samson bringing down the temple, or the Masada zealots jumping to their deaths after exterminating their own families rather than be slaves to the heathen. But instead of showing admiration for these heroes, he argues that their exasperation and despair then was identical to that of today's Palestinians – exactly the kind of argument that enrages the Israeli right, to whom Mograbi, a determined peace activist, is a traitor.

After fiddling for almost two years in the editing rooms, Eyal Halfon finally brought out his ironically titled **What a Wonderful Place**, which ignores the Israeli–Arab conflict in favour of urgent social issues. Yet another compilation of separate intersecting plots, it takes in a flock of Ukrainian hookers pounding the Tel Aviv sidewalks, and their shepherd, a demoted cop (Uri Gavriel), then works its way into the household of a middle-aged farmer using Thai workers on his fields, the farmer's wife and her nasty lover, whose invalid father is looked after by a Filipino with marital problems. It comes full circle with the cop and his pimp employer, whose illegal casinos rip off illegal foreign workers. This is too many stories for one picture, but there is no denying its sincerity, nor the sterling performance of Gavriel, who for once does not play the heavy but offers a moving and perceptive portrait of a complex character.

Also worth mentioning, **Close to Home**, a small, personal, intimate movie, tells the story of two girls in uniforms, both detailed to patrol the streets of Jerusalem and check the documents of "suspect" characters. Based on the experiences of Vidi Bilu, co-writer–director with Dalia Hager, there is a lot to like in this charmingly naïve picture, confirming once again the talent of Hager, who made a strong debut, *Summer at Erica's*, before vanishing from the movie scene for 13 years.

**KAROV LA BAYIT
(Close to Home)**
[Drama, 2005] Script and Dir: Vidi Bilu, Dalia Hager. Phot: Yaron Scharf. Players: Smadar Sayar, Naama Schendar, Irit Suki, Katia Zimbris, Danny Geva, Anna Stephan. Prod: Marek Rozenbaum, Itay Tamir.

MUKHRAKHIM LEHIOT SAMEACH (Joy)
[Family drama, 2005] Script: Omer Tadmor. Dir: Julie Schles. Phot: Itzik Portal. Players: Sigalith Fuchs, Tal Friedman, Keren Mor, Yossi Pollak, Rivka Michaeli, Alexander Senderovich, Dorit Bar-Or. Prod: Amir Harel.
A shy, overweight girl signs up for a reality TV show, hoping to reunite her embattled family and help them overcome a shameful secret from the past.

BEKAROV IKRE LCHA MASHEHU TOV (Comrade)
[Drama, 2005] Script: Uzi Weil. Dir: Eyal Shiray. Phot: Valentin Belonogov. Players: Assi Dayan, Tinker Bell, Adam Hirsch. Prod: Eyal Shiray, David Mandil, Dan Shiray.
Part coming-of-age story, part political allegory, this features a cranky old eccentric who still lives by the codes of the communist revolution, a young boy who rebels against his father and his older sister, whom he adores.

YAMIN KEFUYIM (Frozen Days)
[Drama, 2005] Script and Dir: Danny Lerner. Phot: Ram Shweki. Players: Anat Klauzner, Sandra Sade. Prod: Asaf Rab, Danny Lerner, Alan Lerner.
A young woman drop-out is prevented from reaching a blind date by a suicide bomber blowing himself up in a night-club. She goes through a series of hallucinatory experiences.

LEMAR'IT AYIN (Out of Sight)
[Psychological drama, 2005] Script: Noa Greenberg. Dir: Daniel Syrkin. Phot: Giora Bejach. Players: Tali Sharon, Israel Poliakov, Avigail Harari,

Hadas Yaron, Sandra Sade, Assi Dayan. Prod: Mirit Toovi, Yoram Mandel, Ayelet Imberman.
A blind student returns from the US and tries to find out the truth behind the suicide of her best friend.

LIRKOD (The Belly Dancer)
[Thriller, 2005] Script: Haim Marin. Dir: Marek Rozenbaum. Phot: Valentin Belogonov. Players: Meytal Dohan, Alon Abouboul, Yuval Segal. Prod: Marek Rozenbaum, Itay Tamir.
The lives of a belly dancer, a night-club owner and a petty thief will never be the same again after they carry out a botched heist.

AVIVA AHUVATI (Aviva My Love)
[Drama, 2006] Script and Dir: Shemi Zarhin. Phot: Itzik Portal. Players: Assi Levy, Rotem Abuhav, Dror Keren, Levana Finkelstein, Sasson Gabai. Prod: Eitan Even.

HAB'UA (The Bubble)
[Drama, 2006] Script: Gal Uchovsky. Dir: Eytan Fox. Phot: Yaron Scharf. Players: Ohad Knoler, Alon Friedman, Daniela Wircer, Yousef Sweid, Lior Ashkenazi. Prod: Ronen Ben-Tal, Gal Uchovsky, Amir Feingold.
Three carefree young Israelis living in Tel Aviv's hippest neighbourhood hide a young Arab in their flat.

ADAMA MESHUGA'ATH (Sweet Mud)
[Drama, 2006] Script and Dir: Dror Shaul. Phot: Sebastian Edschmid. Players: Gal Zaid, Henri Garcin, Tomer Steinhof, Ronit Yudkevitch, Shai Avivi. Prod: Edgar Tenembaum, Dror Shaul, Johannes Rexin, Bettina Brokemper, Philippa Kpwarsky, Sharon Shamir.
In 1974, a 12-year-old boy realises his mother is mentally ill and is torn between the egalitarian pretences of the kibbutz on which they live and the fact that the community is turning its back on his mother and himself.

Out of Africa

Whether the two most striking films to be shot in Israel qualify as Israeli films is open to interpretation. Unveiled at Berlin 2005 and a festival favourite ever since (it won Best Film and Best Script at Copenhagen), Radu Mihaileanu's **Live and Become** is basically French, but was shot almost entirely in Israel with a predominantly Israeli cast and crew. It's the emotional tale of a non-Jewish Ethiopian boy brought to Israel under false pretenses who must live down this lie for 20 years.

Hanny Abou Assad's **Paradise Now**, the controversial portrait of two suicide bombers about to leave on their deadly mission, won Best European Film at Berlin and was submitted for the Oscars. Though bearing a Dutch–Palestinian label, it was entirely shot in Israel, the West Bank and Nazareth, with an Israeli outfit, Lama Productions, in charge of production. It was acclaimed all over the world not just for its politics but as an astute psychological drama.

This issue of a film's Israeli identity may well become increasingly prominent, as more films are co-produced, mostly with European partners. Among forthcoming productions, German actress Maria Schrader is directing her first film in Israel, **Love Life**. **Sweet Mud**, a searing account of childhood in a kibbutz by Dror Shaul, has European and Japanese backing. Ra'anan Alexandrowicz (director of *James' Journey to Jerusalem*) is shooting in France **The Miracle of St. Elgendy**, about Israelis living there. There are numerous similar projects under way.

Also worth waiting for will be **Aviva My Love**, Shemi Zarhin's tale of a working woman with literary aspirations and family problems; the new Eytan Fox film, **The Bubble**, about the alienation of Tel Aviv bohemian life from the rest of the country; and Uri Barbash's cinema comeback, **The Salt of the Earth**, after almost a decade of television. Maybe calling 2005 a transitory year isn't that misleading, after all.

DAN FAINARU (dfainaru@netvision.net.il) is co-editor of Israel's only film magazine, *Cinematheque*, and a former director of the Israeli Film Institute. He reviews regularly for *Screen International*.

Italy Lorenzo Codelli

The Year's Best Films

Lorenzo Codelli's selection:
Once You're Born
(Marco Tullio Giordana)
*When Do the Girls Show
Up?* (Pupi Avati)
Crime Novel (Michele Placido)
Mater Natura
(Massimo Andrei)
The Fever
(Alessandro D'Alatri)

Recent Films

BEFORE IT HAD A NAME
*[Drama, 2005] Script: Giada
Colagrande, Willem Dafoe. Dir:
Colagrande. Phot: Ken Kelsch.
Players: Colagrande, Dafoe,
Seymour Cassel. Prod: Nu Image
(US)/Emmett (US)/Bidou Pictures
(US)/Furla Films.*

LA BESTIA NEL CUORE
(Don't Tell)
*[Drama, 2005] Script: Cristina
Comencini, Francesca Marciano,
Giulia Calenda, from
Comencini's novel. Dir:
Comencini. Phot: Fabio
Cianchetti. Players: Giovanna
Mezzogiorno, Alessio Boni, Luigi
Lo Cascio, Giuseppe Battiston.
Prod: Cattleya/Rai Cinema/
Aquarius Film (UK)/Alquimia
Cinema (Spain)/Babe (France).*

THE CLAN
*[Musical comedy, 2005] Script:
Fausto Brizzi, Christian De Sica,
Marco Martani. Dir: De Sica.
Phot: Gian Lorenzo Battaglia.
Players: De Sica, Paolo Conticini,
Sebastian Torchia. Prod: DAP/
Rai Cinema/Victory Media
Group (Germany).*

COSE DA PAZZI
(Sheer Madness)

Another year of decline for Italian cinema peaked with an angry showbusiness strike against the €267m slash in cultural funding threatened by Silvio Berlusconi's government, which would annihilate theatre, music, museums and the film industry, from production to festivals. Some 70 Italian releases secured around 26% of the gross in 2005, similar numbers to 2004. But the gap between the handful of hits and more than 60 fiascos or disappointments widened and total attendance at cinemas fell by eight million.

Family groups are captured by home-brewed blockbusters just once or twice per year, invariably during the Christmas or Easter holidays. Their main hypnotist, producer–distributor–exhibitor Aurelio De Laurentiis, launched **Christmas in Love** for December 2004 and **Christmas in Miami** 12 months later. Both were celluloid panettoni, confections starring Christian De Sica and Massimo Boldi, a stainless, none-too-bright couple, one from the south, the other from the north. For March, that shrewd tycoon squeezed into **Manual of Love** (*Manuale d'amore*) a bunch of slightly brainier jesters from various generations – among them Roman idols Carlo Verdone and Silvio Muccino – multiplying his usual recipe's surefire appeal. Films promising "escape from Hard Times", such as these, propelled the opulent Italian satirical genre decades ago, but now seem reduced to hasty, toothless sketches, anonymously performed. Aldo, Giovanni & Giacomo's **Do You Know Claudia?**, the Milanese trio's warmed-up vaudeville, and, a year later, Tuscan wonderboy Leonardo Pieraccioni's badinage, **I Love You in Any Languages** were cannonades fired by almighty producer–distributor–exhibitor Medusa Film to counter De Laurentiis' at Christmas 2004 and 2005.

Roberto over-reaches; Pupi triumphs

Roberto Benigni's 800 prints of **The Tiger and the Snow**, released in sunny mid-October, did not guarantee his customary instant box-office smash. Are his fans getting blasé about Benigni's metamorphosis from Funnyman to Holyman? This romance between a poet and his ideal girl (Nicoletta Braschi, who else?) starts in a model Italian city where life looks so beautiful and clean, then continues in Baghdad, where US troops, Italian doctors and Iraqi people behave harmoniously despite the bombs. Those backgrounds are merely functional for Benigni's highbrow gags, picked up from Charlot, Pedro Almodóvar, Jorge Luis Borges or even the late Pope

[Comedy, 2005] Script: Vincenzo Salemme, from his play. Dir: Salemme. Phot: Arnaldo Catinari. Players: Salemme, Biagio Izzo, Teresa Del Vecchio. Prod: Cecchi Gori Group.

CUORE SACRO (Sacred Heart)
[Drama, 2005] Script: Ferzan Ozpetek, Gianni Romoli. Dir: Ozpetek. Phot: Gianfilippo Corticelli. Players: Barbora Bobulova, Andrea Di Stefano, Lisa Gastoni. Prod: R&C Produzioni.

FATTI DELLA BANDA DELLA MAGLIANA (Facts About the Magliana Gang)
[Drama, 2005] Script and Dir: Daniele Costantini. Phot: Paolo Ferrari. Players: Francesco Pannofino, Roberto Brunetti, Leo Gullotta. Prod: Istituto Luce/Goodtime.

LA FEBBRE (The Fever)
[Comedy, 2005] Script: Alessandro D'Alatri, Gennaro Nunziante, Domenico Starnone. Dir: D'Alatri. Phot: Italo Petriccione. Players: Fabio Volo, Valeria Solarino, Cochi Ponzoni. Prod: Rodeo Drive/Rai Cinema.

I GIORNI DELL'ABBANDONO (The Days of Abandonment)
[Drama, 2005] Script: Roberto Faenza, Gianni Arduini, Cristiana Del Bello, Diego De Silva, Dino Gentili, Filippo Gentili, Lella Ravasi, Anna Redi. Dir: Faenza. Phot: Maurizio Calvesi. Players: Margherita Buy, Luca Zingaretti, Goran Bregovic. Prod: Jean Vigo Italia/Medusa Film.

LA GUERRA DI MARIO (Mario's War)
[Drama, 2005] Script and Dir: Antonio Capuano. Phot: Luca Bigazzi. Players: Valeria Golino, Andrea Renzi, Nunzio Gallo. Prod: Indigo Film/Fandango.

ALLA LUCE DEL SOLE (Come Into the Light)
[Drama, 2005] Script: Roberto Faenza, Gianni Arduni, Giacomo Maia, Dino Gentili, Filippo Gentili, Cristiana Del Bello. Dir:

Pupi Avati's **When Do the Girls Show Up?**

John Paul. See, for instance, Benigni praying "Our Father…" to Allah! Huge ambitions and a €30m budget – four times the average for an Italian feature – are choking an irresistible talent's capacities.

Established film-makers like Pupi Avati, Alessandro D'Alatri and Marco Tullio Giordana, linked to Rai Cinema's firm auteur policy, devised some of their most personal works. Avati's fertile imagination – he has never used any other writer's scripts – blessed us with two quite different movies back to back. **When Do the Girls Show Up?**, in which two young jazz players in love with the same blonde happen upon totally opposite careers, sounds like a bittersweet slice of autobiography. Running through the desperate 1990s, Avati lyrically revives his own hopeful 1950s. An inspired score by Riz Ortolani and a band of alluring faces energise this dazzling generational fresco. Avati's **The Second Wedding Night** vigorously paints a devastated, starving Italy in 1946, when a widow (famous soprano Katia Ricciarelli) and her grown-up swindler son travel a long way to meet a benefactor. This was unashamed nostalgia for innocent, purer times, most unlike the present.

Alessandro D'Alatri, a virtuoso of irreverent commercials, forges in **The Fever** a stagnant provincial microcosm, inside which a naïve petty clerk tries to cultivate his utopia. A Gogol-like spirit imbues this sugar-coated fairy tale, starring Fabio Volo, an amiable, bearded TV entertainer whose frustrations are typical of the thirty-something breed.

Alessandro D'Alatri's **The Fever**

INTERNATIONAL FILM GUIDE ITALY | 189

Matteo Gadola, left, in Once You're Born

New life after *Youth*

Following his worldwide hit *The Best of Youth*, Marco Tullio
Giordana in **Once You're Born** sails over the Mediterranean to
cross paths with a wealthy child (promising newcomer Matteo
Gadola) saved from the waves by a boat carrying illegal immigrants.
A coming-of-age adventure vaguely inspired by Kipling's *Captains
Courageous*, it boasts Giordana's keen eye for harsh social
confrontations between complex characters. Rising star Alessio
Boni (the soldier brother in *Best of Youth*) plays an industrialist
father, gritty and breakable at the same time. The multi-layered
script, ending on a high note, is the work of the director, with
Stefano Rulli and Sandro Petraglia.

Rulli and Petraglia also crafted Michele Placido's **Crime Novel**, a
sweeping saga covering the last third of the twentieth century in
much darker tones than their script for *Best of Youth*. Here they
focus on the real life Magliana's Gang, a pack of rotten Roman
guys who murder and kidnap to dominate the underworld. Their
flourishing connections with corrupted spies, terrorists and political
bosses shed light on the recent criminalisation of Italy. Placido, an
actor himself, relishes handling his large cast of villains, from
Claudio Santamaria (the trumpet genius of *When Do the Girls Show
Up?*) to Kim Rossi Stuart, Stefano Accorsi and Pierfrancesco
Favino. Warner Bros. deserve praise for daring to sponsor this
committed Cattleya production. The HD docudrama **Facts About
the Magliana Gang**, by Daniele Costantini, deals with the same
mob and is staged inside a jail by actual convicts.

Sermonizing religious thriller **Sacred Heart** and HD detective thriller
Quo Vadis Baby? failed to bring back to fashion Ferzan Ozpetek
and Gabriele Salvatores. With his eye mainly on the home video

Faenza. *Phot: Italo Petriccione.
Players: Luca Zingaretti, Alessia
Goria, Corrado Fortuna. Prod:
Jean Vigo Italia.*

**MANUALE D'AMORE
(Manual of Love)**
*[Comedy, 2005] Script: Giovanni
Veronesi, Ugo Chiti. Dir:
Veronesi. Phot: Tani Canevari.
Players: Carlo Verdone, Silvio
Muccino, Luciana Litizzetto,
Jasmine Trinca, Margherita Buy.
Prod: Filmauro.*

**MA QUANDO ARRIVANO LE
RAGAZZE? (When Do the Girls
Show Up?)**
*[Comedy, 2005] Script and Dir:
Pupi Avati. Phot: Pasquale
Rachini. Players: Claudio
Santamaria, Paolo Briguglia,
Vittoria Puccini, Johnny Dorelli.
Prod: Duea Film/Rai Cinema.*

MATER NATURA
*[Comedy, 2005] Script: Massimo
Andrei, Silvia Ranfagni. Dir:
Andrei. Phot: Vladan Radovic.
Players: Maria Pia Calzone,
Vladimir Luxuria, Enzo
Moscato. Prod: Kubla Khan.*

MON AMOUR
*[Erotic comedy, 2005] Script:
Tinto Brass, Massimiliano Zanin,
Carla Cipriani, from Alina
Rizzi's novel. Dir: Brass. Phot:
Andrea Doria. Players: Anna
Jimskaya, Max Parodi, Nela
Lucic, Riccardo Marino.
Prod: Monamour.*

Max Parodi and Anna Jimskaya in
Mon Amour

MUSIKANTEN
*[Drama, 2005] Script: Franco
Battiato, Manlio Sgalambro.
Dir: Battiato. Phot: Daniele
Baldacci. Players: Alejandro
Jodorowsky, Sonia Bergamasco,
Fabrizio Gifuni. Prod: L'Ottava/
Rai Cinema.*

NATALE A MIAMI
(Christmas in Miami)
*[Farce, 2005] Script and Dir:
Neri Parenti. Phot: Gian
Lorenzo Battaglia. Players:
Massimo Boldi, Christian
De Sica, Massimo Ghini.
Prod: Filmauro.*

L'ORIZZONTE DEGLI EVENTI
(The Horizon of Events)
*[Drama, 2005] Script: Daniele
Vicari, Antonio Leotti, Laura
Paolucci. Dir: Vicari. Phot:
Gherardo Gossi. Players: Valerio
Mastandrea, Gwenaelle Simon,
Lulzim Zeqja. Prod: Fandango/
Medusa Film.*

**LA PASSIONE DI GIOSUÈ
L'EBREO** (The Passion of Joshua
the Jew)
*[Drama, 2005] Script and Dir:
Pasquale Scimeca. Phot: Pasquale
Mari. Players: Leonardo Cesare
Abude, Anna Bonaiuto, Toni
Bertorelli. Prod: Arbash/Poetiche
Cinematografiche/ICC (Spain).*

PROVINCIA MECCANICA
(Smalltown, Italy)
*[Drama, 2005] Script: Silvia
Barbiera, Stefano Mordini. Dir:
Mordini. Phot: Italo Petriccione.
Players: Stefano Accorsi,
Valentina Cervi, Ivan Franeck.
Prod: Medusa Film.*

**QUANDO SEI NATO NON
PUOI PIÙ NASCONDERTI**
(Once You're Born)
*[Drama, 2005] Script: Stefano
Rulli, Sandro Petraglia,
Marco Tullio Giordana. Dir:
Giordana. Phot: Roberto Forza.
Players: Alessio Boni, Matteo
Gadola, Michela Cescon.
Prod: Cattleya/Rai
Cinema/Babe (France)/
Aquarius Film (UK).*

QUO VADIS BABY?
*[Thriller, 2005] Script:
Gabriele Salvatores, Fabio
Scamoni, from Grazia
Verasani's novel. Dir:
Salvatores. Phot: Italo
Petriccione. Players: Elio
Germano, Angela Baraldi,
Gigio Alberti. Prod: Colorado
Film/Medusa Film.*

market, his international domain, veteran Tinto Brass uses HD for **Mon Amour** to exalt juicy sexual contortions in front of Giulio Romano's erotic Renaissance murals. Celebrated singer–composer Franco Battiato's **Musikanten** delivers a solemn Beethoven tribute, starring Mexican magus Alejandro Jodorowsky. Cristina Comencini adapts one of her novels for **Don't Tell**, a nice mix of classic melodrama and topical comedy; Giuseppe Battiston steals the show as a chubby, Wellesian TV hack.

Slaves to TV

Roberto Faenza misfired twice, with a priest-vs,-mafia denunciation, **Come Into the Light**, and a marriage kammerspiel, **Days of Abandonment**. This once-original film-maker yearns to imitate soap opera clichés and rhythms, and is far from alone in this regard, because week after week TV series and miniseries – predominantly hagiographies of saints, housewives or cops – achieve phenomenal ratings on public and private networks. Booming companies like Cattleya invest in these pan-European concoctions, to subsidise their much riskier theatrical ventures. At the same time, leading screenwriters such as Rulli and Petraglia and actor–directors like Placido switch often and freely between media.

Censorship, sadly, rules the networks more than ever, as Sabina Guzzanti exposes in **Viva Zapatero!** This is a brave and funny DV report about her own expulsion from Rai because of her involvement in a parody show vilifying Berlusconi, and is a perfect illustration of the many Mussolini-style rituals that silence uncomfortable voices. Her documentary made a small fortune and deserved to be screened at the European Union. Magnate Vittorio Cecchi Gori came back from the ashes, financing two Vanzina Bros. quickies: **In This World of Thieves** (*In questo mondo di ladri*), a rather biting farce about fraudulent cons, and **Monnezza Is Back**, an abortive sequel to 1970s pulp fictions. Cecchi Gori continues to struggle to recover his multiplexes and other bricks of his dismantled Xanadu.

Domenico Procacci's **Fandango** promoted again some emerging film-makers around the festival circuit but failed to sell enough tickets at home. Fausto Paravidino's debut, **Texas**, premiered at Venice, is an amateurish smalltown lament; Daniele Vicari's sophomore effort, **The Horizon of Events**, launched at Cannes' Critics Week, was a dreary depiction of a scientist's crisis. Antonio Capuano's **Mario's War**, a bland adoption drama, received positive reactions at Locarno, whereas Berlin gave a cool reception to **Tickets**, a triptych set on an express train, for which Ermanno Olmi conceived a luminous parable on altruism, Abbas Kiarostami a witty chat between teenagers, and Ken Loach an exuberant segment about Scottish soccer fans.

The international brigade

Moving abroad, to direct and/or produce, was a positive shift for several Italians this past year. Giada Colagrande and her new husband Willem Dafoe's **Before it Had a Name**, a lustful vehicle baring the authors' bodies and souls, prompts more smiles than climaxes. Actress Ida Di Benedetto backed John Irvin's ballet school intrigue **The Fine Art of Love**, from an old script by unforgettable pioneer Alberto Lattuada, who died in July 2005. Actress Maria Grazia Cucinotta backed **All the Invisible Children**, a multinational Unicef propaganda vehicle, in which only Emir Kusturica succeeds, thanks to his unique vision. Pasquale Scimeca went to Spain to fund **The Passion of Joshua the Jew**, his intense, anti-Mel Gibson epic. Abel Ferrara's **Mary**, Brian De Palma's **The Black Dahlia** and John Boorman's forthcoming **Memoirs of Hadrian** count among the latest Italian co-productions.

Naples could be considered a 'nation' by itself, because of its Bourbon heritage and extremely rich and peculiar culture, still burgeoning from forced underdevelopment. **Mater Natura**, Neapolitan playwright Massimo Andrei's first opus, explodes with joy and colours. A quartet of singing transsexuals sets up an organic farm for depressed males on volcano Vesuvius' slopes; sparkling Maria Pia Calzone embodies **Desiderio** (*Desire*), "an emblem of the transition/transaction of our times", says Andrei.

The transsexual quartet in **Mater Natura**

Neapolitan giant Vittorio De Sica's lookalike scion, Christian, stars in his pansexual musical **The Clan**. Natives Paolo Sorrentino and Mario Martone are at work on their new movies. Neapolitan maestro Francesco Rosi, too long away from cameras, directed for the stage Eduardo De Filippo's *Napoli millonara*, a hymn to the art of surviving catastrophes. And let's not forget that mass-market king Aurelio De Laurentiis also comes from an excellent Neapolitan dynasty.

LORENZO CODELLI (codelli@interware.it) is on the board of Cineteca del Friuli and is a regular contributor to *Positif* and other periodicals.

IL RITORNO DEL MONNEZZA
(**Monnezza Is Back**)
[*Comedy, 2005*] *Script: Enrico Vanzina, Carlo Vanzina, Piero De Bernardi. Dir: Carlo Vanzina. Phot: Claudio Zamarion. Players: Claudio Amendola, Elisabetta Rocchetti, Enzo Salvi. Prod: Cecchi Gori Group.*

TEXAS
[*Drama, 2005*] *Script: Fausto Paravidino, Iris Fusetti, Carlo Orlando. Dir: Paravidino. Phot: Gherardo Gossi. Players: Valeria Golino, Valerio Binasco, Riccardo Scamarcio. Prod: Fandango/ Medusa Film.*

TI AMO IN TUTTE LE LINGUE DEL MONDO
(**I Love You in Any Language**)
[*Comedy, 2005*] *Script: Leonardo Pieraccioni, Giovanni Veronesi. Dir: Pieraccioni. Phot: Italo Petriccione. Players: Pieraccioni, Massimo Ceccherini, Giorgio Panariello. Prod: Levante Film/ Medusa Film.*

TICKETS
[*Comedy, 2005*] *Script: Ermanno Olmi, Abbas Kiarostami, Paul Laverty. Dir: Olmi, Kiarostami, Ken Loach. Phot: Fabio Olmi, Mahmoud Kalari, Chris Menges. Players: Valeria Bruni Tedeschi, Carlo Delle Piane, Silvana De Santis, Filippo Trojano, Martin Compston, William Ruane. Prod: Fandango/Medusa Film/Sixteen Films (UK).*

LA TIGRE E LA NEVE
(**The Tiger and the Snow**)
[*Comedy, 2005*] *Script: Roberto Benigni, Vincenzo Cerami. Dir: Benigni. Phot: Fabio Cianchetti. Players: Benigni, Nicoletta Braschi, Jean Reno. Prod: Melampo Cinematografica.*

TU LA CONOSCI CLAUDIA?
(**Do You Know Claudia?**)
[*Comedy, 2004*] *Script: Aldo Baglio, Giovanni Storti, Giacomo Poretti, Walter Fontana, Valerio Bariletti, Massimo Venier. Dir: Venier. Phot: Marco Pieroni. Players: Baglio, Storti, Poretti, Paola*

Michele Placido's **Crime Novel**

Cortellesi. Prod: A. Gi. Di./ Medusa Film.

ROMANZO CRIMINALE (Crime Novel)
[*Drama, 2005*] *Script: Stefano Rulli, Sandro Petraglia, Gian Carlo De Cataldo, from De Cataldo's novel. Dir: Michele Placido. Phot: Luca Bigazzi. Players: Kim Rossi Stuart, Stefano Accorsi, Pierfrancesco Favino. Prod: Cattleya/*

Warner Bros. Italia/Babe (France)/Aquarius Film (UK).

LA SECONDA NOTTE DI NOZZE (The Second Wedding Night)
[*Comedy, 2005*] *Script and Dir: Pupi Avati. Phot: Pasquale Rachini. Players: Antonio Albanese. Neri Marcorè, Katia Ricciarelli, Marisa Merlini. Prod: Duea Film/ Rai Cinema.*

VIVA ZAPATERO!
[*Documentary, 2005*] *Script and Dir: Sabina Guzzanti. Phot: Paolo Santolini. Players: Guzzanti, Daniele Luttazzi, Michele Santoro, Enzo Biagi. Prod: Studio Uno/Secol Superbo/ Sciocco Produzioni.*

Quotes of the Year

"Audiences going regularly to the movies are all watching 'the same' movie, filling 700 theatres all over Italy. Like in a supermarket, distributors are taking any less wanted products off the shelves."
ERMANNO OLMI, *director.*

"Where are they hiding those good and professional actors so capable of deep feelings? On the stage – that's where!"
MARCO TULLIO GIORDANA, *director.*

David di Donatello Awards 2005

Film: *The Consequences of Love* (*Le conseguenze dell'amore*).
Director: Paolo Sorrentino (*The Consequences of Love*).
Debuting Director: Saverio Costanzo (*Private*).
Producer: Rosario Rinaldo (*Certi bambini/Some Children*).
Actress: Barbora Bobulova (*Cuore sacro/Sacred Heart*).
Actor: Toni Servillo (*The Consequences of Love*).
Supporting Actress: Margherita Buy (*Manuale d'amore/Manual of Love*).
Supporting Actor: Carlo Verdone (*Manual of Love*).
Script: Paolo Sorrentino (*The Consequences of Love*).
Cinematography: Luca Bigazzi (*The Consequences of Love*).
Music: Riz Ortolani (*Ma quando arrivano le*

The Consequences of Love won five Donatellos

ragazze?/When Do the Girls Show Up?*).
Art Direction: Andrea Crisanti (*Sacred Heart*).
Costume Design: Daniela Ciancio (*The Rest of Nothing*).
Editing: Claudio Cutry (*Some Children*).
Sound: Alessandro Zanon (*Le chiavi di casa/ The Keys to the House*).
Feature Documentary: *Un silencio particolare/ A Particular Silence* (Stefano Rulli).
Short Film: *Aria* (Claudio Noce); *Lotta libera* (Stefano Viali).
Foreign Film: *Million Dollar Baby*.
European Film: *The Sea Inside*.

Japan Tomomi Katsuta

The Year's Best Films

Tomomi Katsuta's selection:
Blood and Bone
(Yoichi Sai)
We Shall Overcome
Some Day (Kazuyuki Izutsu)
Maison de Himiko
(Isshin Inudo)
The Milkwoman
(Akira Ogata)
The Hidden Blade
(Yoji Yamada)

Recent and Forthcoming Films

MAISON DE HIMIKO
[Drama, 2005] Script: Aya Watanabe. Dir: Isshin Inudo. Phot: Takahiro Tsutai. Players: Min Tanaka, Joe Odagiri, Kou Shibasaki. Prod: Asmic Ace Entertainment/IMJ Entertainment/ Nippon Television Network/SDP/ Culture Publishers.

KOSHONIN: MASHITA MASAYOSHI (The Negotiator: Mashita Masayoshi)
[Thriller, 2004] Script: Masashi Sogo. Dir: Katsuyuki Motohiro. Phot: Akira Sako. Players: Yusuke Santamaria, Miki Mizuno, Jun Kunimura, Masanori Ishii, Susumu Terajima. Prod: Fuji Television/Robot/ Toho/SPWT.

YOGISHA: MUROI SHINJI (The Suspect: Muroi Shinji)
[Thriller, 2004] Script and Dir: Ryoichi Kimiduka. Phot: Junichiro Hayashi. Players: Toshiro Yanagiba, Rena Tanaka, Sho Aikawa. Prod: Fuji Television/Robot/Toho/SPWT.

The momentum driving Japanese film-making has never been stronger. The government, expecting entertainment revenues to compensate for the decline in manufacturing, injected $22m (2.6 billion yen) into film production and the fostering of new talent in 2005. In 2004, admissions rose by 4.5% to 170 million and the share for domestic films was up by the same amount, to 37.5%. The number of screens also continues to grow. With investors noting the profitability of film in this climate, banks have started to provide new money-raising schemes for producers. Working hand in hand with government and the private sector, the new Visual Industry Promotion Organisation was launched, a counterpart to, for example, France's Centre National du Cinéma.

In the market, Toho, one of the three majors (along with Toei and Shochiku), took more than 60% of the gross for domestic films in 2004. The thriller spin-offs from *Bayside Shakedown* established box-office records for live-action entertainment, while, Katsuyuki Motoki's *Speed*-like thriller, **The Negotiator: Mashita Masayoshi** (*Koshonin: Mashita Masayoshi*), and Ryoichi Kimiduka's suspense drama, **The Suspect: Muroi Shinji** (*Yogisha: Muroi Shinji*), each pulled in $3.5m (4 billion yen) revenue . Kentaro Otani's **Nana**, a girls' buddy-movie adapted from best-selling comics, also reached $3.5m, although all three hits were virtually ignored by the critics. Releasing more than 30 films in this period, Toho could hardly fail to dominate, but there were precious few screens left for medium-sized and small films. There were said to be more than 100 new films sitting on the shelf.

The biggest winner in 2004-05, and another smash for Toho, was Hayao Miyazaki's **Howl's Moving Castle** (*Hauru no ugoku shiro*). His ninth feature animation is a fantasy-adventure, set in an unnamed Europe kingdom, about a girl turned into a 90-year-old by a witch and a handsome wizard. After its release in November 2004, it stayed in the top ten for 21 weeks, grossing more than $174m. Miyazaki's striking imagination and stunning visuals met the audience's high expectations, and his profound view of war, youth and family gave the film a philosophical perspective, as usual. But the story's sudden, uncharacteristic and unconvincing happy ending confused and disappointed the critics.

KAKUSHIKEN ONI NO TUME
(The Hidden Blade)
[Drama, 2004] Script: Yoji Yamada, Yoshitaka Asama. Dir: Yamada. Phot: Mutsuo Naganuma. Players: Masatoshi Nagase, Takako Matsu. Prod: Shochiku/Nippon Television Network/Sumitomo Corporation/ Hakuhodo DY Media Partners.

RINJIN 13 GO
(The Neighbour No. Thirteen)
[Horror, 2004] Script: Hajime Kado, based on the comic by Santa Inoue. Dir: Yasuo Inoue. Phot: Taro Kawazu. Players: Shido Nakamura, Shun Oguri. Prod: Inoue Santa/ Rinjin Partners.
A timid man acquires a Jekyll and Hyde personality and takes revenge on those who bullied him in childhood.

KOI WA 5 ¥7 ¥5!
(*literally,* Love is 5 ¥7 ¥5!)
[Comedy, 2004] Script and Dir: Naoko Ogigami. Phot: Kozo Shibasaki. Players: Megumi Seki, Kinako Kobayashi. Prod: Tohokushinsha Film Corporation/ Cine Qua Non/S.D.P.
A bunch of high-school black sheep enter a haiku championship.

LINDA LINDA LINDA
[Drama, 2005] Script: Nobuhiro Yamashita, Kosuke Mukai. Dir: Yamashita. Phot: Yoshihiro Ikeuchi. Players: Doona Bae, Aki Maeda, Yu Kashii, Shiori Sekine. Prod: Hiroyuki Negishi, Yuji Sadai.

BOKOKU NO AEGIS (Aegis)
[Action, 2005] Script: Yasuo Hasegawa, Kenzaburo Iida, based on the novel by Harutoshi Fukui. Dir: Junji Sakamoto. Phot: Norimichi Kasamatsu. Players: Hiroyuki Sanada, Akira Terao, Koichi Sato, Kiichi Nakai. Prod: Aegis Associates Production.

LORELEI (Lorelei: The Witch of the Pacific Ocean)
[Action, 2005] Script: Satoshi Suzuki, based on the novel by Harutoshi Fukui. Dir: Shinji Higuchi. Phot: Akira Sako. Players: Koji Yakusho,

Sixty years on

The push for producers to make big-budget films, costing more than 1 billion yen ($8.7m), was fuelled in part by the 60th anniversary of the end of the Second World War, which led to a boom in expensive war movies. Shinji Higuchi's **Lorelei: The Witch of the Pacific Ocean** (*Lorelei*) is a fantasy set in August 1945, in which a mysterious Japanese submarine tries to stop a third atomic bomb being dropped on Tokyo. Junji Sakamoto's **Aegis** (*Bokoku no Aegis*) is a contemporary political thriller in which North Korean terrorists hijack a high-tech escort ship. **Samurai Commando: Mission 1549** (*Sengoku jieitai 1549*), directed by Masaaki Teduka, is a sci-fi action movie about a Japanese self defence force squad propelled back to the sixteenth century. All based on novels by Harutoshi Fukui, these films reflected the nationalist sentiment that the Japanese should reconsider its attitudes to post-war peace under the US banner. The films showed a tolerable standard of CGI work and proved that political content is not an obstacle to attracting a mainstream audience – provided that it is not delved into too deeply.

A raging minority

Japan has never been a racially homogeneous nation, partly because of the propaganda of fanatic nationalists. Yoichi Sai's powerful **Blood and Bone** (*Chi to hone*), swept many awards for its shocking portrait of a furiously egotistical Korean–Japanese man who immigrated to Osaka in the 1920s, Shunpei (played brilliantly by Beat Takeshi). He is a greedy and selfish demon, who dominates all those around him, including his family, with pitiless violence. As a Korean–Japanese himself, Sai disclosed the neglected rage of a suppressed people.

Maison de Himiko Prod. Committee

Maison de Himiko

Kazuyuki Izutsu also exposed the harsh situation of the Korean–Japanese in the notable **We Shall Overcome Some Day** (*Pacchigi!*), but in more cheerful style. In 1968 Kyoto, the era of political rattle and hum, a high-school boy falls in love with and pursues in amusing fashion a Korean–Japanese girl whose situation turns out to be far more difficult than he imagined. Izutsu sympathises with this foolish but pure-hearted boy as he tackles the social barrier.

Minorities also appear in Isshin Inudo's **Maison de Himiko**, set in an erratic home for aged homosexuals. Himiko, a retired gay and the founder of the home, is reunited with his daughter Saori after 15 years of separation, at the instigation of his lover, Haruhiko. Saori's obstinate hatred against Himiko, for supposedly abandoning the family, melts in the face of the generosity of the social outcasts at the home. Humbly suggesting the meaning of acceptance and forgiveness, Inudo explores humankind's eternal isolation.

In Nobuhiro Yamashita's **Linda Linda Linda**, three Japanese and one Korean girl form a punk band for a school festival. Starting off awkwardly, the girls slowly show their guts and forge a strong bond. Yamashita has revealed apathetic high-school girls' obscure passion.

Hidden loves

The Hidden Blade (*Kakushi ken oni no tsume*) is veteran Yoji Yamada's second samurai drama, following the highly praised *Twilight Samurai*, and again based on a novel by Shuhei Fujisawa. A lower-class samurai in the mid-nineteenth century harbours a secret love for a married maid, among the turmoil of a conspiracy against his master's regime. With great storytelling skill, Yamada

Tartan Films

Yoji Yamada's **The Hidden Blade**

Kiichi Nkai. Prod: *Aegis Associates Production.*

SENGOKU JIEITAI 1549
(Samurai Commando: Mission 1549)
[*Sci-fi, 2005*] Script: *Kiyoto Takeuchi, Yasushi Matsuura.* Dir: *Masaaki Teduka.* Phot: *Osamu Fujiishi.* Players: *Yosuke Eguchi, Kyoka Suzuki, Takeshi Kaga.* Prod: *Kadokawa Pictures/ Japan Film Fund/Nippon Television Network.*

OPERETTA TANUKIGOTEN
(Princess Raccoon)
[*Musical, 2005*] Script: *Yoshio Urasawa.* Dir: *Seijun Suzuki.* Phot: *Yonezou Maeda.* Players: *Zhang Ziyi, Joe Odagiri, Hiroko Yakushimaru, Saori Yuki, Mikijiro Hira, Hibari Misora.* Prod: *Geneon Entertainment/ Dentsu/Nippon Herald Films/ Shochiku Co./Eisei Gekijo Co./ Ogura Jimusyo Co. Production.*

YOKAI DAISENSO
(The Great Yokai War)
[*Action, 2005*] Script: *Takashi Miike, Mitsuhiko Sawamura, Takehiko Itakura.* Dir: *Miike.* Phot: *Hideo Yamamoto.* Players: *Ryunosuke Kamiki, Hiroyuki Miyasako, Chiaki Kuriyama, Etsushi Toyokawa.* Prod: *Kadokawa Pictures/ Japan Film Fund/Nippon Television Network.* A boy is caught in the battle between traditional Japanese Yokais, or goblins, and an evil spirit.

HAURO NO UGOKU SHIRO
(She and Howl's Moving Castle)
[*Animation, 2004*] Script and Dir: *Hayao Miyazaki.* Voices: *Takuya Kimura, Chieko Baisho.* Prod: *Studio Ghibli.*

PACCHIGI!
(We Shall Overcome Some Day)
[*Drama, 2004*] Script: *Daisuke Habara.* Dir: *Kazuyuki Izutsu.* Phot: *Hideo Yamamoto.* Players: *Shun Shioya, Sosuke Takaoka, Erika Sawajiri.* Prod: *Cine Qua Non.*

ITSUKA DOKUSHO SURU HI
(The Milkwoman)
[Drama, 2005] Script: Kenji Aoki. Dir: Akira Ogata. Phot: Norimichi Kasamatsu. Players: Yuko Tanaka, Ittoku Kishibe, Akiko Nishina. Prod: Paradise Cafe Inc./Pugpoing Japan.

TAKESHIS'
[Drama, 2005] Script and Dir: Takeshi Kitano. Phot: Katsumi Yanagijima. Players: Beat Takeshi, Ren Osugi, Kotomi Kyono. Prod: BandaiVisual/Tokyo FM/TV Asahi/Office Kitano.
A poor actor, Takeshi Kitano's daydreams begin to delude the reality of TV star Beat Takeshi, whom Kitano admires, in this self-referencing fantasy by the renowned actor–director.

HARU NO YUKI (Spring Snow)
[Drama, 2005] Script: Chihiro Ito, Shinsuke Sato, based on the novel by Yukio Mishima. Dir: Isao Yukisada. Phot: Lee Ping-bin. Players: Satoshi Tsumabuki, Yuko Takeuchi. Prod: Spring Snow production committee.

Quote of the Year

"I have such an insatiable desire [to continue producing films]. I want to create movies that inspire children."
HAYAO MIYAZAKI, *receiving the Golden Lion for Lifetime Achievement at Venice in 2005.*

likens the bondage of the historic samurai hierarchy to that of today's white-collar workers. Suppressed love was seen not only 150 years ago. In Akira Ogata's **The Milkwoman** (*Itsuka dokusho suru hi*), Minako (strongly played by Yuko Tanaka), a 50-year-old spinster, delivers milk by bicycle in a hilly town. She and Keita (Ittoku Kishibe), who works for a local municipal office, were high-school sweethearts. Two calm, inert lives are shaken up when Keita's dying wife asks Minako to see her husband again. With minimal expression and quiet narrative, Ogata convincingly generates the tension of long-hidden love.

The tendency to regard films as commercial products more than works of art makes life very difficult for auteur films. However, there have still been a few notable achievements in this area, including Kohei Oguri's poetical fantasy **The Buried Forest** (*Umoregi*). In a mosaic of the dreams and realities of a small town's inhabitants, Oguri sets out to show the possibility of change in the despairing, post-9/11 world. On the other hand, no sign of real-life worries is visible in cult master Seijun Suzuki's bizarre musical, **Princess Raccoon** (*Operetta Tanukigoten*). International Chinese star Zhang Ziyi plays a raccoon princess turned into a woman who sings and dances cheerfully with her beloved human prince, their love overcoming all differences of species. It is all played out in front of CGI backcloths that look like traditional Japanese paintings.

TOMOMI KATSUTA (katsuta.tomomi@mbx.mainichi.co.jp) writes on film for *The Mainichi Shimbun*, one of Japan's major daily newpapers.

Zhang Ziyi, centre, in **Princess Raccoon**

Princess Racoon Production Committee

Kazakhstan Gulnara Abikeyeva

The Year's Best Films:

Gulnara Abikeyeva's selection:

The Hunter (Serik Aprymov)
Rebirth Island (Rustem Abdrashev)
The Nomad (Sergey Bodrov, Talgat Temenov, Ivan Passer)
Shiza (Gulshad Omarova)
Steppe Express (Amanzhol Aytuarov, Satybaldy Narymbetov)

Recent and Forthcoming Films

KUNA
[Drama, 2005] Script and Dir: Bolat Sharip. Phot: Boris Troshev. Players: Alua Kashaganova, Eric Zholzhaksynov. Prod: Sergey Azimov, Kazakhfilm.
A Kazakh village, 1950s. A childless wife decides to get pregnant by another man, with tragic consequences.

TULPAN (Tulip)
[Drama, 2006] Script and Dir: Sergey Dvortsevoi. Phot: Iolanat Dilevska. Players: Ashat Kuncherekov. Prod: Pandora Film (Germany)/Kazakh Inter Cinema.
Ashat returns to his village from army service and decides to become a shepherd, but first he must marry.

KURAK KORPE (Quilt)
[Lyrical comedy, 2006] Script: Ermek Tursunov, Rustem Abdrashev. Dir: Abdrashev. Phot: Murat Nugmanov, Hasan Kadyralieyev. Players: Vladimir Tolokonnikov, Nurzhuman Ihtymbayev, Tamara Kosubayeva, Prod: Sergey Azimov, Kazakhfilm.
Patchwork of stories involving a

One of the biggest events in Kazakh cinema in the past two years has been the production of the $34m mega-project **The Nomad**. Co-directed by Sergey Bodrov, Talgat Temenov and Ivan Passer, this US/Kazakh co-production has all the trappings of Hollywood, including American stars: Kuno Bekker, Jason Scott Lee and Mark Dacascos. The budget included government money, on the initiative of President Nursultan Nazarbaev, with the aim of promoting Kazakhstan as a new independent state. This epic historical drama is set in the early 1700s, when Kazakh tribes united to repel the invading Jungars. It was scheduled for worldwide promotion in March 2006, from Miramax in the United States, Wild Bunch in Europe and Otau-Cinema in Kazakhstan.

Most films in Kazakhstan are made with state support from the national film company, Kazakhfilm, which produces an average of five features per year. The distribution system, however, is private, which is why the promotion of the Kazakh movies in the country is minimal, compared to wide releases for Hollywood films. Only the "Week of Kazakh Cinema", held twice a year, provides a national showcase.

One of the best films of 2004 was **The Hunter**, by Serik Aprymov, winner of the Grand Prix of the National Film Festival, "Bayterek", and two prizes at Locarno IFF. It follows the life of a lonely hunter, who lives up high in the mountains and teaches a teenager how to hunt. The boy has cold hands and looks like a wolf overall. The movie is a parable of the legend of the origin of Turks, who were raised by the blue female wolf. This reference to myths and history is typical of today's Kazakh cinema; it also reflects tendencies that could not be revealed when the country was under Soviet rule and historical movies could not tell stories set before 1917. That is why since independence there are have been so many historical Kazakh movies, many about the self-determination of the nation, as in *The Nomad* and *Sardar* (2004), directed by Bolat Kalymbetov, which also takes place in the times of the Jungar invasion, with two young heroes initiating a revolt against their enemies.

The here and now

There is great local audience interest in movies about modern Kazakh life. For instance, **Shiza** (2004), the feature debut of young female director Gulshad Omarova, enjoyed international success.

village boy, seven, visiting his grandparents in the city.

AINUR

[Drama, 2006] Script and Dir: Darezhan Omirbayev. Prod: Limara Zheksembayeva, Kadam studio.
Love triangle set among the new generation of rich Kazakhs.

KEK

[Historical drama, 2006] Script: Smagul Elybai, Begarys Elubai. Dir: Damie Manabay. Phot: Bulat Suleyev, Murat Aliev. Prod: Sergey Azimov, Kazakhfilm.
Early 1900s. Tragic love story between a Turkmen girl and a Kazakh man.

MUSTAFA CHOKAI

(Historical drama, 2006) Script: Ermek Tursunov, Sergey Bodrov, Akim Tarazi. Dir: Satybaldy Narymbetov. Phot: Hasan Kadyraliev. Prod: Sergey Azimov, Kazakhfilm.

CHAS VOLKA (Wolf's Hour)

[Epic drama, 2006] Script: Anatoly Kim. Dir: Rymbek Alpiev. Phot: Fedor Aranyshev. Players: Tugushpai Dzhamankulov, Abdrashit Abdrakhmanov, Asel Sagatova, Anar Kakenova. Prod: Sergey Azimov, Kazakhfilm.

Wolf's Hour

Quote of the year

"We don't want to shoot ethnographical cinema. Let's speak the same language as the rest of the world."
ABAI KULBAEV, *director, part of the so-called "New-New Kazakh Wave".*

The movie tells the story of a young man employed to find people for bare-knuckle boxing fights, a job that leads to death, pain, suffering and betrayal. **Steppe Express** (2005), directed by Amanzhol Aytuarov and Satybaldy Narymbetov, tells a story about a young Frenchman (Fransua Lenua), who accidentally ends up in the steppes of Kazakhstan for a couple of weeks. He falls in love with Saule (Ayzhan Aytenova), the daughter of the local railway station master, and takes her away to Paris. For the father this is a tragedy that he cannot overcome.

Les Films Christian Fechner

Ayzhan Aytenova, left, and Fransua Lenua in **Steppe Express**

The other discovery of the year was **Rebirth Island**, directed by young Rustem Abdrashev, which won prizes at several international festivals. Shot in black-and-white, it is a poetic elegy about first love, set in 1961. Zharas falls in love with his classmate, Zhibek, but their parents and the school authorities try to block the affair. This youthful tragedy unfolds against the backdrop of the Aral Sea, where the Soviet system destroys both individual fates and the local ecology.

At press time a new national cinematography law was being drafted. Once operational, it should aid the development of a more producer-driven local industry. There are ten independent production companies in Kazakhstan, all ready to produce films, using Kazakhfilm solely as a technical base where they will rent sound stages and equipment, but to achieve this they need greater legislative support.

GULNARA ABIKEYEVA (gabikeyev@mail.ru) is a Director of the Centre of Central Asian Cinematography, Almaty, and Artistic Director of International Film Festival "Eurasia". She has written three books on Kazakh and Central Asian cinema.

Kenya Ogova Ondego

The Year's Best Films

Ogova Ondego's selection:
Broken Monologues
(Willie Owusu)
Two Chicks, One Guy and a Plate of Chips
(Short. Willie Owusu)

Recent and Forthcoming Films

BROKEN MONOLOGUES
[Experimental abstract, 2005]
Dir: Willie Owusu. Players: Nini Wacera, Telly Savalas Otieno. Prod: Telly Savalas Otieno.
Set in urban Africa, this film is about a love relationship gone awry.

TWO CHICKS, ONE GUY AND A PLATE OF CHIPS
[Experimental comedy, 2005]
Dir: Willie Owusu. Players: Aleks Kamau, Velma Mwendwa, Millicent Wambui.
In a Nairobi restaurant, a young man having lunch imagines the conversation that two young women at an adjacent table could be having.

BABU'S BABIES
[Comedy-thriller, 2004] Script and Dir: Christine Bala. Phot: Martin Munyua. Players: Ian Kaburu, Lornah Irungu, Regina Macharia, Ng'ang'a Kirumburu, Toni Njuguna. Prod: Ben Zulu/ Africa Script Development Fund.
Set in Nairobi, the film explores the misplaced notion held by some that cities flow with milk and honey.

REKE TUMANWO
(literally, Let's Part Peacefully)
[Drama, 2004] Script, Dir and Prod: Kibaara Kaugi. Phot:

The year under review saw the emergence of a remarkable low-budget film-making model known as Riverwood. Although a good budget for an East African film is said to be about $100,000, some innovative people based on River Road in downtown Nairobi have since November 2004 been making films on budgets of between $500 and $700. This tiny sum is enough to make a 60-minute comedy, because the film-makers employ one or two hand-held cameras, improvise the script and shoot an entire film in a day or two, and edit it in one more day, before releasing it on VCDs that retail for $3.50.

Lead actors are paid between $30 and $70 per production and there are never more than five characters in each story. On this Riverwood model, one needs to sell just 500 VCDs to break even. The earliest exponents could sell up to 15,000 units, but it appears that a rapid flooding of the market, and piracy, have reduced those figures. Director Wanjiru Kinyanjui is among the advocates of this cheap, convenient and accessible movement, which is dominated by comedies. The most popular actors include Machang'i, Kihoto, Kihenjo, Wandahuhu, Muruna and Kiere.

In March 2005, your correspondent was instrumental in the setting up in Nairobi of ArtMatters Critics Guild (ACG), a national association of film critics and journalists, established to help entrench arts criticism in eastern Africa and raise the standard of arts coverage in the region. By November 2005, ACG had held training workshops for member journalists in Tanzania, Uganda and Zimbabwe. It is affiliated to the International Federation of Film Journalists and Critics (FIPRESCI).

The service industry

Between July 2004 and June 2005, the Department of Film Services issued 392 filming licences, which generated around $1m (Sh732.2m) for the exchequer. Some of the major films to shoot in Kenya were *Die Patriarchin*, *La Isa de los Famosos*, *Spanish Survivor*, *Winter Reise* and *Transit*. The steady inward investment from visiting productions making the most of Kenyan locations is in stark contrast to the struggles of local films at cinemas. Although screened at the 20th Century theatre in Nairobi for three weeks in December 2004, **Babu's Babies**, an urban drama, attracted fewer than a thousand spectators. **Reke Tumanwo**, another local film,

Gadson Waweru. Players:
Simoricious Wangare, Jans
Karsholt, Peter Ndung'u,
Paul Gatonye.
Shot in Kikuyu and launched in
June 2005, this drama examines
the role of the Mau Mau in
Kenya's struggle for independence.

THE WHITE MAASAI
[Fiction, 2004] Script:
Johannes Betz, based on the
novel by Corine Hoffman.
Dir: Hermine Hunthgeburth.
Players: Nina Hoss, Jacky Ido.
Prod: Jurgen Troester/
Constantine Studios, Germany.
A German woman marries a
Samburu and lives with him for
four years, before cultural
differences set them apart.

**MAASAI:
THE RAIN WARRIORS**
[Documentary, 2004] Dir: Pascal
Plisson. Featuring: Ngotiel ole
Mako, Paul Nteri ole Sekenan,
Parkasio ole Muntet, Musurpei
ole Toroge, Swakei Kipilosh,
Kiaki ole Narikae, Peniki ole
Soyiantet.
When drought ravages
Maasailand, it is up to young
warriors to bring rain back by
killing the lion god.

Quote of the Year

"I used to feel so stupid
introducing myself as director
of The Battle of the Sacred
Tree, as I couldn't show
anyone the film while it
was on Beta and 35mm.
However, I am now confident,
as I have put it on VCD."
WANJRU KINYANJUI, on how
she distributed her 10-year-old
film via video halls, on the new
Riverwood model that helps
film-makers overcome the lack
of cinemas.

Babu's Babies struggled to find a local audience

fared even worse in June 2005 at Nu Metro's Prestige Plaza
Theatre in Nairobi.

Kenya has just 21 screens in Nairobi, Mombasa and Kisumu, and two
official film distributors for Hollywood (Fox Film Distributors and Nu
Metro) and three for Bollywood (Fox, Unicine and Nyalimax). The
lowest ticket price is $3, at Fox Theatres' Kenya and 20th Century
cinemas. Nu Metro has upset the monopoly previously enjoyed by
Fox Theatres (EA) Ltd. and targets wealthier patrons, charging $4.50
per head in the evening. Between January and September 2005,
approximately 235,000 people visited Kenyan cinemas.

In January 2005, the Kenya Film Commission was set up hurriedly,
secretively and without any defined structures in place. It is viewed
as being too closely tied to certain special interests to bring general
improvements to the audiovisual sector and was set up at a time
when the industry was already furious at massive increases (at least
500%) in government fees levied on film servicing agencies – a
move that put many people out of business.

Finally, a new film festival, Lola Kenya Children's Screen, was born
in October 2005. With its maiden edition scheduled for August 7–
12, 2006, this festival and market, whose first name is derived from
a Bantu word for "to look", seeks to cultivate sustainable audiences
for cinema and foster a desire among the young to produce quality
films. It will hold annual production workshops, with the aim of
making at least five short films which it will then screen and
showcase around the world.

OGOVA ONDEGO (oondego@artmatters.info) is an arts and lifestyle
writer specialising in African audiovisual productions, who publishes
http://www.artmatters.info and heads Lola Kenya Children's Screen.

Latvia Andris Rozenbergs

The Year's Best Films

Andris Rozenbergs' selection:
Three Musketeeres
(Animation. Janis Cimermanis)
The Hour Is Near
(Docu. Juris Poskus)
The Anatomy of a National Holiday
(Docu. Askolds Saulitis)
Agent Deadly in Love
(Short. Gatis Smits)
The Worm
(Docu. Andis Miziss)

Andris Miziss' **The Worm**

Recent and Forthcoming Films

KILNIEKS (The Hostage)
*[Drama, 2006] Script and Dir:
Laila Pakalnina. Phot: Arko
Okk. Players: Branko Zavrashan,
Kristaps Medins. Prod: Laila
Pakalnina, Hargla (Latvia)/
Arko Okk, Acuba Film (Estonia)/
Igor Pedicek/Casablanca Film
Production (Slovenia).*
A hijacker makes friends with his
hostage, a ten-year-old boy.

**RIGAS SARGI
(Defenders of Riga)**
*[Historical drama, 2006] Script:
Andris Kolbergs. Dir: Aigars
Grauba. Phot: Vladimir Bashta.
Players: Janis Reinis, Elita
Klavina, Andris Keiss, Arturs
Skrastins, Girts Kesteris, Vigo
Roga, Romualds Ancans,
Girts Krumins.*

A Latvian soldier, Martin (Janis Reinis), crosses a bridge at night to meet Elsa (Elita Klavina), his bride, who has been waiting for him to return from the war in 1919. Muffling up in a warm coat, Klavina stands behind the camera to give Reinis the correct eyeline and help complete this, one of the last shots for *Defenders of Riga* (*Rigas sargi*; formerly known as *Guards of Riga*), which finished shooting late in 2005. This war epic's premiere is scheduled for 2006. In 2005, however, the scene was dominated by documentaries.

The Worm (*Tarps*), by Andis Miziss, observes a couple, Karlis, 62 when the film was made, and Inese, 41, who live in appalling conditions. The title is derived from the couple's meagre occupation: selling worms to anglers. The camera follows them closely – to the bathroom, into their bed; it is present at the death of their newborn child. The meticulous searching out of intimate details creates an atmosphere of harsh truthfulness and evokes considerable sympathy. Despite occasional outbreaks of violent talk, one perceives that these people love each other and that only appearances separate them from more refined expression.

In a slightly different style, Gunars Bandens presented **A Streetcar Named Help** (*Tramvajs varda kalpotajs*). A rather special public uses this late night transport, when decent people are fast asleep: men who after copious libations have finally left the bar tables, lovers who cannot stop kissing, bums for whom the vehicle offers shelter against rough weather. Interlaced with beautiful landscapes of Riga at night, the film culminates in a sequence showing a crowd celebrating New Year's Eve, splashing champagne and dancing while the streetcar roams the city. Though Bandens does not get as close to his subjects as Miziss, he still manages to convey the poerty of a city at night, in a style reminiscent of documentaries of the 1960s and 1970s.

Remember, remember the 18th of November

Askolds Saulitis in **Anatomy of a National Holiday** (*Svetku anatomija*) peeks into various aspects of the preparations for the November 18 holiday, the anniversary of the founding of the Republic of Latvia, a day when the state rewards citizens by decorating them with the Order of Lacplesis (a national hero). This is a nationwide ritual in which everybody is supposed to perform

Janis Reinis in **Defenders of Riga**

A love story against the background of November 11, 1919, when 11,000 Latvian riflemen, most of them inexperienced volunteers, defeated 51,000 German and Russian mercenaries.

TUMSIE BRIEZI (Dark Deers)
[Drama, 2006] Script and Dir: Viesturs Kairiss. Phot: Gints Berzins. Players: Kristine Kruze, Elita Klavina, Maija Doveika, Juris Zagars, Kaspars Dimiters, Peteris Martinsons. Prod: Guntis Trekteris, Kaupo Filma.
Ria, 15, clashes with her father when she falls in love for the first time, sparking tragic events.

MONA
[Drama, 2006] Script: Arvis Kolmanis. Dir: Inara Kolmane. Phot: Uldis Jancis. Players: Kristine Belicka, Saulis Balandis, Veleri Yeryomenko Prod: Janis Juhnevics, Studio Devini/Fridrik Thor Fridriksson, Icelandic Film Corporation.
Love triangle set amongst slaughterhouse workers in a provincial town.

SVETKU ANATOMIJA (The Anatomy of a National Holiday)
[Documentary, 2005] Dir: Askolds Saulitis. Phot: Andris Prieditis Prod: Saulitis, Subjektiv Filma.

TARPS (The Worm)
[Documentary, 2005] Script: Elvita Ruka. Dir: Andis Miziss. Phot: Agris Birzulis. Prod: Elvita Ruka, Environment Film Studio, in association with Estonian TV and Latvian TV.

EX-AMEN (Ex-amination)
[Documentary short, 2005] Script and Dir: Inese Klava. Phot: Ivars Zviedris, Valdis Celmins. Prod: Ivars Zviedris, AVE.

his or her appointed role, from the angler catching fish for the feast, right up to the President. At the end, the supervisor of the illuminations slides a wire over electrical contacts, and the sky explodes with fireworks.

Askolds Saulitis' **Anatomy of a National Holiday**

Another kind of ritual is depicted in a short documentary by a debutant director, Inese Klava, *Ex-amination (Ex-amen)*. It deals with the training of people who conduct funeral services, both religious and secular. The central event is the examination taken by public funeral ceremony managers. This is really a test in the art of manipulation. The ceremony manager must know how to evoke sentiments that will satisfy the demands of the deceased's family. Demonstrating their newly acquired skills in a series of close-ups, the managers show by what sort of poetic clichés people can be manipulated, and how they want to be manipulated.

Though neither Klava nor Saulitis make explicit reference to them, their films make one think about election campaigns, about suicide bombers, about many other things that influence human beings and communities. These stories are told with a benevolent smile. Saulitis is more reticent, his subjects are mostly people of high status, while Klava, being enviably young, has on her palette more humour and irony. She represents a new, young generation of Latvian film-makers who are working in an atmosphere of mutual trust and who wish to scrutinise human lives and are aware of how communities tick. Another name to watch is Gatis Smits, who has made a charming graduation short at the University of New York, *Agent Deadly in Love*.

ANDRIS ROZENBERGS (Andris.Rozenbergs@nfc.gov.lv) has directed seven fiction films and a dozen documentaries. He is Head of the Film Registry at Latvia's National Film Centre.

Mexico Carlos Bonfil

The Year's Best Films

Carlos Bonfil's selection:

Battle in Heaven
(Carlos Reygadas)
Distant News
(Ricardo Benet)
The Magician
(Jaime Aparicio)
The Muxes, Authentic, Restless Seekers of Danger
(Docu. Alejandra Islas)
Tropic of Cancer
(Docu. Eugenio Polgovsky)

Recent and Forthcoming Films

CLUB EUTANASIA
(Club Euthanasia)
[Comedy, 2005] Script and Dir: Agustín Oso Tapia. Phot: Javier Morón. Players: Rosita Quintana, Lorenzo de Rodas, Magda Guzmán, Ofelia Medina, Sergio Corona. Prod: Altavista Films/Fidecine/Hartos Indios/ Carlos Taibo Mahojo.

Members of **Club Euthanasia**

EL BAILE DE LA IGUANA
(The Dance of the Iguana)
[Drama, 2005] Script and Dir: Marcel Sisniega. Phot: Jorge Z. López. Players: Ernesto Gómez Cruz, Ester Orozco, Eréndira Dávalos, Emanuel Morales, Norma Angélica. Prod: Patricia Loyo, Astrolabio-Zorry Films.

In 2004 and 2005, Mexican feature production maintained a steady level, averaging 38 features a year, of which half had state support and the rest were largely private ventures. No significant international breakthrough has been made since the widely acclaimed *Amores perros* and *Y tu mamá también*, although Carlos Reygadas' *Battle in Heaven* was the most talked about Mexican film abroad. The political storm created in 2004 by conservative president Vicente Fox's failed bill to dismantle the local film industry has long been forgotten, as has a short-lived initiative to enhance official production funds by levying a small tax on box-office receipts. As a result, Mexican cinema, hardly an industry, barely survives in an unequal battle against US productions and local television.

Despite this grim panorama, local moviegoers have witnessed some stimulating changes. The most relevant has been the creation of new film festivals, in Mexico City and other cities, which broaden the range of international cinematic offerings, while providing an unprecedented platform for local independent productions. Many documentaries and short films would be largely ignored without the Festival Internacional de Guadalajara, the Festival de Morelia or the sophisticated Festival Internacional de Cine de la Ciudad de México.

Equally significantly, official censorship has vanished completely – except for a perverse form of marketing intimidation that still persuades a director or producer to abandon an audacious subject in favour of more commercially rewarding choices. The usual form of negotiation has distributors and exhibitors at the end of the line: thus uncompromising political issues, overt criticism of the church or the army, the display of sexual ambiguities, or off-beat artistic expression are doomed to a restrictive ratings classification or narrow, short-lived exhibition. Added to this situation is the continual invasion of American blockbusters, saturating 80% of box-office. Most private producers favour commercial inanities whose resemblance to television (still a tremendous competitor) guarantees both passive audiences and instant commercial success. Artistic innovation and the search for new subject matter are excluded. Mexico's thriving video piracy market clearly reduces cinema attendance and the recovery of local film investment.

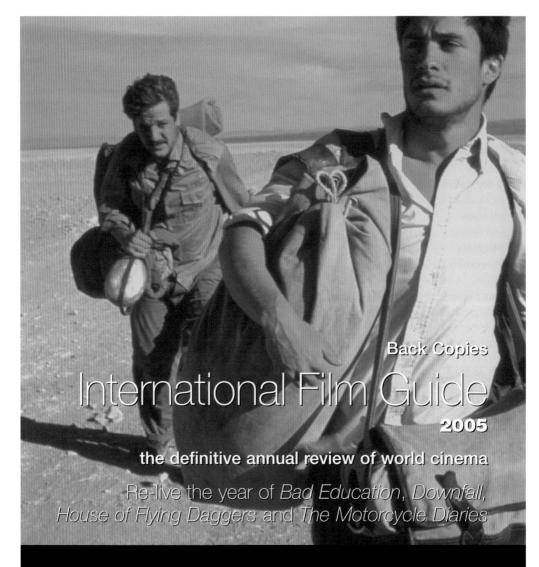

Taking their final exit

Aimed directly at the commercial circuits, **Club Euthanasia** (*Club eutanasia*) was a mild entertainment dealing with recognisable old icons of Mexican cinema: facing illness and approaching death in a retirement home. A small group decides gradually to eliminate other pensioners to get more benefits from the local authorities. Black humour is soon toned down by sentimentality. **The Magician** (*El mago*), an urban melodrama, also deals with death, as a street illusionist faces terminal illness and tries to recover long-lost affections. This is a vivid portrayal of Mexico City slums and a tribute to golden-age Mexican cinema. **The Last Night** (*La ultima noche*) is the final segment of a trilogy featuring the sexual awakening and existential conflicts of urban middle-class teenagers. Dominated by predictable humour for juvenile consumption, it makes some acute comments on cultural alienation.

Erando González as a street illusionist in **The Magician**

Stories of Disenchantment (*Historias del desencanto*) is an imaginative, eclectic fantasy in which love is followed by spiritual initiation. Both naïve and excessive, the film suffers from a relentless accumulation of visual effects and a tedious rhetoric that soon swamps its subject matter with the romantic clichés of juvenile angst. **Two Auroras** (*Dos auroras*), the latest digital experience of veteran film-maker Jaime Humberto Hermosillo, features a hectic love–hate relationship between a famous, wealthy mother and her depressive son. Passion leads here to ritual immolation and cannibalism. Hermosillo has chosen inexpensive digital video to preserve his artistic independence from commercial pressure and hence increase his work rate (as many as four films per year).

Such prolific output is in marked contrast to that of young directors aiming at 35mm productions, who usually have to wait several years to obtain financing. Carlos Reygadas, 35, is an apt example. With little official support for his successful debut, *Japon*, and practically none

HISTORIAS DEL DESENCANTO
(Stories of Disenchantment)
[Comedy-drama, 2005] Script and Dir: Alejandro Valle. Photo: Carlos Arango de Montis. Players: Mario Olivier, Fabiana Perzábal, Ximena Ayala, Jorge Zárate, Teresa Rábago. Prod: Lorenza Manrique, Inna Payán, Las Perlas de la Virgen/Foprocine/Imcine.

EL MAGO (The Magician)
[Drama, 2004] Script: Jaime Aparicio, Enrique Rentería. Dir: Aparicio. Phot: Diego Arizmendi. Players: Erando González, Julissa, Gustavo Muñoz, Maya Zapata, Juan Ángel Esparza. Prod: Mitl Valdez, Cuec/Unam/Foprocine/Imcine.

NOTICIAS LEJANAS
(Distant News)
[Drama, 2005] Script and Dir: Ricardo Benet. Phot: Martin Boege. Players: David Aarón Estrada, Mayahuel del Monte, Martín Palomares, Gina Moret, Lucía Muñoz. Prod: Hugo Rodríguez/CCC/Foprocine/Imcine.

LA ULTIMA NOCHE
(The Last Night)
[Comedy, 2005) Script: Alejandro Gamboa, Marina Stavenhagen. Dir: Gamboa. Phot: Alfredo Kassem. Players: Andrés García, Cecilia Gabriela, Marina Ávila, Elizabeth Valdés, Ricardo Palacio. Prod: Eckehardt von Damm, Coyoacán Films/Warner.

BATALLA EN EL CIELO
(Battle in Heaven)
[Drama, 2005] Script and Dir: Carlos Reygadas. Phot: Diego Martínez Vignatti. Players: Marcos Hernández, Amapola Mushkadiz, Bertha Ruiz, David Bornstien. Prod: Reygadas, Philippe Bober, Susanne Marian.

DOS AURORAS (Two Auroras)
[Drama, 2005] Script and Dir: Jaime Humberto Hermosillo. Phot: Jorge Z. López. Players: María Rojo, Tizoc Arroyo, José Juan Meras, Jesús Hernández,

Rogelio Guerra. Prod:
Raúl Padilla López, José
Antonio Ascensio, Universidad
de Guadalajara.

**LOS MUXES, AUTENTICAS,
INTRÉPIDAS BUSCADORAS
DE PELIGRO**
(The Muxes, Authentic, Restless
Seekers of Danger)
[Documentary, 2005] Script,
Phot and Dir: Alejandra Islas.
Prod: Ra Bancada Films/
Imcine/ Foprocine/Islas, Pacho
Bruce Lane.

**RELATOS DESDE EL
ENCIERRO**
(Tales from the Inside)
[Documentary, 2004] Script and
Dir: Guadalupe Miranda. Phot:
Andrea Borbolla, Lorenza
Manrique. Prod: Ángeles Castro
Gurría, Hugo Rodríguez, Andrea
Gentile. CCC.

TROPICO DE CANCER
(Tropic of Cancer)
[Documentary, 2004] Script, Dir
and Phot: Eugenio Polgovsky.
Prod: Polgovsky, Angeles Castro,
Hugo Rodríguez, Centro de
Capacitación Cinematográfica.

CUATRO LABIOS (Four Lips)
[Documentary, 2004] Script, Dir.
and Phot: Carlos Marcovich.
Players: Ari Borovoy, Erika
Zaba, Mariana Ochoa, Lidia
Ávila, Oscar Shwebel. Prod: El
arroz de diciembre.

VOCES INOCENTES
(Innocent voices)
(Drama) Script: Luis Mandoki,
Oscar Orlando Torres. Dir: Luis
Mandoki. Photo: Juan Ruíz
Anchía. Players: Carlos Padilla,
Leonor Varela, Daniel Giménez
Cacho, José María Yazpik, Ofelia
Medina. Prod: Lawrence Bender,
Federico González Compeán.

for his second long feature, **Battle in Heaven** (*Batalla en el cielo*), he has managed to finance his own films with foreign investment and his own money. His uncompromising new film is a challenging artistic experience, bearing little resemblance to any other film produced in Mexico. Exploring national myths and visual representations, it includes explicit sex between a beautiful young woman and an unappealing middle-aged man, and between him and his obese wife. This is a love story mingling beauty and the grotesque, sex and mysticism, in a context of social realism. It was poorly received in Mexico and very controversial abroad, not least at Cannes.

Carlos Reygadas' controversial **Battle in Heaven**

Tales of the city

Another interesting experience is Ricardo Benet's debut, **Distant News** (*Noticias lejanas*), about the sentimental education of a young man fleeing from his home town in the desert to Mexico City, where he discovers sexual misery, unemployment and moral unrest. The story is told by his young brother in melancholic remembrance of his fallen idol. Marcel Sisniega's **The Dance of the Iguana** (*El baile de la iguana*) is a set of three stories contrasting the lives of a patriarchal landlord in a shabby old town, the mother of a prostitute, and two playful girls. Sisniega, a talented, unpredictable young artist, keeps an enviable freshness in his work that sets him apart from most local film-makers.

Lastly, Luis Mandoki, a director who seemed to have chosen Hollywood as a privileged workplace, returned to Mexico to shoot **Innocent Voices** (*Voces inocentes*), about guerrilla warfare in El Salvador. By choosing a child's viewpoint, instead of his own, Mandoki has managed to turn worn-out melodramatic formulas into a sensitive and honest approach to political violence in Central America during the 1980s. Nonetheless, he proves better as a director of children, in the footsteps of Truffaut and Kiarostami, than as a convincing storyteller – a shortcoming that prevents *Innocent Voices* from being a major work of art.

Documentaries and short films are gaining wide exposure through local festivals and specialised television programmes. Notable recent examples include Alejandra Islas' **The Muxes: Authentic, Restless Seekers of Danger** (*Los Muxes, autenticas, intrépidas buscadoras de peligro*), a moving, funny documentary about an indigenous group of transvestites, and Eugenio Polgovsky's **Tropic of Cancer** (*Tropico de cancer*), about villagers who hunt wild animals and sell them on the road. It offers a challenging view of how this trade allows them to survive harsh social conditions. Guadalupe Miranda's **Tales from the Inside** (*Relatos desde el encierro*) depicts the daily experiences of inmates in a women's prison, their conflicting backgrounds, solitude and unrestrained search for affection.

Many of the films mentioned above are remarkable works that struggle to reach even a limited theatrical audience. Stronger financial support from the state must be found if artistic creation is to prevail. Otherwise, weary commercial formulas will continue their impotent rivalry with American blockbusters, and art film will be reduced to invisibility, leaving frustrated audiences to find lasting refuge in television mediocrity and the thriving video piracy market.

CARLOS BONFIL (bonfil@letraese.org.mx) has been a film critic since 1989 and contributes a weekly article on cinema to *La Jornada*, a leading Mexican newspaper. He is the author of *Through the Mirror: Mexican Cinema and Its Audience* and a book on Cantinflas.

CERO Y VAN CUATRO
[Portmanteau comedy-drama, 2004] Script: Antonio Armonia. Dir: Alejandro Gamboa, Carlos Carrera, Fernando Serrano, Fernando Sariñana. Phot: Chava Cartas, Andrés de León Becker. Players: René Campero, René Iván Dueñas, Alexis Ayala, Gustavo Sánchez Parra, Gastón Melo, Silverio Palacios. Prod: Videocine/Eckehardt von Damme.

Merchant Ivory/Kobal

ISMAIL MERCHANT, *right, with James Ivory and Ruth Prawer Jhabvala during the making of* Howards End. *The 40-year Merchant Ivory partnership came to a premature end when Merchant died on May 25, 2005, aged 68.*

Morocco Roy Armes

Recent Films

LES BANDITS (Crooks)
[Drama, 2004] Script and Dir:
Saïd Naciri. Phot: Beatrice
Mizrahi. Players: Said Naciri,
Abdelkader Moutaâ, Majdouline,
Mohamed Khayari. Prod: Hi-
Com/Short Cut.

CASABLANCA DAYLIGHT
[Drama 2004] Script and Dir:
Mostafa Derkaoui. Phot:
Abdelkrim Derkaoui. Players:
Samira Nour, Bandar Atifi,
Harij Hassan. Prod: Aflam.

TARFYA
[Drama, 2004] Script: Youssef
Fadel. Dir: Daoud Oulad Syad.
Phot: Thierry Lebigre. Players:
Touria Alaoui, Mohamed
Bastaoui, Mohamed Madj,
Mohamed Harraga, Naima Illias.
Prod: Films du Sud.

Saâd Chraïbi's **Prison Child**

JAWHARA (Prison Child)
[Drama, 2003] Script: Youssef
Fadel and Saâd Chraïbi. Dir: Saâd
Chraïbi. Phot: Kamal Derkaoui.
Players: Mouna Fettou, Yassin e
Ahjjam, Latifa Ahrar, Mohamed
Khiyi. Prod: Cinautre.

LA CHAMBRE NOIRE
(The Black Room)
[Drama, 2004] Script and Dir:
Hassen Benjelloun. Phot: Kamal

With a total of ten features released in 2004 and at the beginning of 2005, Morocco continues to be the leading film-producing country in the Maghreb region, and its films receive more and more showings at European festivals. The state system of film support continues to be administered through the National Film Centre (CCM), which now has, as successor to Souheil Benbarka, a new director, the widely respected script-writer and producer Noureddine Sail. The great hit of 2004 was Saïd Naciri's comedy, **Crooks** (*Les bandits*), with an audience of more than a million in Morocco alone. Naciri, celebrated for his one-man stage show, studied film in Los Angeles and had already appeared in Hassen Benjelloun's *The Pal* (which he scripted) and directed a little-seen feature, *Kasbah City* (2002). *Crooks*, shot on HD video to allow a range of special effects, is essentially a breathless series of tiny sketches about a bright and talented pickpocket, Didi (played by Naciri), who sets out on an ambitious scam, imitating a missing heir, but events (and burgeoning love) make him change his ways.

Other established directors active in 2004 included Mostafa Derkaoui, with **Casablanca Daylight**, a commercially successful sequel to 2003's *Casablanca by Night*, using the same child actress, and Daoud Oulad Syad, who brings a characteristically quirky touch to **Tarfya**, dealing with a young woman who arrives in a northern village with nothing more than a bag and a letter.

Hassan's dark legacy

But perhaps the most striking aspect of 2004 Moroccan production were the three features dealing with dark aspects of Morocco's past and, specifically, the persecutions and injustices that took place under the rule of the late King Hassan II. In Hassan Benjelloun's widely seen **The Black Room** (*La chambre noire*), a young couple working at the airport have their lives and plans shattered when the man's past as a Marxist–Leninist student catches up with him. The result is arrest, interrogation and torture. Saâd Chraïbi's **Prison Child** (*Jawhara*) looked at the horror of life in prison through the eyes of a six-year-old girl, who was born and has grown up there. She tells of the sufferings of her parents, wrenched away from their innocent and idealistic lives in a theatre group. Jillali Ferhati's **Imprisoned Memory** (*Mémoire en détention*), by contrast, looks at the problems of young people released from long jail sentences and tormented by what they suffered behind bars.

Three of the younger generation all received their state support after following the now traditional route of first making internationally shown short films, but their choice of subject matter was very varied. Two 'road movies', made as their feature debuts by Paris-based Moroccans, offer young men's reflections on growing up in France and discovering only later the homeland values of their fathers. In Hassan Legzouli's **Tenja**, the son has to drive his father's body for burial in a Morocco he scarcely knows, while in **The Long Journey** (*Le grand voyage*) by Ismaïl Ferroukhi, a non-religious Europeanised young man drives his devout, Arab-speaking father overland to Mecca.

Ismaïl Ferroukhi's **The Long Journey**

By contrast, Yasmine Kassari, after a well-received documentary about Moroccan workers in Europe, turned her attention to the women left behind in rural Morocco in her first fiction feature, **The Sleeping Child** (*L'enfant endormi*), whose title refers to the folk belief that an unborn child can be 'put to sleep', put, as it were, on hold until the husband's return. This is a reticent film, depicting two illiterate, unassertive women who largely submit to the situation to which they are reduced by their husbands' absence. A very different debut was that of Laïla Marrakchi, one of the very youngest Maghrebian film-makers at 30, whose first feature, **Marock**, failed to get state support. It looks at the urban youth of Casablanca, specifically a group of privileged young people who graduate from school to a life of excess: fast cars, pop music, alcohol and first love.

Derkaoui. Players: Mohamed Nadif, Hanane Ibrahimi. Prod: Bentaquela Productions/ Films du Cyclope/Centrale Africaine Cinématographique.

MÉMOIRE EN DÉTENTION
(**Imprisoned Memory**)
[Drama, 2004] Script and Dir: Jillali Ferhati. Phot: Kamal Derkaoui. Players: Mohamed Marouazi, Fatema Loukili. Prod: Heracles Production/MPS.

TENJA
[Drama, 2004] Script: Hassan Legzouli and Emmanuelle Sardou. Dir: Legzouli. Phot: Diego Martinez Vigniatti Players: Roschdy Zem, Aura Atika, Abdou El Mesnaoui. Prod: Why Not Productions/ Videorama/ Soread 2M/Arte/ Mars Films.

LE GRAND VOYAGE
(**The Long Journey**)
[Drama, 2004] Script and Dir: Ismaël Ferroukhi. Phot: Katell Djian. Players: Nicolas Cazale, Mohamed Majd, Jacky Nercessian, Kamel Belgahsi. Prod: Ognon Pictures/Arte France Cinéma/Soread 2M/Casablanca Films Productions/Les Films du Passage.

L'ENFANT ENDORMI
(**The Sleeping Child**)
[Drama, 2004] Script and Dir: Yasmine Kassari. Phot: Yorgos Arvanitis. Players: Mounia Osfour, Rachida Brakni. Prod: Les Coquelicots de l'Oriental.

Quote of the Year

"*The Long Journey* could be a metaphor for Morocco: in a hurry to detach itself from cultural archaism and political authoritarianism, and for Moroccan cinema, which opens its studios and landscapes to big international productions."
TAHAR-CHIKHAOUI, *critic*.

Netherlands Pieter van Lierop

The Year's Best Films

Pieter van Lierop's selection:

Paradise Now
(Hany Abu-Assad)
Paradise Girls (Fow Pyng Hu)
Schnitzel Paradise
(Martin Koolhoven)
Sixth of May (Theo van Gogh)
False Waltz (Marc de Cloe)

Recent and Forthcoming Films

06/05 (Sixth of May)
*[Political thriller, 2004] Script:
Tomas Ross. Dir: Theo van
Gogh. Phot: Thomas Kist.
Players: Thij`s Römer, Tara
Elders, Cahit Olmez, Jack
Wouterse, Johnny de Mol, Carol
Lenssen. Prod: Gijs van de
Westerlaken, Column Producties.*

OFF SCREEN
*[Psychological thriller, 2004]
Script: Hugo Heinen. Dir: Pieter
Kuijpers. Phot: Bert Pot. Players:
Jan Decleir, Jeroen Krabbé,
Astrid Joosten, Theu Boermans,
Gijs de Lange. Prod: Rinkel Film
& TV Productions.*
Based on a real-life hostage
drama in 2002. A disturbed,
armed bus driver protests against
Widescreen TV, which he thinks
gives less to see, not more. He
thought he was attacking Philips'
headquarters, but they had
moved to another building a
week earlier.

PARADISE GIRLS
*[Psychologial triptych, 2005]
Script & Dir: Fow Pyng Hu.
Phot: Benito Strangio. Players:
Kei Katayam, Eveline Wu, Jo
Koo, Guido Pollemans, A.C.
Chaung, Cheng Cheung Lok.*

O n November 2, 2004, Theo van Gogh was murdered by a
Muslim fundamentalist. His artistic legacy is astonishingly
large. One month after this horrific act, the première took
place of **Sixth of May**, the film van Gogh had just completed, about
– irony of ironies – the political assassination of Dutch politician Pim
Fortuyn in 2002. The film's style is reminiscent of the early thrillers of
Yves Boisset, but the suggestion put forward that Fortuyn was the
victim of a conspiracy to persuade the Dutch to buy Joint Strike
Fighter aircraft has not been taken seriously.

This was followed, early in 2005, by a van Gogh-directed TV
adaptation of *Medea*, set in government circles in The Hague. The
end of 2005 brought *Ter Ziele* (*Deceased*), a TV series consisting of
12, 10-minute episodes. Black humour will always be Theo van
Gogh's trademark. This was therefore a prominent ingredient in a
last tribute paid to him by his colleagues in the Dutch film-making
world, in the form of 16 short films, brought together under the title
All Souls (*Allerzielen*).

Hans Teeuwen, one of van Gogh's best friends, made his
directorial debut in October as the director of the heavily van
Gogh-influenced satire, **Masterclass**, which sketches the downfall
of a once-famous director and stage educator (Peer Mascini), who
has shamelessly taken advantage of his students. In the US,
meanwhile, Steve Buscemi, Stanley Tucci and Bob Balaban are
set to make low-budget remakes of three older van Gogh films:
06, *Blind Date* and *Interview*.

Anniversary mourning

Another leading light of the Dutch film world was lost in 2005.
Willem van de Sande Bakhuyzen, born in 1957, had amassed a
great reputation, largely through TV series, and especially through
his collaborations with gifted writer Maria Goos on the acclaimed
Family (*Familie*, 2001) and *Cloaca* (2003). He died of cancer on
September 27, the day before his **Live!** (*Leef!*) had its world
première as opening film of the 25th Netherlands Film Festival in
Utrecht. This kaleidoscopic story of an Amsterdam midwife and her
family's countless intrigues is an exhausting and, ultimately, not very
satisfying experience.

Prod: Motel Films, Pandora Film, NPS.
Three Asian girls (in Holland, Japan and Hong Kong) are victimised by, respectively, a self-centred father, a friend and a lover. They revolt and end up on a tropical island.

PARADISE NOW
[Drama, 2005] Script and Dir: Hany Abu-Assad. Phot: Antoine Heberlé. Players: Kais Nashef, Ali Suliman, Lubna Azabal. Prod: Bero Beyer/Augustus Film/Razor Film/Lumen Films/ Lama Films/Hazazah Film.

HET SCHNITZELPARADIJS
(Schnitzel Paradise)
[Satirical romantic comedy, 2005] Script: Marco van Geffen. Dir: Martin Koolhoven. Phot: Guido van Gennep. Players: Mounir Valentyn, Bracha van Doesburgh, Mimoun Oaïssa, Frank Lammers. Prod: Lemming Film.

LEEF! (Live!)
[Family drama, 2005] Script: Maria Goos. Dir: Willem van de Sande Bakhuyzen. Phot: Joost van Gelder. Players: Monic Hendrickx, Peter Blok, Sarah Jonker, Sophie van Winden, Anne Wil Blankers, Ali Ben Horsting. Prod: IdtV FILM.

LEPEL
[Children's film, 2005] Script: Mieke de Jong. Dir: Willem van de Sande Bakhuyzen. Phot: Guido van Gennep. Players: Joep Truijen, Loes Luca, Carice van Houten, Barry Atsma. Prod: Lemming Film/Zephyr Films.

GUERNSEY
[Psychological drama, 2005] Script and Dir: Nanouk Leopold. Phot: Richard van Oosterhout. Players: Maria Kraakman, Fedja van Huêt, Johanna ter Steege. Prod: Stienette Bosklopper/ Circe Films/Cosmokino.

HET PAARD VAN SINTERKLAAS (Winky's Horse)
[Children's film, 2005] Script: Tamara Bos. Dir: Mischa Kamp. Phot: Lennert Hillige. Players:

It is remarkable how active van de Sande Bakhuyzen was in his last year. Early in 2005, he presented the sparkling and original children's film **Lepel**, about an orphan who runs away from his cruel step-aunt and finds refuge in a department store. 2006 will see the launch of *I Embrace You with a Thousand Arms*, a feature on the topic of euthanasia. In autumn 2005 Paul Verhoeven completed his first film in the Netherlands for 20 years, the €14m **Black Book** (*Zwartboek*), which Verhoeven calls an adventurous detective story. Carice van Houten plays a Jewish former chorus girl whose family is murdered by the Nazis, whereupon she joins the resistance. After the war she sets out to discover who betrayed her relatives.

Guernsey had already screened at Cannes when it took Golden Calves for director Nanouk Leopold and actress Maria Kraakman, as well as the Press Award. It is an unassuming film based around the character of a young wife (Kraakman) who discovers how easily men can be comforted by a new romance after the loss of a partner. She begins to suspect, rightly, that her husband is already looking for a new 'used model'. This leads to marital crisis, culminating in catharsis on the island of Guernsey. A striking feature of the film is how four crucial locations are emphatically and elegantly placed in a series of different, specific architectural movements, without an apparent explanation for this phenomenon.

Johanna ter Steege and Maria Kraakman in **Guernsey**

A time of crisis

These are lean times for the cinemas, as official figures recorded a drop in total attendance from 24.9 million in 2003 to 23 million in 2004, and a further drop of 15% in the first 10 months of 2005. Video rentals have dropped by 17%. Even turnover from legal DVDs is currently static (downloading films from the internet is more common in the Netherlands than elsewhere). These figures are all the more dramatic in light of all the recent efforts to support Dutch cinema, with incentives and higher subsidies. The market share for Dutch films climbed from 9.4% in 2001 to 10% in 2002 and 12.46% in 2003, before falling to 8.8% in 2004. The government has calculated that €41m is currently being pumped into the industry: €20m in tax benefits, €12 million through the Film Fund and €9m by public broadcasters.

A catastrophe looms, as the government has announced that from 2008 it is to scrap the NPS public broadcaster, the Dutch equivalent of the BBC, which invests more than any other company in Dutch films. Documentaries and art films will be hardest hit, and the jury of the Netherlands Film Festival seemed to be drawing attention to this when it gave the most important Golden Calf awards to films from this endangered sector. Best Feature went to **Paradise Now**, about two Palestinian suicide bombers having second thoughts. Directed by Dutch–Palestinian director Hany Abu-Assad, it tooke an award at Berlin for Best European Film, but will compete as the Palestinian entry at the Oscars.

Although there has been a marked increase in horror films in the commercial arena, it is children's films that have continued to dominate the market since 1999, each year bringing a production aimed at the youngest audience and selling around a million tickets. With everyone jumping on this bandwagon, a million children's tickets were still sold, but in 2005 shared between *Pluk and His Tow-Truck*, *Eric in the Land of Insects*, *Floris*, *Lepel*, *Zoop in Africa*, *Knetter*, *Kameleon 2* and *Winky's Horse*. **Winky's Horse**, directed by Mischa Kamp, is the best of the bunch. A six-year-old Chinese girl ends up in the Netherlands and is confused by the folklore of Santa Claus. This disarming story offered a subtle metaphor for immigration, winning Best Screenplay at Utrecht.

Ebbie Tam in **Winky's Horse**

The theme of Holland as multicultural society is treated deftly by Martin Koolhoven in his romantic comedy **Schnitzel Paradise** (*Het schnitzelparadijs*), set in a transport café. Its kitchen staff shared a Golden Calf for Best Supporting Actor and the film became the biggest hit of autumn 2005.

PIETER VAN LIEROP (pvanlierop@gdp.nl) is film editor of the Netherlands Press Association (syndicated in 18 daily papers). He has been a correspondent for *IFG* since 1981.

Ebbie Tam, Jan Decleir, Mamoun Elyounoussi. Betty Schuurman, Aaron Wan, Han-Yi, Anneke Blok. Prod: BosBros Film & TV Productions.

VALSE WALS (False Waltz)
[Ballet film, 2005] Script: Titus Tiel Groenestege, Ria Marks, Marc de Cloe. Dir: Marc de Cloe. Phot: Mick van Rossum, Richard van Oosterhout. Players: Ria Marks, Titus Tiel Groenestege, René van 't Hof, Beppe Costa, Ricky Koole. Prod: Orkater.
Dance/pantomime triptych about a couple in three stages of life: meeting and dancing tangos in a sailor bar; getting bored in front of the TV; roaming around a city in old age.

ZWARTE ZWANEN (Black Swans)
[Drama, 2005] Script: Arend Steenbergen. Dir: Colette Bothof. Phot: Richard van Oosterhout. Players: Carice van Houten, Dragan Bakema, Mohammed Chaara. Prod: Rolf Koot, M+B Film.
Marleen meets Vince on an isolated Spanish beach. Within a week she has tattooed his name on her back, and he gets really scared.

ZWARTBOEK (Black Book)
[War thriller, 2006] Script: Gerard Soeteman. Dir: Paul Verhoeven. Phot: Karl Walter Lindenlaub. Players: Carice van Houten, Halina Reijn, Sebastian Koch, Christian Berkel, Dolf de Vries, Derek de Lint. Prod: Fu Works.

Quote of the Year

"Dutch cinema is a modest garden with a small lawn, a concrete path and a tree in the middle."

JOS STELLING, *director, at the 25th Dutch Film Festival, the event that he founded.*

New Zealand Peter Calder

The Year's Best Films

Peter Calder's Selection:
The World's Fastest Indian
(Roger Donaldson)
Tama Tu (Short. Taika Waititi)

Recent and Forthcoming Films

THE WORLD'S
FASTEST INDIAN
*[Drama, 2005] Script and Dir:
Roger Donaldson Phot: David
Gribble. Players: Anthony
Hopkins, Diane Ladd, Paul
Rodriguez, Aaron Murphy, Annie
Whittle. Prod: Gary Hannam,
Donaldson/WFI Productions.*

RIVER QUEEN
*[Historical drama, 2005]: Script:
Vincent Ward and Toa Fraser. Dir:
Ward. Phot: Alun Bollinger.
Players: Samantha Morton, Kiefer
Sutherland, Cliff Curtis, Temuera
Morrison, Stephen Rea. Prod:
Don Reynolds, Silverscreen Films/
Chris Auty, Film Consortium.*

50 WAYS OF
SAYING FABULOUS
*[Drama, 2004] Script and Dir:
Stewart Main, based on novel by
Graeme Aitken. Phot: Simon
Raby. Players: Andrew Patterson,
Harriet Beattie, Georgia McNeil,
Jay Collins, Michael Dorman,
Rima Te Wiata. Prod:
Michele Fantl.*

Lou (Harriet Beattie) in **50 Ways of Saying Fabulous**

A s the tumult that had surrounded the worldwide success and Oscar triumph of the *Lord of the Rings* trilogy faded, the New Zealand industry was forced glumly to contemplate a huge drop in feature film investment. Appearances were deceptive, of course: the figures plummeted in 2004 to $61m, from a historic high of $155m, because the *Rings* juggernaut had finally come to a halt. Even Peter Jackson's *King Kong* project, in post-production at the time of writing, and the wrapping of *Chronicles of Narnia: The Lion, the Witch and the Wardrobe* could not generate the kind of numbers that *Rings* had. But the year to August 2005 was more than moderately productive, ending with seven local features previewed or waiting in the wings.

By far the most notable is Vincent Ward's **River Queen**, whose fraught genesis generated headlines at home and abroad. Sydney-based Ward, an intense and passionate artist with a reputation for being both temperamental and a micro-manager, has twice had films invited into competition at Cannes – the first New Zealander to be so honoured. He spent five years writing and financing this historical epic about a young Irishwoman who must search desperately for her son when she finds herself with family on both sides during the turbulent land wars between the British colonial army and Maori in the 1860s.

Warriors take to the water in **River Queen**

Ken George/River Queen Prods. Ltd/RQ Film Prod. (UK) Ltd.

The shoot, which took place in rugged and spectacular locations on one of the country's most beautiful rivers, was dogged by rain and unseasonable cold, and production had to be suspended when star Samantha Morton succumbed to flu. When she returned, simmering tensions between her and Ward flared up again and, at the insistence of the production guarantor, Ward was removed as director, although he returned to oversee post-production. The finished film is ravishingly beautiful – the stunning cinematography is by veteran lensman Alun Bollinger, who took the helm when Ward was dumped – but is hampered by a frustratingly opaque and rambling storyline. It explores an important period in New Zealand history and evokes it brilliantly, but its appeal beyond these shores may be limited despite the presence of Morton and co-star Kiefer Sutherland.

The Kiwi need for speed

The year saw a return to New Zealand for another famous expat, Roger Donaldson, to direct a screenplay he wrote before he went to Hollywood. **The World's Fastest Indian** tells the quintessentially Kiwi story of Burt Munro, who took his backyard-built Indian Scout motorcycle to Bonneville Salt Flats in 1967 and set a world record that stands today. Donaldson's interest in Munro began in the early 1970s, when he co-directed a television documentary in which Munro returned to the scene of his triumphs. The film, the first the veteran director has written since 1981's *Smash Palace*, is a light and tender, even slightly Disney-esque, against-the-odds drama about an unlikely hero who embodies much of the can-do ingenuity of the Kiwi character (his bike's petrol tank is stopped with a brandy-bottle cork and he shaves the tread off his tyres with a carving knife).

Set in the carefree 1960s, an affluent golden age in New Zealand's history, it exudes sunlit optimism from every frame, and boasts a generous, warm and utterly likeable performance from Anthony Hopkins. He told Donaldson – and later the local press – that he

Anthony Hopkins as Burt Munro, racing on Salt Flats in **The World's Fastest Indian**

SIONE'S WEDDING
[Comedy, 2005] Dir: Chris Graham. Script: Oscar Kightley, James Griffin. Phot: Aaron Morton. Players: Oscar Kightley, Shimpal Lelisi, Robbie Magasiva, Iaheto Ah Hi, Dave Fane, Madeleine Sami, Teuila Blakely, Nathaniel Lees. Prod: John Barnett, Chloe Smith/ South Pacific Pictures.
Contemporary urban story about four thirty-something Polynesian mates whose friendship is disrupted by the impending marriage of one of the group.

NUMBER 2
[Drama, 2005] Script and Dir: Toa Fraser. Phot: Leon Narbey. Players: Ruby Dee, Tuva Novotny, Taungaroa Emile, Xavier Horan, Rene Naufahu. Prod: Tim White, Lydia Livingstone, Philippa Campbell/ Numero Films.
An ageing, mischievous matriarch prepares to hand over the reins of her dynamic Fijian–New Zealand family.

LUELLA MILLER
[Thriller, 2005] Script and Dir: Dane Giraud. Phot: Paul Tomlins. Players: Sara Wiseman, Sia Trokenheim, Philip Brown, Alistair Browning, Jacqueline Nairn, Kevin J. Wilson. Prod: Rob Rowe.
Digital psychological thriller about a generous, lonely woman who opens her door to an enigmatic stranger.

PERFECT CREATURE
[Sci-fi vampire, 2005] Script and Dir: Glenn Standring. Phot: Leon Narbey. Players: Dougray Scott, Saffron Burrows, Leo Gregory, Madeleine Sami. Prod: James Simpson, Peter James, Movision/ Gary Hamilton, Arclight.

Dougray Scott in **Perfect Creature**

Retelling of the vampire myth, set in an alternative 1960s when vampires are the next step in human evolution, but genetic mutation has caused virulent plagues.

THE KAIPARA AFFAIR
[Documentary, 2005] Script and Dir: Barry Barclay. Phot: Fred Renata. Prod: Don Selwyn/He Taonga Films.

IN MY FATHER'S DEN
[Thriller, 2004] Script and Dir: Brad McGann, based on the novel by Maurice Gee. Phot: Stuart Dryburgh. Players: Matthew MacFadyen, Miranda Otto, Vicky Haughton, Colin Moy, Jodie Rimmer, Emily Barclay, Jimmy Keen. Prod: Trevor Haysom (T.H.E), Dixie Linder (Little Bird).

SPOOKED
[Thriller, 2004] Script and Dir: Geoff Murphy. Phot: Rewa Harre. Players: Cliff Curtis, Chris Hobbs, Miriama Smith, John Leigh, Kelly Johnson. Prod: Don Reynolds, Merata Mita, Geoff Dixon, Murphy.

KAIKOHE DEMOLITION
[Documentary, 2004] Dir: Florian Habicht. Phot: Habicht, Christopher Pryor. Prod: Habicht.

Quotes of the Year

"It is still going to be a Vincent Ward film; it is still his vision."

DON REYNOLDS, *producer of* River Queen, *putting on a brave face after Ward was taken off the shoot.*

"It's one of the most pleasant parts I've ever had to play. I've played so many uptight guys, and I'm not really like that."

ANTHONY HOPKINS,
on starring in The World's Fastest Indian.

had never enjoyed making a film so much, and it shows. Even if he never comes close to mastering the New Zealand accent – and particularly the Southland burr, distinctive to the region where the local sequences are set and filmed – he looks like a man having a good time and it's impossible not to go along with him.

Bathed in *Fabulous* light

The light in the deep south of New Zealand has a distinctive magical quality that attracts local film-makers. Last year's big export, *In My Father's Den*, was shot in Central Otago, an inland basin in southern South Island, and, while the new film from that location is unlikely to make the same impact, it's still visually ravishing. **50 Ways of Saying Fabulous** is the second feature by Stewart Main, who co-directed the very camp and highly stylised *Desperate Remedies* in 1993. The title derives from a child character's sneering assessment of what he hates about homosexuals, and the film observes the coming-of-age of Billy (Andrew Patterson), a chubby young boy in a farming community, as he wrestles with his nascent sexuality. The film lacks a defined audience – it's too confrontational for 'kidult' audiences and too juvenile for adults – but is notable for a cracking performance from Harriet Beattie as Billy's hard-bitten tomboy best friend.

Keenly anticipated at press time was *Perfect Creature*, Glenn Standring's sci-fi vampire flick, which has enjoyed exceptionally strong international sales. *Number 2*, which was born as a sensational solo stage piece about an ageing matriarch and her Fijian–New Zealand family, has been opened out into an ensemble piece by writer Toa Fraser, who co-wrote *River Queen*, and he makes his debut as director with the film version, due for release early in 2006. A New Year release was also planned for the equally promising *Sione's Wedding*, which harnesses the anarchic comic talents of a group of young Polynesian writers and performers whose debut TV show, the animated *bro'Town*, was a well-received indigenous *South Park*.

At the 2005 Oscars Taika Waititi flew the flag for New Zealand when his *Two Cars, One Night* was a nominee in the dramatic short feature category. Waititi's new short, *Tama Tu*, takes place entirely in a foxhole in Italy in the Second World War and is an intimate epic, shot in CinemaScope. A group of Maori soldiers must remain silent to avoid revealing their position and while away the time with wordless communication. It's an utterly charming film, capturing perfectly the Maori sense of humour, and it bodes well for Waititi's feature debut, *Eagle vs Shark*, which was due to start shooting late in 2005.

PETER CALDER (peterc@ihug.co.nz), the New Zealand correspondent for *Variety*, has been a film critic for the country's major daily newspaper, the *New Zealand Herald*, for more than 20 years.

Nigeria Steve Ayorinde

The Year's Best Films

Steve Ayorinde's selection:
Across the Niger (Izu Ojukwu)
Bar Beach Blues
(Short. Femi Odugbemi)
The Morning After
(Jimi Odumosu)
Efunsetan Aniwura
(Tunde Kelani)
Dangerous Twins
(Tade Ogidan)

Recent and Forthcoming Films

GOOD MORNING
[Psycho-thriller, 2005] Script and Dir: Ayo Shonaiya. Phot: Timi Adegbite. Players: Tanjereen Martins, Jim Iyke, Chebe Azih. Prod: Jim Iyke/ Lords Promotions (UK).
A chief is found dead in a Nigerian community in London and there are many suspects.

AMAZING GRACE
[Period drama, 2005] Script and Dir: Jeta Amata. Phot: Joe Taylor. Players: Nick Moran, Scott Cleverdon, Mbong Odungibe, Fred Amata. Prod: Jeta Amata and Alicia Arice/Amazing Grace Productions.
The genesis of the Negro spiritual "Amazing Grace" is traced to the Nigerian city of Calabar.

VIOLENCE
[Thriller, 2005] Script: Ogazi Ofuami based on the novel by Festus Iyayi. Dir: Zack Amata. Phot: Players: Liz Benson, Akume Akume, Ladi Torty, Sunny Williams. Prod: TTL Africa Studios.
A poor couple revolt against their tyrannical boss.

N igeria's film industry is unique because of the quantity of made-for-home-viewing video films produced. This phenomenon, which began in 1992 when economic woes and devaluation rendered celluloid films unattractive, has since become the biggest home-video market in Africa. With more than 7,000 video films made in the last 13 years – around 1,000 of them in the first three quarters of 2005 alone – Nigeria can boast that its "Nollywood" film-makers are the third largest producers of cinema, after Hollywood and Bollywood. The industry generated revenues of $45m in 2004, according to the National Film and Video Censors Board, and Kingsley Ogoro's *Osuofia in London*, a comedy set in 1990s London and Nigeria, sold 400,000 copies on DVD in 2003. Film-making has new meaning for 130 million Nigerians, beyond the usual box-office system.

Most directors use Digital Video to shoot comedies and dramas in English, Yoruba and Hausa, and in 2004–05 won back local audiences from the array of 'outside fare'. London-trained Tunde Kelani is one of the busiest film-makers, known for his cultural candour and quaint political undertones. His *Agogo Eewo* (2003) was an utterly absorbing political satire, but with **The Campus Queen** (2004), an inspired romantic comedy-musical in the vein of Spike Lee's *School Daze*, he surprised many by shooting in English and aiming for the youth market; nevertheless, he retained his trademark candour. He earned a retrospective at the New York African Film Festival in 2004 and swiftly scored another major success with **Efunsetan Aniwura** (*Story of an Amazon*), a historical epic set in nineteenth-century Ibadan city.

Many have disparagingly equated the Nollywood label (coined by US journalist Matt Steinglass in 2002) with 'sub-standard' fare. Izu Ojukwu has sought to correct that impression. His **Across the Niger** (2004), a broad romantic thriller set in the early 1970s during the bloody Nigerian civil war, proved his worth. His latest, **Laviva**, a romantic action-thriller set during the 1990s Liberian civil war, is set to confirm him as perhaps the country's most innovative director.

Widows' peak

After a long absence from mainstream film-making, Jimi Odumosu made a big comeback in late 2004 with **The Morning After**, a broad

PRINCE OF THE SAVANNAH

*[Social drama, 2005] Script:
Yinka Ogun. Dir and Prod:
Bayo Awala. Phot: Leke Badiru.
Players: Chidi Ukwu, Tunde
Laniyan, Najite Dede,
Teni Aofiyebi.*
A presidential candidate faces
his nemesis in the heat of
political battle.

CLAWS OF THE LION

*[Drama, 2004] Script:
Tosin James Atega and Remi
Tereira. Dir: Francis Onwuchei.
Phot: Tunde Adekoya. Players:
Keppy Ekpeyong Bassey,
Ekwi Onwuemene, Empress
Njamah, Alex Lopez. Prod:
Frankochei Productions.*
A retired soldier and sex maniac
becomes a pimp, impregnates his
daughter and infects her with HIV.

Director Tunde Kelani

THE CAMPUS QUEEN

*[Romantic comedy, 2004]
Script: Akinwumi Isola. Dir and
Phot: Tunde Kelani. Players:
Sarah Mbaka, Lanre Fasaasi,
Segun Adefila, Lere Paimo.
Prod: Mainframe Productions.*
A beauty queen faces rival
student organisations on a
mission to sanitise society.

Quote of the Year

"I want you to do just one
thing for me. Move up from
number three to number
two, so that we have just
the USA to contend with."
**CHIEF OLUSEGUN
OBASANJO,** *Nigerian President,
urging the Actors Guild of
Nigeria to overtake Bollywood.*

Sarah Mbaka, left, and Segun Adefila in **Campus Queen**

drama about the plight of widowhood, set in ethnic eastern Nigeria at
the turn of the new century and starring award-winning actresses
Bimbola Akintola and Tina Mba. Odumosu rekindled cinemagoing by
taking the film to theatres. Another 'big boy' of Nollywood is US-
trained Tade Ogidan, whose **Dangerous Twins**, a suspense thriller set
in Lagos and London, was his most ambitious project yet. Nigeria's
answer to Leonardo DiCaprio, Ramsey Noah, plays both twins.

The only 35mm film from Nollywood in many years is from another
young director, Jeta Amata, whose beautiful **Amazing Grace** is a
dramatic historical adventure. Like Ojukwu and other well-trained
newcomers, Amata is trying to show that films that could appeal to
international audiences and festivals are a better option than the
hurriedly shot videos that have taken the DVD market to saturation
point. The distributors who exercise a stranglehold on most films
have started feeling the effects of over-production. Early in 2005,
they "banned" 10 leading actors to avoid paying exorbitant
appearance fees.

Some film-makers, such as Femi Odugbemi, aim strictly for the
arthouse. His latest short, *Bar Beach Blues*, is an expository docu-
drama set at the famous Lagos beach. He also shoots 35mm
commercials and runs the most consistent film event in Nigeria, the
Lagos Film Forum, held in July. Others who share his passion now
take succour in foreign grants, particularly from French agencies;
seven producers shared grants totalling about €500,000 in 2005.
With the advent of new co-production opportunities and a pact
between the state-run Nigerian Film Corporation and the Censors
Board to finance celluloid productions, Nollywood must accept that
it can no longer be insulated from internationally accepted film-
making standards.

STEVE AYORINDE (st_ayorinde@yahoo.com) is Arts Editor of *The
PUNCH*, Nigeria's largest selling daily. He is a member of FIPRESCI
and regularly attends film festivals across the world.

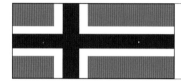

Norway Trond Olav Svendsen

The Year's Best Films

Trond Olav Svendsen's
selection:

Factotum (Bent Hamer)

Kissed by Winter
(Sara Johnsen)

Monsterthursday
(Arild Østin Ommundsen)

Next Door (Pål Sletaune)

Uno (Aksel Hennie)

Annika Hallin in **Kissed by Winter**

Recent and
Forthcoming Films

IKKE NAKEN
(The Colour of Milk)
*[Family film, 2004] Script and
Dir: Torun Lian, based on her
own novel. Phot: John Christian
Rosenlund. Players: Julia Krohn,
Bernhard Naglestad, Andrine
Sæther, Reidar Sørensen, Ane
Dahl Torp. Prod: Catho Bach
Christensen/Painswick Film.*
Selma, 13, wants to win the
Nobel prize instead of letting
boys ruin her life.

MIN MISUNNELIGE FRISØR
(My Jealous Barber)
*[Drama, 2004] Script: Annette
Sjursen, Lars Saabye Christensen,
based on Christensen's short
story. Dir: Sjursen. Phot: Philip
Øgaard. Players: Gard Eidsvold,
Bjørn Sundquist, Hildegun Riise.
Prod: Dag Alveberg/Maipo.*

HAWAII, OSLO
[Drama, 2004] Script: Harald

The feature and documentary film industry in Norway is blossoming. The industry is larger, more productive and better funded than ever before. With an onslaught of 20 cinema releases a year (and I am not complaining), film makes a bigger impact on the Norwegian cultural scene than before, and has on average a significantly larger share of the audience than 20 years ago. Attendance figures were, however, down again in the first half of 2005. It is impossible to tell if a new downward trend is beginning. One source of worry is a weakening of the core group of teenagers and young adults. On the other hand, the figures have been fairly stable for some years, and one or two successful films in a given season always make a difference.

The Film Fund, which has just completed its fourth year, represented a New Deal in Norwegian film history when it arrived on the scene in 2001. It has succeeded in making the industry connect with a broader audience, and helped several new film-makers achieve instant popularity. It has, on the whole, been a source of optimism and self-confidence and, of course, money; Norwegian feature films, today, regularly have as much as 70% of their budget from the government. Some feel that the Fund is too active and detailed in its contribution, dictating to producers what kind of films should be made and how. Perhaps our film culture would benefit if some of the directors whom we have hailed for years as wonderful talents were allowed to make a few films their own way. Some politicians look upon cinema simply as a branch of popular culture, a form of self-financing entertainment for young people. Others feel it is too much like rock'n' roll: too many films made by young male directors whose stories of anger and desire appeal mainly to an audience similar to themselves. An evaluation of the Film Fund will take place over the winter of 2005–06.

Hawaii and surfers

The 2004–05 season brought very mixed but interesting results. It contained above all a great variety of films, some influenced by American directors, though in quite different ways. **Uno** was the solid directorial debut of the popular young actor Aksel Hennie. This story of a young bum coming to terms with his responsibilities after the death of his father mixed realism and genre elements. **Hawaii, Oslo**, Erik Poppe's second feature, gave us the lives of

*Rosenløw Eeg. Dir: Erik Poppe.
Phot: Ulf Brantås. Players: Trond
Espen Seim, Jan Gunnar Røise,
Petronella Barker, Stig Henrik
Hoff, Aksel Hennie. Prod: Finn
Gjerdrum/Torleif Hauge/Paradox.*

MONSTERTORSDAG
(Monsterthursday)
*[Drama, 2004] Script: Gro Elin
Hjelle, Arild Østin Ommundsen.
Dir: Ommundsen. Phot: Trond
Høines. Players: Vegar Hoel, Silje
Salomonsen, Andreas Cappelen,
Kim Bodnia, Christian Skolmen,
Iben Hjeile. Prod: Ingrid Festøy
Ottesen/Muz Film.*

EN FOLKEFIENDE
(An Enemy of the People)
*[Drama, 2005]. Script: Nikolaj
Frobenius, Erik Skjoldbjærg,
based on a play by Henrik Ibsen.
Dir: Skjoldbjærg. Phot: Harald
Paalgård. Players: Jørgen
Langhelle, Sven Nordin,
Kasper Sveen, Trine Wiggen,
Pia Tjelta, Jon Øigarden.
Prod: Aage Aaberge/Nordisk
Film Production.*

UNO
*[Drama, 2004] Script: Aksel
Hennie. Dir: Hennie. Phot: John
Andreas Andersen. Players: Aksel
Hennie, Nicolai Cleve Broch,
Bjørn Floberg, Liv Bernholft
Osa. Prod: Jørgen Storm
Rosenberg/Tordenfilm.*

Kristoffer Joner in **Uno**

LE REGARD
*[Drama, 2005] Script and Dir:
Nour-Eddine Lakhmari. Phot:
Kjell Vassdal. Players: Florian
Cadiou, Jean-Pierre Cassel,
Khalid Benchagra, Hamid
Torchi, Pierre Zaoui. Prod: Egil
Ødegård/Filmhuset.*
An elderly war photographer
looks into his own past.

several Oslo characters with some flair, somewhat in the fashion of a group portrait by Robert Altman or Paul Thomas Anderson.

The strikingly visual **Monsterthursday** (*Monstertorsdag*) was made by a group of independents in the town of Stavanger, headed by talented director Arild Østin Ommundsen, whose second feature this was. It told a tale of jealousy against a backdrop of surfing on the windswept western coastline (with echoes of John Milius' *Big Wednesday*). Two friends love the same woman. She becomes pregnant by one of them and marries him. The rival learns to surf to regain his confidence. All wait for the child – and the big wave. Ommundsen handles the actors very well and is a born storyteller, though he shares the honours with director of cinematography Trond Høines.

Kim Bodnia, left, and Vegar Hoel in **Monsterthursday**

Next Door (*Naboer*), somewhat influenced by David Lynch, showed Pål Sletaune superbly in control, though the subject matter fell a little short of providing a truly engaging film. Kristoffer Joner, now the most popular and consequently the busiest actor in Norwegian films, plays the young man who is lured over to the dark side by the two beautiful women next door. Vibrant camera work and good actors were used to great effect. **Finding Friends** (*Venner for livet*), directed by Arne Lindtner Næss from a script by Ingrid Wiese, was a somewhat old-fashioned, but well acted film for the whole family, with child characters to identify with and a mystery to be solved.

Alone in the world

The winter season also brought a very interesting directorial debut. Sara Johnsen is one of the first graduates of the Norwegian Film School at Lillehammer, and in **Kissed by Winter** (*Vinterkyss*) gives evidence of considerable talent. A woman physician from Stockholm (Annika Hallin) loses her young son and blames herself for his death. She moves to a Norwegian village and reluctantly starts an affair with a charming, divorced man who drives the snow plough (Kristoffer Joner again). A young misfit, the son of Muslim asylum seekers, is found dead in the snow, and she is forced to get involved. The film actually becomes less interesting as the events around the dead man change the focus of the story, but Johnsen achieves a great deal thruogh her very sensitive work with the actors. The underlying tension of the story and the sustained mode of despair are very well handled.

Factotum, Bent Hamer's English-language film, based on a novel by Charles Bukowski, was neither a sensation nor a disappointment. Matt Dillon as Henry Chinaski, Bukowski's alter ego, has adopted some of Bukowskis mannerisms to good effect. There are few down-and-out cronies to be seen, but rather more frustrated employers, who fire Chinaski from various jobs. His relationship with Jan (the excellent Lili Taylor) is both laconic and full of carnal lust.

Matt Dillon and Lili Taylor in Bent Hamer's **Factotum**

Sometimes the takes are very long, as in the scene where Chinaski leaves Jan, yet they stay expressive and interesting. Chinaski keeps getting fired while steadily submitting short stories to a magazine. When one of them is finally accepted, this does not change things a lot, which perhaps is the film art of Bent Hamer in a nutshell. Life is more lyrical than dramatic. Humans are what they are. The poetry is in the situations.

TROND OLAV SVENDSEN (tos@kunnskapsforlaget.no) has worked as a researcher for the Norwegian Film Institute and as a newspaper film critic. Among his publications is a *Theatre and Film Encyclopedia*.

VINTERKYSS (Kissed by Winter)
[Drama, 2005] Script: Sara Johnsen and Ståle Stein Berg. Dir: Johnsen. Phot: Odd Reinhardt Nicolaysen. Players: Annika Hallin, Kristoffer Joner, Linn Skåber, Fritjof Såheim, Michalis Koutsogiannakis, Göran Ragnerstam. Prod: Christian Fredrik Martin/Friland.

VENNER FOR LIVET (Finding Friends)
[Family film, 2005] Script: Ingrid Wiese, Geir Meum Olsen, Arne Lindtner Næss. Dir: Lindtner Næss. Phot: Kjell Vassdal. Players: Magnus Solhaug, Sunaina Jassal, Thorbjørn Harr, Reidar Sørensen, Nina Woxholt. Prod: Ellen Jacobsen/Nordisk Film.

NABOER (Next Door)
[Drama, 2005] Script and Dir: Pål Sletaune. Phot: John Andreas Andersen. Players: Kristoffer Joner, Cecilie Mosli, Julia Schacht, Anna Bache-Wiig, Michael Nyqvist. Prod: Turid Øversveen/4.

FACTOTUM
[Drama, 2005] Script: Bent Hamer, Jim Stark, based on a novel by Charles Bukowski. Dir: Hamer. Phot: Philip Øgaard. Players: Matt Dillon, Lili Taylor, Fisher Stevens, Marisa Tomei, Didier Flamand, Adrienne Shelly. Prod: Jim Stark/Stark Sales/ Bent Hamer/BulBul Films.

IMPORT EKSPORT (Import Export)
[Comedy, 2005] Script and Dir: Khalid Hussain. Phot: Kjell Vassdal. Players: Bjørnar Lisether Teigen, Talat Hussain, Iram Haq, Assad Siddique, Anita Uberoi, Asia Begum. Prod: Egil Ødegård/Filmhuset.
Jan loves Jasmin, but she has been promised to a relative from Pakistan.

Quote of the Year

"In Norway we make too few films for grown-ups!"
NINA GRÜNFELDT, *film-maker, in* Film & Kino *magazine.*

Pakistan Aijaz Gul

Recent and Forthcoming Films

KEWON TUM SEY ITNA PYAR HAI (Love You Why!)
[Urdu. Thriller, 2005] Script and Dir: Ajab Gul. Phot: Waqar Bokhari. Players: Ajab Gul, Babarak, Veena Malik, Nadeem, Talat Hussain. Prod: Saqib Khan.

KOI TUJH SA KAHAN (One and Only)
[Urdu. Drama, 2005] Script: Khalilul Rehman Qamar. Dir and Prod: Reema. Phot: Waqar Bokhari. Players: Reema, Mommar Rana, Veena Malik, Nadeem.

Babrak-Simran in **One and Only**

HOME
[Urdu–English. Short. Drama, 2005] Script and Dir: Faisal Rehman. Phot: Naveed. Players: Uzma Gilani, Faisal Rehman, Uruj, Nasir. Prod: Sultana Siddiqui.

Quote of the Year

"Whoever wants to see me from the inside must go and see my film."

REEMA, *actress, promoting her directorial debut,* One and Only.

In 2004, annual film production stood at 50, with eight Urdu and 17 Punjabi titles. While these two languages declined on screen in 2005, Pushto films jumped from 15 in 2003 to 25 in 2004, largely because Pushto titles are not shown on pirated cable TV channels (known here as CD channels) before reaching cinemas, and are therefore a safer commercial bet. Also, Pushto films were now being made with higher budgets and more attractive production values.

The box-office returns for most films were disappointing. The leftover studios at Lahore are now largely catering to TV productions and commercials. After many cancellations, a large film industry delegation finally met the prime minister, who subsequently directed the Pakistan Electronic Media Regulating Authority and Central Board of Revenue to look into cable piracy and reducing import duty on equipment. He also advised the industry to seek international co-production finance, and promised to support a new Film City in Lahore and Karachi.

Actress Meera caused a sensation by going to India to star in **Vision** (*Nazar*). With plenty of skin and kisses, Meera made tabloid headlines, but this mediocre, low-budget rehash of *The Eyes of Laura Mars* failed at cinemas. Shahzad Rafiq's **Prison Bars** (*Salakhain*) played extremely well nationwide, thanks to highly charged action sequences and an enormously successful multimedia ad campaign. In actor Ajab Gul's second feature, **Love You Why!** (*kewon tum sey itna pyar hai*), he took the juvenile lead in a drama about a corrupt politican (Talat Hussain) and a scrupulously honest retired judge (Nadeem). Reema, who began her career in 1990, was asked to move away from acting and made her directorial debut with **One and Only** (*Koi tujh sa kahan*), partly shot in Malaysia.

Finally, comedian–director–producer Rangilla (born Saeed Khan) passed away in May 2005 after a prolonged illness. He found overnight fame with his directorial debut, *The Storm* (*Diya aur toofan*), in 1969. Composer Amjad Bobby passed away in March 2005. His notable films include *Chief Sahab, It's Yours* (*Yeh dil aap ka huwa*) and *Love Crazy* (*Diwaney terey pyar key*).

AIJAZ GUL (aijazgul@hotmail.com) earned his BA and MA in cinema from USC. He has published numerous articles and three books on cinema. He lives in Islamabad.

Peru Isaac Léon Frías

Recent Films

DIAS DE SANTIAGO
(Days of Santiago)
[Drama, 2004] Script and Dir: Josué Méndez. Phot: Juan Durán. Players: Pietro Sibile, Milagros Vidal, Maricela Puicón. Prod: Chullachaki.

CUANDO EL CIELO ES AZUL
(When the Sky Is Blue)
[Drama, 2005] Script: Sandra Wiese, Talia Jelicic, Antonui Fortunic. Dir: Wiese. Players: Andrea Montenegro, Juan Pablo Gamboa, Cecilia Bernasconi. Prod: Antares.

MAÑANA TE CUENTO
(I Will Tell You Tomorrow)
[Comedy-drama, 2005] Script and Dir: Eduardo Mendoza. Phot: Fergan Chávez-Ferrer. Players: Bruno Ascenzo, Melania Urbina, Jason Day. Prod: Incacine S.A.C./ Aldea Films/Leo Vídeo/ Volcom Producciones.

PIRATAS EN EL CALLAO
(Pirates at Callao)
[Animation, 2005] Script: Pipo Gallo. Dir: Eduardo Schuldt. Prod: Alpamayo Entertainment.

UN DIA SIN SEXO
(A Day Without Sex)
[Comedy-drama, 2005] Script: Frank Pérez-Garland, Christian Buckley, Melania Urbina. Dir: Pérez-Garland. Phot: Christian Declercq. Prod: Luna Llena Films/Fabrizio Aguilar.

EL CAUDILLO PARDO
(The Commander Brownshirt)
[Documentary, 2004] Script and Dir: Aldo Salvini. Phot: Ruben Carpio. Prod: Fauno Films.

A competition organised by Consejo Nacional de Cinematografía (CONACINE) in the first months of 2005 gathered more than 30 feature film scripts, an unprecedented number for this country. Not all of the scripts become films. In fact, three are selected to receive a sum that is just a part of the production budget. Most Peruvian productions need the support of European funds such as the Netherlands' Hubert Bals Foundation, Switzerland's Monte Cinema Veritá, the UK's Film Four or France's TV 5, in addition to the Ibermedia programme, which receives contributions from many Ibero–American countries, and in which Spain has a prominent role. Other than the three victorious CONACINE scripts, few of the other entries will find enough money to be filmed.

In any case, the country seems to be divided these days. In Lima, the capital, production of feature films destined for cinema release continues on a centralised model. Outside Lima, some regional directors make their films on Digital Video and their distribution is aimed at independent theatres, some in Lima, but most in the interior regions.

Four Peruvian features were released in theatres in the first ten months of 2005, all directed by first-time film-makers. **When the Sky Is Blue** (*Cuando el cielo es azul*), directed by Sandra Wiese, deals with a love story in Cuzco, the old capital of the Incan empire. Magic and mysticism are the ingredients in a movie that is very short on inspiration. Eduardo Mendoza's **I Will Tell You Tomorrow** (*Mañana te cuento*), a tale of sexual initiation, follows the line traced by Larry Clark's films, but is not convincing, despite the cast's fine performances. Mendoza is young and, after making two good short films, shows in his first feature considerable skill with actors and narrative fluency, but fails to provide a consistent tone: the initial comedy turns to drama in an unsatisfactory manner. Nevertheless, *I Will Tell You Tomorrow* drew 300,000 admissions, the highest by a Peruvian production in 2005.

More impressive, because its tone and point of view are more coherently developed through action, is Frank Pérez-Garland's **A Day Without Sex** (*Un día sin sexo*), about three couples, one elderly, one middle-aged and one teenaged, which shares common points with Mendoza's film: a low budget, action concentrated in

The Commander Brownshirt

COCA MAMA (Mother Coca)
[Drama, 2004] Script and Dir:
Marianne Eyde. Phot: Mario
Bassino. Players: Milagros del
Carpio, Oscar Carrillo, Miguel
Medina. Prod: Kusi Films.

Gianfranco Brero and Yvonne Fraysinnet in **A Day Without Sex**

time and place, several relationships exposed and an emphasis on ensemble characterisation rather than just one or two leading figures.

Pirates make a killing

The fourth film of the year is the first feature-length animation ever produced in Peru, **Pirates at Callao** (*Piratas en el Callao*), directed by Eduardo Schuldt. It dramatises two historical events that occurred in Callao, a port town near Lima: the 1624 attack by Dutch pirate Jacques L'Hermite, and the Spanish army's assault on the port in 1872, which was repelled by Peruvian forces. The hero is a boy from the present who travels back to both years. The linking of the two events suffers an excess of didacticism. Also, the character design and scenic backgrounds are a little bit elementary and the rhythm does not have the necessary fluency. *Pirates at Callao* did relatively well, not only in theatres but also through merchandising (T-shirts, illustrated books, toys etc.) – a novelty in our small local film history.

Among the documentary films, the one that deserves a special mention is **The Commander Brownshirt** (*El caudillo pardo*), the second long film directed by Aldo Salvini. It is an extended interview with a Peruvian fan of Adolf Hitler and the National Socialist ideology, but the director's approach discovers the personal side of this eccentric character and holds the attention of the spectator throughout.

ISAAC LÉON FRÍAS (ileon@correo.ulima.edu.pe) has been a film critic since 1965 and is Professor of Language and Film History at the University of Lima. From 1965 to 1985 he was director of *Hablemos de Cine* magazine and from 1986 to 2001 ran Filmoteca de Lima.

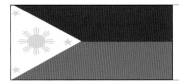

Philippines Tessa Jazmines

The Year's Best Films

Tessa Jazmines' selection:
The Echo (Yam Laranas)
Call of the River
(Cesar Montano)
Magdalena (Laurice Guillen)
I Love You (Joel Lamangan)
Once More (Jeffrey Jeturian)

Recent and Forthcoming Films

ANG PAGDADALAGA NI
MAXIMO OLIVEROS (The
Blossoming of Maximo Oliveros)
*[Drama, 2005] Script: Michiko
Yamamoto, Raymond Lee.
Dir: Aureaus Solito. Phot: Nap
Jamir. Players: Nathan Lopez, Jr.,
Soliman Cruz, Ping Medina,
Bodgie Pascua. Prod:
UFO Pictures.*

PANAGHOY SA SUBA
(Call of the River)
*[War drama, 2004] Script: Cris
Vertido, Cesar Montano. Dir and
Prod: Montano. Phot: Ely Cruz.
Players: Cesar Montano, Juliana
Palermo, Jacky Woo, Joel Torre,
Rebecca Lusterio, Daria Ramirez,
Ronnie Lazaro, Caridad Sanchez,
Suzette Ranillo.*

SIGAW (The Echo)
*[Horror, 2004] Script: Roy
Iglesias and Yam Laranas. Dir
and Phot: Yam Laranas. Players:
Richard Gutierrez, Angel Locsin,
Iza Calzado, Jomari Yllana,
Ronnie Lazaro. Prod: Roselle
Monteverde-Teo (Mega Vision).*

ASHITE IMASU 1941
(I Love You)
*[War/historical drama, 2004]
Script: Ricky Lee. Dir: Joel
Lamangan. Phot: Rolly Manuel.
Players: Judy Ann Santos, Jay*

Philippines cinema put on its adventure cap in 2004–05. "Go indy" was the name of the game. Unitel Pictures' **Magdalena Santa Santita** set the trend in November 2004, giving audiences an edgy, full-length HD feature. This modern-day Magdalene story tackled unconventional subject matter: pray-for-pay ladies who work in Manila's bustling commercial district, with a revered basilica housing a miraculous Black Nazarene image in the background. The film was adult-rated by the Cinema Evaluation Board and lost at the box-office to a rival teen romance, **Bcoz of U**.

This did not faze other indy producers at the Manila Film Festival, which turns the year-end holiday fortnight into a festival of Filipino film. **Call of the River** (*Panaghoy sa suba*), a drama set during the Japanese occupation in 1941, tackled war and peace through the "eyes" of a river that runs through a bucolic southern town, Bohol. Romance, social comment, history, travelogue and action mesh in a three-hour epic that used the native Visayan dialect and English subtitles. Produced, directed and co-written by erstwhile leading man Cesar Montano, who also starred, it won seven awards at Manila, including Best Direction and Screenplay, and screened at Cannes, New York and Toronto.

Even the big studios emerged from their comfort zone of eye-candy movies. Regal Entertainment made what became known as "the other World War II movie": **I Love You** (*Ashite imasu 1941*), the story of a Japanese commanding officer's love for a cross-dressing gay, who becomes torn between this relationship and his loyalty to his Filipino guerilla confrères. Regal also showed the third of its grand Filipino–Chinese family sagas. **Mano Po 3** focused on the forbidden love of a popular and successful Fil–Chi woman for her college sweetheart.

Scary movies

Filipino horror films took on a life of their own. Manila showcased **Spirit of the Glass**, a misadventure set in an old house whose fearsome history is awakened by a ouija board, and **The Echo** (*Sigaw*), an eerie, scream-provoking flick about a rundown apartment that terrifies its residents. It was optioned for a Hollywood remake and its director, Yam Laranas, was signed up by ICM. The horror boom had been kicked off in September by **Feng**

Manalo, Raymart Santiago,
Dennis Trillo, Anita Linda,
Jaclyn Jose, Angelu de Leon.
Prod: Regal Entertainment for
Bas Films.

LA VISA LOCA
[Satirical comedy, 2005] Script
and Dir: Mark Meily. Phot: Lee
Meily. Players: Robin Padilla,
Rufa Mae Quinto, Johnny
Delgado, Paul Holme, Tessie
Tomas, Noel Trinidad, Robert
Sena, Isay Alvarez. Prod: Unitel
Pictures.

PINOY BLONDE
[Funky comedy, 2005] Script:
Lore Reyes. Dir: Peque Gallaga.
Players: Epy Quizon, Boy 2
Quizon, Iza Calzado, Ricky
Davao, Jaime Fabregas, Eddie
Garcia + All Star Cast. Prod:
Tony Gloria, Unitel Pictures.

MANO PO 3
[Drama, 2004] Script: Roy
Iglesias. Dir: Joel Lamangan.
Players: Vilma Santos,
Christopher De Leon, Jay
Manalo, Sheryl Cruz, Angelica
Panganiban, Carlo Aquino,
Patrick Garcia, Eddie Garcia.
Prod: Regal Entertainment.

LASTIKMAN
[Action comedy, 2004] Script:
Mars Ravelo/R.J. Cuevas. Dir:
Mac C. Alejandre. Phot: Regine
Rosanna. Players: Sarah
Geronimo, Mark Bautista, John
Estrada, Danilo Barrios, Cherie
Gil, Elizabeth Oropesa, Joel
Torre, Mark Gil, Bearwin Meily,
Tuesday Vargas, Mikel Campos.
Prod: Viva Films.

Quote of the Year

"I want the audience to
bring home their fear, to be
afraid of being left alone in
their house."
YAM LARANAS, director of The
Echo, on making scary movies.

Shui (ghastly happenings in a suburban neighbourhood are traced to an ancient curse), which outlasted all its box-office competitors – including Hollywood films. **Nine Days** (Pasiyam) also made waves. Its title refers to the traditional novena offered for the soul of the newly deceased so that it will not disturb the living.

Among the comedies and teen romances that made money, **So Happy Together** targeted the teeny-boppers market, **Lastikman** gave us the adventures of a stretchable, comedic superhero, and **Enteng Kabisote** was a romantic fantasy. TV teen idols Richard Gutierrez and Angel Locsin were successfully paired in **Let the Love Begin**, a rich girl–poor boy romance.

The spirit of adventure continued all year. Jeffrey Jeturian's **Once More** (Minsan pa), the maiden venture of independent MLR Films, was acclaimed by the discerning Young Critics Circle. Unitel Pictures released two more out-of-the-box films mid-year: **La Visa Loca**, about the complicated, comedic quest for the American Dream, starred box-office icon Robin Padilla, while Peque Gallaga's **Pinoy Blonde** was a breakthrough for Philippines cinema in form and content. The tale of two cousins who make movies in their minds and get entangled with the underworld was part animation, part MTV, all HD and as surreal as it gets. The marketing campaign, which included rock concerts, fan parties and school tours was equally unconventional.

Overseas, **The Blossoming of Maximo Oliveros** (Ang pagdadalaga ni Maximo Oliveros), the touching and obliquely funny story of a caring, gay pre-teen growing up in an uncaring locale, won Best Picture in the First Films Competitions at the Montreal World Festival. The march of the indy films continued in the second half of 2005. The Cinema One Originals Digital Film Festival in August showcased a wide range of productions, including **Stray Cats** (Mga pusang gala), a provocative story of two neighbours who share a common, uneasy subservience to their respective lovers. The director, Ellen Ongkeko-Marfil, had invested her own savings into the project. Such adventures are now a dime a dozen in Philippines cinema.

TESSA JAZMINES (tjazmines@yahoo.com) is Philippines correspondent for Variety and Asia Image. She is Associate Professor of Journalism at the University of the Philippines College of Mass Communication.

Poland Barbara Hollender

The Year's Best Films

Barbara Hollender's selection:
Persona non grata
(Krzysztof Zanussi)
I Am (Dorota Kedzierzawska)
The Cross-Way Cafe
(Leszek Wosiewicz)
Ode to Joy
(Anna Kazejak-Dawid, Jan
Komasa, Maciej Migas)
The Collector (Feliks Falk)

Recent and Forthcoming Films

DOSKONALE POPOLUDNIE
(The Perfect Afternoon)
*[Drama, 2005] Script and Dir:
Przemysaw Wojcieszek. Phot:
Jola Dylewska. Players: Michal
Czarnecki, Magdalena
Poplawska, Malgorzata
Dobrowolska, Jerzy Stuhr. Prod:
Telewizja Polska SA/Agencja
Produkcji Filmowej/Pawel
Rakowski, Skorpion Art.*

JESTEM (I Am)
*[Drama, 2005] Script and Dir:
Dorota Kedzierzawska. Phot:
Artur Reinhart. Players: Piotr
Jagielksi, Agnieszka Nagorzycka,
Edyta Jungowska, Pawel
Wilczak. Prod: Artur Reinhart,
Kid Film/Andrzej Serdiukow,
Telewizja Polska SA.*

KOMORNIK (The Collector)
*[Drama, 2005] Script: Grzegorz
Loszewski. Dir: Feliks Falk. Phot:
Bartek Prokopowicz. Players:
Andrzej Chyra, Kinga Preis,
Malgorzata Kozuchowska. Prod:
Janusz Morgenstern, Jerzy
Buchwald, Studio Filmowe
Perspektywa/Andrzej Serdiukow,
Telewizja Polska SA/Pawel
Mossakowski, Canal+*

This was a breakthrough year for Polish cinema. In June 2005, after 15 years of push and shove, the Polish Diet passed a new Cinematography Bill, in large part following the French model. In July the Polish Institute of Film Art (PISF) was established, headed by former vice-minister of culture, Agnieszka Odorowicz, 31. Crucially, the Bill ensures that the Institute's budget will come not just from taxpayers but also from a compulsory levy on public and private terrestrial TV stations: 1.5% of their advertising revenue. Cinemas must contribute 1.5 % of box-office receipts, and the same figure applies to the revenues of cable TV operators and video and DVD distributors. From 2006, this should bring the Institute an estimated total of $33m (100m zloty), three or four times more than in recent years, to be spent on scriptwriting, international promotion and, above all, production. Odorowicz has announced a plan to support co-productions, which may receive funding of up to $2m, and a special fund to support debuts. Now the ball is in the producers' court: to take risks by making artistic films, at a time when local directors are demonstrating considerable talent.

In 2005, 30 Polish features were made, financed chiefly by state funds, state-owned TV and Canal Plus Poland. They continued to be "hard times" products, done on the cheap, with some of the cheapness showing. However, after years of stagnation, film-makers are flexing their creative muscles again, particularly younger ones, using the screen to paint today's Poland with stories of people from their circles. This human mosaic is sad to look at: a record of aimlessness, aggression, hopelessness. Sadder still, these young directors do not spin tales about slum dwellers, or uneducated skinheads, but about themselves – boys and girls with university diplomas, but clueless as to what they want to do in life.

For example, in **Ode to Joy** (*Oda do radosci*), by students of the Lodz film school, Anna Kazejak-Dawid, Jan Komasa and Maciej Migas, the main characters, from different backgrounds and parts of Poland, meet on the bus to London. All lacking hope, a girl from Silesia, a Warsaw hip-hop fan and a guy who has just graduated from university share the road to the unknown, having failed to find home – or a job – in their own country. This is an important movie, especially in light of a recent study that showed half of Polish secondary-school pupils to plan to emigrate west after getting a degree.

Polska/WFDiF/Agencja
Produkcji Filmowej.

LAWSTORANT
[Comedy, 2005] Script: Tadeusz
Porebski. Dir: Mikolaj Haremski.
Phot: Zdzislaw Najda. Players:
Zbigniew Buczkowski, Michal
Wisniewski, Malgorzata
Pieczynska. Prod: PDB
EDBUD/AT-FILM.

MASZ NA IMIE JUSTINE
(Your Name Is Justine)
[Drama, 2005] Script: Franco de
Pena, Tomasz Kepski, Chris
Burdza. Dir: Franco de Pena.
Phot: Arek Tomiak. Players:
Anna Cieslak, Arno Frish,
Malgorzata Buczkowska. Prod:
Piotr Dzieciol, Opus
Film/Stephan Carpiaux,
Hemispheres Films/Telewizja
Polska SA/Agencja Produkcji
Filmowej/Eurimages.

MISTRZ (Master)
[2005] Script: Piotr Trzaskalski,
Wojciech Lepianka. Dir: Piotr
Trzaskalski. Phot: Piotr
Sliskowski. Players: Konstantin
Lawronienko, Jacek Braciak,
Monika Buchowiec, Teresa
Branna. Prod: Piotr Dzieciol,
Lukasz Dzieciol, Opus
Film/Telewizja Polska SA/Peter
Rommel Productions/ZDF/Arte/
Agencja Produkcji Filmowej/
Media Plus SA.

ODA DO RADOSCI
(Ode to Joy)
[Drama, 2005] Script and Dir:
Anna Kazejak-Dawid, Jan
Komasa, Maciej Migas. Phot:
Klaudiusz Dwulit, Piotr
Niemyjski, Radoslaw Radczuk.
Players: Malgorzata
Buczkowska, Dorota Pomykala,
Piotr Glowacki, Roma
Gasiorowska, Leslaw Zurek,
Tomasz Lengren. Prod: Michal
Kwiecinski, Akson Studio/
Krzysztof Gierat, Telewizja
Polska SA/Canal+ Polska/
Agencja Produkcji Filmowej.

PERSONA NON GRATA
[Drama, 2005] Script and Dir:
Krzysztof Zanussi. Phot: Edward
Klosinski. Players: Zbigniew

Malgorzata Buczkowska, Michal Zurawski and Dorota Pomykala in Ode to Joy

The heroine of Anna Jadowska's **It's Me, Now** (*Teraz ja*) is another non-achiever, on the run from her boyfriend and everyday life. On a headlong, directionless journey through Poland, she meets petty, spiteful, aggressive, bitter people, who all try to take advantage. Another difficult and unpleasant reality is shown in Przemyslaw Wojcieszek's **The Perfect Afternoon** (*Doskonale popoludnie*), in which three young intellectuals struggle to support a small publishing house. Yet Wojcieszek seeks hope. One character throws away an airline ticket to Ireland. But why do the climactic scenes at a wedding and the characters' promise to build Poland of their dreams look like a caricature?

Older, and just as sad

The older generation of artists gave just as doleful an impression of the country, but the sole representative to relate directly to life today is Krzysztof Zanussi, whose **Persona non grata** is a tale about old age that is as bitter as a tale about the young. At the Polish embassy in Uruguay, we are among people well established in life. Yet the disillusion and incompatibility of the characters are similar to those of the young back in Poland. One loser, an ex-Solidarity activist, cannot come to terms with emptiness and a web of lies, and says farewell to this world.

Others choose allegory over realism. Their movies also portray a Poland not shown by colour magazines, but the directors, who themselves have had ups and downs, escape into morality plays. Named Best Film at the national film festival, Feliks Falk's **The Collector** (*Komornik*) has a hero who wades through wrecked lives, collecting taxes from the destitute, until he experiences a shock and seeks redemption. A social drama becomes a movie about spiritual rebirth. A similar twist is used by Leszek Wosiewicz in **The Cross-Way Café** (*Rozdroze Cafe*), about a bank robbery that kills four people, yet the culprits are no degenerates. Wosiewicz dissects the crime, showing ordinary blokes who had no intention to kill. Despite its harsh social diagnostics, it still meanders into redemptive territory.

Andrzej Chyra, second left, as **The Collector**

Many Polish movies are completely detached from reality. Piotr Trzaskalski's **The Master** (*Mistrz*) is a fairytale about provincial people following their dreams, yet blind to the genuine values and people around them. It also concerns art, and we hear echoes of Fellini and Tarkovsky. A tale of loneliness and love, Dorota Kedzierzawska's **I Am** (*Jestem*), made a beautiful film: clean, full of half-light, without a wasted word.

Love is all around

A bumper crop of love stories included Izabella Cywinska's **The Lovers of Marona** (*Kochankowie z Marony*), a refined psychological study, Jacek Bromski's Sino–Polish co-production, **The Lovers of the Year of the Tiger** (*Kochankowie roku tygrysa*) and the pure fairy story, **An Angel in Love** (*Zakochany aniol*). There also was a serious German–Polish co-production, Roberta Glinskiego's **The Call of the Toad**, and a few pure entertainment titles as well.

What is Polish film like today? Promising is the best word to use. So, after years of hiatus, Polish films reached major festivals again: *My Nikifor* (see *IFG 2005*) took the Grand Prix at Karlovy Vary, *The Master* was shown at San Sebastian and *I Am* at Toronto. Polish cinema is bouncing back from the financial and artistic misery of recent years. Among the most heartening signs are the variety of genres being mined and the crumbling of the artificial, media-created border between "young" and "old" – and both camps came up with interesting productions in the last year.

BARBARA HOLLENDER (b.hollender@rp.pl) is a Warsaw-based journalist and film critic for the daily *Rzeczpospolita* and covers the Berlin, Cannes and Venice festivals. She has co-written, with Zofia Turowska, the books *Stars in Zoom* and *Studio Tor*.

Zapasiewicz, Nikita Michalkow, Jerzy Stuhr, Andrzej Chyra. Prod: Krzysztof Zanussi, Iwona Ziulkowska-Okapiec, Studio Filmowe Tor/Leonid Vereschagin, Nikita Michalkow, Three T Productions/Sintra/ Telewizja Polska SA/ Canal+ Polska.

PO SEZONIE (After the Season)
[Drama, 2005] Script and Dir: Janusz Majewski. Phot: Witold Adamek. Players: Magdalena Cielecka, Leon Niemczyk, Ewa Wisniewska, Malgorzata Socha. Prod: Witold Adamek, Close Up/Wlodzimierz Niderhaus, WFDiF/Agencja Produkcji Filmowej.

RH+
[Thriller, 2005] Script and Dir: Jaroslaw Zamojda. Phot: Tomasz Dobrowolski. Players: Anna Przybylska, Robert Zoledziewski, Katarzyna Bujakiewicz, Michal Figurski. Prod: Ivona Karbowski, Krzysztof Karbowski, MCM Productions/Malgorzata Corvalan, INC(USA)/Da Vinci/ Agencja Produkcji Filmowej.

ROZDROZE CAFE (The Cross-Way Café)
[Drama, 2005] Script and Dir: Leszek Wosiewicz. Phot: Andrzej Ramlau. Players: Robert Olech, Maria Pakulnis, Jacek Rozenek, Dominika Markuszewska. Prod: Leszek Wosiewicz, Odysey Films/Maciej Karpinski, Andrzej Serdiukow, Telewizja Polska SA/Pawel Mossakowski, Malgorzata Retej, Canal+ Polska/Marek Trojak, Ryszard Sibilski, ITI Film Studio/Agencja Produkcji Filmowej.

TERAZ JA (It's Me Now)
[Drama, 2005] Script and Dir: Anna Jadowska. Phot: Robert Mleczko, Aleksander Jaquet. Players: Agnieszka Warchulska, Maciej Marczewski. Prod: Radoslaw Sts, Piotr Reisch, SPI International Poland/Telewizja Polska SA.

Portugal Martin Dale

The Year's Best Films

Martin Dale's selection:
Alice (Marco Martins)
Bullets and Biscuits
(Luís Ismael)
The Murmuring Coast
(Margarida Cardoso)
Magic Mirror
(Manoel de Oliveira)
I'll See You in My Dreams
(Miguel Ángel Vivas)

Sofia Apricio in
I'll See You in My Dreams

Recent and Forthcoming Films

ADRIANA
[Drama, 2004] Script and Dir: Margarida Gil. Phot: Rui Poças. Players: Ana Moreira, Vitor Correia, Bruno Bravo, Isabel Ruth. Prod: Take 2000.

ALICE
[Drama, 2005] Script and Dir: Marco Martins. Phot: Carlos Lopes. Players: Nuno Lopes, Beatriz Batarda, Miguel Guilherme, Ana Bustorff. Prod: Clap Filmes.

BALAS & BOLINHOS
(Bullets and Biscuits)
[Comedy, 2004] Script and Dir: Luís Ismael. Phot: Bruno Carvalho. Players: Fernando Rocha, Jorge Neto, Luís Ismael,

Notwithstanding the continuing dismal performance of Portuguese films at the local box office (a market share of less than 1%), there were definite signs of a new spirit in local cinema in 2004–05. State-funded films still found it hard to generate audiences, but several, in particular Marco Martins' *Alice*, suggested the emergence of a new wave of creative talent. Simultaneously, several micro-budget films produced without state funding sparked creative and commercial interest, including Luís Ismael's *Bullets and Biscuits* (43,000 admissions) and Fernando Fragata's *Rotten Luck* (70,000 admissions), which fared much better at the box-office than films funded by the national institute, ICAM.

Several thematic obsessions have characterised Portuguese cinema over the last three decades, including fatalism, pessimism, despair, solitude and suffering, tempered by eternal hope of redemption. Marco Martins' **Alice** explores such emotions in a highly innovative manner, the fruit of the director's background as assistant to Manoel de Oliveira and Wim Wenders, combined with his more recent experience as a commercials director. A haunting piano score by Bernardo Sassetti and lensing by Carlos Lopes help to transform Lisbon into a shadowy underworld through which anguished father Mario (Nuno Lopes) traipses in search of his missing four-year-old daughter, Alice.

Curiously, another local film, **A Shot in the Dark** (*Um tiro no escuro*), produced by Tino Navarro, also focuses on the search for a lost daughter. Directed by Leonel Vieira, it follows a Brazilian mother, Verónica (Vanessa Machado), whose newborn baby girl has been kidnapped. In order to find her, she moves to Portugal, gets a job in a strip club and becomes involved with bank robbers. However, the film tends towards the formulaic and was far less successful at the box-office than Navarro's string of local blockbusters from the late 1990s.

Branco rebuilds his team

Another key local producer who experienced difficulties was Paulo Branco, obliged to renew his stable of regular directors following the deaths of João Cesar Monteiro (February 2003) and José Álvaro Morais (January 2004), and the loss of talent to rival producers, in particular 96-year-old Manoel de Oliveira and young director Cláudia Tomaz. Branco's main productions in 2005 were *Alice* and **The**

Fatalist (*O Fatalista*) by João Botelho, a slow comedy about whether man or God controls the universe, adapted from an eighteenth-century novel, *Jacques le Fataliste* by Denis Diderot.

For many years now, de Oliveira has been considered the godfather of Portuguese cinema, casting a marked imprint on the pacing, aesthetics, characterisation and subject matter of national films. In 2004 he fell out with Branco, his long-time producer, publicly stating that "our personal relations had reached a point of no return", and switched to the fledgling, Oporto-based Miguel Cadilhe. Trained in London, Cadilhe produced Oliveira's latest work, **Magic Mirror** (*Espelho mágico*), which explores the themes of life, death and the world beyond, based on Agustina Bessa-Luis' novel *The Soul of the Rich*.

The Portuguese–French production team of Maria João Mayer and François d'Artemare is emerging as a powerhouse. Having cut their teeth on shorts, documentaries and line production, they are now responsible for a rising number of feature films. In 2004 the duo released two films, **The Murmuring Coast** (*A costa dos murmúrios*) and **Without Her** (*Sem ela*), both exploring Portuguese emigration. *The Murmuring Coast*, directed by Margarida Cardoso and based on the novel by Lídia Jorge, is an absorbing tale of mystery and violence during the final years of Portuguese colonial rule in Mozambique. It has a wonderful 1960s look and a commanding performance by Beatriz Batarda. *Without Her*, by Anna da Palma, is a vérité portrayal of the breakdown of a symbiotic relationship between two children of Portuguese emigrants to France. Madness, violence and abandonment also feature in João Pedro Rodrigues' *Odete*, about Rui (Nuno Gil), who mourns the death of his gay lover in a car crash, but the film fails to achieve the power of the director's debut work, *Phantom*.

Subsidy, who needs it?

The 2004-05 season saw a rising number of successful local films produced outside the traditional subsidy circuit. US-trained Fernando Fragata had a major box-office success in 1998 with his debut, *Sweet Nightmare*, but since then has found it impossible to secure government support. In desperation, he decided to embark on a self-funded, $150,000 film, **Rotten Luck** (*Sorte nula*). With the help of a major marketing campaign and support from niche cable channel SIC Radical, this rather lightweight tale of a luckless, lovestruck man on the run proved to be the year's biggest local hit.

Luís Ismael mortgaged his house to raise the $150,000 budget for **Bullets and Biscuits** (*Balas & bolinhos*). His "nonsense comedy" charts the adventures of four unlikely lads in search of buried treasure, who pimp, steal from church donation boxes, star in

J.D. Duarte. Prod: Associação de Artes Cinematográficas.

O FATALISTA (The Fatalist)
[Drama, 2005] Script and Dir: João Botelho. Phot: Edmundo Diaz. Players: Rogerio Samora, Andre Gomes, Suzana Borges, Rita Blanco. Prod: Madragoa Filmes.

THE HERO
[Drama, 2005] Script: Carla Baptista. Dir: Zeze Gamboa. Phot: Mario Masini. Players: Oumar Makena Diop, Milton Coelho (Santo), Patricia Bull. Prod: David & Golias.

I'LL SEE YOU IN MY DREAMS
[Horror, 2005] Script: Filipe Melo. Dir: Miguel Angél Vivas. Phot: Pedro J. Márquez. Players: Manuel João Vieira, João Didelet, Rui Unas, Sofia Aparício. Prod: Pato Profissional.

KISS ME
[Drama, 2004] Script: Vicente Alves do Ó. Dir: António de Cunha Telles. Phot: José António Loureiro. Players: Marisa Cruz, Manuel Wiborg, Nicolau Breyner. Prod: Animatográfo.

ESPELHO MÁGICO (Magic Mirror)
[Drama, 2005] Script and Dir: Manoel de Oliveira. Phot: Renato Berta. Players: Ricardo Trepa, Leonor Silveira, Luis Miguel Cintra, Michel Piccoli. Prod: Filbox.

UM SONHO DE UMA NOITE DE SÃO JOÃO (Midsummer Dream)
[Animation, 2005] Script and Dir: Manolo Gómez, Ángel da la Cruz. Players: Gabino Diego, Carmen Machi, Emma Penella, Gemma Cuervo. Prod: Dygra Films (Spa.)/Appia Films (Port.).

ODETE
[Drama, 2005] Script: João Pedro Rodrigues/Raulo Rebelo. Dir: João Pedro Rodrigues. Phot: Rui Pocas. Players: Ana Cristina de Oliveira, Nuno Gil, João Carreira. Prod: Rosa Filmes.

SORTE NULA (Rotten Luck)
[Crime mystery, 2005] Script, Dir and Phot: Fernando Fragata. Players: Helder Mendes, António Feio, Adelaide de Sousa, Rui Unas. Prod: XXX.

A RIVER
[Drama, 2005] Script: António Cabrita. Dir and Phot: José Carlos de Oliveira. Players: Anabela Moreira, Jorge Mota, Cândida Bila, Timótio Manganhela. Prod: Marginal Filmes.

Joaquim de Almeida in **A Shot in the Dark**

**UM TIRO NO ESCURO
(A Shot In The Dark)**
[Drama, 2004] Script: João Nunes. Dir: Leonel Vieira. Phot: Marcelo Durst. Players: Joaquim de Almeida, Vanessa Machado, Ivo Canelas, Miguel Borges. Prod: MGN Filmes.

SEM ELA (Without Her)
[Drama, 2004] Script and Dir: Anna da Palma. Phot: Tony Costa. Players: Aurélien Wiik, Bérénice Bejo, Vítor Norte, Maria Emília Correia. Prod: Filmes do Tejo.

Quote of the Year

"People are fed up with stories about drug-addicted mothers. I won't be the one to transform things, but I hope someone does so soon."
FILIPE DE MELO, *producer of* I'll See You in My Dreams.

cheap porno films and generally wreak havoc on innocent bystanders. With its Bollywood-style soundtrack and manic humour, the film appealed to some, but appalled others.

The motley quartet from **Bullets and Biscuits**

Portugal's first ever zombie movie, the 20-minute *I'll See You in My Dreams*, directed by Spanish-born Miguel Ángel Vivas, actually received a grant at the outset, but the original producer ran off with the money – obliging the film-makers to raise private financing. Slickly produced, with excellent special effects, the film's main twist is that the zombie killer has caged his former lover – now a zombie – and ultimately rejoins her in the realm of the undead.

At the level of film policy, ICAM still promises to launch an investment fund, which at press time looked as if it might be operational early in 2006. But several commentators were sceptical, given the recent change of government and the fact that this idea has been on the back burner for almost 10 years.

MARTIN DALE (formigueiro@mail.telepac.pt) has lived in Lisbon since 1994 and works as an independent media consultant. He has written several books on the film industry, including *The Movie Game* (Continuum, 1997).

Romania Cristina Corciovescu

The Year's Best Films

Cristina Corciovescu's
selection:

**The Death of Mister
Lazarescu** (Cristi Puiu)
**The Great Communist
Bank Robbery**
(Docu. Alexandru Solomon)
The Italian Girls
(Napoleon Helmis)
Ryna (Ruxandra Zenide)
The Children of the Decree
(Docu. Florin Iepan)

Forthcoming Films

INGERUL NECESAR
(The Necessary Angel)
*[Drama, 2006] Script and Dir:
Gheorghe Preda. Phot: Silviu
Stavila. Players: Anca Florea,
Emily Daller, Constantin
Florescu. Prod: MDV Film.*
A beautiful and mysterious
woman is tracked by a
stranger who sends her weird,
blue messages.

PACALA SE INTOARCE
(Pacala Returns)
*[Comedy, 2005] Script and
Dir: Geo Saizescu. Phot: Mihai
Malaimare jr. Players: Denis
Stefan, Anemona Niculescu,
Sebastian Papaiani, Valentin
Teodosiu, Magda Catone,
Georgiana Saizescu. Prod:
Nerv Film.*
The well-known folk hero Pacala
(the main character of a film made
by Saizescu in 1974) returns,
together with his son, Pacala Jr.
Both are silly, muddle-headed
people who constantly get into
trouble, but escape because they
are lucky.

The most important event of the year was the success of Cristi Puiu's **The Death of Mister Lazarescu** (*Moartea domnului Lazarescu*), which took prizes not only at Cannes, in Un Certain Regard, but also at other festivals in Copenhagen, Namur, Motovun, Reykjavik, Cluj, Alba Regia and Chicago. Puiu more than met the expectations created first by his short, *Cigarettes and Coffee* (*Un cartus de Kent si un pachet de cafea*) and then his debut feature, *Stuff and Dough* (*Marfa si banii*). Co-scripted by Puiu with Razvan Radulescu, the new film is an ambitious auteur piece that grips an audience for two hours, despite giving away its dénouement in its title.

Sixty-three-year-old widower Lazarescu (Ion Fiscuteanu) shares a flat with three cats and has only two surviving relatives, a sister in a distant town and a married daughter living in Canada. Puiu makes no attempt to create suspense, and there is no artifice. Rather, he captures the death of his ailing title character almost in a documentary manner. Taken ill one night, Lazarescu is shuttled from pillar to post in an ambulance, as the paramedic and the driver search for a hospital that will treat him, and the film unfolds like a road movie. Each of the three characters is given the space for a nuanced performance.

With cool realism, the film captures the hospital night shift and the routine fight for survival performed by medical personnel who, even if prone to casual inefficiency, still retain humanity. Although essentially a minimalist piece, with great attention to detail, the film

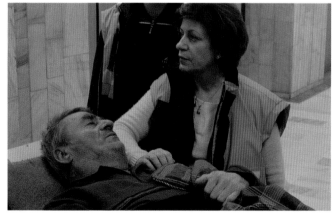

Ion Fiscuteanu, front, as the title character in **The Death of Mister Lazarescu**

LEGATURI BOLNAVICIOASE
(Love Sick)
*[Drama, 2006] Script: Cecilia
Stefanescu, based on her own
novel. Dir: Tudor Giurgiu. Phot:
Alexandru Sterian. Players:
Maria Popistasu, Ioana Barbu,
Tudor Chirila, Virginia Mirea,
Mihaela Radulescu, Tora
Vasilescu. Prod: Libra Film.*
The ambiguous relationships
(friendship, lesbian attraction,
incestuous feelings) between
three students – two girls and a
boy, the brother of one of them.

**CUM MI-AM PETRECUT
SFARSITUL LUMII (The Way
I Spent the End of the World)**
*[Drama, 2006] Script and Dir:
Catalin Mitulescu. Phot: Marius
Panduru. Players: Dorothea
Petre, Timotei Duma, Cristian
Vararu. Prod: Strada Film.*
In a suburb of Bucharest in 1989,
Eva, a beautiful and sensual
teenager, is in love with Vomica,
the spoiled son of a security agent.
When Vomica betrays her, Eva
discovers that the world
surrounding her is rotten.

DUPA EA (After Her)
*[Drama, 2006] Script: Lia Bugnar.
Dir: Cristina Ionescu. Phot:
Tudor Mircea. Players: Dragos
Bucur, Anca Florea, Valentina
Pelinel. Prod: Templefilm.*
A man with an accomplished
career and a happy family life
longs for an unknown woman
who leaves behind her only
suffering and death.

MARGO
*[Drama, 2005] Script: Ion
Carmazan, George Dogaru.
Dir: I. Carmazan. Phot:
Liviu Marghidan. Players:
Cristina Cioran, Paula Chirila,
Ilinca Harnut, Delia Nartea.
Prod: Eurofilm Art.*
Margo is a prostitute who likes
to "note" the most important
events of her life in a video-diary
(conflicts with her father, who is
also her pimp; relationships with
her clients; parties with her
friends). This cassette will
become a dangerous weapon.

finds room for colourful characters and a good deal of dry humour.
The moral balance and Puiu's refusal to judge people or
professions are other crucial qualities; no one is blamed or
absolved. Instead, the audience is left to reflect on how one learns,
often abruptly, that death is part of life.

The *Italian Girls* in tears

The massive success of Puiu's film in the national market is a good
sign for an industry that has recently started to advance more
coherently. As many as 16 Romanian feature premieres were
expected to have taken place by the end of 2005, with 11 more in
advanced stages of production. These have included first films by
younger directors. Names to watch include Napoleon Helmis with
The Italian Girls (*Italiencele*), a tragi-comedy about a group of
young women leaving to work in Italy and ending as prostitutes in
Kosovo, Ruxandra Zenide with **Ryna**, the drama of a teenager
abused by her father in a Danube delta village, and Florin Piersic Jr,
with **Reverse Angle** (*Fix alert*), made in the vein of Tarantino.

Older film-makers have been reasonably productive lately. Awarded
a Silver Lion in Venice in 1992, Dan Pita returns with two films:
Second Hand, about a teenager raped by a high-school
classmate, and **The Lady of My Dreams** (*Femeia visurilor*), the
drama of an ageing film-maker (maybe meant to represent Pita
himself), his women, dreams and nightmares. Consistent with his
"rough" and "angry" approach, Mircea Daneliuc delivers a new
satire of today's Romania, **The Nervous System** (*Sistemul nervos*).
After years spent in politics rather than film-making, Sergiu
Nicolaescu attempts to make up for lost time with two premieres:
Orient Express, the 1930s-set tale of a landowner who has retired
to the countryside after going bankrupt in Paris, and **15**, inspired by
the political events in Timisoara in 1989.

Documentary film-making also shows signs of improvement, with a
number of Romanian titles competing at major documentary festivals
and making an impact on the local market. Notable recent
productions include Alexandru Solomon's **The Great Communist
Bank Robbery** (*Marele jaf communist*), the elaborate reconstruction
of an event that stirred the spirits in 1950s Bucharest, namely the
hold-up of Romania's National Bank by Jewish former apparatchiks,
who were subsequently sentenced to death, and Florin Iepan's **The
Children of the Decree** (*Nascuti la comanda: Decreteii*), a more
journalistic approach to the tragic consequences of Nicolae
Ceausescu's birth-control policy between 1966 and 1989.

CRISTINA CORCIOVESCU (corcio@rnc.ro) is a film critic and the
author of several film dictionaries.

Russia Kirill Razlogov

The Year's Best Films

Kirill Razlogov's selection:
The Sun (Alexandre Sokurov)
4 (Ilja Khrzhanovsky)
First on the Moon
(Alexei Fedorchenko)
Dreaming of Space
(Alexei Uchitel)
Wild Beach
(Alexandre Rastorgujev)

Recent and Forthcoming Films

SOLNTSE (The Sun)
*[Historical drama, 2005] Script:
Yuri Arabov. Dir and Phot:
Alexandr Sokurov. Players: Issey
Ogata, Robert Dawson, Kaori
Momoi, Shiro Sano, Taijiro
Tamura. Prod: Igor Kalenov,
Andrey Sigle, Marco Muller,
Nikola-Film/Proline-Film/
Downtown Pictures (Italy)/Mact
Productions (France)/Riforma
Film (Switzerland).*

**VOKALNYIE PARALLELI
(Vocal Parallels)**
*[Musical drama/opera film, 2005]
Script: Renata Litvinova, Rustam
Khamdamov. Dir: Khamdamov.
Phot: Rifkat Ibragimov, Sergei
Mokritsky. Players: Renata
Litvinova, Erik Salim-Meruert,
Araksia Davtian, Rosa
Dzhamanova, Bibigul Tuligenova.
Prod: Galina Kuzembaeva, Gala-
TV/Kazakhfilm.*

**APOCRIF: MUZYCA DLYA
PETRA I PAVLA (Apocrypha:
Music for Peter and Paul)**
*[Drama, 2004] Script: Yury
Arabov. Dir: Adel Al-Khadad.
Phot: Andrey Shepelev. Players:
Andrei Savostianov, Albert
Filosov, Daria Mikhailova,*

The year 2005 confirmed the growing commercialisation of Russian cinema. The tremendous domestic success of Timur Bekmambetov's *Night Watch* (*Nochnoj dozor*) in 2004 was followed by Fox's large international release of a re-edited English version of the film in late 2005. Meanwhile, a new Russian blockbuster, **Turkish Gambit** (*Turetskij gambit*), grossed $18.5m domestically. This adaptation of Boris Akunin's historical detective story, directed by Dzhanik Fajziev (who, like Bekmambetov, also comes from television and, curiously, came to Moscow from Tashkent, capital of Uzbekistan), will probably have less international appeal than the universal horror of *Night Watch*. Both hits were produced and promoted by Channel One (Pervyj Kanal), Russia's biggest TV station.

The overall picture is dominated by the growth of theatrical distribution. There are now more than 1,000 modernised cinemas, including many multiplexes. From 2000 to 2005, annual box-office has grown from $7m to at least $350m. Even if the market share for Russian films remains relatively modest (around 10%), the regular presence of Russian films at the top of the hit parade is a major advance. Other recent hits include **Counsellor of State** (*Statskij Sovetnik*), another Akunin adaptation, starring Nikita Mikhalkov and filmed by young Filipp Yankovsky (son of the actor Oleg Yankovsky), which took $7.4m. That figure was almost matched by **Shadow Boxing** (*Boy s ten'yu*), a thriller set in the boxing world, by Alexei Sidorov, who became famous after directing the television super-hit *The Brigade* (*Brigada*). **Personal Number** (*Lichnyj nomer*), a political action movie by Evgeny Lavrentiev, made $4.6m, and **Dead Man's Bluff** (*Zhmurki*), a gangster parody by cult director Alexej Balabanov (*Brother, The River, The War*), also starring Nikita Mikhalkov, took $4.2m.

Then came **Reel it in and Split** (*$mat4vaj udochki*), a gangster comedy by Oleg Stepchenko ($3.1m), **The Escape** (*Pobeg*; $2.2m), a contemporary thriller by Egor Konchalovsky (son of Andrey Konchalovsky and nephew of Mikhalkov), Konstantin Bronzit's **Alyosha Popovitch and Tugarin Snake** (*Alyosha Popovitch i Tugarin Zmej*), an animated fantasy ($1.7m) and **From 180 and Higher** (*Ot 180 i vyshe*; $1.3m), a romantic and slightly erotic comedy by Alexandr Strizhenov (son of the famous actor Oleg Strizhenov). It is difficult to calculate the break-even for these films, because public

Alexander Feklistov. Prod:
Galina Melnik, Adel Al-Khadad,
Apocrypha Film Studio/Ministry
of Culture of Russia.
Peter Chaikovsky, a famous
composer, visits his sister at her
country estate.

UDALENNYI DOSTUP
(Remote Access)
[Drama, 2004] Script and Dir:
Svetlana Proscurina. Phot:
Alexandr Burov with the
participation of Sergei
Yurizditsky. Players: Dana
Agisheva, Alexandr Plaksin,
Elena Rufanova, Vladimir Ilyin,
M Fyodor Lavrov. Prod: Yuri
Obukhov, Kinoproba/ Maxim
Gorky's Studio/Ministry of
Culture of Russia.
Several years have passed since a
father rescued his son from the
boat accident that drowned his
wife and daughter.

TREBUETSYA NYANYA
(Babysitter Required)
[Psychological drama, 2005]
Script and Dir: Larisa Sadilova.
Phot: Anatoly Petriga. Players:
Marina Zubanova, Alexei
Makarov, Victori Isakova, Ira
Shipova, Raisa Ryazanova. Prod:
Vladimir Tyurin, Richmond.
A new babysitter causes trouble
for a happy family.

STATSKY SOVETNIK
(Counsellor of State)
[Detective drama, 2005] Script:
Boris Akunin. Dir: Philipp
Yankovsky. Phot: Vladislav
Opelyants. Players: Oleg
Menshikov, Nikita Mikhalkov,
Konstantin Khabensky, Vladimir
Mashkov, Oleg Tabakov,
Oksana Fandera. Prod: Leonid
Vereshchagin, TriTe/Channel
One Russia/Federal Agency for
Culture and Cinematography.
In the late nineteenth century,
the former Governor-General
of Siberia is murdered. Who
killed him?

PERVYIE NA LUNE
(First on the Moon)
[Pseudo-documentary, 2005]
Script: Alexander Gonorovsky,

Dmitry Dyuzhev and Alexey Panin in the comedy **Dead Man's Bluff**

support, private sponsoring and product placement make budgets
relative, and the grosses cited above are given out by producers and
distributors, without any independent verification.

The wave of action movies rolls on, from Vassily Chiginski's
Kremlin-financed political thriller, **Mirror Wars. Reflection 1**
(Zerkal'nye vojny. Otrazhenie 1), to the similar but more professional
Men's Season. Velvet Revolution (Muzhskoj sezon. Barkhatnaja
revolutsija) by Oleg Stepchenko. At press time, cinemas were
primed for the sequels Antikiller 3, Night Watch 2 and Boomer 2
(the release of the last two had been announced for September
2005, but was postponed until early 2006). All these films use
contemporary Russia as a setting, oscillating between Moscow and
the provinces, with occasional episodes in war zones such as
Afghanistan or Chechnya. Only the Akunin adaptations are set in
the distant past, specifically the late nineteenth century.

Arthouse diversity

In contrast to the thrillers and adventures, the arthouse productions
look elsewhere in time and place, with the notable exception of the
comic thriller sequel **Don't Cry, Mummy 2** (Mama ne goryui 2) by
Maxim Pezhemsky. The most ambitious film of the year, Alexander
Sokurov's **The Sun** (Solntse), portrays the Japanese emperor
Hirohito in post-war turmoil. This masterpiece, the best so far in
Sokurov's series devoted to dictators of the twentieth century (after
Hitler and Lenin, with a fourth to follow), was praised by Russian
critics but given a mixed reception elsewhere, sometimes
dismissed as "reactionary".

The winner of the top prize at the Moscow International Film
Festival, Alexei Uchitel's **Dreaming of Space** (Kosmos kak
predchuvstvie) was attacked by Russian critics but pleased the
international jury. This retro portrayal of the Soviet Union in the late
1950s had confused plot links and motivations, and became a
philosophical parable. The black-and-white feature debut of the
internet artist Sergej Loban, **Dust** (Pyl'), a science-fiction anti-

Issey Ogata in Alexander Sokurov's **The Sun**

utopian vision, was praised by young critics as a revolutionary breakthrough in post-modern film-making.

The success of a programme of "alternative" Russian films in Rotterdam (partly repeated at Moscow) stimulated the international success of a pessimistic, blackly comic modern saga about life in the Russian provinces (city and village compared), **4** by Ilya Khrzhanovsky. Other alternative (or "parallel", as they are usually called in Russia) pieces included **Bipedalism** (*Pryamokhozhdenie*), a science-fiction piece on the hybridisation of humans with animals, by Evgeny Yufit, and Tania Detkina's **The Rascal** (*Pakostnik*), a grotesque love and hate story set in a country house. At the other end of the spectrum we find Andrej Kravchuk's **The Italian** (*Ital'janets*), a touching story of a six-year-old boy searching for his real mother to escape being sold to an Italian family.

Soviet aesthetics

The national festival "Kinotavr" was resold by its founder, Marc Rudinstein, to the managers of the STS television network, but few changes were made (the only major one: no international festival at the same time as the Russian competition). As if to compensate for this absence, the main award was given to **Roots** (*Bednye rodstvenniki*) by Pavel Lungin, a Russian Jew living in France, for a tragi-comic story set in a Ukrainian province, identified in the film's synopsis only as "somewhere on the territory of ex-USSR". This was a very Soviet type of satire, indeed. A more conventional form of Soviet (almost socialist realist) aesthetics, still effective in a retro way, was proposed by actor, director and ex-MP Stanislav Govorukhin in **Not Only Bread** (*Ne khlebom jedinym*), an adaptation of a famous novel from the late 1950s by Vladimir Dudintsev.

Valery Ogorodnikov finally released his re-edited film version of a TV serial, **Red Sky. Black Snow** (*Krasnoe nebo. Chernyj sneg*), about wartime conflicts in unoccupied parts of Russia. More recent Near East wars interested Fyodor Bondarchuk (son of Sergei) in his much awaited directorial debut, **The 9th Company** (*Devjataja rota*).

Ramil Yamaleev. Dir: Alexei Fedorchenko. Phot: Anatoly Lesnikov. Players: Boris Vlasov, Victoria Ilyinskaya, Anatoly Otradnov, Alexei Slavnin, Andrey Osipov, Victor Kotov. Prod: Alexei Fedorchenko, Dmitry Vorobyev, Sverdlovsk Film Studio/SFS Films/Deya Toris/ Ministry of Culture of Russia. The heroic deeds and tragedies of the first Soviet cosmonauts.

PAKOSTNIK (The Rascal)
[Romantic tragi-comedy, 2004] Script and Dir: Tania Detkina. Phot: Dobrynya Morgachev. Players: Maxim Roganov, Svetlana Malysheva, Anton Privalov, Alexandra Ilienko, Yana Galina, Sergei Vishnevsky. Prod: Vyacheslav Mayasov, Alexander Gerasimov, Master-Film/Ministry of Culture of Russia.

MAMA NE GORYUI 2 (Don't Cry, Mummy 2)
[Dark comedy, 2005] Script: Maxim Pezhemsky, Konstantin Murzenko. Dir: Pezhemsky. Phot: Andrey Zhegalov. Players: Gosha Kutsenko, Andrey Panin, Evgeny Sidikhin, Alexander Bashirov, Fyodor Bondarchuk, Mikhail Efremov, Ivan Bortnik. Prod: Sergei Selyanov, CTB. Sequel to a popular dark comedy from 1997. In a northern coastal town, rivals fight for supremacy in a mayoral election.

KOSMOS KAK PREDCHUVSTSVIE (Dreaming of Space)
[Drama, 2005] Script: Alexander Mindadze. Dir: Alexei Uchitel. Phot: Yuri Klimenko. Players: Evgeny Mironov, Evgeny Tsyganov, Irina Pegova, Elena Lyadova. Prod: Alexei Uchitel, Rock/Federal Agency for Culture and Cinematography.

ZHMURKI (Dead Man's Bluff)
[Dark comedy, 2005] Script: Stas Mokhnachev, Alexei Balabanov. Dir: Balabanov. Phot: Evgeny Privin. Players: Alexei Panin, Dmitry Dyuzhev, Nikita Mikhalkov, Sergei Makovetsky,

Victor Sukhorukov, Dmitry Pevtsov, Alexander Bashirov. Prod: Sergei Selyanov, CTB. Two young bandits must decide whether to keep or give back a suitcase full of heroin.

BEDNYIE RODSTVENNIKI (Roots)
[Tragicomedy, 2005] Script: Gennady Ostrovsky. Dir: Pavel Lungin. Phot: Mikhail Krichman. Players: Konstantin Khabensky, Sergei Garmash, Leonid Kanevsky, Daniil Spivakovsky, Marina Golub, Natalia Koliakanova. Prod: Pavel Lungin, Catherine Dussart, Olga Vasilyeva, Onix. The hero specialises in tracing lost relatives. If he can't find the real person, he just organises a replacement...

4
[Absurd tragi-comedy, 2004) Script: Vladimir Sorokin. Dir: Ilya Khrzhanovsky. Phot: Alisher Khamidkhodzhaev, Alexander Ilkhovsky, Shandor Berkeshi. Players: Marina Vovchenko, Irina Vovchenko, Svetlana Vovchenko, Sergei Shnurov, Yuri Laguta, Konstantin Murzenko, Anatoly Adoskin. Prod: Elena Yatsura, Filmokom/DAGO-2000/ Hubert Bals Fund IFF Rotterdam/ Ministry of Culture of Russia. Before (or after) an industrial catastrophe, three people meet at a bar – a butcher, a piano tuner and a prostitute. A the same time, going to her sister's funeral, Marina, meets her other sisters.

DEVYATAYA ROTA (The 9th Company)
[Drama, 2005] Script: Yuri Korotkov. Dir: Fyodor Bondarchuk. Phot: Maxim Osadchy. Players: Mikhail Porechenkov, Alexei Chadov, Yuri Kolokolnikov, Dmitri Duhev, Nicolai Fomenko. Prod: Victor Glukhov, Elena Yatsura, Sergei Melkumov, Fyodor Bondarchuk, Stepan Mikhalkov, Art Pictures Group/PK "Slovo". The dramatic events of a young soldier's army life.

A surprise sensation was produced in Yekaterinburg. Alexej Fedorchenko, a documentary film-maker, made his feature debut, **First on the Moon** (*Pervye na Lune*), a pseudo-documentary about a space trip by Russians in the 1930s. It premiered at the Khanty-Mansijsk International Film Festival in Siberia, then went to Venice, where it got a provocative award for Best Documentary and was launched on to the international circuit.

This Yekaterinburg discovery highlighted the emergence of new film production centres, especially in regions rich in natural resources: petrol, gas or precious stones. Oil-rich Tatarstan hosted the first International Festival of Muslim Cinema to mark the 1,000th anniversary of its capital, Kazan. One of the awards here (and at Kinotavr) was given to the first feature film financed in (and by) this autonomous republic, Ildar Yagofarov's **Kuktau**, a sentimental journey of an adult and a child. A war film was produced in **Yakutia-Sakha**, a historic melodrama on Stalin's purges in Bashkortostan. This is a trend to be watched.

A documentary renaissance

Marina Razbezhkina with *Harvest Time* (2004) and Alexej Fedorchenko this year have proved that documentary film-makers can make competitive fiction features. Even if the curious but confusing mixture of genres in Georgi Gabelia's **Ten Commandments** (*Desjat' zapovedej*) was less successful, this trend is supported by a large number of interesting documentaries. The TV producer and director Vitaly Mansky produced a provocative chronicle of a beach near Krasnodar, **Wild Beach. The Heat of the Tender** (*Dikij pljazh. Zhar nezhnykh*), directed by Alexander Rastorgujev: six hours of pathetic horrors, ugly faces and bodies, comedies and tragedies in a popular, cheap holiday resort. Mansky himself directed **Our Motherland** (*Nasha rodina*), a search for his former high-school companions all over Russia and the world, which was more personal but less convincing.

The main award at the national documentary film festival in Yekaterinburg went to **A Season Without War** (*Mirnaja zhizn'*) by Pavel Kostomarov and the Frenchman Antoine Cattin. Their first film, *Transformer* (*Transformator*), had created a scandal in 2003 with its crude portrayal of everyday life and realistic dirty language. The same style dominates their new account of Chechens (father and son) trying to start a new life in a Russian village. It so shocked one of the heads of the Russian Union of Filmmakers that he resigned from the festival's board of management.

We also saw the successful use of more traditional genres, especially biographies of artists Sergej Paradzhanov, Marina Tsvetaeva, Arsenij Tarkovsky and Georgij Zhzhenov. Fiction films, documentaries and, to a lesser extent, animation show a growing diversity – a natural result of industry development and state support aimed at reaching annual production of 100 feature films from 2007. As regional and independent productions are not always included in official statistics, this target might even have been passed in 2005.

KIRILL RAZLOGOV (razlog@hotmail.com) is Director of the Russian Institute for Cultural Research and Programme Director of the Moscow International Film Festival. He has written 14 books on cinema and culture and hosts Kultura's weekly TV show, *Movie Cult*.

Director Ilya Khrzhanovsky found an audience with **4**

KOLYA – PEREKATI POLE (Nick – Roll a Field)
[Melodrama, 2005] Script: Georgy Nikolaev, Nikolay Dostal. Dir: Nikolay Dostal. Phot: Yuri Nevsky. Players: Andrei Zhigalov, Irina Rozanova, Alla Kluka, Sergei Batalov, Vladimir Tolokonnikov. Prod: Fyodor Popov.
The sequel to the film *Cloud-paradise* (1991). One day a casual phrase thrown at the witnesses has forced the main character to leave home and his beloved. 10 years have passed.

BOOMER 2
[Detective drama, 2005] Script and Dir: Piotr Buslov. Phot: Alexander Simonov. Players: Svetlana Ustinova, Vladimir Vdovichenkov, Andrei Merzlikin, Alexander Golubev, Nikolay Olyalin. Prod: Sergei Selyaniov, Sergei Chliyants, CTB/ Pigmalion Production.
Sequel to the hit thriller *Boomer* (2003) picks up on the original film's hero, who must keep his promise to a friend and make a journey.

GARPASTUM
[Historical drama, 2005] Script: Alexander Vainshtein, Oleg Antonov. Dir: Alexei German. Phot: Oleg Lukichev. Players: Chulpan Khamatova, Gosha Kutsenko, Evgeny Pronin, Danila Kozlovsky. Prod: Alexander Vainshtein.
Dramatic story about love, football and revolution during the First World War.

ALYOSHA POPOVITCH I TUGARIN ZMEY (Alyosha Popovitch and Tugarin Snake)
[Animated heroic comedy, 2004] Script: Maxim Sveshnikov, Ilya Maximov, Konstantin Bronzit. Dir: Bronzit. Prod: Alexander Boyarsky, Sergey Selyanov, Melnitsa/CTB.

Serbia & Montenegro Goran Gocic

The Year's Best Films

Goran Gocic's selection:
We Are No Angels 2
(Srdjan Dragojevic)
Red-Coloured Grey Truck
(Srdjan Koljevic)
South by Southeast
(Milutin Petrovic)
Made in Serbia (Docu.
Mladen Djordjevic)

Branislav Lecic as **A Devil's Warrior**

Recent and Forthcoming Films

BALKANSKA BRACA
(Balkan Brothers)
[Thriller, 2005] Script: Obrad Nenezic, Stevan Koprivica. Dir, Phot and Prod: Bozidar Bota Nikolic. Players: Petar Bozovic, Nikola Kojo.
Émigrés from ex-Yugoslavia end up in the Paris criminal underground.

CARLSTON ZA OGNJENKU
(Charleston for Ognjenka)
[Period comedy, forthcoming] Script: Srdjan Dragojevic, Stevan Koprivica, Biljana Srbljanovic, Uros Stojanovic. Dir: Stojanovic.

Even though cinema admissions are continuing to fall in Serbia, 2004 was still relatively stable. Since the price of tickets rose steeply, overall profits were higher than in 2003. A dozen domestic films found their way into production, nine of which entered theatres, and five ended up in the year's top 10, with the sixth, *Fall into Paradise!* being ranked 14th. Audiences, depressed by the problems of a society still in transition, gravitate towards anything that will cheer them up: five out of the six most popular local features were comedies

As a similar distraction from present woes, nostalgic movies are also in high demand, which may explain why a hybrid, the period comedy **Robbery of the Third Reich** (*Pljacka Treceg Rajha*), was 2004's top-grossing film. The only successful Serbian non-comedy of the season, the formulaic tearjerker **Goose Feather** (*Jesen stize dunjo moja*), set during the Second World War, was a period melodrama, high on nostalgia, about two young villagers who fall in love but are tragically separated. A grimmer Second World War drama, **Memo**, written and directed by newcomer Milos Jovanovic and backed by Kusturica's Rasta Films, never even reached theatres.

In the first months of 2005, Srdjan Dragojevic returned in big style with a sequel to his teenage comedy from 1992. In **We Are No Angels 2** (*Mi nismo andjeli 2*), an ageing womaniser, Nikola, once Belgrade's top stud, faces a mid-life crisis and tries to prevent his teenage daughter from dating. This was the only film of the season with a substantial budget (around €1m), 35mm cinematography, solid production values and aggressive advertising. It was Dragojevic's first feature for seven years and attracted more than 800,000 people.

Srdjan Koljevic, an experienced screenwriter, made his directing debut with the road comedy **Red-Coloured Grey Truck** (*Sivi kamion crvene boje*), in which a colour-blind Bosnian truck driver (Srdjan Todorovic) tries to make it through a surreal Serbian countryside. The movie generated good entertainment, reasonable business and an award for Todorovic. **Packing the Monkeys, Again!** (*Opet pakujemo majmune*) a contemporary urban comedy directed by a charming newcomer from Montenegro, Marija Perovic, played moderately in Serbia.

If they won't fund you...

Already in their 40s, Milutin Petrovic and Sasa Radojevic got tired of unsuccessful pitching and decided to make their films as a team on shoestring budgets – and to their taste. The results were two overtly intellectual attempts to change the landscape of local film-making. **Kisses** (*Poljupci*), scripted and directed by Radojevic and produced by Petrovic, is a contemplative, poetic family drama in the style of Eric Rohmer. **South by Southeast** (*Jug-jugoistok*), directed and produced by Petrovic and scripted by Radojevic, is a politically provocative, unusual conspiracy-theory thriller, a paraphrase of *Bunny Lake Is Missing*.

With the opening of the War Crimes Tribunal, Serbia was set on a path of reluctant remorse. **A Midwinter Night's Dream** (*San zimske noci*) directed by Goran Paskaljevic, reflected these events. A war veteran traumatised by the atrocities committed by his comrades during the war in Croatia represents the past, and a real-life autistic girl the future. The film won several awards, including a Special Prize of the Jury in San Sebastian, but its pessimism and national self-flagellation, alas, destroyed its prospects at the box-office. **Victims Are Thankful** (*Zrtve su zahvalne*) is even more pamphlet-like and was not shown in cinemas.

Other war-related features shared a similar commercial fate; audiences seemed by and large to have become tired of such subjects. Even Kusturica's **Life Is a Miracle**, which did well abroad, especially in France (around 800,000 admissions), significantly failed to meet domestic expectations. Likewise, contemporary drama **Awakening from the Dead** (*Budjenje iz mrtvih*) written and directed by experienced Milos Radivojevic, expresses more anger than remorse. Like **Balkan Brothers** (*Balkanska braca*), which focuses on the destinies of war émigrés abroad, caught up in crime, it belongs to a brand-new genre: post-war dramas. **Take a Deep Breath** (*Disi duboko*) was the very first Serbian lesbian melodrama, but audiences were not that impressed.

Svetozar Cvetkovic on location for **Awakening from the Dead**

Phot: Dusan Ivanovic. Players: Katarina Radivojevic, Sonja Kolarcic. Prod: Batric Nenezic, Marko Paljic, Mirjana Tomic/ Blue Pen.
A spell is cast on two village girls to prevent them getting married, but they head for town to find husbands at any cost.

EVROPA PREKO PLOTA (Europe Next Door)
[Docu-drama, 2005] Script, Dir and Prod: Zelimir Zilnik. Phot: Misa Milosevic, Jovan Milinov. Players: Suzana Vukovic, Roko Babickovic.

FLERT (Flirting)
[Omnibus comedy-horror, 2005] Script: Nikola Misic. Dir: Misic, Vladimir Popovic, Mladen Sevic, Radoslav Vojnovic. Phot: Ivana and Radoslav Vladic. Players: Srdjan Todorovic, Branko Vidakovic. Prod: BK Film Academy.
Two dead people visit Belgrade on a mission: bring back four youngsters.

IMAM NESTO VAZNO DA VAM KAZEM (I Have Something Important to Tell You)
[Drama, 2005] Script and Dir: Zeljko Sosic. Phot: Vladimir Vucinic. Players: Bojan Marovic, Dragan Nikolic. Prod: Branko Baletic.
A Montenegran musician says goodbye to friends and family before leaving to work abroad.

IVKOVA SLAVA (Ivko's Home Saint Day)
[Period drama, forthcoming] Script: Miroslav Momcilovic, Zdravko Sotra, from the novel by Stevan Sremac. Dir: Sotra. Players: Enis Beslagic, Dragan Bjelogrlic. Prod: Dragan and Goran Bjelogrlic, Cobra Films.

JESEN STIZE DUNJO MOJA (Goose Feather)
[Period melodrama, 2004] Script: Djordje Milosavljevic, Toni Matulic. Dir and Prod: Ljubisa Samardzic. Phot: Radoslav Vladic. Players: Branislav Trifunovic, Marija Karan.

KROJACEVA TAJNA
(Tailor's Secret)
[Thriller, forthcoming] Script and Dir: Milos Avramovic. Players: Goran Susljik, Marija Vickovic. Phot: Nemanja Jovanov. Prod: Lazar Ristovski, Zillion Films.
A lonesome tailor is haunted by a femme fatale, leading to murder.

OPTIMISTA (The Optimist)
[Drama, forthcoming] Script: Vladimir Paskaljevic, Filip David. Dir: Goran Paskaljevic. Phot: Milan Spasic. Players: Lazar Ristovski. Prod: Ristovski, Zillion Films.
A hypnotist travels around Serbia, selling hope to the desperate.

POGLED SA AJFELOVOG TORNJA (A View from the Eiffel Tower)
[Drama, 2005] Script: Nikola Vukcevic, Irina Kikic-Stojkovic, based on a novel by Branislav Glumac. Dir: Vukcevic. Phot: Nikola Sekeric. Players: Branislav Trifunovic, Lena Bogdanovic. Prod: Vukcevic, Ivan Djurovic, Milko Josifov, Janez Kovic, Novica Samardzic.
A doctor's daughter prostitutes herself to hurt her father.

SEJTANOV RATNIK
(A Devil's Warrior)
[Teen horror, forthcoming] Script: Marko Mrdjenovic, Stevan Filipovic, Natasa Vranjes. Dir: Filipovic. Phot: Katarina Velickovic. Players: Branislav Lecic, Danilo Beckovic, Svetlanda Bojkovic.
A resurrected Turkish warrior starts slaughtering Serbian teens.

Quote of the Year
"I was experimenting heavily with chemicals, but only in order to prepare for the study of technology."
SRDJAN TODOROVIC, *star of* Kusturica's Underground, *when asked about drug use, in magazine* Fama.

Home truths

A few film-makers, however, managed to spice up the season with docu-dramas. **Made in Serbia**, from film student Mladen Djordjevic, depicts the hilarious local porn scene and made it to theatres. Zelimir Zilnik continues to make politically conscious works on budgets similar to those of Petrovic and Radojevic, but with more exposure abroad. This season he launched **Europe Next Door** (*Evropa preko plota*), about the impact of Schengen passports on those living near the border with Hungary. It was to be shown in Cologne in late 2005, as a part of a programme dedicated to German guest-worker sub-culture. Boris Mitic's documentary festival hit, **Pretty Diana**, about resourceful gypsies and their hand-made transport, is still cruising the world, two years after it was shot (50 festivals, 20-plus prizes).

In early 2005, the government introduced strict implementation of PDV (the local version of VAT), which brought an additional 18% of expenses to the film industry. This brought a sudden halt to film-making, as producers expected support and concessions from the state, as in other countries in the region. The government responded quickly, and, in an attempt to fight DVD and CD piracy, reduced PDV to 8% on all newspapers and magazines offering giveaway books, CDs or DVDs. This quickly prompted the launch of several new film magazines, *Fama*, *DVD Mania*, *Neon*, and accompanied by cheap but legal DVDs (€2.5 to €3 euros each, instead of the usual €15). The pirates were partially defeated but the move did nothing to increase cinema admissions. However, the promising fact for the Serbian industry is that every third cinemagoer still chooses a domestic movie over a foreign one.

GORAN GOCIC (gocic@hotmail.com) is a broadcast and print journalist whose works have been published by more than 30 media outlets in seven languages. He is author of monographs on Andy Warhol and Emir Kusturica and is directing his first documentary, *Balkan Diaries: Bulgaria*.

Serbian émigrés are caught up in crime in **Balkan Brothers**

Singapore Yvonne Ng

The Year's Best Films

Yvonne Ng's selection

Be With Me (Eric Khoo)

Singapore GaGa
(Tan Pin Pin)

One More Chance
(Jack Neo)

The Maid (Kelvin Tong)

Bliss (Short. Victric Thng)

Alessandra De Rossi in **The Maid**

Recent and Forthcoming Films

BE WITH ME
*[Drama, 2005] Script: Eric Khoo,
Wong Kim Hoh. Dir: Khoo.
Phot: Adrian Tan. Players:
Theresa Chan, Ezann Lee,
Samantha Tan, Chiew Sung
Ching, Seet Keng Yew. Prod:
Jacqueline Khoo, Zhao Wei Films.*

CAGES
*[Drama, 2005] Script and
Dir: Graham Streeter. Phot:
Mark Lapwood. Players:
Tan Kheng Hua, Dickson Tan,
Makoto Iwamatsu, Zelda
Rubinstein. Prod: Tania Sng,
Aquafire Productions.*

THE MAID
*[Horror, 2005] Script and Dir:
Kelvin Tong. Phot: Lucas
Jodogne. Players: Alessandra De
Rossi, Chen Shucheng, Hong
Huifang, Benny Soh. Prod:*

The year 2005 started on a distressing note when Bertrand Lee, a promising director in his 20s, was seriously injured in January while filming in Mumbai, India. Other film developments were fortunately less tragic. **I Do I Do**, Jack Neo's romantic comedy, ushered in the Chinese New Year in early February with reflections on love, marriage and the country's declining birth rate. It features popular TV actors Sharon Au and Adrian Pang, who excels in his role as a rejected lover, but suffers from a contrived plot.

Neo's second 2005 movie was **One More Chance**, about the tribulations of three released prisoners attempting to re-integrate into the community. Co-directed with Toh Lan Sin, the $600,000 (S$1m) drama stars Neo regulars Mark Lee, Henry Thia and Marcus Chin. Darker than his usual comedies, it was prompted by Neo's discovery that an astounding 11,000 ex-convicts leave Singapore's rehabilitation centres each year, many struggling to gain social acceptance. This topic was addressed in Gerald Lee's *Twilight Kitchen* (2003), followed by a TV movie, *Coming Home* (2004). *One More Chance*, with Neo's characteristic mix of melodrama and comedy, will no doubt generate greater publicity for the cause, and strong ticket sales. At press time, Neo was busy with *I Not Stupid Too*, a sequel to his 2002 runaway hit *I Not Stupid*. Planned for release by the end of 2005, it explores the relationships between parents and their teenaged children.

Mediacorp Raintree Pictures co-produced **The Maid**, a $900,000 horror by former film critic Kelvin Tong, starring Filipino actress Alessandra de Rossi as a young maid working for a Singaporean couple and their mentally handicapped son. Arriving in Singapore at the start of the Chinese Seventh Month, when the souls of the dead roam among the living, she experiences ghostly encounters in her employers' dilapidated house. Less impressive than Raintree's earlier Asian horror co-productions *The Eye* and *The Eye 2*, *The Maid* was nevertheless a big hit, taking a record-breaking $450,000 during its opening weekend.

Unseen Singapore

Tan Pin Pin's 55-minute video featurette **Singapore GaGa** was an unconventional, delightful album of the sights and sounds of everyday life in Singapore – particularly those ignored, forgotten,

Daniel Yun/MediaCorp Raintree
Pictures/Media Development
Authority of Singapore/ Dream
Movie Entertainment Overseas
Limited (HK).

AI DU AI DU (I Do I Do)
*[Romantic comedy, 2005] Script:
Boris Boo. Dir: Jack Neo, Lim
Boon Hwee. Phot: Andy Yuen.
Players: Sharon Au, Adrian Pang,
Marcus Chin. Prod: Daniel
Yun/MediaCorp Raintree Pictures/
J Team Productions/Creative
Motion Pictures/ Kantana Motion
Pictures (Thailand).*

**XIAOHAI BU BEN 2
(I Not Stupid Too)**
*[Social comedy, 2006] Script: Jack
Neo and Rebecca Leow. Dir:
Neo. Phot: Ardy Lam. Players:
Shawn Lee, Joshua Ang, Ashley
Leong. Prod: Daniel Yun/
MediaCorp Raintree Pictures/
Scorpio East Entertainment.*

**SANGE HAO REN
(One More Chance)**
*[Drama, 2005] Script: He Qi An,
Jack Neo. Dir: Neo,
Michael Woo, Toh Lan Sin.
Phot: Chiu Wai Ying. Players:
Mark Lee, Henry Thia, Marcus
Chin. Prod: Boris Boo/J Team
Productions/Community Action
for the Rehabilitation of Ex-
offenders Network.*

SINGAPORE GAGA
*[Documentary, 2005] Script, Dir
and Prod: Tan Pin Pin. Phot:
Ryan Seet, Reu Loh, Tan Pin Pin.*

0430
*[Drama, 2006] Script: Liam Yeo,
Royston Tan. Dir: Tan. Phot:
Lim Ching Leong. Players: Xiao
Li Yuan, Kim Young Jun. Prod:
Zhao Wei Films.*

Quote of the Year

"It's very hard to make
anything critical in Singapore.
You have to say something
without actually saying it. So
it's a sort of shadow dance."

TAN PIN PIN, *on the making of*
Singapore GaGa.

marginalised or taken for granted: street buskers, the city's leading harmonica player, a veteran ventriloquist and radio broadcasters who read the news in Chinese dialects that fewer and fewer Singaporeans understand. This was a well-structured, amusing, yet serious documentary.

Another pleasant surprise was Eric Khoo's third feature in 10 years, **Be With Me**, inspired by an extraordinary and courageous deaf and blind woman in her 60s, Theresa Chan. She plays herself in this $120,000 production, which mixes fact and fiction in separate tales of hope, love and destiny. With less than one minute of dialogue, the stories revolve around an elderly couple separated by death, a security guard obsessed by an attractive woman and two teenagers involved in a lesbian relationship. Despite a certain awkwardness in integrating Theresa's story with the others, it remains a quietly powerful ode to love and chance. It opened the Directors Fortnight in Cannes 2005, where it received a standing ovation.

Director Eric Khoo, filming **Be With Me,** *with Theresa Chan*

New features for 2006 reflect an increasing trend towards international collaboration. *One Last Dance*, by Brazilian director Max Makowski, is a Chinese triad thriller produced by Raintree Pictures and Beijing-based Ming Productions, with a cast from Hong Kong, Singapore and Taiwan, and Harvey Keitel. **Cages**, produced by Singapore film-maker Tania Sng's Aquafire Productions and written and directed by American first-time feature director Graham Streeter, is a HD film about a single mother and her blind son who are forced to reunite with her father. Royston Tan's anticipated drama *0430* centres on the relationship between an 11-year-old Singaporean boy and a Korean man. This strategy of international partnerships seems to be reaping rewards. *One Last Dance* was pre-sold to Japan and France, while *Cages* premiered at the 2005 Pusan International Film Festival.

YVONNE NG (kinema@watarts.uwaterloo.ca) has written on Asian cinema and is on the editorial board of *KINEMA* (published at the University of Waterloo). She is the co-author of *Latent Images: Film in Singapore* (OUP, 2000) and *Latent Images: Film in Singapore CD-ROM* (Singapore, 2003).

Slovakia Miro Ulman

Recent and Forthcoming Films

O DVE SLABIKY POZADU
(Two Syllables Behind)
[Romantic drama, 2004] Script and Dir: Katarína Sulajová. Phot: Alexander Surkala. Players: Zuzana Sulajová, Miki Kren, Anna Ferenczy, Marek Majesky, Ivan Romancík, Richard Stanke, Lucia Hurajová, Matej Landl. Prod: Patrik Pass/Trigon Production/Slovenská Televízia/ Ceská Televize Brno (Czech Republic)/Ateliéry Bonton Zlín (Czech Republic).

KONECNÁ STANICA
(Terminal Station)
[Comedy, 2005] Script: Stanislav Stepka, based on his play. Dir: Jirí Chlumsky. Phot: Tomás Jurícek. Players: Zdena Studenková, Josef Somr, Anna Sisková, Josef Abrhám, Stanislav Stepka, Csongor Kassai, Diana Mórová, Eva Kerekesová, Lubo Paulovic, Katarína Kolníková, Marián Geisberg, Milan Lasica. Prod: Milan Stránava/JMB Film & TV Production/Slovenská Televízia/ Stúdio 727/RND.

SLNECNY STÁT
(The City of the Sun)
[Tragi-comedy, 2005] Script: Marek Lescák, Martin Sulík. Dir: Sulík. Phot: Martin Strba. Players: Oldrich Navrátil, Ivan Martinka, Lubos Kostelny, Igor Bares, Anna Cónová, Petra Spalková, Anna Sisková, Csongor Kassai. Prod: Cestmír Kopecky/První verejnoprávní (Czech Republic)/Titanic/Seská Televize – Televizní Studio Ostrava (Czech Republic)/ Cinemart (Czech Republic).

It seems that after many years of dreaming, Slovak cinema is finally waking up. Since the foundation of independent Slovakia in 1993, three feature films a year has been the average, but six have a copyright for 2005. In additon to the majority Slovak productions metioned below, the country has had a part in distinguished minority co-productions: Petr Zelenka's *Wrong Side Up* and *Lunacy* (see Czech Republic report) and Yvan Le Moine's *Friday or Another Day* (*Piatok alebo iny den*). November 2005 saw the conclusion of the shooting of three films and the launching of six more. This surge was brought about mainly by entry into the European Union, economic reforms and state assistance ($4.6m is promised for 2006).

The Sixth IFF Bratislava premiered and gave its Audience Award to **Two Syllables Behind** (*O dve slabiky pozadu*), the directing debut of Katarína Sulajová. The protagonist is a student of visual arts, who since childhood has earned a living as a dubbing actress. It is an attractive story of a young woman who has lent her identity to strange characters in a recording studio, while missing out on her own life. **Terminal Station** (*Konecná stanica*) is an absurd comedy based on a popular play by Stanislav Stepka. It follows the investigation into a murder commited at a small, abandoned train station and features fine Slovak and Czech actors. However, it would have been more enjoyable if watched on the TV screens for which it was originally made.

The City of the Sun (*Slnecny stát*) is the Slovak nominee for the Oscars in 2006. Martin Sulík's new movie follows four workers who wake up one day jobless. Since they consider it humiliating to register at the Unemployment Board or to retrain, they decide to go into business. But nothing is easy, either in business or in their relationships with their loving, quarrelling, sad wives and difficult offspring. The film holds up a mirror to today's society. The last premiere of 2005 was the full-length documentary **Here We Are** (*My zdes*), about a family who, after the split of the Soviet Union, decide to return to Slovakia, a land they know only from the tales of their parents. The new beginning brings more disilusionment than joy.

MIRO ULMAN (mulman@stonline.sk) is a freelance journalist. He works for the Slovak Film Institute and is a programmer for the Bratislava International Film Festival.

Slovenia Ziva Emersic

The Year's Best Films

Ziva Emersic's selection:
Labour Equals Freedom
(Damjan Kozole)
Gravehopping (Jan Cvitkovic)

Recent and Forthcoming Films

OD GROBA DO GROBA
(Gravehopping)
[Drama, 2005] Script and Dir: Jan Cvitkovic. Phot: Simon Tansek. Players: Gregor Bakovic, Natasa Matjasec, Domen Remskar, Brane Grubar, Zoran Dzeverdanovic, Vlado Novak. Prod: Staragara/ Slovenian Film Fund.
Pero (Bakovic), in his mid-30s, uses his considerable talent as a writer to concoct funeral speeches that reveal his philosophy, which often brings mourners to tears.

DELO OSVOBAJA
(Labour Equals Freedom)
[Black comedy, 2004] Script and Dir: Damjan Kozole. Phot: Ales Belak. Players: Peter Musevski, Natasa Barbara Gracner, Marjuta Slamic, Primoz Petkovsek, Manca Dorrer. Prod: Emotion Film/TV Slovenija/Slovenian Film Fund.
The small, sharply edged story of the mid-life crisis of Pero (Musevski, giving another of his brilliant, heartbreaking performances).

UGLASEVANJE (Tuning)
[Drama, 2005] Script: Igor Sterk, Sinisa Dragin. Dir: Sterk. Phot: Simon Tansek. Players: Peter Musevski, Natasa Burger, Polona Juh, Andraz Polic. Prod: A.A.C. Productions/TV Slovenija/Bela Film/Slovenian Film Fund.
Sterling production values and pitch-perfect performances from

Despite modest production of three or four long feature films per year, Slovenian cinema managed to remain stable and respectable in terms of international acclaim and home box-office results in 2004–05. The stability of production and the growing number of films is the result of new thinking by Slovenian producers, who have become far more daring, experienced and internationally oriented. The modest budget of the Slovenian Film Fund has made them seek co-producers beyond national borders, mainly in the former Yugoslavia and central Europe. The results include films such as *Red-Coloured Grey Truck*, backed by Slovenia, Serbia and Germany and directed by Srdjan Koljevic; *How I Killed a Saint* by Teona Strugar Mitevska, made in partnership with France and Macedonia, and *Well-tempered Corpses*, by director Benjamin Filipovic of Bosnia, made by Slovenia, France, Bosnia and Italy.

Despite some doubts about the justification of Slovenian minority participation in foreign projects (the question being "Where is the national interest if the story does not concern Slovenia?"), this tactic proved to be fruitful, and promising for the future. The post-production of all the films was carried out at Viba Studios in Ljubljana, which provides perhaps the strongest argument in favour of co-productions.

In 2005 three central figures of the middle generation of domestic film-makers presented their new films, which, for the first time in a long while, created a feeling of production continuity. The peak of the season was without doubt the Altadis Award at the San Sebastian Film Festival for Jan Cvitkovic's second movie, **Gravehopping** (*Od groba do groba*). A carefully orchestrated strategy in picking the right festival (Cvitkovic turned down a sidebar slot at Venice) proved successful, and the highest financial award ever for a Slovenian film-maker, €90,000, was his reward. Another internationally established director, Igor Sterk, completed his third feature, **Tuning** (*Uglasevanje*), which had its international premiere at Karlovy Vary. After the success of Sterk's *Express, Express*, which was the first Slovenian film to find German distribution, *Tuning* had been eagerly awaited by both festival selectors and domestic critics.

Damjan Kozole saw his seventh feature, **Labour Equals Freedom** (*Delo osvobaja*), screened at Locarno just after he became the first Slovenian director ever to see a retrospective of his films organised by the American Film Institute, in different parts of the US. He is also the first of his generation to have a film, *Spare Parts*, sold all over Europe for arthouse distribution.

Peter Musevski, centre, and Andrej Natigal in **Labour Equals Freedom**

Memories of Ljubljana

The veteran helmer Matjaz Klopcic finally saw his personal *Amarcord* completed this year: **Ljubljana the Beloved** (*Ljubljana je ljubljena*) is a memoir film, dedicated to Klopcic's native city, and set in the time of Italian and German occupation during the Second World War. Klopcic was one of the leading, then Yugoslav, directors in the 1960s and 1970s, who openly admired and supported modern European film-making, especially the French new wave. His films were often accused of being too hermetically sealed and artistic, but he surprisingly went on to direct the most popular film of Slovenian cinema ever, the drama-turned-national-icon *Flowers of Autumn*.

All in all, 2005 saw some surprising twists and turns in Slovenian cinema, reflecting the enormous hunger for film-making among all generations of directors and scriptwriters. Besides the trend towards increased international co-operation, there is also a noticeable creative movement in alternative, privately funded production, surprisingly backed by the local distributors and cinema owners. For example, the low-budget black drama **Bullets Miss the Fool**, by Mitja Novljan, dared to prove its credibility with domestic audience and was greeted with enthusiasm by the younger generation.

ZIVA EMERSIC (Ziva.Mali@rtvslo.si), a journalist and film critic, is a former director of the Slovenian National Film Festival in Portoroz, and currently commissioning editor of the Documentary Programme at TV Slovenia.

Musevski (again proving himself Slovenia's finest actor) and Burger as a married couple becalmed in the waters of complacency and disguise.

LLUBLJANA JE LLUBLJENA (Ljubljana the Beloved)
[Drama, 2005] Script and Dir: Matjaz Klopcic. Phot: Tomislav Pinter. Players: Kristijan Gucek, Iva Krajnc, Natasa Barbara Gracner, Igor Samobor, Ivanka Mezan, Polde Bibic. Prod: ArsMedia/Slovenian Film Fund.
The first expensive costume drama in Slovenia in many years.

ESTRELITA
[Drama, 2006] Script: Metod Pevec, Abdulah Sidran. Dir: Pevec. Prod: Vertigo/Emotion Film/Media Plus.
After her famous husband's death, a widow discovers that he has been cheating on her.

TRAKTOR, LJUBEZEN IN ROCK'N'ROLL (A Tractor, Love and Rock'n'Roll)
[Comedy, 2005] Script: Branko Djuric, Feri Lainscek, Miroslav Mandic. Dir: Djuric. Phot: Sven Pepeonik. Players: Djuric, Jernej Kuntner, Vlado Novak, Tanja Ribic, Vlado Kreslin. Prod: ATA d.o.o.
A rural love story and some tales of power and prejudice.

KARAULA (Border Post)
[Black comedy 2006] Script: Rajko Grlic, Ante Tomic. Dir: Rajko Grlic. Prod: Vertigo/ Emotion Film.
The story of a border post at the Albanian border in the early 1990s.

L... KOT LJUBEZEN (L... like Love)
[Drama, forthcoming] Script: H. Ambrost, T. Kocynsky, D. Dukovsky. Dir: Janja Glogovac. Phot: Igor Luther. Players: Lucija Serbedzija, Rade Serbedzija, Ksenija Misic, Labina Mitevska, Tommy Flanagan. Prod: Richard Nemec/Fabula/Slovenian Film Fund.

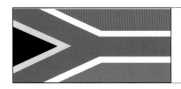

South Africa Martin P. Botha

The Year's Best Films

Martin Botha's selection:
Tsotsi (Gavin Hood)
Hotel Rwanda (Terry George)
Born into Struggle
(Docu. Rehad Desai)
A Trade of Cultures
(Docu. Wynand Dreyer)
Max and Mona
(Teddy Mattera)

*Mpho Lovinga and the goat, Mona,
in* **Max and Mona**

Recent and Forthcoming Films

A TRADE OF CULTURES
*[Documentary, 2004] Script:
Wynand Dreyer, Nina Allchurch.
Dir: Dreyer. Phot: Chris Lotz.
Prod: Wynand Dreyer/
African Mirror.*

A Swahili woman in **A Trade of Cultures**

THE FLYER
*[Drama, 2005] Script: Phillip
Roberts, Revel Fox. Dir: Fox.
Phot: Robert Malpage. Players:
Jarrid Geduld, Ian van der
Heyden, Marcel van Heerden,*

In the 18 months to August 2005, South African features, documentaries and shorts won more than international awards, not to mention the Oscar Nomination for Best Foreign-Language film for Darrell Roodt's *Yesterday* (reviewed in *IFG 2005*). At the 55th Berlinale, Mark Dornford-May's **Carmen in Khayelitsha** (*U-Carmen eKayelitsha*), an adaptation of Georges Bizet's opera set in the Cape Town township of Khayelitsha and sung in Xhosa, was a surprise winner of the Golden Bear. By transferring the larger-than-life characters and their torments to a set of shacks at the Spier Estate near Cape Town, Dornford-May seldom succeeds in integrating documentary-style shooting with the stylised nature of opera. The characterisation is also unconvincing and the acting mediocre. The best ingredient is Giullio Biccari's mobile, inquisitive camerawork.

Apartheid, past and present

South African struck further gold at FESPACO. Zola Maseko's feature debut, **Drum**, a visually stunning chronicle of South Africa during the 1950s, won the Golden Stallion. Drum depicts life in Sophiatown before the apartheid government bulldozed this beacon of non-racialism and focuses on Henry Nxumalo (America's Taye Diggs), a reporter for *Drum* magazine, and his reports on the slave camps at Bethal Farm. Diggs is fine, but the script is spoiled by clichés and anachronisms (local critics questioned the film's claims to historical authenticity) and ultimately the best thing about *Drum* is its wonderful art direction, which deservedly won the Prix du Meilleur Décor at FESPACO. *Drum* also won a Silver Dhow and the FIPRESCI Prize at Zanzibar 2005.

Ramadan Suleman's contemporary drama **Zulu Love Letter** won several awards at FESPACO, including Best Actress for Pamela Monvete Marimbe. Tormented by the haunting images and grief of the apartheid past, single mother and journalist Thandi (Marimbe) has difficulty communicating with her estranged daughter, Mangi, 13, who was born deaf and dumb following the beating that the pregnant Thandi received at hands of the apartheid hit squad who murdered some of her friends. Suleman's film offers some potent drama, but ultimately fails because it tackles too many issues without dealing with all of them adequately.

Far more satisfying on a narrative and aesthetic level is first-time director Teddy Mattera's **Max and Mona**, which won the Prix Oumarou Ganda at FESPACO. It is one of the few black comedies to emerge from South Africa: a perfectly balanced combination of grief, love and death. Max is treasured by his village because he has inherited an extraordinary gift as a professional mourner. Invoking the ancestors, Max can reduce the stoniest heart to tears. He must, however, follow his calling to study medicine in Johannesburg, where he realises that he cannot pay his study fees on time, and is saddled with a complaining sacred goat, Mona. Max tries to get money from his uncle Norman, who agrees on condition that Max uses his talents at various city funerals. Mattera and co-writer Greg Latter deservedly won Best Screenplay at the 2004 Cape Town World Cinema Festival.

Gangs of Jo'burg

The most outstanding two features of the past year were Gavin Hood's *Tsotsi* and Terry George's Oscar-nominated **Hotel Rwanda**. The latter depicts with great power the story of Paul Rusesabagina and his attempts to save the lives of Tutsi refugees during the Rwanda genocide of 1994. Another South Africa/UK co-production, **Tsotsi**, made history at the 2005 Edinburgh Film Festival by becoming the first film in more than seven years to win both the Standard Life Audience Award for most popular film and the Michael Powell Award for Best Film. It then scooped the People's Choice Award at Toronto.

Based on the only novel written by Athol Fugard, it depicts the story of a young boy orphaned at the age of nine and forced to claw his way to adulthood in the sprawling, violent townships of Johannesburg, forever living in the moment. An impromptu car-jacking, which results in the accidental kidnapping of an infant, forces him to confront his own humanity. The film is an emotive and powerful journey in which Tsotsi learns to confront the demons of his past while coming to terms with his destiny. *Tsotsi* was chosen as South Africa's entry for the 2006 Academy Awards.

Left to right: gang members Tsotsi (Presley Chweneyagae), Boston (Mothusi Magano), Butcher (Zenzo Ngqobe) and Die Aap (Kenneth Nkosi) in **Tsotsi**

Kim Engelbrecht. Prod: Jeremy Nathan, Joel Phiri (DV8)/ Michelle Wheatley.

HOTEL RWANDA
[Drama, 2004] Script: Keir Pearson, Terry George. Dir: George. Phot: Robert Fraisse. Players: Don Cheadle, Sophie Okonedo, Joaquin Phoenix, Nick Nolte. Prod: Alex Ho, Terry George/ Miracle Pictures/Seamus Prods/ United Artists.

DRUM
[Period drama, 2004] Script: Jason Filardi, Tim Grimes, Zola Maseko. Dir: Maseko. Phot: Lisa Rinzler. Players: Taye Diggs, Tumisho Masha, Moshidi Motshegwa. Prod: Dumisani Dlamini, Rudolf Wichmann (Nova Films), Chris Sievernich, Matt Milich/Armada Pictures International/Jason Filardi, Andreas Grosch, Andreas Schmid.

FAITH'S CORNER
[Drama, 2005] Script & Dir: Darrell James Roodt. Phot: Michael Brierley. Players: Leleti Khumalo, Thobani Khubeka, Sibonelo Xulu. Prod: Anant Singh, Helena Spring, Videovision/Distant Horizon.

MAX AND MONA
[Comedy, 2004] Script: Teddy Mattera, Greg Latter. Dir: Mattera. Phot: Ivan Leathers. Players: Mpho Lovinga, Jerry Mofokeng, Percy Matsemela, Thumi Melamu, Coco Merckel. Prod: Jeremy Nathan, Joel Phiri/ DV8/Icemedia.

RED DUST
[Drama, 2004] Script: Troy Kennedy-Martin. Dir: Tom Hooper. Phot: Larry Smith. Players: Hilary Swank, Jamie Bartlett, Marius Weyers, Ian Roberts, Chiwetel Ejiofor. Prod: Anant Singh, Helena Spring, Videovision/Ruth Caleb, David M. Thompson, BBC Films.

TSOTSI
[Drama, 2005] Script and Dir: Gavin Hood. Phot: Lance Gewer. Players: Presley Chweneyagae, Mothusi Magano,

Kenneth Nkosi, Ian Roberts.
Prod: Peter Fudakowski/The UK
Film & TV Production Company/
Paul Raleigh/ Moviworld.

Pauline Malefane as the heroine of
Carmen in Khayelitsha

U-CARMEN eKHAYELITSHA
(Carmen in Khayelitsha)
[Musical drama, 2005] Script:
Mark Dornford-May, Andiswa
Kedama, Pauline Malefane.
Based on the opera by Georges
Bizet. Dir: Dorford-May. Phot:
Giullio Biccari. Players: Pauline
Malefane, Andile Tshoni, Zorro
Sidloyi. Prod: Ross Garland,
Mark Dornford-May/Nandi's
Art Institute in association with
Spier Films.

ZULU LOVE LETTER
[Drama, 2004] Script: Bheki
Peterson, Ramadan Suleman.
Dir: Suleman. Phot: Manuel
Teran. Players: Pamela Nomvete,
Mphumi Malatsi, Connie Mfuku,
Patrick Ndlovu, Patty Patience,
Kurt Egelhof. Prod: Bheki Peterson
(South Africa), Jacques Bidou,
Marianne Dumoulin (France).

Quote of the Year

"South Africa's golden age of
film appears to be dawning."
THABO MBEKI, *jubilant South*
African President, after Drum's
success at FESPACO 2005.

Tom Hooper's **Red Dust** is one of three recent features (the others are John Boorman's *In My Country* and *Zulu Love Letter*) to deal with the Truth and Reconciliation Commission. New York lawyer Sarah Barcant (a quite wooden Hilary Swank) becomes the hero when she returns home to represent a local community at a TRC hearing for a former apartheid police officer. As with *In My Country*, American heroes save the day and the traumatic past of South Africa is reduced to a mere backdrop.

The biggest local hit at the box-office in 2004 was once again a slapstick comedy by Leon Schuster. **Oh Schucks I Am Gatvol** consists of loosely structured gags about life in the new South Africa. Any attempt at satire is overshadowed by the lavatory humour and candid camera footage. But South Africans seemed to like it, since it grossed an amazing R23m.

Two outstanding documentaries towered above other local productions: Rehad Desai's **Born into Struggle** and Wynand Dreyer's **A Trade of Cultures**. Desai's film is a very moving, intimate portrait of his relationship with his political activist father, Barney, and brilliantly captures pain, conflict and love across three generations. Dreyer's visually stunning portrait of the Swahili people on the east coast of Africa is greatly enhanced by the glorious images of Mombasa, captured by cinematographer Chris Lotz.

Lastly, some award-winning short films: most notable is the work by Thabang Moleya, a graduate of the City Varsity Film and Television School. His *Case 474* takes a look at the relationship between Siyabonga, a hardened criminal, and his defense lawyer, Kate, a young, white privileged woman. His other short, *Portrait of a Dark Soul*, won the Jameson Award for Best Short at Cape Town 2004. Here, Moleya again examines the impact of our past on our current mental state, through the tale of a group of gangsters in the aftermath of a failed robbery. There is a raw honesty to his short films and he is an important new voice. Equally impressive is the work of another City Varsity student, Nina Mnaya, who won several awards for her short, *Life Is Hard*, a strongly told day-in-the-life of a struggling black man.

Dr MARTIN P. BOTHA (martinbotha@telkomsa.net) has published more than 200 articles and reports and several books on South African and African cinema. He is working on a historical dictionary of African cinemas and a book on director Jans Rautenbach.

South Korea Nikki J. Y. Lee

The Year's Best Films

Nikki J. Y. Lee's selection:
Sympathy for Lady Vengeance (Park Chan-wook)
The President's Last Bang (Im Sang-soo)
Marathon (Jung Yun-chul)
Blood Rain (Kim Dae-seung)
This Charming Girl (Lee Yun-gi)

Cha Seung-won in **Blood Rain**

Recent and Forthcoming films

MUYOUNGGUM
(Shadowless Sword)
[Martial arts epic, 2005] Script: Kim Taeo-Gwan, Shin Jun-hee. Dir: Kim Young-jun. Phot: Seo Gun-hee. Players: Yun So-y, Lee Seo-jin, Shin Hyun-jun. Lee Gi-yong. Prod: Park Soo-yeon, CJ Entertainment/New Line Cinema/ Taewon Entertainment.
In 926 AD, the best female warrior of Balhae, an ancient Korean kingdom, is dispatched to Gueran to bring back a lost prince.

GWANGSIG-I DONGSAENG GWANGTAE (Gwang Brothers)
[Romantic comedy, 2005] Script

The instability and unpredictability accompanying the rapid recent growth of South Korean cinema have kept the local film industry alert to its uncertain future. The statistics for 2004–05 and the list of local box-office hits signal that the industry is entering a relatively stable period, although a handful of problems pose new challenges. The domestic market share reached almost 60% in 2004 and in 2005 maintained levels above 50%. Most worrying for industry executives, however, was the fact that while theatrical admissions grew by 13% in 2004, they fell back by 6.2% during the first three quarters of 2005. This was chiefly because 2005's South Korean films could not match the performance of *Taegukgi* (*Taegukgi hwinalrimyeo*) and *Simildo* (*Shilmido*), which had both drawn more than 10 million admissions each. According to the Korean Film Council, admissions for local films dropped by 13.5% while admissions for foreign films grew by 3.8% between January and September 2005. Yet local films' market share in August, September and October hit 70%.

The big news of 2004–05 may be the success of mid-budget genre films, compared to the relatively low box-office returns of local blockbusters such as Song Hae-sung's **Rikidozan** (*Yeokdosan*), which opened in December 2004, and **Antarctica Journal** (*Namguk ilgi*), released in May 2005. *Rikidozan*, a biopic about the legendary Korean–Japanese pro wrestler Rikidozan, was shot in Japan with a mostly Japanese cast and prominent Korean actor Sol Gyung-gu (*Peppermint Candy*, *Oasis*, *Public Enemy*) in the title role. It drew approximately 1.4 million admissions nationwide. Another big Sidus project, Im Pil-sung's *Antarctica Journal*, about a Korean expedition to the South Pole, drew only 1.1 million admissions.

The Korean War fantasy **Welcome to Dongmakol** *was a huge hit in 2005*

and Dir: Kim Hyun-seok. Phot: Choi Jin-woong. Players: Kim Ju-hyuk, Bong Tae-gyu, Lee Yo-won, Kim A-jung, Jung Gyung-ho. Prod: Shim Jae-myung, Lee Wu-jeong, MK Pictures.
Gwangsik is extremely shy with women, while his younger brother, Gwantae, is a mindless playboy. This sweet, romantic story shows the brothers learning how to love women.

NA-EU GYULHON WONJUNGGI
(My Wedding Campaign)
[Romantic comedy-drama, 2005] Script: Hwang Byung-guk, Yun Sun-yong, Choi Jong-hun. Dir: Hwang. Phot: Lee Du-man. Players: Jung Jae-young, Yu Jun-sang, Su Ae, Park Gil-su, Jeon Sang-jin, Gwon Tae-won, Kim Seong-gyum. Prod: Hwang Wu-hyun, Hwang Jae-woo, Tube Pictures/Don Quixote Holdings.
Mantaek, a single desperate farmer in his late 30s, goes to Uzebekistan on a group tour to find a bride.

YONGSEO BUTJI MOTHAN JA (The Unforgiven)
[Drama, 2005] Script and Dir: Yun Jong-bin. Phot: Kim Byung-chul. Players: Ha Jeong-wu, Seo Jang-won, Yun Jong-bin, Im Hyun-sung, Han Seong-chun. Prod: Yun Jong-bin, A&D Pictures.
A bitter story of conscripted soldiers in an army whose absurd rules and inhumane disciplines eat up young souls.

DASUT-EUN NEMU MANA (Five Is Too Many)
[Drama, 2005] Script and Dir: Ahn Sul-gi. Phot: Kim Han-sol. Players: Cho Si-nae, Yu Hyung-gun, Kim Do-gyun, Choi Ga-hyun. Prod: Ahn Sul-gi, Ssial Film.
Four people who are not tied by any blood relationship live together and get along better as a pseudo-family than many a real family.

TAEPUNG (Typhoon)
[Action epic, 2005] Script and Dir: Gwak Gyung-taek. Phot:

More modest films blossomed, all dealing with diverse themes in refreshing ways. Jung Yun-chul's **Marathon** (*Mal-aton*), about a young runner suffering from autism, was the biggest hit in the first half of 2005, drawing more than five million admissions. Its record was broken by Park Kwang-hyun's **Welcome to Dongmakgol** (*Welcome tu dongmakgol*), set during the Korean War. Like *Shiri* (1999) and *Joint Security Area* (2000), *Welcome to Dongmakgol* touches upon sensitive historical issues, such as the division of North and South Korea. This humanist fantasy entertainment depicts a small village as a utopian space where the peaceful reconciliation of soldiers from both sides is possible.

These unexpected successes enabled distributor Showbox/Mediaflex to take a 21.6% market share, surpassing the two dominant companies, CJ Entertainment (19.7%) and Cinema Service (12.3%), which face another potential competitor in MK Pictures, a leading new production company that has launched a distribution arm and international sales agency.

Best served cold

Internationally established auteur directors also contributed to the blossoming of films from diverse genres. Park Chan-wook's **Sympathy for Lady Vengeance** (*Chinjulhan gumjassi*), the last segment of his revenge trilogy, drew fanatical media attention upon release in July 2005. Attracting 3.6 million admissions, this tale of one young woman's revenge and salvation after 13 years' imprisonment is at times rather unkind to its audience (the literal translation of the Korean title is "Kind Miss Gumja"). This high-ranking box-office position confirms the popularity of Park and the star power of Lee Young-ae, now a pan-Asian TV star, who successfully turned herself into the strange but stylish Gumja.

Tartan Films

Lee Young-ae as the heroine of **Sympathy for Lady Vengeance**

By contrast, Hong Sang-soo's **Tale of Cinema** (*Gukjangjeon*), another strange love story of the type now familiar as Hong's "brand", and Kim Ki-duk's **Bow** (*Hwal*) failed to impress local moviegoers, drawing just 41,000 and 1,500 admissions respectively. Kim Ki-duk Film produced and distributed the latter, screening it in only one venue and neglecting to organise a preview for journalists. At the same time as it was announced that Kim was going to be given the Vittorio De Sica Award in Italy, he seemed to be more detached from local audiences than ever before.

A number of other well-made, modest films also did good business. Taken together, they deal with uneasy Korean men who must fight desperately for love and life. For example, the boxers in Ryu Seung-wan's **Crying Fist** (*Jumuggi unda*) have their own reasons to win. One old and wrecked boxer has to fight his last bout in the hope of being reunited with his son, while his opponent is a young man who discovers the first hope in his life while boxing in prison. In Kim Ji-woon's **A Bittersweet Life** (*Dalcomhan insaeng*), a low-ranking gangster has to fight for survival against the twisted turns of his destiny. In Jang Jin's **The Big Scene** (*Baksu chilttae ttenara*), a prosecutor has to fight against the prime suspect in a murder case, while the proceedings are broadcast on live television. Among a group of melodramas released in the autumn, Park Jin-pyo's **You're My Sunshine!** (*Nenun nae wunmyung*) disarms audiences with its sad story of one farmer's dedicated love for a woman accused of intentionally spreading the HIV virus.

Painting on a vast canvas

Epic historical dramas have also become an important genre in contemporary local cinema. Following the success in 2004 of E.J-yong's *Untold Scandal*, several other attractive period films embellished with imaginative elements were released. Kim Dae-seung's **Blood Rain** (*Hyul-eu nu*) is a mystery thriller set in nineteenth-century Chosun. Its plot, hinging on a series of murders that occur across five consecutive days, and the arguments among the main characters all reveal this as an eloquent adaptation of Umberto Eco's *The Name of the Rose*. The tightly knit narrative structure and the economic editing guarantee intelligent fun through Sherlock Holmes-style investigations. The Chosun period is viewed through the prism of Eco's European Middle Ages, creating a seemingly real but imaginary historical space.

Im Sang-soo's **The President's Last Bang** (*Guttae gusaramdul*) reflects another constant trend of South Korean cinema: its look back at the 1970s and the 1980s – the country's darkest period under military dictatorship. Refusing to adopt a nostalgic or sentimental tone, Im delves into the events that occurred one night

Hong Kyung-pyo. Players: Jang Dong-gun, Lee Jung-jae, Lee Mi-yeon. Prod: Park Sung-gun, Yang Jung-gyung, Jininsa Film.
The conflict between Sin, a pirate, and Kang Se-jong, an officer of the Korean navy.

YASU (Running Wild)
[Action-noir, 2005] Script and Dir: Kim Sung-soo. Phot: Choi Sang-muk. Players: Yu Ji-tae, Kwon Sang-woo, Sohn Byung-ho, Um Ji-won. Prod: Jung Oh-young, Popcorn Film Inc.
A sharp prosecutor and a wild detective pursue a powerful and seemingly untouchable gang boss.

CHEONGYEON (Blue Swallow)
[Biopic, 2005] Script and Dir: Yun Jong-chan. Phot: Yun Hong-sik. Players: Jang Jin-young, Kim Ju-hyuk, Nakamura Toru, Yu Min, Han Ji-min. Prod: Choi Sung-soo, Korea Pictures.
In the 1920s, a Korean woman goes to Japan with a dream of becoming a pilot.

WANG-EU NAMJA (King and the Clown)
[Epic drama, 2005] Script: Choi Suk-hwan. Dir: Lee Jun-ik. Phot: Ji Gil-wung. Players: Gam Woo-sung, Jung Jin-young, Gang Sung-yeon, Lee Jun-gi, Jang Hang-sun, Yu Hae-jin. Prod: Jung Jin-wan, Lee Jun-ik, CineWord Inc./Eagle Pictures.
In the late 1400s, two street clowns become King Yeonsan's private palace entertainers. Every time they perform, blood and death follow.

YUWOL-EU ILGI (Diary of June)
[Detective thriller, 2005] Script: Ko Jung-won. Dir: Im Kyung-soo. Phot: Kim Chul-ju. Players: Shin Eun-gyung, Kim Yun-jin, Moon Jung-hyuk, Yun Joo-sang, Maeng Sae-chang, Kim Sung-ha. Prod: Choi Hyun-sik, Cho Won-jang, Film and Pictures Inc./Boston Media Inc.
A veteran female detective and an inexperienced young male detective track a serial killer.

EUMRAN SEOSAENG
(Forbidden Quest)
[Epic comedy-drama, 2006]
Script and Dir: Kim Dae-woo.
Phot: Kim Ji-yong. Players: Han
Seok-gyu, Lee Bum-soo, Kim
Min-jeong, Oh Dal-soo, Kim
Roe-ha. Prod: Lim Jungha,
Bidangil Younghwasa Inc.
In the late 1400s, Chosun period,
when the conservative Confucian
moral code rules, one noble man
from an aristocratic family writes
pornographic novels.

SARANG-EUL NOTCHIDA
(Lost in Love)
[Melodrama, 2006] Script and
Dir: Chu Chang-min. Phot: Lee
Gi-won. Players: Sol Gyung-gu,
Song Yun-a, Lee Gi-woo, Lee
Hwee-hyang, Jang Hang-sun.
Prod: Paik Sun-hee, Cinema
Service/The Pictures Factory.
A couple who separated 10 years
ago meet again by chance.

Quote of the Year

"The most important thing I
consider in making films is
that first it should differ from
the films of other people and
second it should differ from
any of my previous films."

PARK CHAN-WOOK, *director,*
talking about Sympathy for Lady
Vengeance *in* Premier *magazine.*

in 1979, when long-time dictator Park Jung-hee was assassinated
by one of his close followers, the chief of the Korean Central
Intelligence Agency. As a result of legal opposition by Park's son,
who claimed that Im's film distorts historical fact, the director was
obliged to cut four minutes of documentary footage. Stylistically
cool and dry, the film mockingly depicts how high-ranking officials
sustained Park's dictatorship as if they were a group of greedy and
silly gangsters.

At press time it was too early to declare whether 2005 would be
remembered as the year when the local blockbuster sank. Many
major films were awaiting release in the hot season, starting from
December. *Shadowless Sword* (*Muyounggum*) is a large-scale
martial arts film produced as a multi national project in collaboration
with New Line Cinema. Three big films that were scheduled to join
the fray in mid-December were *Typhoon* (*Taepung*), an ocean
action movie directed by Gwak Gyung-taek (*Friend*), the action noir
Running Wild (*Yasu*), by Kim Sung-soo, and *Blue Swallow*
(*Cheongyeon*), a historical drama about the first Korean female pilot.

As South Korean cinema becomes increasingly well known
internationally, it becomes more international itself, in terms of
location, casting, staffing, co-production and global distribution.
The rising popularity of South Korean popular culture in the Asian
region means that the industry now targets the Asian market, and
even begins to look towards America. Export sales of Korean films
achieved a soaring increase (88%) in 2004, Japan becoming the
biggest overseas market. Hur Jin-ho's **April Snow** (*Oechul*) took
second place at the Japanese box-office.

Encouraged by such success, Korean cinema is undertaking
various forms of international collaboration, making vigorous efforts
to expand its success story into other regions, from Uzbekistan
(My *Wedding Campaign/Na-eu gyulhon wonjunggi*) to Los Angeles
(*Love Talk*). Internal factors also push film-makers further into
international markets, because local films still have to recoup 70%
of their revenue from theatrical sales, following the collapse of the
home-video market and serious depression in the DVD market.

NIKKI J. Y. LEE (naausica@hotmail.com) is a film researcher based
in Seoul and London. She contributed to *Cine21*, a weekly Korean
film magazine, from 2001 to 2005.

Spain Jonathan Holland

The Year's Best Films

Jonathan Holland's selection:

Hard Times
(Manuel Martín Cuenca)

Other Days Will Come
(Eduard Cortés)

Princesses
(Fernando León de Aranoa)

The Secret Life of Words
(Isabel Coixet)

The Sky Turns
(Mercedes Álvarez)

Recent and Forthcoming Films

ALATRISTE
[Historical drama, 2006] Script and Dir: Agustin Díaz Yanes. Players: Viggo Mortensen, Juan Echanove, Eduardo Noriega, Elena Anaya. Prod: Telecinco/ Origen/Universal Studios Networks España.

AZUL OSCURO CASI NEGRO
(*literally,* **Dark Blue, Almost Black**) *[Drama, 2006] Script and Dir: Daniel Sánchez Arévalo. Phot: Juan Carlos Gómez. Players: Quim Gutiérrez, Marta Etura, Antonio de la Torre. Prod: Tesela.*

THE BACKWOODS
[Horror, 2006] Dir: Koldo Serra. Players: Gary Oldman, Virginie Ledoyen, Paddy Considine, Aitana Sanchez-Gijón. Prod: Monfort/Filmax/Holy Cow/ Videntia Frames/Divine.

BAJO LAS ESTRELLAS
(*literally,* **Under the Stars**) *[Drama, 2006] Script and Dir: Felix Viscarret. Phot: Álvaro Gutiérrez. Players: Emma Suárez, Alberto San Juan y Julián Villagrán. Prod:*

At the end of 2004, the atmosphere in the Spanish film industry was upbeat. Alejandro Amenábar's **The Sea Inside** was an early favourite for the Oscar for Best Foreign Film, and the promises to the industry made by José Luis Zapatero's new government still felt fresh. February came, and Amenábar duly won, but as 2005 rolled on, the politicos' promises were not fulfilled. Come the San Sebastián Film Festival in September, parts of Spain's audiovisual sector had drafted a letter of complaint demanding that private TV channels commit 5% of their revenues to Spanish cinema, and seeking tax exemptions that might encourage a more high-risk, high-return climate.

The letter was never delivered, but it revealed that tensions between the film industry and the government, whatever its colour, are here to stay. The promises keep coming, though: among ideas mooted for 2006 by the current Minister of Culture is a fund to support the exhibition of local films, and an increase in funds for independent distribution, up from €900,000 in 2005 to €1.4m in 2006.

Many observers, however, believe that Spanish cinema's difficulties are not a question of economics but of inferior product. In 2004, a record 133 films were produced; in the eyes of some, the available resources – creative, economic and technical – are being spread too thinly, though by the end of 2005 annual production will probably have dropped from the 2004 high. The number of co-productions (41 in 2004) is on the rise, reflecting the local industry's increasingly global outlook. This new internationalism is further demonstrated by export figures. According to producers' body FAPAE, international sales have nearly tripled over the past four years, making €80.5m in 2004 and almost reaching the levels achieved by French and British films.

But all of this conceals some unhappy home truths. After reaching almost 16% in 2003, market share went down to 13.4% in 2004 – a drop of roughly three million spectators. National institute ICAA's annual report puts a brave face on Spain's longstanding inability to attract local cinemagoers by reporting that there were five or more Spanish films in the weekly Top 20 throughout 2004, but this may have been caused by sheer volume, and ignores the fact that most titles appeared between numbers 11 and 20.

Fernando Trueba PC.

BIENVENIDO A CASA
(*literally,* **Welcome Home**)
*[Drama, 2006] Script and Dir:
David Trueba. Phot: Juan
Molina. Players: Alejo Sauras,
Pilar López de Ayala, Ariadna
Gil, Cocha Velasco. Prod:
Fernando Trueba.*

CELIA'S LIVES
*[Drama, 2006] Script and Dir:
Antonio Chavarrias. Phot:
Guillermo Granillo. Players:
Najwa Nimri, Luis Tosar, Daniel
Giménez Castro, Alex Casanovas.
Prod: Oberon Cinematografica
(Spain)/Tau (Mexico).*

DESVIADOS (*literally,* **Diverted**)
*[Thriller, 2006] Script: David
Sarasketa, Javier Etxaniz
Petralanda. Dir: Jesus Ponce.
Phot: Javier Aguirre. Players: Eloy
Azorín, Óscar Jaenada, Beatriz
Segura. Prod: Bainet Zinema.*

EL LABERINTO DE KOVAK
(*literally,* **Kovak's Labyrinth**)
*[Thriller, 2006] Script:
Daniel Monzón, Jorge
Guerricaechevarría. Dir: Monzón.
Phot: Carles Gusi. Players:
Timothy Hutton, Lucía Jiménez,
David Kelly, Gary Piquer. Prod:
Filmax/Estudios Picasso.*

**LA EDUCACION DE LAS
HADAS** (*literally,* **The Education
of the Fairies**)
*[Drama, 2006] Script and Dir:
José Luis Cuerda. Phot: Hans
Burmann. Players: Ricardo
Darín, Irene Jacob, Victor
Valdivia Reina. Prod: Tornasol,
Finales Felices/Messidor Films.*

LA FIESTA DEL CHIVO
(**The Feast of the Goat**)
*[Drama, 2005] Script: Luis
Llosa, Augusto Cabada, Mario
Vargas Llosa. Dir: Luis Llosa.
Phot: Javier Salmones. Players:
Isabella Rossellini, Thomas
Milian, Juan Diego Botto. Prod:
Lolafilms/Future Films.*

FOUR LAST SONGS
*[Drama, 2006] Script and Dir:
Francesca Joseph. Phot: Javier
Salmones. Players: Stanley Tucci,*

Up until summer 2005, the only Spanish movie to appear in the top 25 was Roberto Santiago's **The Longest Penalty in the World** (*El penalti mas largo del mundo*), a vehicle for TV comedian Fernando Tejero, but in the second half of the year help came from a sleeper, Alberto Rodríguez's **7 Virgins** (*7 virgenes*), and Santiago Segura's scatological cop comedy **Torrente 3: The Protector** (*Torrente 3: el Protector*), which broke the all-time first weekend box-office record, before settling down when everyone over the age of 12 realised how bad it was. Segura's policy is to deliver another *Torrente* instalment if each makes more money than the last, so *Torrente 4* will, sadly, be among us some day. The critics hate his formula, but Segura is crying all the way to the bank.

A terrorist in *Wolf*'s clothing

Artistically, as ever, things have ranged from the truly awful to the superb, with little to hold things together apart from a certain depressing conservatism of approach, perhaps economy-driven. Comedies, *Torrente* and *Penalty* apart, were thin on the ground, costly and dreadful, but mostly did decent business. Juan Calvo's debut, **Say I Do** (*Di que si*), was a TV show satire that looked good but had a cliché-laden script, while Enrique Lopez Lavigne and Juan Cavestany's **The Amazing World of Borjamari and Pocholo** (*El asombroso mundo de Borjamari y Pocholo*) was a witless look at a couple of 1980s posh kids who refuse to grow up.

Other genres fared better, particularly the thriller. Miguel Courtois' slick, smart **The Wolf** (*El lobo*), based on the true story of an infiltrator into the Basque terrorist movement, ETA, had a surprisingly sustained theatrical run. Mariano Barroso's **Ants in the Mouth** (*Hormigas en la boca*), featuring corruption aplenty in 1950s Cuba, represented the best work yet from this consistent (and consistently underrated) director. Another forty-something director, Santiago Garcia de Leaniz, delivered an intense, brooding study of murderous sibling rivalry in rural Spain with his confident, nuanced debut, **The Night of the Brother** (*La noche del hermano*). Maverick Pablo Llorca took on a typically outré project with the English-language **The Scar** (*La cicatriz*), a low-budget study of sex and politics behind the former Iron Curtain, while Eduard Cortés wove a compact, thriller plot into a searching family drama in **Other Days Will Come**, which featured the year's finest romantic pairing: the delightful Cecilia Roth and a heartbroken Antonio Resines.

Tracks of their tears

The complications and horrors of twentieth-century Spanish history represent a rich source of material, now being tapped by a growing number of high-quality documentaries. The focus is now less on the Civil War than the repression that followed it. Israel Sanchez-Prieto's affecting **Blue Days** tracks the exhumation of victims of Franco from mass graves, while Marta Arribas and Ana Pérez's **Memory Train** (*El tren de la memoria*) was a reconsideration of the 1960s rail exodus of two million Spaniards to foreign countries in search of work.

Marta Arribas and Ana Pérez's **Memory Train**

The March 2004 Madrid terrorist bombings produced a powerful portmanteau piece, **11M**, while Carlos Benpar made **Cinéastes versus Magnates** (*Cineastas contra magnates*), an endlessly fascinating diatribe against the technical abuses visited on movies when they transfer to TV, featuring testimony from Hollywood heavyweights. Vicente Pérez Herrero's **Skin for Sale** (*La piel vendida*) was a bleak but entertaining study of the Spanish porn industry. The outstanding documentary was Mercedes Álvarez's profound, haunting study of a disappearing way of life in rural Spain, *The Sky Turns* (*El cielo gira*). Inspired by the work of maestro Victor Erice, it trawled the small festivals and rightly picked up many awards.

The films made each year by Spanish women can sadly still be counted on one hand. Marta Balletbò-Coll delivered **Sevigné**, a witty study of the Catalan chattering classes; Chus Gutiérrez's high-energy **El Calentito** looked enthusiastically back to the feverish punk years of Spain's transition from dictatorship to democracy; Patricia Ferreira's **Something to Remember Me By** (*Para que no me olvides*) was a stately family drama about memory; and Isabel Coixet, the female director with the highest international profile, made her most powerful film, the English-language **The Secret Life of Words**. Sarah Polley and Tim Robbins face off in this magnificently intense piece, set on an oil rig. Less successful, perhaps because they were comedies, were **Semen, a Love Story** (*Semen, una historia de amor*) by Inés Paris and Daniela Fejerman, a surrogate birth screwball comedy, and Laura Maña's wilfully off-beat yarn about a village where people go to die, **Dying in San Hilario** (*Morir en San Hilario*).

Marisa Paredes, Emmanuelle Seigner, María Esteve. Prod: Mate Cantero/Last Songs Ltd.

GOYA'S GHOSTS
[*Historical drama, 2006*] Script: Milos Forman, Jean-Claude Carrière. Dir: Forman. Phot: Javier Aguirresarobe. Players: Natalie Portman, Javier Bardem, Stellan Skarsgård, Randy Quaid, Prod: Saul Zaentz.

HOTEL TÍVOLI
[*Comedy, 2006*] Script: Antón Reixa, Xosé Morais, Carlos Portela. Dir: Reixa. Phot: Marcelo Iaccarino. Players: Luis Tosar, Ginés García Millán, Isidoro Fernández. Prod: Filmanova (Spain)/Zentropa (Denmark)/Animatógrafo 2 (Portugal)/Aquafilms (Argentina).

LOS AIRES DIFICILES
(*literally*, **The Difficult Airs**)
[*Drama, 2006*] Script: Ángeles González-Sinde, Albero Macías. Dir: Gerardo Herrero. Players: José Luis García Pérez, Cuca Escribano, Roberto Enriquez. Prod: Tornasol/Continental/Maestranza.

OCULTO (*literally*, **Hidden**)
[*Thriller, 2006*] Script: Antonio Hernández, Enrique Brasó. Dir: Hernández. Phot: Unax Mendía. Players: Laia Marull, Leonardo Sbaraglia, Angie Cepeda. Prod: Zebra.

REMAKE
[*Drama, 2006*] Script: Roger Gual, Javier Calvo. Dir: Gual. Phot: Cobi Migliora. Players: Juan Diego, Silvia Munt, Eusebio Poncela. Prod: Ovideo (Spain)/Patagonik Film Group (Argentina).

RODANDO (*literally*, **Turning**)
[*Drama, 2006*] Script: Martín Román, Sigfrid Monleón. Dir: Monleón. Phot: Alfonso Parra. Players: Sancho Gracia, Pilar Bardem, Barbara Lennie, Javier Pereira. Prod: Wanda Vision/Indigo Media/Fénix.

LA SILLA
[*Drama, 2006*] Script and Dir:

Julio D. Wallovits. Phot: Tomàs Pladevall. Players: Francesc Garrido, Ulises Dumont, Gonzalo Cunill. Prod: Eddie Saeta.

TIRANTE EL BLANCO
[Historical drama, 2005] Script and Dir: Vicente Aranda. Phot: José Luis Alcaine. Players: Gian Carlo Giannini, Jane Asher, Sid Mitchell, Rafael Amargo. Prod: Carolina Films/DeAplaneta/ Future Films Coproductions/ Mikado Films/Talent Films.

TORRENTE 3: EL PROTECTOR (Torrente 3: The Protector)
[Comedy, 2005] Script and Dir: Santiago Segura. Phot: Unax Mendia. Players: Segura, Jose Mota, Javier Gutiérrez, Yvonne Scio. Prod: Amiguetes Entertainment.

LOS 2 LADOS DE LA CAMA
(literally, The 2 Sides of the Bed) [Comedy, 2005] Script: David Serrano. Dir: Emilio Martínez Lázaro. Players: Ernesto Alterio, Guillermo Toledo, Alberto San Juan, María Esteve. Prod: Telespan 2000.

VOLVER (literally, Going Back)
[Drama, 2006] Script and Dir: Pedro Almodóvar. Phot: José Luis Alcaine. Players: Penélope Cruz, Carmen Maura, Lola Dueñas, Blanca Portillo. Prod: El Deseo.

YOUR LIFE IN 65 MINUTES
[Comedy, 2006] Script: Albert Espinosa. Dir: María Ripoll. Phot: Mario Montero. Players: Andrés Gertrudix, Javier Pereira, Nuria Gago. Prod: Alquimia Cinema/Messidor Films.

Quote of the Year

"The red carpet at the Oscars was the worst thing. Nobody talked to me. I felt like the unwanted piece of hake in the fish market."
ALEJANDRO AMENÁBAR,
director of the Academy Award-winning The Sea Inside.

Sarah Polley and Tim Robbins in **The Secret Life of Words**

Málaga vs. San Sebastián

This year's Málaga festival, which aspires to be the nation's premier showcase for Spanish cinema, was mostly disappointing. Many of the best films were on show at San Sebastián, which revealed an increasing awareness among young directors of contemporary social issues. Chema de la Peña and Gabriel Velázquez's **Sud Express** dealt wittily with love and immigration along the high-speed Lisbon–Paris rail line, and Manuel Martín Cuenca's equally well crafted, but dramatically more complex **Hard Times** (Malas temporadas) provided a valuable, gritty study of marginalised lives blighted by politics and passion. Both offered an all too rare combination of heart and brains.

7 Virgins, featuring Spain's highest-profile teen actor, Juan José Ballesta, looks at the 48-hour leave from a Seville reform school of a golden-hearted delinquent, and was a surprisingly solid hit. It suggests that Ballesta is now one of the few Spanish performers whom people will pay to see. Another memorable and popular social critique was Fernando León de Aranoa's **Princesses** (Princesas), a drama about the friendship between two prostitutes, with Candela Peña in one of the year's outstanding performances. If one Spanish film could claim to have a handle on women's experiences, this was it, and it was by a man.

It has been a quiet period for the veterans, though Oscar-winner José Luis García delivered two films to keep his fans happy: an appealing old-time comedy, **Ninette**, and a rangy, cast-of-thousands nostalgia item, **Tiovivo 1950**. Carlos Saura's **Iberia** is an efficient if uninspiring addition to his list of musical documentaries, while Montxo Armendáriz's intelligent, atmospheric reworking of a classic Basque novel, **Obaba**, opened San Sebastián and was chosen as Spain's Oscar submission – though it's unlikely to match Amenábar's success.

In all, 44 debut features were in the 2004 line-up, some of which had yet to see theatrical light by November 2005, and though several showed promise, none truly stood out. Of interest were David Carreras' **Hipnos**, a psychodrama whose solid script was cobbled together from the leftovers of David Fincher and M. Night Shamayalan, and Guillem Morales' **The Uncertain Guest**, which revisited early Polanski in its study of a young man slowly going crazy. Jesus Ponce's **15 Days with You** (*15 días contigo*), a rough-grained study of jailbirds becoming lovebirds, and Ramon Termens and Carles Torras' **Youngsters** (*Jóvenes*), a high-energy amoral youth drama, were more socially oriented.

Telmo Esnal and Asier Altuna's small-town comedy **Go!** (*Aupa Etxebeste*) became the first full-length feature in the Basque language for 13 years, but had little else to recommend it. The best debut of the year was Jose Corbacho and Juan Cruz's gentle, appealing criss-cross study of Barcelona barrio life, **Tapas**, which won Best Film at the otherwise lacklustre Málaga festival.

JONATHAN HOLLAND (jholland@gmail.com) is *Variety*'s film reviewer in Spain.

Juan José Ballesta in **7 Virgins**

Spanish Film Academy Goya Awards 2005

Film: *The Sea Inside/Mar adentro* (Alejandro Amenabar).
Animated Film: *El enigma del chico croqueta*.
Director: Alejandro Amenabar (*The Sea Inside*).
New Director: Pablo Malo, (*Cold Winter Sun*).
Original Screenplay: Alejandro Amenabar, Mateo Gil (*The Sea Inside*).
Adapted Screenplay: Jose Rivera (*The Motorcycle Diaries*)
Actor: Javier Bardem (*The Sea Inside*).
Actress: Lola Duenas (*The Sea Inside*).
Supporting Actor: Celso Bugallo (*The Sea Inside*).
Supporting Actress: Mabel Rivera (*The Sea Inside*).
New Actor: Tamar Novas (*The Sea Inside*).
New Actress: Belen Rueda (*The Sea Inside*).
European Film: *Head-On* (Germany).
Foreign Spanish-Language Film: *Whisky* (Uruguay).

Sri Lanka Amarnath Jayatilaka

The Years Best Films

Amarnath Jayatilaka's selection:

Forsaken Land
(Vimukti Jayasundara)

August Sun
(Prasanna Vithanage)

Butterfly Wings
(Somaratna Dissanayaka)

Guerilla Marketing
(Jayantha Chandrasiri)

Buongiorno Italia
(Vishvanath Buddhika Kirtisena)

Recent and Forthcoming Films

RANDIYA DAHARA
(Showers of Gold)
[Social drama, 2004] Script and
Dir: Udayakantha Warnasuriya.
Phot: K.D. Dayananda, Jayanath
Gunawardhana. Players:
Geetha Kumarasinghe, Kamal
Adduraarachchi, Jackson
Anthony, Sanath Gunatilaka.
Prod: Neil Ranjit Palliyaguru.

MILLE SOYA (Buongiorno Italia)
[Social drama, 2004] Script and
Dir: Vishvanath Buddhika
Kirtisena. Phot: Moshe Ben
Yaash, K.A. Dharmasena.
Players: Mahendra Perera, Kamal
Adduraarachchi, Sangeetha
Weeraratna. Prod: Buddhi
Keertisena, Cinema Buddhi.

IRA MEDIYAMA (August Sun)
[Social drama, 2005] Script and
Dir: Prasanna Vithanage. Phot:
M.D. Mahindapala. Players: Peter
D'Almeida, Nimmi Harasgama,
Namal Jayasinghe, Mohamed
Refiulla. Prod: Soma Edirisinghe,
EAP Films & Theatres Ltd.

Forsaken Land (*Sulanga enu pinisa*), the maiden feature by young Vimukti Jayasunandra won the Camera d'Or award at Cannes 2005, the first time that a Sinhala film has won such a high-profile award at the festival. This drama captures a strange state of limbo between war and peace, set in the country ravaged by civil war and currently wavering in an unstable ceasefire. It follows the aimless, hopeless wandering of a few isolated characters in the vast, desolate region close to the theatre of war. The harsh terrain and the trauma of past violence have left them incapable of finding inner peace. The listless existence of one villager leads to the incomprehensible murder of an unknown victim, under cover of darkness – a haunting reference to Raskolnikov's murder of the money-lender in Dostoyevsky's *Crime and Punishment*. The murder epitomises mankind's gradual descent in to madness and barbarity.

Prasanna Vithanage's **August Sun** (*Ira mediyama*) won several awards on the international festival circuit before its release at home. Set in the mid-1990s, it has three simultaneous narratives about characters looking for what they have lost. Arafath, an 11-year-old Muslim boy, struggles to keep his dog after his family is forced from their home by LTTE terrorists. In Colombo, Chamari looks for her pilot husband, believed to be missing in action. Duminda walks into a brothel in the city of Anuradhapura, only to find that his lost sister is among the sex workers.

Guerilla Marketing, a drama by Jayantha Chandrasiri, provides psychological analysis and political satire. Tisara is an advertising expert, working alongside his wife, Suramya. She is unaware of many aspects of his life, including his teenage bout of schizophrenia. Gregory is a cunning politician who engages Tisara to mastermind his presidential campaign, and we see the relationship between these entirely different characters.

Italia for beginners

Vishvanath Buddhika Keertisena's **Buongiorno Italia** (*Mille soya*) revolves around a group of young unemployed musicians. After friends return from Italy talking about the money to be made there, we see the escapades of the group as they try to enter Italy illegally. *One Shot* was a political parody, the second directorial effort of popular actor Ranjan Ramanayaka, who also wrote the script and played the lead role. It was the highest-grossing film of 2005, playing for more than 100 days and drawing almost 950,000 admissions – a huge figure in local terms.

The audience response was both instant and astounding. The film peeps into the conduct of politicians and their cohorts, satirising them to great effect and introducing the first Sri Lankan cinema superhero. On their own, the people never rise up against corruption, robbery or tyranny. But a hero does just that in *One Shot*, and audiences flocked to see somebody fighting single-handedly on their behalf, providing cinematic escapism from economic, moral and intellectual poverty. While *One Shot* is a one-dimensional film experience, it brought cinema closer to a population who had begun to move away from movies.

Somaratna Dissanayake knows how to customise his product by using children in the main roles, and completed his fourth film, **Butterfly Wings** (*Samanala thatu*). This family melodrama stars child actor Dasun Madhusankha, who played the child Buddhist monk in Dissanayake's *Suriya Arana*, which in 2004 became the biggest Sinhala box-office hit ever. Madhusankha plays Sira, 10, part of a street family who survive by singing and dancing on the streets. Sira dreams of owning a bicycle and has a physically disabled younger sister and a father with heart disease. He is sold to a paedophile foreigner, but manages to rob his captor and run away. He returns home knowing that he has enough money for a bicycle, but finds that his father has been admitted to hospital. Sira gives all his money to save his father, but to no avail. Now obliged to look after his mother and sister, Sira continues his father's work, entertaining people on the street.

AMARNATH JAYATILAKA is a filmologist and a leading film personality in Sri Lanka.

Somaratna Dissanayaka's **Butterfly Wings**

Prasanna Vithanage's **August Sun**

ASANI WARSHA
(Wrath & Rain)
[Social drama, 2005] Script and Dir: Vasantha Obeysekara. Phot: Jayanath Gunawardana. Players: Jagath Chamila, Kamal Adduraarachchi, Meena Kumari. Prod: Soma Edirisinghe, EAP Films & Theatres Ltd.

SULANGA ENU PINISA
(Forsaken Land)
[Social drama, 2005] Script and Dir: Vimukti Jayasundara. Phot: Channa Deshapriya. Players: Mahendra Perera, Kaushalya Fernando, Hemasiri Liyanage, Nilupuli Jayawardena. Prod: Upul Shantha Sannasgala, Dr Chanda Aluthge, Phillippe Avril (France).

GUERILLA MARKETING
[Social drama, 2005] Script and Dir: Jayantha Chandrasiri. Phot: Ruwan Costa. Players: Kamal Addaraarachchi, Jackson Anthony, Sangeetha Weeraratna, Yasohoda Wimaladharma. Prod: European Consultancy Ltd. (UK).

SAMANALA THATU
(Butterfly Wings)
[Family melodrama, 2005] Script and Dir: Somaratna Dissanayake. Phot: Channa Deshapriya. Players: Dasun Madhusanka, Suminda Sirisena, Duleeka Marapana, Dulanjali Ariyatilaka. Prod: Renuka Balasooriya.

ONE SHOT
[Political parody, 2005] Script and Dir: Ranjan Ramanayaka. Phot: Jayanath Gunawardhana. Players: Ramanayaka, Wilson Karu, Anarkali Akarsha, Sriyani Amarasena. Prod: Soma Edirisinghe, EAP Films & Theatres Ltd.

Sweden Gunnar Rehlin

The Year's Best Films

Gunnar Rehlin's selection:
Dalecarlians (Maria Blom)
God Save the King
(Ulf Malmros)
Sandor Slash Ida
(Henrik Georgsson)
**The Queen of Sheba's
Pearls** (Colin Nutley)
Zozo (Josef Fares)

Per-Anders Jörgensen/Memfis Film

Sofia Helin in **Dalecarlians**

Recent and
Forthcoming Films

FYRA VECKOR I JUNI
(Four Weeks in June)
*[Drama, 2005] Script and Dir:
Henry Meyer. Phot: Hakan
Holmberg. Players: Tuva
Novotny, Ghita Norby, Jessica
Zandén, Lukasz Garlicki. Prod:
Peter Kropenin, Omega Film.*
Two disturbed women from
different generations help each other.

SEX, HOPP & KÄRLEK
(Sex, Hope & Love)
*[Drama, 2005] Script and
Dir: Lisa Ohlin. Phot: Dan
Laustsen. Players: Ing-Marie
Carlsson, Krister Henriksson,
Lennart Jahkel, Mira Eklund,
Oliver Loftéen. Prod: Peter
Hiltunen, Illusionfilm.*
The return of a former lover turns
a married woman's life upside-
down in a small country town.

A film that featured prominently in last year's IFG report continued to make an impact into 2005. Kay Pollak's *As it Is in Heaven* drew almost 1.5 million admissions and the initial DVD pressing sold out in a fortnight, making it one of the biggest domestic successes ever. In late January 2005, however, something strange happened. Even though Pollak's film was nominated for many Golden Bug awards, it was totally shunned by the jury. A shocked Pollak tried to understand what had happened, only to be told the very next day that his film had been nominated for the Best Foreign-Language Film Oscar. The film also had a triumphant out-of-competition screening at Berlin, and even though the Academy Award went to *The Sea Inside*, Pollak must have felt he'd had at least partial revenge on the Bugs jurors.

Three films dominated the Golden Bugs. Tomas Alfredson's dark comedy, **Four Shades of Brown** (*Fyra nyanser av brunt*), took the prizes for Director, Actor, Actress and Supporting Actor. Sound and cinematography awards went to Colin Nutley's **The Queen of Sheba's Pearls**, a semi-autobiographical story of a young boy growing up in England in the 1950s, shot in England with just two Swedish actors. Critical response was mostly fine, but the box-office was a disappointment by the standards of Nutley's numerous hits.

Maria Blom's **Dalecarlians** won Best Film, Supporting Actress and Screenplay. An experienced theatre director and playwright, Blom had adapted *Dalecarlians* from her own play about three sisters reunited to celebrate their father's 70th birthday. Starting out as a

The Queen of Sheba's Pearls

comedy but turning darker and darker, it was a deserved critical and box-office success and Blom is a name to watch. *Dalecarlians* opened at Christmas 2004, alongside Jack Ersgård's **Rancid**, an English-language thriller shot in a Stockholm studio but set in New York. It flopped on all levels, its makers failing to realise that if you are going to make an 'American' thriller in Sweden, it had better be at least as good as the genuine article.

When is a Swedish film not Swedish?

The Bugs nominations started a heated debate on the criteria by which a film should be deemed Swedish. Simon Staho's drama, **Day and Night**, had a tour de force by Mikael Persbrandt and everyone regarded his nomination as a formality. But no. Even though all the actors were Swedish and the film was made in Sweden, the fact that the director and lead producer were Danish was enough to have the film labelled Danish and Persbrandt could not be nominated (he won the Ingmar Bergman Prize instead). Later, the film flopped in Denmark, where the audience regarded it as Swedish. Go figure. This debate resumed in autumn 2005, with Staho's new film **Bang Bang Orangutang** (once again starring Swedish actors, once again shot in Sweden) and Klaus Härö's **Mother of Mine** (a mostly Finnish production, shot in Sweden with Swedish actors) as the focus of the debate.

At the Gothenburg festival in February, the biggest domestic success was Henrik Georgsson's teen love story **Sandor Slash Ida**, which unfortunately did not do as well commercially as it should have done. Opening the fest was Mats Aréhn's autobiographical **The Chef**, which deservedly quickly sank into oblivion. With no Swedish films opening between March and August, the new season started promisingly with Lisa Ohlin's drama **Sex, Hope & Love** (*Sex, hopp & kärlek*).

The season continued with Ulf Malmros' very funny and energetic **God Save the King** (*Tjenare kungen*), about two teenage girls starting a punk rock band in Gothenburg in 1984 (this promised to be the director's biggest hit), and Josef Fares' autobiographical **Zozo**. After his funny comedies *Jalla! Jalla!* and *Kops*, Fares in his third film turned his eye to his own history. *Zozo* is about a 10-year-old boy who in the mid-1980s leaves civil war-torn Beirut and moves to Sweden. Although not Fares' own story per se, it is still based on his experiences, a well-told, moving, dramatic and also funny film. It was the sole Swedish entry at Toronto and was the official submission for the Best Foreign-Language Oscar.

Richard Hobert made a strong comeback with **Harry's Daughters** (*Harrys döttrar*), a drama about the rivalry between two adult sisters, when one has a child and the other suffers a still birth. Very well acted, especially by Amanda Ooms as the sister who loses her baby,

Ola Kjelbye/Sonet Film

Ing-Marie Carlsson in
Sex, Hope & Love

CARAMBOLE
[Thriller, 2005] Script: Niklas Rockstrom, Bjorn Carlberg, Stefan Thunberg. Dir: Daniel Lind Lagerlof. Players: Sven Wollter, Eva Rexed, Thomas Hanzon, Philip Zanden, Peter Andersson. Prod: Jan Marnell, Johan Mardell, Svensk Filmindustri.
A retired policeman returns to action after his son is murdered.

ZOZO
[Drama, 2005] Script and Dir: Josef Fares. Phot: Aril Wretblad. Players: Imad Creidi, Antoinette Turk, Viktor Axelsson, Elias Gergi, Carmen Lebbos. Prod: Anna Anthony, Memfis Film.

DEN UTVALDE (The Chosen)
[Thriller, 2005)] Script: Eric Donell. Dir Donell/Martin Söder. Phot: Jari Mutikainen. Players Andreas Wilson, Julia Dufvenius. Prod: Donell, Desperado Films.
A series of brutal murders in the university town of Uppsala.

TJENARE KUNGEN (God Save the King)
[Comedy, 2005)] Script and Dir: Ulf Malmros. Phot: Mats Axby. Players: Josefin Neldén, Cecilia Wallin, Johanna Strömberg, Malin Morgan. Prod: Lena Rehnberg, Sandrew Metronome.

Sandrew Metronome

Cecilia Wallin, left, and Josefin Neldén in **God Save the King**

KIM NOVAK BADADE ALDRIG I GENESARETS SJÖ

(Kim Novak Never Swam in the Lake of Genesaret)

[Drama, 2005] Script: Hakan Nesser, Martin Asphaug. Dir: Asphaug. Phot: Philip Ogaard. Players: Anton Lundqvist, Johan Hson Kjellgren, Jesper Adefeldt, Jonas Karlsson, Helena af Sandeberg. Prod: Valdemar Bergendahl, Svensk Filmindustri. A man thinks back to the murderous childhood summer when he discovered sex.

DOXA

[Drama, 2005] Script and Dir: Leif Magnusson. Phot: Jens Schlosser. Players: Eva Rexed, Cilla Jerf, Torkel Pettersson, Pernilla August. Prod: Matthias Nohrborg, Autro Images. A young woman seeks the truth about her father's illness.

MUN MOT MUN

(Order to Love)

[Drama, 2005] Script and Dir: Björn Runge. Phot: Anders Bohman. Players: Marie Richardson, Pernilla August, Ann Petrén. Prod: Claes Gunnarsson, Zoid Produktion. A dark family drama in the tradition of the director's previous film, Daybreak.

MORENO OCH TYSTNADEN

(Moreno and the Silence).

[Thriller, 2005] Script: Björn Carlström, Stefan Thunberg. Dir: Erik. Leijonborg. Phot: Rolf Lindström. Players: Sven Wollter, Eva Rexed, Björn Bengtsson, Thomas Oredsson.

Per-Anders Jørgensen/Memfis Film

Imad Creidi as the hero fleeing Lebanon in Josef Fares' Zozo

this film re-established Hobert as a force to be reckoned with. On the industry side, overall box-office declined in 2004 and into 2005, but mainly for non-Swedish films. Domestic product still has a faithful audience. Last year's report noted that Svensk Filmindustri had sought to buy competitor Sandrew Metronome's chain of cinemas. A lot of protests were heard, as many thought this would give Svensk an unhealthy monopoly. In the end, new owners emerged, led by successful arthouse distributor Triangelfilm, founded a decade ago by Mattias Nohrborg. The chain was renamed Astoria Cinemas, after the most beautiful and prestigious of the chain's theatres. At press time, Astoria Cinemas was not fully operational, but Nohrborg promised there would be room enough for commercial films from the majors and for small art movies.

GUNNAR REHLIN (rehlin@pressart.se) is a Swedish film critic and journalist, working for different media in Sweden, Norway and Finland. He is the author of a book about Stellan Skarsgård.

Prod: Jan Marnell, Johan Mardell, Svensk Filmindustri. A young woman is burned to death, and when the killer kidnaps a second victim, the police race to save her.

Quote of the Year

"I'd lie if I said it wasn't about me. But he is much prettier and cooler than I ever was."

JOSEF FARES, *on the hero of his semi-autobiographical Zozo.*

Switzerland Michael Sennhauser

The Year's Best Films

Michael Sennhauser's selection:

Snow White (Samir)
Absolut (Romed Wyder)
One Long Winter Without Fire (Greg Zglinski)
November (Luki Frieden)
Precariously in Love (Peter Luisi)

Vincent Bonillo in **Absolut**

Recent and Forthcoming Films

ABSOLUT
[Drama, 2004] Script and Dir: Romed Wyder. Phot: Denis Jutzeler. Players: Vincent Bonillo, Irene Godel, François Nadin, Delphine Lanza, Ulysse Prévost, Véronique Mermoud. Prod: Wyder, Blow-up Film Production/ Télévision Suisse Romande/Almaz Film Productions/Laïka Films.

omething is happening in Swiss cinema, but the question remains: "What, exactly?" From autumn 2005 and spring 2006, there has been more local fare – fiction as well as documentaries – up on the screen than for a long while, yet at press time nobody in the industry was certain whether this was all due to *succès cinéma*, the box-office-dependent system of subsidies, to a (very) slight increase in film funding in general or to a coincidental clustering of productions all reaching the screen after lengthy development.

What is beyond doubt is that autumn 2005 saw the arrival of an unprecedented number of well-tailored, audience-targeted fiction films, most inspired by the mould-breaking success of 2003's teen comedy *Ready, Steady, Charlie!*, which seems to have boosted producers' activities. The first of four crowd-pleasers to hit the screens in late 2005 was Samir's **Snow White** (the director's full name is Samir Jamal-Aldin, but he styles himself by first name only). The 50-year-old director–producer employed his longstanding multi-faceted visual style to tell the melodramatic tale of a coke-snorting, designer-clothes-wearing rich girl from Zurich, who falls in love with a socially over-aware hip-hop star from Geneva. This plotline cleverly attempted to bridge two gaps within Swiss demographics, one the so-called *Rösti-Graben*, the language barrier between the German- and French-speaking parts of the country, the other the age gap between arthouse and teenage audiences. *Snow White* met with fierce criticism, mostly from the foreign press at the Locarno Film Festival, as well as with (mostly) unusually enthusiastic responses from the Swiss media.

Luc Schaedler's **Angry Monk**

**ANGRY MONK –
REFLECTIONS ON TIBET**
*[Documentary, 2005] Script
and Dir: Luc Schaedler. Phot:
Filip Zumbrunn. Prod: Angry
Monk Productions/Schweizer
Fernsehen DRS.*

GAMBIT
*[Documentary, 2005] Script and
Dir: Sabine Gisiger. Phot:
Reinhard Köcher, Helena
Vagnières. Players: Jörg Sambeth.
Prod: Dschoint Ventschr
Filmproduktion/Schweizer
Fernsehen DRS/Télévision Suisse
Romande/Radiotelevisione
Svizzera di Lingua Italiana.*

THE GIANT BUDDHAS
*[Documentary, 2005] Script and
Dir: Christian Frei. Phot: Peter
Indergand. Prod: Christian Frei
Filmproduktionen/Schweizer
Fernsehen DRS/ZDF/arte.*

Hanspeter Müller in **Grounding**

**GROUNDING – DIE LETZTEN
TAGE DER SWISSAIR**
*[Docu-drama, 2006] Script: Jürg
Brändli, Michael Sauter. Dir:
Michael Steiner, Tobias Fueter.
Phot: Filip Zumbrunn. Players:
Hanspeter Müller, Gilles Tschudi,
Rainer Guldener, Jürg Löw,
Stephan Bürgi. Prod: C-Films/
Schweizer Fernsehen DRS/
La petite entreprise.*

JEUNE HOMME
*[Drama, 2006] Script: Maya
Todeschini, Christoph Schaub,
Marcel Hoehn. Dir: Christoph
Schaub. Phot: Stéphane Kuthy.*

The young heroes of Michael Steiner's **Mein Name ist Eugen**

Released only two weeks after *Snow White*, **Mein Name ist Eugen** (literally, *My Name Is Eugen*) was the cinematic retelling of a beloved Swiss classic of entertainment literature, a collection of stories from the 1950s, all revolving around the young boy Eugen and his three friends, wreaking playful havoc among families and neighbours. Michael Steiner's film is a clever mix of boy-brat stories and 1950s nostalgia, thereby, like Samir, linking several audience demographics.

In general, Swiss producers seem to have rediscovered the virtues of producing for broader domestic audiences, while at the same time for going too much tailoring for international markets. This is especially true of the autumn's third big feature film. **Grounding** (*Grounding – Die letzten Tage der Swissair*), again directed by the seemingly omnipresent Michael Steiner, is a docu-fiction covering the hardest blow to Swiss self-esteem in many years: the demise of Swissair. Because of newly discovered facts within the ongoing investigation into the airline's collapse, the film's theatrical release was pushed back to allow for re-shoots.

The most successful Swiss film in 2004 was another comedy. Christoph Schaub's **Sternenberg**, originally made for TV but then released theatrically by Buena Vista Switzerland, reached more than 120,000 viewers. An ageing expatriate comes back to the village of his early love, where his daughter (who does not know him) teaches the kids. When the little school is under threat of closure for lack of children, he enrols as a pupil, alerting the national media and thus saving the day (and his daughter's job).

Absolut power

While the success of these populist films still incites frowning and bickering among old school auteurists, it becomes increasingly clear that these less intellectually ambitious works (and the public funds they obviously require) are not really the harbingers of death for all things of cultural value, but are in fact creating new and younger audiences for smaller and even experimental films. One of the more interesting experiments in 2004–05 was Romed Wyder's hacker-thriller **Absolut**. Two young activists try to interrupt a Geneva summit of world leaders by smuggling a virus into the computer system of an international bank. Their plans are thwarted when one has an accident and is subjected to an experimental brain scan and attempted memory recovery by two corrupt female doctors in the secret employ of said bank.

Absolut was distinguished by the very thorough approach of Wyder and his team. They not only set up a website (www.absolut-film.com) to root their scary docu-fiction deeper in reality, they also mastered their own DVD (Wyder is, among other things, a specialist in digital-to-film transfers), electronic press kits, and more or less even theatrical distribution. Yet the film was made by the simplest means, using psychology and excellent actors rather than digital trickery to build up its futuristic suspense.

A unique kind of film-making was employed by Peter Luisi for his **Precariously in Love** (*Verflixt verliebt*), an improbable docu-fiction about a non-film-maker pretending to make a film just to get close to the principal actress. The flimsy and yet efficient film, complete with an inbuilt fictionalised "making of'" as part of the comic plot, was shot for almost no money and without subsidies in a matter of days.

Cold comforts

An international success – at least festival-wise – was Greg Zglinski's **One Long Winter Without Fire** (*Tout un hiver sans feu*). The Swiss-Polish director won prizes in Venice (2004) and Bolzano, as well as the Swiss Film Prize for best fiction film in early 2005. The story of a couple in the harsh winter of the Swiss Jura mountains, mourning the loss of their young daughter and finally coming to terms with life again through their contact with Kosovan refugees, is told hauntingly and with beautiful minimalism. Similar qualities marked Luki Frieden's **November**, a bleak outlook on a family's life falling apart after the mother wins a lottery and all their long-suppressed problems burst forth on a wave of newfound money.

Players: Matthias Schoch, Alexandra Vandernoot, Didier Flamand, Hans Peter Müller-Drossaart. Prod: Marcel Hoehn, T&C Film.

JO SIFFERT – LIVE FAST/ DIE YOUNG
[Documentary, 2005] Script: Men Lareida, Reto Baumann. Dir: Men Lareida. Phot: Pio Corradi. Prod: Hugofilm/SRG SSR idée suisse.

LENZ
[Drama, 2006] Script and Dir: Thomas Imbach. Phot: Jürg Hassler. Players: Milan Peschel, Barbara Maurer. Prod: Bachim Film/Pandora Film.

MARIA BETHNIA, MÚSICA È PERFUME
[Documentary, 2005] Script and Dir: Georges Gachot. Phot: Matthias Kälin. Prod: Georges Gachot, Pierre-Olivier Bardet, Idéale Audience/France 5/ Schweizer Fernsehen DRS/ Télévision Suisse Romande/ Radiotelevisione Svizzera di Lingua Italiana/SRG SSR idée suisse.

MEIN NAME IST EUGEN
(*literally,* **My Name Is Eugen**)
[Drama, 2005] Script: Michael Sauter, Christoph Frey, Michael Steiner. Dir: Steiner. Phot: Pascal Walder. Players: Manuel Häberli, Janic Halioua, Dominic Hänni, Alex Niederhäuser, Beat Schlatter, Mike Müller, Sabina Schneebeli, Patrick Frey, Stefan Gubser, Jürg Löw, Monika Niggeler, Stephanie Japp. Prod: Kontraproduktion/ C-Films/Schweizer Fernsehen

DRS/Impuls Home Entertainment/Teleclub.

NACHBEBEN
(Scenes from the Aftermath)
[Drama, 2006] Script: Petra Lüschow. Dir: Stina Werenfels. Phot: Piotr Jaxa. Players: Michael Neuenschwander, Susanne-Marie Wrage, Bettina Stucky, Georg Scharegg, Leonardo Nigro, Olivia Frölich, Mikki Levy. Prod: Dschoint Ventschr Filmproduktion.

NOVEMBER
[Drama, 2003] Script and Dir: Luki Frieden. Phot: Frank Blau. Players: Charlotte Heinimann, Max Rüdlinger, Muriel Rieben, Elias Arens, Martin Rapold, Lilian Naef, Oscar Sales Bingisser. Prod: Carac.

RICORDARE ANNA
[Drama, 2005] Script: Walo Deuber, Josy Meier. Dir: Walo Deuber. Phot: Stefan Runge, Knut Schmitz. Players: Mathias Gnädinger, Bibiana Beglau, Pippo Pollina, Margareta von Krauss, Suly Röthlisberger, Giuseppe Cederna, Tanja Onorato, Sebastian Rudolph. Prod: Dschoint Ventschr Filmproduktion/Schweizer Fernsehen DRS/Radiotelevisione Svizzera di Lingua Italiana.

RYNA
[Drama, 2005] Script: Marek Epstein, Ruxandra Zenide. Dir: Zenide. Phot: Marius Panduru. Players: Dorotea Petre, Matthieu Rozé. Prod: Xavier Ruiz, Strada Films/Télévision Suisse Romande/ Elefant Films.

SNOW WHITE
[Drama, 2005] Script: Michael Sauter, Samir. Dir: Samir. Phot: Andreas Hutter, Michael Saxer. Players: Julie Fournier, Carlos Leal, Zoé Miku, Stefan Gubser. Prod: Dschoint Ventschr Filmproduktion/Filmhaus.

Aurélien Recoing and Gabriela Muskala in **One Long Winter Without Fire**

Even though production of fiction films is on the increase, documentaries remain a mainstay of Swiss cinema, keeping a steady audience theatrically within the country and making up the lion's share of international sales – if mostly for TV. The Swiss do come back to the cinema for local fare, it seems – and they are buying DVDs with great enthusiasm. After the generally declining attendance figures in 2003, admissions increased by 4.4% in 2004. American films gained most from this positive development, claiming 68.2% of total gross and 25 of the 30 top titles. With 25.7% of the market, European films maintained a similarly high level.

There were 420 new films released theatrically in 2004, which indicates great diversity, although the 40 new Swiss productions took a market share of only 2.5%. Even if minority co-productions with foreign directors, such as *Les choristes*, were added, that figure rises to just 4.85%, significantly lower than 2003's 5.69%. Yet that high in 2003 was mainly due to the success of *Ready, Steady, Charlie!*, whereas 2004 offered a much broader palette, which augurs well for sustainable success.

MICHAEL SENNHAUSER (info@prevu.ch) is Film Editor at Swiss National Radio and Co-Head of The Critics Week at Locarno International Film Festival.

Carlos Leal and Julie Fournier in
Snow White

STERNENBERG
[Drama, 2004] Script: Micha Lewinsky. Dir: Christoph Schaub. Phot: Peter Indergand. Players: Sara Capretti, Mathias Gnädinger, Walo Lüönd, Stephen Sikder, Daniel Rohr, Hanspeter Müller. Prod: Produktion Langfilm/ Schweizer Fernsehen DRS.

Taiwan Ian Gabriel Rowen

The Year's Best Films

Ian Gabriel Rowen's
selection:

Heirloom (Leste Chen)
Let It Be (Lam-chuan Yen
and Cres Juang)
Respire (Wi Ding Ho)
Splendid Float (Zero Chou)
Stone Dream (Hu Tai-li)

Recent and Forthcoming Films

**FAN GUN BA, NANHAI
(Jump! Boys)**
*[Documentary, 2005] Script,
Dir and Phot: Yu-Hsien Lin.
Prod: Jinh-yi Juang/Jump
Boy Entertainment.*
Several boys from different
families have totally different
characteristics, yet after school
they don't play computer games
or go to McDonald's, but head
straight for gymnastics training.
No matter how demanding the
training, they never quit.

GUI SI (Silk)
*[Horror, 2006] Script and Dir:
Su Chao-pin. Phot: Arthur Wong.
Players: Chang Chen, Yosuke
Eguchi, Karena Lam. Prod:
Huang Chih-ming/CMC.*
A group of scientists and
investigators are probing several
mysterious deaths. They discover
that shortly before expiring all
the victims sprouted silk from
their torsos and limbs.

**GULIAN HUA
(Love's Lone Flower)**
*[Drama, 2005] Script and Dir:
Tsao Jui-yuan. Players: Lee
Sin-je, Hsiao Shu-shen, Anita
Yuen. Prod: Tsao Jui-yuan/
Tsao Films Production.*

With 37 releases, almost as many as in the last two years combined, and the emergence of commercially savvy young production companies, Taiwan cinema continued its slow rebound in 2005. There has been a steady rise in local market share; from 0.3% in 2003 to 1.1% in 2004 and to 1.83% as of October 2005. New releases from auteurs Tsai Ming-liang and Hou Hsiao-hsien and a decent documentary slate were also of considerable help.

Heirloom (*Zhaibian*), the first feature by 24-year-old Leste Chen, scored the year's top opening weekend for a domestic film. The success of this $700,000 horror film buoyed the prospects of Three Dots Productions, which produced 2004's breakout gay comedy **Formula 17** (*17 sui de tiankong*). This year, they also produced a woman-focused fantasy, **The Shoe Fairy** (*Ren yu duoduo*), starring Vivian Hsu, released by Hong Kong's Focus Films as the first of their Focus: First Cuts HD projects. In 2006, Three Dots will release *Catch* (*Guoshi wu shuang*), a caper reuniting *Formula 17* director D.J. Chen with star Tony Yang.

No one could have guessed that Tsai Ming-liang's porn-themed musical, **The Wayward Cloud** (*Tianbian yi duo yun*), would become a blockbuster, bringing in over $3m in Taipei alone. After this bleak, nearly dialogue-free film earned two awards and considerable buzz in Berlin in February, Tsai presented it to Taiwan's censorship board with the caveat that he would not release it if they cut a single frame. The board acquiesced, and the ensuing local media frenzy about the film's sexual explicitness drew unlikely mainstream audiences across Taiwan, who made it the year's top domestic hit – even if they walked away scratching their heads.

Tsai Ming-liang's **The Wayward Cloud** *became a surprise local blockbuster*

This romance follows hostess Yuenfang from Shanghai to Taiwan, where her nostalgic love for lost singer Wubao is reignited when she meets the similarly beautiful but troubled Juan Juan.

LIANREN (Fall… in love)
[Romantic drama, 2005] Script and Dir: Wang Ming-tai. Phot: Chin Ting-chang. Players: Wan fang, Li Kangyi, Hsu Kui-yin. Prod: Liang Hong-zhi/Yu Ching Film Co. Ltd.
Alan and Angel are in love. Belle, whom Alan still has a crush on, coincidentally moves in next to Angel. The girls become close without realising they are in love with the same man.

QIAOKELI RAP (Chocolate Rap)
[Dance musical, 2006] Script and Dir: Chi Y. Lee. Phot: Lawrence Schweich. Players: Chen Hsin-hung, Megan Lai. Prod: Li-fen Chien/Chi & Company.
Under leading manager Pachinko's guidance, break-dancer Choco begins rising to the top of the scene, until a car accident changes their fast lives. When Choco hits rock bottom and agrees to teach an ambitious small-time dancer, he embarks on his battle to regain his confidence.

REN YU DUODUO
(The Shoe Fairy)
[Fantasy, 2005] Script and Dir: Robin Lee. Phot: Ching Ting-chang. Players: Vivian Hsu, Duncan Lai. Prod: Michelle Yeh/Aileen Li/Three Dots Entertainment.
Wheelchair-bound Dodo grew up listening to fairy tales. After an operation allows her to walk, she maintains her girly passion for shoes, annoying her husband, Smiley. When she gives up her shoe-buying she can no longer walk, and becomes the shoe fairy.

TIAN BIAN YI DUO YUN
(The Wayward Cloud)
[Musical, 2005] Script and Dir: Tsai Ming-liang. Phot: Liao Pen-jung. Players: Lee Kang-sheng, Chen Shiang-chyi, Lu Yi-ching.

Tsai won an even unlikelier $323,353 grant from Kaohsiung City, where a quarter of the film was shot, for "contributing to the city's good image". Hou Hsiao-hsien's **Three Times** (*Zui hao de shiguang*), composed of three period pieces and starring Chang Chen and Shu Qi, did not prove quite as marketable, but at least scored a wider release than his last work, 2003's *Café Lumière*.

Beleaguered by problems both political and artistic, Taiwan's oldest studio, Central Motion Picture Company, showed no signs of recovery. Lin Cheng-sheng's family drama, **The Moon Also Rises** (*Yueguangxia, Wo jide*), picked up a few local and international awards, but failed to find much of an audience, and Stan Yin's spooky mountain hotel thriller, **Bad Moon** (*E yue*), fared even worse. CMPC produced only one feature in 2005, **The Song of Spirit**, by first-time director Wu Hong Yi.

Though no documentary came close to 2004's *Gift of Life* (*Shengming*) in box-office or critical reception, **Let it Be** (*Wu mi le*) and **Jump! Boys** (*Fan gun ba, nanhai*) demonstrated the health of the genre. The former took a folksy and personal look at the declining fortunes of southern rice farmers; the latter, made for only $16,000, followed a gymnastics team preparing for a national competition.

Jump! Boys *follows the obsessive training of young gymnasts*

A *Hunter* on the home front

Aboriginal issues and Taiwan's ever-present search for national identity also wove their way into 2005's feature films. Though **The Sage Hunter** (*Shanzhu feishu sankenu*), about a tribal hunter trying to protect his community from highway development, was funded out of Hong Kong and shot by Tony Cheung, it featured a primarily Taiwanese amateur and aboriginal cast, with a script based on the best-selling book by aboriginal Paiwan activist Ahronglong Sakinu, who also starred in the leading role. Aborigines, who number over 450,000 or 2% of the island, largely welcomed the film. A more conventional offering was **Fishing Luck** (*Feiyu*), a love story about a city girl finding love and freedom on the aboriginal Orchid Island, off the southern coast of Taiwan.

In a relatively weak year internationally, with only 51 films selected for competition, two shorts helped to compensate. Lin Chien-ping's *Small Station* (*Xiao zhan*) became the first Taiwanese (and first Chinese-language) film to win the Leone Citroen award for best short film at Venice, and the dystopian *Respire* (*Huxi*), filmed in Taiwan by Malaysian-born Chinese director Wi Ding Ho, picked up the Kodak Discovery Award at the International Critics Week at Cannes. The ensuing buzz resulted in an unusual arrangement, which paired the 15-minute 35mm short with Pedro Almodóvar's *Bad Education* for a two-week Taipei screening, and it later picked up the SITGES Award in Spain.

Not such a "Fantabulous" idea

The Government Information Office (GIO) tried something new in 2005 by holding a first-ever Taiwan Film Expo in Taipei's World Trade Center. As part of the GIO's "Fantabulous [sic] Taiwan" scheme, the Golden Horse Film Festival and awards ceremony were moved up a few weeks to early November, to coincide with the television Golden Bell Awards and the Expo. Alas, no amount of schedule juggling could improve Taiwan's poor performance in the 2005 awards, but this was no surprise. The GIO also announced stricter requirements for production subsidies, including the provision of three years of company accounts, and also announced that applicants for marketing subsidies must first make $15,000 (NT$500,000) at the Taipei box-office to qualify.

While former major players like CMPC may be faltering, films from new and energetic companies should, with luck, pick up the slack. One example is Lee Chi-yuan's upcoming **Chocolate Rap** (*Qiaokeli rap*), produced by the new Chi & Company and billed as Asia's first hip-hop film. Other examples may come from Taiwan Streaming Media Technology (TSMT), which jumped this year from internet media to feature films and released **The Strait Story** (*Fushi guangying*), a historical drama about a Taiwanese artist trained in Japan. TSMT is also handling copyrights for many new film and TV releases.

Meanwhile, at press time, everyone was anxiously anticipating the $5m **Silk** (*Guisi*), a horror film written and directed by Double Vision's Su Chao-pin and starring Chang Chen and Karena Lam. Funded by giant CMC Electronics, the film may serve as a bell-wether for the future viability of (relatively) big-budget film-making in Taiwan.

IAN GABRIEL ROWEN (ian@theory.org) has consulted or interpreted for most of Taiwan's major festivals, translated scripts and subtitles for several Taiwanese features and documentaries, and reported on Taiwan film for *POTS*, Taipei's arts and culture weekly.

Prod: Homegreen Films/Arena Films/Arte France Cinema. As Taipei suffers a serious water crisis, Shiang-chyi begins an affair with watch-seller Hsiao-kang. They meet every day in her apartment. Hsiao-kang keeps his new career as a porn actor secret from Shiang-chyi, even as he shoots a film in a neighbouring apartment.

WU MI LE (Let it Be) *[Documentary, 2005] Script, Dir and Phot: Lam-Chuan Yen, Cres Juang. Prod: Cimage Taiwan Film Co.* A document of the daily lives of three elderly rice farmers in Tainan County's Houbi Township. For 50 years, this is how they have passed their days, shedding a bead of sweat for each grain of rice.

YUEGUANGXIA, WO JIDE (The Moon Also Rises) *[Drama, 2004] Script and Dir: Lin Cheng-sheng. Phot: Song Wen-zhong, Yang Wei-han. Players: Lin Chia-yu, Shih Yi-nan, Yang Kuei-mei. Prod: Lin/Chiu Shun-ching/Central Motion Picture Company.* In the south-eastern countryside, Chen Pao-chai's 20-year-old daughter, Hsi-lien, is about to start work as an elementary-school teacher. Despite opposition from Pao-chai, Hsi-lien wants to marry her cousin, Chen Jun-ming, who secretly meets her.

Quote of the Year

"Young people usually entertain fancy ideas about their future in film industry. Central Motion Picture Company does not."

JENNIFER JAO, *head of international business development at Taiwan's oldest studio.*

Thailand Anchalee Chaiworaporn

The Year's Best Films

Anchalee Chaiworaporn's selection:

Citizen Dog
(Wisit Sasassanathieng)
Worldly Desires
(Apichatphong Weerasethakul)
Ahingsa Jikko Mee Gam
(Leo Kittikorn)

Ahingsa Jikko Mee Gam

Recent and Forthcoming Films

AHINGSA JIKKO MEE GAM
[Thriller, 2005] Script and Dir: Leo Kittikorn. Phot: Thammacharoen Phromphan, Amorn Duangtaweethong, Chat Maneephong. Players: Boriwat Yoo-toh, Theeradanai Suwanhom, Prinya Ngamwongwan. Prod: RS Film.

BUPPHARATREE 2
(Rahtree Returns)
[Horror, 2005] Script and Dir: Yuthlert Sippapak. Phot: Somkid Phukphong. Players: Cherman Boonyasak, Kris Srepoomseth, Dee Dokmadan, Den Dokpradu. Prod: Maeng Pong.

INVISIBLE WAVE
[Film noir, 2005] Script: Prabda Yoon. Dir: Penek Rattanaruang. Phot: Christopher Doyle. Players: Gang Hye-Jang, Asano Tadanobu. Prod: Five Stars Production/Fortissimo.

The year 2005 saw two paradoxical changes in Thai cinema. While the mainstream industry became sluggish, flooded by poor films, the independents grew stronger, with the emergence of feature film newcomers. Total production dropped from 48 in 2003 and 2004 to approximately 37 in 2005, and by September only 26 local films had released, excluding the Hong Kong-directed *The Eye Infinity* and *Ghost of Mae Nak* (from Britain's Mark Duffield).

The top four blockbusters were all low-quality, mass-market flicks. Martial arts action movie **Tom Yum Goong**, the sequel to *Ong Bak: The Muay Thai Warrior*, became the top grosser of 2005, taking $4.9m. It brings Tony Jaa to Australia to fight Vietnamese gangsters. Jaa's stardom has changed several domestic and international distribution methods. Locally, the ticket sales were shared between the producers and five regional distributors, instead of a wholesale rights deal as in the past. Internationally, *Tom Yam Goong* became the first Thai film to be released almost simultaneously in Thailand, Hong Kong, Taiwan and South Korea.

The other three blockbusters, **The Holy Man**, **Hello Yasothorn** and **Dumber Heroes**, were all slapstick efforts starring local TV comedians. Despite poor production and nonsensical plots, they climbed into the all-time list of the top 10 Thai hits. It seems comedy and martial arts have joined horror as surefire hit genres in Thai cinema.

Sasanathieng's *Dog* days

Sadly, most of the artistically impressive Thai films were commercial flops. Wisit Sasanathieng, who with *Tears of the Black Tiger* (2000) directed the first Thai film to appear at Cannes, delivered his second film, **Citizen Dog**, but it earned a pittance at the box-office before being helped by Luc Besson's EuropaCorp for international distribution. This surreal fairytale details the lives of two rural people who try to achieve their dreams in Bangkok. Reminiscent of *Tears of the Black Tiger*, it is another colour-splashed movie, full of fun and life.

The Tin Mine, the second feature of Jira Maligul, tells of the coming of age of a famous local writer whose life was changed after he was sent by his father to work in a tin mine in the south.

Wisit Sasanatieng's **Citizen Dog**

When it opened in May 2005, nationalism spread through film circles again, as respected directors, critics and politicians all praised it as the best Thai film of 2005. While it waited to be selected for a major film festival, the local and international releases of Penek Rattanaruang's **Invisible Wave** were postponed to 2006. *Invisible Wave* features Korean star Gang Hye-Jang (*Old Boy*) as a mafia mistress involved with a sushi chef (Asano Tadanobu), and is set in Hong Kong, Macao, Bangkok and Phuket.

Kittikorn Leosirikul's **Ahingsa Jikko Me Gam** (literally, *Ahingsa, a Junkie Who Has Karma*) was the stylish, punk story of a group of youths who encounter strange incidents and try to find out if they are caused by the drugs they are taking or karma. They discover that karma is no longer an invisible Buddhist principle, but a junkie in red clothes and Nike shoes.

Fortunately, while the mainstream is in decline, the independent sector has moved on to solid ground. Inspired by Apichatphong Weerasethakul, whose fourth feature, *Tropical Malady*, was Thailand's first Cannes prize-winner, two documentaries and one feature – all shot in digital – were made without funding from the major companies. **Three Friends**, by Aditya Assarat, Mingmongkol Sunakul and Pumin Chiradee, follows actress-cum-model Napakapa Nakprasit as she seeks to balance friendships, love and career. The other documentary, **Innocence**, by Nisa Kongsri and former Miss Thailand Areeya Chumsai, details the lives of hill-tribe schoolchildren who constantly dream of seeing the sea. The one independent fiction feature, **Ordinary Love**, shot in black and white on digital by young director Teekhadet Vucharadhanin, explored the reunion of two former lovers who still love each other but decide to remain just friends.

ANCHALEE CHAIWORAPORN (anchalee_chai@yahoo.com) is a film critic based in Thailand. She won the M.L. Bunlua Thepphayasuwan Award for Best Film Critic in 2000 and the M.R. Ayumongkol Award for Best Feature Writer in 2002. She runs a bilingual website on Thai cinema http://www.thaicinema.org

KHOMSAN-RACHANEE (Ordinary Romance)
[Drama, 2005] Dir: Teekhadet Vucharadhanin. Phot: Phumin Chinaradee. Players: Maneeya Herman, Pleo Sirisuwan.

MAMEE (Three Friends)
[Documentary, 2005] Dir: Aditya Assarat, Mingmongkol Sunakul, Pumin Chiradee. Players: Napakapa Nakprasit, Benporn Poonsome, Jitraporn Phanit. Prod: The Dedicate Ltd.

MAHALAI MUENG-RAE (The Tin Mine)
[Drama, 2005] Script and Dir: Jira Maligul. Phot: Charnkij Channiwikaipong. Players: Pichaya Watjitphan, Dolya Matcha, Anthony Howard Gould. Prod: GTH.

The Tin Mine

MAH NAKORN (Citizen Dog)
[Surreal romantic comedy, 2005] Script and Dir: Wisit Sasanatieng. Phot: Rewat Phreeleat. Players: Mahasamuth Boonyarak, Sangthong Keathuthong. Prod: Five Star Productions.

PHUEN SANIT (Dear Dakanda)
[Romance, 2005] Script: Nithid Naphitchayasuthin. Dir: Khomkrit Treewimol. Phot: Prames Chankrasae. Players: Sunny Suwanmethanon, Siraphan Wattanajinda. Prod: GTH.

SUA RONG HAI (Crying Tigers)
[Documentary, 2005] Dir: Santi Taephanich. Players: Phornsak Songsaeng, Luafuea Jokmok, Maen Huapla. Prod: Sahamongkol Film/Baramyoo.

TOM YUM GOONG
[Action, 2005] Script: Khongdej Jaturontrassamee. Dir: Prachya Pinklaew. Players: Tony Jaa, Mam Jokmok. Prod: Sahamongkol Film/Baramyoo.

Tunisia Roy Armes

Recent Films

LA DANSE DU VENT
(The Wind Dance)
[Drama, 2004] Script and Dir:
Taïeb Louhichi. Phot: Franck
Rabel. Players: Mohamed
Choukh, Haifa Bouzouta, Hatem
Berrabeh, Cheikro Rammah.
Prod: Tanit Productions.

LE PRINCE (The Prince)
[Drama, 2004] Script and Dir:
Mohamed Zran. Phot: Tarek
Benabdallah. Players:
Abdelmonem Chouayet, Sonia
Mankai, Mustapha Adouani,
Ahmed Snoussi, Tayeb Weslati.
Prod: Sangho Films/Mandala
Productions/Soread 2M.

PAROLE D'HOMMES
(A Man's Word)
[Drama, 2004] Script and Dir:
Moez Kamoun. Phot: Michel
Baudour. Players: Jamel Sassi,
Fethi Mselmani, Jamila Chichi,
Ramzi Azaïez, Lotfi Dziri. Prod:
Touza Films.

ELLE ET LUI (Him and Her)
[Drama, 2004] Script and Dir:
Elyes Baccar. Phot: Mohamed
Maghraoui. Players: Mohamed
Ali Ben Jemaa, Anissa Daoud.
Prod: CTV Services.

L'ESQUIVE (The Dodge)
[Drama, 2004] Script and Dir:
Abdellatif Kechiche. Phot:
Lubomir Bakchev. Players:
Osman Elkharraz, Sara
Forestier, Sabrina Ouazani,
Hajar Hamlili, Rachid Hami.
Prod: Jacques Ouaniche.

NOCE D'ETE
(Summer Wedding)
[Drama, 2004] Script: Moktar
Ladjimi and Nouri Bouzid. Dir:
Ladjimi. Phot: Jacques Besse.
Players: Mohamed Ali Ben

Despite the total impossibility of Tunisian films recovering their costs in the tiny domestic market, production has actually almost doubled since the beginning of the new millennium. Before 2000, production had been less than two films a year on average: since then we have had 20 Tunisian new films. This output is very irregular, however, with the release dates timed to fit in with the biennial cycle of the Tunisian film festival, the Journées Cinématographiques de Carthage, which remains one of the most significant on the African continent.

Despite the upsurge of production, no one has made more than one feature in the five-year period, though nine of the film-makers have been newcomers. Taïeb Louhichi, whose first and best-known film, *The Shadow of the Earth*, dates back to 1982, though he is still in his 50s, completed his fourth feature in 2004, **The Wind Dance** (*La danse du vent*). His previous film about well-to-do delinquent teenagers, *Moon Wedding*, having aroused little critical attention, Louhichi turned in his new feature to the question of how cinema is possible in Tunisia. His protagonist is a film-maker (played by the great Algerian director Mohamed Chouikh) who becomes lost in the south Tunisian desert and haunted by the vision of a beautiful Berber girl. The dance of the title describes the way images of the girl and the film he is struggling to make haunt his imagination.

The Prince (*Le prince*), the new film by another established (though younger) director, Mohamed Zran, takes place, by contrast, in the all-too-real setting of the Avenue Bourguiba, the main thoroughfare of contemporary Tunis. But it, too, is a tale of impossible love, this time that of a poor flower seller for a rich and beautiful, mature, middle-class woman working at the local bank. In dealing with this little world of loves, hopes and dreams, Zran shows a shrewd insight into the psychology of the Arab male, and a gift for comedy not apparent in his earlier work. As always, his sense of place and awareness of unspoken social divisions are strong.

A novel debut

The first of the newcomers, Moez Kamoun, was trained like the others in France, but returned home to work for many years as an assistant director and production manager on more than 50 films

Sara Forestier in **The Dodge**

by Tunisian and European directors. Though he has directed a number of shorts since 1987, **A Man's Word** (*Parole d'hommes*) is his first feature, and one of the few Maghrebian movies to be adapted from a popular novel. It is a disenchanted look at the lives of three young friends, Abbes, Sassi and Saad, starting with their childhood in a remote oasis settlement, where they are entranced by the passing Mercedes cars driven by people from Tunis. As adults, they all move to the big city, but their lives bring little satisfaction among the complexities and hypocrisies of urban life.

The much younger Elyes Baccar has followed a similar path of French training, assisting on Tunisian and foreign features and directing shorts. His first feature, **Him and Her** (*Elle et lui*), is the claustrophobic tale of a reclusive young man and a female intruder who may or may not be a figment of his imagination. The youngest newcomer, Moktar Ladjimi, who studied film-making in Paris and now lives there, had already made three documentaries widely seen on the festival circuit. His first fiction feature, **Summer Wedding** (*Noce d'été*), is another disillusioned tale of urban life, dealing with a journalist who is frustrated in his professional life and runs away on the night of his loveless arranged marriage.

In a very different vein, the Tunisian-born but Paris-based actor–director Abdellatif Kechiche made **L'Esquive** (variously translated as *The Scam* or *The Dodge*), an amusing and invigorating comedy about young people from the immigrant community in the Paris suburbs in which Kechiche grew up. The film was rewarded with four of the principal Césars (the French Oscars) for 2005, proving how closely the immigrant community in France participates in mainstream cinema.

Jemâa, Fethi Maddaoui, Lofti Abdelli. Prod: CTV Services.

LA VILLA (The Villa)
[Drama, 2003] Script: Mohamed Mahfoudh. Dir: Mohamed Damak. Phot: Khaled Belkiria. Players: Lotfi Abdelli, Mohamed Jabali, Dorra Zarrouk, Lotfi Dziri, Anissa Lotfi, Michket Krifa. Prod: CTV Films.

UNE ODYSSEE (The Odyssey)
[Thriller, 2003] Script and Dir: Brahim Babaï. Players: Saba Moubareck, Jamel Madani, Ezzedinne Gannoun, Noureddine Souli.

MITTERRAND EST MORT (Mitterrand is Dead)
[Short, 2003] Script and Dir: Hedi Sassi. Phot: Florence Levasseur. Players: Sophie Quinton, Mohamed Damraoui, Yann de Monterno, Gilles Carbello. Prod: Capharmaüm Production (France).

Turkey Atilla Dorsay

The Year's Best Films

Atilla Dorsay's selection:

Boats out of Watermelon Rinds (Ahmet Ulucay)
Lovelorn (Yavuz Turgul)
Toss-Up (Ugur Yücel)
Istanbul Tales
(Ümit Ünal et al)
Angel's Fall
(Semih Kaplanoglu)

Olgun Simsek, left, and Kenan Imirzalioglu in **Toss Up**

Recent and Forthcoming Films

ANLAT ISTANBUL
(Istanbul Tales)
[Comedy-drama, 2005] Script: Ümit Ünal. Dir: Ünal, Kudret Sabancı, Selim Demirdelen, Yücel Yolcu, Ömür Atay. Phot: Mehmet Aksin. Players: Altan Erkekli, Özgü Namal, Mehmet Günsür, Cetin Tekindor, Yelda Reynaud. Prod: TMC Film Yapim Ltd.

AYIN KARANLIK YÜZÜ
(The Dark Face of the Moon)
[Drama, 2005] Script: Metin Bilgin. Dir: Biket Ilhan. Phot: Aydin Sarioglu. Players: Ali Poyrazoglu, Sanem Celik, Mehmet Ali Alabora, Metin Belgin. Prod: Sinevizyon Film/Hyperion S.A. (Greece).

The optimistic outlook expressed in last year's *IFG* entry was only partly justified: 22 films were released in 2004, up from 17 in 2003 – not exactly a boom. In terms of quality, however, the year was quite satisfactory, not least in the amazing blend of films from the oldest directors and exceptional newcomers. Atif Yilmaz, 79, finally released **Borrowed Bride** (*Egreti gelin*), dramatising an old and apparently lost tradition according to which wealthy rural families provided 'easy' lower-class women to teach their young sons how to be real men. Yilmaz told this story of love versus tradition with ease, humour and social criticism and was rewarded with a surprise box-office hit.

At 85, Memduh Ün returned to directing 12 years after *Bullshit* (*Zikkimin kökü*), but unfortunately his health prevented him from finishing *Cinema Is a Miracle* (*Bir mucizedir sinema*) and it was completed by his ex-assistant, Tunc Basaran, for release in 2005–06. Ali Özgentürk, 60, once the creator of marvellous personal films such as *Hazal* and *The Guardian*, gave us **The Time of the Heart** (*Kalbin zamani*), a timeless love story between a mysterious woman and her three suitors, set entirely in the legendary Pera Palas hotel in Istanbul, whose guests have included Agatha Christie and Greta Garbo. But the antique décor was the only genuinely good thing about this confused, sometimes amateurish film.

Erden Kiral, 64, once responsible for internationally acclaimed films such as *A Season in Hakkari*, returned with **Yolda** (*On the Road*), a personal film, screened at Venice 2005, about his voyage with the late Yilmaz Güney, discussing the making of the famous *Yol*, which was started by Kiral and then taken over, on Güney's insistence from prison, by Serif Gören. Although not entirely satisfactory, especially for people who knew Güney, it took a fresh, sensitive approach to a legendary creator, and the courage to show both parties' weaknesses.

Yavuz Turgul, 60, the Turkish director most adept at combining mass-market cinema with personal creativity, gave, nine years after the legendary *The Bandit* (*Eskiya*), another beautiful film, **Lovelorn** (*Gönül Yarasi*), depicting a strange and almost impossible love triangle among common people, with a first-class script, convincing characters, a constant melancholy and some unforgettable scenes.

Meltem Cumbul, left, and Sener Sen in **Lovelorn**

Orhan Oguz, 57, who began as a fine cinematographer before directing several prestigious films, returned with **Magic** (*Büyü*), a professional but childish rural horror story.

The always interesting Kutlug Ataman, who works as an *artiste complet*, with works-in-progress combining cinema, video, painting, sculpture and "happenings", returned to pure cinema with **The Story of Two Girls** (*Iki genc kiz*), adapting a successful novel by Perihan Magden, about two girls from opposite sides of society, tackling hidden sexuality and class clashes. Shot on video, in ugly colour, with improvisation and dubious acting, this was nevertheless fresh and heartfelt.

A sci-fi sensation

The young generation seemed more interested in instant popular success than personal vision. Thus, Ömer Faruk Sorak, after *Vizontele*, which he co-directed with the immensely popular actor–writer–director Yilmaz Erdogan, co-operated this time with another TV celebrity, the comedian Cem Yilmaz. They turned **G.O.R.A.**, the first Turkish sci-fi film, into the biggest box-office success ever, with four million tickets sold (and even positive reviews and box-office in the UK). The great stage actor Ferhan Sensoy made a late comeback to cinema in two films. **What a Luck!** (*Sans Kapiyi Kirinca*), by the newcomer Tayfun Güneyer, was about a middle-class Turkish family who, after winning a TV contest, find themselves in Cuba, where the father's uncanny resemblance to a city governor leads to all manner of comic events. What a waste of the first Turkish–Cuban co-production! **Pardon!**, adapted from a bitter stage comedy by Sensoy himself and directed by the first-timer Mert Baykal, his son-in-law, is slightly better, with a theatrical atmosphere concentrating on actors and acting, although this also makes it rather suffocating.

Oguzhan Tercan, 14 years after his first film, gave us **Robbery alla Turca** (*Hirsiz var!*), another busy comedy with characters played by TV, theatre and film celebrities, combining slapstick, Chaplinesque clowning, sitcom and absurdity. Abdullah Oguz, in his second film,

BALANS VE MANEVRA
(Balance and Movement)
[Comedy-drama, 2005] Script and Dir: Teoman. Phot: Gökhan Atilmis. Players: Teoman, Burak Sergen, Bülent Kayabas, Seda Akman. Prod: Project Müzik Film/ Maxximum Film (Germany).

EGRETI GELIN
(Borrowed Bride)
[Comedy-drama, 2005] Script: Atif Yilmaz, Gül Dirican. Dir: Yilmaz. Phot: Kenan Ormanlar. Players: Müjde Ar, Metin Akpinar, Nurgül Yesilcay, Onur Ünsal. Prod: Yesilcam Film/ Cinegram Film & TV Productions.

Nurgül Yesilcay in **Borrowed Bride**

GELIBOLU (Gallipoli)
[Documentary, 2005] Script and Dir: Tolga Örnek. Phot: Volker Tittel. Prod: Ekip Film.

G.O.R.A.
[Sci-fi comedy, 2004] Script: Cem Yilmaz, Muhittin Korkmaz, Engin Günaydin. Dir: Ömer Faruk Sorak. Phot: Veli Kuzlu. Players: Cem Yilmaz, Safak Sezer, Ozan Güven, Rasim Öztekin, Özkan Ugur. Prod: BKM Prod.

GÖNÜL YARASI (Lovelorn)
[Drama, 2005] Script and Dir: Yavuz Turgul. Phot: Soykut Turan. Players: Sener Sen, Meltem Cumbul, Timucin Esen, Güven Kirac. Prod: FilmaCass.

HIRSIZ VAR!
(Robbery alla Turca)
[Comedy, 2005] Script: Haluk Özenc. Dir: Oguzhan Tercan. Phot: Tolga Kutlar. Players: Haluk Bilginer, Mehmet Ali Erbil, Birol Ünel. Prod: Medyapim.

IKI GENC KIZ
(The Story of Two Girls)
[Drama, 2005] Script: Kutlug Ataman, based on the novel by Perihan Magden. Dir: Ataman. Phot: Emre Erkmen. Players: Feride Cetin, Vildan Atasever, Hülya Avsar. Prod: Ataman Film.

KALBIN ZAMANI
(The Time of the Heart)
[Drama, 2005] Script and Dir: Ali Özgentürk. Phot: Ertunc Senkay. Players: Hülya Avsar, Oktay Kaynarca, Halil Ergün, Birol Ünel. Prod: Asya Film.

MELEGIN DÜSÜSÜ
(Angel's Fall)
[Drama, 2005] Script and Dir: Semih Kaplanoglu. Phot: Eyüp Boz. Players: Tülin Özen, Budak Akalin, Musa Karagöz. Prod: Kaplan Film.

O SIMDI MAHKUM
(He's a Convict Now)
[Comedy, 2005] Script: Levent Kazak. Dir: Abdullah Oguz. Phot: Soykut Turan. Players: Yavuz Bingöl, Burhan Öcal, Erkan Can. Prod: Green Pine Studios.

PARDON!
[Comedy-drama, 2005] Script: Ferhan Sensoy. Dir: Mert Baykal. Phot: Ulas Zeybek. Players: Ferhan Sensoy, Rasim Öztekin, Zeki Alasya. Prod: Plato Film.

UZAK (Dur)
[Documentary, 2005] Dir: Kazım Öz. Prod: Mezopotamya Sinema Kolektif Yapim.

Quote of the Year

"For years, it's the same speech: our cinema is getting better, our films are doing better. What I want to hear now is that they are really good and they are doing really well. Not better, just good."

KADRI YURDATAP, *a producer since 1963.*

He's a Convict Now (*O simdi mahkum*), gave us a popular law-against-mafia comedy with good characterisation. The woman director Biket Ilhan's **The Dark Face of the Moon** (*Ayin karanlık yüzü*) was an action film set on the Turkish Gökceada island in the Aegean and offered an interesting take on Turkish–Greek relations.

Tales of the city

The best films came from young, talented directors. The acclaimed singer–composer Teoman made a pleasant debut with **Balance and Movement** (*Balans ve manevra*). **Angel's Fall** (*Melegin düsüsü*) was the second film of Semih Kaplanoglu, a very sober depiction of a bunch of young people caught in the meanderings of modern life. It was so understated as to leave me wholly bored, but there was no denying its visual quality and masterly structure.

All five stories in the portmanteau **Istanbul Tales** (*Anlat Istanbul*) were written by Ümit Ünal, who directed one episode and left the rest to Kudret Sabanci, Selim Demirdelen, Yücel Yolcu and Ömür Atay, most of whom were first-timers. The result is a marvellous, captivating film whose stories are mixed up à la *Amores perros*. Istanbul's most secretive and hidden beauties are revealed.

Two debuts were for me the year's greatest achievements. **Boats out of Watermelon Rinds** (*Karpuz kabugundan gemiler yapmak*), directed by Ahmet Ulucay after many shorts and documentaries, was reviewed last year but reached Turkish cinemas only in 2005. **Toss-Up** (*Yazi tura*), by the multi-talented writer, actor, director and TV celebrity Ugur Yücel, told separately two stories, with a key overlapping scene. It's basically about the "Kurdish problem", which still haunts many Turks, from the authorities to the simple peasant, all told with a digital and moving camera and remarkable acting.

Two exceptional titles stand out in a fine year for documentaries. **Gallipoli** (*Gelibolu*) by Tolga Örnek, who made *The Hittites* (*Hititler*), tackled the famous defence of the Dardanelles by the Turks during the First World War, and surprisingly emphasised the English and Australian points of view more than the Turkish one. Even more surprisingly, it sold an astonishing 650,000 tickets. **Far Away** (*Dur*), by the Kurdish director Kazım Öz, is a touching account of Kurds forced to leave their native villages for unhappy exile in northern Europe.

ATILLA DORSAY (aldorsay@superonline.com) has been a movie critic for daily newspapers since 1966, and is the author of more than 30 books, including biographies of Yilmaz Güney and Türkan Soray. He is founder and president of SIYAD, the Association of Turkish Critics.

Ukraine Volodymyr Voytenko

The Year's Best Films

Volodymyr Voytenko's selection:

Wayfarers
(Docu. short. Ihor Strembitskiy)

Against the Sun
(Docu. Short.
Valentyn Vasyanovych)

Play for Three Actors
(Animated short.
Oleksandr Shmyhun)

Dangerously Free Man
(Docu. Roman Shyrman)

The 9th Company
(Fyodor Bondarchuk)

Recent and Forthcoming Films

PUTEVODITEL (Guidebook)
*[Experimental, 2004] Script
and Dir: Oleksandr Shapiro.
Phot: Pavlo Oleksiyenko.
Players: Oleksiy Horbunov,
Volodymyr Horyanskiy,
Vitaliy Linetskiy, Alla Serhiyko,
Volodymyr Yamnenko.
Prod: Serhiy Baranov/Lazaretty
Reproduction/Channel 1+1.*

**TROYANSKYY SPAS
(Trojan Spas)**
*[Tragi-comedy, 2004] Script:
Tetyana Lyuta, Oleksandr
Denysenko. Dir: Denysenko.
Phot: Anatoliy Khymych.
Players: Anatoliy Hnatyuk,
Oleksandr Denysenko,
Lyubov Bohdan, Sofia Dzhun,
Volodymyr Nikolayenko.
Prod: National O. Dovzhenko
Feature Film Studio/Ministry of
Culture and Arts of Ukraine.*

While Ukrainian feature film production did not increase in the past 12 months, there was a revival in TV series, which, as neighbouring Russia has shown, can become a catalyst for the movie industry. Importantly, following the Orange revolution, there has been reform of the state management of the film industry. For 2005–06, the government has prioritised the funding of 30 short films by first-time directors, in an urgent attempt to bridge the generation gap that opened during the last decade of minimal production, when there were hardly any opportunities for young directors. This initiative has also been spurred by recent festival successes for Ukrainian shorts at international film festivals, in particular the Palme d'Or awarded to the poetic–philosophical documentary **Wayfarers** (*Podorozhni*) by Ihor Strembitskiy at Cannes.

Ukrainian distributors remain dependent on their Russian counterparts, who since the days of the USSR have acquired distribution rights for Ukraine. A key factor in preserving this state of affairs is that Ukrainians understand Russian, and so, unlike in television, which has some powerful and independent local players, the entire international repertoire (mostly Hollywood films) is dubbed into Russian, and American and Russian films dominate the box-office (no official figures are collated). Part of the reason for the low level of national film production is that there are not enough screens for Ukrainian films to make back their budgets from the local market. There are just 140 screens for a population of 47 million and the market share for local films is less than 0.5% (the average ticket price is around $2.20). Although the number of cinemas is expected to rise, it may take at least five years to solve this problem.

Ihor Strembitskiy's **Wayfarers**

Natalya Dolya & Oleksiy Bohdanovych in **Stolen Happiness**

UKRADENE SCHASTYA
(Stolen Happiness)
[Drama, 2004] Script: Serhiy Dyachenko, Maryna Dyachenko, Oles Ulyanenko, after drama by Ivan Franko. Dir: Andriy Donchyk. Phot: Volodymyr Huyevskiy. Players: Natalya Dolya, Anatoliy Pashynin, Oleksiy Bohdanovych, Yevhen Pashyn. Prod: Oleksandr Rodnyanskiy, Volodymyr Oseledchyk, Mykola Shevchenko/Channel 1+1/ UMG/ Ministry of Culture and Arts of Ukraine.

TATARSKYY TRYPTYKH
(Tatar Triptykh)
[Drama, 2004] Script: Oleksandr Muratov, Victoria Muratova, after short stories by Mykhaylo Kotsyubynskiy. Dir: Muratov. Phot: Volodymyr Bass. Players: Elzara Batalova, Akhtem Seytablayev, Iryna Salahayeva, Elmar Ablaye. Prod: National O. Dovzhenko Feature Film Studio/Ministry of Culture and Arts of Ukraine.

SHTOLNYA (Pit)
[Thriller, 2006] Script: Oleksiy Khoroshko, Lyubomyr Kobylchuk. Dir: Kobylchuk. Phot and Prod: Khoroshko. Players: Oleksiy Zabyehayev, Olha Storozhuk, Pavlo Li, Svitlana Artamonova, Serhiy Stasko.

Quote of the Year

"I am a Ukrainian director and wish to make my speech in Ukrainian, not in Russian."
IHOR STREMBITSKIY, *turning down the interpreter's request for him to speak Russian as he receives the Palme D'Or for his short,* Wayfarers, *at Cannes.*

Oleksandr Shapiro's low-budget experimental film **Guidebook** (*Putibnyk*) had post-production support from local television channel 1+1 and was presented in the "Forum of New Cinema" at Berlin 2005. It was admired by the young metropolitan audience at home, not least because Kiev itself is the film's protagonist: a megalopolis in which the opinions and lifestyles of the young generation are depicted. The narrative weaves together several miniature stories, told from many subjective perspectives. There were deservedly harsh reviews for Oleksandr Denysenko's farcical tragi-comedy Trojan Spas (*Troyanskyy spas*), which suffered from a poorly formulated plot and anaemic direction. It takes place in a village in southern Ukraine, where an amateur theatre group produces a stage parody on an ancient subject, against a background of post-Soviet social decline.

Wars, past and recent

The war drama **Iron Sotnia** (*Zalizna sotnya*), directed by Oles' Yanchuk, is a Ukrainian–Australian co-production about the Ukrainian rebel army's struggle against the Nazi and communist occupation of western Ukraine during and after the Second World War. Sketchily written and directed, it had limited regional distribution. The Ukrainian–Russian–Finnish production **The 9th Company** (*9-ya rota*; credits in Russia section) by the debutant director Fyodor Bondarchuk (son of Sergey Bondarchuk) was filmed in the Crimean mountains. Its premiere in September 2005 was the biggest event of the year for Ukrainian film and it was on course for record-breaking box-office. It shows the tragedy of the last days of the war in Afghanistan in 1989: a group of Soviet army recruits fights to take a strategic position and all except for the hero perish – not knowing that the war has already ended. Bondarchuk combines confident and politically correct presentation of individual characters and national types with convincing and technically perfect battle pieces.

Finally, Oleksandr Muratov's **The Tatar Triptych** (*Tatarskyy tryptykh*) is the first ever film to use the Crimean Tatar language. Filmed on the Ukrainian Black Sea peninsula, it depicts the life of Crimean Tatars at the beginning of the twentieth century. We follow the fate of three women in a patriarchal Muslim society: one accepts paternal will and marries an unloved husband, but dreams of another man; the second acts fearlessly against tradition and perishes; the third, afraid of her parents, does not support her sweetheart, who rebels against customary law. The film is directed with an overly literary hand, and the characters' motivation is poorly established.

VOLODYMYR VOYTENKO (kinokolo@base.1plus1.net) studied at the cinema faculty in Kiev. He is a film critic and editor-in-chief of the analytical quarterly *KINO-KOLO* (www.kinokolo.ua) and presents a weekly art cinema programme on the national TV channel 1+1.

United Kingdom Philip Kemp

The Year's Best Films

Philip Kemp's selection:

A Cock and Bull Story
(Michael Winterbottom)

Separate Lies
(Julian Fellowes)

Wallace & Gromit in The Curse of the Were-Rabbit
(Nick Park, Steve Box)

The Descent (Neil Marshall)

The Constant Gardener
(Fernando Meirelles)

Emily Watson and Tom Wilkinson in
Separate Lies

Recent and Forthcoming Films

ASYLUM
[Drama, 2005] Script: Patrick Marber, from the novel by Patrick McGrath. Dir: David Mackenzie. Phot: Giles Nuttgens. Players: Natasha Richardson, Ian McKellen, Marton Csokas, Hugh Bonneville. Prod: Mace Neufeld/ Samson/Seven Arts/ Zephyr.

BULLET BOY
[Social drama, 2004] Script: Saul Dibb, Catherine Johnson. Dir: Dibb. Phot: Marcel Zyskind. Players: Ashley Walters, Luke Fraser, Claire Perkins, Leon Black. Prod: BBC Films/ UK Film Council/Shine.

Every decade, it seems, the rickety superstructure of the British film industry is shaken by a crisis, more often than not the result of government action. When the Treasury put a stop to the tax credit systems known as Sections 42 and 48, many in the industry treated it as something close to a deathblow. Independent producer Jeremy Thomas estimated the resulting loss in production volume to be as high as £235m ($411m), while the ex-Polygram boss, producer Michael Kuhn, warned that "we face the bleakest prospects for UK indigenous production" since he had entered the business in the 1980s, and that the outlook for British film-makers was "darker, I think, than in most years in my lifetime".

The Treasury's far stricter rules as to what does or doesn't count as a UK film for tax purposes have meant that big-budget overseas productions are increasingly enticed away to the lower-cost attractions of new film-making centres in Central and Eastern Europe or the southern hemisphere. Co-productions no longer looked so seductive to overseas companies, now that they could no longer write off upwards of 50% of the budget against tax. The fifth *Harry Potter* movie looked likely to quit the franchise's UK base at Leavesden, while *Casino Royale* has largely abandoned James Bond's traditional home at Pinewood for locations outside the UK. For similar reasons, the complex network of post-production houses based in and around Soho were feeling the pinch.

There were more positive developments in early December 2005, however, when Chancellor Gordon Brown announced the replacements for Sections 42 and 48: a new rate of tax relief of 16% for larger-budget films and 20% for lower-budget productions. John Woodward, the UK Film Council's chief executive, greeted the move as "the best news the industry has received for five years", acknowledging that there had been "real uncertainty as to whether the infrastructure of the British film industry was sustainable, but what the Chancellor has done is unequivocally secured the long-term future of the infrastructure."

Shandy fizzes

Indigenous British production starts had fallen by a third – from 45 in 2003 to only 30 in 2004 – and according to Andrew Eaton of Revolution Films, Michael Winterbottom's regular producer and

Twentieth Century Fox

Shine Films/BBC Films/Kobal

Ashley Walters in **Bullet Boy**

THE BUSINESS
*[Crime thriller, 2005] Script
and Dir: Nick Love. Phot:
Damian Bromley. Players:
Danny Dyer, Tamer Hassan,
Geoff Bell, Georgina Chapman.
Prod: Vertigo.*

THE CONSTANT GARDENER
*[Drama, 2005] Script: Jeffrey
Caine, from the novel by John le
Carré. Dir: Fernando Meirelles.
Phot: César Charlone. Players:
Ralph Fiennes, Rachel Weisz,
Hubert Koundé, Danny Huston,
Bill Nighy. Prod: Focus/Scion/
UK Film Council.*

A COCK AND BULL STORY
[US Title: **TRISTRAM SHANDY:
A COCK AND BULL STORY**]
*[Costume drama, 2005] Script:
Martin Hardy. Dir: Michael
Winterbottom. Phot: Marcel
Zyskind. Players: Steve Coogan,
Rob Brydon, Gillian Anderson,
Keeley Hawes. Prod: Revolution/
BBC Films/East Midlands/Scion.*

THE DESCENT
*[Horror, 2005] Script and Dir:
Neil Marshall. Phot: Sam
McCurdy. Players: Shauna
MacDonald, Natalie Mendoza,
Alex Reid, Saskia Mulder. Prod:
Celador/NorthMen.*

FESTIVAL
*[Satirical comedy, 2005] Script
and Dir: Annie Griffin. Phot:
Danny Cohen. Players: Chris
O'Dowd, Lyndsey Marshal,
Stephen Mangan, Daniela
Nardini. Prod: Young Pirate/
UK Film Council/Channel Four.*

**THE GREAT ECSTASY OF
ROBERT CARMICHAEL**
*[Drama, 2005] Script: Thomas
Clay, Joseph Lang. Dir: Clay.
Phot: Yorgos Arvinitis. Players:*

deputy chair of the Film Council, "the bottom has fallen out of the UK distribution market. Nobody is offering anything, or they are offering a pathetic amount." Eaton had good reason to recall his gloomy words when the main backers pulled out of his latest production, Winterbottom's **A Cock and Bull Story**, on the eve of shooting, taking with them over 50% of the funding. Indomitable as ever, Eaton and Winterbottom carried right on with the shoot, drawing on their own personal savings to replenish the budget and incorporating the vicissitudes of the production into the script itself (this off-the-peg rewriting led to Winterbottom's regular screenwriting partner, Frank Cottrell Boyce, taking his name off the script, which is credited to the pseudonymous Martin Hardy).

Laurence Sterne's mid-18th-century novel *The Life and Opinions of Tristram Shandy* is a gloriously idiosyncratic work that the film's star, Steve Coogan, describes onscreen as "a post-modern classic written way before there was any modernism to be 'post' about". It has sometimes been called "the most unfilmable book ever written". Winterbottom, never one to duck a challenge, has turned Sterne's novel about the impossibility of writing a novel into a film about the impossibility of making a film. The result is quirky, diverting and unashamedly digressive, packed with in-jokes, shaggy-dog stories and enough red herrings for a fish supper. Winterbottom slyly plays off the real-life rivalry between his two male leads, Coogan and Rob Brydon; as the final credits roll the pair are still squabbling over which does a better Al Pacino impersonation.

Redbus Film Distribution

Steve Coogan, left, and Rob Brydon in **A Cock and Bull Story**

No less diverting – in its own very different style – was the long awaited feature-length Wallace and Gromit adventure from Nick Park and his Aardman team of animators. **Wallace & Gromit in The Curse of the Were-rabbit** ("Something wicked this way hops") utterly redeems the relative disappointment of *Chicken Run*. Daffy Lancastrian inventor Wallace and his infinitely resourceful dog, Gromit, tackle marauding bunnies, while Wallace wins the heart of Lady Campanula Tottington away from her arrogant aristo suitor (voiced by Helena Bonham Carter and Ralph Fiennes, sending up their respective images). Park and Steve Box's film cheerfully spoofs horror movie conventions from *King Kong* to *The Incredible Hulk*, and demonstrates how old-fashioned stop-motion animation, complete with visible thumbprints on the models, can still reach out to us in a way that CGI never can.

Horrors below, horrors above

The Descent, Neil Marshall's second feature after *Dog Soldiers*, plays its horror movie conventions fairly straight, but never feels stale. This tale of six young women trapped underground on a potholing expedition in the Appalachians and hunted down by blind albino troglodytes marks an impressive advance on its predecessor. Cool, controlled and luridly atmospheric, it suggests a major British horror director in the making.

Shauna MacDonald comes up for air in **The Descent**

There are intimations of horror, too, about **Asylum**, skilfully adapted by Patrick Marber from a novel by Patrick McGrath. David Mackenzie, who had already explored the shifting borderline between normality and abnormality in *Young Adam*, captures the oppressive claustrophobia of McGrath's novel, as a psychiatrist's bored young wife is drawn dangerously into the orbit of a seductive mental patient.

There is horror of a very different and all too real kind in Michael Caton-Jones' **Shooting Dogs**, a searing account of the first few days of the 1994 Rwandan genocide, when militant Hutus took to the streets to slaughter nearly a million Tutsis and moderate Hutus. Covering much the same ground as Terry George's *Hotel Rwanda*, Caton-Jones' film gains from fluid camera technique, the advantage of shooting in the actual locations involved, and a tough-minded attitude to the horrors on view. It's weakened, though, by filtering events largely through the white sensibilities of its heroes, a wide-eyed young teacher (Hugh Dancy) and an agonised Catholic priest (John Hurt, giving one of his finest performances).

Dan Spencer, Danny Dyer, Lesley Manville, Ryan Winsley. Prod: Boudu/Pull Back Camera.

GUY X
[Black comedy, 2005] Script: Steve Attridge, John Paul Chapple. Dir: Saul Metzstein. Phot: François Dagenais. Players: Jason Biggs, Natascha McElhone, Jeremy Northam, Michael Ironside. Prod: Film & Music Entertainment/Spice Factory/Icelandic Film Fund.

GYPO
[Drama, 2005] Script and Dir: Jan Dunn. Phot: Jacob Kusk. Players: Pauline McLynn, Chloe Sirene, Paul McGann, Rula Lenska. Prod: BBC/ Distant Eye/Molinare/ Spotty Dog/VMI.

THE HITCHHIKER'S GUIDE TO THE GALAXY
[Sci-fi comedy, 2005] Script: Douglas Adams, Carey Kirkpatrick, from Adams' novel. Dir: Garth Jennings. Phot: Igo Jadue-lillo. Players: Martin Freeman, Mos Def, Sam Rockwell, Zooey Deschanel, Bill Nighy. Prod: Touchstone/Spyglass.

THE JACKET
[Thriller, 2005] Script: Marc Rocco, Massy Tadjedin. Dir: John Maybury. Phot: Peter Deming. Players: Adrien Brody, Keira Knightley, Jennifer Jason Leigh, Kris Kristofferson. Prod: Mandalay/Warner/Section Eight.

THE LAST HANGMAN
[Biopic, 2005] Script: Jeff Pope. Dir: Adrian Shergold. Phot: Danny Cohen. Players: Timothy Spall, Juliet Stevenson, Eddie Marsan, Juliet Lewis. Prod: Granada/UK Film Council.

THE LEAGUE OF GENTLEMEN'S APOCALYPSE
[Black comedy, 2005] Script: Jeremy Dyson, Mark Gatiss, Steve Pemberton, Reece Shearsmith. Dir: Steve Bendelack. Phot: Rob Kitzmann. Players: Gatiss, Pemberton, Shearsmith, David Warner, Victoria Wood.

Investing in film across the UK

Regional film agencies across the UK work with the UK Film Council and other partners, investing in local filmmakers, providing film finance and offering a range of services to incoming productions.

Their film activities include:

- Production funding
- Assistance to filmmakers working in the region - location finding, crewing, etc
- Cinema audience development
- Archive development
- Training and education
- Business and skills development

Please contact individual agencies directly for information.

For details on the work of the UK Film Council please visit the website www.ukfilmcouncil.org.uk
Tel: +44 (0) 20 7861 7861

Regional Screen Agency contacts

EM Media
35 - 37 St Mary's Gate
Nottingham NG1 1PU
Tel + 44 (0) 115 934 9090
Fax + 44 (0) 115 950 0988
Email info@em-media.org.uk
www.em-media.org.uk

Film London
20 Euston Centre, Regent's Place
London NW1 3JH
Tel + 44 (0) 20 7387 8787
Fax + 44 (0) 20 7387 8788
Email info@filmlondon.org.uk
www.filmlondon.org.uk

Northern Film & Media
Central Square, Forth Street
Newcastle-upon-Tyne NE1 3PJ
Tel + 44 (0) 191 269 9200
Fax + 44 (0) 191 269 9213
Email info@northernmedia.org
www.northernmedia.org

North West Vision
233 The Tea Factory
Liverpool L1 4DQ
Tel + 44 (0) 151 708 2967
Fax + 44 (0) 151 708 2984
Email info@northwestvision.co.uk
www.northwestvision.co.uk

Screen East
1st Floor, 2 Millennium Plain
Norwich NR2 1TF
Tel + 44 (0) 1603 776 920
Fax + 44 (0) 1603 767 191
Email info@screeneast.co.uk
www.screeneast.co.uk

Screen South
Shearway Business Park
Shearway Road, Folkestone
Kent CT19 4RH
Tel + 44 (0) 1303 298 222
Fax + 44 (0) 1303 298 227
Email info@screensouth.org
www.screensouth.org

Screen West Midlands
9 Regent Place
Birmingham B1 3NJ
Tel + 44 (0) 121 265 7120
Fax + 44 (0) 121 265 7180
Email info@screenwm.co.uk
www.screenwm.co.uk

Screen Yorkshire
Studio 22, 46 The Calls
Leeds LS2 7EY
Tel + 44 (0) 113 294 4410
Fax + 44 (0) 113 294 4989
Email info@screenyorkshire.co.uk
www.screenyorkshire.co.uk

South West Screen
St Bartholomew's Court
Lewins Mead, Bristol BS1 5BT
Tel + 44 (0) 117 952 9977
Fax + 44 (0) 117 952 9988
Email info@swscreen.co.uk
www.swscreen.co.uk

UK FILM | COUNCIL
LOTTERY FUNDED

Metrodome Distribution

Hugh Dancy, left, and John Hurt in **Shooting Dogs**

The adaptation game

As ever, impeccably staged and costumed adaptations of English literature formed a staple of the year's output. Joe Wright's **Pride and Prejudice** looks superb, and novelist Deborah Moggach does a skilled job of filleting Jane Austen, but the film is let down by its casting. The point of Elizabeth Bennett, after all, is that she's not spectacularly pretty, but very bright, making the ubiquitous Keira Knightley rather less than ideal for the role, and Matthew MacFadyen never quite cuts it as Darcy. But the cast does offers one outstanding compensation: Donald Sutherland's Mr. Bennett, drily ironic and effortlessly stealing every scene in which he appears.

Casting weaknesses also marred Roman Polanski's **Oliver Twist**. Jamie Foreman gives us a brutal, sullen Bill Sykes, but misses the demonic malice that both Robert Newton and Oliver Reed brought to the role, and young Barney Clark makes a pallid Oliver. Still, Ben Kingsley brings out the pathos and genuine tenderness underlying Fagin's villainy and there are some relishable cameos, not least Alun Armstrong's apoplectic magistrate, Fang. Polanski, powerfully drawing on memories of his own tormented childhood, effectively eclipses memories of Carol Reed's musical version, even if the shadow of David Lean's classic adaptation still looms large.

As Polanski, and indeed Ang Lee with *Sense and Sensibility* have shown, turning non-English-born directors loose on classic English texts can unleash fruitful creative tensions. John le Carré's **The Constant Gardener** may not yet quite qualify as 'classic', but handing the film adaptation over to Brazilian director Fernando Meirelles (*City of God*) was a stroke of genius. Meirelles cuts through le Carré's sober prose and careful plotting with irresistible energy, jumping nimbly back and forth in time and getting to grips with his Kenyan locations with raw, documentary-like immediacy. His evident identification with the exploited Africans enhances the novel's sense of anger at the arrogant callousness of international pharmaceutical giants.

Prod: Film Four/Hell's Kitchen/ Tiger Aspect/Universal.

THE LIBERTINE
[Costume drama, 2005] Script: Stephen Jeffreys, from his play. Dir: Laurence Dunmore. Phot: Alexander Melman. Players: Johnny Depp, John Malkovich, Samantha Morton, Tom Hollander. Prod: Mr Mudd/ Isle of Man Film/Weinstein Co.

MRS HENDERSON PRESENTS
[Comedy-drama, 2005] Script: Martin Sherman. Dir: Stephen Frears. Phot: Andrew Dunn. Players: Bob Hoskins, Judi Dench, Christopher Guest, Kelly Reilly. Prod: Pathé/BBC Films.

MILLIONS
[Comedy-drama, 2005] Script: Frank Cottrell Boyce. Dir: Danny Boyle. Phot: Anthony Dod Mantle. Players: Alex Etel, Lewis Owen McGibbon, James Nesbitt, Daisy Donovan. Prod: Mission/Pathé/BBC Films/ UK Film Council.

Giles Keyte/Mission Pics/Fox/Kobal

Alex Etel in **Millions**

OLIVER TWIST
[Costume drama, 2005] Script: Ronald Harwood, based on Dickens' novel. Dir: Roman Polanski. Phot: Pawel Edelman. Players: Barney Clark, Ben Kingsley, Jamie Foreman, Harry Eden, Leanne Rowe. Prod: RP Films/RunteamII/Etic.

Guy Ferrandis/Pathé

Barney Clark as **Oliver Twist**

ON A CLEAR DAY

[Drama, 2005] Script: Alex Rose. Dir: Gaby Dellal. Phot: David Johnson. Players: Peter Mullan, Brenda Blethyn, Jodhi May, Jamie Sives. Prod: Forthcoming/InFilm.

PRIDE AND PREJUDICE

[Costume drama, 2005] Script: Deborah Moggach, based on Jane Austen's novel. Dir: Joe Wright. Phot: Roman Osin. Players: Keira Knightley, Matthew MacFadyen, Brenda Blethyn, Donald Sutherland. Prod: Universal/Studio Canal/ Working Title.

Matthew Macfadyen and Keira Knightley in **Pride and Prejudice**

PUFFBALL

[Psychological thriller, 2006] Script: Dan Weldon. Dir: Nicolas Roeg. Phot: Baz Irvine. Players: Donald Sutherland. Prod: Amerique/Grand Pictures/ Tall Stories/UK Film Council.

RAG TALE

[Comedy-drama, 2005] Script and Dir: Mary MacGuckian. Phot: Mark Wolf. Players: Rupert Graves, Malcolm McDowell, Jennifer Jason Leigh, Bill Paterson. Prod: Endgame/ Pembridge/Scion/Carousel.

RED ROAD

[Drama, 2006] Script and Dir: Andrea Arnold. Phot: Robbie Ryan. Players: Nathalie Press, Martin Compston, Tony Curran, Kate Dickie. Prod: Sigma/Zentropa/ UK Film Council.

From left: Hubert Koundé, Ralph Fiennes and Rachel Weisz in **The Constant Gardener**

A far less celebrated novelist than Austen, Dickens or even le Carré, Nigel Balchin, furnishes the source material for actor and *Gosford Park* screenwriter Julian Fellowes' first film as director, **Separate Lies**. Set in one of those plush, leafy Buckinghamshire villages where the 1950s seem never to have died, this is a subtle, complex exploration of moral and emotional dilemmas. Tom Wilkinson, as ever, is nothing less than note-perfect as the overly complacent husband who finds his well-upholstered life and marriage cracking wide open, but he's well matched by Emily Watson as his much younger wife, at once flattered and distressed at finding herself the focus of competing desires. As might be expected, given Fellowes' wealth of acting experience, he brings out the best from his whole cast, and his script constantly keeps us unsure just where our allegiances should lie.

Back on the Boyle?

Ever since he went disastrously off-course with *A Life Less Ordinary*, admirers of Danny Boyle's trenchant early films have been hoping for a return to form. *28 Days Later* seemed to herald it, but with **Millions**, charming and appealing though it is, he seems to be coasting at less than full power. A junior caper movie in which two young brothers find a bagful of stolen currency just before the UK goes over to the Euro, it secures likeably endearing performances from its juvenile leads but can't quite avoid a touch of the cutes.

Bullet Boy seems more like the kind of film Boyle might once have made. Documentary maker Saul Dibb's debut fiction feature is set, and largely shot, around the tough streets of Hackney in East London, where Ricky (Ashley Waters), 20, black and fresh out of jail, is determined to go straight. But his best friend, the all-too-inaptly named Wisdom, has a fatal bent for trouble, something easily found in London's growing gun culture. The plot's nothing new; but the authenticity and immediacy with which Dibb captures his chosen milieu and the macho street-patois of his characters make the film feel fresh and urgent.

Nudes and ruffs and rock'n'roll

Three wildly differing British biopics were released within days of each other towards the end of the year. The least demanding of the three, **Mrs Henderson Presents**, stars Judi Dench (now securely enthroned as a national treasure) and Bob Hoskins (surely heading that way) as respectively the owner of the Windmill Theatre, wartime home of tasteful British female nudity, and her faithful manager. Nothing tasteful, luckily, about the nudity or the sex on offer in **The Libertine**, with Johnny Depp as bawdy Restoration poet and bisexual lecher John Wilmot, Earl of Rochester. Both Depp and John Malkovich (as Charles II) throw themselves into their roles with gusto, but the film suffers from a fractured script (adapted by Stephen Jeffreys from his own stage play) and never quite attains the thrust its subject would surely have appreciated.

Rochester died aged 32, probably of syphilis. Brian Jones, founder member of The Rolling Stones, was even younger, just 27, when he was found drowned in the swimming pool at his country mansion. Producer Stephen Woolley, making his directorial debut, charts Jones' last few months in the punningly titled **Stoned**. Over the years, lurid rumours have circulated about Jones' death, often involving Faustian pacts. Woolley and his screenwriters pin the guilt on Jones' builder, Frank Thorogood, who apparently confessed to the murder on his deathbed. Paddy Considine makes the most of the underwritten role of Thorogood, but as Jones, Leo Gregory never quite convinces as any kind of rock star, fading or otherwise, and the film trails some distance behind Roeg and Cammell's mesmerisingly labyrinthine *Performance*.

Love them or loathe them, no one else makes films quite like Sally Potter's. Her latest, **Yes**, may well be her most defiantly idiosyncratic yet. For a start, it's written entirely in verse – iambic pentameter, Shakespeare's favourite – and entails long passages of internal monologue on abstruse scientific and philosophical matters. The plot

Simon Abkarian and Joan Allen in **Yes**

Nicola Dove/Greenestreet Films/UKFC/Kobal

SEPARATE LIES
[Drama, 2004] Script and Dir: Julian Fellowes. Phot: Tony Pierce-Roberts. Players: Emily Watson, Tom Wilkinson, Rupert Everett. Prod: Fox Searchlight/ Celador/DNA.

SHOOTING DOGS
[Drama-doc, 2006] Script: David Wolstencroft. Dir: Michael Caton-Jones. Phot: Ivan Strasburg. Players: John Hurt, Hugh Dancy, Claire-Hope Ashitey, Dominique Horwitz. Prod: CrossDay/BBC/Egoli Tossell/UK Film Council.

STONED
[Biopic, 2005] Script: Neal Purvis, Robert Wade. Dir: Stephen Woolley. Phot: John Mathieson. Players: Leo Gregory, Paddy Considine, David Morrissey, Monet Mazur. Prod: Intandem/Audley/Number 9.

Vertigo Films

Leo Gregory in **Stoned**

STRAIGHTHEADS
[Thriller, 2005] Script: Dan Reed and Brian Elsley. Dir: Reed. Phot: Chris Seager. Players: Gillian Anderson, Danny Dyer, Anthony Calf. Prod: FilmFour/Screen West Midlands/UK Film Council.

WALLACE & GROMIT IN THE CURSE OF THE WERE-RABBIT
[Animation, 2005] Script and Dir: Nick Park, Steve Box. Phot: Dave Alex Riddett, Tristan Oliver. Voices: Peter Sallis, Ralph Fiennes, Helena Bonham Carter. Prod: Aardman/DreamWorks Animation.

DreamWorks Animation/Aardman

Wallace & Gromit in The Curse of the Were-Rabbit

A WOMAN IN WINTER
[Drama, 2006] Script and Dir: Richard Jobson. Phot: Simon Dennis. Players: Jamie Sives, Julie Gayet, Jason Flemyng, Brian Cox. Prod: HanWay/ Tartan/UK Film Council/Vestry.

YES
[Romantic drama, 2004] Script and Dir: Sally Potter. Phot: Alexei Rodionov. Players: Joan Allen, Simon Abkarian, Sam Neill, Sheila Hancock. Prod: Greenestreet/UK Film Council/Adventure.

Quotes of the Year

"Actors understand no more about acting than bus conductors, in terms of what's good and bad."
RUFUS SEWELL, *actor.*

"Anything that's adventurous, different, groundbreaking or original is completely ignored by the distribution fraternity. Having dull and witless distributors means that the agents dictate."
STEPHEN WOOLLEY,
producer-director

– an erotic triangle between an Irish-American scientist (Joan Allen), her English politician husband (Sam Neill) and her lover, a Lebanese chef (Simon Abkarian) – risks getting lost beneath the director's self-indulgent musings. Still, you have to admire her audacity.

Such diversity and creative energy might seem to back the arguments of those who maintain the UK industry is basically on a sound footing and will weather the latest storm, as it's weathered so many others. Among these optimists – perhaps not surprisingly – is John Woodward of the Film Council, which had come in for stinging criticism from Michael Kuhn early in 2005 (he called it "a Janus-like body… not hearing criticism because it is the most powerful dispenser of patronage") and was blamed by director Terence Davies for scuppering his long-cherished adaptation of Lewis Grassic Gibbon's classic Scots novel, *Sunset Song*, by withdrawing its support not long before shooting was due to start.

One scheme by which the UKFC sets considerable store is its $20m Digital Screen Network, scheduled to reach 209 cinemas across the UK, starting from late 2005. Funded by National Lottery cash, the scheme is intended to revolutionise both distribution and exhibition. In the long term, say the UKFC and its partner, Arts Alliance Digital Cinema, distributors will no longer be saddled with the cost of striking multiple 35mm prints. Visual and sound quality will be vastly improved, increasing audience satisfaction. And cinemas equipped with the new technology – at no cost to the exhibitor – will be required to commit to screening a minimum of "specialised" films (arthouse, indie or foreign-language). This, the Council believes, will massively broaden the range of films on offer nationwide.

Audiences aren't likely to be lacking, whether for celluloid or digital screenings. In early 2004, gloomy predictions were made that UK admission figures would be badly down on the previous year, some pointing to the poor quality of major releases, others to the ever-inflating price of seats (Leicester Square ticket prices in London's West End are now the highest in Europe, with an eye-watering top whack of almost $30), and some to the booming DVD market. UK prices for DVD players, it was noted, are the second *lowest* in Europe. Yet admissions for 2004 reached 171.3m, up 2.4% on the previous year and the second highest total since 1972.

PHILIP KEMP is a freelance writer and film historian, and a regular contributor to *Sight & Sound*, *Total Film* and *DVD Review*.

United States Eddie Cockrell

The Year's Best Films

Eddie Cockrell's selection:

A History of Violence
(David Cronenberg)

Transamerica
(Duncan Tucker)

Good Night, and Good Luck. (George Clooney)

No Direction Home: Bob Dylan
(Docu. Martin Scorsese)

Brokeback Mountain
(Ang Lee)

Recent and Forthcoming Films

AMERICAN DREAMZ
[Satire, 2006] Script and Dir: Paul Weitz. Players: Hugh Grant, Dennis Quaid, Mandy Moore, Willem Dafoe, Marcia Gay Harden, Chris Klein, Jennifer Coolidge. Prod: NBC Universal/Depth of Field.

ART SCHOOL CONFIDENTIAL
[Comedy-drama, 2006] Script: Dan Clowes. Dir: Terry Zwigoff. Players: John Malkovich, Anjelica Huston, Jim Broadbent, Max Minghella, Steve Buscemi. Prod: Malkovich, Liane Halfon, Russell Smith, United Artists Pictures.

ASK THE DUST
[Romantic drama, 2006] Script: Robert Towne, from the novel by John Fante. Dir: Towne. Players: Colin Farrell, Salma Hayek, Justin Kirk, Donald Sutherland, Val Kilmer. Prod: Paula Wagner, Tom Cruise, Jonas McCord, Cruise-Wagner Productions.

Last year in this space it was reported that a *New York Times* headline had asked "Where, Oh Where, Are the Oscar Contenders?" for the year 2004. As it happens, for all the typical smoke and fury generated in the unusually crowded year-end Academy Award race, the quiet, controversial film that eventually won Best Picture had yet to open when the *Times* piece ran, and would in fact not do so – even in limited release – until December 15, 2004.

On the surface, Clint Eastwood's **Million Dollar Baby** is about a grizzled old fight trainer (Eastwood) who takes on a cocky young woman with a hunger for the ring (Hilary Swank, who earned her second Best Actress award). For long-time Clint watchers, however, the film is a quiet yet firm continuation of his spare, no-nonsense, seemingly effortless approach to moviemaking. Mix a surprising plot twist involving euthanasia into the stealth release pattern, and the resulting word-of-mouth was enough to carry the day (intriguingly, after 35 years making movies exclusively for Warner Bros., their resistance to the project sent Eastwood to DreamWorks, where he's making *Flags of Our Fathers* with Steven Spielberg).

Flash forward nearly 12 months, and this strategy was once again being utilised by at least three films of potential Oscar calibre. Spielberg's hotly-anticipated *Munich* flew well under the pre-release radar and did not open until two days before Christmas; Ang Lee's sublime drama, *Brokeback Mountain*, was thrilling critics with its level-headed look at two 1960s cowboys who share a special love; and Duncan Tucker's audaciously funny *Transamerica* – one of the first high-profile releases from the newly-minted Weinstein Company – was proving a comic showcase for long-time critics' favourite and *Desperate Housewives* co-star Felicity Huffman.

Merie W. Wallace/Warner Bros./Kobal

Hilary Swank and Morgan Freeman both won Oscars for **Million Dollar Baby**

BABEL

[Drama, 2006] Script: Guillermo Arriaga. Dir: Alejandro Gonzalez Iñarritu. Players: Brad Pitt, Cate Blanchett, Gael García Bernal, Elle Fanning, Koji Yakusho. Prod: Iñarritu, Steve Golin, Jon Kilik, Anonymous Content.

BASIC INSTINCT 2: RISK ADDICTION

[Thriller, 2006] Script: Henry Bean, Leora Barish. Dir: Michael Caton-Jones. Players: Sharon Stone, David Morrissey, Charlotte Rampling, David Thewlis. Prod: Mario Kassar, Andrew G. Vajna, Moritz Borman, Sony Pictures Entertainment/InterMedia Film/ C-2 Pictures.

THE BLACK DAHLIA

[Mystery thriller, 2006] Script: Josh Friedman, from the novel by James Ellroy. Dir: Brian De Palma. Players: Josh Hartnett, Scarlett Johansson, Hilary Swank, Aaron Eckhart, Mia Kirschner. Prod: Art Linson, Rudy Cohen, Moshe Diamant, Avi Lerner, Signature Films/ Nu Image.

BORDERTOWN

[Thriller, 2006] Script and Dir: Gregory Nava. Players: Antonio Banderas, Jennifer Lopez, Martin Sheen, Sonia Braga, Juan Diego Botto. Prod: Jennifer Lopez, Simon Fields, Gregory Nava, Mobius Entertainment/El Norte Productions/Nuyorican/Mosaic Media Group.

BREAKING AND ENTERING

[Drama, 2006] Script and Dir: Anthony Minghella. Players: Jude Law, Vera Farmiga, Juliette Binoche, Robin Wright Penn, Martin Freeman. Prod: Anthony Minghella, Sydney Pollack, Timothy Bricknell, Miramax/ Mirage Enterprises.

THE CHILDREN OF MEN

[Sci-fi adventure drama, 2006] Script: Alfonso Cuarón, David Arata, Timothy J. Sexton, from the novel by P.D. James. Dir: Cuarón. Players: Michael Caine,

Yet the news is not all good. Home theatres are on the rise, theatrical attendance is down and Hollywood has the digital jitters. After years of steady growth, the American motion picture industry is in upheaval – if not outright crisis. The numbers support this alarming trend. According to the Motion Picture Association of America, domestic box-office revenue for 2004 was nearly $9.54 billion, a $500m increase over 2003. Look closer, however, and even that slim profit is an illusion: ticket prices rose 3%, even as total admissions fell 2.5% to 1.481 billion (to be fair, this last number halved 2003's precipitous 5% erosion in attendance).

While the number of films passing the less and less significant $100m mark at the box-office was down to 21 in 2004, from 29 the previous year, five of those were the engines pulling the train: *Shrek 2* (nearly $437m), *Spider-Man 2* ($373m) *The Passion of the Christ* ($370m), *The Incredibles* ($252m) and *Harry Potter and the Prisoner of Azkaban* ($249m). That's out of 483 films released, a paltry 10 more than in 2003.

Summertime blues

The downward spiral continued into the soft summer of 2005. By early May, the month that has evolved into the opening of the hopefully lucrative summer tentpole season, receipts for the year were nearly $2.8 billion (6% behind the same point in 2004). Nevertheless, the industry was upbeat: "You can quote me on this," Revolution partner and industry vet Tom Sherak told *Variety*. "Give us some rain on Memorial Day, and Katie, bar the door!"

Nearly four months later, as Hurricane Katrina was breaking up over the Midwest after laying waste to New Orleans, Hollywood surveyed the wreckage of its summer. Sure, there were hits, including *Revenge of the Sith*, *War of the Worlds*, *Batman Begins*, *Charlie and the Chocolate Factory*, *Madagascar* and *Wedding Crashers*. Even the overly glib *Mr. & Mrs. Smith*, the remake of *The Longest Yard* and the quirky superhero saga *Fantastic Four* caught on with audiences. But the real story here is a continuation of the insidious Big Event syndrome, which posits that fewer people pay more money at more theatres to see a growing number of pre-sold blockbusters, low-brow entertainments and one-off zeitgeist surprises (think *Passion of the Christ* and *Fahrenheit 9/11*). What suffers are the mid-range pictures, which still cost a lot of money to make but are passed over by moviegoers in favour of, well, the Big Event.

Thus, aside from the record 2005 Labor Day weekend performance of left-field actioner *Transporter 2* ($20.3m in four days on 3,303 screens), business as a whole for the season was down 9% to $3.53 billion, from 2004's $3.86 billion. This despite there being nine films grossing $150m-plus, compared to only five in 2004.

Why? "I honestly think you have a combination of things," Paramount distribution president Wayne Lewellen told *Variety*, "not the least of which is the quality of the product." He may have been obliquely referencing the one major dramatic disappointment of the season, Ron Howard's **Cinderella Man**. Competent and pretty, but utterly conventional, the Capra-ized story of Depression-era boxer Jim Braddock (Russell Crowe) holds little dramatic tension or surprise.

Russell Crowe, left, and Paul Giamatti in **Cinderella Man**

Despite all this uncertainty, good pictures continue to be made, and in many cases marketed well. Two prominent examples of this synergy were **Wedding Crashers** and **The 40-Year-Old Virgin**, which combined high-concept ideas with genuinely well-written situational blue humour into recipes that had the movie press heralding the return of the R-rated comedy. By the end of 2005, *The 40-Year-Old Virgin* had earned close to $109m, while *Wedding Crashers* was the year's fourth most popular film with just over $209m (and, significantly, the highest-grossing movie without a strong fantasy element: only *Sith*, *War of the Worlds* and *Harry Potter and the Goblet of Fire* had earned more at press time).

Knowing me, knowing you

Among the ever-growing crop of Amerindies were two little films that satisfied in very different ways. **Me and You and Everyone We Know** marked a narratively startling but profoundly humanist directorial debut for Miranda July. Responding to the news that his wife is leaving him and their two children, forlorn shoe salesman Richard (John Hawkes, so good in the HBO series *Deadwood*) sets his hand on fire but can't quite figure out why. Meanwhile, struggling video artist Christine (July herself) makes ends meet by driving a cab for the elderly. Finally, Richard's mixed-race kids, 14-year-old Peter (Miles Thompson) and seven-year-old Robbie (the cherubic Brandon Ratcliff), are confronted by provocative questions relating to teenage sex and internet chatrooms, respectively.

Clive Owen, Julianne Moore, Chiwetel Ejiofor, Peter Mullan. Prod: Marc Abraham, Eric Newman, Hilary Shor, Iain Smith, Strike Entertainment/ Beacon Communications/ Hit & Run Productions/ Quietus Productions.

CLICK
[Comedy fantasy-drama, 2006] Script: Steve Koren, Mark O'Keefe, Tim Herlihy, Adam Sandler, Jack Giarraputo. Dir: Frank Coraci. Players: Adam Sandler, Sean Astin, Kate Beckinsale, Christopher Walken, Henry Winkler. Prod: Jack Giarraputo, Neal H. Moritz, Steve Koren, Mark O'Keefe, Columbia Pictures/ Revolution Studios.

THE DEPARTED
[Drama, 2006] Script: William Monahan. Dir: Martin Scorsese. Players: Leonardo DiCaprio, Matt Damon, Jack Nicholson, Mark Wahlberg, Alec Baldwin, Ray Winstone, Gerard McSorley, Vera Farmiga. Prod: Graham King, Warner Bros.

FIERCE PEOPLE
[Drama, 2006] Script: Dirk Wittenborn, from his book. Dir: Griffin Dunne. Players: Diane Lane, Anton Yelchin, Donald Sutherland, Kristen Stewart, Elizabeth Perkins. Prod: Nick Wechsler, Lions Gate.

FIND ME GUILTY
[Crime drama, 2006] Script: Sidney Lumet, J.J. Mancini, Robert McCrea. Dir: Sidney Lumet. Players: Vin Diesel, Peter Dinklage, Annabella Sciorra, Linus Roache, Ron Silver, Alex Rocco. Prod: Sidney Lumet, Robert Greenhut, Diesel, George Zakk, Robert DeBrino, Bob Yari Productions.

FLAGS OF OUR FATHERS
[Historical war drama, 2006] Script: Paul Haggis, from the book by James Bradley. Dir: Clint Eastwood. Players: Adam Beach, Jamie Bell, Judith Ivey, Robert Patrick, Barry Pepper.

Prod: Eastwood, Steven Spielberg,
DreamWorks SKG/Warner Bros./
Malpaso.

FLIGHT 93
[Drama, 2006] Script and Dir:
Paul Greengrass. Players: David
Alan Basche, Liza Colon-Zayas,
Denny Dillon. Prod: Eric Fellner,
Tim Bevan, Working Title/
Universal Pictures.

FRIENDS WITH MONEY
[Drama, 2006] Script and
Dir: Nicole Holofcener.
Players: Jennifer Aniston,
Catherine Keener, Frances
McDormand, Joan Cusack,
Scott Caan. Prod: Anthony
Bregman, Ted Hope, Anne
Carey, Sony Pictures Classics.

FUR
[Biographical drama, 2006]
Script: Erin Cressida Wilson.
Dir: Steven Shainberg.
Players: Nicole Kidman, Robert
Downey Jr. Prod: Bill Pohlad,
Laura Bickford, Bonnie
Timmermann, Andrew Fierberg,
River Road Entertainment.

THE GOOD GERMAN
[Mystery drama, 2006] Script:
Paul Attanasio, from the novel
by Joseph Kanon. Dir: Steven
Soderbergh. Players: George
Clooney, Cate Blanchett, Tobey
Maguire, Beau Bridges, Jack
Thompson. Prod: Soderbergh,
Gregory Jacobs, Ben Cosgrove,
Section 8.

THE GOOD SHEPHERD
[Romantic mystery thriller, 2006]
Script: Eric Roth. Dir: Robert
De Niro. Players: Matt Damon,
Angelina Jolie, De Niro, John
Turturro, William Hurt, Alec
Baldwin, Billy Crudup. Prod:
James G. Robinson, Jane
Rosenthal, De Niro, Morgan
Creek Productions/Tribeca
Productions/Universal Pictures.

GRIND HOUSE
[Horror, 2006] Script and Dir:
Robert Rodriguez, Quentin
Tarantino. Players: John Jarratt.
Prod: Elizabeth Avellan,
Rodriguez, Tarantino,

Phoebe Sudrow/FilmFour/IFC Films/Kobal

John Hawkes and Miranda July in **Me and You and Everyone We Know**

In their eccentric ways, each of these decent yet confused characters yearns for love – just like *Me and You and Everyone We Know*. If this sounds dangerously close to Todd Solondz territory, blame the inherent dryness of a written plot synopsis: July's immensely assured style and innate humanism elevate these characters out of the interpersonal muck to the level of graceful and poignant morality play. Winner of the Special Jury Prize at Sundance and no fewer than four awards at Cannes (including the Critics' Week nod), *Me and You and Everyone We Know* stands as one of the year's most original American films.

More conventional, but every bit as resonant, writer-director Josh Sternfeld's **Winter Solstice** is built around a quietly magnificent performance from Australian-born vet Anthony LaPaglia, now best known for his star turn on the TV show *Without a Trace*. In a leafy New Jersey suburb, pensive widower Jim Winters (LaPaglia), who still wears his wedding ring even when he washes dishes, tends to his landscaping business while raising teenaged sons Gabe (Aaron Stanford) and Pete (Mark Webber). Though the two boys are close, change is at hand: Gabe seems restless despite the love of girlfriend Stacey (Michelle Monaghan), while Pete is becoming alarmingly lax in his schoolwork. When Gabe abruptly announces he's moving to Florida, even as new neighbour Molly (Allison Janney) begins to draw Jim out of his shell, the Winters' days seem short indeed.

The feature debut of NYU alumnus Sternfeld, *Winter Solstice* is an extraordinarily perceptive family drama, played with exquisite restraint not only by LaPaglia but also Stanford (*Spartan*, *Tadpole*), Webber (*Jesus' Son*) and Janney (*The West Wing*). A deeply optimistic film, despite a title that may be read as the exact opposite (note the name of Jim's business: Terra Firma), *Winter Solstice* circles around to reaffirm the hard-fought bonds of family even as it brings out the quiet, profound truths of life.

Cold, comforting?

On the still-hot documentary front, one title ruled the roost. Mysteriously sold as a feelgood family film, **March of the Penguins** follows the yearly migration of the Emperor Penguins to their mass breeding ground. The film has an odd history, having originally been made in France with each penguin voiced by a different actor to a pop score. For the US market, distributor Warner Independent Pictures scrapped the music and dialogue, commissioned a more conventional score and hired the ever dependable Morgan Freeman to narrate in his patented rueful mode. While immensely popular, the resulting film is a freakish anthropomorphisation of a mysterious and cruel ritual.

Infinitely more interesting was Martin Scorsese's reverential and revelatory **No Direction Home: Bob Dylan**. Though he shot precious little fresh footage for the three-and-a-half-hour film, Scorsese's genius lay in the way in which he juxtaposed Dylan's galvanising music to the social upheaval of early 1960s America. It's a proud, brave, riveting film that at once enlightens and confounds the viewer – much the visual equivalent of Dylan's vivid, eternal body of work.

Genre films were led by the welcome return of George A. Romero with **Land of the Dead**, extending the trilogy that began with 1968's black-and-white classic, *Night of the Living Dead*, then commented wryly on consumer culture with 1979's *Dawn of the Dead* and took on a chilling militaristic tone with the vastly underrated *Day of the Dead* (1985).

Michael Gibson/Universal/Kobal

George A. Romero's **Land of the Dead**

For the fourth installment, Romero is in fighting form, with an elaborate metaphor of privilege and persuasion, as the island enclave of Fiddler's Green is run by greedy businessman Kaufman (Dennis Hopper) as a haven against the now-dominant zombies. With a performance from Hopper that was reportedly modeled after US Secretary of Defense Donald Rumsfeld and action sequences both

A Band Apart/Troublemaker Studios/The Weinstein Company.

IN THE LAND OF WOMEN
*[Romantic comedy-drama]
Script and Dir: Lawrence Kasdan. Players: Meg Ryan, Adam Brody, Kristen Stewart, Olympia Dukakis, Clark Gregg. Prod: Steve Golin, David Kanter, Land Films.*

INSIDE MAN
[Thriller, 2006] Script: Russell Gerwitz, Menno Meyjes. Dir: Spike Lee. Players: Denzel Washington, Clive Owen, Jodie Foster. Prod: Brian Grazer, Universal Pictures/ Imagine Entertainment.

KILLSHOT
[Action thriller, 2006] Script: Hossein Amini, from the novel by Elmore Leonard. Dir: John Madden. Players: Diane Lane, Mickey Rourke, Thomas Jane, Joseph Gordon-Levitt, Rosario Dawson, Johnny Knoxville. Prod: Richard Gladstein, FilmColony/Weinstein Company.

LADY IN THE WATER
[Fantasy mystery thriller, 2006] Script and Dir: M. Night Shyamalan. Players: Paul Giamatti, Bryce Dallas Howard, Bob Balaban, Sarita Choudhury, Jared Harris, Mary Beth Hurt, Bill Irwin, Jeffrey Wright. Prod: Shyamalan, Sam Mercer, Rebellion Pictures.

LUCKY YOU
[Drama, 2006] Script: Eric Roth, Curtis Hanson. Dir: Hanson. Players: Eric Bana, Drew Barrymore, Robert Duvall, Debra Messing, Robert Downey Jr. Prod: Hanson, Carol Fenelon, Denise DiNovi, Lucky You Pictures.

MARIE-ANTOINETTE
[Historical drama, 2006] Script and Dir: Sofia Coppola. Players: Kirsten Dunst, Jason Schwartzmann, Rip Torn, Molly Shannon, Judy Davis, Marianne Faithfull, Steve Coogan. Prod: Coppola, Ross Katz, Columbia

Pictures/American Zoetrope.

THE MARTIAN CHILD
[Comedy drama, 2006] Script:
Seth E. Bass, Jonathan Tolins.
Dir: Menno Meyjes. Players:
John Cusack, Bobby Coleman,
Amanda Peet, Sophie Okonedo,
Joan Cusack, Oliver Platt. Prod:
David Kirschner, Corey Sienega,
Ed Elbert, Hannah Rachel
Production Services.

THE MESSENGERS
[Sci-fi action thriller, 2006] Script:
Stuart Beattie, Todd Farmer,
Mark Wheaton. Dir: Oxide Pang
Chung, Danny Pang. Players:
John Corbett, Dylan McDermott,
Penelope Anne Miller, Kristen
Stewart. Prod: Sam Raimi,
William Sherak, Jason Shuman,
Robert G. Tapert, Scarecrow
Productions/Bluestar
Entertainment/Ghost House
Pictures/Mandate Pictures.

MIAMI VICE
[Action comedy, 2006] Script
and Dir: Michael Mann. Players:
Colin Farrell, Jamie Foxx, Gong
Li, Naomie Harris, Luis Tosar.
Prod: Mann, Wayne Morris,
Universal Pictures.

THE PAINTED VEIL
[Drama, 2006] Script: Ron
Nyswaner, from the novel by
W. Somerset Maugham. Dir: John
Curran. Players: Naomi Watts,
Edward Norton, Liev Schreiber.
Prod: Stratus Film Company/
Warner Independent Pictures.

POSEIDON
[Adventure, 2006] Script: Akiva
Goldsman, Mark Protosevich,
Paul Attanasio. Dir: Wolfgang
Petersen. Players: Josh Lucas,
Kurt Russell, Jacinda Barrett,
Richard Dreyfuss. Prod: Mike
Fleiss, Petersen, Duncan
Henderson, Warner Bros.

A PRAIRIE HOME
COMPANION
[Comedy, 2006] Script: Garrison
Keillor. Dir: Robert Altman.
Players: Keillor, Meryl Streep,
Lily Tomlin, Lindsay Lohan,
Woody Harrelson, Kevin Kline,

elaborate and imaginative, this horror triumph prompted genre director Guillermo Del Toro to proclaim: "It should be a cause of celebration among all of us that Michelangelo has started another ceiling."

A slightly more mainstream success story was **Crash**, the competent and provocative multi-character story of race and redemption in modern-day Los Angeles that marked the fine directorial debut of Million Dollar Baby screenwriter Paul Haggis. Riding good press from the 2004 Toronto festival, the film proved a surprise hit with upscale audiences during its spring 2005 release.

Don Cheadle, centre, as a cop in **Crash**

Return of the Oscar-hunters

As 2005 headed into the home stretch, a number of titles emerged from the pack as potential Oscar contenders. Though known primarily as the director of such so-called "body horror" titles as Scanners (1981), The Fly (1986), Naked Lunch (1991) and the other Crash (1996), Canadian-born and Toronto-based David Cronenberg (profiled as a Director of the Year at the front of this edition) has refined and matured his vision in recent years, primarily with the little-seen but sublimely constructed and acted Spider (2002).

Yet there's little in Cronenberg's œuvre to prepare one for the subtlety and restraint inherent in **A History of Violence**. With small-town Canada standing in for small-town America (Cronenberg has yet to make a film in the United States), this is essentially a B-Western transposed and pared down to its essence: humble diner owner Tom Stall (Viggo Mortensen) may or may not be a reformed mob killer trying to turn over a new leaf, and a big-city hitman (Ed Harris) arrives to call him out.

"I've killed a lot of people in my movies," Cronenberg told the film magazine Uncut, "but the first time I ever saw a fistfight, it was a truly horrific thing." This is precisely the feeling captured by the film, as Stall's obvious distaste for the nuts-and-bolts of close-in violence is overrun by his instinct to survive. Perhaps the film's greatest achievement is the delicate balance between suspense and sly comedy, legendarily prompting one patron at the film's first Cannes festival press show to howl: "Stop laughing, you fucking piece-of-shit critics and take this film serious!" Cronenberg's first mature masterpiece to date, in a career spanning more than three decades, *A History of Violence* is not to be missed.

Each year, Hollywood seems more and more obsessed with historical biopics, many of which feature bona fide star turns embedded in otherwise pedestrian and/or overblown movies. In late 2004 it was controversial sex researcher Alfred Kinsey (Bill Condon's earnest **Kinsey**), obsessive recluse Howard Hughes (Martin Scorsese's kinetic **The Aviator**) and ba-da-bing "Mack the Knife" crooner Bobby Darin (Kevin Spacey's weird **Beyond the Sea**).

A year later the Hollywood historians were at it again. Yet while Joaquin Phoenix's visceral turn as Johnny Cash in James Mangold's **Walk the Line** and Philip Seymour Hoffman's letter-perfect essaying of author Truman Capote in Bennet Miller's **Capote** both hew closely to the "great performance, questionable film" model, one fall release that examines a troubled time in America through the actions of one man is George Clooney's **Good Night, and Good Luck**. Note the period in the title, which was the phrase early TV newsman Edward R. Murrow (David Strathairn) used to sign off his broadcasts. Increasingly troubled over the anti-Communist stance of Wisconsin Republican senator Joseph McCarthy, Murrow takes a stand and publicly challenges the politician.

George Clooney and David Strathairn in **Good Night, and Good Luck.**

Produced with the same feel for early live television Clooney displayed in his live broadcast remake of *Fail Safe* a few years ago, the film has been burnished to a black-and-white glow by cinematographer Robert Elswit. The perfect casting of Straithairn, nearly a dead ringer for Murrow, extends to all the supporting players in a movie as absorbing as it is relevant (many will find a direct corollary to current US policy).

Virginia Madsen, John C. Reilly. Prod: Robert Altman, Sandcastle 5/Green Street/River Road Entertainment.

RUNNING WITH SCISSORS
[Comedy-drama, 2006] Script and Dir: Ryan Murphy. Players: Annette Bening, Brian Cox, Joseph Fiennes, Evan Rachel Wood, Alec Baldwin, Jill Clayburgh. Prod: Ryan Murphy, Brad Grey, Jennifer Aniston, Brad Pitt, Dede Garnier, TriStar Pictures.

A SCANNER DARKLY
[Animated sci-fi drama, 2006] Script: Richard Linklater, from the novel by Philip K. Dick. Dir: Linklater. Players: Keanu Reeves, Winona Ryder, Robert Downey Jr., Woody Harrelson, Rory Cochrane. Prod: Jonah Smith, Palmer West, George Clooney, Steven Soderbergh, Anne Walker McBay, Tommy Pallotta, Warner Independent Pictures/Thousand Words.

THE SENTINEL
[Political thriller, 2006] Script: George Nolfi, from the novel by Gerald Petievich. Dir: Clark Johnson. Players: Michael Douglas, Kiefer Sutherland, Kim Basinger, Eva Longoria, David Rasche, Martin Donovan, Clark Johnson. Prod: Michael Douglas, Arnon Milchan, Marcy Drogin, 20th Century Fox/ Regency Enterprises.

SPINNING INTO BUTTER
[Drama, 2006] Script: Rebecca Gilman, Doug Atchison, based on Gilman's play. Dir: Mark Brokaw. Players: Sarah Jessica Parker, Beau Bridges, Miranda Richardson, Mykelti Williamson, James Rebhorn. Prod: Norman Twain, Lou Pitt, Sarah Jessica Parker, Spinning Into Butter.

STRANGER THAN FICTION
[Dramatic comedy, 2006] Script: Zach Helm. Dir: Marc Forster. Players: Will Ferrell, Dustin Hoffman, Maggie Gyllenhaal, Emma Thompson, Queen Latifah, Linda Hunt, Tom Hulce,

Redbus Film Distribution

*Kristin Chenoweth. Prod:
Lindsay Doran, Crick Pictures.*

SUPER EX-GIRLFRIEND
*[Romantic sci-fi comedy, 2006]
Script: Don Payne. Dir: Ivan
Reitman. Players: Uma
Thurman, Luke Wilson, Anna
Faris, Eddie Izzard. Prod: Gavin
Polone, 20th Century Fox.*

WORLD TRADE CENTER
*[Drama, 2006] Script: Andrea
Berloff. Dir: Oliver Stone.
Players: Nicolas Cage, Michael
Pena, Maria Bello, Maggie
Gyllenhaal. Prod: Michael
Shamberg, Stacey Sher, Moritz
Borman, Debra Hill, Double
Feature Films.*

ZODIAC
*[Thriller, 2006] Script: James
Vanderbilt, from the book by
Robert Graysmith. Dir: David
Fincher. Players: Jake Gyllenhaal,
Mark Ruffalo, Robert Downey
Jr., Anthony Edwards. Prod:
Mike Medavoy, Arnold W.
Messer, Bradley J. Fischer, James
Vanderbilt, Cean Chaffin,
Phoenix Pictures.*

Quotes of the Year

"My problem is I'm like a
junkie. I want a good movie
fix, and I never get that fix.
I want to be taken into some
place, some world, some
idea that I haven't thought
of or imagined. And it
doesn't happen."
TERRY GILLIAM, *director,
speaking about his career in*
Time *magazine, August 2005.*

"They were like the beta-
testing guys. They've had to
go through the endless
questions about 'So, what
was it like to kiss a guy?'"
JAMES SCHAMUS, *co-president
of Focus Features, on the
challenges confronting*
Brokeback Mountain *stars Jake
Gyllenhaal and Heath Ledger,
November 2005.*

Cowboys in love

Another early bet to figure in the end-of-year kudos race is
Brokeback Mountain, Ang Lee's exquisitely modulated adaptation
of E. Annie Proulx's short story about two loner outdoorsmen
whose friendship veers into an intimacy that informs the balance of
their heterosexual lives. As thought-provoking as the premise is, the
film wouldn't work without the intuitive performances of Heath
Ledger and Jake Gyllenhaal as the star-crossed lovers; the mixture
of rough and tender is eye-opening.

Focus Features/Kobal

Jake Gyllenhaal, left, and Heath Ledger in **Brokeback Mountain**

In much the same way that Lee's film subverts the audience's
expectations of exactly what a relationship between two people can
be, the brashly funny **Transamerica** toys audaciously with the
fundamental idea of what a person is, and how that sense of self
dictates behaviour. Playing like *Sideways* turned inside out, this
represents a triumphantly genre-bending big-screen bow for writer-
director Duncan Tucker: a laugh-out-loud funny, tartly off-colour and
ultimately touching road movie involving the cross-country adventures
of a persnickety transsexual (Felicity Huffman) and the runaway street
hustler son (Kevin Zegers) whose existence is news to her. An
outspoken comedy that feels like vintage John Waters scripted by
Alexander Payne and Jim Taylor, *Transamerica* takes a touchy subject
and renders it not only approachable, but accessible.

At press time, the 500-pound gorilla on the release schedule was
Peter Jackson's three-hour-plus remake of **King Kong**, a Big Event
picture if there ever was one, in a crowded holiday season of equal
parts popcorn and prestige. Somewhere between Manhattan and
Munich, Hollywood continues to battle the forces of change.

Uruguay Jorge Jellinek

The Year's Best Films

Jorge Jellinek's selection:
Alma Mater (Álvaro Buela)
Orlando Vargas
(Juan Pittaluga)
A Dios Momo
(Leonardo Ricagni)
Crónica de un sueño
(Docu. Mariana Viñoles,
Stefano Tononi)
Vientos de Octubre
(Docu. Adriana Nartallo,
Daniel Amorin)

Recent and Forthcoming Films

A DIOS MOMO
[Comedy-drama, 2005] Script and Dir: Leonardo Ricagni. Phot: Pablo Vera. Players: Matías Acuña, Jorge Esmoris, Canario Luna, Mauricio Rosencof. Prod: Raúl Pochintesta.
A black 11-year-old street kid, called Obdulio, who sells newspapers for a living, befriends the night watchman of a newspaper, who introduces him in the magical world of the "murgas" (Carnival chorus groups) under the spell of God Momo, who reigns during the Uruguayan Carnival.

ORLANDO VARGAS
[Drama, 2004] Script and Dir: Juan Pittaluga. Phot: Christel Fournier. Players: Aurélien Recoing, Elina Löwensohn, Rosa Simonelli, Héctor Guido, Eduardo Amaro, Jorge Bolani, William Triest, Ernesto Liotti. Diego Bernabé. Prod: Gemini Films (France)/Laroux Cine (Uruguay).
A French diplomat gets involved in a dangerous affair that

After the exhilarating effects in 2004 of *Whisky*, the Uruguayan film that received global recognition, and the Oscar in March 2005 for Best Song to Uruguay's Jorge Drexler for "The Other Side of the River", from *The Motorcycle Diaries*, it was back to normal for Uruguayan cinema in 2005. The new, leftist government arrived promising help for the developing movie industry, but the tough reality proved hard to change, and long-mooted plans for a film law were still being debated in Parliament late in 2005.

However, the impetus created in recent years by the awarding of more than 40 international prizes to local productions continued to stimulate new projects, and at least five new films were in post-production at press time. This ensures continuity, and although the effects of the 2002 economic crisis were still visible, three new long feature films were released in 2005, and many shorts produced on video and documentaries found their way on to the cultural circuit.

With a general drop of about 20% at the box-office, these new productions could not reach the same size of audience as other recent films, and they were also received with less enthusiasm by the press. But with promising titles on the horizon, like the imaginative comedy *The Pope's Toilet* (*El baño del Papa*), directed by Enrique Fernández and photographer César Charlone (who shot *City of God*), Uruguayan cinema should be here to stay.

The most acclaimed film of the year was **Alma Mater**, an ambitious, risk-taking and mysterious voyage to the frontiers of mysticism. Pitched somewhere between reality and the supernatural, it follows the experience of a shy and religious supermarket cashier (Roxana

Roxana Blanco, left, dances in **Alma Mater**

involves the dictatorial regime of the country. He decides to escape with his family to a seaside resort near the frontier with Brazil, but there he mysteriously disappears.

Juan Pittaluga's **Orlando Vargas**

ALMA MATER
[Drama, 2004] Script and Dir: Álvaro Buela. Phot: Daniel Rodriguez Maseda. Players: Roxana Blanco, Nicolás Becerra, Walter Reyno, Werner Schünemann, Beatriz Massons, Humberto de Vargas, Jenny Galván. Prod: José Pedro Charlo, Austero Producciones/ Xerxes Indies Films (Brazil).

RUIDO *(literally,* **Noise***)*
[Comedy, 2004] Script and Dir: Marcelo Bertalmío. Phot: Daniel Machado. Players: Jorge Visca, Jorge Bazzano, Mariana Olazabal, Lucía Carlevari, Eva Santolaria, Fermín Casado, Miquel Sitjar, Joseph Linuesa. Prod: Lavorágine Films/ Zeppelin Films (Spain)/Jorge Rocca (Argentine).
Basílio is an unhappy man with a golden heart and a tendency to get involved in other people's problems. Depressed and on the brink of suicide, he is rescued by a 12-year-old girl who asks for his help in a strange mission.

EL BAÑO DEL PAPA
(The Pope's Toilet)
[Comedy, 2005] Dir: Enrique Fernández and César Charlone. Script: Fernández. Phot: Charlone. Players: César Troncoso, Virginia Méndez, Mario Silvia, Virginia Ruiz. Prod: Elena Roux, Laroux Cine/Chaya Films (France)/O2 Films (Brazil).
In 1988, during the Pope's visit

Blanco) assaulted by mystic visions that convince her she is pregnant, and perhaps expecting the new messiah.

This second work by former critic Álvaro Buela, who almost a decade ago impressed with the thirty-something comedy *Una formade bailar* (literally, *A Certain Form to Dance*), enters new territory for Uruguayan cinema. With Bresson and Jacques Tourneur as declared influences, Buela investigates the profound influence of popular religion in an apparently agnostic society. With suggestive images and music, and impressive work from newcomer Blanco (named Best Actress at Biarritz), the film overcomes the limitations of a script that never decides if the visions are real or the hallucinations of a troubled mind.

Carnival time

Less impressive than *Alma Mater*, but more appealing to the general public was Leonardo Ricagni's **A Dios Momo** (literally, *Goodbye Momo*), a colourful musical trip into the magic of the Uruguayan Carnival tradition, based on the chants of the "murgas" (satirical choral groups) and the rhythm of black candombe. It follows the initiation of a kid, Obdulio (Matías Acuña), named after the famous Obdulio Varela, captain of the 1950 World Cup-winning Uruguayan football team. With experience in advertising, Ricagni confirms his elaborate visual style, already shown in *El Chevrolé* (1997), but also his weakness in constructing credible situations. Acuña is very good, however, as is the music.

The most disappointing note was struck by Marcelo Bertalmío with **Ruido** (literally, *Noise*), a low-key, surreal comedy that failed to be funny, surprising or irreverent. This absurd story of a depressed clerk rescued from suicide by a series of bizarre characters, including a municipal inspector of noises, lacks rhythm and is unevenly cast. After making the charming *Los dias con Ana* (literally, *Days with Ana*) a funny, lighthearted student comedy, Bertalmío misfires completely with a work that seems distantly

Jorge Visca, left, and Jorge Bazzano in **Ruido**

to Uruguay, the news that he will visit the little town of Melo inspires Beto, an ambitious local smuggler, to build a public toilet and make money from the thousands of visitors expected.

LA PERRERA (Dog Pound)
[Comedy-drama, 2005] Script and Dir: Manuel Nieto. Phot: Guillermo Nieto. Players: Pablo Riera, Martín Adjemian, Sergio Gorfain, María Sofía Dabarca. Prod: Fernando Epstein, Control Z Films/Hernán Musaluppi (Argentine).
After losing his scholarship, David, a failed student, must return to the family house in the small, isolated beach town of La Perrera. He'll have to stay for the year, but is forced by his authoritarian father to build his own home, on a piece of land that he gave him some years before.

CRÓNICA DE UN SUEÑO
(*literally,* **Chronicle of a Dream**)
[Documentary, 2004]. Script and Dir: Mariana Viñoles and Stefano Tononi. Prod: Viñoles and Tononi.
During the national elections in October 2004, Mariana returns from abroad to her home town of Melo, where she finds relatives and friends, while the new political climate agitates the peaceful place.

VIENTOS DE OCTUBRE
(*literally,* **October Winds**)
[Documentary, 2004]. Script and Dir: Adriana Nartallo and Daniel Amorín. Prod: Nartallo and Amorín.
The story investigates how the triumph of the left in the national elections brings hope and enthusiasm to the life of different people affected by the crisis.

Quote of the Year

"This is the best film ever produced by Uruguayan cinema."
JORGE VISCA, *star of* Noise, *defending this critically savaged flop.*

influenced by the Spanish black comedies, such as those by Santiago Segura and Alex de la Iglesia.

More interesting was **Orlando Vargas**, by Juan Pittaluga, an Uruguayan based in Paris, who presented this feature debut in the Critics Week at Cannes. Enigmatic, and with a charged atmosphere, this political thriller revolves around a French diplomat who resists pressures from powerful interests, and then disappears after fleeing with his family to a seaside resort near the Brazilian frontier. Well constructed, but with too many unsolved clues in its climax, the film is sustained by the acting of France's Aurélien Recoing and Romania's Elina Löwensohn as the diplomat and his wife.

Uruguay vs. Steven Seagal

Political changes in the country were reflected in a series of very interesting documentaries, including **Crónica de un sueño** (literally, *Chronicle of a Dream*), by Mariana Viñoles and Stefano Tononi, and **Vientos de octubre** (literally, *October Winds*), by Adriana Bartallo and Daniel Amorín, which both offered personal and critical accounts of the triumph of the Frente Amplio in the national elections, without hiding their sympathies.

Politics and cinema were also mixed in the fervent reactions produced by Steven Seagal's submarine adventure, *Submerged*, which offers a distorted image of Uruguay. Directed by Britain's Anthony Hickox, the film presents a country governed by a corrupt dictator, with terrorists, a hidden nuclear submarine and blond peasants with goats! Actually filmed in Bulgaria, this low-budget rubbish was a surprising success in video stores, and received formal protests by the government.

The real Uruguay will be presented in a better light to cinemagoers by Hollywood in Michael Mann's forthcoming *Miami Vice*, in which the sea resort of Atlantida is made to resemble Havana! This film could open the door for other visiting productions, which might discover the benefits of filming at low cost in a friendly and quite safe country.

JORGE JELLINEK (jorjelli.com.uy) has been a film critic and journalist for over 20 years, contributing to newspapers, magazines and radio. He writes for the Pan-American weekly *Tiempos del Mundo* and is vice-president of the Uruguayan Critics' Association.

Uzbekistan Gulnara Abikeyeva

The Year's Best Films:

Gulnara Abikeyeva's selection:

Shepherd (Yusuf Razykov)

Boys in the Sky 2
(Zulfikar Musakov)

Giant and a Squab
(Jakhangir Kasymov)

Teenager (Yelkin Tuichiev)

The Well
(Turaniyaz Kalimbetov)

Yusuf Razykov's **Shepherd**

Recent and Forthcoming Films

HOTIRA RASHKI
(Jealousy of Memory)
[Drama, 2005] Dir: Fatih
Dzhalalov. Prod: Uzbekfilm.

VATAN (Motherland)
[Drama, 2006] Script and
Dir: Zulfikar Musakov.
Prod: Uzbekfilm.

JOL BUDSIN (Happy Journey)
[Drama, 2006] Dir: Kamara
Kamalova. Prod: Uzbekfilm.

VATANI BIR PARCHASI
(Piece of Motherland)
[Detective drama, 2006]
Script: Murad Muhhamad Dost.
Dir: Jakhongir Kasymov.
Prod: Uzbekfilm.

SEKRET KRASOTI
(The Secret of Beauty)
[Comedy, 2006] Dir: Dzhamilya
Pulatova. Prod: Uzbekfilm.

In Uzbekistan, film production is directly connected with the local audience's appetite for national cinematography. Some six or seven feature films are produced on 35mm each year and a similar number are made on video, and they receive wide distribution in cinemas and video salons. Whatever the international concerns about his policies in other areas, there is no doubting that the government of President Islam Karimov is positively directed towards the development of cinematography. In March 2004, Karimov signed a Decree "About the Development of the Management of Cinematography", which committed resources to the development of national production, aiming to increase this to 15 productions shot on 35mm each year. The government is also helping to provide new equipment and technical support for cinemas. A further aim is for the national cinema to increase the production of films to 15 per year.

The runaway local hit of 2004–05 was Zulfikar Musakov's **Boys in the Sky 2**, the sequel to his *Boys in the Sky* (2003). Both are comedies providing warm, kind stories about friendship, love and youth. Adolescents Hamdam, Hurshid, Djavokhir and Bakhtier have been friends since the cradle. In the sequel they experience first love – all falling for their classmate, Lola. This causes them temporarily to break apart, but their friendship eventually becomes stronger.

Another popular comedy was **Giant and a Squab**, directed by Jakhangir Kasymov. A giant man (Nadir Saidaliyev) comes from his village to the city to find work, but is fired from every job that he finds. Even though he works hard, he eats for three people and no one in the city is able to cope with his appetite. His tortures are finally over when he meets a manager (Obid Asomov) who is half his size and understands better than others the significance of height and weight when it comes to getting something out of life.

Shepherd, directed by Yusuf Razykov, is completely different. While his married, older brother is earning money abroad, 13-year-old village boy Jamshid takes care of his sister-in-law, Mastura, because according to traditional rules she cannot be left alone. At the beginning this is a burden for him, but then he realises that he is in charge not only of Mastura, but also of the whole house where he becomes the master. He develops from "woman's shepherd" into a real man – and there are not many real men in the village. Razikov is

Obid Asomov, left, and Nadir Saidaliyev in **Giant and a Squab**

one of the most serious directors in Uzbekistan. Between 1998 and 2004, he was director of the Uzbekfilm studio, nurturing the development of many young film-makers and generally playing an influential role in national production.

An interesting debut was made by Yelkin Tuichiev with **Teenager**, shot at the experimental youth cinema facility, "Studio-5". Ilkhom is the only male in a family of women who are always arguing about everything and pay no attention to him. That is why he independently tries to find the meaning of everything that he observes in his life. In general in Uzbek cinema, directors are striving to work in commercial genres that will draw the public, so we see comedies like those mentioned above, historical movies and also melodramas like **The Tortures of Love**.

LOLAZORDAGI KAPLAKLAR
(Butterflies of the Blooming Field)
[Drama, 2006] Dir: Melis Abzalov. Prod: Uzbekfilm.

FAKAT GALABA (Only Victory)
[Drama, 2006] Dir: Yusuf Razikov. Prod: Uzbekfilm.

Boys in the Sky 2

Quote of the Year

"I don't want to spend all my life shooting the continuation of *Boys in the Sky*, because I don't want to be a hostage to its success."
ZULFIKAR MUSAKOV, *on the perils of directing a hit franchise, at the premiere of* Boys in the Sky 2.

Venezuela Martha Escalona Zerpa

The Year's Best Films

Martha Escalona Zerpa's
selection:
Florentino y el diablo
(Michael New)
Punto y raya (Elía Schneider)
Yotama Flies Away
(Luis Armando Roche)
Kidnap Express
(Jonathan Jakubowics)
Puente Llaguno
(Docu. Àngel Palacios)

Recent and Forthcoming Films

[CNAC denotes Centro Nacional de Cinematografía.]

FLORENTINO Y EL DIABLO
(*literally,* Florentino and the Devil)
[Drama, 2004] Script: Edilio Peña, Michael New. Dir: New. Phot: Cezary Jaworski. Players: Pastos González, José Montilla, José Torres, Juanita New, F. Reyna. Prod: Michael New Productora Cinematográfica/ Centro de Cinematografía of Universidad de los Andes/ CNAC/Hubert Bals Fund (Rotterdam).

PUNTO Y RAYA
(*literally,* Point and Stroke)
[Comedy-drama, 2004] Script: Henry Herrera. Dir: Elia Schneider. Phot: Oscar Pérez. Players: Roque Valero, Edgar Ramírez, Ramiro Meneses, Daniela Alvarado, Pedro Lander, Dora Mazzone. Prod: José R. Novoa, Cnac-Unity Films-Jiresco/Xenon-regalo Light/ CNAC/Viriato Films (Spain)/ Cinecorp (Chile)/BFS Producciones (Uruguay).

Generally, Venezuelan cinema has been and remains a site for contemporary debate, and its most recent productions denounce the realities of social and economic injustice. Caracas, one of the most violent cities in South America, emerges as the primary setting. Extreme poverty, class contrasts, armed criminality and political polarisation are at the heart of films exploring the daily, almost warlike violence of urban life: the so-called "express kidnappings" (crudely portrayed in *Kidnap Express*), armed robberies (in *Yotama Flies Away*), poverty and segregation in children's shelters (*Maroa*) and the violent 2002 coup attempt (the documentary *Puente Llaguno*).

In this context, does Jonathan Jakubowics' **Kidnap Express** (*Secuestro Express*) complement, justify or exaggerate the tendency towards violence? Or does it help audiences to understand and exorcise it? This question is vitally important, because *Kidnap Express* promises to be the greatest ever Venezuelan blockbuster, and the first Venezuelan film ever distributed by Miramax in New York, Los Angeles and Miami as well as Venezuela. Martin and Carla, a wealthy couple engaged to be married, are kidnapped in Las Mercedes (a well-to-do neighbourhood in Caracas) by three criminals in search of easy money and social revenge. Carla's father has 24 hours to pay the ransom. It was filmed in digital video in Caracas during the 2003 oil strike, against the backdrop of demonstrations for and against the government. Jakubowics commented that he "wanted to make a social experiment by putting people from different social classes in the same car". Clearly influenced by Tarantino and Robert

The poster for Jonathan Jakubowics' crime hit **Kidnap Express**

Rodriguez, it is an exciting, hard-hitting, gruesome film in a climate of constant psychological tension. By July 2005, it had sold more than 200,000 tickets at Venezuelan cinemas.

Stepping away from recurrent social themes, Michael New's **Florentino y el diablo** (literally, *Florentino and the Devil*), which represents the Venezuelan folklore version of Faust in his archetypical confrontation with evil, can be qualified as a landmark in Venezuela film history, both in its subject matter and in its exceptionally beautiful use of music and photography. Florentino is the mythological representation of the *llanero* (man of the plains), the young singer who challenged the Devil to a duel of improvised verses. Combining folklore and the poem by Venezuelan writer Alberto Arvelo Torrealba, New shot in Barinas, highlighting the beauty of the *llanos* (plains) and their inhabitants' language.

New law, new hope

With the passing of the National Cinematography Law in August 2005, it appears that Venezuelan cinema may at least emerge from crisis. As in previous years, the 10 most popular movies in Venezuelan screens in 2004 were Hollywood blockbusters and the market share of Venezuelan movies is only 1%, making a local movie industry almost unsustainable. The 20-plus international awards for films such as **Punto y Raya** (14 international awards), **Yotama Flies Away** (*Yotama se va volando*, four prizes), **Puente Llaguno, claves de una masacre** and **Love in Concrete** (*Amor en concreto*, four international awards) are proof of the outstanding creative efforts of the Venezuelan film-makers, who have somehow overcome all internal restrictions and obstacles.

According to Juan Carlos Lossada, director of CNAC (the Centre for National Cinematography), the new law creates a screen quota for Venezuelan movies, which involve between three and 12 weeks of screening, regardless of box-office performance. Another innovation is a quota insisting that at least 20% of prints of foreign movies are made in Venezuela, as opposed to Mexico, where the process has been based. In addition, special grants will be used to finance a Fund for the Promotion of Cinematography (Fonprocine), supported by movie and home video distributors, laboratories, producers and terrestrial and cable television channels. The money will be used for the production, distribution and screening of Venezuelan movies and the preservation of Venezuela's film heritage.

MARTHA ESCALONA ZERPA (Dr.M_Escalona_Z@web.de) is a freelance journalist with a PhD from Humboldt University. She has been a film critic since 1995 and lives in Berlin.

Enemy soldiers meet in **Punto y Raya**

PUENTE LLAGUNO, CLAVES DE UNA MASACRE
(*literally,* **Puente Llaguno, Clues to a Massacre**)
[*Documentary, 2005] Script and Dir: Àngel Palacios. Prod: Asociación Nacional de Medios Comunitarios Libres y Alternativos (ANMCLA).*

YOTAMA SE VA VOLANDO
(**Yotama Flies Away**)
[*Drama, 2003] Script: Carlos Brito, Jacques Espagna, Luis Armando Roche. Dir: Roche. Phot: Vitelbo Vásquez. Players: Asdrúbal Meléndez, Beatriz Vásquez, Oriana Meléndez, Edgar Ramírez. Prod: Marie-Françoise Roche (Arsiete)/CNAC.*

AMOR EN CONCRETO
(**Love in Concrete**)
[*Comedy-drama, 2003] Script: Franco de Peña, Tomasz Kepski, Antoine Vivas, Andrés Schaffer. Dir: de Peña. Players: Alejandro Chabán, Eric Wildpret, Beatriz Valdés, Carlos Miranda. Prod: Cameo Films/Caracas Acrobates Film/Zyga Films/Paris ZDF/ Anette Pisacane (ARTE).*

SECUESTRO EXPRESS
(**Kidnap Express**)
[*Crime drama, 2005] Script and Dir: Jonathan Jakubowics. Phot: David Chalker. Players: Mia Castro, Carlos Julio Molina, Pedro Pérez, Carlos Madera, Jean Paul Leroux, Ruben Blades. Prod: Elizabeth Avellan, Sandra Condito, Salomon Jakubowicz, Jonathan Jakubowicz, Eduardo Jakubowicz.*

Other Countries

BENIN

Benin has just two active directors, both resident in Paris. Their preoccupations are very different, however, with Jean Odoutan concentrating on immigrant life in Paris (see *IFG 2005*), while his compatriot Idrissa Mora Kpaï, one of the few African film-makers trained in Germany, continues to look with fresh eyes at novel aspects of African life. In his first feature, *Si-Gueriki*, Kpaï explored his family history, discovering that his mother, who leads the conventional domestic life of an African woman, was in fact descended from the royal family of his tribe, being literally the 'queen mother'.

In **Arlit: A Second Paris** (*Arlit: deuxième Paris*, 2004), Kpaï returns to the desert town in northern Niger from which he left for Europe, exploring its paradoxical development. In the 1970s it was a boom town, its prosperity based in the French-owned uranium mine, drawing workers from all over Africa. Arlit is still a magnet, but now the young men are all passing through, struggling to make their way across the Sahara to the promised land of Europe. – *Roy Armes*

BURKINA FASO

Burkina Faso is in many ways the film capital of Francophone Africa: the site of its major film festival, FESPACO (the Festival Panafricain du Cinéma de Ougadougou), and home of the African film-makers' federation (FEPACI). It has also produced more features than any of its West African neighbours, except Senegal. Four new features, three by newcomers, were shown at the 19th FESPACO in 2005. Boubakar Diallo, a novelist and self-taught director, showed **Sofia**, the story of a girl who quarrels with her boyfriend when out driving in the bush and is left in the middle of nowhere. But she manages to hitch a lift and embarks on a new affair with a young musician heading for town, where he hopes to make his name.

Another newcomer, Apolline Traoré, studied film in Boston, where she moved when she was 17, and made several shorts before embarking on her first feature. **Under the Moonlight** (*Sous la clarté de la lune*) shows the return to a Burkinabè village of a young Frenchman and his seven-year-old daughter, Martine, who discovers the mother from whom she was separated at birth and who is now deaf and dumb. The mother, disapproving of the way Martine has been brought up, kidnaps her and attempts to flee, with unfortunate results.

By far the best debut was made by Fanta Régina Nacro, who studied at both the Burkinabè film school, INAFEC, and in Paris, and who had already earned an international reputation with a series of lively and inventive short films shown at various festivals. **The Night of Truth** (*La Nuit de la vérité*) is a hugely ambitious study of African genocide, set in an imaginary state but full of real contemporary relevance. It shows the difficulties experienced by the president and his rival, the chararismatic Colonel Théo, in trying to re-establish peace and harmony after ten years of civil war in their ethnically divided country. The focus is on the two leaders and their wives, and

Fanta Régina Nacro's **The Night of Truth**

the story culminates when the president's wife, driven mad by the murder of her only son, arranges for the man responsible, Théo, to be burned alive over an open fire (a fate which, it seems, befell the director's own uncle).

The Night of Truth is a passionately sincere film, but it is perhaps over-ambitious. The writing and directing both have an over-explicit theatricality, and the acting cannot quite rise to the heights needed to capture these extraordinary personal stories, which try to encapsulate the complete horror of ethnic hatred. Though flawed, *The Night of Truth* is immensely apposite and courageous, and a reminder that the ambitious new generation of African women directors are no longer willing simply to chronicle women's domestic oppression.

Didier Bergounhoux

Dani Kouyate's **OuagaSaga**

Two established directors were also active. **OuagaSaga** was a fresh departure for its director, Dani Kouyaté, son of the distinguished actor Sotigui Kouyaté (who works with Peter Brook in Paris). Where Kouyaté's first two features were very much concerned with tradition and rooted in African oral storytellling, *OugaSaga* is a contemporary tale of urban youth, tracing the adventures of a gang of boys on the verge of delinquency, whose lives are transformed by a lottery win. Using video for the first time, Kouyaté makes excellent use of both the fluidity of shooting and the special effects that the medium allows, and the film is well suited to its intended popular African television audience.

One of Burkina Faso's real veterans, S. Pierre Yaméogo, whose feature film-making career began in the 1980s, showed his sixth film, **Get Up and Walk** (*Delwende*), at Cannes in 2005. This is a typical example of Yaméogo's social commitment, a passionate denunciation of certain traditional beliefs and practices, which put the blame for village disasters on helpless old women who, as a result, are accused of witchcraft and driven into exile. Such practices are used by the men to hide their own very real transgressions. The project began as a television documentary, which Yaméogo subsequently developed as a fiction feature so that it would reach a wider audience.
– *Roy Armes*

CAMEROON

One of the major Cameroonian directors is Jean-Marie Teno, who trained in Paris, where he now lives, and has worked largely in documentary since 1984 (making just a single fiction feature, *Clando*, about illegal taxi drivers in 1996). His aim, in works like *Africa, I Will Fleece You*, on colonial misrule, and *Chief!*, about the nature of male authority – has always been to utter "a great cry of rage against injustice in Cameroon and show elements allowing the understanding and eventual untangling of the complex threads of oppression in Africa".

This 1990s work established Teno as a major voice in contemporary African cinema. His latest feature, **The Colonial Misunderstanding** (*Le Malentendu colonial*, 2004), examines the role of religion in colonial rule, taking as its theme Desmond Tutu's celebrated dictum: "When the first missionaries reached Africa, they had the bible and we had the land. They asked us to pray. So we closed our eyes to pray. When we opened them again, the situation was reversed. We had the bible and they had the land." – *Roy Armes*

COSTA RICA

Young director Esteban Ramírez's **Caribe** (2004), his debut feature, is the first Costa Rican film to receive international acclaim. The country had already set a record by producing four features in only three years: Oscar Castillo's *Murder at the Meneo* (*Asesinato en El Meneo*, 2001), Andrés Heidenreich's *Password, a Look into Darkness* (*Password. Una mirada en la oscuridad*, 2002) Maureen Jiménez's *Passionate Women* (*Mujeres apasionadas*, 2003) and Mauricio Mendiola's *Marasmo* (2003).

Building on this foundation, *Caribe* was able to obtain national critical acclaim, wide acceptance by the public (about 60,000 admissions) and international recognition, after Ramírez was awarded Best Director at the Latin American Film Festival in Trieste. His film also won four other awards, including the audience prize at the 30th Iberoamerican Film Festival in Huelva, Spain.

Ramírez aimed for international appeal by casting three foreign actors: Jorge Perugorría (Cuba), Cuca Escribano (Spain) and Maya Zapata (Mexico). Nevertheless, the film's plot is placed within a distinctly Costa Rican framework, never losing its local touch. It interweaves a love triangle involving Perugorría's married plantation owner, his wife (Escribano) and her half-sister (Zapata), with a current ecological issue: the resistance of a group of inhabitants against potential petroleum exploitation in the area, set against a picturesque Caribbean backdrop.

Jorge Perugorría and Cuca Escribano in **Caribe**

However, although *Caribe* participated in more than 20 festivals, no Costa Rican film has yet obtained proper commercial distribution in the domestic market, nor recouped its budget. The initial investment in films always comes from private sources, because, like the rest of Central America, Costa Rica has no laws, funds or subsidies to support audiovisual art. The only support in the region is from Cinergia, a fund for supporting films in Central America and Cuba, which was set up in 2004 and provides funds from international co-operation.

Costa Rican films are currently undergoing an exceptional moment of effervescence. Hilda Hidalgo has obtained the rights to adapt the novel *About Love and Other Demons* from Colombian Nobel Prize-winner Gabriel García Márquez, and is scheduled to begin filming in September 2006. Ishtar Yasin and Isabel Martínez are also preparing films for 2006. Yasin's film, *The Path* (*El camino*), deals with Nicaraguan immigration to Costa Rica. Martínez's *The Cha Cha Cha King* (*El rey del cha cha cha*) tells the story of a former Nicaraguan guerrilla who, in his old age, becomes a dance instructor. All three films are first works.

The Cha Cha Cha King and another film, the documentary *Searching for My Guerilla Godmother* (*Buscando a mi madrina guerrillera*), by Santiago Martínez, which deals with the Sandinista Revolution and its aftermath in Nicaragua, obtained their main financial support from Cinergia.

By **MARIA LOURDES CORTÉS** (marialcortes@correo.co.cr), who teaches film at the Universidad de Costa Rica and directs The Film and Television School of the Veritas University and the Cinergia audiovisual foundation. The most recent of her numerous books on Costa Rican and Central American cinema is *La pantalla rota. Cien años de cine en Centroamérica* (2005).

CYPRUS

The most talked about Cypriot film of 2005 was not even released last year. *Akamas*, directed by Panicos Chrysanthou, is due for completion in early 2006, but drew fire in sections of the right-wing press for its controversial politics. The film has a Turkish Cypriot hero, which is unprecedented in a film made by Greek Cypriots.

It is also set partly during the years of 'EOKA' – the island's struggle for independence from Britain between 1955 and 1960 – and allegedly shows the freedom fighters in an unflattering light. Chrysanthou himself has rejected the accusations, and called on critics to wait until they had seen the completed film before attacking it.

Akamas was one of only two films nearing completion in late 2005, the other being *Hi! Am Erica!*, directed by Yiannis Ioannou. The Ministry of Culture (via the Cinema Advisory Committee) remains the main source of funding in Cyprus, and a number of films that received funding in 2004 went into production in 2005. These include *Little Crime* (*Mikro Englima*) from Christos Georgiou, who had a success with *Under the Stars*, and *Wooden Man* (*Xilinos*), by Yiannis Economides, who previously made *Matchbox*. Both directors are based in Greece.

No new Cypriot features emerged in 2005. More worryingly, the list of future projects approved for funding by the Advisory Committee included no features, only shorts and medium-length films (known as "debouta"). The only exceptions are a couple of titles approved for script development money – but these may not be filmed for years, if at all. It remains to be seen if 2005 was an aberration, or if the Cyprus film industry, which seemed quite promising a couple of years ago, has been stymied by a dearth of good scripts and the tiny size of the local market. A proposed transfer of the Advisory Committee from the Ministry of Culture to the Ministry of Commerce and Industry – whether or not it happens – reflects the belief in some quarters that more commercial films are needed to kick-start the industry.

By **THEO PANAYIDES**, who reviews films for the *Cyprus Mail*.

EL SALVADOR

El Salvador is one of the most violent countries in Latin America and has one of the highest homicide rates. The average number of violent deaths each year exceeds the death toll in the country's civil war. Given this reality, Jorge Dalton was at press time working on the documentary *Until Life Do Us Part* (*Hasta que la vida nos separe*, 2006), which combines popular legends with testimony from various members of a community that has lived in a cemetery since 1958 – and feels more secure living among the dead than the living. The cemetery is like a village, and offers such diverse services as plumbing, carpentry, a convenience store and a soccer field. The children play among the graves, unleashing their adventures and imagination.

Dalton was also preparing another documentary, *Things About Life or Heroes Grazing in My Garden* (*Cosas de la vida o En mi jardín pastan los héroes*), a Cuban co-production that reunites two injured war veterans, Maximiliano Navarro, a farmer, and Luis Galdámez, a Reuters photographer. The documentary is narrated by the protagonists themselves and uses interviews, photographs and archive footage.

The recent civil war and gang violence are two topics addressed by Salvadoran film-makers. Veteran José David Calderón, who produced *Fish out of Water* (*Los peces fuera del agua*, 1969), one of the first Salvadoran films, is currently preparing *Of the Same Blood* (*De la misma sangre*), which deals with the confrontation of two friends during the Civil War. Noé Valladares, who made a short film, *A Saint's Virtue* (*La virtud de un santo*, 1997), is preparing his first feature, *Fourteen Crazy Aprils* (*Catorce abriles locos*), which deals with gangs.

Rolando Medina was scheduled to shoot *Ulysses with a Y* (*Ulises con y*) early in 2006, also a debut feature. It narrates the life of a man who after being released from jail discovers that his country is no longer the place he left behind when he was convicted. Medina already has contracts with Mexico and the United States to distribute the film. As co-screenwriter of Luis Mandoki's *Innocent Voices* (*Voces inocentes*; see Mexico section), Salvadoran Oscar Torres has projected the recent conflicts of Central America into the international arena. The film, which has received much public and critical acclaim, views the El Salvador civil war from the perspective of a little boy, who is converted into adulthood by violence. – *Maria Lourdes Cortés*

FIJI

Many festivals, from Sundance to Singapore, have acclaimed **The Land Has Eyes** (2004), the first fiction feature produced in Fiji, the Polynesian archipelago independent from the UK since 1970. Costing under $1m, it was shot on Rotuma Island by Vilsoni Hereniko (born in Mea, 1954), a playwright, teacher and documentary maker who used mostly locals for his cast and crew. The story follows Viki (Sapeta Taito), a poor but lovely girl who is haunted by the mythical Warrior Woman (Rena Owen from *Once Were Warriors*) and fights for justice and her freedom.

Influenced by *Whale Rider* and Murnau's *Tabu*, Hereniko unveils an extraordinary Eden, wavering between past, present and future. The resounding appeal of this movie has set in motion an infant industry. The Fiji Audio Visual Commission (www.fijiaudiovisual.com) offers several incentives to productions shooting or investing in the islands. US movies *Anacondas: The Hunt for the Blood Orchid* and *Straight Edge* were recently shot here. Various facilities are in development, while an animation school and studio launched in 2004 at the Fiji Institute of Technology has contributed to Miramax's *The Great North Pole Elf Strike*. – *Lorenzo Codelli*

GUATEMALA

Rafael Rosal's **Las Cruces, the Next Village** (*Las Cruces, poblado próximo*, 2005) is the fourth Guatemalan film produced in the last two years and the director's first feature. The jungle is the backdrop for war. A squad of six men and a woman decide to protect a village, Las Cruces, which is to be attacked by the army. The Indians do not know if they should trust this group of young mountain soldiers or if they should flee. The group itself faces many contradictions; the same emotions that propelled the recent civil war.

Rosal, along with Elias Jiménez, heads the production company Casa Comal and created the Icarus Central American Film Festival, now in its eighth year. In 2003, Jiménez made **The House Across the Street** (*La casa de en frente*), a film about political corruption, prostitution and the *maras* (delinquent gangs). It was seen by some 200,000 spectators and participated in a dozen international film festivals. Also in 2003, Mexican director Carlos García Agraz's *Where the Roads End* (*Donde acaban los caminos*), adapted from a novel by Mario Monteforte Toledo, addressed the issue of racism towards the Indians.

Elias Jiménez's **The House Across the Street**

Though it had yet to find a commercial release by late 2005, **What Sebastián Dreamt** (*Lo que soñó Sebastián*), by Rodrigo Rey Rosa, is undoubtedly one of the best Central American films of recent years. Adapted by Rey Rosa from his own novel, it addresses the issue of protecting nature. Sebastián is a writer who forbids others from hunting on his land, an activity which, ironically, the inhabitants of the region depend on. The film was shot entirely in the Petén jungle also featured in *Las Cruces, the Next Village*, and this is the film's

A poster for **What Sebastián Dreamt**

true protagonist, with a lake at its heart and an overabundance of nature. Cinematographer Guillermo Escalón makes sure to take care of nature as well as portray it as a victim of mankind's progress. The film has a sparse narrative language, yet is full of tension and ambiguity, as the natural world confronts progress and modernity.

Guatemalan cinema is experiencing something of a rebirth, and although there is no government support private film and television production is undergoing an exceptional burst of creativity, especially considering that no theatrical features were produced in the decade following Luis Argueta's *The Silence of Neto* (*El silencio de Neto*, 1994). – *Maria Lourdes Cortés*

HONDURAS

Katia Lara presented her documentary **Open Heart** (*Corazón abierto*, 2005) in Tegucigalpa, Honduras, as well as at international film festivals. It traces the remarkable story of the only theatrical Honduran film produced to date, Sami Kafati's *No Land Has an Owner* (*No hay tierra sin dueño*), which began filming in 1986 and was completed in 2002, six years after the director's death. *No Land Has an Owner* was shown at Cannes and at the Tribeca Film Festival. It addresses the issue of rural discrimination, through the story of a rich landowner who "legally" steals land from the peasants. Although the film deals with the issue rather tritely, it touches on problems that are still prevalent: territorial conflicts, political corruption, alcoholism and lack of education. *Open Heart* exposes the

Katia Lara's **Open Heart**

difficulties of the film-maker and her family in producing and finishing the film, and presents it as a metaphor for perseverance, and the need for more films to be produced in Central America.

During 2002, two other films were produced, on video, something unheard of for Honduras, which has had a rather sparse film history. Hispano Durón produced **Anita the Insect Hunter** (*Anita la cazadora de insectos*), addressing the consumer aspirations of the middle-class, and the young director Juan Carlos Fanconi filled movie theatres for more than three straight months with **Midnight Souls** (*Almas de la medianoche*), a mix of horror and Honduran legends. Fanconi is currently preparing his second film, *El Xendra*, a co-production with Guatemala and Costa Rica whose plot combines Indian legends and extra-terrestrials.
– *Maria Lourdes Cortés*

KYRGYZSTAN

In Kyrgyzstan, a nation of four million people, a record-breaking four features were shot in 2004–05, thanks to local film-makers, investors and foreign producers' interest in Central Asia. Two of the four are co-productions. **Saratan** (2004), directed by Ernest Abdizhaparov, was shot with half its budget provided by the government of the Republic of Kyrgyzstan and half from German company Icon-Film. The film anticipated the revolutionary events of March 2004, with a story about the head of a village, who in times of collapse and chaos decides to take matters into his own hands, regulating the planting of crops and inspiring villagers to work hard for a tomorrow that will provide them with a rich harvest.

The Wedding Chest (2005), directed by Nurbek Egen, is a Russia–Kyrgyzstan–Germany–France co-production, produced by Evgeniya Tirdatova. Young Aidar returns back to his home village on the coast of lake Issyk-Kul with a beautiful French girl, Isabelle. Isabelle is amazed by the natural beauty and the harmonious life in this remote land and is ready to marry Aidar, but something holds him back, perhaps the voices of his ancestors.

Another important production for Kyrgyzstan is **Mother's Lament of Mankurt** (2004), directed by Bakhyt Karagulov and based on the tenth-century legend of the fighting tribes of Zhuan-zhaun, who turned local warriors into slaves, or *mankurts*. This legend, explored in the novel by famous writer Chingyz Aitmatov, is very important for the national identity of the whole Central Asian region.

A very important trend in the development of Kygryz cinematography is the recent appearance of local producers. In 2004, a private company, Oy Art, led by Tolondo Toichubayev, was established. It aims to unite Central Asian film-makers for the "10+" programme, whose goal is to produce 10 masterpieces by the year 2010. The production of each film will begin only after the confirmed participation of European partners – producers or distributors. The production of two "10+" films has already begun: Ernest Abdizhaparov's *Boz Salkyn*, the story of a kidnapped bride, and Aktan Arym Kubat's *Light*, about a village electrician. – *Gulnara Abikeyeva*

LITHUANIA

The artistic situation of Lithuanian cinema remains dynamic, despite the ongoing shortage of finance for film production. The industry continues to lobby for the creation of a national film institute, at a time when state support (currently € 1.27m per year) for film production has not risen for almost 10 years. So it is hardly surprising that from 1988 to 2004, only eight features were made in Lithuania. The sole advantage is that because Lithuanian feature premieres are so rare, the audience always looks forward to them eagerly.

Sarunas Bartas' **Seven Invisible Men** (*Septyni nematomi vyrai*) became the first Lithuanian film to be screened at Cannes (in the Directors' Fortnight) in 2005. It portrays the USSR, and despair in the faces of people who understand that there is no

escape from their situation. The film's Lithuanian premiere was scheduled to follow in 2006. **Forest of the Gods**, by Algimantas Puipa, had its world premiere in Toronto and enjoyed record-breaking success in Lithuania, attracting 17,500 viewers in just 10 screening days. The film is based on the book of the same name, written by a Lithuanian, Balys Sruoga, after he had spent three years in a Nazi concentration camp in Stuthoff. He died shortly after his release and the novel was published only 10 years after his death.

Puipa's film tells of an artist and intellectual who somehow survived being a prisoner of the two most monstrous totalitarian regimes of the last century, fascism and Stalinism. The Professor (Valentinas Masalskis) is a very special person who abides by his own Decalogue, his own rules of truth and morality. At the German concentration camp, death seems inevitable, but irony helps him survive and dissociate himself from cruel reality. On his release, he writes a play and a book of memoirs, painting Stuthoff in sarcastic colours. However, this type of work is not acceptable to the Soviet government and he faces a new challenge scarcely less extreme than the camp. Puipa has successfully continued the tradition of films based on Lithuanian literature.

In December 2005, Audrius Juzenas was still completing post-production on *Ghetto*, based on Joshua Sobol's play about the Jewish Ghetto in Vilnius in 1942–43. Also forthcoming is the second feature from Kristijonas Vildziunas, following *The Lease Agreement. You Am I* is a contemporary adventure about a visionary architect building a futuristic tree-house in a gloomy forest. His resolution to create a new model of life is tested in many ways. However, his braveness, sincerity and simplicity help him to reach a happy ending.

Among the younger generation of film-makers, Ignas Miskinis, Ignas Jonynas, Giedre Beinoriute and Donatas Vaisnoras seem certain to enrich Lithuanian cinema. At press time, Miskinis was filming *Diring*, a black comedy about the exaggerated importance of image in modern society, centred around a fierce competition to promote a fictitious commercial brand.

By **Dr. GRAZINA ARLICKAITE** (info@kino.lt), who lectures in the cinema and theatre faculty of the Lithuania Music and Theatre Academy. She is a member of the European Film Academy and artistic director of International Film Festival "Vilnius Spring".

MADAGASCAR

Film-making in Madagascar is almost synonymous with Raymond Rajaonarivelo, who has directed its two fictional features, *Tabataba* and *When the Stars Meet the Sea*, as well as a number of documentaries. His latest non-fiction work, **Mahaleo** (2004), co-directed with the woman documentarist César Paes, paints a portrait of the past 30 years of Madagascan life through the work of the country's most popular pop group, Mahaleo, which has dominated the musical scene throughout this period. The group's title means 'free' and the seven musicians have always tried to present an independent view of national developments through their music. – *Roy Armes*

MALTA

Rarely can the introduction of financial incentives for film and television production have brought such instant, high-profile dividends. By the time the Malta Film Commission Act came into effect in July 2005, the island had already welcomed Steven Spielberg's *Munich* for what became a five-week shoot. The Act empowered the Malta Film Commission to provide financial incentives for visiting production, via a cash rebate of up to 20% of eligible expenditure (labour, hotels, equipment hire, props, catering etc.) spent on the island. Feature film and television productions, animation and documentaries that are at least partially produced on Malta can all qualify.

Spielberg and his 360-strong crew (190 visiting, 170 Maltese) used a total of 42 locations around the island, which represented Israel, the West Bank, Beirut, Cyprus, Athens, Spain and Italy.

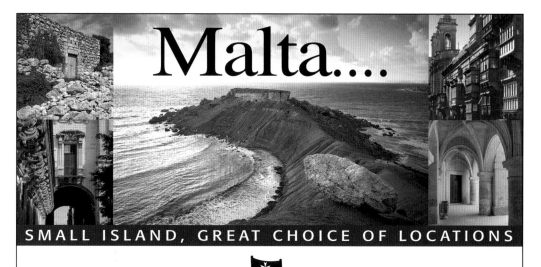

Karen Ballard/DreamWorks/Universal Studios

Malta's Sliema seafront doubles for Israel in **Munich,** *starring Eric Bana, centre, and Geoffrey Rush*

Though Malta has hosted large-scale shoots in the past, most recently *Troy*, this was the first time that a major production had been shot on the island's roads and in urban areas, rather than in a controlled location, such as the Mediterranean Film Studios (MFS) water tanks, or the neighbouring coastal 'backlot' at Fort Riccasoli (where large sets for *Troy* were built in 2003).

The incentive scheme also contributed to the arrival in November 2005 of the second unit from Ron Howard's *The Da Vinci Code*, with Malta doubling for the ancient Middle East. Other projects shot on the island last year included a piratical two-hour television drama-documentary, *Blackbeard*, made by the UK's Dangerous Films for the BBC in co-production with American, German and French channels. *Blackbeard* used the MFS water tanks, as did the German feature film *Godspeed*, a German mini-series, *Pamir*, and a British submarine TV drama, *Ghostboat*. A BBC docu-drama about the life of Elizabeth David saw Malta doubling for Italy and France. – *Daniel Rosenthal*

NAMIBIA

The Namibia Film Commission (NFC) has been mandated by government to build the film industry and attract foreign film producers to use Namibia as a location. Following NFC's promotional trip to Cannes in 2004, in March 2005 Namibia was also represented at the pan-African FESPACO festival. Most of the commission's efforts are geared towards the development of local talent through the Film and Video Development Fund, which offers training, fellowships and attachments, and organises scriptwriting competitions. Its goal is "a vibrant and sustainable film industry by the year 2030, in line with the National Vision of government."

Some $8m (Nam$50m) of government funding was assigned through NFC in 2005 for *Nujoma: Where Others Wavered*. Directed and written by Charles Burnett, the film will depict Namibia's history of national liberation and celebrate the country's landscapes, by dramatising the life of Sam Nujoma, the first president of Namibia and former president of the South West African People's Organisation (SWAPO). The film stars Danny Glover and Carl Lumby and is produced by Uazuva Kaumbi and the Pan African Centre of Namibia. It will be released in 2006.

The most notable production of the past year was Swiss director Peter Liechti's documentary, **Namibia Crossings**. It focuses on a trip through Namibia by the Hambana Sound Company, 12 musicians and singers gathered from Namibia, Zimbabwe, Angola, Switzerland and Russia. They tour a country that is in the process of reinventing itself. The shared search for the deeper sources of music becomes a testing experience for each individual, taking them to the edge at times. Some encounters with local music groups in remote provinces trigger a range of emotions – euphoric as well as sad. The film was included in various festivals, including FESPACO, Visions du Réel at Nyon and the Zimbabwe International Film Festival. – *Martin P. Botha*

Peter Liechti's **Namibia Crossings**

NEPAL

In the last decade, Nepalese cinema has faced many obstacles. The number of films produced has fallen sharply and 60% of cinemas have closed down. Institutionally, not a single distributor has made efforts to take Nepali films to the international market, even in India, where Nepali is widely spoken in many states. Despite this situation, an inaugural, week-long National Film Festival was organised by the government to encourage people to engage with the film industry. It was opened by the Queen, and the King participated in the closing ceremony.

However, few films were made in 2005, and most of these were of very limited quality. An exception was the comedy-drama **Jalpari**, directed by and starring Madankrishna Srestha and Haribamsa Acharaya, which found a wide audience with its relevant tale, touching on the real-life shortage of drinking water for the people of Kathmandu. One day, a man (played by Madankrishna) is trekking in the hills and meets a young girl by the riverside, Jalpari (Neha Karki). They have a nice conversation and she invites him home for a cup of tea, where Madankrishna's character tells Jalpari's father (Haribamsa) that he would like her to marry his son, a hydro-engineer.

Haribamsa goes to Kathmandu as a guest of his prospective in-laws. He is shocked by the misery of the people he sees queuing for drinking water and decides not to marry his daughter into life in such a wretched city. But the young engineer shows him how he can convert rainwater for drinking at his own home and convinces the father to let him marry Jalpari. This is a very simple, low-budget story, but well composed and full of comedy. The people of Kathmandu felt they were part of the film as they watched it, which is something very rare in Nepali cinema.

By **UZZWAL BHANDARY**, who appears as a comedian and satirist on Nepal TV.

NICARAGUA

The last Nicaraguan fiction film, Ramiro Lacayo's *The Spectrum of War* (*El espectro de la guerra*) was produced in 1988. Since then, Nicaragua has produced many internationally acclaimed documentaries, most recently **The Immortal** (*El immortal*, 2005), by Mercedes Moncada. Moncada, the daughter of a Spanish mother and Nicaraguan father, lived in Nicaragua for more than a decade. Her film, a co-production between Nicaragua, Spain and Mexico, deals with the Nicaraguan civil war from the point of view of the Rivera family, who were separated by the armed conflict and whose children were forced to fight on opposing sides. At the end of the war, the Riveras return home to find that their country is impoverished and continues to divide them. The film shows how division, religious manipulation, chauvinism and poverty are part of the legacy of violence in contemporary Nicaragua. Critics praised Moncada for her narrative style, which has mythic elements and a spiritual circularity that reflects her vision of the world.

Mercedes Moncada's **The Immortal**

Moncada's first documentary, *The Passion of Maria Elena* (*La pasión de María Elena*, 2002), also obtained international acclaim. Other non-fiction directors with international reputations include María José Alvarez and Martha Clarissa Hernández, who directed *From the Mud to the South* (*Desde el barro al sur*, 2002), about Nicaraguan immigration to Costa Rica. The film has helped make both countries' governments more sensitive on this issue. Florence Jaugey's *From Girlhood to Motherhood* (*De niña a madre*, 2004) became the first local documentary to be screened commercially. It addresses the issue of adolescent mothers in Nicaragua.

Jaugey also made **The Story of Rosa** (*La historia de Rosa*, 2005), about a nine-year-old Nicaraguan girl who becomes pregnant in Costa Rica, and the conflict surrounding her proposed abortion. Jaugey had earlier been praised for her feature documentary, *The Island of Lost Children* (*La isla de los niños perdidos*, 2001), and at press time was preparing her first fiction film, *La Yuma*, about a girl who devotes herself to boxing as her only route out of poverty. – *Maria Lourdes Cortés*

NIGER

With just one feature, Djingarey Maiga's *Black Friday*, in the last 15 years, Niger is the one country in Francophone West Africa to have missed out on the recent revival in sub-Saharan African film production. This gap is remedied to some extent by the first feature-length documentary to be directed by a woman in Niger, Rahmatou Kéita's **Al'lèèssi, An African Actress** (*Al'lèèssi, une actrice africaine*), which has been shown at several European and North American festivals. It is a study of the life of Zalika Souley, who in her mid-50s lives in poverty with her four children in a suburb of Niamey, but who was, in the 1960s and early 1970s, the first star of what seemed then a burgeoning Niger cinema, appearing in the films of such pioneers as Oumarou Ganda. – *Roy Armes*

PANAMA

Some people say that heroes are not born, but made. This phenomenon tends to happen by accident and, often, those people considered to be least heroic assume the role of heroes. **The Fists of a Nation** (*Los puños de una nación*, 2005), a documentary by Pituka Ortega, explores this phenomenon through the life of famed Panamanian boxer Roberto "Mano de Piedra" Durán. It presents a parallel between Panama's fight for sovereignty from the US during the 1970s, led by General Omar Torrijos, and the rise of Durán, who became a five-time world champion. This parallel reached epic proportions in 1980 when "Mano de Piedra" challenged and beat the Olympic champion, America's "Sugar" Ray Leonard. After this victory, Durán became a national hero and a Latin American icon.

However, the glory did not last, and the hero as well as the country again fell to the Americans. The village of El Chorrillo, Duran's birthplace, was invaded by the Americans in 1989. Through news and sports archive footage, *The Fists of a Nation* shows how smaller nations, with their low self-esteem, cling to erratic and unpredictable heroes who have the courage to make their dreams come true – a feat that the country itself cannot match.

Roberto Durán in **The Fists of a Nation**

Another parallel between Panamanian history and individual history is made by Enrique Castro Ríos, who directed a short film, *Memories of the Old Man's Son* (*Memorias del hijo del viejo*, 2003), about his father. He is currently working on a longer feature documentary, *Aqua Yala* (2006), which, from a poetic perspective, tries to raise awareness about the dangers of extending the locks from the Panama Canal into lands farmed by peasants. He also made the documentary *Ebo* (2004). Filmed entirely in the Dulegaya Indian language, it deals with the issue of intercultural bilingual education in the township of Kuna Yala.

Finally, Panamanian cinema's international profile was raised by the international acclaim for **One Dollar, The Price of Life** (*One Dollar. El Precio de la vida*, 2002), by Hector Herrera, which looks at the urban ghettos where youngsters once played together and now organise gangs for control of the drug business. – *Maria Lourdes Cortés*

PARAGUAY

Slowly but surely, Paraguay seems to be joining its Latin American neighbours in the audiovisual field. At least three new Paraguayan features were in different stages of production in December 2005, and new projects were expected to be completed soon, while the much-needed introduction of a Cinema Law was still being discussed. Although Paraguayan cinema began a few years after the first imported films were shown in the country at the beginning of the 20th century, production was always feeble and erratic. Modern sources indicate that Paraguay's first feature was produced in 1937: a co-production with Argentina, *Paraguay, tierra de promisión*, directed by James Bauer, who was born in Germany.

In 1976, Guillermo Vera directed the historial drama *Cerro Corá*, which was produced by the state to flatter President and dictator Alfredo Stroessner. In 1994, the satirical *Miss Ameriguá*, a comedy about a beauty contest in a little town ruled by a military despot, was made in co-production between Paraguay, Sweden and Chile, and directed by the Chilean Luis Vera. In 1998, Claudio MacDowell directed *The Call of the Oboe* (*El toque del oboe*), a co-production between Paraguay and Brazil, and one of its screenwriters, Hugo Gamarra, directed the documentary *The Gate of Dreams* (*El portón de los sueños*), about Augusto Roa Bastos, probably Paraguay's greatest writer. Gamarra also runs the annual Asunción International Film Festival, whose 14th edition took place in October 2005.

Since 2000, there has been a revitalisation of local cinema, mostly in digital format. One of the emerging directors is Galia Giménez who has already made three movies: *Requiem for a Soldier* (*Réquiem por un soldado*) and *María Escobar* (both 2002) and now **Gunter's Winter** (*El invierno de Gunter*, 2005), set in the 1970s, during the Stroessner dictatorship. Gunter, the President of

the World Bank, learns that his niece is in jail in Paraguay and tries desperately to save her life.

Another feature was directed in 2002 by Enrique Collar. The title, *Miramenometokei*, is a "Spanish-Guarani" expression that may be translated as "thorns of the soul", and reflects the experiences of Victoria, a young and beautiful woman who tries to escape from a depressing environment. Also interesting was *Estudio para una siesta paraguaya* (literally, *Study for a Paraguayan Nap*, 2003), directed by Argentinean Lía Dansker, who gave an accurate and sensitive portrait of the difficult situation of Paraguayan inmigrants in Buenos Aires.

Documentary production is also on the rise, and one brilliant example is **Cándido López: The Battle Fields** (2004), directed by Argentinean José Luis García, who explores the work of a painter who accompanied the Argentine army that participated in the War of the Triple Alliance (1865–70), which devastated Paraguay. In **Rechts Links** (literally, *Right Left*), directed by Rafael Kohan, the testimony of seven of the last survivors of Auschwitz, who live in Paraguay, is reflected in an absorbing and moving way. Another documentary, **Saint Balthasar's Route**, co-produced by Vimark Studios and Uruguayan Odair Tabárez, explores the roots of a little rural community of black people, through the rhythm of the *candombe*.

Historical events are also evident in two other forthcoming films. Manuel Cuenca's *The Earth Was Burning* (*La tierra ardía*) is based on Jorge Ritter's novel about an episode in the war with Bolivia in 1932–35. *Elisa*, directed by Augusto and Galia Giménez is about Elisa Lynch, the lover of the Paraguayan President, Marshall Francisco Solano López. Finally, well-known Argentinean producer Lita Stantic (*The Holy Girl*) has engaged young María Paz Encina to direct *Paraguayan Hammock* (*Hamaca Paraguaya*), a co-production with Argentina, France and Netherlands. It's the story of Candida and Ramón, an elderly peasant couple waiting for their son to come back from the battlefield durig the Chaco War in 1935. They also wait for the rain, for the wind, for the heat to pass, for the dog to stop barking, and for better times to come. – *Alfredo Friedlander and Jorge Jellinek*

PUERTO RICO

Local production has continued to flourish under the auspices of the new Production Fund at the Puerto Rico Film Commission, which contributes up to 80% of a film's budget (up to a maximum of $1.5m). In October 2005, Vicente Juarbe's **Cayo** became the first fund-sponsored film to open and was submitted as Puerto Rico's entry for the Oscars. The main character is a man with cancer, who goes for picnics to a small bay near the town of Culebra until the US authorities stop him, prompting the town's inhabitants to rally round.

Gerardo Rodriguez and Joshua Rosado in **Cayo**

Two other films were in post-production at press time. In Iván Dariel's historical drama, *The Runaway Slave* (*Cimarrón*), the title character leads a revolt in 17th-century Puerto Rico. Ricardo Matta's drama, *Thieves and Liars* (*Ladrones y mentirosos*), tells three interconnecting stories of drugs and corruption, featuring Steven Bauer and Elpidia Carrillo.

Two co-productions, one with the US and another with Spain, also benefited from the Fund: *Yellow* stars and is produced by Puerto Rican, Hollywood-based actress Roselyn Sánchez (*Rush Hour 2*); *Salt Water* (*Agua con sal*), was mainly shot in Spain. Nine other projects are in development and the call for entries that ended on November 30, 2005 will add a few productions in

2006. There was even a privately financed production, *The Comeback Dream* (*El sueño del regreso*), the fourth film of Puerto Rican director Luis Molina, which was due to open in January 2006. It is a comedy about a diverse group of Puerto Ricans who return to the island after spending many years in the US.

Luis A. Riefkohl, Executive Director of the Film Commission, has embarked on an international initiative that includes deals to develop feature co-productions with Buena Onda Films and the International Film Collective. Co-production agreements with Argentina and the Dominican Republic are in the works. Also, the Commission is promoting tax credits under Law 362, for local and foreign production. The establishment of a digital cinema circuit sponsored by the government is being studied and, for the first time, the Film Commission is giving incentives for short films.

Digitally shot movies keep coming up on commercial television, mostly melodramas. Public broadcaster Channel 6 screened a three-part mini-series, *It Seems Like Yesterday* (*Parece que fue ayer*), that chronicles the life of a family during the second half of the last century. The Lucy Boscana Dramatic Project of Channel 6 also had a call for entries in September, so more projects, especially mini-series, are expected in 2006.

Hollywood continued coming to the island for its locations and financial incentives. Most prominent were *The Hoax*, a CIA story with Richard Gere, directed by Lasse Hallström, and *The Reaping*, with Hilary Swank. Linda Carter, of *Wonder Woman* fame on TV, came down for a low-budget vampire flick, *Slayer*.

By **JOSÉ ARTEMIO TORRES**, a San Juan-based critic and film-maker.

RWANDA

The year 2005 will probably come to be remembered for the birth of a Rwandan film industry, because more than 10 films – an unprecedented number – were produced.

In January 2005, Eric Kabera, director and producer of the award-winning documentary, *Keepers of Memory*, co-produced with Radio Canada a documentary film, **Mères Courage** (literally, *Mothers Courage*), on women who became high-ranking decision-makers in the Rwandan government after their tragic experiences in the 1990s genocide. The film was directed by Leo Kalinda, a famous Rwandan-Canadian journalist based in Montreal, and selected for several festivals.

Also in January, Rwanda Cinema Centre (RCC) launched the first Films on Youth by Youth (FYY) programme, which aims to give practical training to young Rwandan screenwriters and directors. After a call for scripts was issued on local radio, more than 35 young people submitted their short film projects, and the result was the production of seven short films after two months of intensive training and production. These films focused on public health, the environment, street children and other topics.

RCC also organised the second meeting of the East African Films Forum, to discuss challenges faced by the new and still fragile film industry in the region, and the inaugural Rwanda Film Festival. This was held from March 17 to 30, under the banner of "Regional Co-operation for Audiovisual Excellence in East and Central Africa". It showcased 100 films, including fiction features, documentaries, shorts and animation. Rwandan audiences were delighted to meet members of the African film elite for the first time, including Rudolf Wichmann, producer of *Drum* (South Africa), and Mahamat Saleh Haroun, director of *Abouna* (Chad/France), who both presented their films. Attendance exceeded expectations. The festival's five provincial locations attracted 11,000 people and a further 5,150 attended the Kigali screenings.

Two acclaimed new features on the genocide, *Sometimes in April* by Raoul Peck, and *Hotel Rwanda*, by Terry George, both premiered in Rwanda, respectively in February and March, at the National Stadium, which was totally full on both occasions. Many Rwandans were assistants and extras in Peck's stunning film, and this is one of the

reasons why Rwandans are more and more interested in cinema. Also attracting great public attention was Jacques Favreau's *Sunday by the Pool in Kigali*, a story of love between a Rwandan waitress at the famous Hotel des Mille Collines and a Canadian journalist. The film, entirely shot in Rwanda with some Rwandan actors, is based on the novel by Gil Courtemanche.

In July, Eric Kabera was awarded with the Unicef Mention Award at the Zanzibar International Film Festival for **Through My Eyes**, a Rwandan–Kenyan documentary on Rwandan youth's perspectives for the future. Another notable project is **Isugi** (literally, *The Virgin*), a medium-length film by the promising Jacques Rutabingwa, about the psychological struggle of a young girl orphaned by the genocide and living with her aunts. She gets into trouble when her uncle starts to court her behind her aunt's back. The film is intelligent and beautifully shot. Rutabingwa is now collaborating with RCC to produce four short films by debuting directors on HD, as part of the second FYY Training Programme. The films will be launched at the second Rwanda Film Festival in March 2006. One is *Scars of Days* by Omar Moukhtar, about two village boys who come to Kigali to get rich. One becomes a businessman and the other a gigolo. The second film is *The Silent Epidemic* by Ayubu Kasasa Mago, which tackles drug abuse among local youths.

By **DADDY YOUSSOUF RUHORAHOZA** (admilink@yahoo.co.uk), who is production manager at Eric Kabera's Kigali-based company, Link Media Production.

Omar Moukhtar's **Scars of Days**

TAJIKISTAN

Movie production in Tajikistan almost stopped completely during the Civil War from 1992–97, as many film-makers moved to Russia, Uzbekistan or western Europe. However, in the past two to three years there has been a revival of sorts. The Tajikfilm studio shoots one full-length feature film per year and five to six documentaries on video. Cinemas are operating, but show films only on video or DVD.

In 2004, in the capital, Dushanbe, the first Didor Film Festival was held. The competition included movies from Central Asia, Iran, Afghanistan and Russia. The closing ceremony saw grants awarded to young Tajik directors to make their first short films. The money was provided by the famous Iranian director Mohsen Makhmalbaf, who has a family home in Dushanbe. This strong link between Tajik and Iranian film-makers is not accidental; both nationalities share the same Persian cultural identity and speak almost the same form of Farsi.

Moreover, Makhmalbaf in 2005 made his own film, **Love**, in Dushanbe, with a Tajik copyright. It tells the story of a man who on his 40th birthday arranges a date with four of his beloved women at the same time and place. As the story unfolds, we find out that the protagonist does not search only kisses and hugs in his love affairs. He pursues the rarest moments of happiness that make the soul melt and gain wings, that make one want to live and create.

In 2004 and 2005, two features were shot on video by Tajik directors. Umedsho Mirzoshirinov's **The Statue of Love** follows a teenager's unhappy love for a slightly older young woman and his disappointments in life. Guland Mukhabbatova and Dalera Rakhmatova's **Rover** (*Ovora*) tells the story of Abdullo, who lives in a mountain village. His life changes dramatically during preparations for his ritual circumcision. Among Tajik documentaries, one of the best recent examples is Orzu Sharipov's **11,000 Kilometres from New York**, which focuses on the life of refugees on the border of Afghanistan and Tajikistan. They find shelter on the islands of the river Pyanjh. – *Gulnara Abikeyeva*

Mohsen Makhmalbaf's Love

TANZANIA

Tanzania has no film production infrastructure, nor an institutional framework to support film-making. Most cinemas have been turned into shopping malls, centres of worship, embassies or university buildings. All the cinemas in Zanzibar have closed down and there are just three screens in the one functioning cinema in Dar es Salaam, where between January and September 2005 some 47,000 viewers paid around $5 per head to watch the latest Hollywood imports.

Nevertheless, production continues, and in July 2004, the Zanzibar International Film Festival of the Dhow Countries (ZIFF) hosted the launch of the Tanzania Independent Producers Association (TAIPA). Its mission is "to establish solidarity amongst independent producers, to facilitate the growth of a sustainable, viable, and dynamic television and film industry in Tanzania." It is seen as filling the gap left by the demise of the Tanzania Film Company and the Audiovisual Institute. ZIFF provides vital opportunities for interaction between media professionals, policy makers and individuals working towards cultural and economic development through regional and international collaboration.

Tanzania has more than 20 television stations. Although there is a statutory requirement that at least 60% of broadcast content should be 'local', broadcasters have ignored this requirement, which further limits opportunities for local film-makers. Nevertheless, 2004 saw the completion of Beatrix Mugishagwe's debut feature, *Tumaini: Childood Robbed*, and in 2005, Mwangaza Kang'anga wrote, directed and produced a one-woman film, *Kizunguzungu*. – *Ogova Ondego*

UGANDA

An international film festival and screenwriters' laboratory were established in Kampala in 2004. Amakula Kampala International Film Festival is co-directed by American Lee Ellickson and Alice Smits, from the Netherlands. Two successful editions have already taken place and attracted film buffs from all over the world to the Ugandan capital. In August 2005, Kampala hosted the first ever Maisha Film Laboratory, the brainchild of Mira Nair, director of the *Salaam Bombay* and *Monsoon Wedding* fame. Its aim is to train film-makers in East Asia and East Africa.

The first event focused on screenwriting and the next one, in August 2006, will tackle directing. Another positive development in Kampala in 2005 was the launch of the Uganda International Film Foundation (UIFF), an organisation that brings together players in the audiovisual sector.

Kevin McDonald shot scenes in Uganda for *The Last King of Scotland*, based on Giles Foden's book about the regime of Idi Amin. Indigenous production is limited to short films and Uganda-based Congolese film-maker, Petna Ndaliko Katondolo, makes experimental shorts including *Lamokowang* (2004) and *Twaomba amani* (2005). Together with Kenya's Willie Owusu and Nigeria's Newton Aduaka, Katondolo is viewed by critics as representing a new wave of film-making in Africa. Other Ugandan shorts made recently include *Heart of Kampala* (2005), co-directed by Winnie Gamisha and Andreas Frowein, and *Gang Obong Obur: Our Homes Have Become Ghost Villages* (2005), directed by Robbie Wodomal.

Director Petna Ndaliko Katondolo

Cinemagoing in Kampala is very limited, with only two public cinemas, the larger and more modern of which is Cineplex Cinema, with two screens and 395 seats. By contrast, the video halls, known in the widely spoken Luganda language as *bibanda* (shacks), take in an estimated 120,000 viewers each day at around $0.07 per head – compared to prices of more than $7 a ticket at Cineplex.

Viewers sit on wooden benches inside dark structures made of reeds, wood, cardboard and stone, watching videos of violent action films on television monitors. Electric wiring often hangs dangerously above the audience. Kampala is home to around 600 of Uganda's estimated 2,000 *bibanda*, which offer affordable and convenient entertainment to Ugandans who cannot afford to watch films at commercial theatres. Many are situated in densely-populated neighbourhoods of Kampala.

The most remarkable aspect of this market is that most videos shown are in English and viewers lack a good grasp of the language – so the films are translated or voiced-over live in Luganda by VJs (video jockeys). The VJs claim copyright to their work. Among the popular VJs are Jingo and Prince Joe Nakibinge, who is also an elected councilor. The VJs' 'translation' may not necessarily be accurate, but they hold great sway with video operators, and viewers hang on their every word.

The government of Uganda had tried to close down the video halls in 2002, arguing they were unsafe, havens for thieves and drug addicts, and that they distracted children from their studies. Their livelihood thus threatened, investors came together and formed the self-regulatory Video Owners & Operators Association. Benon Tibanyendera, its general secretary, says that it has the power to enter and inspect any video library and screening hall. He admits that many of these halls screen pirated videos, and owners have only recently started paying statutory taxes to the exchequer. – Ogova Ondego

ZIMBABWE

Since last year's report on Zimbabwe, the political situation in the country has become even worse. Amid the prolonged political and economic crisis, the local film industry is, inevitably, in the doldrums. Yet 2005 should be remembered for three remarkable Zimbabwean short films.

Based on an old Shona folk tale, Tsitsi Dangarembga's *Mother's Day* (*Kare Kare Zvako*), celebrates the diversity of contemporary Zimbabwean music. The narrative deals with an African village, where famine has severely hit one family. The father decides to kill his wife and eat her flesh. He sets a trap for her, but eliminating the mother of his children proves harder than expected.

The film successfully reinterprets the macabre and magical elements of popular tradition through music, song and dance. At the 15th Festival of African, Asian and Latin American Cinema in Milan it won first prize in the African Short Film competition and its quality was confirmed at the 2005 Zanzibar Film festival, where it won the Golden Dhow for Best Short Film.

Equally impressive is *Killer October*, a South Africa–Zimbabwe co-production by Garth Meyer, a graduate of the CityVarsity Film and Television School in Cape Town. By means of stunning visuals and an evocative sound design, Meyer tells the story of a young boy who loses a loved one due to an unknown disease. The film hints at AIDS, which currently ravages Zimbabwe. The boy embarks on a mythical journey to find a resting place for the ashes of his parent. Documentary and African myth are impressively integrated.

Inger Smith's *The One That Fits Inside the Bathtub* was selected for competition at the Locarno, Commonwealth, Apollo and Durban film festivals in 2005. Striving to find her place in the world around her, the principal character (Smith) in this poetic short is forced to reappraise her lifestyle after her sense of security is destroyed.

Inger Smith in **The One That Fits Inside the Bathtub**

In the context of the current racial situation in Zimbabwe, Smith, who was born and raised there but is currently studying at CityVarsity, raises very relevant questions about cultural identity and whether being white can also mean being African. Her film is ultimately a very moving experience and deservedly received much praise at Locarno. – Martin P. Botha

World Box-Office Survey 2004

ARGENTINA

	Admissions
1. Shrek 2	3,122,000
2. The Passion of the Christ	2,807,000
3. The Return of the King	1,950,000
4. Patoruzito (Argentina)	1,896,000
5. Troy	1,683,000
6. The Day After Tomorrow	1,592,000
7. Spider-Man 2	1,589,000
8. The Prisoner of Azkaban	1,268,000
9. The Incredibles	1,180,000
10. Something's Gotta Give	1,094,000

Population:	38 million
Admissions:	44 million
Total box-office:	$90m
Screens:	800
Avge. ticket price:	$2.00

$1 = ARS 2.97. Source: INCAA/SICA.

AUSTRALIA

	$m
1. Shrek 2	37.07
2. The Return of the King	36.36
3. The Prisoner of Azkaban	24.40
4. Meet the Fockers	20.22
5. Spider-Man 2	17.96
6. Troy	17.45
7. The Incredibles	17.26
8. The Day After Tomorrow	14.89
9. Love Actually (UK/US)	13.79
10. The Edge of Reason	13.43

Population	20.27 million
Admissions:	91.45 million
Total box-office:	$668m
Local films' market share:	1%
Screens:	1,909

$1 = A$1.28. Sources: Motion Pic. Distributors' Assoc./ Australian Film Commission.

AUSTRIA

	Admissions
1. (T)Raumschiff Surprise (Germany)	1,135,758
2. Finding Nemo	1,029,273
3. The Return of the King	662,138
4. The Prisoner of Azkaban	649,072
5. Shrek 2	596,176
6. 7 Dwarfs (Germany)	554,798
7. Troy	493,538
8. Something's Gotta Give	468,575
9. Brother Bear	469,535
10. The Day After Tomorrow	380,251

Population:	8.2 million
Admissions:	19.4 million
Local films' market share:	2.1%
Sites/screens:	176/560

$1 = €0.74
Source: Association of the Audiovisual & Film Industry.

BELGIUM

	Admissions
1. The Prisoner of Azkaban	1,108,663
2. Shrek 2	951,124
3. Troy	772,468
4. Podium (France/Belgium)	668,834
5. The Day After Tomorrow	662,782
6. The Last Samurai	577,933
7. The Incredibles	568,825
8. Brother Bear	487,127
9. Spider-Man 2	453,820
10. Shark Tale	450,148

Population:	10.39 million
Admissions:	23.79 million
Sites/screens:	123/515
Avge. ticket price:	$7.43

$1 = €1.24
Source: Moniteur du Film.

BOLIVIA

	$
1. The Passion of the Christ	466,028
2. The Return of the King	288,987
3. Spider-Man 2	233,379
4. The Day After Tomorrow	197,735
5. Troy	190,465
6. The Robbery (Bolivia)	189,182
7. The Prisoner of Azkaban	179,558
8. Garfield	85,278
9. I, Robot	84,026
10. Brother Bear	83,325

Population:	9.40 million
Admissions:	1.57 million
Total box-office	$3,418,395
Local films' market share	9%
Screens:	33
Avge. ticket price:	$2.6

$1= Bs 7.95. Source: Manfer Films.

BRAZIL

	Admissions
1. Spider-Man 2	7,737,714
2. The Passion of The Christ	6,883,895
3. Shrek 2	4,672,046
4. The Return of the King	4,268,649
5. Troy	4,177,660
6. The Prisoner of Azkaban	3,355,659
7. The Day After Tomorrow	3,264,034
8. Garfield	3,226,512
9. Cazuza (Brazil)	3,082,522
10. Olga (Brazil)	3,075,749

Population:	181 million
Admissions:	114.73 million
Total box office:	$647.59m
Local films' market share:	14.3%
Screens:	1,997
Avge. ticket price:	$2.46

US$ 1 = R$ 2.72 Source: Filme B.

BULGARIA

	Admissions
1. Troy	286,955
2. The Return of the King	223,622
3. The Last Samurai	161,515
4. The Day After Tomorrow	156,019
5. Welcome to the Jungle	92,729
6. I, Robot	97,694
7. The Prisoner of Azkaban	83,936
8. Ocean's Twelve	59,807
9. King Arthur	60,260
10. The Passion of the Christ	55,868

Population:	7.8 million
Admissions:	3.12 million
Total box-office:	$8.01m
Local films' market share:	0.22%
Sites/screens:	61/85
Avge. ticket price:	$2.56

$1 = BGN 1.57. Source: Geopoly Ltd.

CHILE

	Admissions
1. Shrek 2	1,116,275
2. The Passion of the Christ	824,964
3. The Day After Tomorrow	661,747
4. Machuca (Chile)	654,169
5. Spider-Man 2	589,004
6. Troy	546,401
7. The Prisoner of Azkaban	492,788
8. The Incredibles	468,310
9. The Last Samurai	347,838
10. Garfield	297,161

Population:	15.11 million
Admissions:	11.44 million
Total box-office:	$39.1m
Local films' market share:	8.96%
Screens:	273
Avge. ticket price:	$4.14

$1 = Ch$535. Source: Cámara Chilena de Comercio Cinematográfico.

COLOMBIA

	Admissions
1. The Passion of the Christ	1,365,872
2. Shrek 2	1,034,534
3. Spider-Man 2	938,097
4. The Return of the King	859,294
5. Troy	649,368
6. The Day After Tomorrow	577,890
7. The Prisoner of Azkaban	513,778
8. Brother Bear	469,770
9. The Last Samurai	451,793
10. Garfield	433,802

Population:	46 million
Admissions:	18 million
Total box-office:	$74.01m
Screens:	412
Avge. ticket price:	$3.40

$1 = COP 2,468. Source: Proimágenes en Movimiento.

CROATIA

	Admissions
1. The Return of the King	269,597
2. The Passion of the Christ	260,899
3. Troy	139,179
4. The Prisoner of Azkaban	102,830
5. Shrek 2	100,188
6. Alexander	87,721
7. The Day After Tomorrow	74,215
8. The Last Samurai	72,825
9. The Edge of Reason	66,457
10. Spider-Man 2	63,702

Population:	4.38 million
Admissions:	2.9 million
Local films' market share:	3%
Screens:	64
Avge. ticket price:	$4

$1 = Kunas 6.00. Source: Central Bureau of Statistics/ Hollywood magazine.

CZECH REPUBLIC

	Admissions
1. The Return of the King	778,852
2. The Prisoner of Azkaban	703,219
3. Troy	608,765
4. Shrek 2	588,244
5. Up and Down (Czech)	555,928
6. Snowboarders (Czech)	484,949
7. The Poets Never Lose Hope (Czech)	407,406
8. Kamenak 2 (Czech)	400,848
9. Finding Nemo	264,091
10. Spider-Man 2	236,287

Population:	10.2 million
Admissions:	2.87 million
Total box-office:	$10.72m
Local films' market share:	23.5%
Screens:	756
Avge. ticket price:	$3.35

$1 = CZK 24.54. Source: Czech Film Centre.

DENMARK

	Admissions
1. The Prisoner of Azkaban	629,000
2. The Return of the King	544,000
3. King's Game (Denmark)	501,000
4. Brother Bear	486,000
5. Shrek 2	462,000
6. My Sister's Kids in Egypt (Denmark)	456,000
7. Brothers (Denmark)	422,000
8. Terkel in Trouble (Denmark)	376,000
9. Troy	370,000
10. Spider-Man 2	347,000

Population:	5.4 million
Admissions:	12.8 million
Total box-office:	€105,2m
Local films' market share:	24%
Sites/screens:	163/380
Avge. ticket price:	€8.72

€1 = DKK 7.45. Source: Danish Film Institute.

EGYPT

	Admissions
1. Okal	21,019,536
2. Groom from Security Area	16,192,584
3. Tito	12,167,074
4. The Great Fuul of China	11,246,701
5. Pauper of the Sea	7,672,356
6. The Pasha Is Student	7,396,146
7. Totally Stupid	6,384,448
8. My Aunt Faransa	5,870,447
9. First Year of Embezzlement	5,505,125
10. Girls' Love	4,937,212

All films are Egyptian.

Population:	72 million
Local films' market share:	73%
Sites/screens:	167/249
Avge. ticket price:	$3.47

$1 = LE 6.50. Source: Motion Pictures Cairo.

ESTONIA

	Admissions
1. The Return of the King	73,100
2. Shrek 2	59,218
3. The Day After Tomorrow	55,835
4. Troy	52,484
5. The Prisoner of Azkaban	49,177
6. Garfield	32,707
7. Revolution of Pigs (Estonia/Finland)	26,345
8. Spider-Man 2	24,621
9. The Edge of Reason	22,628
10. Set Point (Estonia)	22,532

Population:	1.35 million
Admissions:	1.19 million
Total box-office:	$5.95m
Local films' market share:	5.39%
Sites/screens:	12/81
Avge. ticket price:	$5.0

$1 = EEK 12.59. Source: Estonian Film Foundation.

FINLAND

	Admissions
1. The Prisoner of Azkaban	343,176
2. The Return of the King	329,727
3. Brother Bear	269,596
4. The Day After Tomorrow	229,308
5. Spider-Man 2	229,207
6. Shrek 2	207,106
7. Vares (Finland)	201,151
8. Dognail Clipper (Finland)	195,169
9. Troy	179,975
10. Home on the Range	160,235

Population:	5.2 million
Admissions:	7.9 million
Total box-office:	$71.34m
Local films' market share:	21%
Sites/screens:	340
Avge. ticket price:	$8.97

Source: Finnish Film Foundation.

FRANCE

	Admissions (millions)
1. The Chorus (France/Switz.)	8.36
2. Shrek 2	7.09
3. The Prisoner of Azkaban	6.89
4. Spider-Man 2	5.20
5. The Incredibles	4.75
6. A Very Long Engagement (France)	4.23
7. Podium (France/Belgium)	3.55
8. Brother Bear	3.50
9. Two Brothers (France/UK)	3.28
10. The 11 Commandments (France)	2.89

Population:	59 million
Admissions:	194.8 million
Total box-office:	$1.33 billion
Local films' market share:	39%
Sites/screens:	2,128/5,302
Avge. ticket price:	$6.85

$1 = €0.85. Source: Centre National du Cinéma.

GERMANY

	Admissions
1. (T)Raumschiff Surprise (Germany)	9,165,335
2. The Prisoner of Azkaban	6,536,641
3. 7 Dwarfs (Germany)	6,516,658
4. Downfall (Germany)	4,523,573
5. Troy	3,834,346
6. Shrek 2	4,111,337
7. The Return of the King	3,282,125
8. The Day After Tomorrow	3,008,449
9. Spider-Man 2	3,451,820
10. Something's Gotta Give	2,601,043

Population:	82.52 million
Admissions:	156.7 million
Total box-office:	$1.06 billion
Local films' market share:	23.80%
Sites/screens:	1,831/4,868
Avge. ticket price:	$4.80

$1 = €1.18. Source: Federal Film Board.

GREECE

	Admissions
1. Brides (Greece)	700,000
2. Ocean's Twelve	460,000
3. The Prisoner of Azkaban	400,000
4. Alexander	370,000
5. King Arthur	352,000
6. War of the Worlds	345,000
7. Meet the Fockers	330,000
8. Mr. & Mrs. Smith	300,000
9. National Treasure	295,000
10. Million Dollar Baby	270,000

August 2004 to July 2005. Figures unconfirmed officially.

Population:	10.9 million
Admissions:	15 million
Screens:	490
Avge. ticket price:	$8.0

$1 = €0.80. Source: Cinema Department, Ministry of Culture.

HUNGARY

	Admissions
1. Shrek 2	769,034
2. Revenge of The Sith	670,123
3. Fateless (Hungary)	443,435
4. Garfield	361,403
5. The Edge of Reason	329,042
6. Meet the Fockers	324,602
7. Hitch	242,638
8. Spider-Man 2	222,172
9. Shark Tale	219,685
10. Alexander	212,148

Population:	10.1 million
Admissions:	13.60 million
Total box-office:	$53.7m
Local films' market share:	9.77%
Screens:	531
Avge. ticket price:	$3.95

$1 = Forints 200. All figs. for Aug. 2004 to Aug. 2005. Sources: Assoc. of Hungarian Film Distribs./ Magyar Filmunio.

ICELAND

	Admissions
1. The Return of the King	53,288
2. The Prisoner of Azkaban	47,012
3. Shrek 2	46,484
4. Spider-Man 2	40,349
5. The Day After Tomorrow	34,665
6. The Edge of Reason	29,596
7. Garfield	31,394
8. In Tune with Time (Iceland)	20,966
9. Cold Light (Iceland)	19,900
10. The Bourne Supremacy	19,847

Population:	293,577
Admissions:	1.45 million
Total box-office:	$13.5m
Local films' market share:	4%
Avge. cinema ticket price:	$9.60

$1 = ISK 71.85. Source: Statistics Iceland.

IRAN

	$
1. The Duel	693,552
2. Girls' Dormitory	485,910
3. Engagement Party	458,757
4. The Charlatan	457,145
5. A Candle in the Wind	410,628
6. The Bachelors	428,878
7. A Rose for the Bride	374,965
8. The Weeping Willow	366,666
9. The Extra Wife	342,222
10. Top of the Tower	311,111

All titles are Iranian.

Population:	70 million
Admissions:	4.5m
Total box-office:	$6.9 m
Screens:	290
Avge. ticket price:	$1.07

$1 = Rials 8,800. Source: Farabi Cinema Foundation.

IRELAND

	$m
1. Shrek 2	6.3
2. The Prisoner of Azkaban	3.7
3. The Edge of Reason	3.7
4. The Day After Tomorrow	3.2
5. Spider-Man 2	2.8
6. The Incredibles	2.7
7. Shark Tale	2.6
8. The Passion of the Christ	2.6
9. Man About Dog (Ireland)	2.5
10. Troy	2.4

Population:	3.91 million
Admissions:	17.3 million
Total box-office:	$124.56m
Local films' market share:	2.5%
Screens:	373
Avge. ticket price:	$6.75

$1 = €1.20. Source: AC Nielsen EDI/Carlton Screen Advertising.

ISRAEL

	Admissions
1. Shrek 2	570,000
2. Turn Left at the End of the World (Israel)	450,000
3. The Return of the King	405,000
4. The Prisoner of Azbakan	300,000
5. Troy	290,000
6. The Incredibles*	275,000
7. Shall We Dance*	250,000
8. Shark Tale*	250,000
9. Something's Gotta Give	250,000
10. The Day After Tomorrow	221,000

*Still on release in 2005. Source: Ha-Ir (Tel Aviv weekly newspaper).

Population:	6.5 million
Admissions:	9.8 million
Local films' market share:	13.2%
Avge. ticket price:	$7.5

ITALY

	$m
1. Madagascar	24.7
2. Meet the Fockers	16.7
3. Manual of Love (Italy)	16.7
4. The Tiger and the Snow (Italy)	15.6
5. War of the Worlds	15.4
6. Charlie and the Choclate Factory	12.2
7. The Edge of Reason	11.7
8. Shark Tale	10.2
9. Fantastic Four	10.5
10. Alexander	12.1

Jan. 2005 to Nov. 2005 (approx. 75% of annual gross).

Population:	58.4 million
Admissions:	62 million
Total box-office:	$424.11m
Local films' market share:	26.3%
Screens:	3,628
Avge. ticket price:	$8.5

$1= €0.85. Sources: Cinetel/Agis.

JAPAN

	$m
1. Howl's Moving Castle (Japan)	173.9m
2. The Last Samurai	119.1m
3. The Prisoner of Azkaban	117.4m
4. Finding Nemo	95.7m
5. The Return of The King	89.7m
6. Crying Out Love… (Japan)	73.9m
7. Spider-Man 2	58.2m
8. The Day After Tomorrow	45.2m
9. Be with You (Japan)	41.7m
10. Pokemon: Destiny Deoxys (Japan)	38.1m

Population:	127.7 million
Admissions:	170.1 million
Total box-office:	$1.83 billion
Local films' market share:	37.5%
Screens:	2,825
Avge. ticket price:	$10.78

$1 = Yen 115. Source: Japan Motion Picture Producers' Association.

KENYA

	Admissions
1. The Passion of The Christ	60,070
2. Spider-Man 2	36,145
3. The Prisoner of Azkaban	17,460
4. The Day After Tomorrow	17,452
5. Troy	15,683
6. The Last Samurai	14,172
7. White Chicks	12,024
8. The Bourne Supremacy	10,419
9. Shrek 2	9,830
10. Alexander	9,360

Population:	34 million
Total box-office:	$597,551
Screens:	21
Local films' market share:	less than 1%
Avge. ticket price:	$2.5

$1 = KES 8.2. Sources: ComMattersKenya Ltd./ ArtMatters.Info/African Cine Week.

LATVIA

	Admissions
1. Troy	247,871
2. The Return of the King	247,485
3. Shrek 2	214,475
4. The Day After Tomorrow	209,402
5. The Return of the King	153,619
6. The Last Samurai	137,059
7. The Passion of the Christ	136,987
8. King Arthur	125,413
9. Garfield	111,769
10. Van Helsing	111,379

Population:	2.31 million
Admissions:	1.68 million
Total box-office:	$3.50m
Local films' market share:	2.7%
Sites/screens:	61/78
Avge. ticket price:	$4.30

$1 = LVL 0.57. Source: Film Registry of the National Film Centre.

MEXICO

	$m
1. Shrek 2	28.79
2. Spider-Man 2	20.95
3. The Day After Tomorrow	19.68
4. The Passion of the Christ	19.00
5. Troy	15.76
6. The Prisoner of Azakaban	15.19
7. The Incredibles	10.64
8. Shark Tale	9.69
9. Scooby Doo: Monsters Unleashed	9.25
10. The Last Samurai	8.70

Population:	105 million
Admissions:	162 million
Total box-office:	$486m
Local films' market share:	5.5%
Sites/screens:	499/3,491
Avge. ticket price:	$3.25

$1 = M$11.30. Sources: Instituto Mexicano de Cinematografía/Cineteca Nacional.

NETHERLANDS

		Admissions
1.	The Prisoner of Azkaban	1,230,000
2.	The Return of the King	1,064,000
3.	Shrek 2	977,000
4.	Troy	703,000
5.	The Day After Tomorrow	654,000
6.	The Edge of Reason	631,000
7.	Shark Tale	611,000
8.	Brother Bear	518,000
9.	The Last Samurai	482,000
10.	The Incredibles	416,000

Population:	16.3 million
Admissions:	26 million
Total box-office:	$195m
Local films' market share:	9.2%
Screens:	614
Avge. ticket price:	$7.97

Source: Netherlands Cinematographic Federation.

NEW ZEALAND

		$m
1.	Shrek 2	7.56
2.	The Prisoner of Azkaban	4.22
3.	Spider-Man 2	3.06
4.	The Edge of Reason	2.74
5.	Troy	2.60
6.	The Day After Tomorrow	2.38
7.	The Passion of the Christ	1.96
8.	The Last Samurai	1.94
9.	Shark Tale	1.81
10.	50 First Dates	1.67

Population:	4.06 million
Admissions:	17.17 million
Total box-office:	$106.97m
Local films' market share:	5%
Screens:	343
Avge. ticket price:	$6.23

$1 = NZ$1.3. Source: Motion Picture Distributors'
Association of New Zealand.

NORWAY

		Admissions
1.	Shrek 2	610,747
2.	The Prisoner of Azkaban	591,462
3.	The Return of the King	488,096
4.	The Junior Olsen Gang Goes Rock'n'Roll (Norway)	407,500
5.	Spider-Man 2	379,716
6.	Brother Bear	334,411
7.	The Day After Tomorrow	308,554
8.	Uno (Norway)	287,566
9.	Troy	272,990
10.	The Edge Of Reason	265,376

Population:	4.5 million
Admissions:	11.97 million
Total box-office:	$122.85m
Local films' market share:	13.7%
Screens:	632
Avge. ticket price:	$10.26

$1 = NOK 6.37.
Source: National Association of Municipal Cinemas.

PAKISTAN

1. Commando
2. Punjabi Girl
3. Blessing
4. The Boy
5. Remand
6. Rascal
7. Soldier
8. Scoundrel
9. Warlord
10. Sacrifice

All films are Pakistani. Individual figures N/A.

Population:	140 million
Admissions:	20 million
Total box-office:	$10m
Local films' market share:	80%
Screens:	300
Avge. ticket price:	$1

$1 = Rs. 60.

PERU

		Admissions
1.	The Passion of the Christ	896,757
2.	The Day After Tomorrow	737,580
3.	Spider-Man 2	709,821
4.	Shrek 2	579,472
5.	Troy	579,229
6.	Garfield	402,262
7.	The Prisoner of Azkaban	375,129
8.	The Last Samurai	296,312
9.	Shark Tale	285,185
10.	Exorcist: The Beginning	254,439

Population:	28 million
Screens:	175 (Lima only)

POLAND

		Admissions
1.	Shrek 2	3,390,922
2.	Passion of the Christ	3,451,908
3.	The Return of the King	2,089,415
4.	Never Again (Poland)	1,620,307
5.	Troy	1,184,083
6.	Brother Bear	1,170,602
7.	The Prisoner of Azakaban	1,040,789
8.	The Edge of Reason	831,238
9.	Shark Tale	911,933
10.	The Day After Tomorrow	789,222

Population:	38.23 million
Admissions:	33.40 million
Total box-office:	$22.83m
Local films' market share:	8.69%
Sites/screens:	730/1122
Avge. ticket price:	$4.29

$1 = Zloty 14.2.

ROMANIA

		Admissions
1.	Troy	249,949
2.	The Passion of the Christ	216,998
3.	The Return of the King	214,870
4.	The Last Samurai	121,525
5.	The Prisoner of Azkaban	120,056
6.	Spider-Man 2	102,681
7.	The Day After Tomorrow	97,785
8.	Van Helsing	82,695
9.	King Arthur	66,313
10.	Scary Movie 3	65,902

Population:	21.73 million
Admissions:	4.00 million
Total box-office:	$8.02m
Local films' market share:	7.0%
Screens:	183
Avge. ticket price:	$2

$1 = ROL 28,249. Source: Statistical Report of Romanian Cinematography.

RUSSIA

		$m
1.	Night Watch (Russia)	16.22
2.	The Return of the King	14.02
3.	Troy	12.45
4.	The Day After Tomorrow	10.06
5.	Spider-Man 2	9.09
6.	The Prisoner of Azkaban	7.97
7.	Van Helsing	7.50
8.	I, Robot	6.08
9.	King Arthur	5.61
10.	Shrek 2	5.15

Population:	144.2 million
Admissions:	160 million
Total box-office:	$262m
Local films' market share:	12.4%
Sites/screens:	457/785
Avge. ticket price:	$3 (in modernised cinemas)

$1 = Rubles 28.6. Source: Rossiiskaya Kinematografia.

SERBIA & MONTENEGRO

		Admissions
1.	Robbery of the Third Reich (Serbia)	338,836
2.	Troy	224,138
3.	When I Grow Up, I'll Be Kangaroo (Serbia)	212,225
4.	The Return of the King	194,333
5.	Life Is a Miracle (Serbia)	165,881
6.	Goose Feather (Serbia)	145,990
7.	The Passion of the Christ	121,749
8.	The Last Samurai	110,494
9.	Red-Coloured Grey Truck (Serbia)	95,854
10.	The Day After Tomorrow	85,659

Population:	8.5 million
Admissions:	3.01 million
Total box-office:	$7.8m
Local films' market share:	34.8%
Sites/screens:	180/200
Avge. ticket price:	$2.60

$1 = Dinars 59.81. Source: Film Distribs.' Assoc. of Serbia.

SINGAPORE

		$m
1.	Spider-Man 2	3.11
2.	The Prisoner of Azkaban	2.70
3.	The Incredibles	2.17
4.	The Day After Tomorrow	1.85
5.	Kung Fu Hustle (Hong Kong)	1.75
6.	Shrek 2	1.70
7.	Troy	1.68
8.	The Best Bet (Singapore)	1.50
9.	The Passion of the Christ	1.43
10.	Van Helsing	1.41

Population:	4.24 million
Admissions:	16 million
Total box-office:	$71m
Local films' market share:	4%
Screens:	151
Avge. ticket price:	$4.44

$1 = SG$1.68. Sources: S'pore Film Soc./ Film Exhibs.' Assoc./S'pore Film Commission.

SLOVAKIA

		Admissions
1.	The Prisoner of Azkaban	194,996
2.	Shrek 2	164,097
3.	The Return of the King	160,797
4.	Troy	148,353
5.	Spy Kids 3D – Game Over	115,333
6.	The Passion of the Christ	98,188
7.	Brother Bear	91,775
8.	Garfield	89,667
9.	Shark Tale	79,522
10.	Dirty Dancing: Havana Nights	65,066

Population:	5.4 million
Admissions:	2.97 million
Total box-office:	$8.01m
Local films' market share:	0.34%
Sites/screens:	265/281
Avge. ticket price:	$2.76

$1 = Crowns 33. Source: Slovak Distributors' Association.

SLOVENIA

		Admissions
1.	Troy	186,381
2.	The Return of the King	128,953
3.	The Prisoner of Azkaban	87,953
4.	The Last Samurai	87,646
5.	Garfield	86,286
6.	The Day After Tomorrow	79,521
7.	The Edge of Reason	70,334
8.	The Passion of the Christ	64,309
9.	Shrek 2	57,218
10.	King Arthur	53,381

Population:	1.98 million
Admissions:	3 million
Total box office:	$11m
Screens:	111
Avge. ticket price:	$4

$1 = SIT 195. Source: Slovenian Film Fund.

SOUTH AFRICA

	$m
1. Shrek 2	4.35
2. The Passion of the Christ	3.53
3. Oh Schucks I Am Gatvol (South Africa)	3.35
4. Spider-Man 2	2.63
5. Troy	2.19
6. The Day After Tomorrow	2.18
7. The Prisoner of Azkaban	2.16
8. Shark Tale	1.96
9. Ocean's Twelve	1.94
10. Something's Gotta Give	1.88

Population:	45 million
Total box-office:	$25m
Local films' market share:	4%
Sites:	70/562 (excluding independents)
Avge. ticket price:	$5.00

*$1 = R 7. Source: National Film and Video Foundation/
Ster-Kinekor.*

SOUTH KOREA

	Admissions
1. Tae Guk Gi (South Korea)	3,509,563
2. Silmido (South Korea)	2,569,826
3. Troy	1,513,408
4. Shrek 2	1,285,594
5. Spirit of Jeet Kune Do (South Korea)	1,023,601
6. The Day After Tomorrow	959,010
7. The Passion of the Christ	940,230
8. The Prisoner of Azkaban	892,900
9. My Little Bride (South Korea)	876,600
10. A Moment to Remember (South Korea)	797,593

Population:	48.5 million
Admissions:	119 million
Total box-office:	$810m
Local films' market share:	59.3%
Sites/screens:	302/1,451
Avge. ticket price:	$6

$1 = Won 1,107. Source: Korean Film Council.

SPAIN

	$m
1. Shrek 2	28.77
2. Troy	20.54
3. The Sea Inside (Spain)	19.35
4. The Last Samurai	18.65
5. The Incredibles	16.91
6. The Prisoner of Azkaban	16.29
7. Spider-Man 2	15.59
8. I, Robot	14.55
9. The Day After Tomorrow	14.50
10. The Return of the King	12.58

Population:	40.3 million
Admissions:	143.9 million
Total box-office:	$833.7m
Local films' market share:	13.4%
Sites/screens:	1,194/4,253
Avge. ticket price:	$6.50

*$1 = €1.20. Source: Instituto de la Cinematografía
y de las Artes Audiovisuales.*

SWEDEN

	Admissions
1. As It Is in Heaven (Sweden)	1,158,415
2. The Return of the King	902,039
3. The Prisoner of Azkaban	712,578
4. Brother Bear	611,526
5. Spider-Man 2	495,162
6. The Day After Tomorrow	429,425
7. Troy	428,514
8. Shrek 2	419,449
9. The Incredibles	388,330
10. King Arthur	352,383

Population:	9.01 million
Admissions:	16.60 million
Local films' market share:	22.3%
Sites/screens:	815/1,178
Avge. ticket price:	$10.14

$1 = SEK 7.56. Source: Swedish Film Institute.

SWITZERLAND

	Admissions
1. The Prisoner of Azkaban	608,204
2. Shrek 2	553,360
3. Troy	453,869
4. Something's Gotta Give	396,039
5. The Return of the King	392,114
6. (T)Raumschiff Surprise (Germany)	391,029
7. The Day After Tomorrow	381,723
8. Spider-Man 2	353,728
9. Fahrenheit 9/11	350,695
10. Brother Bear	342,512

Population:	7.40 million
Admissions:	16.96 million
Total box-office:	$199.74m
Local films' market share:	4.85%
Sites/screens:	326/528
Avge. ticket price:	$11.60

$1 = SF1.23
Source: State Secretariat of Economic Affairs.

TAIWAN

	$m
1. The Day After Tomorrow	5.397
2. Kung Fu Hustle (Hong Kong)	4.438
3. The Prisoner of Azkaban	3.998
4. Spider-Man 2	3.955
5. The Last Samurai	3.052
6. The Incredibles	2.864
7. National Treasure	2.849
8. Troy	2.801
9. I, Robot	2.536
10. Shrek 2	2.286

Population:	2.6 million
Admissions:	11.05 million
Total box-office:	$83.70m
Local films' market share:	1.10%
Sites/screens:	188/694
Avge. ticket price:	$8.07

$1 = NT$32.15. Source: Government Information Office.

TURKEY

	Admissions
1. G.O.R.A. (Turkey).	4,000,358
2. Hello Lazy Class (Turkey)	2,581,587
3. Robbery Alla Turca (Turkey)	934,126
4. Lovelorn (Turkey)	891,198
5. The School (Turkey)	836,521
6. Gallipoli (Turkey)	664,213
7. Kingdom of Heaven	640,106
8. Borrowed Bride (Turkey)	637,281
9. War of The Worlds	594,740
10. Shrek 2	553,916

Population:	70 million
Admissions:	29.70 million
Total box-office:	$140m
Local films' market share:	55%
Sites/screens:	550/1270
Avge. ticket price:	$3.50

$1 = TRL 1,406,000. Source: Antrakt-Sinema magazine. Figures for Sept. 2004 to Aug. 2005.

UNITED KINGDOM

	$m
1. Shrek 2*	84.17
2. The Prisoner of Azkaban	80.62
3. The Edge of Reason*	62.89
4. The Return of the King	61.95
5. The Incredibles*	51.10
6. Spider-Man 2	46.72
7. The Day After Tomorrow	43.96
8. Shark Tale*	39.91
9. Troy	31.50
10. I, Robot	31.46

* Still in release in 2005.

Population:	59.8 million
Admissions:	171.25 million
Total box-office:	$1.46 billion
Local films' market share:	16%
Screens:	646/3,342
Avge. ticket price:	$8.52

$1 = £0.51. Sources: Film Distribs.' Assoc./UK Film Council.

UNITED STATES AND CANADA

	$m
1. Shrek 2	436.7
2. Spider-Man 2	373.3
3. The Passion of the Christ	370.2
4. The Incredibles*	251.6
5. The Prisoner of Azkaban	249.3
6. The Day After Tomorrow	186.7
7. The Bourne Supremacy	176.1
8. Meet the Fockers*	162.4
9. Shark Tale*	160.7
10. The Polar Express*	155.1

Source: Variety. *Still in release in 2005. Figures for Jan 5, 2004 to Jan 2, 2005.

US population:	295.7 million
Total US box-office:	$9.54 billion
Total US admissions for 2004:	1.536 billion
US sites/screens:	6,012/36,594
Avge. US ticket price:	$6.21

Source: MPAA.

URUGUAY

	Admissions
1. Shrek 2	193,979
2. The Passion of the Christ	129,268
3. Spider-Man 2	113,800
4. The Prisoner of Azkaban	107,700
5. Troy	107,188
6. Something's Gotta Give	102,204
7. The Day After Tomorrow	96,893
8. Garfield	80,166
9. The Incredibles	75,556
10. Home on the Range	65,878

Population:	3.24 million
Total box-office:	$6.85 million
Admissions:	2.34 million
Local films' market share:	2.4%
Screens:	52
Avge. ticket price:	$3.00

$1= UYU 25.5. Source: RBS Distribution Company.

VENEZUELA

	$m
1. Shrek 2	2.68
2. The Passion of the Christ	2.41
3. The Day After Tomorrow	2.24
4. The Incredibles*	1.93
5. Troy	1.48
6. Spider-Man 2	1.38
7. The Polar Express	1.37
8. The Prisoner of Azkaban	1.35
9. Garfield	1.05
10. Ocean's Twelve	1.04

Population:	25 million
Total box-office:	$48.97 million
Admissions:	20.34 million
Screens:	353
Avge. ticket price:	$2.41

Source: Rodrigo Llamozas.

WORLDWIDE

	$m
1. Shrek 2**	903
2. The Prisoner of Azkaban	789
3. Spider-Man 2	783
4. The Passion of the Christ	609
5. The Day After Tomorrow	540
6. The Return of the King	517
7. The Incredibles**	515
8 Troy	497
9. I, Robot	346
10. The Last Samurai*	319

Source: Variety. *Excludes 2003 gross.
**Still in international release in 2005.

Unless otherwise indicated, all titles are majority-US productions and all figures are for January to December 2004. Figures for The Lord of the Rings: The Return of the King *(US/New Zealand) and* The Last Samurai *exclude 2003 grosses.* Harry Potter and the Prisoner of Azkaban *and* Bridget Jones: The Edge of Reason *are both (US/UK).*

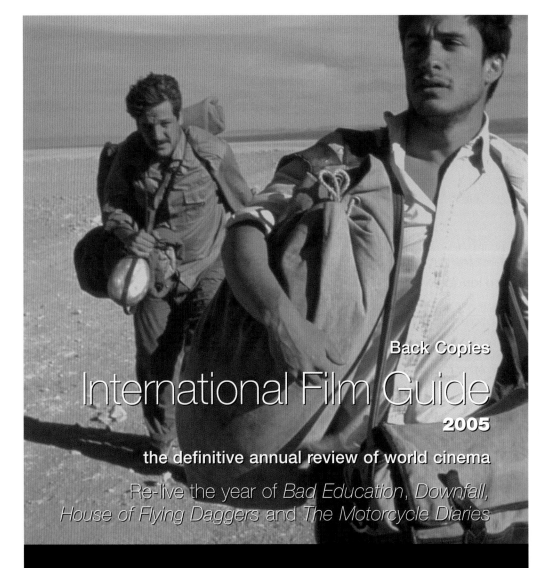

Film Festivals Calendar

WELCOME TO THE BERLINALE

→ Wettbewerb
→ Panorama
→ Perspektive Deutsches Kino
→ Kinderfilmfest / 14plus
→ Forum
→ Retrospektive
→ European Film Market
→ Berlinale Co-Production Market
→ Berlinale Talent Campus

56.
Internationale
Filmfestspiele
Berlin 09. –19.02.06

www.berlinale.de

Berlinale 2002-06:
New Sections, New Ventures, New Synergy

By Ed Meza & Andrew Horn

Berlinale Facts & Figures

• The Berlin International Film Festival was established by the western allied forces in post-war Berlin, to serve as a showcase for the culture of the free world in the divided city.

• The first festival opened on June 6, 1951 with Alfred Hitchcock's *Rebecca*.

• The film programme is divided into six sections: Competition, Panorama, Forum, Kinderfilmfest/14plus, Perspektive Deutsches Kino and Retrospective.

• Almost 17,000 film industry and media professionals, representing 80-plus countries, now attend the Berlinale each year, including 3,800 journalists.

• In 2005, total attendance for festival screenings exceeded 396,000.

The Competition

The 10-day Competition is the centrepiece of the Festival. The screenings for the premieres are held in the 1,600-seat Berlinale Palast, the main Festival venue. The films are chosen by Festival Director Dieter Kosslick, assisted

Dieter Kosslick

The Talent Campus, the Co-Production Market, the World Cinema Fund, the Perspektive Deutsches Kino section, the new 14plus programme within the Kinderfilmfest and the expansion of the European Film Market (EFM) have transformed the Berlinale since Dieter Kosslick took charge for the 2002 Festival.

Kosslick, a former head of the Hamburg Film Office and the Filmstiftung North Rhine–Westphalia, succeeded Moritz de Hadeln, Director from 1980 to 2001. De Hadeln had overseen the Festival's move from the Zoo Palast and other cinemas scattered around the Zoo Station, in what used to be downtown West Berlin, to its grander new home at the newly-built Potsdamer Platz in 2000. The move helped to cement the Festival's status as one of the most prestigious meeting places of the new, reunified German capital. The new venue, an architectural wonder bridging former East and West Berlin, offered a more central location, including the impressive Berlinale Palast for red-carpet premieres, two multiplexes for section screenings and the Debis (now Daimler-Chrysler) tower to house the EFM.

Kosslick's start also saw a renewed commitment to German film, with four homegrown features in the Competition, including Tom Tykwer's opening night film, *Heaven*, and Andreas Dresen's *Grill Point* (*Halbe Treppe*). The focus on Germany was strengthened further by the introduction of the Perspektive Deutsches Kino (Perspectives of German Cinema) sidebar for up-and-coming national talent.

"What Dieter Kosslick in his first five years very clearly achieved, and very different from the last 20 years, is the accent on German films," says Josef Schnelle, of the Association of German Film Critics. "Perspektive is showcasing German films by new directors. In addition, the presence of German films in the Competition and the other sections has become very strong. Kosslick has established a real platform for German cinema." The Berlinale has encouraged other major festivals like Cannes to pay more attention to German movies, Schnelle adds.

Synergy in action

Since 2002, the Berlinale has become more cohesive than ever – a model of synergy, where films are born, financed and later presented. The Talent Campus helps train new generations of film-makers, the by an advisory committee, which consists of the programme section directors and international film experts. Competition films celebrate their world or international premieres in Berlin, judged by an international jury of between seven and nine members, who represent a range of professional, artistic and cultural backgrounds.

International Jury Awards 2005

Golden Bear:
Carmen in Khayelitsha
(*U-Carmen eKhayelitsha*),
Mark Dornford-May.
Jury Grand Prix – Silver Bear:
Kong Que (*Peacock*),
Gu Changwei.
Silver Bear for Best Director:
Marc Rothemund (*Sophie Scholl
– The Final Days/Sophie Scholl –
Die letzten Tage*).
Silver Bear for Best Actress:
Julia Jentsch (*Sophie Scholl –
The Final Days*).
Silver Bear for Best Actor:
Lou Taylor Pucci (*Thumbsucker*,
Mike Mills).
**Silver Bear for an Outstanding
Single Achievement:** Tsai Ming
Liang (*The Wayward Cloud/
Tian Bian Yi Duo Yun*).
Silver Bear (Best Film Music):
Alexandre Desplat (*The Beat
That My Heart Skipped/
De battre mon coeur s'est arête*,
Jacques Audiard).
Alfred-Bauer Prize:
The Wayward Cloud.
Blue Angel Award: *Paradise Now*
(Hany Abu-Assad).

*Julia Jentsch with her Silver Bear
in 2005*

Full house: the Berlinale Palast auditorium

Co-Production Market and the World Cinema Fund help international producers secure sometimes elusive financing. Andres Gomez, president of the International Federation of Film Producers Association (FIAPF), says: "Dieter Kosslick has revitalised the Festival in ways that FIAPF would like to see happen at other festivals."

Despite recent changes, some Berlinale traditions remain – not least the political edge that gave the Festival its unique identity during the Cold War. "I think the new identity is the old identity," says Kosslick, "and there is a simple reason: the Festival was built in the 1950s by the Americans and the other Allies to break the [city's] isolation. The Festival was always about international understanding. It was always politically outspoken and the people who came here were outspoken. Golden Bear-winners like *Bloody Sunday* and *In This World* show that we are still very young and fresh in terms of political sentiment. And as long as I am here we will continue with it."

Panorama

Showcasing cutting-edge arthouse fare and independent cinema, Panorama seeks to bridge the gap between artistic vision and commercial interests by also presenting major studio productions and genre-extending work such as Brad Anderson's *The Machinist* and Kevin Spacey's *Beyond the Sea*. The section has always sought to reflect world cinema, especially with a strong political slant and films addressing queer themes, such as Duncan Tucker's *Transamerica*, Eytan Fox's *Yossi & Jagger* and Sebastien Lifshitz's *Wild Side*.

"It's fun because the Berlin audience loves challenges," says Wieland Speck, director of the Panorama. "I can bring in films which professionals would not dare to touch if they were shown in professionals-only events, but here, with the support of the urban audience, I can convince the buyers to think twice about daring subject matter or aesthetics." Panorama titles are in general available to buyers, making it an especially attractive section for distributors. "That was the idea from the beginning," adds Speck, "to broaden the mainstream's diversity and to serve distributors looking to find arthouse fare."

International Forum of New Cinema

In 2001, Christoph Terhechte became director of the Forum, succeeding Ulrich and Erika Gregor, who had founded the section more than 30 years ago. The Forum had seen itself as a more rebellious alternative to the "official" Berlinale, but that changed with Kosslick's arrival, says Terhechte. "The Forum is now a part of the whole." It pays special attention to new trends and fresh voices in world cinema. In recent years the Forum premiered Jia Zhang-ke's *Xiao Wu*, Angela Schanelec's *Mein langsames Leben* and David Gordon Green's George *Washington*.

Directorial debuts and innovative works by young film-makers are presented alongside films from well-known maverick directors, such as Catherine Breillat's *Anatomy of Hell*. New Festival initiatives have helped bring the sections closer together. Young film-makers have greater opportunities to come together to realise projects at the Talent Campus, to find financing via the Co-Production Market and possibly to get their film screened at the Forum. "Directors who are discovered in the Forum and get their chance to become known on an international stage might later be welcomed in the Competition," adds Terhechte.

Kinderfilmfest/14plus

The Kinderfilmfest competition makes the world of film, in all its many forms, accessible to young audiences. Children can see the best national and international shorts and features, giving them a look at the lives of their peers in other cultures, as well as a chance to see themselves from different perspectives.

Actress Corinna Harfouch and Berlinale Director Dieter Kosslick at the opening of the Kinderfilmfest in 2005

Panorama
The Panorama's stated mission is "to discover the arthouse programme of the next film season and present the latest developments in independent cinema". Its selection attempts "to bridge the gap between artistic vision and commercial interests", presenting shorts, fiction features and feature documentaries, ranging from debuts to the latest work of experienced directors. The Panorama Special feature allows also major studio presentations.

Wieland Speck

"The great challenge every year," says Panorama director Wieland Speck, "is to create anew the symbiosis between film buyers, festival programmers, the press and the urban audience itself."

International Forum of New Cinema
The Forum aims to challenge the mainstream. Programme director Christoph Terhechte says: "Avant-garde and experimental films and essays, long-term observations, political reportage, undiscovered cinematographies –

Christoph Terhechte

in this section one finds films that playfully and colourfully beat new paths in film-making." Directorial debuts and innovative works by young film-makers are the main focus. The emphasis is firmly on cultural exchange and there is always passionate discussion in post-screening debates between audiences and visiting film-makers.

Kinderfilmfest/14plus

Since 1978, this competitive section has fostered the emerging generation of cinemagoers. The Kinderfilmfest makes the fullest possible range of films accessible to viewers aged four and above, presenting German and international shorts and features that mirror the important concerns of young people worldwide. The youth film competition, 14plus, provides a special insight for teenagers in multi-faceted coming-of-age films. Moderated post-screening discussions with directors and actors encourage greater understanding. section director Thomas Hailer says: "Meeting our special target groups of children or teenagers is always a great experience that definitely widens a director's point of view on his or her film."

Thomas Hailer

In 2003, Kinderfilmfest/14plus director Thomas Hailer and co-director Maryanne Redpath launched the 14plus competition for teen viewers who were too old for the children's films and restricted from watching films in the other age-controlled sections of the Berlinale. "In the past we felt that there was a gap for all the adolescents who we had already made curious as children about Berlinale films," says Hailer. 14plus now provides insight into the experiences of young people around the globe. Real life is mirrored in often unconventionally crafted coming-of-age-films.

Kinderfilmfest/14plus premieres around 25 features yearly and has earned its reputation as an excellent platform for films suitable not only for the younger generations. "For me, a cinema with more than a thousand eager children, teenagers *and* adults is the best proof that challenging films easily cross the boundaries set by age", says Hailer.

Perspektive Deutsches Kino
(Perspectives of German Cinema)

This section was set up to integrate German cinema more fully into the Berlinale. It offers a dozen films from new talent that might have not yet been picked up by a distributor or had a theatrical run. Unlike other sections that carry German titles, Perspektive will even screen films that have played at other festivals. "It's a platform for new German film-makers to gain exposure to local and international audiences, and that includes buyers and scouts for other festivals," says Perspektive director Alfred Holighaus.

He recalls how audiences immediately embraced the section: "In the first year it took us by surprise. All the shows were completely over-booked. We had twice the [anticipated] attendance and had to schedule more shows." Two of the section's biggest successes were Marcus Mittermeier's *Quiet Like a Mouse* (*Muxmäuschenstill*), which was a big arthouse hit in Germany, and Robert Thalheim's *Netto*, which went on to win several national and international awards.

"We have achieved our goal," says Holighaus, "in that every year we put together a programme that the audience wants to see. It is also very well received by the press and helps to integrate a generation of exciting German film-makers into the Festival."

Berlinale Special

Based in the Filmpalast on Kurfürstendamm, one of Berlin's classic movie theatres, and curated by Dieter Kosslick, the Berlinale Special was established in 2004. It casts its spotlight on individual productions that have earned special attention. With this programme the Festival invites audiences to watch extraordinary new productions and also brings back classics of cinema history. It honours deserving film personalities while also presenting movies that are interesting for contemporary reasons.

The Special complements the thematic highlights of other sections. Other selections, such as the current Marshall Plan Film series, "Selling Democracy", complement the main programme with their own focal points, exploring new film territory and creating new connections to the contemporary world.

Short Films

The Berlinale shows a diverse selection of around 60 short films, not only in the Competition but also in the Panorama, the Perspektive Deutsches Kino and the Kinderfilmfest/14plus. An International short Film Jury awards several prizes.

Award-winners and jury members at the climax of the 2005 Berlinale

The World Cinema Fund By Ed Meza & Andrew Horn

The World Cinema Fund (WCF) was founded as a joint initiative of the German Federal Cultural Foundation and the Berlinale in 2004. Its goal is to support film-makers from Africa, Latin America, the Near and the Middle East and Central Asia. In 2005, the Goethe Institut became a partner in the fund, which has an annual budget of €550,000. It is co-managed by Vincenzo Bugno and Sonja Heinen, who also heads the Berlinale Co-Production Market.

Some 367 projects from 52 countries were submitted in the first three rounds of funding; 20 projects had received production or distribution funding by December 2005. "The WCF has had a great start," comments Bugno. Three films have been completed: Hany Abu-Assad's Palestinian suicide bomber drama, *Paradise Now*, winner of the Blue Angel Award at the 2005 Berlinale and nominated for the Golden Globe for Best Foreign Film, Ernest Abdyjaparov's Kyrgyz title, *Saratan*, which was screened at 35

Perspektive Deutsches Kino (Perspectives of German Cinema)
This section's slogan is "Discover the Competition directors of tomorrow." It was launched by Dieter Kosslick in 2002, to give the international audience a chance to see the self-confident work of the new generation of German directors: features, medium-length, experimental and documentary films. The focus is on "personal styles, unconventional forms and individual attitudes towards life and cinema".

Alfred Holighaus

Programme director Alfred Holighaus also sees the section as a springboard, and facilitates important contacts between young film-makers and industry personnel.

Retrospective and Hommage

The Retrospective presents carefully selected series of films from around the world, centred around cultural-historical issues, technical aspects or specific directors and styles. Archive discoveries of previously unknown material play alongside once-popular films now ripe for rediscovery. Every year, the section focuses on a different area of film history; the Retrospective for 2006 was dedicated to the screen heroines of the 1950s.

SONJA HEINEN, *World Cinema Fund (WCF) Manager:*

"WCF is not only [about] the financial support, but also giving the local industry a chance to develop."

Sonja Heinen

VINCENZO BUGNO, *WCF Adviser:*

"We support German producers and are trying to support their need to develop new links with producers abroad."

Vincenzo Bugno

Paradise Now: *backed by the World Cinema Fund*

international festivals, and *A Perfect Day*, from Lebanese directors Khalid Joreige and Joana Hadjithomas, which won the FIPRESCI Award at Locarno in 2005.

The WCF requires that beneficiaries have a German partner, although the funds should be spent in their home region. The German producer or the foreign company can apply, but not the film-makers themselves. "We want to bring people together. If they don't already have a German producer, we can help them find one," explains Heinen. Projects can receive up to €100,000 – a substantial figure, given that a recent WCF-backed production's budget was just €200,000.

Bugno says the fund's "lighthouse strategy" supports countries that can help their neighbours. "South Africa can have a lighthouse function in the whole southern part of Africa," he explains, "because of some very professional producers and well-developed production facilities. Through them we are starting to receive projects from Zambia and Mozambique." Heinen says the WCF also encourages cross-border co-operation. "In Ecuador, there are no post-production facilities, so you can't even make prints there. But you can go to Chile or Peru. WCF is not only [about] the financial support, but also giving the local industry a chance to develop. When such a film is shown at an international festival, people become interested. This is the lighthouse effect."

WCF also provides distribution support in Germany. It backed the German release of Daniel Burman's *A Lost Embrace*, which picked up two Silver Bears in 2004. WCF works with the Berlinale Co-Production Market, presenting three or four selected projects annually in its World Cinema section. All the 2004 projects, *Waiting for an Angel*, *A Perfect Day*, *Barca!* and *El Otro*, found co-production or financing partners in this way.

The Berlinale Talent Campus By Ed Meza & Andrew Horn

Campus Mentors

KEN ADAM –

The Oscar-winning production designer (*Dr. Strangelove*, the 007 films) began as one of the first Campus mentors in 2003, and has returned every year since, doing both lectures and seminars. "I think the Campus is one of the most imaginative new schemes," he says. "It's always nice to be surrounded by enthusiasm and it's great for these young people to meet some of the greats in the film industry. I feel it's a duty of anybody who can be of some help to take part in something like this. In any case, I find nothing more exciting than talking to young people. It's stimulating and it keeps me young."

STEPHEN FREARS –

The British director of *High Fidelity* and *Dirty Pretty Things* has been a popular figure at the Campus since its first year, giving workshops on acting and directing. "I've just always enjoyed going there. It's always interesting meeting young people and at the Campus they're from such a variety of backgrounds." For Frears, a lot of the experience of working with the Talents seems to be about demystification. "They're all looking for a secret and most of the time is spent telling them there isn't a secret. They learn that all directors are different and there are no set rules."

Stephen Frears

Since its launch in 2003, the Berlinale Talent Campus has become one of the Festival's most popular and crowded events. The brainchild of Dieter Kosslick, the Campus was part of his plan to open up the Berlinale, make it more relevant to young film-makers and create "a place where people could learn the state of the art". Kosslick appointed Christine Dorn as programme manager, and, along with Thomas Struck and Christine Tröstrum, she organised and co-ordinated the new event. In 2005, Cathy Rohnke became programme manager; Dorn remained as a Campus consultant.

Based at Berlin's House of World Cultures and providing ample opportunity to learn from international film-makers, the 2006 Campus selected some 500 'Talents' (from around 3,500 applications), representing more than 100 countries, to take part in workshops, lectures, screenings and discussions. Visiting film-makers coach the Talents. In 2005, for example, Walter Salles (*The Motorcycle Diaries*) acted as mentor to young directors selected for the "Talent Movie of the Week", in which Talents make short films, working with local production companies, like Berlin-based Sabotage Films.

Campus participants usually include film-makers or actors with films in the Berlinale. Participants have included Ken Adam, John Boorman, Stephen Frears, Frances McDormand, Anthony Minghella, Walter Murch, Alan Parker, David Puttnam, Tom Tykwer and Wim Wenders. In 2006, producer Jeremy Thomas (*The Last Emperor*) and editor Jim Clark (*The World Is Not Enough*) were among the guest lecturers.

Though educational, the Campus "is not a beginners' workshop", says Struck. It demands a certain level of professionalism from participants to help ensure that it continues to receive sufficient sponsorship. It is privately financed via the EU's MEDIA programme, regional film subsidy organisation Medienboard Berlin-Brandenburg and Skillset, which oversees all government-supported media industry training in the UK, and came on board through the involvement of the UK Film Council, one of the Campus' founding partners. Additional partners include Volkswagen and the Euromed Programme.

Campus participation is not limited to film students, although applicants must provide a one-minute film, based on a designated theme. Rohnke says this requirement makes it possible for a greater diversity of people to apply. In 2005, the theme was soccer ("Shoot Goals Shoot Films"), while the 2006 event focused on

Walter Salles, left, in conversation with Peter Cowie at the 2005 Talent Campus

"Films on Hunger, Food and Taste", through a partnership with the Slow Food movement, whose official aim is "to protect the pleasures of the table from the homogenisation of modern fast food". The best shorts were screened at the Berlinale and invited to the Short Film Festival in Bra, Italy, in April 2006. The Campus also has an annual focus on a creative craft; this year it was Editing.

By providing more Talents with the opportunity to get creative, and not just during the Berlinale, the Campus has taken on a life of its own. "This is something which is really building up," says Struck. "We were not even aware in the beginning how sustainable the whole programme would be, how the Talents would respond to the opportunity to communicate and even set up productions together." Explains Kosslick: "After the 2006 event we'll have 2,000 Talents around the world who are still connected, and many are developing joint projects." Rohnke adds: "It is also about having the Campus alive all year long. Our website, www.berlinale-talentcampus.de, is the very core of our worldwide network."

Global horizons

In 2004, Talent Campuses debuted at the Molodist Festival in Kiev, the Osian's Cinefan Film Festival in New Delhi and the Sithengi Film & TV Market section of the Cape Town World Cinema Festival. Other campuses have since been set up at the Universidad del Cine, Buenos Aires, and the Pusan International Film Festival, South Korea. "The Talent Campus decided to support only developing countries whose film industry would benefit the most" says Skillset's Sandy Lieberson.

Struck says the international spin-offs have given the Berlin Campus the opportunity to help regions "that need more support, and where we want to encourage more people to apply". While international Campuses are organised locally, they are overseen by Berlin staff to ensure that they follow certain criteria. "This is an intellectual franchise system," says Rohnke. "If it says Talent Campus it has to be of the same quality as Berlin."

Campus Talents

ATSUSHI FUNAHASHI –
A Japanese director based in the US, who was a Talent in 2004, Funahashhi is a prime example of Campus synergy. For his feature, *Big River*, Funahashi met his co-producer Mohammed Naqvi and co-writer and cinematographer Eric Van Den Brulle when both were fellow Talents at the 2005 Campus. They managed to find the rest of the film's budget from Japanese producer-distributor Office Kitano, via the Co-Production Market.

"I think that attending the Talent Project Market gave the project huge credibility, so that Office Kitano got interested and trusted its quality." *Big River* had its European premiere in the Forum in 2006.

MYRNA MAAKARON –
Maakaron came to the Campus in 2004 as both a film-maker and actress, having studied and performed in her native Lebanon and later in Paris. Her "Berlin Today" film, *Berlin, Beirut*, went on to be a multiple prize-winner in many international festivals.

"The Campus changed my way of thinking," she says. "I was naïve in the beginning and I thought film-making was kind of 'mafia' and actually it's not. These people who make beautiful films started just like us and it was positive for me to see it's just me, how much I can work and give to this work.

"We were all from so many different cultures and it was very good to know more about each other. I'm still in touch with some of them and we talk to each other and give each other tips." Her new film project is a French–German–Lebanese co-production.

The new
European Film Market
welcomes you
to Berlin.

The first international Market of the year.

56.
Internationale
Filmfestspiele
Berlin 09. –19.02.06

eFm
European Film Market

The European Film Market By Ed Meza & Andrew Horn

BEKI PROBST, *Director, European Film Market (EFM):*

"Our aim is to keep our structure, to keep our well-known name for being an organised market."

Beki Probst

KAREN ARIKIAN, *Deputy Director, EFM:*

"Now that we have this lead position at the front of the year, it necessitates that we be able to grow."

Karen Arikian

Industry Views

MICHAEL BARKER, *President, Sony Pictures Classics:*

"We've been going to the Market since 1989 and every year it's grown incrementally. It is also very well organised, very well run. I think being the first major

The European Film Market (EFM) faced the biggest change in its history with the February 2006 move into Berlin's Martin Gropius Bau exhibition hall, a flagship location reflecting the Market's new prominence as the year's first major stop for international film buyers.

EFM has come a long way since 1978, when the Berlinale's move from June to February gave the fledgling Film Fair, as it was then known, a chance to blossom. That shift in dates was made for the sake of the Film Fair, because Wolf Donner, the Berlinale's then Director, argued that late winter was a comparatively fallow period on the film industry calendar, so the Berlinale stood a good chance of establishing itself as an industry meeting place between Cannes, in May, and the Mifed in Milan, in October.

In 1980, when Moritz de Hadeln succeeded Donner as Director, he appointed Aina Bellis to head the Film Fair. Eight years later, current EFM Director Beki Probst took over. Renaming the Film Fair was one of her first decisions. "I didn't like the name because in Berlin you have so many fairs: furniture and food or whatever," she recalls. "The idea behind calling it the European Film Market was that we had the American Film Market (AFM) in another part of the world and our name acted as a counterbalance. When we first started out with this name, some people wondered if it was just for European films. But now the message is clear: we are an international film market based in Europe."

The EFM logo projected onto the front of the Martin Gropius Bau

The industry imperative

The EFM remains integral to the Berlinale. Up to 40% of the films screened in the Market come from the different sections of the Festival. That, says Probst, adds great value to both events. "Every film festival, no matter how big or small, is interested in having the industry there. The press is important, of course, but you need the industry because those films that are in a festival should afterwards see the light… or the darkness of a movie theatre."

One of EFM's major milestones was its move in 2000 to the Debis (now Daimler-Chrysler) building at Potsdamer Platz. The Market, along with the Festival, grew with the move. "Everything took on another dimension," says Probst. "The Debis building was much bigger than the old Cinecentre and we had more screening facilities."

EFM's new home: the Martin Gropius Bau

This year's transfer to the Martin Gropius Bau was even more significant. The building is one of Germany's most striking exhibition spaces, located within a few minutes' walk of Potsdamer Platz. It offers twice as much exhibition space as the Daimler-Chrysler and organisers say it allows EFM to accommodate the increasing demands of the industry. The Renaissance-style building, built between 1877 and 1881, has a 200-seat cinema, an impressive atrium and plenty of rooms filled with natural light for the exhibitors.

Berlinale Director Dieter Kosslick explains: "We don't want necessarily to have the biggest market, but we would like to have the most beautiful and effective market. The most beautiful we have, thanks to the building, which is one of the most striking in Germany."

market of the year all the major players are present and the Market really captures what's going on in every film industry around the world – not only the films that are there at Berlin, but also the projection of what's coming out the rest of the year."

Michael Barker

ADRIANA CHIESA DI PALMA, *Adriana Chiesa Enterprises:*

"I think there is one characteristic very special to Berlin: a human dimension. It's not just a commercial place, it's everything. I think we talk about cinema in Berlin. You have the possibility of meeting with the press, with the director, with the authors, with the producers and there is a whole atmosphere which is very favourable for making sales, because I think [when] selling films it's very important to have human dialogue, human connections."

Adriana Chiesa Di Palma

PIERS HANDLING,

Director, Toronto International Film Festival:

"As a programmer, I primarily go to the curated sections of the Festival now, so for me the Market has become a networking opportunity. You could sit and talk to the sales agents and get an early fix on what the rest of the year was going to hold in store. We value our European contacts and all the Europeans are there in force, so it's a very efficient way for us to touch base with everyone."

Piers Handling

CLAUDIA LANDSBERGER,

Managing Director, Holland Film:

"I think it's good for everybody that this market is expanding. With AFM moving to November there will be more people coming to Berlin. It's all about meeting each other and if that is organised I'm not worried.

Claudia Landsberger

AFM's move, EFM's gain

The AFM's move from February to November in 2004 contributed to the demise of Milan's Mifed, which had been traditionally held in October–November. This change in the industry calendar provided a unique opportunity for EFM, according to Kosslick. "Now we are suddenly the first and only market at the start of the year. As companies plan their marketing and sales strategies, we think they will take a serious look at Berlin in its new position."

The new-look market calendar provided EFM with a major challenge. Karen Arikian, its Deputy Director, says: "Now that we have this lead position at the front of the year, it necessitates that we be able to grow. In the [Daimler-Chrysler], we were full up to the seams, and the Martin Gropius Bau offers space to accommodate many more companies."

A further advantage was the fact that the Martin Gropius Bau is part of the Kulturveranstaltungen des Bundes in Berlin, the umbrella organisation for film, theatre, music and literary festivals, including the Berlinale. Being under the same roof made arrangements more convenient, adds Arikian.

The new location gives EFM two full floors, plus the 200-seat cinema, which will be equipped with HD. On the ground floor, half of the Central Hall is designed as the EFM Lounge, offering a bar and bistro seating. The other half is divided between the MEDIA Programme, which had a significant presence, and the Spanish umbrella stand. Other companies were based in the exhibition rooms around the Central Hall.

Along with extensive exhibition space, the first floor featured a second lounge in the Gallery, with tables and seating for up to 60 people. A large room on the second floor was dedicated to the Arts Alliance Media "Screenings on Demand Lounge". This space featured two "mini-cinemas" for the Market's on-demand screenings as well as a number of internet viewing stations. The on-demand screenings are part of a new partnership between the Berlinale and London-based Arts Alliance Media.

Other regular Market screenings were held at the Cinemaxx and CineStar multiplexes at Potsdamer Platz, the Arsenal, the German Film and Television Academy (DFFB) in the Sony Center and a 60-seat video screening room in the House of Representatives (also the base for the Co-Production Market), just across the road from the Martin Gropius. In total, this gave EFM 100 more screening slots than in 2005, when titles sold in Berlin included Jacques Audiard's *The Beat That My Heart Skipped* and Kay Pollack's *As It Is In Heaven*.

As It Is in Heaven: *screened and sold at EFM 2005*

The makeover was not cheap. "Our costs were higher this year due to the move and increase in staff, as well as certain upgrades which we are implementing," says Arikian. "For example, we've re-designed the official EFM catalogue, purchased a scanning system which generates a buyers list following screenings, and renovated the cinemas in the Martin Gropius Bau to bring it up to standard."

Product and initiatives

As for the actual product at EFM, Arikian says it retains the usual high quality of arthouse films, but its new position in the industry calendar has resulted in "a slightly more commercial aspect to the Market in general". EFM also set up different programmes within the event, such as "Straight from Sundance" and its partnership with the Frankfurt Book Fair, which offers a platform for publishers and producers to meet and deal.

The German Cinema section, officially part of the EFM, again highlighted films that have been theatrically released in Germany and are deemed strong enough for further international release. An initiative in its second year in 2006 was the "Works in Progress" series, highlighting Argentinian films, which offers a forum for films still in production, and opportunities to meet potential partners.

While EFM experienced a major growth spurt with the move, the new location, new participants and new sections, Probst cautions:

Berlin is a very important market for films from the Netherlands because it's a market that is very much focused on arthouse film and smaller, fragile films, not necessarily big audience films – it's our kind of people who are at that market."

HENGAMEH PANAHI,
President, Celluloid Dreams sales agency:

"This is where we like to premiere our films and, coming before Cannes, it's the first market of the year. And I think the new [location] is stating that even louder.

Hengameh Panahi

New things like the Talent Campus or Co-Production Market say a lot about the [organisers'] real interest in helping the market and the industry people. They are always taking it further and adjusting to the needs of the marketplace, not just repeating a recipe every year."

THORSTEN SCHAUMANN,
Head of Sales, Bavaria Film International:

"The connection between the Market and the Festival works very well for us. We've had *Good Bye, Lenin!, Head-On, A Lost*

Embrace – international films which we've premiered in Berlin and went on to a very strong market. People arrive fresh from their Christmas holidays so they have a lot of energy to look for new projects, and they're open. Coming back from AFM in 2005, one of the things I heard most was 'See you in Berlin.'"

Director Beki Probst, left, with Soojin Jung, Project Manager at Mirovision

Thorsten Schaumann

"I am against a wild growth. Growth has to go together with structure and if you don't have the structure to go with it, then this growth becomes absolutely chaotic. So that's our aim, to keep our structure, to keep our well-known name for being an organised market. We don't want to lose that."

The Berlinale Co-Production Market By Ed Meza & Andrew Horn

In 2004, the Berlinale Co-Production Market made its debut, with 32 official projects in development. Among them was Russian director Alexandr Sokurov's *The Sun* (*Solntse*). Sokurov already had an Italian co-producer and was looking for a French partner. The new market brought him together with Paris-based Mact Productions. A year later, *The Sun* screened in Competition at the Berlinale.

The Co-Production Market is a prime example of how the Berlinale has evolved from a presentational platform for films into a prime mover in helping international film-producers make movies. The market offers international producers, film financiers, distributors, sales agents, representatives of funding organisations and TV broadcasters a place to come together.

Lenfilm/Nikola Film/Kobal

The Sun: *co-financed in Berlin*

Producers can apply with projects of budgets between €1m and €10m, which have already secured at least 30% of their financing. Around 30 projects are selected from more than 300 submissions, and presented in a catalogue prior to the event. Meetings are scheduled in advance between project representatives and financiers. Some 1,000 meetings are held during the event, which is based in the Berlin House of Representatives, and for 2006 was extended from two to three days' duration. At least 20 films that participated at the market in 2004 or 2005 have since been produced.

Sonja Heinen, head of the Co-Production Market, says that although the event is similar in concept to Rotterdam's CineMart, held in late January–early February, it is more producer-driven, adding that Berlin is not in competition with Rotterdam. On the contrary, Berlin and Rotterdam have joined forces, creating the "Rotterdam–Berlinale Express", which selects three projects from CineMart to be presented in Berlin. Berlin also has rather higher-budgeted projects than CineMart.

The market's burgeoning partnership with the Frankfurt Book Fair aims to bring producers and financiers into contact with the publishing industry. Ten literary works were specially presented in 2006 as strong candidates for film adaptation.

Unlike other co-production markets, which may fly in financiers to meet with film-makers, the Berlin mart seeks to exploit the high-calibre personnel already gathered for the Festival and EFM. "We benefit from the Berlinale in that everyone is already there," says Heinen. The market is financed through sponsorship from regional public film fund MDM (Mitteldeutsche Medienförderung Leipzig) and the EU's MEDIA programme. It has developed organically, but has strong links to EFM and the Talent Campus and now the World Cinema Fund.

The EFM's new location at the Martin Gropius Bau is just a stone's throw from the House of Representatives. The market offers EFM

participants a Producers' Lounge where they can have meetings and access Co-Production Market panel discussions and case studies. Co-Production attendees have the opportunity to be in contact with EFM delegates and find out who might be interested in their projects. "Basically, it's like an interactive tool of the EFM," says Heinen.

One of hundreds of meetings at the 2005 Co-Production Market

Talent for sale

The Berlinale Co-Production Market and Talent Campus also operate the Talent Project Market, in which between 15 and 20 young film-makers participating in the Campus can present their feature film projects. Industry insiders, such as Ido Abram from the Maurits Binger Institute and Ida Martins of sales agents Media Luna, serve as mentors, coaching young participants on how best to take meetings. The Talent Project Market has become a hit with producers, some of whom have begun to focus mainly on the Talent meetings.

In 2005, producer Annette Pisacane met Talent Campus participant Javier Fuentes-Leon and picked up his project, *Undertow*, the story of a young Peruvian fisherman grappling with his sexuality and the ghost of his departed lover while trapped in a backward fishing village. Maybe it will become an entry for the Berlinale 2007.

American Film Market
November 1-8, 2006

The business of independent motion picture production and distribution reaches a peak at AFM. More than 7,000 acquisition and development executives, agents, attorneys, directors, financiers, film commissioners, producers and writers converge in Santa Monica for screenings, deal-making and hospitality. Each year, hundreds of films are financed, packaged, licensed and greenlit, sealing over $500min business for both completed films and those in pre-production. And now, with the AFM/AFI FEST alliance, attendees will capitalise on the only festival-market combination in North America. *Inquiries to:* 10850 Wilshire Blvd, 9th Floor, Los Angeles, CA 90024-4311, USA. Tel: (1 310) 446 1000. Fax: 446 1600. e: afm@ifta-online.org. Web: www.americanfilmmarket.com.

Amiens
November 2006

Discovery of new talents, new cinematography and reassessment of film masters. A competitive festival in northern France for shorts, features, animation and documentaries. Also retrospectives, tributes and the "Le monde comme il va" series, which includes works from Africa, Latin America and Asia. "Europe, Europes", an expanding section for more than 10 years, presents new works from Young European Talents (Shorts, Documentaries and Animation). *Inquiries to:* Amiens International Film Festival, MCA, Place Léon Gontier, 80000 Amiens, France. Tel: (33 3) 2271 3570. Fax: 2292 5304. e: contact@filmfestamiens.org. Web: www.filmfestamiens.org.

Amsterdam – International Documentary Film Festival (IDFA)
November 23-December 3, 2006

The world's largest documentary festival, built up over two decades, IDFA screens 200 films and sells more than 120,000 tickets. The programme offers creative documentaries, organises numerous debates and special events and includes numerous awards. Also the Forum, a market for international co-financing. *Inquiries to:* International Documentary Film Festival-Amsterdam, Kleine-Gartmanplantsoen 10, 1017 RR Amsterdam, Netherlands. Tel: (31 20) 627 3329. Fax: 638 5388. e: info@idfa.nl. Web: www.idfa.nl.

Austin Film Festival
October 19-26, 2006

Celebrating its 13th year, an internationally-recognised Film Festival and Screenwriters' Conference – one of the select few in the US accredited by the Academy of Motion Picture Arts and Sciences. It brings together a broad range of established and up-and-coming directors, writers and industry professionals for screenings, panels and high-profile networking. *Inquiries to:* Austin Film Festival, 1604 Nueces, TX 78701, USA. Tel: (1 512) 478 4795. Fax: 478 6205. e: info@austinfilm.com. Web: www.austinfilmfestival.com.

Bergen
October 2006

Norway's beautiful capital of the fjords launches the 7th BIFF in 2006. The festival has a main International Competition of about 15 films, as well as an International Documentary Competition; sidebars with international arthouse films, Norwegian shorts, gay and lesbian shorts, videorama, as well as premieres of the upcoming Christmas theatrical releases, through extensive collaboration with Norway's

distributors. Also hosts seminars and other events. *Inquiries to:* Bergen International Film Festival, Georgernes verft 12, NO-5011 Bergen, Norway. Tel: (47) 5530 0840. Fax: 5530 0841. e: biff@biff.no. Web: www.biff.no.

Berlin –
Internationale Filmfestspiele Berlin
February 2007

Situated at the Potsdamer Platz, the Berlinale has increased its popularity with the public and film professionals. In 2005, it had more than 16,000 accredited guests and sold a remarkable 396,000 tickets for more than 1,100 screenings in 12 cinemas. The website registered 128,264 million hits between December 15, 2004 and February 25, 2005. Some 3,815 journalists from 81 countries reported on the programme and visits by the likes of Cate Blanchett, Kevin Spacey, Keanu Reeves and Tilda Swinton. The European Film Market recorded another increase in participants (up to 4,284, from 70 countries), screenings and turnover. The third Berlinale Talent Campus offered panels and workshops on film-making, theory and marketing, with a special focus on "Designing Your Future", and involved 530 young film-makers from 90 countries (see www.berlinale-talentcampus.de). The second Berlinale Co-Production Market was a great success and was expanded for 2005. Inquiries to: Internationale Filmfestspiele Berlin, Potsdamer Str 5, D-10785 Berlin, Germany. Tel: (49 30) 259 200. Fax: 2592 0299. e: info@berlinale.de. Web: www.berlinale.de.

AWARDS 2005 [see page 336]

Bermuda International Film Festival
March 17-25, 2006

Features the best of independent film from around the world in three competition categories: features, documentaries and shorts. Q&A sessions with directors, and the festival's popular lunchtime "Chats with…" sessions give filmgoers and film-makers a chance to mix. A competition victory earns each film's director an invitation to sit on the festival jury the following year. AMPAS recognises the festival as a qualifying event for the Short Films Oscars. Submission deadline: October 1. Inquiries to: Bermuda International Film Festival, Broadway House, PO Box 2963, Hamilton HM MX, Bermuda. Tel: (441) 293 3456. Fax: 293 7769. e: bda@biff.bm. Web: www.bermudafilmfest.com.

Bilbao International Documentary and Short Film Festival
November 27-December 2, 2006

Long-running competitive festival for shorts and documentaries, heading for its 48th edition in 2006. At the 2005 event, the Festival Grand Prize was awarded to *Obreras saliende de la fabrica*

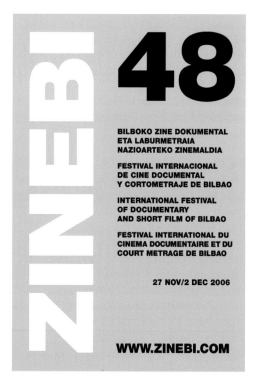

48

BILBOKO ZINE DOKUMENTAL
ETA LABURMETRAIA
NAZIOARTEKO ZINEMALDIA

FESTIVAL INTERNACIONAL
DE CINE DOCUMENTAL
Y CORTOMETRAJE DE BILBAO

INTERNATIONAL FESTIVAL
OF DOCUMENTARY
AND SHORT FILM OF BILBAO

FESTIVAL INTERNATIONAL DU
CINEMA DOCUMENTAIRE ET DU
COURT METRAGE DE BILBAO

27 NOV/2 DEC 2006

WWW.ZINEBI.COM

(Chile), directed by José Luis Torres, and the Grand Prize for Spanish Cinema went to Igor Legarreta and Emilio Pérez's *El Gran Zambini*. The deadline for entries is mid-September. *Inquiries to:* Bilbao International Documentary and Short Film Festival, Colón de Laurreátegui, 37-4° Derecha, 48009 Bilbao, Spain.
Tel: (34 94) 424 8698. Fax: 424 5624.
e: info@zinebi.com. Web: www.zinebi.com.

Brisbane International Film Festival
Late July-early August 2006

The BIFF is in its 14th year and is Queensland's leading film event. Presented annually by the Pacific Film and Television Commission, it provides a focus for film culture in Queensland by showcasing the best and most interesting world cinema. Screening more than 300 films, the diverse non-competitive programme includes features, documentaries, shorts, experimental work, animation and some video. Each year the festival draws film enthusiasts to view the entertaining mix of local and international films, retrospectives and colourful events that capture the imagination and embrace the vibrant art of film-making. *Inquiries to:* Brisbane International Film Festival, GPO Box 909, Brisbane, QLD, 4001, Australia. Tel: (61 7) 3007 3003. Fax: 3007 3030.
e: biff@biff.com.au. Web: www.biff.com.au.

Buenos Aires International Independent Film Festival (BAFICI)
April 11-23, 2006

The Buenos Aires International Independent Film Festival was created in 1999. Sections include the two Official Competitions, for features and shorts. "Argentina – Brand-New Novelties" has, since 2001, highlighted the increasing production of independent films in Argentina, complemented by the "Work in Progress" section. BAFICI also programmes sections dedicated to outstanding directors. *Inquiries to:* Buenos Aires Festival Internacional de Cine Independiente, Av Corrientes 1530, Piso 8, Oficina 7, 1042 Buenos Aires, Argentina. Tel: (54 11) 4373 8930.
Fax: 4374 0320. e: produccion@bafici.gov.ar.
Web: www. bafici.gov.ar.

Cannes
May 17-28, 2006

Cannes remains the world's top festival, attracting key films, personalities and industry personnel. The official selection includes the Competition, films out of competition, "Un Certain Regard", Cinéfondation and Cannes Classics (created 2004). The Marché du Film, with facilities improved and extended since 2000 (Riviera–Producers network, Short Film Corner) is part of the official organisation. The 2005 festival jury, presided over by Emir Kusturica, included Toni Morrison, Salma Hayek, Nandita Das, Agnès Varda, Javier Bardem, Fatih Akin, Benoit Jacquot and John Woo. *Inquiries to:* Festival de Cannes, 3, rue Amélie 75007 Paris, France. Tel: (33 1) 5359 6100. Fax: 5359 6110.
e: festival@festival-cannes.fr.
Web: www.festival-cannes.org.

AWARDS 2005
Palme d'Or: **L'Enfant** (Belgium/France), Luc and Jean-Pierre Dardenne.
Grand Prix: **Broken Flowers** (USA), Jim Jarmush.
Best Director: Michael Haneke, **Caché** (Austria/France/Germany/Italy).
Best Actor: Tommy Lee Jones, **The Three Burials of Melquiades Estrada** (USA).
Best Actress: Hanna Laslo, **Free Zone** (Belgium/France/Israel/Spain).
Best Screenplay: Guillermo Arriaga, **The Three Burials of Melquiades Estrada** (USA).
Jury Prize: **Shangaï Dreams** (China), Wang Xiaoshuai.
Caméra d'Or: **Me and You and Everyone We Know** (USA), Miranda July; **The Forsaken Land** (France/Sri Lanka), Vimutkthi Jayasundara.

Cartagena
March 3-10, 2006

Ibero-Latin American films, including features, shorts, documentaries, tributes to Latin American directors and a film and TV market. A competitive section for Colombian films was added in 2000. *Inquiries to:* Victor Nieto Nuñez, Director, Cartagena International Film Festival, Centro, Calle San Juan de Dios, Baluarte San Francisco Javier, Cartagena, Colombia.

Tel: (57 5) 660 1037. Fax: 660 0970.
e: info@festicinecartagena.com.
Web: www.festicinecartagena.com.

Chicago
October 2006

The Chicago International Film Festival is among the oldest competitive events in North America. It spotlights the latest work by established international directors and newcomers showcasing more than 100 features and 40 shorts during the festival. It bestows its highest honour, the Gold Hugo, on the best feature in the International Competition, with separate prizes for documentaries, student films and shorts. Chicago is one of two US sites to award the FIPRESCI prize for first- and second-time directors, judged by top international critics. *Inquiries to:* Chicago International Film Festival, 30 E Adams St, Suite 800, Chicago, IL 60603, USA. Tel: (1 312) 683 0121. Fax: 683 0122. e: info@chicagofilmfestival.com. Web: www.chicagofilmfestival.com.

Cinéma Tout Ecran
November 2006

Cinéma Tout Ecran looks beyond audiovisual boundaries and focuses on the artistic quality of works made for television or cinema, the unique skills of the film-maker and the representation of life through fiction. With its selection orientated towards the artistic quality and the talent of the film-maker, the festival wishes to promote the research and support of new films and writers. *Inquiries to:* Adrian Stiefel, Press Manager, Cinéma Tout Ecran, International Cinema & Television Festival, Maison des Arts du Grütli, 16 rue Génèral Dufour, CP 5759 CH-1211 Geneva 11, Switzerland. Tel: (41 22) 809 6918. Fax: 329 3747. e: presse@cinema-tout-ecran.ch. Web: www.cinema-tout-ecran.ch.

Clermont-Ferrand Short Film Festival
Late January-early February 2007

International, National and "Lab" competitions for 16mm, 35mm films and digital works on DigiBeta, all completed after January 1, 2006, of 40 minutes or less. All the entries will be listed in the Market

catalogue. Many other side programmes (retrospectives and panoramas). *Inquiries to:* Clermont-Ferrand Short Film Festival, La Jetée, 6 place Michel-de L'Hospital 63058 Clermont-Ferrand Cedex 1, France. Tel: (33 473) 916 573. Fax: 921 193. e: info@clermont-filmfest.com. Web: www.clermont-filmfest.com.

Denver
November 9-19, 2006

The Starz Denver International Film Festival presents approximately 200 films from around the world and plays host to more than 100 film-makers. Includes new international features, cutting-edge independent fiction and non-fiction works, shorts and a variety of special programmes. Also pays tribute to established film artists with retrospective screenings of their works. Entry fee: $40 ($20 for students). The Denver Film Society also programmes the Starz FilmCenter, Colorado's only cinematheque, daily throughout the year, and produces the Starz First Look Student Film Festival in April and the Aurora Asian Film Festival in June. *Inquiries to:* Denver Film Society, 1725 Blake St, Denver,

STARZ DENVER
INTERNATIONAL
FILM FESTIVAL

Celebrating 29 years
November 9 - 19 • 2006

"The best kept secret on the US Film Festival circuit may well be the Starz Denver International Film Festival."
--*Indiewire*, 2005

Inquiries to:
303.595.3456
www.denverfilm.org
dfs@denverfilm.org

Denver Film Society • Starz FilmCenter

Colorado 80202, USA. Tel: (1 303) 595 3456. Fax: 595 0956. e: dfs@denverfilm.org. Web: www.denverfilm.org.

AWARDS 2005
Mayor's Lifetime Achievement Award: Ang Lee.
John Cassavetes Award for Maverick Film-making: Philip Baker Hall.
Stan Brakhage Vision Award: Robert Breer.
Emerging Film-maker Award: **Laura Smiles** (USA), Jason Ruscio.
The Maysles Brothers Documentary Award: **El perro negro: Stories from the Spanish Civil War** (Hungary/The Netherlands), Peter Forgacs.
Krzysztof Kieslowski Award for Best Foreign Feature: **My Nikifor** (Poland), Krzysztof Krauze.
Kids First! Best of Fest Award: **Barbie and the Magic of Pegasus** (USA), Greg Richardson.
Starz People's Choice Award (Feature): **Mrs. Henderson Presents** (UK), Stephen Frears and **Tsotsi** (South Africa/UK), Gavin Hood.
Starz People's Choice Award (Documentary): **Music Is My Life, Politics My Mistress: The Story of Oscar Brown Jr.** (USA), Donnie L. Betts.
Starz People's Choice Award (Short): **The Mantis Parable** (USA), Josh Staub.

Edinburgh International Film Festival
August 2006

The world's longest continually running film festival, Edinburgh is also one of the most accessible. The emphasis is on new films, innovation and excellence worldwide, UK films and young directors, retrospectives and seminars. There's an offbeat sparkle to the mix of local audiences and visitors. Edinburgh also encapsulates Film UK, a focus for all matters concerning UK Film. *Inquiries to:* Edinburgh International Film Festival, 88 Lothian Rd, Edinburgh EH3 9BZ, Scotland. Tel: (44 131) 228 4051. Fax: 229 5501. e: info@edfilmfest.org.uk. Web: www.edfilmfest.org.uk.

Espoo Ciné International Film Festival
August 22-27, 2006

Espoo Ciné has established itself as the annual showcase of contemporary European, primarily long feature, cinema in Finland. The traditional

section should appeal to every movie buff in Finland, and the growing fantasy selection should attract those hungry for stimulation of the imagination. It is a member of the European Fantastic Film Festivals Federation and organises the Méliès d'Or fantastic film competition final this year. Also US indies, new films from other continents, the best of contemporary Finnish cinema, outdoor screenings, retrospectives, sneak previews, seminars and distinguished guests. *Inquiries to:* Espoo Ciné, PO Box 95, FIN-02101 Espoo, Finland.
Tel: (358 9) 466 599. Fax: 466 458.
e: office@espoocine.org.
Web: www.espoocine.org.

Fajr International Film Festival
Late January-early February 2007
Iranian International Market for Films and TV Programmes
Late January 2007

The festival will celebrate its 25th edition in 2007. Apart from the International Competition, the Fajr programmes include "Festival of Festivals" (a selection of outstanding films presented at other international festivals), "Special Screenings" (films of documentary or narrative content which introduce cinema or cultural developments in certain geographical regions) and retrospectives. The newly-created Competition of Spiritual Cinema emphasises cinema's role as a rich medium for the expression of the essence of religious faith. Another new addition is the Competition of Asian Cinema, organised with the aim of promoting film art and industry in Asian countries. Festival Director: Alireza Rezadad. During the festival, the Farabi Cinema Foundation also organises the Iranian International Market for Films and TV Programmes, which will have its 10th edition in 2007. *Inquiries to:* Fajr International Film Festival, 2nd Fl., No. 19, Delbar Alley, Toos

Organized by:
FARABI CINEMA FOUNDATION
International Affairs:
1st Floor, No. 19, Delbar Alley, Toos St., Valiye-Asr Ave., Tehran 19617, Iran.
Tel: +98 21 22734939, 22741252-4 / Fax: +98 21 22734953
E-mail#1: fcf1@dpi.net.ir E-mail#2: intl@fcf.ir http://www.fcf.ir
Festival Office:
2nd Fl., No. 19, Delbar Alley, Toos St., Valiye Asr Ave., Tehran 19617, Iran,
Tel: +9821 , 22734801,22735090, Fax: +9821 22734801,
E-mail: office@fajrfestival, Website: www.fajrfestival.ir
For any information about the 2007 edition, please contact Farabi Cinema Foundation.

January 20-30, 2006 , Tehran

St. Valiye Asr Ave., Tehran 19617, Iran.
Tel: (98 21) 2273 4801/5090. Fax: 2273 4953.
e: fcf2@dpi.net.ir. Web: www.icff-ir.com.
Market inquiries: International Affairs, 1st Floor,
No. 19, Delbar Alley, Toos St., Valiye-Asr Ave.,
Tehran 19617, Iran. Tel: (98 21) 2273 4939/2274
1253/2274 1254. Fax: 2273 4953.

AWARDS 2005
International Competition
Best Feature Film: **The Ninth Day**
(Germany/Luxembourg), Volker Schlöndorff.
Special Jury Prize: **Wake Up, Arezu** (Iran),
Kianoush Ayari.
Best Director: Volker Schlöndorff (**The Ninth Day**).
Best Script: Dennis Gansel and Maggie Peren
for **Napola** (Germany), Dennis Gansel.
Best Performance: Ulrich Matthes for
The Ninth Day.
Best Technical or Artistic Achievement:
Kianoush Ayari for **Wake Up, Arezu**.
Best Short Narrative Film: **The Telegram**
(France), Coralie Fargeat.
Diploma of Honour: **The Wet Corner of the
Street** (Iran), Payam Azizi.

Fantasporto
February 24-March 4, 2006

The 26th edition of the Oporto International Film
Festival takes place in theatres of Oporto, mostly
at the Rivoli – Teatro Municipal, Cinema Passos
Manuel, Palácio de Cristal – Biblioteca Almeida
Garret and the AMC Theatres at the Arrábida
Shopping (a total of about 2,100 seats). Apart
from the Competitive Sections (Fantasy, Directors
Week, Orient Express) the festival will also include
the "Porto em Curtas" for short films, "Panorama
of the Portuguese Cinema", "Anima-te" for
younger audiences, "Première" for previews and
vintage features, "Love Connection" and a
Bollywood section. The Retrospectives will include
German Expressionism, Shaw Brothers, and the
Official Retrospective of Hungarian Films to
celebrate the 50th anniversary of the Republic of
Hungary. Director: Mário Dorminsky. *Inquiries to:*
Fantasporto, Rua Anibal Cunha 84, Sala 1.6,
4050-048 Porto, Portugal. Tel: (35 1) 222 076 050
Fax: 222 076 059. e: info@fantasporto.online.pt.
Web: www.fantasporto.com.

AWARDS 2005

Fantasy Section
Film: **Nothing** (Canada), Vincenzo Natali.
Special Jury Award: **Bubba Ho-Tep** (USA),
Don Coscarelli.
Director: Robin Campillo, **Les Revenants**
(France).
Actor: Bruce Campbell, **Bubba Ho-Tep** (USA).
Actress: Karen Black, **Firecracker** (USA).
Screenplay: James Wan, **Saw** (USA).
Best Visual Effects: Byung-Chun Min,
Natural City (South Korea).
Best Short: **Le dernière minute** (France),
Nicolas Salis.
Directors' Week
Film: **Old Boy** (South Korea), Park Chan-Wook.
Director: Naoto Kamazawa, "Birthday" episode
from **Tokyo Noir** (Japan).
Special Jury Award: Sideways (USA),
Alexander Payne.
Actor: Paul Giamatti, **Sideways** (USA).
Actress: Kate Elliot, **Fracture** (New Zealand).
Screenplay: Hwang Go-Yun, Lim Jun-Hyeong,
Park Chan-Wook, **Old Boy**.
Orient Express Competitive Section
Film: **My Mother the Mermaid** (South Korea),
Heung-Shik Park.
Special Jury Award: **Vital** (Japan),

Shynia Tsukamoto.
Méliès Awards
Méliès D'Argent: **Les revenants** (France),
Robin Campillo.
Méliès D'Argent Short Film: **Le dernière minute**.
Critics Jury Award: **Vinzent**, Ayassi.
Audience Award: **Constantine** (USA),
Francis Lawrence.

Report 2005

The 25th edition had a long list of guests,
including Karen Black (USA), Guillermo del Toro
(Mexico), Doug Bradley (UK), Vincenzo Natali
(Canada), John Hurt (UK) and Dario Argento
(Italy). The festival had worldwide coverage, with
330 journalists attending. *Variety* called it one of
the 20 best film festivals in the world. Total
attendance was about 120,000. There were also
exhibitions and several workshops.
– Áurea Ribeiro.

Far East Film Festival
April 21-29, 2006

Annual themed event which, since 1998, has
focused on Eastern Asian cinema. *Inquiries to:*
Centro Espressioni Cinematografiche, Via Villalta
24, 33100 Udine, Italy. Tel: (39 04) 3229 9545.
Fax: 3222 9815. e: fareastfilm@cecudine.org.
Web: www.fareastfilm.com.

AWARDS 2005

Audience Award First Prize: **Peacock** (China),
Gu Changwei.
Audience Award Second Prize: **Kamikaze Girls**
(Japan), Nakashima Tetsuya.
Audience Award Third Prize: **Someone Special**
(Korea), Jang Jin.

Paolo Jacob

Chinese actress and director Xu Jinglei at Far East Film 2005, where she presented her **Letter from an Unknown Woman**

Report 2005

Far East Film attracted a record audience of more than 50,000. Around 2,500 joined the regular morning screenings at the new venue Visionario – Visual Arts Centre, for the acclaimed retrospective on the world of Nikkatsu Action. There were 900 accredited guests from more than 20 countries, plus more than 60 VIP guests (film directors, stars, producers and Asian experts), 200 journalists, 50 buyers, and representatives of 31 international film festivals. The festival previewed the best releases from China, Hong Kong, Japan, Korea, Thailand, Malaysia, Philippines. Closing film was *Love Battlefield* by Hong Kong director Soi Cheang.

Festival des 3 Continents, Nantes
November 21-28, 2006

The only annual competitive festival in the world for films originating solely from Africa, Asia and Latin and Black America. It's one of the few festivals where genuine discoveries may still be made. From Hou Hsiao-hsien or Abbas Kiarostami in the 1980s, to Darejan Omirbaev or Jia zang Ke more recently, unknown great authors have been shown and acknowledged in

28TH FESTIVAL DES 3 CONTINENTS
Cinemas from Africa, Latin America and Asia
Nantes - 21>28 nov. 2006
www.3continents.com

Nantes. For 27 years, F3C has also charted the film history of the southern countries through retrospectives (genres, countries, actors and actresses), showing more than 1,200 films and bringing to light large pieces of an unrecognised part of the world's cinematographic heritage. *Inquiries to:* Alain and Philippe Jalladeau, Directors, Festival des 3 Continents, BP 43302, 44033 Nantes Cedex 1, France.
Tel: (33 2) 4069 7414. Fax: 4073 5522.
e: festival@3continents.com.
Web: www.3continents.com.

Filmfest Hamburg
September 22-29, 2006

Under the direction of Albert Wiederspiel, around 100 international films are screened as German or world premieres in the following sections: Main Programme, Children Film Festival ,TV Movies in Cinema and Eurovisuell. The Douglas Sirk Prize honours outstanding contributions to film culture and business. There are more than 30,000 admissions and about 1,000 industry professionals attend. Filmfest Hamburg also sees itself as a platform for cultural exchange and dialogue: in the past years, the festival has shed light on productions from Asia (from Iran to Japan and Korea) and Europe (from the UK and Scandinavia to France, Spain and Eastern Europe). *Inquiries to:* Filmfest Hamburg, Steintorweg 4, D-20099 Hamburg, Germany.
Tel: (49 40) 3991 9000. Fax: 3991 90010.
e: info@filmfesthamburg.de.
Web: www.filmfesthamburg.de.

Flanders International Film Festival – Ghent
October 10-21, 2006

Belgium's most prominent annual film event attracts attendance of 100,000-plus. Principally focused on "The Impact of Music on Film", this competitive festival awards grants worth up to $120,000 and screens around 150 features and 80 shorts, most without a Benelux distributor. Other sections include the World Cinema spectrum (World, European, Benelux or Belgian premieres), film music concerts, retrospectives, seminars and a tribute to an important film-maker. The festival's Joseph Plateau Awards are the highest film honours in Benelux. Presented for the first time in 2001, the World Soundtrack Awards, judged by some 220 international composers, celebrate excellence in film scoring. *Inquiries to:* Flanders International Film Festival-Ghent, 40B Leeuwstraat, B-9000 Ghent, Belgium. Tel: (32 9) 242 8060. Fax: 221 9074. e: info@filmfestival.be. Web: www.filmfestival.be.

AWARDS 2005

Grand Prix for Best Film: **The Three Burials of Melquiades Estrada** (USA), Tommy Lee Jones.
Georges Delerue Prize for Best Music: Stephen Warbeck, **Proof** (USA).
SABAM Award for Best Screenplay: Eric Khoo and Wong Kim Hoh, **Be with Me** (Singapore).
Robert Wise Award for Best Director: Li Yu, **Dam Street** (China).
Xplore! Award: **Kammerflimmern** (Germany), Hendrik Hölzemann.
Best Belgian Short: **Meander**, Joke Liberge.
Ace Competition for Flemish Student Shorts: **Ureca**, Kenneth Taylor.
Prix UIP/Ghent: **Delivery** (Germany), Till Nowak.
FNAC Audience Award: **Het Paard Van Sinterklaas** (Belgium/Netherlands), Mischa Kamp.
Canvas Audience Award: **Crossing the Bridge** (Germany/Turkey), Fatih Akin.

Fort Lauderdale International Film Festival
Mid October-mid November 2006

FLIFF features more than 150 films from 40 countries during the world's longest film event, with screenings in Miami, Palm Beach and Fort Lauderdale. Awards include Best Film, Best Foreign-Language Film, Best American Indie, Best Director, Actor, Screenplay, Best Florida Film and Kodak Student prizes for Narrative (over 25 minutes), Short Narrative (25 minutes or under), Documentary and Experimental. The Festival has a fun party side, too, with a Beach Party, Sunday Brunch Cruise, Champagne Starlight Sail, a Fashion show aboard a 300-passenger luxury barge, and a gala featuring South Florida's top restaurants. The Sundance Channel Festival Café has daily and nightly parties. Attendance topped 60,000 in 2005. The deadlines for entries are: July 1 (Professional Early Deadline 1st Call), August 15 (Final Professional Deadline), Sept 15 (Student Deadline for catalogue) and Sept 30 (Final Deadline). *Inquiries to:* The Fort Lauderdale International Film Festival, 1314 East Las Olas Blvd. Suite 007, Fort Lauderdale, FL 33301, USA. Tel: (1 954) 760 9898. Fax: 760 9099. e: info@fliff.com. Web: www.fliff.com.

Freedom Film Festival
Late January 2007

Founded in 1997 by the American Cinema Foundation, this showcase of films from Eastern and Central Europe is dedicated to illuminating Europe's recent history and creating opportunities for its film-makers. The films relate to the struggle for personal, political, economic and artistic freedom during Stalin's times and in the wake of the Cold War. It has activities at Karlovy Vary and Moscow. *Inquiries to:* American Cinema Foundation, 9911 W Pico Blvd, Suite 1060, Los Angeles, CA 90035, USA. Tel: (1 310) 286 9420. Fax: 286 7914. e: acinema@cinemafoundation.com. Web: www.cinemafoundation.com.

Fribourg
March 12-19, 2006

Features, shorts and documentaries from Asia, Africa and Latin America unspool at this Swiss event, with a competitive section. *Inquiries to:* Fribourg Film Festival, Rue Nicolas-de-Praroman 2, Case Postale 550, 1701 Fribourg, Switzerland. Tel: (41 26) 347 4200. Fax: 347 4201. e: info@fiff.ch. Web: www.fiff.ch.

AWARDS 2005
Le Regard d'Or: **The Night of Truth** (Burkina Faso/France), Fanta Régina Nacro. *Special Jury Award:* **The Sleeping Child** (Belgium/Morocco), Yasmine Kassari. *Ecumenical Jury Award:* **The Black and White Milk Cow** (China), Yang Jin. *E-Changer Award:* **Turtles Can Fly** (Iran/Iraq), Bahman Ghobadi. *FICC Award:* **The Black and White Milk Cow**. *FIPRESCI Award:* **The Sleeping Child**. *Audience Award:* **Turtles Can Fly**. *Documentary Award:* **Repatriation** (South Korea), Kim Dong-won; **Darwin's Nightmare** (Austria/Belgium/France), Hubert Sauper.

Giffoni
July 15-22, 2006

Located in Giffoni Valle Piana, a small town about 40 minutes from Naples, the Giffoni International Film Festival for Children and Young People was founded in 1971 by Claudio Gubitosi to promote films for youthful audiences and families. Now includes four competitive sections: Kidz (animated and fiction shorts that tell fantastic stories, juried by 225 children aged six to nine); First Screens (fiction features and animated shorts, mainly fantasy and adventure, juried by 400 children aged 9 to 12); Free 2 Fly sees 380 teenagers (aged 12 to 14) assessing features and shorts about the pre-adolescent world; Y GEN has 250 jurors (aged 15 to 19) and takes a curious look at cinema for young people. *Inquiries to:* Giffoni Film Festival, Cittadella del Cinema, Via Aldo Moro 4, 84095 Giffoni Valle Piana, Salerno, Italy. Tel: (39 089) 802 3001. Fax: 802 3210. e: info@giffoniff.it. Web: www.giffoniff.it.

The Free to Fly and Y Gen juries at Giffoni 2005

AWARDS 2005
Free 2 Fly-Golden Gryphon: **Innocent Voices** (Mexico), Luis Mandoki. *Y Gen-Golden Gryphon:* **Napola** (Germany), Dennis Gansel. *First Screens-Golden Gryphon:* **Duma** (USA), Carroll Ballard. *Kidz-Golden Gryphon Animation:* **The Golden Blaze** (USA), Bryon E. Carson. *Kidz-Golden Gryphon Feature:* **The Wild Soccer Bunch** (Germany), Joachim Masannek.

Report 2005
The 35th GFF, which revolved around "Emotion" as its main theme, was attended by more than 80,000 people. More than 80 movies were screened. More than 1,500 jurors from all over the world gathered together to watch the movies and get to know each other. Among the guests nearly all of the directors of the films in competition and also celebrities such as Haley Joel Osment and Claire Danes.
– **Tony Guarino**, International Relations.

Gijón International Film Festival
Late November-early December 2006

One of Spain's oldest festivals (43rd edition in 2005), Gijón is now at the peak of its popularity. Having firmly established itself as a barometer of new film trends worldwide, it draws a large and enthusiastic public. Gijón has built on its niche as a festival for young people, programming innovative and independent films made by and for the young, including retrospectives, panoramas, exhibitions and concerts. Alongside the lively Official Section, sidebars celebrate directors who have forged new paths in film-making. *Inquiries to:* Gijón International Film Festival, PO Box 76, 33201 Gijon, Spain. Tel: (34 98) 518 2940. Fax: 518 2944. e: festivalgijon@telecable.es. Web: www.gijonfilmfestival.com.

Le Giornate del Cinema Muto
October 7-14, 2006

The world's first and largest festival dedicated to silent cinema. Officially based in Pordenone, for the past seven years it has taken place in the nearby historic town of Sacile. The festival sees an international invasion by archivists, historians, scholars, collectors and enthusiasts, along with cinema students chosen to attend the internationally recognised "Collegium". The Film Fair features books, CD-ROMs and DVDs, and provides a valued meeting place for authors and publishers. Festival Director: David Robinson. *Inquiries to:* Le Giornate del Cinema Muto, c/o La Cineteca del Friuli, Palazzo Gurisatti, Via Bini 50, 33013 Gemona (UD), Italy. Tel: (39 04) 3298 0458. Fax: 3297 0542. e: info.gcm@cinetecadelfriuli.org. Web: www.cinetecadelfriuli.org/gcm/.

Report 2005
Highlights of the 24th edition were a major programme of Japanese silent cinema, featuring impressive new restorations by the National Film Centre, Tokyo, and a complete retrospective of the surviving films of André Antoine. Greta Garbo was remembered on her centenary and tributes were also paid to Lillian Gish, Laurel and Hardy, Valentino and Gloria Swanson. A special

Paolo Jacob

Australian director Bruce Beresford, left, and festival President Livio Jacob at the Giornate 2005

festival guest was Australian director Bruce Beresford, who presented the 1919 Australian blockbuster *The Sentimental Bloke* and his own 2003 feature, *And Starring Pancho Villa as Himself*, starring Antonio Banderas and reconstructing Pancho Villa's involvement with film-makers such as D.W. Griffith, W.C. Cabanne and Raoul Walsh in the making of the now lost silent biopic *The Life of General Villa*.
– **Giuliana Puppin**, Press Office.

goEast Festival of Central and Eastern European Film in Wiesbaden
April 5-11, 2006

Established in 2001 for audiences interested in Eastern European film, with a mix of current productions and historical series, an academic symposium, student competition and related events. Member of FIAPF and European Coordination of Film Festivals; hosts FIPRESCI jury. *Deadline:* mid-Jan. *Inquiries to:* Deutsches Filminstitut, Schaumainkai 4, 60596 Frankfurt. Tel: (49 69) 9612 2025. Fax: 6637 2947. e: kopf@filmfestival-goeast.de. Web: www.filmfestival-goeast.de.

goEast ➡ **FESTIVAL OF CENTRAL AND EASTERN EUROPEAN FILM**
05.04. TO 11.04.2006 IN WIESBADEN

Deutsches Filminstitut – DIF
Tel. +49(0)69-9612 2027 / Fax +49(0)69-6637 2947
info@filmfestival-goEast.de / www.filmfestival-goEast.de

Göteborg
Late January-early February 2007

Now in its 29th year, Göteborg Film Festival is one of Europe's key film events. Large international programme and a special focus on Nordic films, including the Nordic Competition. International seminars and the marketplace Nordic Event attract buyers and festival programmers to the newest Scandinavian films. Some 1,500 professionals attend and more than 110,000 tickets are sold. *Inquiries to:* Göteborg Film Festival, Olof Palmes Plats, S- 413 04 Göteborg, Sweden. Tel: (46 31) 339 3000. Fax: 410 063. e: goteborg@filmfestival.org. Web: www.filmfestival.org.

Haugesund – Norwegian International Film Festival

August 18-25, 2006

Held in Haugesund, on the West Coast of Norway, the festival is Norway's major event for film and cinema and the Norwegian and Scandinavian film industry is represented by more than 1,000 participants, as well as several hundred international buyers, producers and directors. The New Nordic Films market runs at the beginning of the festival period. The Amanda Awards (the Norwegian "Oscars") take place at the start of the week. Festival Director: Gunnar Johan Løvvik. Programme Director: Håkon Skogrand. Honorary President: Liv Ullmann. *Inquiries to:* PO Box 145, N-5501 Haugesund, Norway.
Tel: (47 52) 743 370. Fax: 743 371.
e: info@filmfestivalen.no.
Web: www.filmfestivalen.no.

AWARDS 2005

Amanda Award Best Film: **Hawaii, Oslo** (Norway), Erik Poppe.
Amanda Award Best Director: Aksel Hennie, **Uno** (Norway).
Amanda Award Best Script: Harald Rosenløw-Eeg, **Hawaii, Oslo**.
Best Nordic Debut: **Vinterkyss**, Sara Johnsen.
Best International Feature: **Der Untergang** (Germany), Oliver Hirschbiegel.

Helsinki Film Festival – Love & Anarchy

September 14-24, 2006

An important festival for current cinema in Finland, now in its 19th year, Helsinki promotes high-quality international film-making to Finnish audiences and distributors. True to its subtitle, "Love and Anarchy", the event uncompromisingly challenges limits of cinematic expression and experience. Non competitive. *Submission deadline:* June 30. *Inquiries to:* Helsinki Film Festival, Mannerheimintie 22-24, PO Box 889, 00101 Helsinki, Finland.
Tel: (358 9) 6843 5230. Fax: 6843 5232.
e:office@hiff.fi. Web: www.hiff.fi.

Hong Kong

April 4-19, 2006

The Hong Kong International Film Festival (HKIFF) is one of Asia's most reputable platforms for film-makers, film professionals and filmgoers from all over the world to launch new works and experience outstanding cinema. Established in 1977, the 16-day event showcases more than 200 new films and several retrospective programmes. HKIFF is now officially an independent, charitable organisation, Hong Kong International Film Festival Society Limited. *Inquiries to:* Hong Kong International Film Festival Society Office, 21/F, Sunshine Plaza, 353 Lockhart Road, Wan Chai, Hong Kong.
Tel: (852) 2970 3300. Fax: 2970 3011.
e: info@hkiff.org.hk. Web: www.hkiff.org.hk.

AWARDS 2005

Golden DV Award: **The Soup, One Morning** (Japan), Izumi Takahashi; Oxhide (China), Liu Jiayin.
Humanitarian Award for Best Documentary: **Before the Flood** (China), Li Yi-fan and Yan Yu.
Humanitarian Award for Outstanding Documentary: **Asshak, Tales from the Sahara** (Switzerland/Germany), Ulrike Koch. *Special*

Mention: **Shape of the Moon** (Netherlands), Leonard Retel Helmrich.
SIGNIS Award: **Turtles Can Fly** (Iran/Iraq), Bahman Ghobadi.
FIPRESCI Award: **Lost in Wu Song** (China), Lu Yi-tong.
Skyy Vodka Short Film Competition: **A Fish with a Smile** (Taiwan), C Jay Shih.

Report 2005

Both international and local film celebrities graced the 29th HKIFF. Apart from the celebrities mentioned in the Awards, the directors and cast members of the Opening, Closing, Gala Premiere and Special Presentation films attracted much attention. HKIFF was proud of the increased support from its overseas guests, more than 400 of whom flew in.
– **Raymond Yeung**.

Huelva
November 2006

The main aim of Huelva Latin American Film Festival is to show and promote films of artistic quality that contribute to a better knowledge of Latin American production, including works from the Hispanic US. Huelva has become a key rendezvous, enabling European buyers and film buffs to catch up with the latest developments. It includes a competition for films from Latin America and the Hispanic US, tributes and round-table discussions. *Inquiries to:* Casa Colon, Plaza del Punto s/n, 21003 Huelva, Spain.
Tel: (34 95) 921 0170/0299. Fax: 921 0173.
e: prensa@festicinehuelva.com.
Web: www.festicinehuelva.com.

IFP Market
September 17-22, 2006

If you are seeking financing, sales, completion funding or production partners, IFP Market is the place to begin accessing industry executives through screenings, business and pitch meetings, targeted networking and social events. An essential networking opportunity, the IFP Market attracts hundreds of financiers, buyers, distributors, broadcasters, development executives, agents, managers and festival programmers from the US and abroad. *Inquiries to:* Pooja Kohli, Managing Director, IFP Market and Conference, 104 West 29th St, 12th Floor, New York, NY 10001, USA.
Tel: (1 212) 465 8200. Fax: 465 8525.
e: ifpny@ifp.org. Web: www.ifp.org.

India
October 2006

Annual, government-funded event recognised by FIAPF and held in Goa under the aegis of India's Ministry of Information and Broadcasting. Comprehensive "Cinema of the World" section, foreign and Indian retrospectives and a film market, plus a valuable panorama of the year's best Indian films, subtitled in English. *Inquiries to:* The Director, Directorate of Film Festivals, Sirifort Auditorium 1, August Kranti Marg, Khel Gaon, New Delhi 110049, India. Tel: (91 11) 2649 9371/9356. Fax: 2649 7214/9357).
e: dir.dff@hub.nic.in or ddiffi.dff@hub.nic.in.
Web: www.mib.nic.in/iffi.

Internationale Hofer Filmtage/Hof International Film Festival
October 24-29, 2006

Dubbed "Home of Film" (HOF) by Wim Wenders, Hof is famous for its thoughtful selection of some 50 features. Founded by the directors of the New German Cinema, Hof enjoys a high reputation among German film-makers and international luminaries such as Peter Jackson, Mike Leigh and Atom Egoyan. Directed by one of the most respected German film enthusiasts, Heinz Badewitz, Hof has enjoyed a rising reputation these past 39 years. A screening here often results in a distribution deal. *Inquiries to:* Postfach 1146, D-95010 Hof, Germany or Heinz Badewitz, Lothstr 28, D-80335 Munich, Germany. Tel: (49 89) 129 7422. Fax: 123 6868. e: info@hofer-filmtage.de. Web: www.hofer-filmtage.de.

Istanbul
April 1-16, 2006

The only film festival that takes place in a city where two continents meet, the Istanbul International Film Festival, recognised as a specialised competitive event by FIAPF, acts as a valuable showcase for distributors internationally. Attendance exceeds 90,000. Now in its 25th edition, this dynamic event focuses on features dealing with the arts, tributes, selections from world festivals, with other thematic sections such as "A Country – A Cinema", "The World of Animation", "Favourites of a Master", "The Eccentrics of Cinema", "Mined Zone", "Human Rights in Cinema" and a panorama of Turkish cinema. *Inquiries to:* Ms. Hulya Ucansu, Istanbul Foundation for Culture and Arts, Istiklal Caddesi 146, Beyoglu 34435, Istanbul, Turkey. Tel: (90 212) 334 0700 exts. 721 & 724. Fax: 334 0702. e: film.fest@iksv.org. Web: www.iksv.org.

Please contact:
Heinz Badewitz, Director

FAX: ++49 89 123 68 68
eMail: h.badewitz@hofer-filmtage.de

40th HOF international film festival
October, 24th to 29th, 2006

THE HOF SOCCER DREAM TEAM:
1. ATOM EGOYAN
2. JOHN SAYLES
3. VOLKER SCHLOENDORFF
4. HERBERT ACHTERNBUSCH
5. GEORGE A. ROMERO
6. TERENCE DAVIES
7. ROBERTO BENIGNI
8. VINCENT WARD
9. DAVID CRONENBERG
10. JIM JARMUSCH
11. JOHN CARPENTER
12. ROGER CORMAN
13. NEIL JORDAN
14. WERNER HERZOG
15. WIM WENDERS
16. PAUL COX
COACH: SAM FULLER

SUBSTITUTES:
MONTE HELLMAN | PAUL BARTEL
MELODY CHAREF | DETLEV BUCK
DORIS DÖRRIE | ALEX COX
BRIAN DE PALMA | SÖNKE WORTMANN
JOHN WATERS | PERCY ADLON

http://www.hofer-filmtage.de

Sophia Loren at Istambul 2005, with Sakir Eczacibasi, chair of the city's Foundation for Culture and Arts

AWARDS 2005

International Competition
Golden Tulip ex aequo: **Gilles' Wife**
(Belgium/France/Italy/Luxembourg/Switzerland),
Frédéric Fonteyne; **Café Lumière** (Japan),
Hou Hsiao-hsien.
FIPRESCI Award: **Innocence**
(Belgium/France/UK), Lucile Hadzihalilovic.
Peoples Choice Awards: **Innocence**.
National Competition
Turkish Film of the Year: **Istanbul Tales**,
Umit Unal, Kudret Sabanci, Selim Demirdelen,
Yucel Yolcu and Omur Atay.
Turkish Director of the Year: Ugur Yucel, **Toss-Up**.
Turkish Actor: Olgun Simsek, **Toss-Up**.
Turkish Actress: Yelda Reynaud, **Istanbul Tales**.
Special Prize of the Jury: Eyup Boz, **Angel's Fall**.
FIPRESCI Award: **Angel's Fall**.

Semih Kaplanoglu.
People's Choice Awards: **Toss-Up**, Ugur Yucel.

Report 2005

The 2005 Istanbul International Film Festival
was one of the most successful editions of
recent years, with the total number of films
screened at 166 and an attendance of 90,000.
Sophia Loren honoured the opening gala with
a special appearance. Harvey Keitel, Neil
Jordan and French novelist-film-maker Alain
Robbe-Grillet received awards, and gave
master classes and panel discussions. The
international competition jury, presided over by
acclaimed director Jane Campion, shared the
grand prize of the Festival, the Golden Tulip,
between Frédéric Fonteyne's *Gilles' Wife* and
Hou Hsiao-hsien's *Café Lumiere*.
– **Yusuf Pinhas**, Festival Editor.

Jerusalem International Film Festival
July 6-15, 2006

More than 70,000 people increase their
awareness of contemporary world cinema at
Israel's most prestigious cinematic event, housed
in a beautiful cinematheque, with screenings in
four additional venues. The Opening Gala attracts
more than 7,000 spectators, under the stars, in
the shadow of the Ancient City walls. The festival
continues to receive warm praise worldwide for its
intimate atmosphere, unique setting and efforts to
promote the appreciation and distribution of
quality films in Israel. More than 200 films are
presented in several sections, including: Best of
International Cinema; Israeli Cinema;

Documentaries; Animation; Jewish Themes; Human Rights; Retrospectives; Avant Garde; Restorations; Television; Special Tributes and Classics. The festival presents several prizes and awards, including Wim van Leer in Spirit of Freedom (International Competition), Mayor's Award for Jewish Experience (International Competition), Wolgin Awards for Israeli Cinema. *Inquiries to:* Jerusalem Film Festival, Hebron Road 11, Jerusalem 91083, Israel. Tel: (972 2) 565 4333. Fax: 565 4334. e: festival@jer-cin.org.il. Web: www.jff.org.il.

Director: Lia van Leer

JERUSALEM FILM FESTIVAL

July 6 – 15 2006

Karlovy Vary International Film Festival
June 30-July 8, 2006

Founded in 1946, Karlovy Vary is one of the most important film events in Central and Eastern Europe. It includes Official Selection (competition of full-length feature films, documentary films in competition, East of the West) and other programme sections highlighting production from all around the world. Film Entry deadline: April 14, 2006. *Inquiries to:* Film Servis Festival Karlovy Vary, Panská 1, CZ 110 00 Prague 1, Czech Republic. Tel: (420 2) 2141 1011. Fax: 2141 1033. e: festival@kviff.com. Web: www.kviff.com.

AWARDS 2005
Grand Prix- Crystal Globe: **My Nikifor** (Poland), Krzysztof Krauze.
Special Jury Prize: **What a Wonderful Place** (Israel), Eyal Halfon.
Best Director: Krzysztof Krauze, **My Nikifor**.
Best Actress: Krystyna Feldman, **My Nikifor**.
Best Actor (Ex-aequo): Luca Zingaretti, **Come into the Light** (Italy); Uri Gavriel, **What a Wonderful Place** (Israel).

Award-winners Eyal Halfon, Sébastien Rose, Uri Gavriel, Krystyna Feldman, Krzysztof Krauze and Juliusz Machulski at Karlovy Vary 2005

Special Jury Mention: **Noriko's Dinner Table** (Japan), Sion Sono.
Audience Award: **Life with My Father** (Canada), Sébastien Rose.
Best Documentary Film Under 30 Minutes: **My God** (Belarus), Galina Adamovich.
Best Documentary Film Over 30 Minutes: **Estamira** (Brazil), Marcos Prado.
East of the West: **Ragin** (Russia/Austria), Kirill Serebrennikov.
Award for Outstanding Contribution to World Cinema: Robert Redford (USA) Jiri Krejcik (Czech Republic), Sharon Stone (USA) and Liv Ullmann (Norway).

Report 2005
During the 40th edition, 142,500 people saw 242 feature films. Among the festival guests were Robert Redford, Sharon Stone, Liv Ullmann, Gael Garcia Bernal, Atom Egoyan, Michael Madsen, Alexander Payne, Michael Pitt and Walter Salles. The programme featured tributes to Kihachiro Kawamoto, Jiri Krejcik, Sam Peckinpah, Liv Ullmann and Robert Redford, and retrospectives: Nature and Landscape in Norwegian Cinema, Focus on Canadian Film, 2005: A Musical Odyssey, Worried About Work, World War II: 60 Years After. A new film industry event was introduced at the festival: the East of the West Panel, which presented new films from Central and Eastern Europe that were in post-production or awaiting release.
– **Andrea Szczukova**, Head of Film Industry Office.

La Rochelle
June 30–July 10, 2006

The festival includes retrospectives for directors
or actors and tributes to important but unjustly
neglected directors or actors. Films for children
are shown every morning. Special Events, such
as film previews, silent films with piano
accompaniment, are open to all. The festival
ends with an all-night programme of five films,
followed by breakfast in cafés overlooking the
old port. *Inquiries to:* La Rochelle International
Film Festival, 16 rue Saint Sabin, 75011 Paris,
France. Tel: (33 1) 4806 1666. Fax: 4806 1540.
e: info@festival-larochelle.org.
Web: www.festival-larochelle.org. Director: Mrs.
Prune Engler; Artistic Director: Mrs. Sylvie Pras.

Las Palmas de Gran Canaria
International Film Festival
March 2006

The Festival Internacional de Cine de Las
Palmas de Gran Canaria is the Canary Islands'
principal forum for independent productions that
would not otherwise be picked up by the
mainstream distribution circuit. Competitive
Official Selection in which feature films, mainly
from Europe and Latin America, compete for the
top prize, the Golden Lady Harimaguada, and
other awards. The 7th edition, in 2006, will also
feature retrospectives on Chris Marker and Jia
Zhangke (winner of the Golden Lady
Harimaguada for *The World* in 2005), a Euronoir
section and a focus on Japanese anime.
Inquiries to: C/ León y Castillo 322, 4ª Planta,
35007 Las Palmas de Gran Canaria.
Tel: (34 928) 446 833/446 644. Fax: 446 651.
e: laspalmascine@hotmail.com. Web: (?)

Leeds
November 2006

The Leeds International Film Festival is the largest
regional film festival in the United Kingdom. In
addition, Leeds Film organises the year-round
Leeds Film Quarter and education programmes
and delivers the Leeds Young People's Film
Festival. Inquiries to: Leeds International Film
Festival, The Town Hall, The Headrow, Leeds, LS1

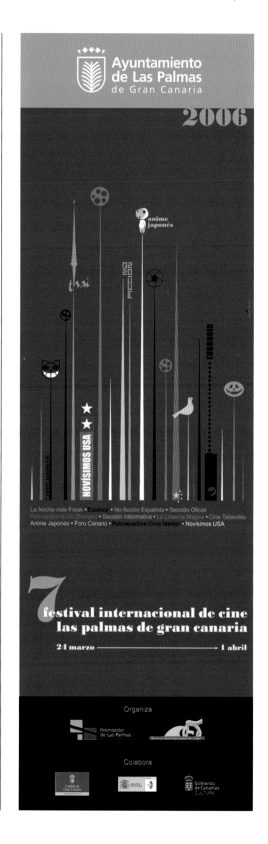

3AD, UK. Tel: (44 113) 247 8398. Fax: 247 8494.
e: filmfestival@leeds.gov.uk.
Web: www.leedsfilm.com.

Locarno
August 2-12, 2006

The Locarno International Film Festival, one of the world's top cinematic all-feature events, traditionally aims to promote personal film-making of artistic merit, to provide a showcase for major new films of the year from around the world and to take stock, in its competitive section, of the new perspectives of film-making expression, concentrating especially on such new film directors and industries as command international attention. The festival's ongoing process of cultural inquiry, has contributed to revealing or confirming directors who are currently enjoying very wide recognition. In recent years the festival has also become an important industry showcase for auteur film-making, a strong networking opportunity for distributors, buyers and producers from around the world, with over 3,000 film professionals and 1,000 journalists attending. *Inquiries to:* Festival Internazionale del Film Locarno, Via Ciseri 23, CH-6601 Locarno, Switzerland. Director: Frédéric Maire. Tel: (41 91) 756 2121. Fax: 756 2149. e: info@pardo.ch. Web: www.pardo.ch.

AWARDS 2005
International Competition
Golden Leopard: **Nine Lives** (USA), Rodrigo García.
Special Jury Prize: **Un couple parfait** (France/Japan), Nobuhiro Suwa.
Silver Leopards: **Fratricide** (France/Germany/Luxembourg), Yilmaz Arslan; **3 Grad Kaelter** (Germany), Florian Hoffmeister; **We Are All Fine** (Iran), Bizhan Mirbaqeri.
Actress Leopard: The ensemble of actresses, **Nine Lives** (USA).
Actor Leopard: Patrick Drolet, **La Neuvaine** (Canada).
Special Mention: The Quay Brothers, **The Piano Tuner of Earthquakes**; Marco Grieco, **La guerra di Mario**; Xevat Gectan, **Fratricide**.
Video Competition
Golden Leopards: **Les États Nordiques**

(Canada), Denis Coté; **Masahista** (Philippines), Brilliante Mendoza.
Special Jury Mention: **Between the Devil and the Wide Blue Sea** (Germany), Romuald Karmakar.

London
October 18–November 2, 2006

The UK's largest and most prestigious festival, sponsored by the *Times* newspaper and presented at the National Film Theatre and in the West End, and at cinemas throughout the capital. The programme comprises around 200 features and documentaries, as well as a showcase for shorts. There is a British section and a very strong international selection from Asia, Africa, Europe, Latin America, US independents and experimental and avant-garde work. More than 1,200 UK and international press and industry representatives attend and there is a buyers/sellers liaison office. *Inquiries to:* Sarah Lutton, London Film Festival, National Film Theatre, South Bank, London SE1 8XT, UK. Tel: (44 20) 7815 1322. Fax: 7633 0786. e: sarah.lutton@bfi.org.uk. Web: www.lff.org.uk.

Málaga
March 17-25, 2006

Some 1,800 professionals attend: 800 accredited journalists, 87 buying companies representing 31 countries; 413 accredited assistants to the European and Latin-American documentary market (MercaDoc), 61 companies representing a total of 24 countries at the Spanish Film Market (Market Screenings). Some 110,000 spectators attended the screenings and parallel activities. *Inquiries to:* Salomon Castiel, Director, Málaga Festival–Spanish Cinema, Calle Carcer 6, 29012, Málaga, Spain. Tel: (34 95) 222 8242. Fax: 222 7760. e: info@festivaldemalaga.com. Web: www.festivaldemalaga.com.

Mannheim-Heidelberg
November 2006

The Newcomers' Festival: for young independent film-makers from all over the

world. Presents around 35 new features and around 10 shorts in two main sections, International Competition and International Discoveries (entry deadline: August 4). The Newcomers' Market & Industry Screenings: reserved for international buyers and distributors. The Mannheim Meetings: Part 1 is one of only four worldwide co-production meetings for producers and runs in parallel to the main event (entry deadline: July 31). Part 2 is the unique European Sales & Distribution Meetings for theatrical distributors and sales agents. The Distribution Market will take place during the festival. More than 60,000 filmgoers and 1,000 film professionals attend. *Inquiries to:* Dr. Michael Koetz, International Filmfestival Mannheim-Heidelberg, Collini-Center, Galerie, D-68161 Mannheim, Germany.
Tel: (49 621) 102 943. Fax: 291 564.
e: ifmh@mannheim-filmfestival.com.
Web: www.mannheim-filmfestival.com.

Mar del Plata International Film Festival
March 9-19, 2006

The festival was first held in 1954, but because of a 26-year hiatus is only celebrating its 21st edition in 2006. Held annually since 1996. The festival's President is acclaimed film-maker Miguel Pereira. It is the only A-grade film festival in Latin America with an Official Competition, usually comprising around 15 movies, generally two from Argentina. Key sections include "Latin American Films" and "Women and Film". Also important is the Mercosur Film Market (MFM; Director: Gabriel Giandinotto). *Inquiries to:* Mar del Plata International Film Festival, Avenida de Mayo 1222, 3er, (1085) Cap Fed, Argentina.
Tel: (54 11) 4383 5115.
e: info@ mardelplatafilmfest.com.
Web: www.mardelplatafilmfest.com.

Melbourne International Film Festival
Late July-early August 2006

MIFF is widely regarded as the most significant film event in Australia. It has the largest and most diverse programme of screenings and special events in the country, in addition to the largest audience. There is also growing

international regard for MIFF as a film market place, with a steady increase in sales agents attending. The longest-running festival in the southern hemisphere showing more than 400 features, shorts, documentaries and new media works, presented in five venues. *Inquiries to:* PO Box 2206, Fitzroy Mail Centre 3065, Melbourne, Victoria, Australia.
Tel: (61 3) 9417 2011. Fax: 9417 3804.
e: miff@melbournefilmfestival.com.au.
Web: www.melbournefilmfestival.com.au.

Mill Valley
October 5-15, 2006

The Mill Valley Film Festival presents a wide variety of international programming, shaped by a commitment to cultural and artistic excellence. This intimate, welcoming event of unusually high calibre and dedication is set in a beautiful small town just north of San Francisco. The non-competitive festival includes the innovative VFest, as well as the Children's Film Fest, tributes, seminars and special events. *Inquiries to:* Mill Valley Film Festival, California Film Institute, 38 Miller Ave, Suite 6, Mill Valley, CA 94941, USA.
Tel: (1 415) 383 5256. Fax: 383 8606.
e: zelton@cafilm.org. Web: www.mvff.com.

Montreal World Film Festival
Late August-early September 2006

The goal of the festival is to encourage cultural diversity and understanding between nations, to foster the cinema of all continents by stimulating quality, to discover and encourage new talents, and to promote meetings between cinema professionals from around the world. Apart from the "Official Competition" and the "First Films Competition", the festival presents "Hors Concours" (World Greats), a "Focus on World Cinema" and "Documentaries of the World", plus tributes to established film-makers and a section dedicated to Canadian student films. *Inquiries to:* Montreal World Film Festival 1432 de Bleury St, Montreal, Quebec, Canada H3A 2J1.
Tel: (1 514) 848 3883. Fax: 848 3886.
e: commandites@ffm-montreal.org.
Web: www.ffm-montreal.org.

AWARDS 2005

Grand Prix of the Americas (Best Film): **Off Screen** (Belgium/Netherlands), Pieter Kuijpers.
Jury Awards: **The Milkwoman** (Japan), Akira Ogata; Snowland (Germany), Hans W Geissendörfer.
Director: Claude Gagnon, **Kamataki** (Canada/Japan).
Artistic Contribution: Arek Tomiak, director of photography on **Your Name Is Justine** (Luxembourg/Poland).
Actress: Adrian Ozores, **Heröina** (Spain).
Actors: Jan Decleir, **Off Screen** (Belgium/Netherlands).
Best Screenplay: Jose Corbacho, Juan Cruz, **Tapas** (Spain).
Innovation Award: **Sex, Hope & Love** (Sweden)/ for the direction of actors and particularly Mira Eklund.
Air Canada People's Choice Award: **Kamataki**.
Award for the Most Popular Canadian Film: **Kamataki**.
Glauber Rocha Award for the Best Latin American Film: **Play** (Argentina/Chile), Alicia Scherson.
Award for the Best Documentary Film: **The Ninth** (Canada), Pierre-Henry Salfati.
FIPRESCI Prize: **Kamataki**.
Ecumenical Prize: **Kamataki**.

Moscow International Film Festival
June 16-25, 2006

Biannual from 1959-98, the festival provided an open window on world cinema, with an international competition for domestic productions and many from Eastern Europe and developing countries, and a non-competitive panorama of commercial hits absent from regular local distribution. Since going annual in 1999, the programme has become more arthouse-oriented (Hollywood now dominates mainstream cinemas) and there are visits by A-list stars and directors (Jack Nicholson, Meryl Streep, Fanny Ardant, Quentin Tarantino, William Friedkin, Emir Kusturica) attracted by the Life Achievement and Stanislavsky acting awards. The large competition remains international in scope and genres, covering Europe and the CIS, South East Asia, Latin and North America. A new competitive

section, Perspectives, started in 2004. The Media-Forum (panorama and competition) is devoted to experimental films and video art. *Inquiries to:* Moscow International Film Festival, 10/1 Khokhlovsky Per, Moscow 109028, Russia. Tel: (7 095) 917 2486. Fax: 916 0107. e: info@miff.ru. Web: www.miff.ru.

Napa Sonoma Wine Country Film Festival
Late July-Early August 2006

World cinema, culture and conscience converge in the heart of Northern California's premium wine region, Napa and Sonoma Valleys. The festival is gently paced, mainly non-competitive and accepts features, documentaries, shorts, and animation. All genres are welcome. Programme sections are: World Cinema, American Independents, EcoCinema (environment), Food on Food, Music and Film, Arts in Film and Cinema of Conscience (social issues). Many of the films are shown outdoors. *Inquiries to:* PO Box 303, Glen Ellen, CA 95442, USA. Tel: (1 707) 935 3456. e: wcfilmfest@aol.com. Web: www.wcff.us.

AWARDS 2005

Best of the Fest: **Unconscious** (Spain), Joaquin Oristrell and **Mix** (USA), Stephen Low.
Best First Feature: **Sinfonia de Ilegales** (Spain), Jose Luis de Damas.
Best US Cinema: **Duma**, Carroll Ballard.
Best Eco Cinema: **Earth from Above** (France), Renaud Delourme and **The Real Dirt on Farmer John** (USA), Taggart Siegel.
Best Cine Latino: **Bombon El Perro** (Argentina), Carlos Sorrin.

Netherlands Film Festival, Utrecht
September 27-October 9, 2006

Since 1981, Holland's only event presenting an overview of the year's entire output of Dutch film-making. The festival opens the new cultural season with Dutch retrospectives, seminars, talk shows and premieres of many new Dutch films. Dutch features, shorts, documentaries and TV dramas compete for local cinema's grands prix, the Golden Calf, in 18 categories. The Holland Film Meeting, the sidebar for international and national film professionals, includes a Market Programme and the Netherlands Production Platform for Dutch and European producers. *Inquiries to:* Nederlands Film Festival, PO Box 1581, 3500 BN Utrecht, Netherlands. Tel: (31 30) 230 3800. Fax: 230 3801. e: info@filmfestival.nl. Web: www.filmfestival.nl.

New York
September 29–October 15, 2006

Highlights the best of American and international cinema. Deadline around July 10. Application forms and details available from late May. No entry fee. Non-competitive. All categories and lengths accepted. Formats accepted: VHS (NTSC or PAL), u-matic, DVD (all regions), 16mm, 35mm. For acceptance, you must have a 16mm or 35mm print available. Works must be New York City premieres. *Inquiries to:* Sara Bensman, Film Society of Lincoln Center, 70 Lincoln Center Plaza, New York, NY 10023-6595, USA. Tel: (1 212) 875 5638. Fax: 875 5636. e: festival@filmlinc.com. Web: www.filmlinc.com.

Nordische Filmtage Lubeck
November 1-5, 2006

Held in the charming medieval town of Lubeck, north of Hamburg, the festival spotlights Scandinavian and Baltic cinema, enabling members of the trade, critics and other filmgoers to see the best new productions. Also features a large documentary section. Attendance exceeds 18,000 for more than 130 screenings. *Inquiries to:* Janina Prossek, Nordische Filmtage Lubeck, Schildstrasse 12, D-23539 Lubeck, Germany. Tel: (49 451) 122 1742. Fax: 122 1799. e: info@filmtage.luebeck.de. Web: www.filmtage.luebeck.de.

AWARDS 2005
NDR Film Prize: **Manslaughter** (Denmark), Per Fly.
Baltic Film: **Mother of Mine** (Finland), Klaus Härö.
Audience Prize: **Mother of Mine** (Finland), Klaus Härö.
Children's and Youth Film Prize: **Mat the Cat** (Estonia), René Vilbre.
Interfilm Church Prize: **Homesick** (Finland),

Petri Kotwica.
Children's Jury: **We are the Champions** (Denmark), Martin Hagbjer.

Report 2005
The NDR Film Prize jury, including German actor Axel Milberg, Turkish-German director Buket Alakus and former head of Swiss culture David Streiff, gave Special Mentions to Aku Louhimies' innovative Finnish *Frozen Land* and Maria Blom's Swedish debut *Dalecarlians*, but awarded its € 12,500 prize to *Manslaughter*, the third episode of Per Fly's trilogy on Danish society, the first two parts of which won the prize in 2000 and 2003. "Star" of the festival was 11-year-old Topi Majaniemi, the lead in Klaus Härö's *Mother of Mine*. Armin Mueller-Stahl was honoured with a tribute.
– **Stephen Locke**, Press Officer.

Armin Mueller-Stahl at the 2005 Nordische Filmtage

Nyon
April 24-30, 2006

Since 1994, Visions du Réel, International Film Festival in Nyon (a few miles from Geneva), aims to promote independent films and audiovisual productions classified as creative documentaries, where film-makers deliver their own personal vision of today's world in all its aspects (social issues, intimate portraits, enquiries, journey diaries, experimental movies). All these films are treated as a specific and committed form of cinema. The works (irrespective of length or format) are divided into six sections: Competition International; Regards Neufs (international competition for first

21st
INTERNATIONAL ODENSE FILM FESTIVAL

[AUGUST 2006]

Imaginative and surprising shorts
All 16 mm, 35 mm and BetaSP can compete

Entry deadline April 1st 2006

Download entryform at www.filmfestival.dk

www.filmfestival.dk

Vindegade 18 · DK-5000 Odense C · Denmark
Tel: + 45 6613 1372 / +45 6551 4044
Fax: +45 6591 4318 / E-mail: off.ksf@odense.dk

films); Tendances; Investigations; Helvétiques; Ateliers; Séances Spéciales. Since 2002, Visions du Réel organised also its own official international market (Doc Outlook). Entry deadline: mid-January (regulations and entry form available each autumn on festival website). *Inquiries to:* Visions du Réel, 18, rue Juste Olivier, PO Box 1430, CH-1260 Nyon 1, Switzerland.
Tel: (41 22) 365 4455. Fax: 365 4450.
e: docnyon@visionsdureel.ch.
Web: www.visionsdureel.ch.

AWARDS 2005
International Competition
Grand Prix Visions du Réel: **The Pipeline Next Door** (France), Nino Kirtadzé.
Prix SRG SSR Idée Suisse: **Massaker** (France/Germany/Lebanon), Monika Borgmann, Lokman Slim and Hermann Theissen.
Audience Prize: **Frozen Angels** (Finland/France/Germany/USA), Eric Black and Frauke Sandig.
Inter-religious Jury Prize: **Fata Morgana** (Finland), Anastasia Lapsui and Markku Lehmuskallo.
Young Audience Prize: **Jimmywork** (Canada), Simon Sauvé.
Regards Neufs
Canton Vauds: **Farewell** 1999 (Taiwan), Ching-Yi Wu; **The North Star** (Finland), Erkko Lyytinen.
Prix Kodak Suisse: **Carnogica** (Switzerland), Martina Jacoma.
Prix Egli Swiss Effects SA: **Made in Italy** (Belgium/Italy), Fabio Wuytack
From All Sections
Prix Télévision Suisse Romande: **Melodias**

Bianca Dugaro

The festival's Natalie Böhler with Thai director Apichatpong Weerasethakul at Visions du Réel 2005

(Switzerland), François Bovy.
*Prix Suissimage/Société Suisse des Auteurs
SSA:* **Brother Yusef** (Germany/Switzerland),
Nicolas Humbert and Werner Penzel.
Prix "Regards Sur le Crime": **Melodias**
(Switzerland), François Bovy.
Prix John Templeton Foundation: **The Pipeline
Next Door** (France), Nino Kirtadzé.

Oberhausen
May 4-9, 2006

In May 2005, Oberhausen once more became
the centre of the short film world. The traditional
competitions of the 51st edition – International,
German, children's shorts and music video –
once again provided an over-view of current
international short film and video production; the
thematic programme "The Fallen Curtain" looked
at the search for new identities after 1989. A
special focus day on mobile shorts met with
great interest. Closing date for entries: mid
January. Entry forms and regulations can be
downloaded at www.kurzfilmtage.de from
September. Festival Director: Dr. Lars Henrik
Gass. *Inquiries to:* Oberhausen International
Short Film Festival, Grillostrasse 34, D-46045
Oberhausen, Germany. Tel: (49 208) 825 2652.
Fax: 825 5413. e: info@kurzfilmtage.de.
Web: www.kurzfilmtage.de.

Odense
August 2006

Denmark's only international short film festival
invites the best international unusual short films
with original and imaginative content. Besides
screenings of more than 200 national and
international short films and Danish
documentaries, Odense Film Festival offers a
number of exciting retrospective programmes and
viewing of all competition films in the Videobar.
The festival hosts a range of seminars for film
professionals, librarians and teachers, educates
children and youth in the field of forceful,
alternative film experiences and is a meeting place
for international film directors and other film
professionals in the field of short films and
documentaries. *Inquiries to:* Odense Film Festival,
Vindegade 18, DK-5000 Odense C, Denmark.

Tel: (45) 6613 1372, ext 4044. Fax: 6591 4318.
e: off.ksf@odense.dk. Web: www.filmfestival.dk.

AWARDS 2005
International Grand Prix: **A Good Day** (Sweden),
Per Hanefjord.
International Grand Prix Special Prize:
Panorama (France), Marinca Villanova.
International Special Prize: **Eye Level** (Georgia),
George Ovashvili.
International Special Prize: **Autobiographical
Scene Number 6882** (Sweden), Ruben Östlund.
National Grand Prix: **The German Secret**
(Denmark), Lars Johansson.
National Special Prize: **Angie** (Denmark),
Tine Katinka Jensen.
National Special Prize: **Pas På Nerverne**
(Denmark), Rene Bo Hansen.
National Special Prize: **Min Fars Sind**
(Denmark), Vibe Mogensen.
National Special Mention: **I Danmark Er Jeg
Født** (Denmark), Peter Klitgaard.
Hans Christian Andersen Prize: **The Hidden
Face** (Netherlands), Elbert Strien.
Hans Christian Andersen Special Mention:
The Swenkas (Denmark), Jeppe Rønde.
International Prize of the Juvenile Jury: **Never an
Absolution** (Iran/Sweden), Cameron B Alyasin.
National Prize of the Juvenile Jury: **Can You Die
in Heaven?** (Denmark), Erlend E Mo.

Oulu International Children's
Film Festival
November 13-19, 2006

Annual festival with competition for full-length
feature films for children, it screens recent titles
and retrospectives. Oulu is in northern Finland, on
the coast of the Gulf of Bothnia. *Inquiries to:* Oulu
International Children's Film Festival, Torikatu 8,
90100 Oulu, Finland.
Tel: (358 8) 881 1293/94. Fax: 881 1290.
e: oek@oufilmcenter.inet.fi. Web: www.ouka.fi/lef.

Palm Springs
January 11-22, 2007

Each year, Palm Springs honours individuals and films with a variety of International awards. Last year's honorees included Nicole Kidman, Kevin Spacey, Laura Linney, Samuel L. Jackson, Liam Neeson, Alexander Payne and Howard Shore. The festival has more than 600 entries and 105,000 attendees. *Inquiries to:* Darryl MacDonald, 1700 E. Tahquitz Canyon Way, Suite 3, Palm Springs, CA 92262, USA. Tel: (1 760) 322 2930. Fax: 322 4087. e: info@psfilmfest.org. Web: www.psfilmfest.org.

Pesaro
June 24-July 2, 2006

The Mostra Internazionale del Nuovo Cinema, or Pesaro Film Festival (founded in Pesaro in 1965 by Bruno Torri and Lino Miccichè), in 2005 celebrated its 40th birthday. Since 2000, Giovanni Spagnoletti has directed the Festival. The festival is synonymous with discoveries, re-readings and special events. *Inquiries to:* Mostra Internazionale del Nuovo Cinema (Pesaro Film Festival), Via Villafranca 20, 00185 Rome, Italy. Tel: (39 06) 445 6643/491 156. Fax: 491 163. e: pesarofilmfest@mclink.it. Web: www.pesarofilmfest.it.

Report 2005
There were eight outdoor evening screenings in the main square in Pesaro. The spectators chose *Mountain Patrol* by Lu Chuan (Hong Kong) as Best Film. A complete retrospective was dedicated to Spanish director Victor Erice, who attended. A complete retrospective of Marco Bellocchio's work provided an extraordinary trip through 40 years of Italian cinema, completed by a round table discussion. – **Maria Grazia Chimenz**, the Secretariat.

Portland
February 11-26, 2007

The 30th Portland International Film Festival will be an invitational event presenting more than 100 films from 30-plus countries to 35,000 people from throughout the Northwest. Along with new international features, documentaries and shorts, the 2007 festival will feature showcases surveying Hispanic film and literature, Pacific Rim cinema and many of the year's foreign-language Oscar submissions. *Inquiries to:* Northwest Film Center, 1219 SW Park Ave, Portland, OR 97205, USA. Tel: (1 503) 221 1156. Fax: 294 0874. e: info@nwfilm.org. Web: www.nwfilm.org.

30th Portland International Film Festival
February 9-25, 2007

NORTHWEST FILM CENTER
www.nwfilm.org   503-221-1156

Pusan International Film Festival (PIFF)
Mid-October 2006

Established in 1996 in Busan, Korea, PIFF has been voted as "The Best Film Festival in Asia" (*Time Asia*, November 2004). It promotes Asian and Korean cinema, as well as introducing quality films from all corners of the world. In addition, its project market – Pusan Promotion Plan – has been a platform for moving Asian film projects forward in the international marketplace, along with its own talent campus, Asian Film Academy, offering various film-making programmes for young talent from all over Asia. *Inquiries to:* 3rd Floor, 1-143, Shinmunno 2-Ga, Jongro-Gu, Seoul, 110-062, Korea. Tel: (82 2) 3675 5097. Fax: 3675 5098. e: publicity@piff.org. Web: www.piff.org.

Raindance
October 2006

Raindance is the largest independent film festival in the UK and aims to reflect the cultural, visual and narrative diversity of international independent film-making, specialising in first-time film-makers. The festival screens around 100 feature films and 200 shorts as well as hosting a broad range of workshops and masterclasses. *Inquiries to:* Oli Harbottle,

Festival Producer, Raindance Film Festival, 81 Berwick St, London, W1F 8TW, UK. Tel: (44 20) 7287 3833. Fax: 7439 2243. e: festival@raindance.co.uk. Web: www.raindance.co.uk/festival.

AWARDS 2005

Official Selection Feature: **Canary** (Japan), Akihiko Shiota.
Official Selection Short: **A Monk's Awakening** (France), Lou Ma Ho.
UK Feature: **Rollin' with the Nines**, Julian Gilby.
UK Short: **Six Shooter**, Martin McDonagh.
Debut Feature: **The Gingerbread Man** (USA), Jonathan Spirk.
Documentary: **Punk: Attitude** (UK), Don Letts.
Diesel Film of the Festival: **Right Place** (Japan), Kosai Sekine.
Tiscali Short Film Award: **Cricker Crack** (UK), Rob Heppell.
The Big Issue Short Film Award: **The Ends** (UK), Justin Edgar.

Report 2005

The 13th Raindance saw admissions rise for the fourth consecutive year, to 18,000 people. Highlights included a lively lecture by Vanessa Redgrave. The festival jury included Natalie Press, Richard Jobson and Tommy Ramone. Many films were bought at the festival, including two US debut features, *Buy It Now* and *The Gingerbread Man*.
– **Oli Harbottle**, Producer.

Reykjavik International Film Festival
September 28-October 8, 2006

Now in its third year, RIFF was conceived to promote Icelandic Cinema culture and nurture a diverse and fruitful film industry. National and international film-makers compete for creative awards. Festival Director Hronn Marinosdottir promises a fascinating festival organised with a programming committee drawn from Iceland's most talented film-makers and critics. The honorary chairman is former Director of the Toronto Film Festival, Helga Stephenson. Festival Programming Director is Dimitri Eipides. The New Visions category reflects the most contemporary and noteworthy international film-making. The Open Sea category showcases independent and award-winning films from around the world. In co-operation with the University of Iceland and others, RIFF runs seminars and courses hosted by national and international film-makers. Reykjavik's vibrant nightlife complements the festival, with special events in bars, clubs, galleries and museums. *Inquiries to:* Reykjavik International Film Festival, Hellusund 3, 101 Reykjavík, Iceland. Tel: (354) 861 7374. Web: www.filmfest.is.

International Film Festival Rotterdam
January 24-February 4, 2007

For 35 years, Rotterdam has showcased the best of contemporary independent and experimental film. With more than 200 features, including over 60 world or European premieres, it supports diversity, discoveries and film talent worldwide. It also hosts the leading co-production market, the CineMart. Rotterdam's Hubert Bals Fund (HBF) supports film-makers from non-Western countries. *Inquiries to:* International Film Festival Rotterdam, PO Box 21696, 3001 AR Rotterdam, Netherlands. Tel: (31 10) 890 9090. Fax: 890 9091. e: tiger@filmfestivalrotterdam.com. Web: www.filmfestivalrotterdam.com.

Festival dates:
28. 8. – 8. 10. 2006
www.filmfest.is

REYKJAVIK INTERNATIONAL FILM FESTIVAL

Report 2005

The festival drew attendance of 358,000. Russian, Southeast Asian and Iraqi films and their makers were at the centre of the audience's and media's interest. The VPRO Tiger Awards for best first or second feature in competition went to Daniele Gaglianone (Italy) for *Changing Destiny*, Ilya Khrzhanovsky (Russia) for *4* and Mercedes Alvarez (Spain) for *The Sky Turns*. Well received first films were Ismaël Ferroukhi's *Le grand voyage* (France/Morocco), Maria Blom's *Dalecarlians* (Denmark/Sweden) and Pascale Breton's *Illumination* (France).
– **Bert-Jan Zoet**, Press.

San Francisco International Film Festival

April 20-May 6, 2006

The oldest film festival in the Americas, in its 49th year, San Francisco continues to grow in importance and popularity. It presents more than 175 international features and shorts. Special awards include the Skyy Prize ($10,000 cash for an emerging director), The Golden Gate Awards and the FIPRESCI Prize. *Inquiries to:* San Francisco International Film Festival, San Francisco Film Society, 39 Mesa St, Suite 110, The Presidio, San Francisco, CA 94129, USA. Tel: (1 415) 561 5000. Fax: 561 5099. e: publicity@sffs.org. Web: www.sffs.org.

AWARDS 2005

Skyy Prize: **Me and You and Everyone We Know** (USA), Miranda July.
FIPRESCI Prize: **Private** (Italy), Saverio Costanzo.
Golden Gate Awards
Best Short: **The Ecstatic** (Germany/Pakistan), Till Passow.
Best Documentary: **Czech Dream** (Czech Republic), Vit Klusak and Filip Remunda.
Best Bay Area Short: **The Life of Kevin Carter** (USA), Dan Krauss.
Best Bay Area Documentary: **The Real Dirt on Farmer John** (USA), Taggart Siegel.
New Visions: **Phantom Foreign Vienna** (Austria), Lisl Ponger.
Best Narrative Short: **Twilight** (USA), Victoria Gamburg.
Best Bay Area Non-Documentary Short:

Torchlight (USA), Kerry Laitala.
Best Animated Short: **Ryan** (Canada), Chris Landreth.
Best Youth Work: **Inertia** (USA), Erica Eng.
Best Work for Kids and Families: **A Slippery Tale** (Germany), Susanne Seidel.
Audience Award Narrative: **Me and You and Everyone We Know**.
Audience Award Documentary: **Pursuit of Equality** (USA), Mike Shaw and Geoff Acallan.

San Sebastián

Mid-September 2006

Held in an elegant Basque seaside city known for its superb gastronomy and beautiful beaches, the Donostia-San Sebastian Festival remains Spain's most important event in terms of glamour, competition, facilities, partying, number of films and attendance (more than 1,600 production and distribution firms, government agencies and festival representatives from 40 countries, and more than 1,100 journalists from 39 countries). Events include the Official Competitive section, Zabaltegi, with its 90,000 cash award, Altadis-New Directors, Horizontes Latinos and meticulous retrospectives. In partnership with the Rencontres Cinémas Amérique Latine in Toulouse, the Films in Progress industry platform aims to aid the completion of six Latin American and two Spanish projects. *Inquiries to:* San Sebastián International Film Festival, Apartado de Correos 397, 20080 Donostia, San Sebastian 20080, Spain. Tel: (34 943) 481 212. Fax: 481 218. e: ssiff@sansebastianfestival.com. Web: www.sansebastianfestival.com.

AWARDS 2005

Golden Shell for Best Film: **Something Like Happiness** (Czech Republic/Germany), Bohdan Sláma.
Special Jury Award: **Iluminados por el fuego** (Argentina), Tristán Bauer.
Silver Shell for Best Director: Zhang Yang, **Sunflower** (China).
Silver Shell for Best Actress: Ana Geislerová, **Something Like Happiness**.
Silver Shell for Best Actor: Juan José Ballesta,

7 Virgins (Spain).
Jury Award for Best Photography: Jong Lin,
Sunflower (China).
Jury Award for Best Screenplay: Wolfgang
Kohlhasse, **Summer in Berlin** (Germany).

Santa Barbara
February 2007

Established in 1986 in the glamorous seaside
resort 90 minutes north of LA, Santa Barbara
International Film Festival has received
worldwide recognition for its diverse
programming. A jury of industry professionals
selects winners in several categories, including
Best US Feature, Best Foreign Feature, Best
Director, Best Documentary Feature and Best
Short. *Inquiries to:* SBIFF, 1528 Chapala Street
203, Santa Barbara, CA 93101, USA.
Tel: (1 805) 963 0023. Fax: 962 2524.
e:info@sbfilmfestival.org.
Web: www.sbfilmfestival.org.

AWARDS 2005
The American Spirit Award: **Mail Order Wife**
(USA), Andrew Gurland and Huck Botko.
Best International Feature: **Deadlines** (France),
Michael Lerner and Ludi Boeken.
*Special Jury Award for Best Actor in an
International Film:* Bruno Ganz.
*Special Jury Award for Best Actress in an
International Film:* Sibell Kekilli.
Special Jury Award for Cinematic Originality:
Alone Across Australia (Australia), Jon Muir.
*Nueva Vision Award for Best Spanish or Latin
American Film:* **The Other Side of the Street**
(Brazil/France), Marcos Bernstein.
Best Documentary Film: **A Hard Straight** (USA),
Goro Toshima.
Fund for Santa Barbara Social Justice Award:
Homeland: Four Portraits of Native Action
(USA), Roberta Grossman.

Sarasota
March 31-April 9, 2006

Ten days of independent film, symposiums and
events in a beautiful location; hospitable, inquisitive
audiences plus a well-organised and publicised
programme. *Inquiries to:* Tracy Kelley, Marketing

Director, Sarasota Film Festival, 635 S Orange
Ave, Suite 10B, Sarasota, Florida 34236, USA.
Tel: (1 941) 364 9514. Fax: 364 8411.
e: info@sarasotafilmfestival.com.
Web: www.sarasotafilmfestival.com.

Seattle International Film Festival
May 25-June 18, 2006

One of the largest festivals in the US, Seattle
presents more than 220 features, 50
documentaries and 100 shorts. There are cash
prizes for the juried New Directors Competition,
New American Cinema Competition,
Documentary Competition, Short Film: Live
Action, Short Film: Documentary and Short Film:
Animation. Also: Contemporary World Cinema,
Emerging Masters, Asian Tradewinds, Women in
Cinema, Tributes, New Pioneers and Archival
Films. *Inquiries to:* Seattle International Film
Festival, 400 Ninth Avenue North, Seattle, WA
98109, USA.
Tel: (1 206) 464 5830. Fax: 264 7919.
e: info@seattlefilm.com.
Web: www.seattlefilm.com.

Report 2005
The festival continued to break box-office
records, with an audience exceeding 150,000,
including such eminent Seattleites as Microsoft's
Bill Gates, Eddie Vedder of Pearl Jam and Ann
Wilson of Heart. The festival closed with the
North American premiere of Gus Van Sant's Last

*Peter Sarsgaard, Maggie Gyllenhaal, Festival Director
Helen Loveridge and Artistic Director Carl Spence at
Seattle 2005*

Days. Peter Sarsgaard received an award for Outstanding Achievement in Acting and the festival honoured Joan Allen with a special award created by glass artist Dale Chihuly.
– **Beth Barrett**, Programming Coordinator.

seattle international film festival
May 25 - June 18, 2006   www.seattlefilm.org

Seville Film Festival
November 2006

The Sevilla Festival de Cine presents the best of European and contemporary cinema, with a Competition for European features and documentaries, plus a panorama of films produced with Eurimages support, and a non-competitive section for European shorts. Sixth edition in 2006. Registration deadline: mid-Sept. *Inquiries to:* Seville Film Festival, Pabellón de Portugal, Avenida Cid 1, 41004 Seville, Spain.
Tel: (34 954) 297 833. Fax: 297 844.
e: prensa@festivaldesevilla.com.
Web: www.festivaldesevilla.com

Singapore International Film Festival
April 2006

Founded in 1987, SIFF is one of the leading festivals in Southeast Asia. Some 300 films from more than 40 countries are shown to 50,000 viewers through the main, fringe and special programmes and retrospectives. Fringe screenings are free and begin a week before the main programme. The festival,s Asian focus and film selection attract programmers from all over the world. The Silver Screen Awards honour the best in Asian cinema, including the unique, combined NETPAC/FIPRESCI prize, co-ordinated by the Network for Promotion of Asian Cinema and the International Federation of Film Critics. *Inquiries to:* Singapore International Film Festival, 45A Keong Saik Rd, Singapore 089149, Singapore.
Tel: (65) 6738 7567. Fax: 6738 7578.
e: filmfest@pacific.net.sg. Web: www.filmfest.org.sg.

Sitges International Film Festival of Catalonia
October 2006

Now approaching its 39th edition in a pleasant town on the Catalan coast, 30 kilometres from Barcelona, Sitges focuses on fantasy films and is considered one of Europe's leading specialised festivals, but is also open to new trends. The one official category, "Fantàstic", brings together the year's best genre productions. Other wide-reaching categories include Gran Angular (contemporary cinema with a language of its own), Orient Express (Asian genre films), Anima't (animation), Seven Chances (seven discoveries made by film critics), Audiovisual Català (Catalan productions) and Retrospectives. Sitges 2006 will be commemorating the 20th anniversary of the festival's screening of David Lynch's *Blue Velvet*. *Inquiries to:* Sitges Festival Internacional de Cinema de Catalunya, Avenida Josep Tarradellas, 135 Esc A 3r 2a, 08029 Barcelona, Spain.
Tel: (34 93) 419 3635. Fax: 439 7380.
e: info@cinema.sitges.com.
Web: www.sitges.com/cinema.

Sithengi, Film & TV Market/ Part of the Cape Town World Cinema Festival (CTWCF).
November 17-26, 2006

The year 2005 marked the tenth Anniversary of the Sithengi Film & TV Market. The Market is the business component of the CTWCF and is aimed at industry professionals, "talent" and aspirants. The Market components are the Product Market (Product Library; Market Screenings and Exhibition Centre); Co-production Forums; Documentary Co-production Forum; Feature Film Co-production Forum; Writers' Forum; Talent Campus; and Conferences. Inquiries to: Sithengi, PO Box 52120, Waterfront 8002, Cape Town, South Africa.
Tel: (27 21) 430 8160. Fax: 430 8186.
e: info@sithengi.co.za.
Web: www.sithengi.co.za.

Solothurn Film Festival
January 22-28, 2007

Being the most important forum for Swiss film-making, Solothurn is a popular rendezvous. For 40 years, it has been the place to see the results of Swiss film production, to make discoveries and form opinions. A selection of films and videos by Swiss authors and foreign authors residing in Switzerland is on the programme, but also co-productions between Switzerland and other countries. A retrospective of prominent film-makers or actors refreshes memories of Swiss cinema history. Young talent can be discovered in the film school section. Screenings are accompanied by a variety of daily round-table discussions and seminars. The presentation of the Swiss Film Prizes guarantees an atmosphere of suspense and the appearance of well-known faces. *Inquiries to:* Solothurn Film Festival, Postfach 1564, CH-4502 Solothurn, Switzerland.
Tel: (41 32) 625 8080. Fax: 623 6410.
e: info@solothurnerfilmtage.ch.
Web: www.solothurnerfilmtage.ch.

Report 2005
The 40th edition welcomed 1,200 Swiss professionals and 140 guests from 25 countries. A total of 257 films and videos were presented to 44,000 spectators; 179 Swiss films were shown in the main programme, 78 international films/videos in different special programmes. The retrospective was dedicated to the actor Bruno Ganz. Another special programme presented a selection of recent films from former Yugoslavia. The Swiss Film Prize for the best fiction film went to *Tout un hiver sans feu*, by Greg Zglinski, and the best documentary was *Accordion Tribe*, by Stefan Schwietert.
– **Ivo Kummer**, Festival Director.

42nd Solothurn Film Festival
January 22 – 28 2007   www.solothurnfilmfestival.ch

Stockholm
November 16-26, 2006

The Stockholm International Film Festival will this year celebrate its 17th anniversary as one of Europe's leading cinema events. Recognised by FIAPF and hosting a FIPRESCI jury, it is also a member of the European Coordination of Film Festivals. The festival welcomes 85,000 visitors, more than 500 accredited media and business representatives and more than 80 international guests every year. In 2005, some 160 films from 40 different countries were presented. Oliver Stone, David Cronenberg, Park Chan-wook, Ang Lee and Lauren Bacall are some of the last few years more distinguished guests. Some 200 films have gained distribution in connection with the festival, which recently launched the distribution company Edge Entertainment and introduced the Scandinavian audience to films by directors such as François Ozon, Gaspar Noé and David Gordon Green. *Inquiries to:* Stockholm International Film Festival, PO Box 3136, S-103 62 Stockholm, Sweden. Tel: (46 8) 677 5000. Fax: (46 8) 200 590. e: info@stockholmfilmfestival.se. Web: www.stockholmfilmfestival.se.

AWARDS 2005
Film: **Nordeste** (Argentina/France), Juan Diego Solanas.
First Feature: **Me and You and Everyone We Know** (USA), Miranda July.
Short Film: **Sons of Tû – The God of War** (New Zealand), Taika Waititi.
Actress: Carole Bouquet and Aymará Rovera, **Nordeste** (France).
Actor: Vincent d'Onofrio, **Thumbsucker** (USA).
Screenplay: Annie Griffin, **Festival** (UK).
Cinematography: Adrian Tan, **Be with Me** (Singapore).
Lifetime Achievement: David Cronenberg.
Visionary Award: Terry Gilliam.
Audience Award: **Storm** (Sweden), Björn Stein and Måns Mårlind.
FIPRESCI Award for Best Film: **Be with Me** (Singapore), Eric Khoo.
FIPRESCI Award Northern Light: **Accused** (Denmark), Jacob Thuesen.

Sundance Film Festival
January 18-28, 2007

Long known as a celebration of the new and unexpected, Sundance puts forward the best in independent film from the US and around the world: 125 feature films and 80 shorts. The critically acclaimed Independent Feature Film Competition and the World Cinema Competition present features and documentaries, and competition films are combined with nightly premieres of works by veteran film artists. There are also archive gems by early independent film-makers, animation of every kind, cutting edge experimental works, midnight cult films, and a jam packed schedule of panel discussions. *Inquiries to:* Geoffrey Gilmore, Director, Festival Programming Department, Sundance Institute, 8530 Wilshire Blvd, 3rd Floor, Beverly Hills, CA 90211-3114, USA. Tel: (1 310) 360 1981. Fax: 360 1969. e: institute@sundance.org. Web: www.sundance.org.

AWARDS 2005
Grand Jury Prize (Documentary): **Why We Fight** (USA), Eugene Jarecki.
Grand Jury Prize (Dramatic): **40 Shades of Blue** (USA), Ira Sachs.
Audience Award (Documentary): **Murderball** (USA), Henry Alex Rubin and Dana Adam Shapiro.
Audience Award (Dramatic): **Hustle & Flow** (USA), Craig Brewer.
World Grand Jury Prize (Documentary): **Shape of the Moon** (The Netherlands), Leonard Retel Helmrick.
World Grand Jury Prize (Dramatic): **The Hero** (Angola/France/Portugal), Zeze Ganboa.
World Audience Award (Documentary): **Shake Hands with the Devil: The Journey of Romeo Dallaire** (Canada), Peter Raymont.
World Audience Award (Dramatic): **Brothers** (Denmark), Susanne Bier.

Tampere
March 8-12, 2006

This is the 36th year of one of the world's leading short film festivals. Famous for its international sauna party, it attracts entries from

more than 60 countries. The 850 professionals and nearly 30,000 spectators can see 500-plus shorts in some 100 screenings: international competition (with a Grand Prix and other awards); international retrospectives and tributes; training seminars for professionals. The market includes shorts and documentaries from. *Inquiries to:* Tampere Film Festival, PO Box 305, 33101 Tampere, Finland.
Tel: (358 3) 213 0034. Fax: 223 0121.
e: office@tamperefilmfestival.fi.
Web: www.tamperefilmfestival.fi.

Telluride
September 1-4, 2006

Each Labor Day weekend, Telluride triples in size. More than 5,000 passionate film enthusiasts flood the town for four days of total cinematic immersion. This is a unique, friendly gathering in a historic mining town, spectacularly located in the mountains of Colorado. Telluride remains one of the world's most influential festivals, as famous directors, players and critics descend on the Sheridan Opera House and other theatres. The dedication of organisers and participants to

cinema gives Telluride a sincere, authentic feel – not forgetting the "surprise" element: the programme is only announced on the first day. There are several tributes each year (Laura Linney, Theo Angelopoulos and Jean-Claude Carrière in 2004; Mickey Rooney, Charlotte Rampling, and the Dardenne brothers in 2005). Each year one of the world's great film lovers is invited to collaborate on the festivals programming; past Guest Directors include Salman Rushdie, Stephen Sondheim, and in 2005, author Don Delillo.
Inquiries to: The Telluride Film Festival, 379 State St, Portsmouth, NH 03801, USA.
Tel: (1 603) 433 9202. Fax: 433 9206.
e: mail@telluridefilmfestival.org.
Web: www.telluridefilmfestival.org.

Thessaloniki International Film Festival
November 2006
Thessaloniki Documentary Festival
March 10-19, 2006

In its 47th year, the oldest and one of the most important film events in south eastern Europe targets a new generation of film-makers as well as independent films by established directors.

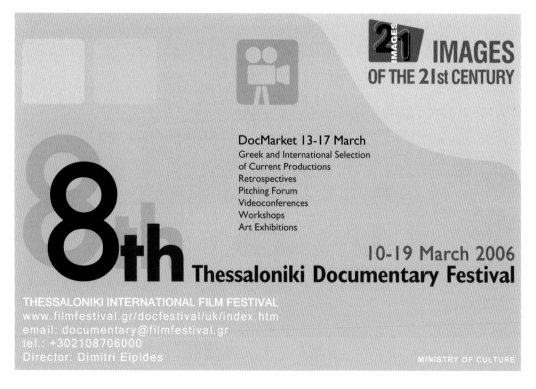

21 IMAGES
IMAGES
OF THE 21st CENTURY

DocMarket 13-17 March
Greek and International Selection of Current Productions
Retrospectives
Pitching Forum
Videoconferences
Workshops
Art Exhibitions

8th
10-19 March 2006
Thessaloniki Documentary Festival

THESSALONIKI INTERNATIONAL FILM FESTIVAL
www.filmfestival.gr/docfestival/uk/index.htm
email: documentary@filmfestival.gr
tel.: +302108706000
Director: Dimitri Eipides

MINISTRY OF CULTURE

The International Competition (for first or second features) awards the Golden Alexander (€37,000) and the Silver Alexander (€22,000). Other sections include Greek Film Panorama, retrospectives, Balkan Survey, the new informative section Independence Days, plus masterclasses, galas and exhibitions.

The Thessaloniki Documentary Festival – Images of the 21st Century is Greece's major annual non-fiction film event. Its sections include "Views of the World" (subjects of social interest), "Portraits – Human Journeys" (highlighting the human contribution to cultural, social and historical developments) and "Recording of Memory" (facts and testimony of social and historic origin). The festival also hosts the International Documentary Market. *Inquiries to:* Thessaloniki International Film Festival, 9 Alexandras Ave, 114 73 Athens, Greece. Tel: (30 210) 870 6000. Fax: 644 8143. e: info@filmfestival.gr. Web: www.filmfestival.gr. Director: Despina Mouzaki. *Inquiries to:* Thessaloniki Documentary Festival (address and Tel/Fax numbers as above). Director: Dimitri Eipides. e: eipides-newhorizons@filmfestival.gr.

Tokyo International Film Festival
October 2006

Major competitive international event; cash prize of $100,000 awarded for the Tokyo Grand Prix and $20,000 for the Special Jury Prize. Other sections include: Special Screenings, Winds of Asia and Japanese Eyes. Chairman: Tsuguhiko Kadokawa. *Inquiries to:* Tokyo International Film Festival, 5F Tsukiji Yasuda Building, 2-15-14 Tsukiji Chuo-ku, Tokyo 104-0045, Japan. Tel: (81 3) 3524 1081. Fax: 3524 1087. e: info@tiff-jp.net. Web: www.tiff-jp.net.

Torino Film Festival
November 2006

Dubbed second only to Venice on the crowded Italian festival circuit, and known for its discoveries as well as for its unique retrospectives, Torino constitutes a meeting point for contemporary international cinema. The festival pays particular attention to emerging cinemas and film-makers and promotes awareness of new directors whose work is marked by strong formal and stylistic

research. Its programme includes competitive sections for international features, Italian documentaries and Italian shorts, as well as spotlights and premieres. *Inquiries to:* Torino Film Festival,
Via Monte di Pietà 1, 10121 Torino, Italy.
Tel: (39 011) 562 3309 Fax: 562 9796.
e: info@torinofilmfest.org.
Web: www.torinofilmfest.org.

Toronto International Film Festival
September 7-16, 2006

The Toronto International Film Festival is one of the most successful public festivals in the world and a must-attend event for the public, industry, and press alike. It remains committed to supporting Canadian film-makers and showcasing the best in global film. *Inquiries to:* Toronto International Film Festival, 2 Carlton St, 16th Floor, Toronto, Ontario, M5B 1J3, Canada.
Tel: (1 416) 967 7371. Fax: 967 3595.
e: tiffg@torfilmfest.ca. Web: www.e.bell.ca/filmfest.

Tribeca Film Festival
April 25-May 7, 2006

The first Tribeca Film Festival was held in May 2002, having been assembled in only four months by a group headed by Robert De Niro, Jane Rosenthal and Craig Hatkoff, with the invaluable support of Martin Scorsese. Its goal was the spiritual and economic revitalization of lower Manhattan after the devastating events of 9/11. The upcoming 5th edition will continue to present competitions with cash prizes totalling more than $100,000, open to feature-length narrative features and documentaries made anywhere in the world, to short films by both professionals and students, and to NY-produced films of any length, as well as out-of-competition screenings of films that may have screened elsewhere, of new restorations and rediscoveries, and of films for a family audience. *Inquiries to:* Peter Scarlet, 375 Greenwich St, New York, NY 10013, USA.
Tel: (1 212) 941 2400. Fax: 941 3939.
e: festival@tribecafilmfestival.org.
Web: www.tribecafilmfestival.org.

AWARDS 2005
Best Narrative Feature: **Stolen Life** (China), Li Shao Hong.
Best Narrative Filmmaker: Alicia Scherson, **Play** (Argentina/Chile).
Best Documentary Feature: **El Perro Negro: Stories from the Spanish Civil War** (Hungary/Netherlands), Peter Forgacs.
Best New Documentary Film-makers: Jeff Zimbalist and Matt Mochary, **Favela Rising** (Brazil/USA).
Best Actress in a Narrative Feature: Felicity Huffman, **Transamerica** (USA).
Best Actor in a Narrative Feature: Cees Geel, **Simon** (Netherlands).
Best Narrative Feature Made in New York: **Red Doors** (USA), Georgia Lee.
Best Documentary Feature Made in New York: **Rikers High** (France/USA), Victor Buhler.
Audience Award: **Street Fight** (USA), Marshall Curry.
Best Family Short (Kid's Jury): **Spandex: A Father's Tale** (USA), Matthew Manson.
Best Narrative Short: **Cashback** (UK), Sean Ellis.
Best Documentary Short: **The Life of Kevin Carter** (USA), Dan Krauss.
Best Student Short: **Dance Mania Fantastic** (USA), Sasie Sealy.

Report 2005
More than 150 features and 100 shorts from 45 countries were screened, to a total audience of over 250,000. The festival featured panels on the film-making, the business of film, politics and film, and intimate conversations with established film-makers; special events such as art exhibits of acclaimed New York artists, drive-in screenings of both premieres and classic films, gala premieres, the ASCAP Music Lounge and the Family Festival.
– **Casey Baltes**, Assistant to the Executive Director.

Tromsø International Film Festival
January 16-21, 2007

The world's northernmost film festival is also Norway's best attended, with 42,000 admissions in 2005. Tromsø is known for presenting the best of current international art cinema,

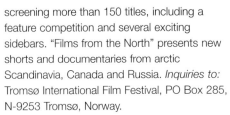

Welcome to Tromsø International Film Festival, Norway

January 16th – 21st 2007

The world's northernmost film festival invites you to an exotic week in the polar night and a cutting edge selection of fresh quality feature films.

screening more than 150 titles, including a feature competition and several exciting sidebars. "Films from the North" presents new shorts and documentaries from arctic Scandinavia, Canada and Russia. *Inquiries to:* Tromsø International Film Festival, PO Box 285, N-9253 Tromsø, Norway. Tel: (47) 7775 3090. Fax: 7775 3099. e: filmfestival@tiff.no. Web: www.tiff.no.

AWARDS 2005
Norwegian Peace Film Award: **Beautiful City** (Iran), Asghar Fahadi.
Aurora Prize: **Turtles Can Fly** (Iran/Iraq), Bahman Ghobadi.
FIPRESCI Prize: **Midwinter Night's Dream** (Yugoslavia), Goran Paskaljevic.
Don Quijote: **Le Regard** (Norway), Nour-Eddine Lakhmari.
Tromsø Palm: **Fragile** (Sweden), Jens Jonsson.
Audience Award: **As It Is In Heaven** (Sweden), Kaj Pollack.

Report 2005
Attendance records were once again broken at the 15th festival, confirming its status as the largest audience festival in Norway, with almost 42,000 admissions. The programme

offered the best of current international arthouse features in addition to shorts and documentaries from the circumpolar North. Guest Mike Leigh met the audience to discuss his work, as did Kurdish film-maker Bahman Ghobadi, awarded the main prize, for *Turtles Can Fly*.
– **Martha Otte**, Festival Director.

Umeå
September 14-20, 2006

Umeå International Film Festival, now in its 21st year, is a competitive event screening around 100 features and 100 shorts. It has considerable standing as a gateway for distribution in Sweden and the Nordic countries and is the largest film festival in northern Scandinavia. The lively programme includes an international competitive panorama, innovative shorts, Swedish and Nordic documentaries, seminars, workshops and special guests. The popular "Camera Obscura" section includes obscure films and restored or neglected classics. In 2005 the festival presented a Japanese theme showcasing the best in Japanese features and short films. Artistic Director: Thom Palmen.

21st Umeå International Film Festival
14 - 20 September 2006
Umeå, Sweden

www.filmfest.se

Masako Kurihara, director, Kousuke Sakoda, director, and Arata Ito, producer, at Umeå 2005

Inquiries to: Umeå International Film Festival, Box 43, S-901 02 Umeå, Sweden.
Tel: (46 90) 133 388. Fax: 777 961.
e: info@ff.umea.com. Web: www.ff.umea.com.

AWARDS 2005
Best National Short Film
Filmblick Award: **Time Out**, Jorgen Bergmark.
Young Filmblick Award: **Julia**, Daniel Wirtberg.

Valencia International Film Festival – Mediterranean Cinema
October 2006

Launched in 1980 and organised by the Valencia Municipal Film Foundation, the Valencia Mostra/Cinema del Mediterrani aims to promote greater understanding among people and culture in the Mediterranean area, stressing its historical roots by showing high-quality films that contribute to a better critical awareness of each country's film industry and art. *Inquiries to:* Valencia Mostra/Cinema del Mediterrani, Plaza de Arzobispo 2, 46003 Valencia, Spain.

Tel: (34 96) 392 1506. Fax: 391 5156.
e: festival@mostravalencia.com.
Web: www.mostravalencia.org.

Valladolid
October 20-28, 2006

Valladolid moves on to its 51st edition. One of Spain's key events, the festival spotlights the latest work by established directors and newcomers. Competitive for features, shorts and documentaries. Also offers retrospectives, a selection of recent Spanish productions and a congress of new Spanish directors. *Inquiries to:* Valladolid International Film Festival Office, Teatro Calderón, Calle Leopoldo Cano, s/n 4ª Planta, 47003 Valladolid, Spain.
Tel: (34 983) 426 460. Fax: 426 461.
e:festvalladolid@seminci.com.
Web: www.seminci.com.

AWARDS 2005
International Jury Awards
Prix UIP Valladolid: **Vincent** (Germany), Giulio Ricciarelli.
Golden Spike for Short Film: **Don't Say a Word** (Australia), Marek Blaha.
Silver Spike for Short Film: **9.20am** (Mexico), Roberto Aguilera.
50th Anniversary Prize: **The Mysterious Geographic Explorations of Jasper Morello** (Australia), Anthony Lucas.
Best Director of Photography Award to: **Mongolian Ping Pong** (China), Hao Ning.
Actress: Krystyna Feldman, **My Nikifor** (Poland), Krzysztof Krauze.
Actor: Melvil Poupaud, **Time to Leave** (France), François Ozon.
Pilar Miró Prize for Best New Director: Daniel

Cebrián, **Second Round** (Spain).
Golden Spike for Feature Film: **In Bed**
(Chile/Germany), Matías Bize.
Silver Spike for Feature Film: **Time to Leave**.
50th Anniversary Prize: **Manderlay**
(Denmark/France/Germany/The Netherlands/
Sweden/USA) Lars von Trier; **Hidden**
(Austria/France/Germany/Italy), Michael Haneke.

Vancouver
September 28-October 13, 2006

Now in its 25th year, this festival has grown into
an event of considerable stature. Approximately
150,000 people attend more than 300
international films. Vancouver also hosts an
Annual Film & Television Trade Forum. *Inquiries
to:* Alan Franey, 1181 Seymour St, Vancouver,
British Columbia, Canada V6B 3M7.
Tel: (1 604) 685 0260. Fax: 688 8221.
e: viff@viff.org. Web: www.viff.org.

AWARDS 2005
Audience Awards
*People's Choice for Most Popular International
Film:* **Live and Become** (France/Israel),
Rahu Mihaileanu.
*Federal Express Award for the Most Popular
Canadian Feature:* **Eve and the Fire Horse**
(British Columbia), Julia Kwan.
*National Film Board Award for Best
Documentary Feature:* **A Particular Silence**
(Italy), Stefano Rulli.
Dragons and Tigers Award for Young Cinema:
Ox Hide (China), Liu Jiayin.
City TV Western Canada Feature Film Award:
Lucid (USA), Sean Garrity.
*Bravo! Fact Award for Best Young Western
Canadian Director of a Short Film:* Jamie Travis
for **Patterns**.
*Women in Film and Video Vancouver's Artistic
Merit Award:* Carly Pope for **The Hamster**.
Trade Forum One-Minute Motion Picture Contest:
Maryam Najafi and Nima Soofi for **La casa**.

Venice
Early September 2006

Under Marco Müller's trendy regime, the 63-year-
old Mostra d'Arte Cinematografica is trying to
overcome problems such as its old-fashioned
facilities on expensive Lido Island, a vanishing
market and heavy political interference.
Retrospectives, tributes and parties galore, plus
exquisite art exhibitions around downtown Venice,
make a visit here essential, especially if you need
to meet Italian business partners. Dante Ferretti
was president of the 2005 jury, alongside Edgar
Reitz, Amos Gitai and Christine Vachon. Stefania
Sandrelli and Hayao Miyazaki received Golden
Lion Career Awards. The independently run
'Venice Days' (www.venice-days.com) are growing
into an alternative festival. *Inquiries to:* La Biennale
di Venezia, San Marco, 1364, Cà Giustinian,
30124 Venice, Italy.
Tel (39 041) 521 8711. Fax: 521 8810.
e: ufficiostampa@labiennale.org.
Web: www.labiennale.org/en/cinema.

AWARDS 2005
Golden Lion for Best Film: **Brokeback
Mountain** (USA), Ang Lee.
Grand Jury Prize: **Mary** (France/Italy/USA),
Abel Ferrara.
Best Direction: **Les amants réguliers** (France),
Philippe Garrel.
Coppa Volpi for Best Actor: David Strathairn,
Good Night, and Good Luck.
Coppa Volpi for Best Actress: Giovanna
Mezzogiorno, **La bestia nel cuore**.

Victoria Independent Film &
Video Festival
Late January-early February 2007

From the mainstream to the original, the festival
offers up the finest contemporary international
independent cinema. It has a strong interest in
putting programmers, media and industry
professionals together with emerging film-
makers and is dedicated to raising awareness of
film and its artistic insights. Set in beautiful
Victoria, it includes a film forum, new media
event, discussions, family day, lectures and a
film-related art exhibition. Trigger Points Pacific
Co-Production Conference brings together
producers and funders to help make projects
happen. *Inquiries to:* Victoria Independent Film &
Video Festival, 808 View St, Victoria, British
Columbia, V8W 1K2, Canada.

Tel: (1 250) 389 0444. Fax: 389 0406.
e: festival@vifvf.com. Web: www.vifvf.com.

AWARDS 2005
Star! TV Award for Best Feature: **Two Great Sheep** (China), Liu Hao.
Famous Players Award for Best Canadian Feature: **White Skin** (Quebec), Daniel Roby.
Best Short: **Milo 55160** (Canada), David Ostry.
Best Short Animation: **Ryan** (Ontario, Canada), Chris Landreth.
Audience Favourite: **Being Cariboo** (British Columbia, Canada), Leanne Allison and Diana Wilson.
CBC Newsworld Award for Best Documentary: **Sneakers** (Netherlands), Femke Wolting.
InVision Award for Best Student Film: **Tahara** (Egypt/USA), Sarah Rahsad.
CHUM Television Award for Best Canadian First Feature: **Jimmywork** (Quebec, Canada), Simon Sauve.

Report 2005
The 11th festival opened with Simone Sauve's award-winning *Jimmywork*. Featuring more than 175 features and shorts in all kinds of genres,

the festival drew more than 14,000 visitors. Legendary DoPs Laszlo Kovacs (*Easy Rider*) and William Fraker (*Jaws*) taught a highly informative session at the Film Forum. Interactive Futures continued to bring new media artists in from to think, show and see technology. At the inaugural Trigger Points Pacific Co-Production Conference, 28 producers met 19 broadcasters, distributors, funders and acquisitions executives from all around the Pacific Rim.
– **Kathy Kay**, Festival Director.

**VIENNALE –
Vienna International Film Festival**
October 13-25, 2006

The VIENNALE is Austria's most important international film event, as well as being one of the oldest and best-known festivals in the German-

ViENNALE

VIENNA INTERNATIONAL FILM FESTIVAL

OCTOBER 13–25, 2006

www.viennale.at

speaking world. It takes place in beautiful cinemas in Vienna's historic centre, providing a festival with an international orientation and a distinctive urban flair. A high percentage of the approximately 86,000 visitors to the festival are a decidedly young audience. In its main programme, the VIENNALE shows a carefully picked selection of new films from all over the globe as well as new films from Austria. The choice of films offers a cross section of bold film-making that stands apart from the aesthetics of mainstream conventionality and is politically relevant. Aside from its focus on the newest feature films of every genre and form imaginable, the festival gives particular attention to documentaries, international shorts, experimental works and crossover films. The VIENNALE receives international acclaim for its annual, large-scale historical retrospectives, in collaboration with the Austrian Film Museum, plus numerous special programmes and tributes to prominent personalities and institutions. *Inquiries to:* Siebensterngasse 2, 1070 Vienna, Austria. Tel: (43 1) 526 5947. Fax: 523 4172. e: office@viennale.at. Web: www.viennale.at.

Wellington International Film Festival
July 2006

Wellington launched its 34th annual programme of more than 140 features from more than 30 countries in 2005 with Michael Haneke's *Hidden*. The festival provides a non-competitive New Zealand premiere showcase and welcomes many international film-makers and musicians. Brimming with animation, arthouse, documentaries and retrospective programmes, this year's festival along with its 37-year-old Auckland sibling matched last year's record-breaking attendance. Festival Director: Bill Gosden. *Inquiries to*: Wellington Film Festival, Box 9544, Marion Square, Wellington 6037, New Zealand. Tel: (64 4) 385 0162. Fax: 801 7304. e: festival@nzff.co.nz. Web: www.nzff.co.nz.

WorldFest–Houston
April 21-30, 2006

The 39th WorldFest–Houston International Film Festival continues its totally dedicated independent film screening format and will screen around 60 feature premieres. There are special sidebars of Foreign, Children's and Family Film Sections. All 35mm and DVD films are screened at the AMC Meyer Park Theatre. Also includes Short Film Showcase, a special review of 100 new short and student films from the festival that gave early honours to Spielberg, Lucas, The Coen Brothers, Ridley Scott, Oliver Stone and Ang Lee, among many others. WorldFest offers more than $25,000 in cash grants and film and equipment awards, including the $2,500 Eastman Kodak Student Award. Deadline: mid-December. *Inquiries to:* WorldFest–Houston, PO Box 56566, Houston, TX 77256-6566, USA. Tel: (1 713) 965 9955. Fax: 965 9960. e: mail@worldfest.org. Web: www.worldfest.org.

AWARDS 2005
Best Feature Film: **Frontier Dream** (Japan), Tetsuya Matsushima.
Best Film & Video Production-Documentary: **The Biology of Prenatal Development, The Endowment for Human Development** (USA), Brian J Stillwell, MD.
Best Television & Cable Production: **The Question of God: Sigmund Freud & CS Lewis** (USA), Catherine Tatge.
Best Short Subject: **I Spy With My Little Eye** (Germany/USA), Mattias Emcke.
Best Music Video: **Super Troupers: Thirty Years of ABBA** (UK), Steve Cole.
Best TV Commercial: **Napkin** (USA), Baker Smith.
Best Student Production: **Natural Selection** (USA), Monte Zajicek.
Best Experimental: **Of Burning Hills** (Canada), Jason White.
Best Unproduced Screenplay: **The Seer** (USA), Kathleen Behun.
HP Crystal Vision Award for Feature Films: **The Civilization of Maxwell Bright** (USA), David Beaird.
HP Crystal Vision Award for Short Films: **Silent Warrior** (Germany), Alex Dierbach.
Eastman Kodak Cinematography Award: **Die Uberraschung** (Germany), Florian Deyle.

Other Festivals and Markets of Note

Alcalá de Henares/Comunidad de Madrid Film Festival, Plaza del Empecinado 1, 28801 Alcalá de Henares, Madrid, Spain. Tel: (34 91) 879 7380. Fax: 879 7381. e: festival@alcine.org. Web: www.alcine.org. (*Competition for Spanish shorts, new directors and Madrid-made videos, plus international shorts and Spanish director sidebars – Nov 11-18, 2006.*)

Almería International Short Film Festival, Diputación de Almería, Departamento de Cultura y Juventud, Calle Navarro Rodrigo 17, 04071 Almeria, Spain. Tel: (34 950) 211 100. Fax: 211 547. e: coordinador@almeriaencorto.net. Web: www.almeriaencorto.net. (*Competition for international shorts – May/June.*)

Angelus Awards Student Film Festival, 7201 Sunset Blvd., Hollywood, CA 90046, USA. Tel: (1 323) 874 6635. Fax: 874 1168. e: info@angelus.org. Web: www.angelusawards.org. (*International competition honouring college level student films of uncommon artistic calibre that reflect compassion and respect for the human condition. Screening and awards ceremony held at the Directors' Guild of America, Hollywood – late Oct/early Nov.*)

Anima: The Brussels Animation Film Festival, Folioscope, Avenue de Stalingrad 52, B-1000 Brussels, Belgium. Tel: (32 2) 534 4125. Fax: 534 2279. e: info@folioscope.be. Web: www.awn.com/folioscope. (*Showcase for the newest, most interesting animation – Feb 24-March 5, 2006.*)

Animerte Dager, Fredrikstad Animation Festival, Kasernen Gamlebyen, Box 1405, N-1602 Fredrikstad, Norway. Tel: (47) 6930 6071. e: ad@animertedager.no. Web: www.animertedager.no. (*Nordic, Baltic and international animation, with retrospectives and student films. Competitive – Nov.*)

Ann Arbor Film Festival, PO Box 8232, Ann Arbor, MI 48107, USA. Tel: (1 734) 995 5356. Fax: 995 5396. e: info@aafilmfest.org. Web: www.aafilmfest.org. (*Experimental films from all over the world – March 21-26, 2006.*)

Annecy/International Animated Film Festival and International Animated Film Market (MIFA), Centre International du Cinéma d'Animation, 18 Avenue du Trésum, BP 399, 74013 Annecy Cedex, France. Tel: (33 4) 5010 0900. Fax: 5010 0970. e: info@annecy.org. Web: www.annecy.org. (*Long-established international and competitive festival with a useful sales/distribution market (MIFA) – Festival: June 5-10, 2006; MIFA: June 7-9, 2006.*)

Asian Film Festival, c/o Prabhat Chitra Mandal, Sharda Cinema Bldg, 1st Floor, Dadar, Mumbai 400 014, India. Tel: (91 22) 2413 1918. e: director@affmumbai.com. Web: www.affmumbai.com. (*Established in 2002, with the sole aim of propagating Asian film culture in India and creating an audience for Asian cinema. Full-length feature films only. Sections: Spectrum Asia, Focus on One Country, Award Winners, Seminars, Asian Film Culture Award, DVD Section, Competition of Diploma Films from Asian Film Schools. Entry form and other information available online – Oct 20-27, 2006.*)

Aspen Shortsfest & Filmfest, 110 E Hallam, Ste 102, Aspen, CO 81611, USA. Tel: (1 970) 925 6882. Fax: 925 1967. e: filmfest@aspenfilm.org. Web: www.aspenfilm.org. (*Shortsfest: Short subject competition – April 5-9, 2006; Filmfest: Feature-length invitational – Sept/Oct.*)

Atlantic Film Festival, PO Box 36139, Suite 220, 5600 Sackville St, Halifax, NS, B3J 3S9, Canada. Tel: (1 902) 422 3456. Fax: 422 4006. e: festival@atlanticfilm.com. Web: www.atlanticfilm.com. (*Film and video features, shorts, documentaries and animation;*

*also includes industry workshops and panels –
Sept 14-23, 2006.)*

Auckland International Film Festival, PO Box
9544, Marion Sq, Wellington 6037, New Zealand.
Tel: (64 4) 385 0162. Fax: 801 7304.
e: festival@nzff.co.nz. Web: www.nzff.co.nz.
*(The festival provides a non-competitive New
Zealand premiere showcase and welcomes
many international film-makers and musicians.
Twinned with the Wellington Film Festival – July.)*

Augsburg Children's Film Festival,
Filmbüro Augsburg, Schroeckstrasse 8, 86152
Augsburg, Germany. Tel: (49 821) 153 078.
Fax: 155 518. e: filmbuero@t-online.de.
Web: www. filmtage-augsburg.de. *(International
features for children – March 26-April 2, 2006.)*

Banff Mountain Film Festival, The Banff Centre
for Mountain Culture, Box 1020, Station 38,
Banff, AB, T1L 1H5, Canada.
Tel: (1 403) 762 6675. Fax: 762 6277.
e: cmc@banffcentre.ca.
Web: www.banffmountainfestivals.ca.
*(International competition for films and videos
related to mountains and the spirit of adventure –
Oct 28-Nov 5, 2006.)*

Bite the Mango Film Festival, National
Museum of Photography, Film & TV, Bradford,
BD1 1NQ, UK. Tel: (44 1274) 203311.
Fax: 394540. e: irfan.ajeeb@nmsi.ac.uk.
Web: www.bitethemango.org.uk. *(A celebration
of cultural cinema from China and Japan, to
Malaysia and Pakistan – Sept 22-28, 2006.)*

Bogotá Film Festival, Residencias
Tequendama, Centro Internacional Tequendama,
Bogotá, Colombia. Tel: (57 1) 341 7562.
Fax: 341 7504. e: direccion@bogocine.com.
Web: www.bogocine.com. *(Competitions for new
directors; feature films and documentaries –
Oct 4-12, 2006.)*

Boston Film Festival, 9B Hamilton Place,
Boston, MA 02108, USA. Tel: (1 617) 482 0200.
e: info@bostonfilmfestival.org. Web:
www.bostonfilmfestival.org. *(Approximately 50*

*films, including studio releases, American
independents, documentaries and shorts – Sept.)*

Bradford Animation Festival, National Museum
of Photography, Film & Television, Bradford, BD1
1NQ, UK. Tel: (44 1274) 203364. Fax: 394540.
e: lisa.kavanagh@nmsi.ac.uk.
Web: www.baf.org.uk. *(Industry-based animation
festival; masterclasses, seminars, workshops and
screenings with some of animation's top names.
Home to the BAF Awards, which open for entries
in March – Nov.)*

Bradford Film Festival, National Museum of
Photography, Film & TV, Bradford, BD1 1NQ,
UK. Festival Director: Tony Earnshaw.
Tel: (44 1274) 203 320. Fax: 394 540.
e: tony.earnshaw@nmsi.ac.uk.
Web: www.bradfordfilmfestival.org.uk. *(Includes
the BFF Lifetime Achievement Award, director
showcase, Screentalk interviews and
Masterclasses, retrospectives and the
Widescreen Weekend – March 3-18, 2006.)*

British Silent Cinema, Broadway, 14-18 Broad
St, Nottingham, NG1 3AL, UK. Tel: (44 115) 952
6600. Fax: 952 6622. e: laraine@broadway.org.uk.
Web: www.britishsilentcinema.co.uk. *(Screenings
and presentations – April.)*

**Brussels International Festival of Fantastic
Film,** 8 Rue de la Comtesse de Flandre 1020
Brussels, Belgium. Tel: (32 2) 201 1713.
Fax: 201 1469. e: info@bifff.org. Web: www.bifff.org.
*(Competitive international and European selection
for shorts and features. Special side events
include the International Body Painting contest –
March 10-25, 2006.)*

**Cph:Dox – Copenhagen International
Documentary Festival,** Store Kannikestraede 6,
1169 Copenhagen K, Denmark. Tel: (45) 3312
0005. Fax: 3312 7505. e: info@cphdox.dk. Web:
www.cphdox.dk. Producer: Niels Lind Larsen.
Programmer: Tine Fischer. *(early Nov.)*

Cairo International Film Festival, 17 Kasr el
Nile St, Cairo, Egypt. Tel: (20 2) 392 3562.
Fax: 393 8979. e: info@cairointernationalfilmfest.com.

Web: www.cairofilmfest.com. (*Organized by the General Union of Arab Artists. Competitive – late Nov-early Dec.*)

Cambridge Film Festival, Cambridge Arts Picturehouse, 38-39 St Andrew's Street, Cambridge CB2 3AR, UK. Tel: (44) 1223 500 082. Fax: 462 555. Web: www.cambridgefilmfest.org.uk (*Heading for its 26th edition, a leading non-competitive UK showcase for British, American and world cinema, including Retrospectives and Revivals, Documentary; based at the three-screen Arts Picturehouse – mid-July 2006*).

Camerimage, Rynek Nowomiejski 28, 87-100 Torun, Poland. Tel: (48 56) 621 0019. Fax: 652 2197. e: office@camerimage.pl. Web: www.camerimage.pl. (*Competition, Special Screenings, William Fraker's Retrospective, Student Festival, World Panorama Retrospective, seminars, workshops, press conferences, exhibitions – late Nov-early Dec.*)

Cartoons on the Bay, Rai Trade, Via Umberto Novaro 18, 00195 Rome, Italy. Tel: (39 06) 3749 8315. Fax: 3751 5631. e: cartoonsbay@raitrade.it. Web: www.cartoonsbay.com. (*International Festival and Conference on television animation, organised by RAI Trade – April.*)

Chicago International Children's Film Festival, Facets Mulimedia, 1517 W Fullerton, Chicago, IL 60614, USA. Tel: (1 773) 281 9075. Fax: 929 0266. e: kidsfest@facets.org. Web: www.cicff.org. (*Largest and oldest festival of children's films in US – Oct 26-Nov 5, 2006.*)

Chicago Latino Film Festival, International Latino Cultural Center of Chicago, c/o Columbia College Chicago, 600 S Michigan Ave, Chicago, IL 60605-1996, USA. Tel: (1 312) 431 1330. Fax: 344 8030. e: info@latinoculturalcenter.org. Web: www.latinoculturalcenter.org. (*ILCC promotes awareness of Latino culture through the arts, including this festival – April 21-May 3, 2006.*)

Cinekid, Korte Leidsedwarstraat 12, 1017 RC Amsterdam, Netherlands. Tel: (31 20) 531 7890. Fax: 531 7899. e: info@cinekid.nl.

Web: www.cinekid.nl. (*International film, TV and new media festival for children and young people – Oct 21-29, 2006.*)

Cinema Jove International Film Festival, Calle La Safor 10, Despacho 5, 46015 Valencia, Spain. Tel: (34 96) 331 1047. Fax: 331 0805. e: programcinemajove@gva.es. Web: www.gva.es/cinemajove. Festival Director: Rafael Maluenda. (*Specialises in the work of young film-makers aged 35 and under and has a feature and short film international competition. Deadline for submission: April 15 – June 17-24, 2006.*)

Cinéma Méditerranéen Montpellier, 78 Avenue du Pirée, 34000 Montpellier, France. Tel: (33 4) 9913 7373. Fax: 9913 7374. e:info@cinemed.tm.fr. Web: www.cinemed.tm.fr. (*Competitive festival for fiction works by directors from the Mediterranean Basin, the Black Sea states, Portugal or Armenia. Categories: Feature, Short, Documentary, Panorama. Formats: 16mm, 35mm. Preview on VHS and DVD – Oct.*)

Cinéma Italien Rencontres D'Annecy, Bonlieu Scène Nationale, 1 rue Jean Jaures, BP 294, 74007 Annecy Cedex, France. Tel: (33 450) 334 400. Fax: 518 209. e: com@annecycinemaitalien.com. Web: www.annecycinemaitalien.com. (*Feature films from Italy, with tributes and retrospectives. Competitive – early Oct.*)

Cinemagic World Screen Festival for Young People, 49 Botanic Avenue, Belfast, BT7 1JL, Northern Ireland. Tel: (44 28) 9031 1900. Fax: 9031 9709. e: joan@cinemagic.org.uk. Web: www.cinemagic.org.uk. (*Children's films in competition, screenings and masterclasses – late Nov/early Dec.*)

Cinemayaat (Arab Film Festival), 2 Plaza Ave, San Francisco, CA 94116, USA. Tel (1 415) 564 1100. Fax: 564 2203. e: info@aff.org. Web: www.aff.org. (*Showcases works by independent film-makers that provide insightful and innovative perspectives on Arab people, culture, art, history and politics. Deadline for entries: April 16 – Sept.*)

Cinequest, PO Box 720040, San Jose, CA
95172-0040, USA. Tel: (1 408) 995 5033.
Fax: 995 5713. e: info@cinequest.org.
Web: www.cinequest.org. (*Maverick films, film-
makers and technologies. Competition for features,
documentaries and shorts, plus tributes, seminars,
entertainment – March 1-12, 2006.*)

Cleveland International Film Festival, 2510
Market Ave, Cleveland, OH 44113-3434, USA.
Tel: (1 216) 623 3456. Fax: 623 0103.
e: cfs@clevelandfilm.org.
Web: www.clevelandfilm.org. (*International
"World Tour" progamme with specials such as
family films, American independents and lesbian
and gay films – March 16-26, 2006.*)

Cognac International Thriller Film Festival,
Le Public Système Cinéma, 40, rue Anatole
France, 92594 Levallois-Perret Cedex, France.
Tel: (33 1) 4134 2033. Fax: 4134 2077.
e: kbeunel@le-public-systeme.fr.
Web: www.festival.cognac.fr. (*International
thrillers and "films noir"; competitive for features
and French-speaking shorts – April 6-9, 2006.*)

Cork Film Festival, Emmet House, Emmet
Place, Cork, Republic of Ireland.
Tel: (353 21) 427 1711 Fax: 427 5945.
e: info@corkfilmfest.org. Web: www.corkfilmfest.org.
(*Features, documentaries, competitive shorts,
animation, retrospectives, special programmes;
51st edition in 2006. Deadline: July – Oct.*)

**Cottbus Film Festival – Festival of East
European Cinema,** Werner-Seelenbinder-Ring
44/45, D-03048 Cottbus, Germany.
Tel: (49 355) 431 070. Fax: 4310 720.
e: info@filmfestivalcottbus.de.
Web: www.filmfestivalcottbus. (*International
festival of East European films: features and
shorts (competitive), children's and youth film,
spectrum, national hits – Nov.*)

Deauville Festival of American Film, Le Public
Système Cinéma, 40, rue Anatole France, 92594
Levallois-Perret Cedex, France. Tel: (33 1) 4134
2033. Fax: 4134 2077. e: jlasserre@le-public-
systeme.fr. Web: www.festival-deauville.com.

(*Showcase for US features and independent
films – Sept 1-10, 2006.*)

Deauville Festival of Asian Film, Le Public
Système Cinéma, 40, rue Anatole France,
92594 Levallois-Perret Cedex, France.
Tel: (33 1) 4134 2033. Fax: 4134 2077.
e: jlasserre@le-public-systeme.fr.
Web: www.festival-deauville.com. (*Showcase for
Asian feature films – March 8-12, 2006.*)

Dhaka International Film Festival, 75 Science
Laboratory Road, Dhanmondi, Dhaka-1205,
Bangladesh. Tel: (880 2) 862 1062.
e: amzamal@bdcom.com. (*Competitive section
for Asian cinema. Also non-competitive sections,
including 'Retrospective', 'Cinema of the World',
'Children's Film' and 'Bangladesh Panorama'.
Festival Director: Ahmed Muztaba Zamal – Jan.*)

Divercine, Calle Lorenzo Carnelli 1311, 11200
Montevideo, Uruguay. Tel: (59 82) 418 2460/5795.
Fax: 419 4572. e: cinemuy@chasque.apc.org.
Web: www.cinemateca.org.uy. (*July.*)

Dubai International Film Festival,
PO Box 53777, Dubai, United Arab Emirates.
Tel: (971 4) 391 3378. Fax: 391 4589.
Web: www.dubaifilmfest.com. (*The Dubai
International Film Festival, which held its second
edition in 2005, seeks to celebrate true
excellence in Arab cinema while also screening
films from across the world that reflect Dubai's
cosmopolitan character and help to build bridges
between cultures. The non-competitive
programme includes the following sections:
Arabian Nights, Arabian Shorts, Cinema from the
Subcontinent, Insights from Asia, Contemporary
World Cinema and "Operation Cultural Bridge".
Festival Director: Neil D. Stephenson. – Dec.*)

Dublin International Film Festival,
13 Merrion Sq, Dublin 2, Ireland. Tel: (353 1) 661
6216. Fax: 661 4418. e: info@dublIniff.com.
Web: www.dubliniff.com. (*Founded in 2002 and
aimed squarely at the cinemagoing public.
Non-competitive, largely composed of new
international feature films (120 in 2005, including
10 Irish productions or co-productions). Daily*

Talking Pictures events offer lunchtime panel discussions on a variety of film-making topics – Feb 17-26, 2006.)

Duisburg Film Week, Am König Heinrich Platz, D-47049 Duisburg, Germany. Tel: (49 203) 283 4187. Fax: 283 4130. e: info@duisburger-filmwoche.de. Web: www.duisburger-filmwoche.de. *(German-language documentaries from Germany, Switzerland and Austria – early Nov.)*

Durban International Film Festival, University of KwaZulu-Natal, Centre for Creative Arts, Durban 4001, South Africa. Contact: Nashen Moodley. Tel: (27 31) 260 1145. Fax: 260 1055. e: diff@ukzn.ac.za; moodleyn@ukzn.ac.za. Web: www.cca.ukzn.ac.za. *(An important forum for South African and international cinema – June 14-25, 2006.)*

Edmonton International Film Festival, Edmonton International Film Society, Suite 201, 10816A-82 Avenue, Edmonton, Alberta, T6E 2B3, Canada. Tel: (1 780) 423 0844. Fax: 447 5242. e: info@edmontonfilmfest.com. Web: www.edmontonfilmfest.com. *(Feature films, documentaries and shorts – Sept 29-Oct 7, 2006.)*

Emden International Film Festival, An der Berufschule 3, 26721 Emden, Germany. Tel: (49) 4921 9155-0. Fax: 4921 915599. e: filmfest@vhs-emden.de. Web: www.filmfestemden.de. *(Focus on northwest European films, particularly Germany and UK. Deadline for entries: March 27-June.)*

L'Etrange Festival, 81 Boulevard de Clichy, 75009 Paris, France. Tel (33 1) 5320 4860. Fax: 5320 4869. e: aurore.cresson@wanadoo.fr. *(Created in 1993 and dedicated to international features, documentaries and shorts by maverick directors – Sept.)*

European First Film Festival (Premiers Plans), Festival d'Angers, 54 rue Beaubourg, 75003 Paris, France. Tel: (33 1) 4271 5370. Fax: 4271 0111. e: paris@premiersplans.org. Web: www.premiersplans.org. *(Competitive festival for European debut features, shorts and student works – Jan.)*

Femme Totale International Women's Film Festival, Dortmund, c/o Kulturbüro Stadt Dortmund, Küpferstrasse 3, D-44122 Dortmund, Germany. Tel: (49 231) 502 5162. Fax: 502 5734. e: info@femmetotale.de. Web: www.femmetotale.de. *(Biennial festival with changing themes, highlighting films made by women. International feature film competition for women directors: €5,000; Advancement Camera Award for German women cinematographers: €5,000 – April 2007.)*

Festival International du Film Francophone de Namur, 175, Rue des Brasseurs, 5000 Namur, Belgium Tel: (32 81) 241 236. Fax: 224 384. e: info@fiff.be. Web: www.fiff.be. *(Sept 22-29, 2006.)*

Festival Dei Popoli, Borgo Pinti 82 Rosso, 50121 Firenze, Italy. Tel: (39 055) 244 778. Fax: 241 364. e: fespopol@dada.it. Web: www.festivaldeipopoli.org. *(Partly competitive and open to documentaries on social, anthropological, historical and political issues – late Nov/early Dec.)*

Festival du Cinema International en Abitibi-Temscamingue, 215 Mercier Avenue, Rouyn-Noranda, Quebec J9X 5WB, Canada. Tel: (1 819) 762 6212. Fax: 762 6762. e: info@festivalcinema.ca. Web: www.festivalcinema.ca. *(International shorts, medium and full-length features; animation, documentary and fiction – late Oct/early Nov.)*

Festroia, Forum Luisa Dodi, 2900-461 Setúbal Codex, Portugal. Tel: (351 265) 525 908. Fax: 525 681. e: geral@festroia.pt. Web: www.festroia.pt. *(Held in Setúbal, near Lisbon. Official section for countries producing fewer than 30 features per year – June 2-11, 2006.)*

Film & Literature Week, 667 Ponce de León Ave, Box 367, San Juan 00907, Puerto Rico.

Tel: (787) 723 2362. Fax: 723 6412.
e: llmagica@tld.net. President: José Artemio
Torres. (*International films based on literary works – April 20-26, 2006.*)

Filmfest München, Sonnenstr 21, D-80331,
Munich, Germany. Tel: (49 89) 381 9040.
Fax: 381 90426. e: info@filmfest-muenchen.de.
Web: www.filmfest-muenchen.de. (*International screenings and retrospectives – July 15-22, 2006.*)

Filmfestival Max Ophüls Prize, Mainzerstrasse 8,
66111 Saarbruecken, Germany. Tel: (49 681) 906
8910. e: cruth@max-ophuels-preis.de.
Web: www.max-ophüls-preis.de. (*Competitive event for young directors from German-speaking countries – Jan 16-21, 2007.*)

Florida Film Festival, Enzian Theatre,
1300 South Orlando Ave, Maitland, Florida 32751,
USA. Tel: (1 407) 644 6579. Fax: 629 6870.
e: filmfest@gate.net.
Web: www.floridafilmfestival.com. (*Specialises in independent American films: features, shorts, documentaries and non-competitive spotlight films*

– March 24-April 2, 2006.)

**Focus on Asia Fukuoka International Film
Festival,** c/o Fukuoka City Hall, 1-8-1, Tenjin,
Chuo-ku, Fukuoka 810 8620, Japan.
Tel: (81 92) 733 5170. Fax: 733 5595.
e: info@focus-on-asia.com.
Web: www.focus-on-asia.com. (*Dedicated to promoting Asian film. Non-competitive – Sept.*)

Fort Myers Beach Film Festival, Town of Fort
Myers Beach, 2523 Estero Blvd., Fort Myers
Beach, Fl 33931, USA. Festival Director: Janeen
Paulauskis. Tel: (1 239) 765 0919 ext. 131.
e: janeen@fmbeach.org.
Web: www.fmbfilmfest.org. (*Presented by the Town of Fort Myers Beach, the 6th annual Fort Myers Beach Film Festival is Southwest Florida's only event dedicated to bringing audiences and independent film-makers together to celebrate the visual arts and cultivate the talents of the film-makers of tomorrow. The four-day festival will feature events and films that appeal to multi-generational audiences. Activities include a Kids Fest, two nights of film screenings on the*

beaches along the Gulf of Mexico, film-making workshops and parties. Dramas, comedies, documentaries and short films screened during the festival have a chance to win the $1,000 Northern Trust People's Choice Award – April 27-30, 2006.)

Future Film Festival, Via del Pratello 21/2, 40122 Bologna, Italy. Tel: (39 051) 296 0664. Fax: 656 7133. e: future@futurefilmfestival.org. Web: www.futurefilmfestival.org. (*Jan.*)

Galway Film Fleadh, Cluain Mhuire, Monivea Road, Galway, Ireland. Tel: (353 91) 751 655. Fax: 735 831. e: gafleadh@iol.ie. Web: www.galwayfilmfleadh.com. (*Documentary features, independent features, short films and Irish films – July 11-16, 2006.*)

Gerardmer International Fantasy Film Festival, Le Public Système Cinéma, 40, rue Anatole France, 92594 Levallois-Perret Cedex, France. Tel: (33 1) 4134 2033. Fax: 4134 2077. e: kbeunel@le-public-systeme.fr. Web: www.gerardmer-fantasticart.com. (*International fantasy, sci-fi, psychological thriller and horror films, with competition for features and French-speaking shorts – Jan.*)

Haifa International Film Festival, 142 Hanassi Ave, Haifa 34 633, Israel. Tel: (972 4) 8353 520/3. Fax: 8384 327. e: film@haifaff.co.il. Web: www.haifaff.co.il. (*Broad spectrum of new international films, special tributes and retrospectives – end Sept/early Oct.*)

Hawaii International Film Festival, 1001 Bishop St, ASB Tower, Suite 745, Honolulu, Hawaii 96813, USA. Tel: (1 808) 528 3456. Fax: 528 1410. e: info@hiff.org. Web: www.hiff.org. (*Seeks to promote cultural understanding between East and West through film – Oct.*)

Heartland Film Festival, 200 S Meridian, Suite 220, Indianapolis, Indiana 46225-0176, USA. Tel: (1 317) 464 9405. Fax: 464 9409. e: info@heartlandfilmfestival.org. Web: www.heartlandfilmfestival.org. (*Established in 1991 to honour film-makers whose work expresses hope and respect for positive values. Call for entries: April – Oct 19-27, 2006.*)

Holland Animation Film Festival, Hoogt 4, 3512 GW Utrecht, Netherlands. Tel: (31 30) 233 1733. Fax: 233 1079. e: info@haff.nl. Web: www.haff.nl. (*International competitions for independent and applied animation; special programmes, retrospectives, student films, exhibitions – Nov 1-5, 2006.*)

Hometown Video Festival, Alliance for Community Media, 666 11th Street NW, Suite 740, Washington, DC 20001, USA. Tel: (1 202) 393 2650. Fax: 393 2653. e: acm@alliancecm.org. Web: www.alliancecm.org. (*US and international community productions – July.*)

Huesca Film Festival, Avenida del Parque 1,2, 22002 Huesca, Spain. Tel: (34 974) 212 582. Fax: 210 065. e: info@huesca-filmfestival.com. Web: www.huesca-filmfestival.com. (*Well-established competitive shorts festival in country town, with features sidebars – June 8-17, 2006.*)

Hungarian Film Week, Magyar Filmunió, Városligeti, Fasor 38, 1068 Budapest, Hungary. Tel: (36 1) 351 7760. Fax: 352 6734. e: filmunio@filmunnio.hu. Web: www.filmunio.hu. (*Competitive national festival showcasing Hungarian production from the previous year – late Jan-early Feb 2007.*)

Il Cinema Ritrovato, Mostra Internazionale del Cinema Libero, Cineteca del Comune di Bologna, Via Riva di Reno 72, 40122 Bologna, Italy. Tel: (39 051) 219 4814. Fax: 219 4821. e: cinetecamanifestazioni1@comune.bologna.it. Web: www.cinetecadibologna.it. Press office: Patrizia Minghetti at cinetecaufficiostampa@comune.bologna.it. (*International festival of film archives dedicated to cinema history. Selection made among the best film restorations from all over the world; 40,000 spectators, 350 films, 700 guests. Held in four different theatres, plus open-air screenings with live music – July 1-8, 2006.*)

Imago – International Young Film & Video Festival, Apartado 324 Avenida Eugénio de Andrade, Bloco D, 3° Drt-Trás, 6230-909 Fundão, Portugal. Tel/Fax: (00351) 275 771 607. e: info@imagofilmfest.com. Web: www.imagofilmfest.com. (*Oct 2-9, 2006.*)

Independent Film Days, Filmbuero Augsburg, Schroeckstrasse 8, 86152 Augsburg, Germany. Tel: (49 821) 153 078. Fax: 155 518. e: filmbuero@t-online.de. Web: www.filmtage-augsburg.de. (*International event for documentary and independent features, with retrospectives, national focus and student symposium – Nov.*)

International Documentary Festival of Marseille (FID Marseille), 14 Allée Léon Gambetta, 13001 Marseille, France. Tel: (33 4) 9504 4490 Fax: 9504 4491. e: welcome@fidmarseille.org. Web: www.fidmarseille.org. (*The best international documentaries – July.*)

International Film Camera Festival "Manaki Brothers", 8 Mart #4, 1000 Skopje, Republic of Macedonia. Tel/Fax: (389 2) 211 811. e: office@manaki.com.mk. Web: www.manaki.com.mk. (*Held in remembrance of Yanaki and Milton Manaki, the first cameramen of the Balkans – Sept.*)

International Film Festival Innsbruck, Museumstrasse 31, A-6020 Innsbruck, Austria. Tel: (43 512) 5785 0014. Fax: 5785 0013. e: info@iffi.at. Web: www.iffi.at. Director: Helmut Groschup. (*Films about Africa, Latin America and Asia. International competition, Public Award, Francophonie Award and Doc Award. Deadline Feb 25 – May 24-28, 2006.*)

International Film Festival of Uruguay, Lorenzo Carnelli 1311, 11200 Montevideo, Uruguay. Tel: (59 82) 419 5795. Fax: 419 4572. e: cinemuy@chasque.net. Web: www.cinemateca.org.uy. (*Presents independent and documentary films – April 1-16, 2006.*)

International Film Forum "Arsenals",

International Centre of Cinema, Marstalu 14, Riga, LV-1050, Latvia Tel: (371) 721 0114. Fax: 782 0445. e: arsenals@latnet.lv. Web: www.arsenals.lv. (*Biennial competitive festival with $10,000 international competition and latest releases from Latvia, Lithuania and Estonia in features, documentary, shorts and animation – Sept 16-24, 2006.*)

International Women's Film Festival, Maison des Arts, Palace Salvador Allende, 94000 Créteil, France. Tel: (33 1) 4980 3898. Fax: 4399 0410. e: filmsfemmes@wanadoo.com. Web: www.filmsdefemmes.com. (*Features, shorts and animation made by women – March 10-19, 2006.*)

Inverness Film Festival, 17 Old Edinburgh Rd, Inverness, IV2 3HF. Tel: (44 1463) 239 841. Fax: 713 810. e: info@invernessfilmfestival.com. Web: www.invernessfilmfestival.com. Director: Michael McDaid. (*International features, documentaries and shorts, plus workshops – early Nov 2006.*)

Israel Film Festival, Israfest Foundation, 6404 Wilshire Blvd, Suite 1240, Los Angeles, CA 90048, USA. Tel: (1 323) 966 4166. Fax: 658 6346. e: info@israelfilmfestival.com. fest@earthlink.net. Web: www.israelfilmfestival.com. (*US showcase for Israeli features, shorts, documentaries and TV dramas – 2006 dates: Feb 23-March 9 in New York City; March 22-29 in Miami; Nov 30-Dec 15 in LA.*)

Kidfilm/USA Film Festival, 6116 N Central Expressway, Suite 105, Dallas, Texas 75206, USA. Tel: (1 214) 821 6300. Fax: 821 6364. e: usafilmfestival@aol.com. Web: www.usafilmfestival.com. (*Non-competitive; oldest and largest family film festival in the US. Accepts US and international shorts and features – Jan.*)

Kracow Film Festival, Ul Pychowicka 7, 30-364 Krakow, Poland. Tel: (48 12) 267 1355. Fax: 267 4440. e: festiwal@apollofilm.pl. Web: www.cracowfilmfestival.pl. (*Poland's oldest international film festival, showcasing*

documentary, experimental, fiction and short
films – end May/early June.)

London Lesbian & Gay Film Festival, National
Film Theatre, South Bank, London SE1 8XT, UK.
Tel: (44 20) 7815 1323. Fax: 7633 0786.
e: becky.shaw@bfi.org.uk. Web: www.llgff.org.uk.
(Films of special interest to lesbian and gay
audiences. Selected highlights tour regional film
theatres April to Sept – March 29-April 12, 2006.)

Lucas International Children's Film Festival,
c/o Deutsches Filmmuseum, Schaumainkai 41,
60596 Frankfurt/Main, Germany. Tel: (49 69)
9637 6380/81. Fax: 9637 6382.
e: lucas@deutsches-filmmuseum.de.
Web: www.lucasfilmfestival.de. (Germany's
oldest children's film festival. An FIAPF 'A'-
festival. Competition for international productions
for children aged five to 12 – end Sept, 2006.)

Marrakech International Film Festival, Le
Public Système Cinéma, 40, rue Anatole France,
92594 Levallois-Perret Cedex, France.
Tel: (33 1) 4134 2033. Fax: 4134 2077.
e: jlasserre@le-public-systeme.fr.
Web: www.festival-marrakech.com. (Showcase
for international feature films – December.)

Margaret Mead Film & Video Festival,
American Museum of Natural History, 79th St
at Central Park W, New York, NY 10024-5192,
USA. Tel: (1 212) 769 5000. Fax: 769 5329.
e: meadfest@amnh.org.
Web: www.amnh.org/mead. (International
documentaries, shorts and animation – Nov.)

**"Message to Man" International
Documentary,** Short and Animated Film Festival,
Karavannaya 12, 191011, St Petersburg, Russia.
Tel: (7 812) 972 1264. Fax: 449 6572.
e: info@message-to-man.spb.ru.
Web: www.message-to-man.spb.ru.
(International competition, international debut
competition, national documentary competition
and special programmes – June.)

Miami International Film Festival, Miami Dade
College, 300 NE 2nd St, Room 5521, Miami,

Florida 33132-2204, USA. Tel: (1 305) 237 3456.
(1 305) 237 7344. e: info@miamifilmfestival.com.
Web: www.miamifilmfestival.com. (The best of
world cinema; special focus on Ibero-American
films – March 3-12, 2006.)

Midnight Sun Film Festival, Kansanopistontie
5, 99600 Sodankylä, Finland.
Tel: (358 16) 614 525. Fax: 614 522.
e: office@msfilmfestival.fi.
Web: www.msfilmfestival.fi. (International and
silent films, plus award-winners from Cannes,
Berlin, Locarno and Stockholm – June.)

**Minneapolis/St Paul International Film
Festival,** Minnesota Film Arts, 309 Oak St Ave
SE, Minneapolis, MN 55414, USA.
Tel: (1 612) 331 7563. Fax: 378 7750.
e: info@mnfilmarts.org.
Web: www.mnfilmarts.org. (Presents more than
150 films from more than 50 countries –
April 7-22, 2006.)

**Montreal International Festival of New
Cinema,** 3805 Boulevard St-Laurent, Montreal,
Quebec, Canada H2W 1X9.
Tel: (1 514) 282 0004. Fax: 282 6664.
e: info@nouveaucinema.ca.
Web: www.nouveaucinema.ca. (Seeks to explore
quality experimental films as an alternative to
conventional commercial cinema –
Oct 12-22, 2006.)

Mumbai International Film Festival, Rajkamal
Studio, Dr S S Rao Road, Parel, Mumbai 400
012, India. Tel: (91 22) 2413 6571.
Fax: 2412 5268. e: iffmumbai@yahoo.com.
Web: www.iffmumbai.org. (Established in 1997,
the only independent film festival in India,
organised by Mumbai Academy of the Moving
Image; feature films only. Sections: Global Vision,
with a FIPRESCI award, Retro, Tribute, Focus on
Film-maker, Focus on One Country, Film India
Worldwide & Competition for Indian Films – Jan.)

Munich International Festival of Film Schools,
Sonnenstrasse 21, D-80331 Munich, Germany.
Tel: (49 89) 3819 040. Fax: 3819 0426.
e: info@filmfest-muenchen.de.

Web: www.filmfest-muenchen.de. (*Competition for student productions from about 30 film schools – Nov 19-25, 2006.*)

NatFilm Festival, Store Kannikestraede 6, 1169 Copenhagen, Denmark. Tel: (45) 3312 0005. Fax: 3312 7505. e: info@natfilm.dk. Web: www.natfilm.dk. Producer: Andreas Steinmann. Programmer: Kim Foss. (*Off-beat international retrospectives and tributes – March 26-April 9, 2006.*)

New Directors/New Films, Film Society of Lincoln Center, 70 Lincoln Center Plaza, New York, NY 10023, USA. Tel: (1 212) 875 5610. Fax: 875 5636. e: festival@filmlinc.com. Web: www.filmlinc.com. (*Celebrating its 35th year, the festival presents works by new directors; co-sponsored by the Film Society and MOMA – March 22-April 2, 2006.*)

New Orleans Film Festival, 843 Carondelet St, New Orleans, LA 70130, USA. Tel: (1 504) 523 3818. Fax: 975 3478. e: admin@neworleansfilmfest.com. Web: www.neworleansfilmfest.com. (*Competition for all lengths, genres and formats and non-competitive programme that includes remastered classics and cutting-edge new releases – Oct 12-19, 2006.*)

New York EXPO of Short Film and Video, 224 Centre St, New York, NY 10013, USA. Tel: (1 212) 505 7742. e: nyexpo@aol.com. Web: www.nyexpo.org. (*America's longest-running independent shorts festival seeks fiction, animation, documentary and experimental works under 60 minutes and completed in the previous two years. Student and international entries welcome – Dec.*)

Nordic Film Festival, 75 rue General le Clerc, 76000 Rouen, France. Tel: (33 232) 767 322. Fax: 767 323. e: festival-cinema-nordique@festival-cinema-nordique.asso.fr. Web: www.festival-cinema-nordique.asso.fr. (*Competitive festival of Nordic cinema, including retrospectives – March.*)

Northwest Film and Video Festival, Northwest Film Center, 1219 SW Park Ave, Portland, Oregon 97205, USA. Tel: (1 503) 221 1156. Fax: 294 0874. e: info@nwfilm.org. Web: www.nwfilm.org. (*A juried annual survey of new moving image arts by independent Northwest film- and video-makers; features, shorts and documentaries – Nov.*)

OFFICINEMA, Cineteca del Comune di Bologna, Via Riva di Reno 72, 40122 Bologna, Italy. Tel: (39) 051 219 4814. Fax: 219 4821. e: cinetecamanifestazioni1@comune.bologna.it. Web: www.cinetecadibologna.it. (*Competition for final projects from European schools. Press office: Patrizia Minghetti atcinetecaufficiostampa@comune.bologna.it. Visioni Italiane; Italian short film competition: contact Anna Di Martino at visionitaliane@libero.it. 9,000 spectators, 250 films, 200 guests, 10 awards – Nov 23-26, 2006.*)

OKOMEDIA – International Environmental Film Festival, Oekomedia Institute for Environmental Media, Nussmannstr 14, D-79098 Freiburg, Germany. Tel: (49 761) 52 024. Fax: 555 724. e: info@oekomedia-institut.de. Web: www.oekomedia-institut.de. (*International features, documentaries, shorts and animated films about contemporary ecological/environmental issues – Oct.*)

Open Air Filmfest Weiterstadt, Postfach 1164, D-64320 Weiterstadt, Germany. Tel: (49 61) 501 2185. Fax: 501 4073. e: filmfest@weiterstadt.de. Web: www.filmfest-weiterstadt.de. (*Aug.*)

Oxford International Festival of Films, Church Lands House, 417 Henley Avenue, Oxford OX4 4DJ. Tel: (01865) 747 777. e: patriciaterrell@oxfordfestivalfilms.com. Web: www.oxfordfestivalfilms.com. (*May 2-12, 2006.*)

Palm Beach International Film Festival, 289 Via Naranjas, Royal Palm Plaza, Suite 48, Boca Raton, Florida 33432, USA. Tel: (1 561) 362 0003. Fax: 362 0035. e: info@pbifilmfest.org.

Web: www.pbifilmfest.org. (*More than 80 films: American and international features, shorts, documentaries and large format. Competitive – April 20-28, 2006.*)

Palm Springs International Festival of Short Films & Film Market, 1700 E Tahquitz Canyon Way, Suite 3, Palm Springs, CA 92262, USA. Tel: (1 760) 322 2930. Fax: 322 4087. e: info@psfilmfest.org. Web: www.psfilmfest.org. Contact: Darryl Macdonald. (*Largest competitive shorts festival and market in US. Student, animation, documentary, live-action and international competition with Audience and Juried Awards – August 29-Sept 4, 2006.*)

Philadelphia International Film Festival, Philadelphia Film Society, 4th Floor, 234 Market St, Philadelphia, PA 19106, USA. Tel: (1 267) 765 9700. e: info@phillyfests.com. Web: www.phillyfests.com. (*International features, documentaries and shorts – March 30-April 12, 2006.*)

Prix Italia, Via Monte Santo 52, 00198 Rome, Italy. Tel: (39 06) 372 8708. e: prixitalia@rai.it. Web: www.prixitalia.rai.it. (*International competition for radio, TV programmes and multi-media; open only to 75 member organisations – late Sept.*)

RAI Trade Screenings, Rai Trade, Via Umberto Novaro 18, 00195 Rome, Italy. Tel: (39 06) 3749 8257. Fax: 3701 343. e: eleuteri@raitrade.it. Web: www.raitrade.rai.it. (*International programming buyers view RAI productions for broadcast, video and other rights – April.*)

St Louis International Film Festival, 394A Euclid Ave, St Louis, MO 63108, USA. Tel: (1 314) 454 0042. Fax: 454 0540. e: chris@cinemastlouis.org. Web: www.cinemastlouis.org. (*Showcases approximately 180 US and international independent films, documentaries and shorts. Competitive. Entry deadline: July 15 – Nov 9-19, 2006.*)

St Petersburg Festival of Festivals, 10 Kamennostrovsky Ave, St Petersburg 197101, Russia. Tel: (7 812) 237 0072. Fax: 237 0304.

e: info@filmfest.ru. Web: www.filmfest.ru. (*International and local productions – June 23-29, 2006.*)

San Fernando Valley International Film Festival, 5504 Cleon Ave, North Hollywood, CA 91601, USA. Tel: (1 818) 623 9122. e: festival@viffi.org. Web: www.viffi.org. (*Competition for films and screenplays; showcase for film-makers and writers who believe in entertainment that should not contain gratuitous violence or profanity – March 17-26, 2006.*)

San Francisco International Asian American Film Festival, c/o NAATA, 145 9th Street, Suite 350, San Francisco, CA 94103, USA. Tel: (1 415) 863 0814. Fax: 863 7428. e: festival@naatanet. Web: www.naatanet.org. (*Screens over 130 films and videos by Asian-American and Asian artists – March.*)

San Francisco International Lesbian and Gay Film Festival, Frameline, 145 9th St, Suite 300, San Francisco, CA 94103, USA. Tel: (1 415) 703 8650. Fax: 861 1404. e: info@frameline.org. Web: www.frameline.org. (*June 15-25, 2006.*)

San Juan Cinemafest of Puerto Rico, PO Box, San Juan 00902-0079, Puerto Rico. Tel: (787) 723 5015. Fax: 724 4333. President: Mario L. Paniagua. (*International features, Caribbean features and shorts – Nov.*)

San Sebastián Horror and Fantasy Film Festival, Donostia Kultura, Plaza de la Constitucion 1, 20003 Donostia-San Sebastián, Spain. Tel: (34 943) 481 197. Fax: 430 621. e: cinema_cinema@donostia.org. Web: www.donostiakultura.com/terror. (*Short film and feature competition – Oct 28-Nov 4, 2006.*)

San Sebastián Human Rights Film Festival, Donostia Kultura, Plaza de la Constitucion 1, 20003 Donostia-San Sebastián, Spain. Tel: (34 943) 481 197/53/57. Fax: 430 621. e: cinema_cinema@donostia.org. Web: www.cineyderechoshumanos.com. (*March 24-31, 2006.*)

Sao Paulo International Film Festival,
Rua Antonio Carlos, 288 2° Andar, 01309-010
Sao Paulo, Brazil. Tel: (55 11) 3141 1068/2548.
Fax: 3266 7066. e: info@mostra.org.
Web: www.mostra.org. (*Competitive event for
new film-makers and international panorama –
Oct 20-Nov 2, 2006.*)

Siberian International Festival – Spirit of Fire,
Festival Committee, 1 Mosfilmovskaya St,
Moscow, 119992 Russia. Tel: (7 095) 143 9484.
Fax: 938 2312. e: festival@spiritoffire.ru.
Web: www.spiritoffire.ru. (*Showcases 15 films
directed by young talents – late Feb-early March.*)

Sydney Film Festival, PO Box 96, Strawberry
Hills, NSW 2012, Australia.
Tel: (61 2) 9280 0511. Fax: 9280 1520.
e: info@sydneyfilmfestival.org. (*Broad-based,
non-competitive event screening new Australian
and international features and shorts – June.*)

Taormina International Film Festival, Corso
Umberto 19, 98039 Taormina Messina, Italy.
Tel: (39 094) 221 142. Fax: 223 348.
e: info@taormina-arte.com.
Web: www. taorminafilmfest.com. (*Films by
English-language directors; Restorations; Silver
Ribbon awards – June 25-July 2, 2006.*)

Tel-Aviv International Student Film Festival,
Cinema & Television Dept, The Yolanda & David
Katz Faculty of the Arts, Tel Aviv University, Ramat
Aviv 69978, Israel. Tel: (972 3) 640 9936.
Fax: 640 9935. e: filmfest@post.tau.ac.il. Web:
www.taufilmfest.com. (*Workshops, retrospectives,
tributes, premieres – June 3-10, 2006.*)

Tudela First Film Festival, Centro Cultural
Castel Ruiz, Plaza Mercadal 7, 31500, Tudela,
Navarra, Spain. Tel: (34 948) 825 868.
Fax: 412 003. Web: www.geocities.com.
(*late Oct-early Nov.*)

Uppsala International Short Film Festival, PO
Box 1746, SE-751 47 Uppsala, Sweden.
Tel: (46 18) 120 025. Fax: 121 350.
e: info@shortfilmfestival.com.
Web: www.shortfilmfestival.com. (*Sweden's only
international shorts festival. Competitive – Oct.*)

USA Film Festival, 6116 N Central Expressway,
Suite 105, Dallas, Texas 75206, USA.
Tel: (1 214) 821 6300. Fax: 821 6364.
e: usafilmfestival@aol.com.
Web: www.usafilmfestival.com. (*Non-competitive
for US and international features. Academy-
qualifying National Short Film/Video competition
with cash awards – April 20-27, 2006.*)

Valdivia International Film Festival, Cine Club,
Universidad Austral de Chile, Campus Isla Teja
s/n, Valdivia, Chile. Tel: (56 63) 221 961.
Fax: 221 209. e: produccionfestival@uach.cl.
Web: www.festivalcinevaldivia.com. (*International
feature contest, plus Chilean and international
shorts, documentaries and animation – Sept 29-
Oct 6, 2006.*)

**Viewfinders International Film Festival for
Youth,** PO Box 36139, Halifax, NS, B3J 3S9,
Canada. Tel: (1 902) 422 6965. Fax: 422 4006.
e: festival@atlanticfilm.com. Web:
www.atlanticfilm.com. (*Family-oriented films and
videos from all over the world – April 18-22, 2006.*)

Vila do Conde, Festival Internacional de Curtas
Metragens Auditório Municipal, Praa da
República, 4480-715 Vila do Conde, Portugal.
Tel: (351 252) 646 516. Fax: 248 416.
e: festival@curtasmetragens.pt.
Web: www.curtasmetragens.pt. (*National and
International shorts competitions. Special
programme and retrospectives – July 8-16, 2006.*)

Warsaw International Film Festival, PO Box
816, 00-950 Warsaw 1, Poland. Tel: (48 22) 621
4647. Fax: 621 6268. e: festiv@wff.pl. Web:
www.wff.pl. (*Key event in Poland. Fiction and
documentary features. New Films' and New
Directors' competition – Oct 6-15, 2006.*)

**Washington, DC International Film Festival
(Filmfest DC),** PO Box 21396, Washington,
DC 20009, USA. Tel: (1 202) 628 3456.
Fax: 724 6578. e: filmfestdc@filmfestdc.org.
Web: www.filmfestdc.org. (*Celebrates the best
in world cinema – April 19-30, 2006.*)

The Global Directory

AFGHANISTAN

All Tel/Fax numbers begin (93)

Archive

Afghan-Film, Grand Masood Ave 2, Kabul. Tel: 20 210 0279.

Magazine

Afghan Film, Grand Masood Ave 2, Kabul. Tel: 79 314303. cinema_mag@yahoo.com.

Useful Addresses

Aina, Malik Asghar Crossroad, Kabul. Tel: 79 110 667. www.ainaworld.org. Director: Dr Ernst Fassbender

Barmak-Film, sbf@barmakfilm.com. www.barmakfilm.com.

CACA-Kabul, Tel: 79 345 962. cacakabul@hotmail.com. www.cacakabul.org. Contact: Azra Jafari, Malek Shafi'i.

Filmmakers Union, Kabul. Tel: 79 375530. cinemaf@hotmail.com. Contact: Jawan Shir Haidari.

Saba Film, Tel: 70 246 827. Contact: Saba Sahar.

ALGERIA

Useful Address

Cinémathèque Algérienne, 49 rue Larbi Ben M'Hidi, Algiers. Tel: (213 2) 737 548/50. Fax: 738 246. www.cinematheque.art.dz/.

ARGENTINA

All Tel/Fax numbers begin (54 11)

Archive

Pablo Hicken Museum and Library, Defensa 1220, 1143 Buenos Aires. Tel: 4300 5967. Fax: 4307 3839. museodelcinedb@yahoo.com.ar.

Film School

Film University, Pasaje Giufra 330, 1064 Buenos Aires. Fax: 4300 1413. Fax: 4300 1581. fuc@ucine.edu.ar. www.ucine.edu.ar.

Useful Addresses

Critics Association of Argentina, Maipu 621 Planta Baja, 1006 Buenos Aires. Tel/Fax: 4322 6625. cinecronistas@yahoo.com.

Directors Association of Argentina (DAC), Lavalle 1444, 7° Y, 1048 Buenos Aires. Tel/Fax: 4372 9822. dac1@infovia.com.ar. www.dacdirectoresdecine.com.ar.

Directors of Photography Association, San Lorenzo 3845, Olivos, 1636 Buenos Aires. Tel/Fax: 4790 2633. adf@ba.net. www.adfcine.com.ar.

Exhibitors Federation of Argentina, Ayacucho 457, 1° 13, Buenos Aires. Tel/Fax: 4953 1234. empcinemato@infovia.com.ar.

General Producers Association, Lavalle 1860, 1051 Buenos Aires. Tel/Fax: 4371 3430. argentinasonofilm@impsat1.com.ar.

National Cinema Organisation (INCAA), Lima 319, 1073 Buenos Aires. Tel: 6779 0900. Fax: 4383

0029. info@incaa.gov.ar.

Producers Guild of Argentina (FAPCA), Godoy Cruz 1540, 1414 Buenos Aires. Tel: 4777 7200. Fax: 4778 0046. recepcion@patagonik.com.ar.

Sindicato de la Industria Cinematográfia de Argentina (SICA), Juncal 2029, 1116 Buenos Aires. Tel: 4806 0208. Fax: 4806 7544. sica@sicacine.com.ar. www.sicacine.com.ar.

ARMENIA

All Tel/Fax numbers begin (374 1)

Useful Addresses

Armenian National Cinematheque, 25A Tbilisyan Highway, 375052 Yerevan. Tel: 285 406. filmadaran@yahoo.com.

Armenia Film Studios CJSC #1 Eghvard Highway, 375054 Yerevan. Tel: 366 845. afstudios@mail.ru.

Armenian Union of Filmmakers, 18 Vardanants, Yerevan. Tel: 540 528. Fax: 540 136.

Association of Film Critics & Cinema Journalists, 5 Byron Str, 374009 Yerevan. Tel/Fax: 564 484. aafccj@arminco.com. www.arm-cinema.am. www.arvest.am.

Hayfilm Studio, 50 Gevork Chaush, 375088 Yerevan. Tel: 343 000. Fax: 393 538. hayfilm@arminco.com.

Hayk Documentary Studio, 50 Gevork Chaush, 375088 Yerevan. Tel: 357 032.

Paradise Ltd, [Production & Distribution], 18 Abovyan Str, 375010 Yerevan. Tel: 521 271. Fax: 521 302. paradi@arminco.com.
Yerevan Studio, 26 Hovsepyan Str, 47 Nork, 375047 Yerevan. Tel: 558 022. tx-yes@media.am. http://home.media.am/yestudio.

AUSTRALIA

Archive
Screensound Australia, The National Screen and Sound Archive, GPO Box 2002, Canberra ACT 2601. Tel: (61 2) 6248 2000. Fax: 6248 2222. enquiries@screensound.gov.au. Stock: 3,800 Western Australian titles.

Bookshop
Electric Shadows Bookshop, City Walk, Akuna St, Canberra ACT 2601. Tel: (61 2) 6248 8352. Fax: 6247 1230. esb@electricshadowsbookshop.com.au. www.electricshadowsbookshop.com.au.

Film School
Australian Film Television & Radio School (AFTRS), Postal address: PO Box 126, North Ryde NSW 2113. Tel: (61 2) 9805 6611. Fax: 9887 1030. direct.sales@syd.aftrs.edu.au.

Magazine
AFC News, GPO Box 3984, Sydney NSW 2001. Tel: (61 2) 9321 6444. Fax: 9357 3737. info@afc.gov.au. www.afc.gov.au/newsandevents.

Useful Addresses
Australian Entertainment Industry Association (AEIA), 8th Floor, West Tower, 608 St Kilda Rd, Melbourne VIC 3004. Tel: (61 3) 9521 1900. Fax: 9521 2285. aeia@aeia.org.au.
Australian Film Commission (AFC), 150 William St, Woolloomooloo NSW 2011. Postal address: GPO Box 3984, Sydney NSW 2001. Tel: (61 2) 9321 6444. Fax: 9357 3737. info@afc.gov.au. www.afc.gov.au.
Australian Film Finance Corporation (AFFC), 130 Elizabeth St, Sydney NSW 2000. Postal address: GPO Box 3886, Sydney NSW 2001. Tel: (61 2) 9268 2555. Fax: 9264 8551. www.ffc.gov.au.
Australian Screen Directors Association (ASDA), Postal address: PO Box 211, Rozelle NSW 2039. Tel: (61 2) 9555 7045. Fax: 9555 7086. www.asdafilm.org.au.
Film Australia, 101 Eton Rd, Lindfield NSW 2070. Tel: (61 2) 9413 8777. Fax: 9416 9401. www.filmaust.com.au.
Office of Film & Literature Classification (OFLC), 23 Mary St, Surry Hills NSW 2010. Tel: (61 2) 9289 7100. Fax: 9289 7101. oflcswitch@oflc.gov.au.
Screen Producers Association of Australia (SPAA), Level 7, 235 Pyrmont St, Pyrmont NSW 2009. Tel: (61 2) 9518 6366. Fax: 9518 6311. www.spaa.org.au.

More information can be found via the web on www.nla.gov.au/oz/gov/. Also www.sna.net.au for Screen Network Australia, which is a gateway to more than 250 film and television sites.

AUSTRIA
All Tel/Fax numbers begin (43 1)

Archives
Austrian Film Museum, Augustinerstr 1, A-1010 Vienna, Tel: 533 7054-0. Fax: 533 7054-25. office@filmmuseum.at. www.filmmuseum.at.
Filmarchiv Austria, Obere Augartenstr 1, A-1020 Vienna. Tel: 216 1300. Fax: 216 1300-100. augarten@filmarchiv.at. www.filmarchiv.at.

Film School
University of Music & Performing Arts, Dept of Film & TV, Anton-von-Webern-Platz 1, A-1030 Vienna. Tel: 7115 5290. Fax: 7115 5299. filmakademie@mdw.ac.at. www.mdw.ac.at.

Magazine
RAY Kinomagazin, c/o PVS Verleger, Friedmanngasse 44, A-1160 Vienna. Tel: 407 2497. Fax: 407 4389. www.ray-kinomagazin.at. Austria's leading international movie magazine.

Useful Addresses
Association of Austrian Film Directors, c/o checkpointmedia Multimediaproduktionen AG, Seilerstätte 30, A-1010 Vienna. Tel/Fax: 513 0000-0. Fax: 513 0000-11. www.austrian-directors.com.
Association of Austrian Film Producers, Speisingerstrasse 121, A-1230 Vienna. Tel/Fax: 888 9622. aafp@austrian-film.com. www.austrian-film.com.
Association of the Audiovisual & Film Industry, Wiedner Hauptstrasse 53, PO Box 327, A-1045 Vienna. Tel: 5010 53010. Fax: 5010 5276. film@fafo.at. www.fafo.at.
Austrian Film Commission, Stiftgasse 6, A-1070 Vienna. Tel: 526 3323 0. Fax: 526 6801. office@afc.at. www.afc.at.
Austrian Film Institute (OFI), Spittelberggasse 3, A-1070 Vienna. Tel: 526 9730-400. Fax: 526 9730-440. office@filminstitut.at. www.filminstitut.at.
Location Austria, Opernring 3, A-1010 Vienna. Tel: 588 5836. Fax: 586 8659. office@location-austria.at. www.location-austria.at.
ORF, Austrian Broadcasting Corporation, Würzburggasse 30,

A-1136 Vienna. Tel: 878 780.
www.orf.at.
Vienna Film Fund,
Stiftgasse 6, A-1070 Vienna.
Tel: 526 5088. Fax: 526 5088 20.
office@filmfonds-wien.at.
www.filmfonds-wien.at.

AZERBAIJAN
All Tel/Fax numbers begin (994 12)

Useful Addresses
Azerbaijan Film Fond & Museum,
69 H Zardabi St, 370122 Baku.
Tel: 328 975.
Azerbaijanfilm J Jabbarly,
1 Tbilisi Avenue, 370012 Baku.
Tel: 312 960.
Filmmakers Union,
The Government House,
16 U Hajybayov St, Baku.
Tel: 932 727. Fax: 939 620.
Studio Azerbaijanfilm,
Tbilisi ave. 1, 370012 Baku.
Tel: 312 960.

BELARUS

Useful Addresses
All Tel/Fax numbers begin (375 17)

Belarusfilm, Scaryna Prospect 98,
220023 Minsk. Tel: 233 8820.
Ministry of Culture,
Film & Video Department,
Masherov Avenue 11, 220004
Minsk. Tel: 223 7114.
Fax: 223 9045.

BELGIUM

Archive
Royal Film Archive, 23 Rue
Ravenstein, B-1000 Brussels.
Tel: (32 2) 507 8370.
Fax: 513 1272.
cinematheque@ledoux.be.
www.ledoux.be. Founded 1938.

Film School
Institut National des Arts du
Spectacle et Techniques de
Diffusion (INSAS),
8 Rue Thérésienne, B-1000
Brussels. Tel (32 2) 511 9286.
Fax: 511 0279. sec@insas.be
www.insas.be

Magazines
FilmMagie, Cellebroerstraat 16
Bus 2, B-1000 Brussels.
Tel: (32 2) 546 0810.
Fax: 546 0819. info@filmmagie.be.
www.filmmagie.be.

Useful Addresses
A Private View, Vaderlandstraat 47,
B-9000 Ghent. Tel: (32 9) 240 1000.
Fax: 240 1009.
Communauté Française de
Belgique, Centre du Cinéma et de
l'Audiovisuel, Bld Léopold II, 44,
B-1080 Brussels. Tel: (32 2) 413
2519. Fax: 413 2415.
Corridor, Handelskaai 40/4,
B-1000 Brussels. Tel: (32 2) 219
6076. Fax: 219 6595.
silentface@planetinternet.be.
Corsan, Verversrui 17-19,
B-2000 Antwerp.
Tel: (32 3) 234 2518. Fax: 226 2158.
severinewillems_corsan@belgacom.net.
De Filmfabriek, Hoogstraat 33,
B-3360 Bierbeek.
Tel: (32 16) 460 100. Fax: 461 276.
areyouvital@filmfabriek.com.
Entre Chien et Loup, [Producer],
28 Rue de l'Amblève, B-1160
Brussels. Tel: (32 2) 736 4813.
Fax: 732 3383.
dianna.elbaum@brutele.be.
Era Films, Werfstraat 2, B-1000
Brussels. Tel: (32 2) 229 3780.
Fax: 219 6686. erafilms@online.be.
Favourite Films, [Producer],
Vandenbusschestraat 3, B-1030
Brussels. Tel: (32 2) 242 4510. Fax:
242 1408. info@favouritefilms.be.

Flanders Image, Handelskaai
18/3, B-1000 Brussels.
Tel: (32 2) 226 0630. Fax: 219 1936.
flandersimage@vaf.be.
Contact: Christian De Schutter.
cdeschutter@vaf.be.
Flemish Audiovisual Fund (VAF),
Handelskaai 18/3, B-1000
Brussels. Tel: (32 2) 226 0630.
Fax: 219 1936. info@vaf.be.
www.vaf.be.
Fobic Films, Nieuwe Vaart 118,
Bus 48, B-9000 Ghent.
Tel: (32 9) 329 0052. Fax: 329
0052. info@fobicfilms.com.
Help Desk for the Audiovisual Arts
in Flanders (IAK), Bijlokekaai 7E,
9000 Ghent. Tel: (32 9) 235 2260.
Fax: 233 0709. info@iak.be.
Radowsky Films, [Producer], 13
Rue de Belgrade, B-1190 Brussels.
Tel: (32 2) 534 5261. Fax: 538 5571.
radowsky.films@online.be.
Wallonie Bruxelles Image (WBI),
Place Flagey 18, B-1050 Brussels.
Tel: (32 2) 223 2304. Fax: 218 3424.
wbimages@skynet.be.
www.cfwb.be.

BOLIVIA
All Tel/Fax numbers begin (5912)
unless otherwise indicated

Archive
Cinemateca Boliviana,
Calle Rosendo Gutiérrez,
esq. Prolongación Federico Suazo,
s/n, Casilla 9933, La Paz.
Tel: 244 4090.
info@cinematecaboliviana.org.

Useful Addresses
Consejo Nacional del Cine
(CONACINE), Calle Montevideo,
Edificio Requima, Piso 8, La Paz.
Tel: 215 3207/211 7316.
conacine@entelnet.bo.
www.conacine.net.

Fundación Jorge Ruiz
Casilla 4336,
Cochabamba. (591 4) 445 0756.
siempremarina@yahoo.com.
Iconoscopio S.R.L. [Producer]
PO Box 3-12112 sm, La Paz.
marcosloayza@yahoo.es.
Imagen Propia [Producer]
Diaz Romero 1699, La Paz.
Tel: 222 8970.
Imagenpropia@acelerate.com.
Grupo Ukamau [Producer]
Casilla M-10373, Calle Sanauja
651, Zona Riosiño, La Paz.
Tel: 228 1027.
ukamau@entelnet.bo.
Red PAT [Producer]
Calle Posnasky 1069
Miraflores, La Paz.
Pegaso Producciones
P. O. Box 7171, La Paz.
Tel/Fax: 241 7542/214 0690
pegafilm@entelnet.bo.
www.pegasofilms.com.

BOSNIA & HERZEGOVINA

All Tel/Fax numbers begin (387 33)
unless otherwise indicated

Useful Addresses
Academy for Performing Arts,
Obala, Sarajevo. Tel/Fax: 665 304.
Association of Filmmakers,
Strosmajerova 1, Sarajevo.
Tel: 667 452.
Cinemateque of Bosnia & Herzegovina, Alipasina 19,
Sarajevo. Tel/Fax: 668 678.
kinoteka@bih.net.ba.
Deblokada Production, Sarajevo.
Tel: 668 559. deblok@bih.net.ba.
Forum Production, Mis Irbina 2,
Sarajevo. forum@bih.net.ba.
Refresh Production, Sarajevo.
Tel: 211 093. fresh@bih.net.ba.
Sarajevo Film Festival
Zelenih beretki 121, 71 000
Sarajevo. programmes@sff.ba.
Tel/Fax: 209 411.

Academy of Perfoming Arts
Obala Kulina Bana 11, 71 000
Sarajevo.Tel/Fax: 215 277.
Asu_sa@utic.net.ba.
Refresh Production
Splitska 11, 71 000 Sarajevo.
Tel/Fax: 211 093.
produkcija@refresh.ba.
www.refresh.ba.
SAGA Prod.
H.Kulenovica 7, 71 000 Sarajevo.
Tel/Fax: 666 811. saga@sagafilm.ba.
FIST Prod.
Kemalbegova 13, 71 000 Sarajevo.
Tel/Fax: 670 431. Fist@fist.co.ba.
PORTA MOSTAR
Zagrebacka 16, Mostar.
Tel/Fax: 443 526.
miro.barnjak@tel.net.ba.
Studio Animation Neum
Stepeniste Agava 4, Neum.
Tel: 387 63 350 149.
Fax: 387 63 884 334.

BRAZIL

Archives
Cinemateca Brasileira, Largo
Senador Raul Cardoso, Vila
Clementino 207, 04021-070 São
Paulo. Tel: (55 11) 5084 2318
Fax: 5575 9264.
info@cinemateca.com.br.
www.cinemateca.com.br.
Cinemateca do Museu de Arte Moderna, Ave Infante Dom
Henrique 85, Parque do Flengo,
20021-140 Rio de Janeiro.
Tel: (55 21) 2240 4913.
cinemateca@mamrio.com.br.

Useful Addresses
ANCINE (National Agency for Cinema), Praça Pio X, 54, 10th
Floor, 22091-040 Rio de Janeiro.
Tel: (55 21) 3849 1339.
www.ancine.gov.br.

Brazilian Cinema Congress (CBC), ([Federation of Cinema
Unions/Associations], Rua Cerro
Cora 550, Sala 19, 05061-100 São
Paulo. Tel/Fax: (55 11) 3021 8505.
congressocinema@hotmail.comww
w.congressocinema.com.br.
Grupo Novo de Cinema,
[Distributor], Rua Capitao Salomao
42, 22271-040 Rio de Janeiro.
Tel: (55 21) 2539 1538.
braziliancinema@braziliancinema.com.
www.gnctv.com.br.
Ministry of Culture,
Films & Festivals Dept, Esplanada
dos Ministerios, Bloco B, 3rd Floor,
70068-900 Brasilia.
www.cultura.gov.br.

BULGARIA

All Tel/Fax numbers begin (359 2)

Archive
Bulgarian National Film Library,
36 Gurko St, 1000 Sofia.
Tel: 987 0296. Fax: 987 6004.
bmateeva@bnf.bg.

Useful Addresses
Borough Film Ltd, [Producer],
3A Murgash St, 1000 Sofia.
Tel: 445 880. Fax: 943 4787.
borough@mbox.cit.bg.
Bulgarian Film Producers Association, 19 Skobelev,
17A Tzar Osvoboditel Blvd,
1000 Sofia. Tel: 943 4849.
Fax: 943 3703.
Bulgarian National Television,
29 San Stefano St, 1000 Sofia.
Tel: 985 591. Fax: 987 1871.
www.bnt.bg.
Gala Film Ltd, [Producer],
3 Uzundjovska St, 1000 Sofia.
Tel: 981 4209. Fax: 981 2971.
gala@techno-link.com.
Geopoly Ltd, [Producer],
16 Kapitan Andreev St, 1421 Sofia.
Tel/Fax: 963 0661.
geopoly@mail.techno-link.com.

Ministry of Culture,
17 Stamboliiski St, 1000 Sofia.
Tel: 980 6191. Fax: 981 8559.
www.culture.government.bg/.
National Film Centre,
2A Dondukov Blvd, 1000 Sofia.
Tel: 987 4096. Fax: 987 3626.
nfc@mail.bol.bg.
Union of Bulgarian Film Makers,
67 Dondukov Blvd, 1504 Sofia.
Tel: 946 1068. Fax· 946 1069.
sbfd@bitex.com.

BURKINA FASO

Magazine
Fespaco News,
01 BP 2524 Ouagadougou 01.
www.fespaco.bf/news.
Monthly newsletter of the Pan-
African Federation of film-makers.

CANADA

Archives
La Cinémathèque Québécoise,
335 Blvd de Maisonneuve E,
Montréal, Quebec, H2X 1K1.
Tel: (1 514) 842 9763. Fax: 842
1816. info@cinematheque.qc.ca.
www.cinematheque.qc.ca.
National Archives of Canada,
Visual & Sound Archives, 344
Wellington St, Ottawa, Ontario,
K1A 0N3. Tel: (1 613) 995 5138.
Fax: 995 6274. www.archive.ca.

Bookshop
Theatrebooks, 11 St Thomas St,
Toronto, Ontario, M5S 2B7.
Tel: (1 416) 922 7175. Fax: 922
0739. action@theatrebooks.com.
www.theatrebooks.com.

Film Schools
Queen's University, 160 Stuart St,
Kingston, Ontario, K7L 3N6.
Tel: (1 613) 533 2178. Fax: 533
2063. film@post.queensu.ca.
www.film.queensu.ca.

Sheridan College, School of
Animation, Arts & Design, 1430
Trafalgar Rd, Oakville, Ontario, L6H
2L1. Tel: (1 905) 845 9430.
infosheridan@sheridanc.on.ca.
www.sheridanc.on.ca.
Simon Fraser University,
School for the Contemporary Arts,
8888 University Drive, Burnaby,
British Columbia, V5A 1S6.
Tel: (1 604) 291 3363.
Fax: 291 5907.
ca@sfu.ca. www.sfu.ca/sca.
University of Manitoba,
Film Studies Program, 367 University
College, Winnipeg, Manitoba, R3T
2N2. Tel: (1 204) 474 9581.
Fax: 474 7684. film@umanitoba.ca.
www.umanitoba.ca.
University of Windsor,
401 Sunset Ave, Windsor, Ontario,
N9B 3P4. Tel: (1 519) 253 3000.
Fax: 973 7050. register@uwindsor.ca.
www.uwindsor.ca. Film, radio, TV.
Vancouver Film School,
198 West Hastings St, Suite 200,
Vancouver, British Columbia, V6B
1H2. Tel: (1 604) 685 5808.
Fax: 685 5830.
admissions@vfs.com. www.vfs.com.
York University,
Film & Video Dept, 4700 Keele St,
Toronto, Ontario, M3J 1P3.
Tel: (1 416) 736 5149.
Fax: 736 5710. www.yorku.ca.

Magazines
Ciné-Bulles, 4545 Ave Pierre-de-
Coubertin, CP 1000, Succursale M,
Montréal, Quebec, H1V 3R2.
cinebulle@loisirquebec.qc.ca.
www.cinemasparalleles.qc.ca.
Film Canada Yearbook,
Moving Pictures Media, Box 720,
Port Perry, Ontario, L9L 1A6.
Tel (1 905) 986 0050.
Fax: 986 1113.
deborah@filmcanadayearbook.com.
www.filmcanadayearbook.com.

Kinema, Fine Arts & Film Studies,
University of Waterloo, 200
University Ave, Waterloo, Ontario,
N2L 3G1. Tel: (1 519) 888 4567
ext. 3709. Fax: 746 4982.
kinema@watarts.uwaterloo.ca.
www.kinema.uwaterloo.ca.
A journal of history, theory and
aesthetics of world film and audio-
visual media. Twice yearly.
Séquences, 1850 rue Joliette,
Montréal, Quebec, H1W 3G3.
Tel: (1 514) 598 9573.
Fax: 598 1789. cast49@hotmail.ca.

Useful Addresses
**Academy of Canadian Cinema &
Television,** 172 King St E, Toronto,
Ontario, M5A 1J3.
Tel: (1 416) 366 2227. Fax: 366
8454. www.academy.ca.
**Canadian Association of Film
Distributors & Exporters,** 30
Chemin des Trilles, Laval, Quebec,
H7Y 1K2. Tel: (1 450) 689 9950.
Fax: 689 9822. cic@total.net.
**Canadian Film & Television
Production Association,**
151 Slater St, Suite 605, Ottawa,
Ontario, K1P 5H3.
Tel: (1 613) 233 1444.
Fax: 233 0073. ottawa@cftpa.ca.
**Canadian Motion Picture
Distributors Association
(CMPDA),** 22 St Clair Ave E,
Suite 1603, Toronto, Ontario, M4T
2S4. Tel: (1 416) 961 1888.
Fax: 968 1016.
Directors Guild of Canada,
1 Eglinton Ave E, Suite 604,
Toronto, Ontario, M4P 3A1.
Tel: (1 416) 482 6640.
Fax: 486 6639. www.dgc.ca.
**Motion Picture Theatre
Associations of Canada,**
[Exhibitors], 146 Bloor St W,
2nd Floor, Toronto, Ontario, M5S
1P3. Tel: (1 416) 969 7057.
Fax: 969 9852. www.mptac.ca.

National Film Board of Canada, PO Box 6100, Station Centre-Ville, Montréal, Quebec, H3C 3H5. Tel: (1 514) 283 9246. Fax: 283 8971. www.nfb.ca.
Telefilm Canada, 360 St Jacques St W, Suite 700, Montréal, Quebec, H2Y 4A9. Tel: (1 514) 283 6363. Fax: 283 8212. www.telefilm.gc.ca.

CHILE

All Tel/Fax numbers begin (56 2)

Useful Addresses
Arauco Films, Silvina Hurtado 1789, Providencia, Santiago. Tel: 209 2091. Fax: 204 5096. araucofi@entelchile.net.
Departamento de Creación y Difusión Artística, Consejo Nacional de la Cultura y las Artes, Edificio Centenario, Piso 20, Bellavista 168, Valparaíso. Tel: 326 612. cgutierrez.cultura@mineduc.clwww. consejodelacultura.cl.
Chilefilms, La Capitanía 1200, Las Condes, Santiago. Tel: 220 3086. Fax: 229 6406/212 9053. info@chilefilms.cl. www.chilefilms.cl.
Corporación de Fomento de la Producción (CORFO), Moneda 921, Santiago. Tel: 631 8597. Fax: 671 7735. lordonez@corfo.cl. www.corfo.cl.
Filmosonido, Rodolfo Lenz 3399, Ñuñoa, Santiago. Tel: 341 2110. Fax: 204 2054. marcos@filmosonido.cl. www.filmosonido.cl.
PWI, Cruz del Sur 133, Of. 403-404, Las Condes, Santiago. Tel: 207 2883/2760. Fax: 207 2963. marketing@pwimedia.com. www.pwimedia.com.

CHINA

Archive
China Film Archive, 3 Wenhuiyuan Lu, Xiao Xiao Xitian, Haidian District, Beijing 100088. Tel: (86 10) 6225 4422. chinafilm@cbn.com.cn.

Magazines
Film Art, (Dianying yishou), 77 Beisanhuan Zhonglu, Beijing 100088. Quarterly.
Popular Cinema, (Dazhong dianying), 22 Beisanhuan Donglu, Beijing. Official popular film magazine, published fortnightly.
New Cinema Magazine, (Xin dianying), 55 Xingfu Yi Cun, Chaoyang District, Beijing 100027. Tel: (86 10) 6417 6943. www.wfj.cc/magazine/200303/index.htm.

Useful Addresses
August First Film Studio, A1, Beili, Liuliqiao, Guang'anmenwai, Beijing 100073. Tel: (86 10) 6681 2329. Fax: 6326 7324.
Beijing Film Academy, 4 Xitucheng Rd, Haidian District, Beijing 100088. Tel: (86 10) 8204 8899. www.bfa.edu.cn.
Beijing Film Studio, 77 Beisanhuan Central Rd, Haidan District, Beijing 100088. Tel: (86 10) 6200 3191. Fax: 6201 2059.
Beijing Forbidden City Film Company, 67 Beichizi Street, Dongcheng District, Beijing 100006. Tel: (86 10) 6513 1275. Fax: 6513 1275.
China Film Group Corp, 25 Xinjiekouwai St, Beijing 100088. Tel: (86 10) 6225 4488. Fax: 6225 0652. cfgc@chinafilm.com. www.chinafilm.com.
China Film Co-Production Corp, 5 Xinyuan South Rd, Chaoyang District, Beijing 100027. Tel: (86 10) 6466 3330. Fax: 6466 3983. www.cfcc-film.com.cn.

Meishi Film Academy of Chongqing University, Chongqing 400044. Tel: (86 23) 6510 6258/6511 1919. Fax: 6510 5671. meishi@public.cta.cq.c. www.msfilm.cqu.edu.cn/eng/index.aspx.
Poly-Asian Union Film, Building B, 5 Shuguang Tower, Jingshun Road, Chaoyang District, Beijing 100028. Tel : (86 10) 8440 9919. Fax: 8440 9918. service@asian-union.com.
Shanghai Film Studio/Shanghai Film Group, 595 Caoxi Beilu, Shanghai 200030. Tel: (86 21) 6438 7100. www.sfs-cn.com/.

COLOMBIA

Archive
Colombian Film Archives, Carrera 13, No 13-24, Piso 9, Bogotá. Tel: (57 1) 281 5241. Fax: 342 1485. patfilm@colnodo.apc.org. www.patrimoniofilmico.org.co.

Magazine
Kinetoscopio, Carrera 45, No 53-24, Apartado 8734, Medellin. Tel: (57 4) 513 4444, ext 178. Fax: 513 2666. kineto@colomboworld.com. www.colomboworld.com/kinetoscopio. Quarterly covering international and Latin American cinema, Colombian directors and festival news.

Useful Addresses
Association of Film & Video Producers & Directors, Calle 97, No 10-28, Bogotá. Tel: (57 1) 218 2455. Fax: 610 8524. gustavo@centauro.com.
Colombian Association of Cinemas, Calle 23, No 5-85, Int 202, Bogotá. Tel: (57 1) 284 5752. Fax: 334 0809. e-mail: acocine@hotmail.com.

Colombian Association of Documentary Film Directors, Calle 35, No 4-89, Bogotá. Tel: (57 1) 245 9961. aladoscolombia@netscape.net. www.enmente.com/alados.

Colombian Association of Film Directors, Carrera 6, No 55-10, Apartado 202, Bogotá. Tel: (57 1) 235 9798. Fax: 212 2586. lisandro@inter.net.co.

Colombian Association of Film Distributors, Carrera 11, No 93A-22, Bogotá. Tel: (57 1) 610 6695. Fax: 618 5417. fabogado@impsat.net.co.

Film Promotion Fund, Calle 35, No 4-89, Bogotá. Tel: (57 1) 287 0103. Fax: 288 4828. claudiatriana@proimagenescolombia.com. www.proimagenescolombia.com.

Ministry of Culture, Film Division, Calle 35, No 4-89, Bogotá. Tel: (57 1) 288 2995. Fax: 285 5690. cine@mincultura.gov.co. www.mincultura.gov.co.

National Film Council, Calle 35, No 4-89, Bogotá. Tel: (57 1) 288 4712. Fax: 285 5690. cine@mincultura.gov.co. www.mincultura.gov.co. Director: Claudia Aguilera.

CROATIA
All Tel/Fax numbers begin (385 1)

Useful Addresses
Alka Film, 10000 Zagreb, Dedici 12. Tel: 467 4187.

Croatia Film d.o.o, Katanciceva 3, 10000 Zagreb. Tel: 481 3711. Fax: 492 2568.

Croatian Film Directors Guild, Britanski Trg 12, 10000 Zagreb. Tel: 484 7026. info@dhfr.hr. www.dhfr.hr.

Croatian Film Clubs' Association, Dalmatinska 12, 10000 Zagreb. Tel: 484 8764. vera@hfs.hr. www.hfs.hr.

DA Film d.o.o, Juriciceva 16A., 10000 Zagreb. Tel: 954 3362.

Druzba d.o.o, B Magovca 147, 10000 Zagreb. Tel/Fax: 668 1261.

Gama studio d.o.o, Tuckanac 63, 10000 Zagreb. Tel: 483 4168. Fax: 299 3545.

Gral Film, Ilica 42, 10000 Zagreb. Tel: 484 7575.

HRT (Croatian Television), Prisavlje 3, 10000 Zagreb. Tel: 634 3683. Fax: 634 3692.

Interfilm Produkcija, Nova Ves 45, 10000 Zagreb. Tel: 466 7296. Fax: 466 7291.

Jadran Film, Oporovecka I2, Dugi dol 13, 10000 Zagreb. Tel: 298 7222. Fax: 285 1394.

Maxima Film d.o.o, Belostenceva 6, 10000 Zagreb. Tel: 618 4731.

M.B.M. d.o.o, 10000 Zagreb. Tel: 487 3292.

Zagreb Film, Vlacka 72, 10000 Zagreb. Tel: 455 0489.

CUBA

Archives
Archivo Fílmico, Calle 23 No 1109, Entre 8 & 10, Vedado, Havana. Tel: (53 7) 833 6321. archivo@icaic.inf.cu.

Cinemateca de Cuba, Calle 23 No 1155, Entre 10 & 12, Vedado, Havana. Tel: (53 7) 552 844. cinemateca@icaic.inf.cu.

Film Schools
Escuela Internacional de Cine y TV, Finca San Tranquilino, Carretera Vereda Nueva, KM 4.5, San Antonio de Los Baños, Havana. Tel: (53 650) 383 152. Fax: 382 366. eictv@eictv.org.cu. www.eictv.org.

Instituto Superior de Arte, Facultad de Comunicación Audiovisual, 5ta, Avenida Esq A20, Miramar, Playa, Havana. Tel: (53 7) 209 1302. isafaud@cubarte.cult.cu.

Magazines
Cine Cubano, Calle 23 No 1115, El Vedado, Havana. Tel: (53 7) 552 865. publicaciones@icaic.inf.cu.

ECOS, Arzobispado de La Habana, Calle Habana No 152, Esq Chacón, La Habana Vieja. Tel: (53 7) 862 4009. Fax: 338 109. signis@cocc.co.cu.

Useful Addresses
Cinematografía Educativa, Calle 7MA 2802, Entre 28 & 30, Miramar, Playa, Havana. Tel: (53 7) 202 6971. cined@ceniai.inf.cu.

National Film Institute (ICAIC), Calle 23, No 1155, Entre 8 & 10, Vedado, Havana. Tel: (53 7) 552 859. Fax: 833 3281. omar@icaic.inf.cu. www.cubacine.cu.

Televisión Serrana, San Pablo de Yao, Buey Arriba, Granma. Tel: (53 23) 23548. cip214@enet.cu.

CYPRUS
All Tel/Fax numbers begin (357 22)

Cyprus Cinema Advisory Committee, Cultural Services, Ministry of Education & Culture, Kimonos & Thoukididou Street, 1434 Nicosia. Tel: 809 507. Fax: 809 506. echristo@cytanet.com.cy.

Directors Union, 11 Pente Pygadion Street, Flat 4, Ayioi Omologites, 1076 Nicosia. Tel: 458 717. Fax: 458 718. artvision@cytanet.com.cy.

CZECH REPUBLIC
All Tel/Fax numbers begin (420 2)

Archive
National Film Archive, Malesická 12, 130 00 Prague 3. Tel: 7177 0509. Fax: 7177 0501. nfa@nfa.cz. www.nfa.cz.

Film School

FAMU, Film & Television Faculty, Academy of Performing Arts, Smetanovo 2, 116 65 Prague 1. Tel: 2422 9176. Fax: 2423 0285. kamera@f.amu.cz.

Useful Addresses

Association of Czech Filmmakers (FITES), Pod Nuselskymi Schody 3, 120 00 Prague 2. Tel: 691 0310. Fax: 691 1375. **Association of Producers**, Národní 28, 110 00 Prague 1. Tel: 2110 5321. Fax: 2110 5303. www.apa.iol.cz. **Czech Film & Television Academy**, Na Îertvách 40, 180 00 Prague 8. Tel: 8482 1356. Fax: 8482 1341. **Czech Film Centre**, Národní 28, 110 00 Prague 1. Tel: 2110 5302. Fax: 2110 5303. www.filmcenter.cz. **Ministry of Culture**, Audiovisual Dept, Milady Horákové 139, 160 00 Prague 6. Tel: 5708 5310. Fax: 2431 8155. **Union of Czech Film Distributors**, Národní 28, 110 00 Prague 1. Tel: 2494 5220. Fax: 2110 5220.

DENMARK

All Tel/Fax numbers begin (45)

Archive

Danish Film Institute/Archive & Cinemateque (DFI), Gothersgade 55, DK-1123 Copenhagen K. Tel: 3374 3400. Fax: 3374 3401. dfi@dfi.dk. www.dfi.dk. Also publishes the film magazine, *Film*.

Film Schools

European Film College, Carl Th Dreyers Vej 1, DK-8400 Ebeltoft. Tel: 8634 0055. Fax: 8634 0535. administration@efc.dk. www.efc.dk.

National Film School of Denmark, Theodor Christensens Plads 1, DK-1437 Copenhagen K. Tel: 3268 6400. Fax: 3268 6410. info@filmskolen.dk. www.filmskolen.dk.

Magazine

FILM, Gothersgade 55, DK-1123 Copenhagen K. Tel: 3374 3400. susannan@dfi.dk and agnetes@dfi.dk. Published by the Danish Film Institute. Eight issues per year (some English).

Useful Addresses

Danish Actors' Association (DSF), Sankt Knuds Vej 26, DK-1903 Frederiksberg C. Tel: 3324 2200. Fax: 3324 8159. dsf@skuespillerforbundet.dk. www.skuespillerforbundet.dk. **Danish Film Directors (DF)**, Vermundsgade 19, 2nd Floor, DK-2100 Copenhagen Ø. Tel: 3583 8005. Fax: 3583 8006. mail@filmdir.dk. www.filmdir.dk. **Danish Film Distributors' Association (FAFID)**, Sundkrogsgade 9, DK-2100 Copenhagen Ø. Tel: 3363 9684. Fax: 3363 9660. www.fafid.dk. **Danish Film Institute**, Gothersgade 55, DK-1123 Copenhagen K. Tel: 3374 3400. Fax: 3374 3401. dfi@dfi.dk. **Danish Film Studios**, Blomstervaenget 52, DK-2800 Lyngby. Tel: 4587 2700. Fax: 4587 2705. ddf@filmstudie.dk. www.filmstudie.dk. **Danish Producers' Association**, Bernhard Bangs Allé 25, DK-2000 Frederiksberg. Tel: 3386 2880. Fax: 3386 2888. info@pro-f.dk. www.producentforeningen.dk.

ECUADOR

All Tel/Fax numbers begin (59 32)

Film School

Universidad San Francisco de Quito, Contemporary Arts Department, Film and TV, Via Interoceánica & Jardines del Este, Cumbayá. Tel: 289 5723. www.usfq.edu.ec.

Useful Addresses

Cabeza Hueca Producciones, Foch 265 & Plaza Edif. Sonelsa 1er piso, Quito. Tel: 223 9090. cabezahueca@hoy.net. **Cine Ocho y Medio**, Valladolid N24 353 & Vizcaya, Quito. Tel: 290 4720. Fax: 256 5524. rbarriga@ochoymedio.net. www.ochoymedio.net. **Corporación Cine Memoria**, Venezuela N6-09 & Mejía–Of A1, Quito. Tel: 295 9132. cinememoria@andinanet.net. www.cinememoria.com. **Sapo Inc**, juan@sapoinc.com. www.sapoinc.com.

EGYPT

All Tel/Fax numbers begin (20 2)

Archive

National Egyptian Film Archive, c/o Egyptian Film Centre, City of Arts, Al Ahram Rd, Guiza. Tel: 585 4801. Fax: 585 4701. President: Dr Mohamed Kamel El Kalyobi.

Film School

Higher Film Institute, Pyramids Rd, Gamal El-Din El-Afaghani St, Guiza. Tel: 537 703. Fax: 561 1034. aoarts@idsc.gov.eg.

Useful Addresses

El-Arabia Cinema, [Producer/Distributor], 21Ahmed Orabi St, Mohanesseen, Cairo. Tel: 344 4788. Fax: 344 5040.

Central Audio-Visual Censorship Authority, Opera Ground, Gezira, Cairo. Tel: 738 1674.
Fax: 736 9479.

Chamber of Film Industry, 1195 Kornish El Nil, Industries Union Bldg, Cairo. Tel: 578 5111. Fax: 575 1583.

Egyptian Radio & TV Union, Kornish El Nil, Maspero St, Cairo. Tel: 576 0014. Fax: 579 9316.

Media City, [Producer/Distributor], Al Haram Ave, City of Cinema, Giza. Tel: 584 4217. Fax: 584 4219.

National Film Center, Al-Ahram Ave, Giza. Tel: 585 4801.
Fax: 585 4701.

Oscar for Distribution & Theatres, Ramsis Hilton, Cairo.
Tel: 574 7436. Fax: 574 7437.

Shoa's Cultural Media Arab Co, [Producer/Distributor], Marwa St, Dokki, Cairo. Tel: 336 9510.
Fax: 336 9511.

ESTONIA

Archive
Estonian National Archive, Ristiku 84, 10318 Tallinn. Tel: (372 6) 938 613. Fax: 938 611.
filmiarhiiv@ra.ee. www.filmi.arhiiv.ee.

Film School
Department of Audiovisual Arts, Faculty of Fine Arts, Tallinn Pedagogical University, Lai 13, 10133 Tallinn. Tel: (372 6) 411 627. Fax: 412 525. kultuur@tpu.ee. www.tpu.ee.

Useful Addresses
Association of Professional Actors of Estonia, Uus 5, 10111 Tallinn. Tel: (372 6) 464 512. Fax: 464 516. enliit@delfi.ee. www.enliit.ee.

Estonian Association of Film Journalists, Narva Mnt 11E, 10151 Tallinn. Tel: (372 5) 533 894. Fax: 698 154. jaan@ekspress.ee.

Estonian Film Foundation, Vana-Viru 3, 10111 Tallinn.
Tel: (372 6) 276 060. Fax: 276 061. film@efsa.ee. www.efsa.ee.

Estonian Film Producers Association, Rävala pst 11-12, 10143 Tallinn. Tel: (372 6) 67 8 270. Fax: 67 8 721.
produtsendid@rudolf.ee.

Estonian Filmmakers Union, Uus 3, 10111 Tallinn. Tel/Fax: (372 6) 464 068. kinoliit@online.ee.

Union of Estonian Cameramen, Faehlmanni 12, 15029 Tallinn. Tel: (372 5) 662 3069. Fax: 568 401. bogavideo@infonet.ee.

FINLAND

Archive
Finnish Film Archive, Pursimiehenkatu 29-31A, PO Box 177, FIN-00151, Helsinki. Tel: (358 9) 615 400.

Film School
University of Art & Design Helsinki (UIAH), Dept of Film, Hämeentie 135 C, FIN-00560, Helsinki. Tel: (358 9) 756 31.

Magazines
Filmihullu, Malminkatu 36, FIN-00100, Helsinki.
Tel: (358 9) 685 2242.

Filmjournalen, Finlandssvenskt Filmcentrum, Nylandsgatan 1, FIN-20500, Åbo. Tel: (358 2) 250 0431. www.fsfilmcentrum.fi/fj/.

Useful Addresses
Artista Filmi Oy, [Producer], Post Box 69, FIN-28401, Ulvila. Tel: (338 2) 647 7441.
timo.koivusalo@ artistafilmi.com.

Blind Spot Pictures Oy, [Producer], Kalliolanrinne 4, FIN-00510, Helsinki.
Tel: (358 9) 7742 8360.

Dada Filmi Oy, 3 Linja 5, FIN-00530 Helsinki. Tel: (358 9) 774 4780. fennada@dada.pp.fi.

Helsinki-filmi Oy
Vanha Talvitie 11 A, FIN 00580 Helsinki.
Tel. (3589) 7740 300.
aleksi.bardy@iki.fi.
www.helsinkifilmi.fi.

Juonifilmi Oy
Urho Kekkosen katu 4-6 A, 00100 Helsinki.
Tel. (35820) 7300 451.
jarkko.hentula@juonifilmi.fi.
www.juonifilmi.fi.

Kinotar Oy, [Producer], Meritullinkatu 33E, FIN-00170, Helsinki. Tel: (358 9) 135 1864. kinotar@kinotar.com.

MRP Matila & Röhr Productions, [Producer], Tallbrginkatu 1A 141, FIN-00180, Helsinki.
Tel: (358 9) 540 7820. Fax: 685 2229. mrp@matilarohr.com.

Solar Films Oy, [Producer], Kiviaidankatu 1, FIN-00210, Helsinki. Tel: (358 9) 417 4700.

FRANCE

Archives
Archives du Film, 7 bis rue Alexandre Turpault, 78395 Bois d'Arcy. Tel: (33 1) 3014 8000. Fax: 3460 5225.

Cinémathèque de Toulouse, BP 824, 31080 Toulouse Cedex 6. Tel: (33 5) 6230 3010.
Fax: 6230 3012.
contact@lacinemathequedetoulouse.com. www.lacinemathequedetoulouse.com. President: Martine Offroy.

Cinémathèque Française, 4 rue de Longchamp, 75116 Paris. Tel: (33 1) 5365 7474. Fax: 5365 7465. contact@cinemathequefrancaise.com. www.cinemathequefrancaise.com.

Institut Lumière, 25 rue du Premier-Film, BP 8051, 69352 Lyon Cedex 8. Tel: (33 4) 7878 1895. Fax: 7878 3656. contact@institut-lumiere.org. www.institut-lumiere.org.

Bookshops

Atmosphère, Libraire du Cinema, 10 rue Broca, 75005 Paris. Tel: (33 1) 4331 0271. Fax: 4331 0369. librairie.atmosphere@frisbee.fr.

Gilda, 36 rue de Boudonnais, 75001 Paris. Tel: (33 1) 4233 6000. Videos, books, film magazines, compact disc videos, CDs, CD Roms.

Librairie Contacts, 24 rue du Colisée, 75008 Paris. Tel: (33 1) 4359 1771. Fax: 4289 2765. librairiecontacts@wanadoo.fr. www.medialibrarie.com.

Film Schools

Conservatoire Libre du Cinéma Français, 9 quai de l'Oise, 75019 Paris. Tel: (33 1) 4036 1919. Fax: 4036 0102. info@clcf.com. www.clcf.com.

ESEC (Ecole Superieure d'Etudes Libres Cinematographique), 21 rue de Citeaux, 75012 Paris. Tel: (33 1) 4342 4322. Fax: 4341 9521. esec@esec.edu. www.esec.edu.

Femis (École Nationale Supérieure des Métiers de L'Image et du Son), 6 rue Francoeur, 75018 Paris. Tel: (33 1) 5341 2100. Fax: 5341 0280. femis@femis.fr. www.femis.fr.

Magazines

Cahiers du Cinema, 9 passage de la Boule Blanche, 75012 Paris. Tel: (33 1) 5344 7575. Fax: 4343 9504. cducinema@lemonde.fr. Celebrated French monthly journal.

Le Film Français, 150 rue Gallieni, 92514 Boulogne Cedex. Tel: (33 1) 4186 1600. Fax: 4186 1691. lefilmfrancais@emapfrance.com. www.lefilmfrancais.com. Lightweight weekly.

Positif, 3 rue Lhomond, 75005 Paris. Tel: (33 1) 4432 0590. Fax: 4432 0591. www.johnmichelplace.com.fr In-depth interviews, articles, all immaculately researched and highly intelligent.

Premiere, 151 rue Anatole France, 92534 Levallois-Perret. Tel: (33 1) 4134 9111. Fax: 4134 9119. www.premiere.fr. France's familiar movie monthly.

Useful Addresses

Centre National de la Cinématographie, 12 rue de Lubeck, Paris 75016. Tel: (33 1) 4434 3440. Fax: 4755 0491. webmaster@cnc.fr. www.cnc.fr.

Ile de France Film Commission, 11, rue du Colisée, Paris 75008. Tel: (33 1) 5688 1280. Fax: 5688 1219. idf-film@idf-film.com. www.iledefrance-film.com.

Unifrance, 4 Villa Bosquet, Paris 75007. Tel: (33 1) 4753 9580. Fax: 4705 9655. info@unifrance.org. www.unifrance.org.

GEORGIA

All Tel/Fax numbers begin (995 32)

Archive

Central Film Photo Archive, Vaja-Pshavelas Gamziri 1, Tbilisi. Tel: 386 529.

Film School

Georgian State Institute of Theatre & Film, Rustavelis Gamziri 37, 380004 Tbilisi. Tel: 997 588. Fax: 991 153.

Useful Addresses

National Film Centre, Rustavelis Gamziri 37, 380008 Tbilisi. Tel: 984 201. Fax: 999 037. www.kinocentre.myweb.ge.

Society of Audiovisual Authors & Producers, Dzmebi Kakabadzeebis Qucha 2, 380008 Tbilisi. Tel: 998 995. Fax: 932 820. www.itic.org.ge.

GERMANY

Archives

Deutsches Filminstitut-DIF, Schaumainkai 41, 60596 Frankfurt am Main. Tel: (49 69) 961 2200. Fax: 620 060. info@deutsches-filminstitut.de. www.deutsches-filminstitut.de.

Deutsches Filmmuseum Frankfurt am Main, Schaumainkai 41, 60596 Frankfurt am Main. Tel: (49 69) 2123 8830. Fax: 2123 7881. info@deutsches-filmmuseum.de. www.deutsches-filmmuseum.de.

Filmmuseum Berlin-Deutsche Kinemathek, Potsdamer Str 2, 10785 Berlin. Tel: (49 30) 300 9030. Fax: 3009 0313. info@filmmuseum-berlin.de. www.filmmuseum-berlin.de.

Kino Arsenal/Home of Independent Cinema, Potsdamer Str 2, 10785 Berlin. Tel: (49 30) 2695 5100. Fax: 2695 5111. fdk@fdk-berlin.de. www.fdk-berlin.de.

Münchner Stadtmuseum/ Filmmuseum, St Jakobsplatz 1, 80331 Munich. Tel: (49 89) 2332 2348. Fax: 2332 3931. filmmuseum@muenchen.de. www.stadtmuseum-online.de/filmmu.htm.

Bookshops

Buchhandlung Langenkamp,
Beckergrube 19, 23552 Lübeck.
Tel: (49 451) 76479. Fax: 72645.

Buchhandlung Walther König,
Ehrenstr 4, 50672, Cologne.
Tel: (49 221) 205 9625.
Fax: 205 9625.
order@buchhandlung-walther-
koenig.de. www.buchhandlung-
walther-koenig.de.

H Lindemann's Bookshop,
Nadlerstr 4 & 10, 70173 Stuttgart 1.
Tel: (49 711) 2489 9977.
Fax: 236 9672.
fotobuecher@lindemanns.de.
www.lindemanns.de.

Sautter & Lackmann,
Filmbuchhandlung, Admiralitädstr
71/72, 20459 Hamburg.
Tel: (49 40) 373 196. Fax: 365 479.
info@sautter-lackmann.de. Mainly
books, but also videos etc.

Marga Schoeller Buecherstube,
Knesebeckstr 33, 10623 Berlin.
Tel: (49 30) 881 1122. Fax: 881
8479. schoeller.buecher@gmx.net.

**Verlag fur Filmschriften Christian
Unucka**, Postfach 63, 85239
Hebertshausen.
Tel: (49 8131) 13922. Fax: 10075.
order@unucka.de. www.unucka.de.

Film Schools

**Deutsche Film und
Fernsehakademie Berlin,**
Potsdamer Str 2, 10785 Berlin.
Tel: (49 30) 257 590. Fax: 257
59161. info@dffb.de. www.dffb.de.

Filmakademie Baden-Würtenberg,
Mathildenstr 20, 71638
Ludwigsburg. Tel: (49 7141) 969
108. Fax: 969 292.
info@filmakademie.de.
www.filmakademie.de.

**Hochschule für Fernsehen und
Film**, Frankenthaler Str 23, 81539
Munich. Tel: (49 89) 689 570.
Fax: 689 57189. Info@hff-muc.de
www.hff-muc.de.

Magazines

Blickpunkt Film, Einsteinring 24,
85609 Dornach. Tel: (49 89) 4511
4124. Fax: 4511 4451.
hspoerl@e-media.de.
www.blickpunktfilm.de.
Strong on box-office returns and
marketing, weekly.

EPD Medien, Postfach 50 05 50,
60439 Frankfurt am Main.
Tel: (49 69) 5809 8141.
Fax: 5809 8261. medien@epd.de.
www.epd.de/medien. Highbrow.

Entertainment Markt, Einsteinring
24, 85609 Dornach.
Tel: (49 89) 451 140.
Fax: 4511 4444. emv@e-media.de.
www.e-mediabiz.de.
Bi-weekly business magazine.

Film-Echo/Filmwoche,
Marktplatz 13, 65183 Wiesbaden.
Tel: (49 611) 360 980.
Fax: 372 878. info@filmecho.de.
www.filmecho.de. Doyen of the
German trade. Weekly.

Kino, Export-Union des Deutschen
Films GmbH, Sonnenstr 21, 80331
Munich. Tel: (49 89) 599 7870.
Fax: 5997 8730.
export-union@german-cinema.de.
www.german-cinema.de. Published
four times a year in English;
yearbook also available.

**Kino German Film & Intl.
Reports**, Helgoländer Ufer 6,
10557 Berlin. Tel: (49 30) 391
6167. Fax: 391 2424.
ronaldholloway@aol.com. Excellent
magazine published twice a year.

Useful Addresses

Association of Distributors,
Kreuzberger Ring 56, 65205
Wiesbaden. Tel: (49 611) 778 920.
Fax: 778 9212. vdfkino@aol.com.

Association of Exhibitors, Grosse
Praesidentenstr 9, 10178 Berlin.
Tel: (49 30) 2300 4041. Fax: 2300
4026. info@kino-hdf.de.

**Association of German Film
Exporters**, Tegernseer Landstr 75,
81539 Munich. Tel: (49 89) 692
0660. Fax: 692 0910.
vdfe@kanziel-wedel.de.

Export Union, Sonnenstr 21,
80331 Munich. Tel: (49 89) 599
7870. Fax: 5997 8730.
export-union@german-cinema.de.
www.german-cinema.de.

Federal Film Board (FFA), Grosse
Praesidentenstr 9, 10178 Berlin.
Tel: (49 30) 275 770.
Fax: 2757 7111. www.ffa.de.

**New German Film Producers
Association**, Agnesstr 14, 80798
Munich. Tel: (49 89) 271 7430. Fax:
271 9728. ag-spielfilm@t-online.de.

**Umbrella Organisation of the
Film Industry**, Kreuzberger Ring
56, 65205 Wiesbaden.
Tel: (49 611) 778 9114. Fax: 778
9169. statistik@spio-fsk.de.

GREECE
All Tel/Fax numbers begin (30 210)

Useful Addresses
AMA Films, 54 Themistokleous,
106 81 Athens. Tel: 383 3118/381
2640. Fax: 384 2559.
amafilms@amafilms.gr.

**Association of Independent
Producers of Audiovisual Works
(SAPOE)**, 30 Aegialias, 151 25
Maroussi. Tel: 683 3212. Fax: 683
3606. sapoe-gr@otenet.gr.

Cinema Department,
5 Metsovou, 106 82 Athens. Tel:
825 0767/0720. Fax: 825 3604.

Film Trade, 130A Kifissias,
115 26 Athens. Tel: 698 1083. Fax:
698 3430. vassilis@filmtrade.gr.

Greek Film Centre, President &
Managing Director: Diagoras
Chronopoulos, 10 Panepistimou,
106 71 Athens. Tel: 367 8500. Fax:
364 8269. info@gfc.gr. www.gfc.gr.

Greek Film, Theatre & Television Directors Guild, 11 Tossitsa, 106 83 Athens. Tel: 822 8936/3205. Fax: 821 1390. ees@ath.forthnet.gr.

Hellas Film, 10 Panepistimiou, 106 71 Athens. Tel: 367 8500. Fax: 361 4336. info@gfc.gr. www.gfc.gr.

Hellenic Ministry of Culture, 20 Bouboulinas, 106 82 Athens. Tel: 820 1100. w3admin@culture.gr. http://culture.gr.

Odeon SA, (Public Performance Enterprise for the Production & Exploitation of Audiovisual Works), 275 Mesogion, 152 31 Halandri. Tel: 678 6511/6600. Fax: 672 8927. distribution@hvh.com.gr.

Play Time, 11 Mitropoleos, 2nd Floor, 105 56 Athens. Tel: 331 5175. Fax: 331 1309. theoni@infoplaytime.com.gr.

Prooptiki SA, 40-42 Koleti, 106 82 Athens. Tel: 330 7700. Fax: 330 7798. prooptiki@prooptiki.gr.

Rosebud SA Motion Picture Enterprises, 275 Mesogion, 152 31 Halandri. Tel: 678 6511. Fax: 672 8927.

Spentzos Films, 9-13 Gravias, 106 78 Athens. Tel: 382 5953. Fax: 380 9314. festival@otenet.gr.

Union of Greek Film Directors and Producers, 33 Methonis, 106 83 Athens. Tel: 825 3065. Fax: 825 3065.

Union of Greek Film, TV & Audiovisual Sector Technicians (ETEKT-OT), 25 Valtetsiou, 106 80 Athens. Tel: 360 2379/361 5675. Fax: 361 6442. etekt-ot@ath.forthnet.gr.

HONG KONG

All Tel/Fax numbers begin (852)

Archive

Hong Kong Film Archive, 50 Lei King Rd, Sai Wan Ho. Tel: 2739 2139. Fax: 2311 5229. www.filmarchive.gov.hk.

Film School

Hong Kong Academy for Performing Arts, School of Film & Television, 1 Gloucester Rd, Wan Chai. Tel: 2584 8500. Fax: 2802 4372. www.hkapa.edu.

Magazine

City Entertainment, Flat B2, 17/F, Fortune Factory Bldg, 40 Lee Chung Rd, Chai Wan. Tel: 2892 0155. Fax: 2838 4930. www.cityentertainment.com.hk. Indispensable Hong Kong bi-weekly in Chinese for anyone interested in Chinese cinema.

Useful Addresses

Film Services Office, 40/F, Revenue Tower, 5 Gloucester Rd, Wan Chai. Tel: 2594 5745. Fax: 2824 0595. www.fso-tela.gov.hk.

Hong Kong Film Academy, Room 906 Sunbeam Commercial Building, 469-471 Nathan Road, Kowloon. Tel: 2786 9349. Fax: 2742 7017. www.filmacademy.com.hk.

Hong Kong Film Awards Association, Room 1601-2 Austin Tower, 22-26A Austin Ave, Tsim Sha Tsui, Kowloon. Tel: 2367 7892. Fax: 2723 9597. ww.hkfaa.com.

Hong Kong Film Critics Association, 4G, Hoi To Court, 275 Gloucester Rd, Causeway Bay. Tel: 2573 7498. Fax: 2574 6726. www.hkfca.org.

Hong Kong Film Critics Society, Unit 104, 1/F, Corn Yan Centre, 3 Jupiter St, Tin Hau. Tel: 2575 5149. Fax: 2891 2048. www.filmcritics.org.hk.

Hong Kong Film Directors Guild, 2/F, 35 Ho Man Tin St, Kowloon. Tel: 2760 0331. Fax: 2713 2373. www.hkfdg.com.

Hong Kong Film Institute, 6/F, Pak Cheung Building, 295 Lai Chi Kok Rd, Kowloon. Tel: 2728 2690. Fax: 2728 5743. www.hkfilm.com.

Hong Kong, Kowloon and New Territories Motion Picture Industry Association, 13/F, Tung Wui Commercial Bldg, 27 Prat Ave, Tsim Sha Tsui, Kowloon. Tel: 2311 2692. Fax: 2311 1178. www.mpia.org.hk.

Hong Kong Theatres Association, 21/F, Hong Kong Chinese Bank, 42 Yee Woo St, Causeway Bay. Tel: 2576 3833. Fax: 2576 1833.

HUNGARY

All Tel/Fax numbers begin (36 1)

Archive

Hungarian National Film Archive, Budakeszi Ut 51B, H-1021 Budapest. Tel: 200 8739. Fax: 398 0781. filmintezet@ella.hu. www.filmintezet.hu.

Film School

Academy of Drama & Film, Szentkiralyi Utca 32A, H-1088, Budapest. Tel: 338 4855.

Magazine

Filmvilag, Hollan Ernö Utca 38A, H-1137 Budapest. filmvilag@chello.hu. www.filmvilag.hu. Monthly with reviews and interviews.

Useful Addresses

Association of Hungarian Film Artists, Városligeti Fasor 38, H-1068 Budapest. Tel/Fax: 342 4760. filmszovetseg@axelero.hu.

Association of Hungarian Producers, Szinhaz Utca 5-9, H-1014 Budapest. Tel: 355 7049. Fax: 355 7639. producer@mpsz.axelerol.net.

Hungarian Film Union, Városligeti Fasor 38, H-1068 Budapest. Tel: 351 7760/1. Fax: 352 6734. filmunio@filmunio.hu. www.filmunio.hu.

Hungarian Motion Picture Foundation, Városligeti Fasor 38, H-1068 Budapest. Tel: 351 7696. Fax: 352 8789. www.mma.hu.

Hungarian Independent Producers Assocation, Róna Utca 174, H-1145 Budapest. Tel: 220 5421. Fax: 220 5420. eurofilm@axelero.hu.

National Film Office, Wesselenyi Utca 16, H-1075 Budapest. Tel: 327 7070. Fax: 321 9224. info@filmoffice.hu.

ICELAND
All Tel/Fax numbers begin (354)

Archive
National Film Archive, Hvaleyrarbraut 13, 220 Hafnarfjordur. Tel: 565 5993. Fax: 565 5994. kvikmyndasafn@kvikmyndasafn.is. www.kvikmyndasafn.is.

Film Schools
Icelandic Film School, Laugarvegur 176, 105 Reykjavík. Tel: 533 3309 Fax: 533 3308. kvikmyndaskoli@kvikmyndaskoli.is. www.kvikmyndaskoli.is.

Useful Addresses

Association of Icelandic Film Directors, Leifsgata 25, 101 Reykjavík. Tel: 588 6003/898 0209. ho@ismennt.is.

Association of Icelandic Film Distributors, SAM-Bíóin, Álfabakka 8, 109 Reykjavík. Tel: 575 8900. Fax: 587 8910. thorvaldur@sambio.is.

Association of Icelandic Film Producers, Túngötu 14, PO Box 5367, 125 Reykjavík. Tel: 863 3057. Fax: 555 3065. sik@producers.is. www.producers.is.

Film Censor, Túngötu 14, 101 Reykjavík. Tel: 562 8020. kvikmynd@mmedia.is. www.mmedia.is/~kvikmynd/.

Icelandic Film Centre, Túngötu 14, 101 Reykjavík. Tel: 562 3580. Fax: 562 7171. info@icelandicfilmcentre.is. www.icelandicfilmcentre.is.

Icelandic Film Makers Association, PO Box 5162, 128 Reykjavík. Tel: 562 6660. Fax: 562 6665. bjorn@spark.is.

Icelandic Film & Television Academy/EDDA Awards, Túngötu 14, 101 Reykjavík. Tel: 562 3580. Fax: 562 7171. beta@cutandpaste.is

INDIA

Archive
National Film Archive of India, Law College Rd, Pune 411 004. Tel: (91 020) 565 8049. Fax: 567 0027. nfai@vsnl.net.

Film School
Film & Television Institute of India, Law College Rd, Pune 411 004. Tel: (91 020) 543 1817/3016. www.ftiindia.com.

Magazine
Film India Worldwide, Confederation of Indian Industry, 105 Kakad Chambers, 132 Dr Annie Besant Rd, Worli, Mumbai 400 018. Tel: (91 22) 2493 1790. Fax: 2493 9463. www.ciionline.org. www.ciiwest.org. In addition to news, views and reviews, *FIWW* offers an interactive databank service.

Useful Addresses
Film Federation of India, B/3 Everest Bldg, Tardeo, Bombay 400 034. Tel/Fax: (91 22) 2351 5531. Fax: 2352 2062. supransen22@hotmail.com.

Film Producers Guild of India, G-1, Morya House, Veera Industrial Estate, OShiwara Link Road, Andheri (W), Mumbai 400 053. Tel: (91 22) 5691 0662/2673 3065. Fax: 5691 0661. tfpgoli1@vsnl.net. www.filmguildindia.com.

Mukta Arts, 6 Bashiron, 28th Rd, Bandra (W), Mumbai 400 050. Tel: (91 22) 2642 1332. Fax: 2640 5727. muktaarts@vsnl.com. www.muktaarts.com.

National Film Development Corporation Ltd, Discovery of India Bldg, Nehru Centre, Dr Annie Besant Rd, Worli, Bombay 400 018. Tel: (91 22) 2492 6410. www.nfdcindia.com.

INDONESIA
All Tel/Fax numbers begin (62 21)

Archive
Pusat Perfilman H Usmar Ismail, Jalan H.R. Rasuna Said Kav C-22, Kuningan, Jakarta 12940. Tel: 526 8458. Fax: 526 8456. www.pphui.or.id/.

Film Schools

Jakarta Institute of The Arts, Faculty of Film & TV, Jalan Cikini Raya 73, Jakarta 10001. Tel/Fax: 392 4018.

Science, Aesthetics and Technology Foundation (SET), Jalan Bacang III No 5, Gandaria Mayestik, Jakarta Selatan 12130. Tel: 725 1095. Fax: 722 9638. set@indo.net.id.

Useful Addresses

Bali Film Commission [Foreign Production Assistance] Jl. Mertasari 10B, Sanur 80228. Tel. +62361-7444246 Fax. +62361-286425 contact@balifilm.com www.balifilm.com

Boemboe, [Distributor], Jalan Mampang Prapatan XVI No 28, Jakarta 12760. Tel/Fax: 7919 8858. boemboeforum@yahoo.com.

Kalyana Shira Film, [Producer], Jalan Bunga Mawar No 9, Cilandak, Jakarta 12410. Tel: 750 3225. Fax: 769 4318. kalyana@kalyanashira.com.

Ministry of Information for Film & Video, Departemen Penerangan RI, Jalan Merdeka Barat 9, Gedung Belakang, Jakarta Pusat. Tel: 384 1260. Fax: 386 0830.

Ministry of Tourism, Art and Culture, Jalan Medan Merdeka Barat 17, Jakarta 10110. Tel: 383 8000/381 0123. Fax: 386 0210. http://gateway.deparsenibud.go.id.

Offstream Production, Jalan Kelud No 23, Guntur, Setiabudi, Jakarta 12980. Tel/Fax: 829 6185. email@offstream.net. www.offstream.net.

PT Multi Inter Media, Komplek Perkantoran Roxi Mas, Jalan KH Hasyim Ashari Blok C2 No 40, Jakarta 12140. Tel: 633 5103. redaksi@multivisionplus.com.

PT Soraya Intercine Films, Jalan Pintu Air Raya 20, Jakarta 10710. Tel: 380 9126/384 2371. Fax: 384 7538.

Rexinema, [Producer], Jalan Pangeran Antasari No 20, Jakarta 12410. Tel: 769 6071. Fax: 766 1267. www.rexinema.com.

Salto Films [Producer] Jl. Sutan Syahrir 1C/Blok 3-4, Jakarta 10350, Indonesia. Tel: 3192 5113, 3192 5139 Fax: 3192 5360 Email: salto@cbn.net.id, sharmayn@cbn.net.id Homepage: www.saltofilms.com.

Sinemart [Producer/Distributor] Jl. Raya Kebayoran Lama no. 17D Jakarta Selatan, Indonesia. Tel: +6221-5812591. Fax: +6221-5309247. www.sinemart.com.

Tit's Film Workshop, [Producer/Distributor], Jalan Jatipadang-Kebagusan Raya Gg, Damai No 61C, Pasar Minggu, Jakarta 12520. Tel/Fax: 7884 3307.

IRAN

All Tel/Fax numbers begin (98 21)

Archive

National Film Archive of Iran, Baharestan Sq, Tehran 11365. Tel: 3851 2583. Fax: 3851 2710. crb@kanoon.net. Director: Mohammad Hassan Koshneviss.

Film Schools

Institute for Intellectual Development of Children & Young Adults. Tel: 871 0661. Fax: 872 9290. Info@kanoonparvaresh.com.

Sahra Film Cultural Institute, 39 Corner of 6th Alley, Eshqyar St, Khorramshahr Ave, Tehran. Tel: 876 5392/6110. Fax: 876 0488. modarresi@dpir.com.

Tamasha Cultural Institute, 124 Khorramshahr Ave, Tehran 15537. Tel: 873 3844/876 9146. Fax: 873 3844/9146. info@tamasha.net.

Useful Addresses

Behnegar, [Producer/Distributor], 3rd Floor, 9 Bahman 22nd Alley, Yakhchal St, Shariatie Ave, Tehran. info@behnegar.com.

Cima Film, [Producer/Distributor], 53 Kuhyar Alley, Fereshte St, Tehran. Tel: 221 8116/7. Fax: 221 5889.

Farabi Cinema Foundation, [Producer/Distributor], 1st Floor, No.19, Delbar Alley, Toos St, Valise-Asr Avr, Tehran 19617. Tel: 273 4939/4891. Fax: 273 4953. fcf1@dpi.net.ir. www.fcf-ir.com.

Fardis Co, [Producer/Distributor], 113 Shahid Malayeri Pour St, Fath Ave, Haftetir Sq, Tehran. Tel: 830 7732. Fax: 882 5522.

Hedayat Film, [Producer/Distributor], 15 7th St, Khaled Estamboli Ave, Tehran 15137. Tel: 872 7188/89. Fax: 871 4220. info@hedayatfilm.net.

Jozan Film, 20 Razmandegan Alley, Fajr St, Motahhari Ave, Tehran. Tel: 883 7271/83 02704. Fax: 882 6876.

Sureh Cinema Development Organisation, [Producer/Distributor], 213 Somayeh Ave, Tehran 15998-19613. Tel: 880 5294/6682. Fax: 880 5998. international@surehcinema.com.

IRELAND

Film Schools

Ballyfermot College of Further Education, Ballyfermot Rd, Dublin 10. Tel: (353 1) 626 9421. Fax: 626 6754. info@bcfe.cdvec.ie. www.bcfe.ie.

National Film School, Institute of Art, Design & Technology, Kill Ave, Dun Laoghaire, Co Dublin. Tel: (353 1) 214 4600. Fax: 214 4700. donald.taylorblack@iadt.ie. www.iadt.ie.

Useful Addresses

Abbey Films, [Distributor], 29 Lower Georges St, Dun Laoghaire, Co Dublin. Tel: (353 1) 236 6686. Fax: 236 6668. www.abbeyfilms@eircom.net.

Eclipse Pictures, [Distributor], 6 Eustace St, Dublin 2. Tel: (353 1) 633 6002. Fax: 633 6000. www.eclipsepictures.ie.

Film Censor's Office, 16 Harcourt Terrace, Dublin 2. Tel: (353 1) 799 6100. Fax: 676 1898. info@ifco.gov.ie.

Film Institute of Ireland, 6 Eustace St, Dublin 2. Tel: (353 1) 679 5744. Fax: 679 9657. www.fii.ie.

Irish Film Board, Rockfort House, St Augustine St, Galway, Co Galway. Tel: (353 91) 561 398. Fax: 561 405. www.filmboard.ie.

Screen Directors Guild of Ireland, 18 Eustace St, Temple Bar, Dublin 2. Tel: (353 1) 633 7433. Fax: 478 4807. info@sdgi.ie.

Screen Producers Ireland, The Studio Bldg, Meeting House Sq, Temple Bar, Dublin 2. Tel: (353 1) 671 3525. Fax: 671 4292. www.screenproducersireland.com.

ISRAEL

Archive

Israel Film Archive, Jerusalem Film Centre, Derech Hebron, PO Box 8561, Jerusalem 91083. Tel: (972 2) 565 4333. Fax: 565 4335. jer-cin@jer-cin.org.il. www.jer-cin.org.il. Director: Lia van Leer.

Film School

Department of Cinema & Television, David & Yoland Katz Faculty of the Arts, Tel Aviv University, Mexico Bldg, Tel Aviv. Tel: (972 3) 640 9483. Fax: 640 9935. www.tau.ac.il/arts.

Useful Addresses

Israel Film Fund, 12 Yehudith Blvd, Tel Aviv 67016. Tel: (972 2) 562 8180. Fax: 562 5992. info@filmfund.org.il. www.filmfund.org.il.

Israeli Film Council, 14 Hamasger St, PO Box 57577, Tel Aviv 61575. Tel: (972 3) 636 7288. Fax: 639 0098. etic@most.gov.il.

ITALY

Archives

Cineteca del Comune, Via Riva di Reno, 40122 Bologna. Tel: (39 051) 204 820. www.cinetecadibologna.it.

Cineteca del Friuli, Via Bini 50, Palazzo Gurisatti, 33013 Gemona del Friuli, Udine. Tel: (39 04) 3298 0458. Fax: 3297 0542. cdf@cinetecadelfriuli.org. http://cinetecadelfriuli.org. Stock: 3,000 film titles, 3,300 newsreels, 18,000 books. Director: Livio Jacob; Deputy Director: Lorenzo Codelli; Librarian: Piera Patat.

Cineteca Nazionale, Via Tuscolana 1524, 00173 Rome. Tel: (39 06) 722 941. Fax: 721 1619. www.snc.it.

Fondazione Cineteca Italiana, Villa Reale, Via Palestro 16, 20121 Milan. Tel: (39 02) 799 224. Fax: 798 289. info@cinetecamilano.it. www.cinetecamilano.it/.

Fondazione Federico Fellini, Via Oberdan 1, 47900 Rimini. Tel (39 0541) 50085. Fax: 57378. fondazione@federicofellini.it. www.federicofellini.it/.

Museo Nazionale del Cinema, Via Montebello 15, 10124 Turin. Tel: (39 011) 812 2814. www.museonazionaledelcinema.org.

Bookshop

Libreria Il Leuto, Via Di Monte Brianzo 86, 00186 Rome. Tel: (39 06) 686 9269.

Film Schools

Accademia dell'Immagine Parco di Collemaggio, 67100 L'Aquila, Tel: (39 0862) 487 11. Fax: 487 148. accademia@accademiaimmagine.org, www.accademiaimmagine.org

Magica (Master Europeo in Gestione di Impresa Cinematografica e Audiovisiva), Via Lucullo 7 Int 8, 00187 Rome. Tel: (39 06) 420 0651. Fax: 4201 0898. magica@mediamaster.org. www.mediamaster.org.

Scuola Nazionale di Cinema, Via Tuscolana 1524, 00173 Rome. Tel: (39 06) 722 941. Fax: 721 1619. snccn@tin.it. www.snc.it.

Magazines

Box Office, Via Donatello 5/B, 20131 Milan. Tel: (39 06) 277 7961. Fax: 2779 6300. www.e-duesse.it. Bi-monthly.

Cineforum, Via G. Reich 49, 24020 Torre Boldone, Bergamo. Tel: (39 035) 361 361. Fax: 341 255. www.cineforum.it. Monthly.

Griffithiana, Cineteca del Friuli, Via Bini 50, Palazzo Gurisatti, 33013 Gemona, Udine. Tel: (39 04) 3298 0458. Fax: 3297 0542. cdf@cinetecadelfriuli.org. www.cinetecadelfriuli.org. Quarterly devoted exclusively to silent cinema and animation – in English and Italian.

Nocturno, Via Trieste 42, 20064 Gorgonzola, Milan. Tel: (39 02) 9534 0057. www.nocturno.it.

Rivista del Cinematografo, Via Giuseppe Palombini 6, 00165 Rome. Tel: (39 06) 663 7514. Fax: 663 7321. ariccobene@cinematografo.it. www.cinematografo.it.

Useful Addresses

Anica, Viale Regina Margherita 286, 00198 Rome. Tel: (39 06) 442 5961. Fax: 440 4128. anica@anica.it. www.anica.it.

Associazione Generale Italiana Dello Spettacollo (AGIS), Via di Villa Patrizi 10, 00161 Rome. Tel: (39 06) 884 731. Fax: 4423 1838. www.agisweb.it.

Audiovisual Industry Promotion-Filmitalia, Via Aureliana 63, 00187 Rome. Tel: (39 06) 4201 2539. Fax: 4200 3530. www.aip-filmitalia.com.

Bianca Film, via Lampertico 7, 00191 Rome. Tel: (39 06) 329 6791. Fax: 329 6790. biancafilm@flashnet.it.

Cattleya, Via della Frezza 59, 00186 Rome. Tel: (39 06) 367 201. Fax: 367 2050. www.cattleya.it.

Cinecittà Holding Spa, Via Tuscolana 1055, 00173 Rome. Tel: (39 06) 722 861. Fax: 722 1883. direzione@cinecitta.it. www.cinecitta.com.

Duea Film, Piazza Cola di Rienzo 69, 00192 Rome. Tel: (39 06) 321 4851. Fax: 321 5108. www.dueafilm.it.

Fandango, Via Ajaccio 20, 00198 Rome. Tel (39 06) 8535 4026. Fax: 8535 3790. www.fandango.it.

Filmauro, Via XXIV Maggio 14, 00187 Rome. Tel: (39 06) 699 581. Fax: 6995 8410. www.filmauro.it.

Istituto Luce, Via Tuscolana 1055, 00173 Rome. Tel: (39 06) 729 921. Fax: 722 1127. luce@luce.it. www.luce.it.

Medusa Film, Via Aurelia Antrica 422/424, 00165 Rome. Tel: (39 06) 663 901. Fax: 6639 0450. www.medusa.it.

Mikado Film, Via Vittor Pisani 12, 20124 Milan. Tel: (39 02) 6707 0665. Fax: 6671 1488. www.mikado.it.

Rai Cinema, Piazza Adriana 12, 00193 Rome. Tel: (39 06) 684 701. Fax: 687 2141. info@01distribution.it. www.raicinema.it.

Sacher Film, Viale Piramide Cestia 1, 00153 Rome. Tel: (39 06) 574 5353. Fax: 574 0483. sacher.film@flashnet.it.

JAPAN

All Tel/Fax numbers begin (81 3)

Archives

Kawakita Memorial Film Institute, Kawakita Memorial Bldg, 18 Ichiban-cho, Chiyoda-ku, Tokyo 102-0082. Tel: 3265 3281. Fax: 3265 3276. info@kawakita-film.or.jp. www.kawakita-film.or.jp.

National Film Center, 3-7-6 Kyobashi, Chuo-ku, Tokyo 104-0031. Tel: 5777 8600. www.momat.go.jp.

Film School

Japan Academy of Moving Images, 1-16-30 Manfukuji, Aso-ku, Kawasaki-shi, Kanagawa 215-0004. Tel: 951-2511. Fax: 951-2681 www.eiga.ac.jp

Nihon University College of Art, 4-8-24 Kudanminami, Chiyoda-ku, Tokyo 102. Tel: 5275 8110. Fax: 5275 8310. adm@cin.nihon-u.ac.jp. www.nihon-u.ac.jp.

Useful Addresses

Gaga Communications, East Roppongi Bldg, 16-35 Roppongi 3-Chome, Minato-ku, Tokyo 106-0032. Tel: 3589 1026. Fax: 3589 1043. fujimura@gaga.co.jp.

Kadokawa Pictures, Daiichikangin-Inagaki Bldg 6F, 2-1 Shimomiyabicho, Shinjuku-ku, Tokyo 162 0822 Tel: 5229 2073. Fax: 5229 2093. www.kadokawa-pictures.com

Motion Picture Producers Association of Japan, Tokyu Ginza Bldg 3F, 2-15-2 Ginza, Chuo-ku, Tokyo 104 0061. Tel: 3547 1800. Fax: 3547 0909. eiren@mc.neweb.ne.jp.

Shochiku Co Ltd, Intl Business Division, Togeki Bldg, 1-1 Tsukiji, 4-Chome, Chuo-ku, Tokyo 104 8422. Tel: 5550 1623. Fax: 5550 1654. ibd@shochiku.co.jp.

Studio Ghibli International Distribution, 1-4-25 Kajino-cho, Koganei-shi, Tokyo 184-0002. Tel: 4225 35674. Fax: 4225 35721. mikko@tintl.co.jp.

Toei Co Ltd, Intl Dept, 2-17 Ginza, 3 Chome, Chuo-ku, Tokyo 104-8108. Tel: 3535 7621. Fax: 3535 7622. international@toei.co.jp. www.international@toei.co.jp.

Toho International Co Ltd, 15th Floor, Yurakucho Denki Bldg, 1-7-1 Yurakucho, Chiyoda-ku, Tokyo 100-0006. Tel: 3213 6821. Fax: 3213 6825. tohointl@toho.co.jp. www.toho.co.jp.

Tokyo International Anime Fair,
29F No 1 Bldg, 2-8-1 Nishi-
Shinjuku, Shinjuku-ku, Tokyo 163-
8001. Tel: 5320 4786. Fax: 5388
1463. tokyo-anime-fair@nifty.com.
UniJapan Film, 11-6 Ginza,
2-Chome, Chuo-ku, Tokyo 104-
0061. Tel: 5565 7511. Fax: 5565
7531. office@unijapan.org.

KENYA
All Tel/Fax numbers begin (254 2)

Useful Addresses
Alliance Francaise.
Tel: 336 263/4/5. Fax: 336 253.
visualfr@accesskenya.com.
ArtMatters Info, PO Box 842,
00208 Nairobi.Tel: 021 3318/733
703 374. sayit@artmatters.info.
www.artmatters.info/.
Broadcast Automation
Technologies Limited (BATL), PO
Box 25639, Nairobi. Tel: 057 3571.
kenny@batl.net.
ComMatters Kenya Ltd,
PO Box 842, 00208 Nairobi.
Tel: 021 3318/733 703 374.
commatters@artmatters.info.
www.artmatters.info/.
Development Through Media,
PO Box 34696, 00100 Nairobi.
Tel: 022 8459. Fax: 022 8464.
dtm@nbnet.co.ke.
Film Production Department,
PO Box 74934, 00200 Nairobi.
Tel: 065 0120. Fax: 055 3003.
fpd@skyweb.co.ke.
Kenya Film & Television
Professional Association,
PO Box 315, 00600 Nairobi.
Tel/Fax: 027 30388.
kftvpa@hotmail.com.
The Show Company Ltd,
PO Box 25639, Nairobi.
Tel: 057 3571. Fax: 057 5360.
kenny@batl.net.

Themescape Movies EPZ
Limited/Themescape Media Ltd,
PO Box 10078, 00100 Nairobi.
Tel: 057 7121.
themescape@wananchi.com.
Viewfinders Ltd, Nairobi.
Tel: 058 3582/580 869.
Fax: 058 0424.
viewfinders@africaonline.co.ke.

LATVIA
All Tel/Fax numbers begin (371 7)

Archive
Riga Film Museum,
3 Smerla St, Riga LV-1006.
Tel: 755 4190. Fax: 754 5099.
kinomuz @com.latnet.lv.

Useful Addresses
FA-Filma, Kalku 6-4a, Riga,
LV-1006. Tel: 944 3254.
fafilm@re-lab.com.
www.re-lab.lv/fafilma.
Hargla, Valtaiku 19, Riga, LV-1029.
Tel: 923 5618. Fax: 577 686.
laila_pakalnina@diena.lv.
Kaupo Filma, Stabu 17, Riga,
LV-1011. Tel: 291 720.
Fax: 270 542. kaupo@latnet.lv.
Media Desk. Tel: 505 079.
lelda.ozola@nfc.gov.lv.
www.mediadesk.lv.
National Film Centre of Latvia,
Peitavas 10/12, Riga LV-1050.
Tel: 735 8878. Fax: 735 8877.
nfc@nfc.gov.lv. www.nfc.lv.
Platforma Filma,
Dzintaru Prospekts 19,
Jurmala LV-2015. Tel: 754 647.
Fax: 811 308.
grauba@platformafilma.lv
Subjektiv Filma, Kurzemes
Prospekts 2-6, Riga, LV-1067.
Tel: 929 9564. Fax: 843 072.
subjektivfilma@inbox.lv.
Vides Filmu Studija, Pils 17,
Riga, LV-1050. Tel: 503 588.
Fax: 508 589. vfs@vfs.lv.

LITHUANIA
All Tel/Fax numbers begin (370 5)

Archive
Lithuanian State Archive of
Vision & Sound, O. Milaлiaus g. 19
LT-10102 Vilnius, Lithuania
Tel.: +370 5 247 78 19
E-mail: lvga@takas.lt

Film School
Centre of Cinema & Theatre
Information & Education,
Bernandine G 10, 01124 Vilnius.
Tel: 262 6502. audral@theater.it.

Useful Addresses
Lithuanian Filmmakers Union,
Birutes G 18, 08117 Vilnius.
Tel/Fax: 212 0759.
lks1@auste.elnet.lt.
Ministry of Culture,
J Basanaviciaus G 5, 01118 Vilnius.
Tel: 261 2932. culture@muza.lt.
www.muza.lt.
Media Desk, J Basanaviciaus G 5,
01118 Vilnius. Tel: 212 7187.
info@mediadesk.lt.
Lithuanian Theatre, Music and
Cinema Museum
Vilniaus g.. 41
LT-2001, vilnius, lithuania
Tel.: +370 5 2622406.?E-mail:
ltmkm@takas.lt

MEXICO
All Tel/Fax numbers begin (52 5)

Archive
Cineteca Nacional, Avenida
México-Coyoacán 389, Col Xoco,
México DF. Tel: 1253 9314.
www.cinetecanacional.net.

Useful Addresses
Alameda Films [Distributor].
Tel: 5688 7318. Fax: 5605 8911.
Contact: Daniel Birman.
alamedafilms@iserve.net.mx.

Altavista Films [Distributor],
Insurgentes Sur 1898, Piso 12,
Col Florida, CP 03900, México DF.
Tel: 5322 3358. Contact: Francisco
González Compéan.
frago@altavista films.com.mx.
Artecinema de México
[Distributor], Gobernador Ignacio
Esteve 70, Col San Miguel
Chapultepec, CP 11850, México DF.
Tel: 5277 8999.
Arthaus Films [Distributor],
Alfonso Esparza Oteo 144-702,
Col Guadalupe Inn, CP 01020,
México DF. Tel: 5661 1430/0709.
**Association of Mexican Film
Producers & Distributors**, Avenida
División del Norte 2462, Piso 8,
Colonia Portales, México DF.
Tel: 5688 0705. Fax: 5688 7251.
**Cinema Production Workers
Syndicate (STPC),**
Plateros 109 Col San José
Insurgentes, México DF.
Tel: 5680 6292.
cctpc@terra.com.mx.
Dirección General de Radio,
Televisión y Cinematografía (RTC),
Roma 41, Col Juárez, México DF.
Tel: 5140 8010.
ecardenas@segob.gob.mx.
**Instituto Mexicano de
Cinematografía (IMCINE),**
Insurgentes Sur 674 Col del Valle,
CP 03100, México DF. Tel: 5448
5300. Contact: Susana López
Aranda: suslopez@hotmail.com or
Miguel Ángel Ortega:
mercaint@institutomexicanodecine
matografía.gob.mx.

MOROCCO

**Moroccan Cinematographic
Centre**, Quartier Industriel,
Ave Al Majd, BP 421, Rabat.
Tel: (212 7) 798 110. Fax: 798 105.
www.mincom.gov.ma/cinemaroc/ccm.

NETHERLANDS

Archives
Filmmuseum, Rien Hagen,
Vondelpark 3, PO Box 74782,
1070 BT Amsterdam.
Tel: (31 20) 589 1400. Fax: 683
3401. info@filmmuseum.nl.
www.filmmuseum.nl.
**Netherlands Institut voor Beeld
en Geluid**, PO Box 1060, 1200 BB
Hilversum. Tel: (31 35) 677 2672/7.
Fax: 677 2835.
klantenservice@naa.nl. www.naa.nl.

Bookshop
Ciné-Qua-Non, Staalstraat 14,
1011 JL Amsterdam.
Tel: (31 20) 625 5588. Books about
film; specialty vintage posters.

Film Schools
Maurits Binger Film Institute,
Nieuwezijds Voorburgwal 4-10,
1012 RZ Amsterdam.
Tel: (31 20) 530 9630. Fax: 530
9631. binger@binger.ahk.nl.
www.binger.ahk.nl. Contact: Dick
Willemsen.
**Netherlands Film & Television
Academy (NFTA)**, Markenplein 1,
1011 MV Amsterdam. Tel: (31 20)
527 7333. Fax: 527 7344.
info@nfta.ahk.nl. www.nfta.ahk.nl.
Contact: Marieke Schoenmakers.

Magazines
Holland Animation Newsbrief,
Hoogt 4, 3512 GW Utrecht.
Tel/Fax: (31 30) 240 0768.
info@holland-animation.nl.
www.holland-animation.nl.
Published twice yearly.
Skrien, Vondelpark 3, 1071 AA
Amsterdam. Tel: (31 20) 689 3831.
skrien@xs4all.nl. An excellent,
enthusiastic monthly.

Useful Addresses
**Circle of Dutch Film Critics
(KNF)**, PO Box 10650, 1011 ER
Amsterdam. Tel: (31 6) 2550 0668.
Fax: 627 5923. knfilm@xs4all.nl.
Cobo Fund, PO Box 26444,
Postvak M54, 1202 JJ Hilversum.
Tel: (31 35) 677 5348.
Fax: 677 1995. cobo@nos.nl.
Contact: Jeanine Hage.
Dutch Film Fund,
Jan Luykenstraat 2, 1071 CM
Amsterdam. Tel: (31 20) 570 7676.
Fax: 570 7689. info@filmfund.nl.
Contact: Toine Berbers.
Holland Film, Jan Luykenstraat 2,
1071 CM Amsterdam. Tel: (31 20)
570 4700. Fax: 570 7570.
hf@hollandfilm.nl. www.hollandfilm.nl.
**Ministry of Education, Culture &
Science**, Arts Dept, Sector Film,
Europaweg 4, PO Box 25000,
2700 LZ Zoetermeer. Tel: (31 79)
323 4321. Fax: 323 4959.
j.j.cassidy@minocw.nl.
**Netherlands Cinematographic
Federation (NFC),**
Jan Luykenstraat 2, PO Box 75048,
1070 AA Amsterdam. Tel: (31 20)
679 9261. Fax: 675 0398.
info@nfc.org.
Contact: Wilco Wolfers.
**Netherlands Institute For
Animation Film**, PO Box 9358,
5000 HJ Tilburg. Tel: (31 13) 535
4555. Fax: 580 0057. niaf@niaf.nl.
Contact: Ton Crone.
Rotterdam Film Fund,
Rochussenstraat 3C, 3015 EA
Rotterdam. Tel: (31 10) 436 0747.
Fax: 436 0553. info@rff.rotterdam.nl.
Contact: Jacques van Heijnigen.

More information can be found
on www.hollandfilm.nl (click on
Who's Where).

NEW ZEALAND

Archive
New Zealand Film Archive, PO Box
11449, Wellington. Tel: (64 4) 384 7647.
Fax: 382 9595. nzfa@actrix.gen.nz.
www.filmarchive.org.nz.

Magazine
Onfilm, PO Box 5544, Wellesley
St, Auckland. Tel: (64 9) 630 8940.
Fax: 630 1046. nick@onfilm.co.nz.
www.profile.co.nz.

Useful Addresses
Film New Zealand,
PO Box 24142, Wellington.
Tel: (64 4) 385 0766.
Fax: 384 5840. info@filmnz.org.nz.
www.filmnz.com.
New Zealand Film Commission,
PO Box 11546, Wellington.
Tel: (64 4) 382 7680. Fax: 384
9719. marketing@nzfilm.co.nz.
**Ministry of Economic
Development**, 33 Bowen St, PO
Box 1473, Wellington.
Tel: (64 4) 472 0030. Fax: 473 4638.
www.med.govt.nz. Chief Executive:
Geoff Dangerfield.
**Office of Film & Literature
Classification**, PO Box 1999,
Wellington. Tel: (64 4) 471 6770.
Fax: 471 6781.
information@censorship.govt.nz.
**Screen Production &
Development Association
(SPADA)**, PO Box 9567,
Wellington. Tel: (64 4) 939 6934.
Fax: 939 6935. info@spada.co.nz.

NORWAY
All Tel/Fax numbers begin (47)

Archive
Henie-Onstad Art Centre, Sonja
Henie Vei 31, 1311 Høvikodden.
Tel: 6780 4880. post@hok.no.
www.hok.no.

Norwegian Film Institute
(full details below)
Collection: 22,000 films, 22,000
books, 2,500 cameras, props and
technical equipment, some of
them exhibited in a fine film
museum.

Magazine
Film & Kino, PO Box 446 Sentrum,
0104 Oslo. Tel: 2247 4628.
Fax: 2247 4698.
www.filmweb.no/filmogkino/tidsskriftet.
Editor: Kalle Løchen. Wide-
ranging with expressive layout.

Useful Addresses
**National Association of
Municipal Cinemas (Film & Kino)**,
PO Box 446 Sentrum, 0104 Oslo.
Tel: 2247 4500. Fax: 2247 4699.
Contact: Lene Løken.
www.filmweb.no/filmogkino.
**Norwegian Film & TV Producers
Association**,
Dronningens Gt 16, 0152 Oslo.
Tel: 2311 9313. Fax: 2311 9316.
produsentforeningen@produsentfor
eningen.no.
Contact: Tom G Eilertsen.
**Norwegian Board of Film
Classification**,
PO Box 371 Sentrum, 0102 Oslo.
Tel: 2247 4660. Fax: 2247 4694.
post@filmtilsynet.no.
Contact: Tom Løland.
Norwegian Film Development,
PO Box 904 Sentrum, 0104 Oslo.
Tel: 2282 2400. Fax: 2282 2422.
mail@norskfilmutvikling.no.
Contact: Kirsen Bryhni.
Norwegian Film Fund,
PO Box 752 Sentrum, 0106 Oslo.
Tel: 2247 8040. Fax: 2247 8041.
post@filmfondet.no.
Contact: Stein Slyngstad.
Norwegian Film Institute,
Dept of International Relations,
PO Box 482 Sentrum, 0105 Oslo.
Tel: 2247 4500. Fax: 2247 4597.
int@nfi.no.

**Norwegian Film Workers
Association**,
Dronningens Gt 16, 0152 Oslo.
Tel: 2247 4640.
Fax: 2247 4689. nff@filmenshus.no.
Contact: Kjetil Hervig.

PAKISTAN

Useful Addresses
Ministry of Culture,
Block D, Pak Secretariat,
Islamabad. Tel: (92 51) 921 3121.
Fax: 922 1863.
**Pakistan Film Producers
Association**,
Regal Cinema Bldg,
Sharah-e-Quaid-e-Azam, Lahore.
Tel: (92 42) 732 2904.
Fax: 724 1264.

PERU
All Tel/Fax numbers begin (51 1)

Useful Addresses
**Asociación de Cineastas del
Peru**, Calle Manco Capac 236,
Lima-18. Tel: 446 1829.
cineperu@chavin.rcp.net.pe.
**Cine Arte del Centro Cultural de
San Marcos**,
cinearte.ccsm@unmsm.edu.pe.
**Consejo Nacional de
Cinematografía (Conacine)**,
Museo de la Nación,
Avenida Javier Prado 2465, Lima.
Tel/Fax: 225 6479.
**Encuentro Latinoamericano de
Cine**, Centro Cultural de la
Universidad Católica, Avenida
Camino Real 1075, Lima-27.
Tel/Fax: 616 1616.
elcine@pucp.edu.pe.

POLAND

Archives

Muzeum Kinematografi,
Pl Zwyciestwa 1, 90 312 Lódz. Tel:
(48 42) 674 0957. Fax: 674 9006.
National Film Library,
Ul Pulawska 61, 00 975 Warsaw.
Tel: (48 22) 845 5074.
filmoteka@filmoteka.pl.
www.fn.org.pl.

Film Schools

**National Film, Television &
Theatre School**, 63 Targowa Str,
90 323 Lódz. Tel: (48 42) 634
5800. info@film.lodz.pl.
www.filmschool.lodz.pl.
**Silesian University Radio &
Television Faculty**, 40-955
Katowice, Ul Bytkowska 1B.
Tel/Fax: (48 32) 258 7070.
doktorow@us.edu.pl.

Magazines

Film, Ul Pruszkowska 17, 02 119
Warsaw. Tel: (48 22) 668 9083.
Fax: 668 9183. film@film.com.pl.
www.film.com.pl. Popular monthly
Kino, Ul Chelmska 21, 00 724
Warsaw. Tel: (48 22) 841 6843.
Fax: 841 9057. http//.kino.onet.pl.
Culturally inclined monthly designed
to promote European cinema.

Useful Addresses

**Association of Polish
Filmmakers**, Ul Pulawska 61, 02-
595 Warsaw. Tel: (48 22) 845 5132.
Fax: 845 3908. biuro@sfp.org.pl.
www.sfp.org.pl.
Film Polski, Ul Mazowiecki 6/8, 00
048 Warsaw. Tel: (48 22) 826 0849.
Fax: 826 8455.
info@filmpolski.com.pl.
www.filmpolski.com.pl.
Film Production Agency,
Ul Pulawska 61, 02-595 Warsaw.
Tel: (48 22) 845 5324.
info@pakietyfilmowe.waw.pl.

www.pakietyfilmowe.waw.pl.
**National Board of Radio and
Television (KRRIT)**, Skwerks
Wyszynskiego 9, 01-015 Warsaw.
Tel: (48 22) 635 9925.
Fax: 838 3501. krrit@krrit.gov.pl.
www.krrit.gov.pl.
**National Chamber of Audiovisual
Producers**, Ul Pulawska 61,
02-595 Warsaw. Tel: (48 22 845
6570. Fax: 845 5001. kipa@org.pl.
Polish TV Film Agency (TVP),
Ul JP Woronicza 17, 00-999
Warsaw. Tel: (48 22) 547 9167.
Fax: 547 4225. www.tvp.pl.
WFDIF Film Studio,
Ul Chelmska 21, 00-724 Warsaw.
Tel: (48 22) 841 1210-19.
Fax: 841 5891. wfdif@wfdif.com.pl.
www.wfdif.com.pl.

PORTUGAL

Archive

Cinemateca Portuguesa,
Rua Barata Salgueiro 63, 1269-059
Lisbon. Tel: (351 21) 359 6200.
Fax: 352 3180.
www.cinemateca.pt.

Magazine

Estreia, Rua de Anibal Cunha 84,
Sala 1.6, 4050-846 Porto. Tel: (351
22) 207 6050. Fax: 207 6059.
www.estreia.online.pt. Bi-monthly.

Useful Addresses

Animatógrafo, Rua da Rosa 252,
2°, 1200-391 Lisbon. Tel: (351 21)
347 5372. Fax: 347 3252.
animatografo@mail.telepac.pt.
Costa de Castelo, Avenida
Engenheiro Arantes e Oliveira 11A,
1°, 1900-221 Lisbon. Tel: (351 21)
843 8020. info@costacastelo.pt.
www.costacastelo.pt.
Filmes Castelo Lopes,
Rua Castilho 90, 1250-071 Lisbon.
Tel: (351 21) 381 2600. Fax: 386
2076. www.castelolopes.com.

**Institute of Cinema, Audiovisual
& Multimedia (ICAM)**, Rua de S
Pedro de Alcântara 45, 1°, 1250
Lisbon. Tel: (351 21) 323 0800.
Fax: 343 1952. mail@icam.pt.
www.icam.pt.
Lusomundo Audiovisuais,
Avenida da Liberdade 266, 3°,
1250 Lisbon. Tel: (351 21) 318
7300. Fax: 352 3568.
www.lusomundo.pt.
MGN Filmes, Rua de S Bento 644,
4° Esq, 1250-223 Lisbon. Tel:
(351 21) 388 7497. Fax: 388 7281.
mgnfilmes@mail.telepac.pt.
**Madragoa Filmes/Atalanta
Filmes**, Rua da Palmeira 6,
1200-313 Lisbon. Tel: (351 21) 325
5800. Fax: 342 8730.
geral.madragoa@madragoafilmes.com.
www.madragoafilmes.pt or
www.atalantafilmes.pt.
Rosa Filmes, Largo Maria Isabel
Aboim Inglês 2B, 1400-244 Lisbon.
Tel: (351 21) 303 1810.
Fax: 303 1819. rosafilmes@vianw.pt.
www.rosafilmes.pt.
Short Film Agency,
Apartado 214, 4481-911 Vila do
Conde. Tel: (351 25) 264 6683.
Fax: 263 8027.
agencia@curtasmetragens.pt.
www.curtasmetragens.pt.

PUERTO RICO

All Tel/Fax numbers begin (1 787)

Useful Addresses

**Corporation for Public
Broadcasting of Puerto Rico
(Channel 6)**, Sonya Canetti,
Director, PO Box, San Juan 00919-
0909. Tel: 766 0505. Fax: 753
9846. Contact: Victor Montilla,
www.tutv.puertorico.pr

Film & Audiovisual Producers Association, PO Box 190399, San Juan 00919-0399.
Tel: 725 3565. Fax: 724 4333.
tvegsjpr@prtc.net
Contact: Ramón Almodóvar
President

Puerto Rico Film Commission, PO Box 2350, San Juan 00936-2360. Tel: 754 7110. Fax: 756 5706. lriefkohl@pridco.com.
Contact: Luis A. Riefkohl, Executive Director.

National Association of Latino Independent Producers -Puerto Rico Chapter
PO Box 6813, Loiza Station. San Juan, Puerto Rico 00914-6813.
Tel: 268-0063. islafilms@coqui.net

ROMANIA
All Tel/Fax numbers begin (40 1)

Archive
Arhiva Nationala de Filma,
4-6 Dem I Dobrescu Str, Sector 1, Bucharest. Tel: 313 4904.
Fax: 313 4904. anf@xnet.ro.

Film School
Universitatea de Arta Teatrala si Cinematografica, Str Matei Voievod 75-77, Bucharest. Tel: 252 8001. www.edu.ro/uatcb.htm.

Useful Addresses
National Centre of Cinematography, Str Dem I Dobrescu 4-6, Bucharest.
Tel: 310 4301. Fax: 310 4300.
cncin@pcnet.ro.

Romania Film, Str Henri Coanda 27, Bucharest . Tel: 310 4499. Fax: 310 4498. coresfilm@hotmail.com.

Uniunea Cineastilor, Str Mendeleev 28-30, Sector 1, Bucharest 70169. Tel: 316 80 84. Fax: 311 1246. czucin@rnc.ro.

RUSSIA
All Tel/Fax numbers begin (7 095)

Archive
Gosfilmofond of Russia, Belye Stolby, Moskovskaya Oblast 142050. Tel: 546 0520. Fax: 548 0512. www.gosfilmofond.ru.

Magazine
Iskusstvo Kino, 9 Ul Usievich, Moscow 125319.
Tel: 151 5651. Fax: 151 0272.
filmfilm@mtu-net.ru.
www.kinoart.ru.

Useful Addresses
Alliance of Independent Distribution Companies.
Tel: 243 4741. Fax: 243 5582.
felix_rosental@yahoo.com.

Double D Research & Information Group,
13 Vassilyevskaya St, Moscow 123825/Postal address: 28-2-16 Bol Polyanka St, Moscow 119180.
Tel/Fax: 238 2984. vengern@df.ru.
Contact: Daniil Dondurei, Head of Research.

Empire Cinema,
[Major Cinema Chain], Komsomolsky Ave 21-10, Moscow 119146. Tel: 241 4626. Fax: 241 4104. general@formulakino.ru.

Federal Agency of Culture & Cinema of the Russian Federation, Film Service, 7 Maly Gnezdnikovsky Lane, Moscow 103877. Tel: 923 8677/229 7055. Fax: 299 9666.

Karo Premier Film Co, Pushkin Sq, Moscow 103006.
Tel: 209 4585. Fax: 209 3812.
bessedin@karo.ru.

Ministry of Culture & Mass Communication of the Russian Federation, 7 Kitaisky Proezd, Moscow. Tel: 975 2420.
Fax: 975 2420/928 1791.

National Academy of Cinema Arts & Sciences,
13 Vassilyevskaya St, Moscow 123825. Tel: 200 4284.
Fax: 251 5370. unikino@aha.ru.

Russian Guild of Film Directors,
13 Vassilyevskaya St, Moscow 123825. Tel: 251 5889. Fax: 254 2100. stalkerfest@mtu-net.ru.

Russian Guild of Producers,
1 Mosfilmovskaya St, Moscow 119858. Tel: 745 5635/143 9028.
plechev@mtu-net/ru.
Contact: Vladimir Dostal.

Union of Filmmakers of Russia,
13 Vassilyevskaya St, Moscow 123825. Tel: 250 4114. Fax: 250 5370. unikino@aha.ru.

RWANDA

Useful Addresses
Future Production (Music4Films), BP 2401, Kigali. Tel 0864 8562. bizab@hotmail.com.

Image Media, KBC Building, BP 4556, Kigali. Tel: 517 978.
imagesmedia@rwanda1.com.

Kemit, BP 1936. Tel: 502 468. kemit01@yahoo.fr.

Link Media Production, BP 4065, Kigali. erickabera@yahoo.com. admilink@yahoo.co.
www.linkmedia.co.rw. Tel: 0830 6480/0883 1324.

Nord Sud International, Avenue de la Paix, BP183. Tel: 575 810. iraja99@yahoo.com.

Rwanda Cinema Centre, BP 4065, Kigali. ccr_rwanda@yahoo.fr. erickabera@yahoo.com. Tel: 0830 6480/0883 1324.

SERBIA & MONTENEGRO
All Tel/Fax numbers begin (381 11)

Archive
Yugoslav Film Archive,
Knez Mihailova 19, 11000
Belgrade. Tel/Fax: 622 555.
kinoteka@eunet.yu.
www.kinoteka.org.yu.

Film School
Faculty of Dramatic Arts, Bulevar
Umetnosti 20, 11070 Belgrade.
Tel: 214 0419. Fax: 213 0862.
fduinfo@eunet.yu.

Useful Addresses
Association of Film Producers,
Kneza Viseslava 88, 11000
Belgrade. Tel: 323 1943. Fax: 324
6413. info@afp.yu. www.afp.co.yu.
Avala Film International,
[Production Facilities], Kneza
Viseslava 88, 11000 Belgrade.
Tel: 354 8284. Fax: 354 8410.
office@avalafilm.com.
www.avalafilm.com.
Beograd Film, [Chain of Theatres],
Terazije 40, 11040 Belgrade.
Tel: 688 940. Fax: 687 952.
www.beogradfilm.com.
Yugoslav Film Institute, Cika
Ljubina 15/II, 11000 Belgrade.
Tel: 625 131. Fax: 634 253.
ifulm@eunet.yu.

SINGAPORE
All Tel/Fax numbers begin (65)

Film School
School for Film & Media Studies,
Ngee Ann Polytechnic, Block 52,
535 Clementi Rd, Singapore 599489.
Tel: 6460 6992. Fax: 6462 5617.
vtv@np.edu.sg. www.np.edu.sg.

Useful Addresses
Cathay Organisation,
[Distributor & Exhibitor],
#02-04, 11 Unity St, Robertson
Walk, Singapore 237995.
Tel: 6337 8181. Fax: 6334 3373.
www.cathay.com.sg.
**Cinematograph Film Exhibitors
Association,** 13th & 14th Storey,
Shaw Centre, 1 Scotts Rd,
Singapore 228208.
Tel: 6235 2077. Fax: 6235 2860.
Mega Media, [Producer],
32 Maxwell Rd, 01-05,
Whitehouse, Singapore 069115.
Tel: 6536 9140. Fax: 6536 9154.
Raintree Pictures, [Producer],
Caldecott Broadcast Centre,
Andrew Rd, Singapore 299939.
Tel: 6350 3759. Fax: 6251 1916.
puiyin@raintree.com.sg.
www.raintree.com.sg.
Shaw Organisation, [Distributor &
Exhibitor], 1 Scotts Rd, #14-01
Shaw Centre, Singapore 228208.
Tel: 6235 2077. Fax: 6235 2860.
www.shaw.com.sg.
Singapore Film Commission,
140 Hill St, Mita Bldg #04-01,
Singapore 179369. Tel: 6837 9943.
Fax: 6336 1170. www.sfc.org.sg.
Singapore Film Society,
Golden Village Marina, 5A Raffles
Ave, #03-01 Marina Leisureplex,
Singapore 039801.
Fax: 6250 6167. ktan@sfs.org.sg.
www.sfs.org.sg.
Substation, 45 Armenian St,
Singapore 179936.
Tel: 6337 7535. Fax: 6337 2729.
wenjie@substation.org.
www.substation.org.

SLOVAKIA
All Tel/Fax numbers begin (421 2)

Film School
**Academy of Music & Dramatic
Art (VSMU),** Ventúrska 3, 813 01
Bratislava. Tel: 5443 2306.
www.vsmu.sk.

Useful Addresses
**Association of Slovak Film & TV
Directors,** Konventná 8, 811 03
Bratislava. Tel: 5441 9479.
artfilm@artfilm.sk.
**Association of Slovak Film
Distributors,** Senická 17, 811 04
Bratislava. Tel: 5479 1936. Fax:
5479 1939.
dusan.hajek@saturn.sk.
**Association of Slovak Film
Producers,** Grösslingova 32, 811
09 Bratislava. Tel: 5556 5643. Fax:
5296 1939. sapa@webdesign.sk.
Slovak Audiovisual Producers'
Association (SAPA), Tekovská 7,
821 09 Bratislava. Tel: 5556 5643.
Fax: 5296 1045.
sapa@webdesign.sk.
www.sapa.cc.
Slovak Film Institute,
Grösslingova 32, 811 09 Bratislava.
Tel: 5710 1501/27. Fax: 5296
3461. sfu@sfu.sk. www.sfu.sk.
Slovak Film and Television
Academy (SFTA), Ventúrska 3,
813 01 Bratislava. Tel: 5930 3573.
Fax: 5930 3575.
tatarova@vsmu.sk. www.sfta.sk.

SLOVENIA
All Tel/Fax numbers begin (386 1)

Useful Addresses
**Association of Slovenian Film
Makers,** Miklosiceva 26, Ljubljana.
e-mail. dsfu@guest.arnes.si.
**Association of Slovenian Film
Producers,** Brodisce 23, Trzin,
1234 Menges.
dunja.klemenc@guest.arnes.si
Film Studio Viba, Stegne 5,
1000 Ljubljana. Tel: 513 2402.
viba.film@siol.net.
Slovenian Cinematheque,
Miklosiceva 38, Ljubljana. Tel: 434
2520. silvan.furlan@kinoteka.si.
Slovenian Film Fund, Miklosiceva
38, 1000 Ljubljana. Tel: 431 3175.
info@film-sklad.si.

SOUTH AFRICA

Film School
CityVarsity Film, Television & Multimedia School,
32 Kloof St, Cape Town 8000.
Tel: (27 21) 423 3366. Fax: 423 6300. amanda@cityvarsity.co.za.
www.cityvarsity.co.za.
Contact: Amanda Solomon.
Eight departments including film, animation, acting, multimedia and sound under one roof.

Useful Addresses
Aland Pictures, 155 Buitenkant St, Gardens 8001. Contact: Carina Rubin. Tel: (27 21) 462 3306.
Fax: 462 3308. carina@gem.co.za.
www.fosterbrothers.co.za.
Big World Cinema,
PO Box 2228, Cape Town 8000.
Tel: (27 21) 488 0608. Fax: 448 1065. steven@bigworld.co.za.
Contact: Steven Markovitz or Trakoshis Platon.
Cape Film Commission,
6th Floor, NBS Waldorf Bldg, 80 St George's Mall, Cape Town 8001. Tel: (27 21) 483 9070.
Fax: 483 9071.
martin.cuff@capetown.gov.za.
Film Afrika, PO Box 12202, Mill St, Cape Town 8010.
Tel: (27 21) 461 7950.
Fax: 461 7951. info@filmafrika.com.
www.filmafrika.com.
Gauteng Film Office,
88 Fox St, Johannesburg/
PO Box 61840, Marshalltown 2107. Tel: (27 11) 833 8750.
Fax: 834 6157. themba@gfo.co.za.
Independent Producers Organisation,
PO Box 2631, Saxonwold 2132.
Tel: (27 11) 726 1189.
Fax: 482 4621. info@ipo.org.za.
www.ipo.org.za.

M-Net Local Productions,
PO Box 2963, Randburyg 2123.
Tel: (27 11) 686 6123. Fax: 686 6643. cfischer@mnet.co.za.
www.mnet.co.za.
National Film & Video Foundation, 87 Central St, Houghton, Private Bag x04, Northlands 2116.
Tel: (27 11) 483 0880.
Fax: 483 0881. info@nfvf.co.za.
www.nvfv.co.za.
Nu Metro, [Distributor],
Gallo House, 6 Hood Ave, Rosebank, Johannesburg 2196.
Tel: (27 11) 340 9300.
Fax: 442 7030.
South African Broadcasting Co (SABC), Private Bag 1, Auckland Park, Johannesburg 2006. Tel: (27 11) 714 9797.
Fax: 714 3106. www.sabc.co.za.
Videovision Entertainment,
134 Essenwood Rd, Berea, Durban 4001. Contact: Anant Singh. Tel: (27 31) 204 6000. Fax: 202 5000.
nilesh@videovision.co.za.
www.videovision.co.za.

SOUTH KOREA
All Tel/Fax numbers begin (82 2)

Archive
Korean Film Archive,
700 Seocho-dong, Seocho-gu, Seoul 137-718. Tel: 521 3147.
Fax: 582 6213. www.koreafilm.or.kr.

Useful Addresses
CJ Entertainment,
[Producer/Distributor], 26th Floor, Star Tower, 737 Yeoksam-dong, Kangnam-gu, Seoul 100-802.
Tel: 2112 6559. Fax: 2112 6549.
www.cjentertainment.co.kr.
Cineclick Asia,
[Producer/Distributor], Incline Bldg, 3rd Floor, 891-37 Daechi-Dong, Kangnam-gu, Seoul 135-280.
Tel: 538 0211 ext 212. Fax: 538 0479. www.cineclickasia.com.

Cinema Service,
[Producer/Distributor], 5th Floor, Heungkuk Bldg, 43-1 Juja-dong, Jung-gu, Seoul 100-240.
Tel: 2192 8734. Fax: 2192 8790.
www.cinemaservice.com.
Korea Pictures, 5th Floor, Isoni Plaza, 609 Shinsa-dong, Kangnam-gu, Seoul 135-120.
Tel: 544 4312. Fax: 3444 9831.
www.koreapictures.com.
Korean Film Council (KOFIC),
206-46, Cheongnyangni-dong, Tongdaemun-gu, Seoul 130-010.
Tel/Fax: 958 7582. www.kofic.or.kr.
MK Pictures, 6th Floor,
Cowell Bldg, 66-1 Banpo-dong, Seocho-gu, Seoul 137-804.
Tel: 2193 2050. Fax: 2193 2197.
www.mkbuffalo.com.
Mirovision, [Producer/Distributor],
1-151 Shinmunro, 2 Ga,
Jongno-gu, Seoul 110-062.
Tel: 737 1185. Fax: 737 1184.
www.mirovision.com.
Show East,
10th Floor, New Seoul Bldg, 618-3 Shinsa-dong, Kangnam-gu, Seoul 135-894.
Tel: 3445 9688. Fax: 3446 9620.
www.showeast.co.kr.
Showbox/Mediaplex,
16th Floor, Hansol Bldg, 736-1 Yeoksam-dong, Kangnam-gu, Seoul 135-983.
Tel: 3218 5639. Fax: 3444 6688.
www.showbox.co.kr.
Tube Entertainment,
[Producer/Distributor],
664-21 Shinsa-dong, Kangnam-ku, Seoul 135-897.
Tel: 547 8435. Fax: 547 3279.
www.tube-entertainment.co.kr.

SPAIN

Archives

Filmoteca de la Generalitat de Catalunya, Carrer del Portal de Santa Madrona 6-8, Barcelona 08001. Tel: (34 93) 316 2780. Fax: 316 2783. filmoteca.cultura@gencat.net.

Filmoteca Espanola, Calle Magdalena 10, 28012 Madrid. Tel: (34 91) 467 2600. Fax: 467 2611. www.cultura.mecd.es/cine/film/filmoteca.isp.

Filmoteca Vasca, Avenida Sancho el Sabio, 17 Trasera, Donostia, 20010 San Sebastian. Tel: (34 943) 468 484. Fax: 469 998. www.filmotecavasca.com. andaluciafilmcom@fundacionava.org.

Bookshop

Ocho y Medio, Martin de los Heros 23, 28008 Madrid. Tel: (34 91) 559 0628. Fax: 540 0672. libros@ochoymedio.com. www.ochoymedio.com.

Film Schools

Academia de las Artes y las Ciencias Cinematograficas de Espana, Sagasta 20, 3º Derecha, 28004 Madrid. Tel: (34 91) 593 4648. Fax: 593 1492. inforaca@infonegocio.com.

Centre d'Estudis Cinematogràfics de Catalunya, Casp 33 Pral, 08010 Barcelona. Tel: (34 93) 412 0484. Fax: 450 4283. info@cecc.es. www.cecc.es. Three-year course.

Escola Superior de Cinema Audiovisuals de Catalunya (ESCAC), Inmaculada 25-35, 08017 Barcelona. Tel: (34 93) 212 1562. www.escac.es. Four-year course.

Escuela de Cinematografía y de la Audiovisual de la Comunidad de Madrid (ECAM), Centra de Madrid a Boadilla, Km 2200, 28223 Madrid. Tel: (34 91) 411 0497. escuelacine@ecam.es. www.ecam.es. Director: C de la Imagen. Popular three-year course.

Instituto de la Cinematografía y de las Artes Audiovisuales (ICAA), Plaza del Rey S/N, 28070 Madrid. Tel: (34 91) 701 7000. www.cultura.mecd.es/cine.

Media Business School, Velazquez 14, 28001 Madrid, Spain. Tel: (34 91) 575 9583. Fax: 431 3303. fcm@mediaschool.org. www.mediaschool.org.

Magazines

Academia & Boletín, Sagasta 20, 3º Derecha, 28004 Madrid. Tel: (34 91) 593 4648/448 2321. Fax: 593 1492. www.sie.es/acacine/boletin. Excellent twice yearly.

Cine & Tele Informe, Gran Via 64, 4º Derecha, 28013 Madrid. Tel: (34 91) 541 2129. Fax: 559 4282. cineinforme@cineytele.com. www.cineytele.com.

Cinevideo 20, Calle Pantoja, 10 - 4ª Planta, 28002 Madrid. Tel: (34 91) 519 6586. Fax: 519 5119. cinevideo@cinevideo20.es. www.cinevideo20.es.

Fotogramas, Gran Via de les Corts Catalanes 133, 08014 Barcelona. Tel: (34 93) 223 2790. Fax: 432 2907. fotogramas@hachette.es. www.fotogramas.es.

Nickelodeon, Bárbara de Braganza 12, 28004 Madrid. Tel: (34 91) 308 5238. Fax: 308 5885. revista@nickel-odeon.com. www.nickel-odeon.com.

Useful Addresses

Andalucia Film Commission, Avenida Matemáticos Rey Pastor y Castro s/n, 41092 Seville. Tel: (34 95) 446 7310/3. Fax: 446 1516. andaluciafilmcom@fundacionava.org. www.andaluciafc.org/afc.

Catalan Films & TV, Portal Santa Madrona 6-8, 08001 Barcelona. Tel: (34 93) 316 2780. Fax: 316 2781.

Federación de Entidades de Empresarios de Cine de España, Alberto Aguilera, 10 7º Derecha, 28003 Madrid. Tel/Fax: (34 91) 448 8211. feece@feece.com. www.feece.com.

Federation of Associations of Spanish Audiovisual Producers (FAPAE), Calle Luis Bunuel 2-2º Izquierda, Ciudad de la Imagen, Pozuelo de Alarcón, 28223 Madrid. Tel: (34 91) 512 1660. Fax: 512 0148. web@fapae.es. www.fapae.es.

Federation of Cinema Distributors (FEDICINE), Orense 33, 3ºB, 28020 Madrid. Tel: (34 91) 556 9755. Fax: 555 6697. www.fedicine.com.

SRI LANKA

All Tel/Fax numbers begin (94 1)

Magazine

Cinesith, Asian Film Centre, 118 Dehiwala Rd, Boralesgamuwa. Fax: 509 553. afc@sri.lanka.net. www.lanka.net/asianfilm/. Sri Lanka's only serious film magazine.

Useful Addresses

Ceylon Theatres Ltd, [Producer, Exhibitor & Importer], 8 Sir C Gardiner Mawatha, Colombo 02. Tel: 431 242/109.

Eap Film & Theaters (PVT) Ltd,
[Producer, Distributor, Exhibitor &
Importer], Savoy Bldg, 12 Galle Rd,
Wellawatta, Colombo 06.
Tel: 552 877. Fax: 552 878.
eapfilms@sltnet.lk.
National Film Corporation,
[Distributor & Importer], 303
Bauddhaloka Mawatha,
Colombo 07. Tel: 580 247.
Fax: 585 526. filmcorp@sltnet.lk.
Winson Films,
[Producer & Importer], 215/2 Park
Rd, Colombo 05. Tel: 503 451.
Fax: 588 213. winfilms@dynanet.lk.

SWEDEN

Archives
Cinemateket, Swedish Film
Institute, Box 27126, SE-102 52
Stockholm. Tel: (46 8) 665 1100.
Fax: 666 3698. info@sfi.se.
www.sfi.se.
Swedish National Archive for
Recorded Sound & Moving
Images, Box 24124, SE-10451
Stockholm. Tel: (46 8) 783 3700.
Fax: 663 1811.
info@ljudochbildarkivet.se.

Bookshop
Movie Art Gallery,
Sodra Hamngatan 2, SE-411 06
Goteborg. Tel/Fax: (46 31) 151
412. www.movieartofsweden.com.

Film Schools
University College of Film,
Radio, Television & Theatre,
Box 27090, SE-102 51 Stockholm.
Tel: (46 8) 665 1300.
Fax: 662 1484. kansli@draminst.se.
www.draminst.se.
University of Stockholm,
Department of Cinema Studies,
Borgvägen 1-5, Box 27062,
SE-102 51 Stockholm.
Tel: (46 8) 674 7000.

Magazines
Film International,
Lilla Fiskaregatan 10, SE-222 22
Lund. Tel/Fax: (46 46) 137 914.
michael.tapper@filmint.nu.
www.filmint.nu.
Ingmar, Hantverkargatan 88,
SE-112 38 Stockholm. Tel: (46 8)
652 4806. redrum@ingmar.se.
Stardust Magazine,
Holländargatan 22, 113 59
Stockholm. Tel: (46 8) 690 0580.
seo@stardustmagazine.se.
www.stardustmagazine.se.
Eleven issues per year.
Teknik & Mnniska (TM), Borgvgen
1-5, PO Box 27126, SE-102 52
Stockholm. Tel: (46 8) 665 1100.
Fax: 662 2684. tm@sfi.se.
www.sfi.se/tm. Six issues per year.
News of Swedish production from
the Swedish Film Institute.

Useful Addresses
Swedish Film Distributors
Association, Box 23021,
SE-10435 Stockholm.
Tel: (46 8) 441 5570. Fax: 343 810.
Swedish Film Institute,
Box 27126, SE-10252 Stockholm.
Tel: (46 8) 665 1100.
Fax: 666 3698. info@sfi.se.
Swedish Film Producers
Association, Box 27298,
SE-102 53 Stockholm.
Tel: (46 8) 665 1255.
Fax: 666 3748. info@frf.net.

SWITZERLAND

Archives
Cinémathèque Suisse,
Casino de Montbenon,
3 Allée Ernest Ansermet, CP 5556,
1002 Lausanne. Tel: (41 21) 315
2171. Fax: 315 2189.
lausanne@cinematheque.ch.
www.cinematheque.ch.

Cinémathèque Suisse,
Dokumentationsstelle Zürich,
Neugasse 10, Postfach, CH-8031
Zürich. Tel: (41 43) 818 2465.
www.cinematheque.ch.

Bookshops
Filmbuchhandlung Rohr,
Oberdorfstrasse 3, CH-8024, Zurich.
Tel: (41 1) 251 3639. Fax: 251 8922.
Librairie du Cinema,
9 rue de la Terrassiere, CH-1207,
Geneva. Tel: (41 22) 736 8888.
Fax: 736 6616.
www.librairieducinema.ch.

Film Schools
Hochschule Für Gestaltung Und
Kunst, Studienbereich Film/Video,
Limmatstrasse 65, CH-8031
Zürich. Tel: (41 43) 446 3112.
Fax: 446 2355. film.video@hgkz.ch,
www.hgkz.ch.
Hochschule Für Gestaltung Und
Kunst Luzern, Rössligasse 12,
CH-6003 Lucerne.
Tel: (41 41) 228 5460.
Fax: 410 8084. www.hgk.fhz.ch.
Ecole Cantonale d'Art de
Lausanne,
Unité cinéma,
46 Rue de l'Industrie, CH-1030
Bussigny-Lausanne.
Tel: (41 21) 316 9223.
Fax: 316 9266. ecal@ecal.ch,
www.ecal.ch.
Ecole Supérieure des Beaux Arts,
Section Cinéma/Vidéo,
2 Rue Général Dufour,
CH-1204 Geneva.
Tel: (41 22) 317 7820.
Fax: 310 4636.
info.esba@etat.ge.ch,
www.hesge.ch/esba.

Magazines
Ciné-Bulletin, Rue du Maupas 10,
CP 271, CH-1000 Lausanne.
Tel: (41 21) 642 0303. Fax: 642
0331. redaction@cine-bulletin.ch,
www.cine-bulletin.ch.

Film Bulletin,
Hard 4, Postfach 68, CH-8408
Winterthur. Tel: (41 52) 226 0555.
Fax: 226 0556. info@filmbulletin.ch,
www.filmbulletin.ch.

Hors-Champ, Revue de cinéma,
Rue de la Vigie 3, CH-1003
Lausanne. Tel: (41 24) 441 0870.
Fax: 323 9253. Twice-
yearly.contact@hors-champ.ch
www.hors-champ.ch

Swiss Audiovisual Guide,
c/o Avant Première, Rédaction 35,
Rue des Bains, CH-1205 Geneva.
Tel: (41 22) 809 9455.
Annual publication.

Useful Addresses
Federal Office of Culture & Film,
Hallwylstrasse 15, CH-3003 Bern.
Tel: (41 31) 322 9271.
Fax: 322 5771.
cinema.film@bak.admin.ch,
www.kultur-schweiz.admin.ch.

Film Location Switzerland,
Place de la Gare 3, CH-1800 Vevey.
Tel: (41 21) 648 0380.
Fax: 648 0381. info@filmlocation.ch.
www.filmlocation.ch.

Gruppe Autoren, Regisseure,
Produzenten (GARP),
Postfach 1211, CH-8034 Zürich.
Tel/Fax: (41 43) 344 5945.
info@garp-cinema.ch.
www.garp-cinema.ch.

ProCinema, Schweizerischer
Verband Für Kino Und Filmverleih,
Schwarztorstrasse 56, CH-3000
Berne 14. Tel: (41 31) 387 3700.
Fax: 387 3707. www.procinema.ch.

Swiss Film Assocation,
Theaterstrasse 4, CH-8001 Zürich.
Tel: (41 1) 258 4110. Fax: 258 4111.
info@swissfilm.org.
www.swissfilm.org.

Swiss Film Producers
Association (SFP),
Zinggstrasse 16, CH-3007 Bern.
Tel: (41 31) 370 1060. Fax: 372
4053. info@swissfilmproducers.ch.
www.swissfilmproducers.ch.

Swiss Filmmakers Association,
Clausiusstrasse 68, Postfach,
CH-8033 Zürich.
Tel: (41 1) 253 1988. Fax: 253 1948.
info@realisateurs.ch,
www.realisateurs.ch.

Swiss Films, Neugasse 6,
Postfach, CH-8031 Zürich.
Tel: (41 43) 211 4050.
Fax: 211 4060. info@swissfilms.ch.
www.swissfilms.ch.

TAIWAN
All Tel/Fax numbers begin (886 2)

Archive
Chinese Taipei Film Archive,
4F, 7 Chingtao East Rd, Taipei.
Tel: 2392 4243. Fax: 2392 6359.
www.ctfa.org.tw.

Useful Addresses
Central Motion Picture Corp,
6/F, 116 Hanchung St, Taipei 108.
Tel: 2371 5191. Fax: 2331 9241.
www.movie.com.tw.

Chang Tso-chi Film Studio,
2F, 1 Yuying St, Taipei.
Tel: 8663 5179. Fax: 8663 5182.
www.changfilm.com.tw.

Digital Content Industry
Promotion Office, Suite 1105, 18
Chang'an E Rd, Sec 1, Taipei 104.
Tel: 2536 1226. Fax: 2536 2100.
www.digitalcontent.org.tw.

Government Information Office,
Department of Motion Picture Affairs,
2 Tientsin St Taipei 100.
Tel: 3356 7870. Fax: 2341 0360.
www.gio.gov.tw.

Motion Picture Association of
Taipei, 5F, 196 Chunghwa Rd,
Sec 1, Taipei. Tel: 2331 4672.
Fax: 2381 4341.

Nan Fang Film Productions,
2F, No 33, 290 Lane, Kuangfu
South Rd, Taipei.
Tel: 2771 1622. Fax: 2731 9983.

Public Television Service
Foundation, No 70, Lane 75,
Kangning Rd, Sec 3, Taipei.
Tel: 2630 1892. Fax: 2633 8050.
www.pts.org.tw.

Taipei Golden Horse Film Festival,
3F, 37 Kaifeng St, Sec 1, Taipei
100. Tel: 2388 3880. Fax: 2388
3874. www.goldenhorse.org.tw.

Three Dots Entertainment, 3F,
189 Minsheng West Rd, Taipei 103.
Tel: 2557 5157. Fax: 2557 5094.
www.3dots-entertainment.com.

Yen Ping Films Production
Pte Ltd, 1F, 178-1 Sungteh Rd,
Taipei 110. Tel: 8780 6086.
Fax: 8780 6040.

Zoom Hunt International
Production Co, 12F-1, 140 Sec 2,
Roosevelt Rd, Taipei 100.
Tel: 2364 2020. Fax: 2367 0627.
www.zoomhunt.com.tw.

THAILAND
All Tel/Fax numbers begin (66 2)

Archive
National Film Archive,
93 Moo 3, Phutthamonton 5 Rd,
Salaya, Nakorn Prathom 73170.
Tel: 441 0263/4 ext 116.

Useful Addresses
Cinemasia,
73/5 Ladprao 23, Ladyao, Jatujak,
Bangkok 10900.
Tel: 939 0693-4.
office@cinemasia.co.th.

Film Board Secretariat, 7th Floor,
Public Relations Dept, Soi Aree
Samphan, Rama VI Rd, Bangkok
10400. Fax: 618 2364/72.
thaifilmboard@hotmail.com.

Five Star Production Co Ltd,
[Producer/Distributor],
61/1 Soi Thaweemit 2, Rama 9 Rd,
Huaykwang, Bangkok 10310.
Tel: 246 9025-9.
info@fivestarent.com.
www.fivestarent.com.

GMM Tai Hub Co Ltd,
[Producer/Distributor], 92/11 Soi
Taweesuk Sukhumvit 31, Klongton
Nua Wattana, Bangkok 10110. Tel:
662 6223. www.gmmtaihub.com.
Matching Motion Pictures,
16th Sriayudthaya Bldg, 487/1
Sriayudthya Rd, Rajchathewi,
Bangkok10400. Tel: 248 8071-6.
chalermkiat_mmp@matchinggroup.com.
www.matchinggroup.com.
RS Film International,
[Producer/Distributor], 419/1
Ladphrao 15, Jatujak, Bangkok
10900. Tel: 511 0555 ext 85.
pomrudee@rs-film.com.www.rs-film.com.
Sahamongkol Film, SP (IBM) Bldg,
338 Room 3B, Phaholyothin Rd,
Phyathai, Bangkok 10400.
Tel: 273 0930-9.
www.sahamongkolfilm.com.

TURKEY
All Tel/Fax numbers begin (90 212)

Archive
Turkish Film & Television Institute,
80700 Kislaönü-Besiktas, Istanbul.
Tel: 266 1096. Fax: 211 6599.
sinematv@msu.edu.tr.

Useful Addresses
Association of Actors (CASOD),
Istiklal Caddesi, Atlas Sinemasi,
Pasaj-C Blok 53/3, Beyoglu,
Istanbul. Tel: 251 9775.
Fax: 251 9779. casod@casod.org.
Association of Directors (FILM-YON), Ayhan Isik Sokak 28/1,
Beyoglu, Istanbul. Tel: 293 9001.
**Association of Film Critics
(SIYAD),** Hakki Sehithan Sokak-Barlas Apt 33/13, Ulus, Istanbul.
Tel: 279 5998. Fax: 269 8284.
al.dorsay@superonline.com.
Contact: Atilla Dorsay.
**Istanbul Culture & Arts
Foundation (IKSV),**
Istiklal Caddesi, Louvre Apt 146,
800070 Beyoglu, Istanbul.
Tel: 334 0700. Fax: 334 0702.

film.fest@istfest-tr.org.
Özen Film,
[Producer/Distributor], Sakizaggaci
Caddesi, 21 Beyoglu, Istanbul.
Tel: 293 7070/1. Fax: 244 5851.
ozenfilm@superonline.com.
**Turkish Cinema & Audiovisual
Culture Foundation (TÜRSAK),**
Gazeteci Erol Dernek Sokak,
11/ 2 Hanif Han, Beyoglu, Istanbul.
Tel: 244 5251. Fax: 251 6770.
tursak@superonline.com.
Umut Sanat,
[Producer/Distributor], Akasyali
Sokak 18, 4 Levent, Istanbul.
Tel: 325 8888. Fax: 278 3282.
info.umut@umutsanat.com.tr.

UKRAINE
All Tel/Fax numbers begin (380 44)

Archive
Central State Archives of Film,
Photo & Sound Documents,
24 Solomyanska St, Kiev 252601.
Tel: 277 3777. Fax: 277 3655.

Useful Addresses
Dovzhenko National Film Studio,
Prospekt Peremogy 44,
Kiev 252057.
Tel: 446 9231. Fax: 446 4044.
**Karpenko-Kary Kiev State
Institute of the Theatre Arts,**
40 Yaroslaviv St, Kiev 252034.
Tel: 212 1142. Fax: 212 1003.
Ministry of Culture & Art,
19 Franka St, Kiev 252030.
Tel: 226 2645. Fax: 225 3257.
Odessa Film Studio,
Frantsuzky Bulvar 33, Odessa
270044. Tel: 260 0355.
Fax: 260 0355.

Studio 1+1,
14/1 Mechnikova St,
1st Entrance, 5th Floor, Kiev
252023. Tel: 246 4600.
Fax: 246 4518.
Ukrainian Filmmakers Union,
6 Saksaganskogo St, Kiev 252033.
Tel: 227 7557. Fax: 227 3130.

UNITED KINGDOM

Archives
Imperial War Museum,
Lambeth Rd, London SE1 6HZ.
Tel: (44 20) 7416 5320. Fax: 7416
5374. filmcommercial@iwm.org.uk.
www.iwmcollections.org.uk.
**National Film & Television
Archive,** British Film Institute,
21 Stephen St, London W1P 1LN.
Tel: (44 20) 7255 1444.
Fax: 7436 0439.
cataloguing.films@bfi.org.uk.
www.bfi.org.uk.
Scottish Screen Archive,
1 Bowmont Gardens, Glasgow
G12 9LR. Tel: (44 141) 337 7400.
Fax: 337 7413.
archive@scottishscreen.com.
www.scottishscreen.com.

Bookshops
Cinema Bookshop,
13-14 Great Russell St, London
WC1B 3NH. Tel: (44 20) 7637 0206.
Fax: 7436 9979.
Friendly service and an eye for rare
items.
Cinema Store, Unit 4B/C,
Orion House, Upper Saint Martin's
Lane, London WC2H 9NY.
Tel: (44 20) 7379 7838. Fax: 7240
7689. cinemastor@aol.com.

www.thecinemastore.com.

Flashbacks, 6 Silver Place, Beak St, London, W1F 0JS. Tel/Fax: (44 20) 7437 8562. shop@flashbacks.freeserve.co.uk www.dacre.org/.

Greenroom Books, 9 St James Rd, Ilkley, West Yorkshire LS29 9PY. Tel: (44 1943) 607 662. greenroombooks@blueyonder.co.uk. Mail order service for second-hand books on the performing arts.

Ed Mason, Room 301, Riverbank House, 1 Putney Bridge Approach, London, SW6 3JD. Tel: (44 20) 7736 8511. Organises the Collector's Film Convention. Held six times a year at Westminster Central Hall, London.

Movie Boulevard, 3 Cherry Tree Walk, Leeds LS2 7EB. Tel: (44 113) 242 2888. Fax: 243 8840. rick@movieboulevard.co.uk. www.movieboulevard.co.uk.

Offstage Film & Theatre Bookshop, 37 Chalk Farm Rd, London, NW1 8AJ. Tel: (44 20) 7485 4996. Fax: 7916 8046. offstagebookshop@aol.com.

Rare Discs, 18 Bloomsbury St, London WC1B 3QA. Tel: (44 20) 7580 3516. masheter@softhome.net.

Reel Poster Gallery, 72 Westbourne Grove, London W2 5SH. Tel: (44 20) 7727 4488. Fax: 7727 4499. info@reelposter.com. www.reelposter.com.

Shipley Media, 80 Charing Cross Rd, London WC2H 0BB. Tel: (44 20) 7240 4157. Fax: 7240 4186. www.artbooks.co.uk.

Film Schools

London International Film School, 24 Shelton St, London WC2H 9UB. Tel: (44 20) 7836 9642. Fax: 7497 3718. info@lfs.org.uk. www.lfs.org.uk.

Principal: Ben Gibson. Offers a practical, two-year MA course to professional levels.

Middlesex University, School of Arts, Cat Hill, Barnet, Herts EN4 8HT. Tel: (44 20) 8411 5066. Fax: 8411 5013. www.mdx.ac.uk.

National Film & Television School, Station Rd, Beaconsfield, Bucks, HP9 1LG. Tel: (44 1494) 671 234. Fax: 674 042. admin@nftsfilm-tv.ac.uk. www.nftsfilm-tv.ac.uk. MA Courses in: Directing (Animation, Documentary or Fiction); Cinematography; Editing; Post-production Sound; Producing; Production Design; Composing for Film & TV; Screenwriting. Diploma in Sound Recording. Project Development Labs for experienced professionals. Short courses for freelancers. Short courses in digital post-production.

School of Art, Media & Design, University of Wales College, Newport, Caerleon Campus, PO Box 179, NP18 3YG. Tel: (44 1633) 432 643. Fax: 432610. florenceayisi@newport.ac.uk. www.newport.ac.uk.

Surrey Institute of Art & Design, Farnham Campus, Falkner Rd, Farnham, Surrey GU9 7DS. Tel: (44 1252) 722441. Fax: 892616. bfoulk@surrart.ac.uk. www.surrart.ac.uk.

University of Bristol, Dept of Drama, Film & Television Studies, Cantocks Close, Woodland Rd, Bristol BS8 1UP. Tel: (44 117) 928 7838. Fax: 928 7832. kate.withers@bristol.ac.uk. www.bris.ac.uk.

University of Derby, School of Arts, Design & Technology, Kedleston Rdk Derby DE22 1GB. Tel: (44 1332) 591736. Fax: 597739. artdesign@derby.ac.uk. www.derby.ac.uk.

University of Stirling, Dept of Film & Media Studies,

Stirling FK9 4LA. Tel: (44 1786) 467520. Fax: 466855. stirling.media@stir.ac.uk. www.fms.stir.ac.uk.

University of Westminster, Media Art & Design, Watford Rd, Northwick Park, Harrow, HA1 3TP. Tel: (44 20) 7911 5903. Fax: 7911 5955. hunninj@wmin.ac.uk. www.wmin.ac.uk.

Magazines

Empire, 4th Floor, Mappin House, 4 Winsley St, London W1W 8HF. Tel: (44 20) 7436 1515. Fax: 7343 8703. empire@emap.com. www.empireonline.co.uk.

Image Technology – Journal of the BKSTS, Pinewood Studios, Iver Heath, Buckinghamshire, SL0 0NH. Tel: (44 1753) 656656. Fax: 657016. info@bksts.com. www.bksts.com.

Screen International, 33-39 Bowling Green Lane, London, EC1R 0DA. Tel: (44 20) 7505 8080/8099. Fax: 7505 8117. www.screendaily.com.

Sight & Sound, British Film Institute, 21 Stephen St, London W1T 1LN. Tel: (44 20) 7255 1444. Fax: 7436 2327. s&s@bfi.org.uk. www.bfi.org.uk/sightandsound. Established in 1932, the UK's leading film journal.

Total Film, Future Publishing, 99 Baker St, London W1U 6FP. Tel: (44 20) 7317 2600. Fax: 7486 5678. totalfilm@futurenet.co.uk.

Useful Addresses

British Academy of Film & Television Arts (BAFTA), 195 Piccadilly, London, W1V 0LN. Tel: (44 20) 7734 0022. Fax: 7734 1792. www.bafta.org.

British Actors Equity Association, Guild House, Upper St Martins Lane, London, WC2H 9EG. Tel: (44 20) 7379 6000.

Fax: 7379 7001. info@equity.org.uk. www.equity.org.uk.

British Board of Film Classification (BBFC), 3 Soho Sq, London, W1D 3HD. Tel: (44 20) 7440 1570. Fax: 7287 0141. webmaster@bbfc.co.uk. www.bbfc.co.uk.

British Council, Films & Literature Dept, 10 Spring Gardens, London, SW1A 2BN. Tel: (44 20) 7389 3051. Fax: 7389 3175. filmandliterature@britishcouncil.org. www.britishcouncil.org.

British Film Institute, 21 Stephen St, London, W1T 1LN. Tel: (44 20) 7255 1444. Fax: 7436 7950. sales.films@bfi.org.uk. www.bfi.org.uk.

Cinema Exhibitors Association, 22 Golden Sq, London, W1F 9JW. Tel: (44 20) 7734 9551. Fax: 7734 6147. cea@cinemauk.ftech.co.uk.

Directors Guild of Great Britain (DGGB), Acorn House, 314-320 Grays Inn Rd, London, WC1X 8DP. Tel: (44 20) 7278 4343. Fax: 7278 4742. guild@dggb.org. www.dggb.org.

Film Distributors' Association, 22 Golden Square, London, W1F 9JW. Tel: (44 20) 7437 4383. Fax: 7734 0912. info@fda.uk.net. www.launchingfilms.com

Film London, 20 Euston Centre, Regent's Place, London, NW1 3JH. Tel: (44 20) 7387 8787. Fax: 7387 8788. info@filmlondon.org.uk. www.filmlondon.org.uk.

PACT, 45 Mortimer St, London, W1W 8HJ. Tel: (44 20) 7331 6000. Fax: 7331 6700. enquiries@pact.co.uk. www.pact.co.uk.

Scottish Screen, 249 West George St, 2nd Floor, Glasgow, G2 4QE. Tel: (44 141) 302 1700. Fax: 302 1711. info@scottishscreen.com. www.scottishscreen.com.

The Script Factory, 66–67 Wells Str, London W1T 3PY. Tel: (44 20) 7323 1414. Fax: 7323 9463. general@scriptfactory.co.uk. www.scriptfactory.co.uk. Film-makers' organisation. Runs UK and international screenwriting, production and development training, in partnership with the UK Film Council and MEDIA.

UK Film Council, 10 Little Portland St, London, W1W 7JG. Tel: (44 20) 7861 7861. Fax: 7861 7862. info@ukfilmcouncil.org.uk. www.ukfilmcouncil.org.uk.

UK Film Council International, 10 Little Portland St, London, W1W 7JG. Tel: (44 20) 7861 7860. Fax: 7861 7864. internationalinfo@ukfilmcouncil.org.uk. www.ukfilmcouncil.org.uk.

UNITED STATES

Archives

Academy of Motion Picture Arts & Sciences, Academy Film Archive, Pickford Center, 1313 North Vine St, Los Angeles, CA 90028. Tel: (1 310) 247 3000. Fax: 657 5431. lmehr@oscars.org. www.oscars.org.mhl/index.

American Film Institute/National Center for Film & Video Preservation, 2021 North Western Ave, Los Angeles, CA 90027-1657. Tel: (1 323) 856 7600. Fax: 467 4578. info@afi.com. www.afi.com.

George Eastman House/International Museum of Photography & Film, 900 East Ave, Rochester, NY 14607. Tel: (1 585) 271 3361 Fax: 271 3970. film@geh.org. www.eastman.org.

Getty Images Motion Collections, 75 Varick St, 5th Floor, New York, NY 10013. Tel: (1 646) 613 4100. Fax: 613 3601. www.gettyimages.com.

Harvard Film Archive, Carpenter Center for the Visual Arts, Harvard University, 24 Quincy St, Cambridge, MA 02138. Tel: (1 617) 496 6046. Fax: 496 6750. rmeyers@fas.harvard.edu. www.harvardfilmarchive.org.

Library of Congress, Motion Picture, Broadcasting and Recorded Sound Division, 101 Independence Ave SE, James Madison Bldg, LM 336, Washington, DC 20540-4690. Tel: (1 202) 707 8572. Fax: 707 2371. mpref@loc.gov. www.loc.gov/rr/mopic.

Museum of Modern Art, Dept of Film and Video, 11 West 53rd St, New York, NY 10019. Tel: (1 212) 708 9400. Fax: 333 1145. info@moma.org. www.moma.org.

Human Studies Film Archives, National Museum of Natural History, Room MSC G1300, 4210 Silver Hill Rd, Suitland, MD 207460. Tel: (1 301) 238 1315. hsfa@nmnh.si.edu. www.nmnh.si.edu/naa.

Pacific Film Archive, University of California and Berkeley Art Museum, 2621 Durant Ave, Berkeley, CA 94720-2250. Tel: (1 510) 642 0808. bampfa@berkeley.edu. www.bampfa.berkeley.edu.

UCLA Film & Television Archive, Commercial Services Division, 1015 North Cahuenga Blvd, Hollywood, CA 90038. Tel: (1 323) 466 8559. Fax: 461 6317. footage@ucla.edu. www.cinema.ucla.edu.

Wisconsin Center for Film & Theater Research, 816 State St, Madison, WI 53706. Tel: (1 608) 264 6466. Fax: 264 6472. wcftrref@whs.wisc.edu. www.wisconsinhistory.org/wcftr.

Bookshops

Cinema Books, 4753 Roosevelt Way NE, Seattle, WA 98105. Tel: (1 206) 547 7667. Info2@cinemabooks.net. www.cinemabooks.net.

Cinemonde, 478 Allied Drive, Suite

105, Nashville, TN 37211. Tel: (1 615) 832 1997. Fax: 832 2082. cinemonde@earthlink.net. www.cinemonde.com. Cinemonde is a poster store for movie buffs.

Déja Vu Enterprises Inc, 2934 Beverly Glen Circle, Suite 309, Los Angeles, CA 90077. Tel: (1 818) 996 6137. Fax: 996 6147. dejavugallery@socal.rr.com. www.dejavugallery.com.

Dwight Cleveland, PO Box 10922, Chicago, IL 60610-0922. Tel: (1 773) 525 9152. Fax: 525 2969. posterboss@aol.com. www.movieposterbiz.com.

Larry Edmund's Bookshop, 6644 Hollywood Blvd, Hollywood, CA 90028. Tel: (1 323) 463 3273. Fax: 463 4245. info@larryedmunds.com. www.larryedmunds.com.

Samuel French's Theatre & Film Bookshop, (3 Locations) 7623 Sunset Blvd, Hollywood, CA 90046. Tel: (1 323) 876 0570. Fax: 876 6822. 45 West 25th St, New York, NY 10010. Tel: (1 212) 206 8990. Fax: 206 1429. Extended evening hours at 11963 Ventura Blvd, Studio City, CA 91604. Tel: (1 818) 762 0535. www.samuelfrench.com. The world's oldest and largest play publisher (est 1830) operates a separate film and performing arts bookshop.

Gotham Book Mart, 16 East 46th St, New York, NY 10017. Tel: (1 212) 719 4448. Fax: 719 3481. gbmorders@horizon.net.

Limelight Books, 1803 Market St, San Francisco, CA 94103. Tel: (1 415) 864 2265. limelightbooks@limelightbooks.com. www.limelightbooks.com.

Movie Star News, 134 West 18th St, New York, NY 10011. Tel: (1 212) 620 8160. www.moviestarnews.com.

Jerry Ohlinger's Movie Material Store Inc, 253 West 35th St, New York, NY 10001. Tel: (1 212) 989 0869. Fax: 989 1660. jomms@aol.com. www.moviematerials.com.

Film Schools

Information on the thousands of US film schools and courses available can be obtained in the American Film Institute's Guide to College Courses in Film and Television, which can be ordered from Publications, The American Film Institute, 2021 North Western Ave, Los Angeles, CA 90027. Tel: (1 323) 856 7600. Fax: 467 4578. www.afi.com.

Magazines

American Cinematographer, ASC Holding Corp, 1782 North Orange Drive, Hollywood, CA 90028. Tel: (1 323) 969 4333. Fax: 876 4973. customerservice@theasc.com. www.theasc.com.

Animation Journal, 108 Hedge Nettle, Crossing, Savannah, GA 31406-7220. Tel: (1 912) 352 9300. editor@animationjournal.com. www.animationjournal.com. Quarterly.

Animation Magazine, 30941 West Agoura Rd, Suite 102, Westlake Village, CA 91361. Tel: (1 818) 991 2884. Fax: 991

Box Office, 155 South El Molino Ave, Suite 100, Pasadena, California, 91101. Tel: (1 626) 396 0250. Fax: 396 0248. editorial@boxoffice.com; advertising@boxoffice.com. www.boxoffice.com. Business monthly.

Cineaste, 304 Hudson St, 6th Floor, New York, NY 10013-1015. cineaste@cineaste.com. www.cineaste.com. Quarterly.

Classic Images, 301 E 3rd St, Muscatine, IA 52761. Tel: (1 563) 263 2331. Fax: 262 8042. classicimages@classicimages.com. www.classicimages.com.

Film Comment, Film Society of Lincoln Center, 70 Lincoln Center Plaza, New York, NY 10023. Tel: (1 212) 875 5614. Fax: 875 5636. editor@filmlinc.com.

Film Criticism, Allegheny College, Box D, Meadville, PA 16335. Tel: (1 814) 332 4333/43. Fax: 332 2981. lmichael@allegheny.edu.

Film Literature Index, Film & Television Documentation Centre, State University of New York, 1400 Washington Ave, Albany, NY 12222. Tel: (1 518) 442 5745. Fax: 442 5367. fatdoc@albany.edu. www.albany.edu/sisp/fatdoc/index.html.

Film Quarterly, University of California Press, 2000 Center St, Suite 303, Berkeley, CA 94704-1223. Tel: (1 510) 642 9740. Fax: 642 9917. ann.martin@ucpress.edu. www.filmquarterly.org.

Filmmaker Magazine, 501 5th Ave, Room 1714, New York, NY 10017. Tel: (1 212) 983 3150. Fax: 973 0318. publisher@filmmakermagazine.com. www.filmmakermagazine.com.

Hollywood Reporter, 5055 Wilshire Blvd, Los Angeles, CA 90036-4396. Tel: (1 323) 525 2000. Fax: 525 2377. www.hollywoodreporter.com. Daily.

International Documentary Magazine, International Documentary Association, 1201 West 5th St, Suite M320, Los Angeles, CA 90017. Tel: (1 213) 534 3600. Fax: 534 3610. info@documentary.org. www. documentary.org.

Movieline's Hollywood Life, 10537 Santa Monica Blvd, Suite 250, Los Angeles, CA 90025. Tel: (1 310) 234 9501. Fax: 234 0332. andre@movieline.com.

www.movieline.com.

Variety,
5700 Wilshire Blvd, Suite 120,
Los Angeles, CA 90036.
www.variety.com.
The world's foremost
entertainment industry newspaper
(daily and weekly).

Useful Addresses
Directors Guild of America,
7920 Sunset Blvd, Los Angeles,
CA 90046. Tel: (1 310) 289 2000.
Fax: 289 2029. www.dga.org.
Independent Feature Project,
104 W 29th St, 12th Floor, New
York, NY 10001. Tel: (1 212) 465
8200. Fax: 465 8525. ifpny@ifp.org.
www.ifp.org.
**International Documentary
Association,** 1201 W 5th St,
Suite M320, Los Angeles, CA
90017-1461. Tel: (1 213) 534 3600.
Fax: 534 3610.
info@documentary.org.
www.documentary.org.
**Motion Picture Association of
America,** 15503 Ventura Blvd, Encino,
CA 91436. Tel: (1 818) 995 6600.
Fax: 382 1784. www.mpaa.org.
ShoWest, 770 Broadway, 5th
Floor, New York, NY 10003-9595.
Tel: (1 646) 654 7680. Fax: 654 7693.
rsunshine@vnuexpo.com.
www.showest.com.

URUGUAY
All Tel/Fax numbers begin (598 2)

Archive
Cinemateca Uruguaya, Lorenzo
Carnelli 1311, 11200 Montevideo.
Tel: 418 2460. Fax: 419 4572.
cinemuy@chasque.net.
www.cinemateca.org.uy.

Useful Addresses
**Asociación de Críticos de Cine
del Uruguay (ACCU),**
Canelones 1280, Montevideo.
Tel: 622 0085. Fax: 908 3904.

criticosuruguay@yahoo.com.
**Asociación de Productores y
Realizadores de Cine y Video del
Uruguay (ASOPROD),**
Maldonado 1792, Montevideo.
Tel: 418 7998. info@asoprod.org.uy.
www.asoprod.org.uy.
**Fondo Para el Fomento y
Desarrollo de la Producción
Audiovisual Nacional (FONA),**
Palacio Municipal, Piso 1º,
Montevideo. Tel: 902 3775.
fona@prensa.imm.gub.uy.
www.montevideo.gub.uy/cultura/c_fona.
htm.
**Instituto Nacional del Audiovisual
(INA),** Reconquista 535, 8º Piso,
11100 Montevideo. Tel/Fax: 915
7489/916 2632. ina@mec.gub.uy.
www.mec.gub.uy/ina.

VENEZUELA
All Tel/Fax numbers begin (+58 212)

Archives
Cinemateca Nacional
Plaza de los Museos, Galeria de
Arte Nacional, Los Caobos
Caracas. www.cinemateca.org.ve.
**Cine Archivo Bolivar Films
(Cinesa)**
Avenida Luis Guillermo Villegas
Blanco, Edificio Bolívar Films,
Sta. Eduvigis, Caracas.
Tel: 2838455. Fax: 2857561.
cinearchivo@grupocinesa.com.
www.grupocinesa.com.
**Colección de Cine y Video de la
Biblioteca Nacional**
Parroquia Altagracia, Final Avda.
Panteón, Foro Libertador. Edificio
Sede, Nivel Ap-3, Cuerpo 1, Caracas
1010. Tel: 505 9227. www.bnv.bib.ve.

Useful Adresses
**Centro Nacional Autónomo de
Cinematografía (CNAC)**
Avenida Diego Cisneros,
Edificio Centro Monaca, Ala Sur,
Piso 2, Oficina 2-B
Urb. Los Ruices,

1071 Caracas.
comunicación@cnac.org.ve.
www.cnac.org.ve.
**Consejo Nacional de la Cultura
(CONAC)**
Dirección General Sectorial de Cine
y Medios Audiovisuales,
Centro Simón Bolivar, Torre Norte,
Piso 15, El Silencio, Caracas.
Fax: 4829693.
www.conac.org.ve.

ZIMBABWE
All Tel/Fax numbers begin (263 4)

Archive
National Archives of Zimbabwe,
Borrowdale Road, Gunhill, Private
Bag 7729, Causeway, Harare.
Tel: 792 741. archives@gta.gov.zw.
www.gta.gov.zw.

Magazine
Africa Film & TV,
10 Jewry St, Winchester, Hants,
SO23 8RZ, United Kingdom.
Tel: (44 1962) 861 518. Fax: 863
516. www.africafilmtv.com.

Useful Addresses
**African Script Development
Fund,** 43 Selous Ave, Harare.
Tel: 724 673. Fax: 733 404.
asdf@mweb.co.zw.
www.icon.co.zw/asdf.
**Media for Development Trust
(MFD),** 19 Van Praagh Ave Milton
Park PO Box 6755, Harare.
Tel: 701 323/4. Fax: 729 066.
mfd@mango.zw. www.mfd.co.zw.
Contact: John Riber.
**Zimbabwe Broadcasting
Corporation.** Broadcasting Center,
Pockets Hill, PO Box HG444,
Highlands, Harare. Tel: 498 630.
Fax: 498 613. info@zbc.co.zw.
www.zbc.co.zw.
Zimmedia, 26 Cork Rd, Harare.
Tel: 708 426. Fax: 708 425.
info@zimmedia.com.
www.zimmedia.com.

Index to Advertisers